CREATE YOUR ACCOUNT TODAY!

① Ask your instructor for the Course Key for your course.
(Skip this step if you are not enrolled in an instructor-led course.)

COURSE KEY *from your instructor*

② Go to www.nelsonbrain.com.

③ Register as a new user OR sign in, if you already have an account, using your email address and password.

④ In the box labelled "Register," enter the Access Code printed below.

ACCESS CODE

⑤ To access your online resource, click on the "Open" button.

⑥ Enter the Course Key provided by your instructor. (Skip this step if you are not enrolled in an instructor-led course.)

ACCESS CODE

SAVE THIS!

Record your username (your email address) and password for future visits. To access CourseMate, you will always need to return to www.nelsonbrain.com and enter your email address and password to log in.

KEEP ME

YOUR ONLINE STUDY TOOLS ARE NOW ONLY A CLICK AWAY

NELSON / EDUCATION

1 800 268 2222
email: nelson.her@nelson.com
www.nelson.com

Mean square within

$$\text{MSW} = \frac{\text{SSW}}{\text{dfw}}$$

Mean square between

$$\text{MSB} = \frac{\text{SSB}}{\text{dfb}}$$

F ratio

$$F = \frac{\text{MSB}}{\text{MSW}}$$

CHAPTER 10

Chi square

$$\chi^2 \text{ (obtained)} = \sum \frac{(f_o - f_e)^2}{f_e}$$

CHAPTER 11

Phi

$$\phi = \sqrt{\frac{\chi^2}{n}}$$

Cramer's *V*

$$V = \sqrt{\frac{\chi^2}{(n)(\text{Minimum of } r - 1, c - 1)}}$$

Lambda

$$\lambda = \frac{E_1 - E_2}{E_1}$$

CHAPTER 12

Gamma

$$G = \frac{n_s - n_d}{n_s + n_d}$$

Spearman's rho

$$r_s = 1 - \frac{6 \sum D^2}{n(n^2 - 1)}$$

CHAPTER 13

Least-squares regression line

$$Y = a + bX$$

Slope

$$b = \frac{n \sum XY - (\sum X)(\sum Y)}{n \sum X^2 - (\sum X)^2}$$

Y intercept

$$a = \overline{Y} - b\overline{X}$$

Pearson's *r*

$$r = \frac{n \sum XY - (\sum X)(\sum Y)}{\sqrt{[n \sum X^2 - (\sum X)^2][n \sum Y^2 - (\sum Y)^2]}}$$

CHAPTER 14

Partial correlation coefficient

$$r_{yx.z} = \frac{r_{yx} - (r_{yz})(r_{xz})}{\sqrt{1 - r_{yz}^2} \sqrt{1 - r_{xz}^2}}$$

Least-squares multiple regression line

$$Y = a + b_1 X_1 + b_2 X_2$$

Partial slope for X_1

$$b_1 = \left(\frac{s_y}{s_1}\right)\left(\frac{r_{y1} - r_{y2} r_{12}}{1 - r_{12}^2}\right)$$

Partial slope for X_2

$$b_2 = \left(\frac{s_y}{s_2}\right)\left(\frac{r_{y2} - r_{y1} r_{12}}{1 - r_{12}^2}\right)$$

Y intercept

$$a = \overline{Y} - b_1 \overline{X}_1 - b_2 \overline{X}_2$$

Beta-weight for X_1

$$b_1^* = b_1 \left(\frac{s_1}{s_y}\right)$$

Beta-weight for X_2

$$b_2^* = b_2 \left(\frac{s_2}{s_y}\right)$$

Standardized least-squares regression line

$$Z_y = b_1^* Z_1 + b_2^* Z_2$$

Coefficient of multiple determination

$$R^2 = r_{y1}^2 + r_{y2.1}^2 (1 - r_{y1}^2)$$

Statistics

A TOOL FOR
SOCIAL RESEARCH

Second Canadian Edition

Joseph F. Healey

Christopher Newport University

Steven G. Prus

Carleton University

NELSON EDUCATION

NELSON / EDUCATION

**Statistics: A Tool for Social Research,
Second Canadian Edition**

by Joseph F. Healey and Steven G. Prus

**Vice President, Editorial
Higher Education:**
Anne Williams

Acquisitions Editor:
Maya Castle

Marketing Manager:
Terry Fedorkiw

Developmental Editor:
Jessica Freedman

Permissions Coordinator:
Natalie Barrington

Production Service:
Integra Software Services Pvt. Ltd.

Copy Editor:
Cheryl Turner

Proofreader:
Integra Software Services Pvt. Ltd.

Indexer:
Integra Software Services Pvt. Ltd.

**Senior Production
Coordinator:**
Ferial Suleman

Design Director:
Ken Phipps

Managing Designer:
Franca Amore

**Interior Design
Modifications:**
Eugene Lo

Cover Design:
Greg Devitt

Cover Image:
Enjoynz/Getty Images

Compositor:
Integra Software Services Pvt. Ltd.

Printer:
RR Donnelley

**Library and Archives Canada
Cataloguing in Publication Data**

Healey, Joseph F., 1945–
    Statistics : a tool for social research /
Joseph F. Healey, Steven G. Prus.—2nd
Canadian ed.

Includes index.
ISBN 978-0-17-665136-7

1. Social sciences—Statistical methods.
2. Statistics. I. Prus, Steven G. (Steven Gerald),
1967– II. Title.

HA29.H42 2012   519.5
C2011-907345-5

PKG ISBN-13: 978-0-17-665136-7
PKG ISBN-10: 0-17-665136-5

Brief Contents

Detailed Contents

Preface to the Second Canadian Edition

Sociology and the other social sciences (including political science, social work, public administration, criminology, and gerontology) are research-based disciplines, and statistics are part of their everyday language. To join the conversation, you must be literate in the vocabulary of research, data analysis, and scientific thinking. Knowledge of statistics will enable you to understand the professional research literature of your discipline as well as the research reports you encounter in everyday life. Knowledge of statistics will enable you to conduct quantitative research and to contribute to the growing body of social science knowledge. Statistical literacy will move you closer to reaching your full potential as a social scientist.

Although essential, learning (and teaching) statistics can be a challenge. Students in statistics courses typically have a wide range of mathematical backgrounds and an equally diverse set of career goals. They are often puzzled about the relevance of statistics for them, and, not infrequently, there is some math anxiety to deal with.

This textbook introduces statistical analysis for the social sciences while addressing these challenges. The textbook makes minimal assumptions about mathematical background (the ability to read a simple formula is sufficient preparation for virtually all of the material in the textbook), and a variety of special features help students analyze data successfully. The textbook is sufficiently flexible to be used in any program with a social science base.

The textbook is written at a level intermediate between a strictly mathematical approach and a mere "cookbook." We have not sacrificed comprehensive coverage or statistical correctness, but theoretical and mathematical explanations are kept at an elementary level, as is appropriate in a first exposure to social statistics. For example, we do not treat formal probability theory per se. Rather, the background necessary for an understanding of inferential statistics is introduced, informally and intuitively, in Chapters 4 and 5 while considering the concepts of the normal curve and the sampling distribution. The textbook makes no claim that statistics are "fun" or that the material can be mastered without considerable effort. At the same time, students are not overwhelmed with abstract proofs, formula derivations, and mathematical theory, which can needlessly frustrate the learning experience at this level.

GOALS AND FEATURES OF THE TEXTBOOK

The goal of this textbook is to develop basic statistical literacy. The statistically literate person *appreciates* the role of statistics in the research process, is *competent* to perform basic calculations, and can *read* the professional research literature in his or her field as well as any research reports he or she may encounter in everyday life.

The textbook provides various features to develop statistical literacy. We have grouped the main features of the textbook into three categories for the following discussion:

1. An Appreciation of Statistics. A statistically literate person understands the relevance of statistics for social research, can analyze and interpret the meaning of a statistical test, and can select an appropriate statistic for a given purpose and a given set of variables. This textbook develops these qualities, within the constraints imposed by the introductory nature of the course, in the following ways:

- *The relevance of statistics.* The textbook stresses the usefulness of statistics as a means of analyzing and manipulating data and answering research questions. This central theme of usefulness is reinforced by a series of boxes labelled "Application," each of which illustrates some specific way statistics can be used to answer questions.

  Further, the end-of-chapter problems are labelled by the social science discipline or subdiscipline from which they are drawn: SOC for sociology, SW for social work, PS for political science, CJ for criminology and criminal justice, PA for public administration, and GER for gerontology. By identifying problems with specific disciplines, students can more easily see the relevance of statistics to their own academic interests. (Not incidentally, they will also see that the disciplines have a large subject matter in common.)

- *Interpreting statistics.* For most students, interpretation—saying what statistics mean—is a big challenge. The ability to interpret statistics can be developed only by exposure and experience. To provide exposure, we have been careful, in the example problems, to express the meaning of the statistic in terms of the original research question. To provide experience, the end-of-chapter problems almost always call for an interpretation of the statistic calculated. To provide examples, many of the answers to odd-numbered computational problems in the back of the textbook are expressed in words as well as numbers. The "Interpreting Statistics" sections provide additional, detailed examples of how to express the meaning of statistics.

- *Using statistics: Ideas for research projects.* Appendix E offers ideas for independent data-analysis projects for students. The projects require students to use SPSS to analyze a data set. They can be assigned at intervals throughout the semester or at the end of the course. Each project provides an opportunity for students to practise and apply their statistical skills and, above all, to exercise their ability to understand and interpret the meaning of the statistics they produce.

2. Computational Competence. Students should emerge from their first course in statistics with the ability to perform elementary forms of data analysis—to execute a series of calculations and arrive at the correct answer. To be sure, computers and calculators have made computation less of an issue today. Yet, computation and statistics are inseparable, and since social science majors frequently do not have strong quantitative backgrounds, we have included a number of features to help students cope with these challenges:

- *Step-by-step computational algorithms* are provided for each statistic.

- *Extensive problem sets* are provided at the end of each chapter. Most of these problems use fictitious data and are designed for ease of computation.

- *Cumulative exercises* are included at the end of each part to provide practice in choosing, computing, and analyzing statistics. These exercises present only data sets and research questions. Students must choose appropriate statistics as part of the exercise.

- *Solutions* to odd-numbered computational problems are provided so that students may check their answers.

3. The Ability to Read the Professional Social Science Literature. The statistically literate person can comprehend and critically evaluate research reports written by others. The development of this quality is a particular problem at the introductory level since (1) the vocabulary of professional researchers is so much more concise than the language of the textbook, and (2) the statistics featured in the literature are more advanced than those covered at the introductory level. To help bridge this gap, we have included a series of boxes labelled "Reading Statistics" beginning in Chapter 1. In each box, we briefly describe the reporting style typically used for the statistic in question and try to alert students about what to expect when they approach the professional literature. These inserts include excerpts from the Canadian research literature and illustrate how statistics are actually applied and interpreted by social scientists.

Additional Features. A number of other features make the textbook more meaningful for students and more useful for instructors in helping to develop statistical literacy:

- *Readability and clarity.* The writing style is informal and accessible to students without ignoring the traditional vocabulary of statistics. Problems and examples have been written to maximize student interest and to focus on issues of concern and significance. For the more difficult material (such as hypothesis testing), students are first walked through an example problem before being confronted by formal terminology and concepts. Each chapter ends with a summary of major points and formulas and a glossary of important concepts. A list of frequently used formulas inside the front cover and a glossary of symbols inside the back cover can be used for quick reference.

- *Organization and coverage.* The textbook is divided into four parts. Overview sections have been included with each of the four parts of the textbook. These provide a "road map" of the material that follows and help students see why the chapters are organized as they are. Most of the coverage is devoted to the first three parts of the textbook: descriptive statistics, inferential statistics, and bivariate measures of association. The distinction between description and inference is introduced in the first chapter and maintained throughout the textbook. In selecting statistics for inclusion, we have tried to strike a balance between the essential concepts with which students must be familiar and the amount of material students can reasonably be expected to learn in their first (and perhaps only) statistics course, while bearing in mind that different instructors will naturally wish to stress different aspects of the subject. Thus, the textbook covers the full gamut of the usual statistics, with each chapter broken into subsections so that instructors may choose the particular statistics they wish to include.

- *Flow charts.* Flow charts that help students select appropriate statistics are provided in the textbook. The flow charts depict the selection process in more general terms at the beginning of each of the four parts of the textbook and in more detailed form at the beginning of each chapter.

- *Learning objectives.* Learning objectives are stated at the beginning of each chapter. These are intended to serve as "study guides" and to help students identify and focus on the most important material.

- *Review of mathematical skills.* A comprehensive review of all of the mathematical skills that will be used in this textbook (Prologue) is included. Students who are inexperienced or out of practice with mathematics may want to study this review early in the course and/or refer to it as needed. A self-test is included so that students may check their level of preparation for the course.

- *Statistical techniques and end-of-chapter problems are explicitly linked.* After a technique is introduced, students are directed to specific problems for practice and review. The "how-to-do-it" aspects of calculation are reinforced immediately and clearly.

- *End-of-chapter problems are organized progressively.* Simpler problems with small data sets are presented first. Often, explicit instructions or hints accompany the first several problems in a set. The problems gradually become more challenging and require more decision making by the student (e.g., choosing the most appropriate statistic for a certain situation). Thus, each problem set develops problem-solving abilities gradually and progressively.

- *Computer applications.* To help students take advantage of the power of the computer, this textbook integrates Version 20 of SPSS for Windows, though Versions 10 through 19 are completely compatible with the textbook. SPSS (Statistical Package for the Social Sciences) is a leading, state-of-the-art computerized statistical package. Alternatively, students can download a full working evaluation copy of SPSS for Windows. This free 14-day trialware can be downloaded after registering at www.ibm.com/software/analytics/spss/downloads.

   The last part of each chapter, labelled "SPSS for Windows," offers demonstrations and exercises in using SPSS to produce the statistics presented in the chapter. All SPSS outputs from the demonstrations are shown in the textbook, and are unedited. Students choosing to replicate the demonstration will see the same output on their computer screen. SPSS exercises are provided below the demonstrations and give students the opportunity to actually use SPSS to compute statistics. Appendix E provides additional SPSS exercises, and Appendix F gives a general introduction to SPSS.

   Overall, detailed instructions and demonstrations on how to use SPSS for each exercise are provided in this textbook. SPSS can be taught at a basic level from this textbook without the aid of an SPSS supplementary text.

- *Real data.* Four databases for SPSS application give students a wide range of opportunities to practise their statistical skills on "real-life" data: 1) a shortened version of the 2009 Canadian General Social Survey (labelled *GSS.sav*); 2) a shortened version of the 2006 Census of Canada (*Census.sav*); 3) the full version of the 2009 Canadian General Social Survey (*GSSFull.sav*); and 4) the full version of the 2006 Census of Canada (*CensusFull.sav*). The databases are described in Appendix G and are available in SPSS format (i.e., the ".sav" file format) on the website for the textbook.

- *Companion website.* The website for this textbook includes additional material and some less frequently used techniques, additional end-of-chapter problems, supplements containing a detailed discussion of probability, and various other features.

- *Instructor's Manual.* The Instructor's Manual includes chapter summaries, a test item file of multiple-choice questions, answers to even-numbered computational problems, and step-by-step solutions to selected problems.

- *Study Guide.* The Study Guide contains additional examples to illuminate basic principles, review problems with detailed answers, SPSS projects, and multiple-choice questions and answers that complement but do not duplicate the test item file.

KEY CHANGES IN THE SECOND CANADIAN EDITION

This edition of the textbook remains focused on developing the skills necessary for students to become statistically literate. It is written for students with varying levels of mathematical proficiency, providing an accessible yet comprehensive examination of statistics, and continues to expose students to statistics from a uniquely Canadian perspective. With this in mind, various changes were made in this edition. Some of the key changes are:

- Many chapters have been streamlined to focus on the most essential material, and other chapters merged to enhance clarity. Measures of central tendency and dispersion have been merged into a single chapter (Chapter 3), as have basic concepts of bivariate association and measures of association for nominal-level variables (Chapter 11).

- Several new statistics have been added, including the variation ratio (Chapter 3) and Kendall's tau and Somers' *d* (Chapter 12). Other statistical techniques have been moved to the website for the textbook including multivariate analysis for nominal- and ordinal-level variables.

- Regression analysis with nominal- and ordinal-level variables, such as dummy variable and logistic regression analysis, is now covered on the website for the textbook.

- Ordinal measures of association (Chapter 12) are now discussed in the context of the logic of "pairs" that underlies the computation of gamma, Kendall's tau, and Somers' *d.*

- Several sections have been expanded including Section 3.3 on the calculation of the interquartile range and Section 5.4 on the construction of the sampling distribution.

- The textbook, at the time of printing, uses the latest versions of SPSS (version 20) and the Canadian General Social Survey (2009) and Census of Canada (2006).

STUDENT RESOURCES

The **CNOW (0176627731)** includes Learning Objectives, Chapter Summaries, and 15 multiple-choice questions per chapter. In addition, Work Problems and SPSS Work Problems test students' knowledge, with detailed answers so they can verify that they've understood and solved the problems accurately.

SPSS Datasets for *Statistics* can be found at www.healeystatistics. nelson.com. These datasets were written for use with Version 20 of SPSS, but Versions 10 through 19 are completely compatible.

The *Statistics* website at www.healeystatistics.nelson.com is a comprehensive, resource-rich location for students to find pertinent information. As well as SPSS Datasets, they'll find additional review and study materials, including quizzes, glossary flashcards, tables of frequently used formulas and random numbers, and more!

InfoTrac® College Edition is automatically bundled FREE with every new copy of this textbook! InfoTrac College Edition is a world-class online university library that offers the full text of articles from over 5000 scholarly and popular publications—updated daily and going back as far as 20 years. Students (and their instructors) receive unlimited access for four months.

INSTRUCTOR RESOURCES

The **Instructor's Resource CD (0176616209)** gives instructors the ultimate tool for customizing lectures and presentations. These ancillaries include:

- *Instructor's Manual.* The Instructor's Manual contains a chapter summary, a guide to changes in the second Canadian edition, answers to even-numbered end-of-chapter problems, detailed answers to selected textbook problems, and answers to even-numbered textbook cumulative exercises.

- *Test Bank.* The Test Bank consists of multiple-choice, problem, and essay questions. Correct answers and page references are provided for more than 650 multiple-choice questions. Answers are also provided for the problems and essay questions. Files are provided in rich text format for easy editing and printing with all common word-processing formats.

- *ExamView.* All Test Bank questions are included in the ExamView computerized version. The easy-to-use software is compatible with Microsoft Windows and Mac. Create tests by selecting questions from the question bank, modifying these questions as desired, and adding new questions you write yourself. You can administer quizzes online and export tests to WebCT, Blackboard, and other formats.

- *PowerPoint Lecture Presentation.* The PowerPoint Lecture Presentation enables instructors to customize their own multimedia classroom presentations. Key concepts from each chapter are presented in an average of 20 slides per chapter. Material can be modified or expanded for individual classroom use. PowerPoints are also easily printed to create customized transparency masters.

- *Day One*. Day One—Prof InClass is a PowerPoint presentation that instructors can customize to orient their students to the class and textbook at the beginning of the course.

- *SPSS Datasets*. For the convenience of instructors, the SPSS datasets created for the textbook are available on the Instructor's Resource CD. These datasets were written for use with version 20 of SPSS, but versions 10 through 19 are completely compatible.

 The instructor's page of the *Statistics* website at www.healeystatistics. nelson.com contains downloads for the Instructor's Manual, PowerPoint, SPSS datasets, and Day One—Prof InClass presentation. For security reasons, the Test Bank is not offered as a download; contact your Nelson Education sales representative to obtain a copy of it on the Instructor's Resource CD.

ACKNOWLEDGMENTS FOR THE SECOND CANADIAN EDITION

I would like to first and foremost acknowledge and thank Dr. Teresa Abada, University of Western Ontario; Dr. Alex Bierman, University of Calgary; Dr. Stephen Gyimah, Queen's University; Owen Temby, Carleton University; and Dr. Michael Weinrath, University of Winnipeg for their very helpful comments and guidance in writing this textbook. The textbook has also greatly benefitted from the reviews and suggestions provided by many others.

Along with others who prefer to remain anonymous, they include:

Silvia Bartolic, *University of British Columbia*
Tuna Baskoy, *Ryerson University*
Gerald Bierling, *McMaster University*
Jonah Butovsky, *Brock University*
James Frideres, *University of Calgary*
David A. Hay, *University of Saskatchewan*
Robert Hiscott, *University of Waterloo*
Carl Keane, *Queen's University*
Sean Lauer, *University of British Columbia*
Nikolaos Liodakis, *Wilfrid Laurier University*
William Marshall, *University of Western Ontario*
Brenda O'Neill, *University of Calgary*
Thomas Varghese, *University of Alberta*
Weiguo Zhang, *University of Toronto*

Maya Castle, Jessica Freedman, and Kamilah Reid Burrell at Nelson Education provided the utmost effort and dedication to this project, and

I am very thankful for their support. Finally I would like to thank my family: my wife, Deborah Prus, three wonderful children, Laura, Mandy, and Michael, and my parents, Gerry and Tina Prus. I dedicate this textbook to them.

We lastly acknowledge and are grateful to the Literary Executor of the late Sir Ronald A. Fisher, F.R.S., to Dr. Frank Yates, F.R.S., and to Longman Group Ltd., London, for permission to reprint Appendixes B, C, and D from their book *Statistical Tables for Biological, Agricultural and Medical Research* (6th ed., 1974). We are also grateful to the many people at Statistics Canada, namely Belia Velho, Judy Cotterill, Sandra McIntyre, and Marie-Josée Lalonde, for providing the General Social Survey and Census data sets used in this textbook.

Steven G. Prus

Prologue: Basic Mathematics Review

You will probably be relieved to hear that first courses in statistics are not particularly mathematical and do not stress computation per se. While you will encounter many numbers to work with and numerous formulas to use, the major emphasis will be on understanding the role of statistics in research and the logic by which we attempt to answer research questions empirically. You will also find that, at least in this textbook, the example problems and many of the homework problems have been intentionally simplified so that the computations will not unduly distract you from the task of understanding the statistics themselves.

On the other hand, you may regret to learn that there is, inevitably, some arithmetic that y ou simply cannot avoid if you want to master this material. It is likely that some of you haven't had any math in a long time, others have convinced themselves that they just cannot do math under any circumstances, and still others are just rusty and out of practice. All of you will find that even the most complex and intimidating operations and formulas can be broken down into simple steps. If you have forgotten how to cope with some of these steps or are unfamiliar with these operations, this appendix is designed to ease you into the skills you will need to do all of the computation in this textbook.

CALCULATORS AND COMPUTERS

A calculator is a virtual necessity for this textbook. While you could do all the arithmetic by hand, the calculator will save you time and effort and is definitely worth the small investment. Incidentally, you do not need to invest in any of the sophisticated, more expensive models you might see for sale. A square root function is the only extra feature you really need. Of course, if you want the additional features, such as memories and preprogrammed functions, by all means spend the extra money and learn how to use them. However, a simple, inexpensive calculator will work fine for all of the problems in this textbook.

Along the same lines, many of you probably have access to computers and statistical packages. If so, take the time now to learn how to use them, because they will eventually save you time and effort. This textbook includes a guide to a 1statistical package called SPSS (Statistical Package for the Social Sciences), but many other programs are available that will help you accomplish the goals of saving time and avoiding drudgery while generating precise and accurate results.

In summary, you should find a way at the beginning of this course—with a calculator, a statistical package, or both—to minimize the tedium and hassle of mere computing. This will permit you to devote maximum effort to the truly important goal of increasing your understanding of the meaning of statistics in particular and social research in general.

VARIABLES AND SYMBOLS

Statistics are a set of techniques by which we can describe, analyze, and manipulate variables. A variable is a trait that can change values from case to case or from time to time. Examples of variables would include height, weight, level of prejudice, and political party preference. The possible values associated with a given variable might be numerous (e.g., income) or relatively few (e.g., gender). We will often use symbols, usually the letter X, to refer to variables in general or to a specific variable.

Sometimes we will need to refer to a specific value or set of values of a variable. This is usually done with the aid of subscripts. So, the symbol X_1 (read "X-sub-one") would refer to the first score in a set of scores, X_2 ("X-sub-two") to the second score, and so forth. Also, we will use the subscript i to refer to all the scores in a set. Thus, the symbol X_i (read "X-sub-eye") refers to all of the scores associated with a given variable (e.g., the test grades of a particular class).

OPERATIONS

You are all familiar with the four basic mathematical operations of addition, subtraction, multiplication, and division and the standard symbols ($+$, $-$, $\times$, $\div$) used to denote them. Some of you may not be aware, however, that the latter two operations can be symbolized in a variety of ways. For example, the operation of multiplying some number a by some number b may be symbolized in (at least) six different ways:

$$a \times b$$
$$a \cdot b$$
$$a * b$$
$$ab$$
$$a(b)$$
$$(a)(b)$$

In this textbook, we will commonly use the "adjacent symbols" format (i.e., ab), the conventional times sign ($\times$), or adjacent parentheses to indicate multiplication. On most calculators and computers, the asterisk (*) is the symbol for multiplication.

The operation of division can also be expressed in several different ways. In this textbook, we will use either of these two methods:

$$a/b \quad \text{or} \quad \frac{a}{b}$$

Several of the formulas with which we will be working require us to find the square of a number. To do this, simply multiply the number by itself. This operation is symbolized as X^2 (read "X squared"), which is the same thing as $(X)(X)$. If X has a value of 4, then

$$X^2 = (X)(X) = (4)(4) = 16$$

or we could say that "4 squared is 16."

The square root of a number is the value that, when multiplied by itself, results in the original number. So the square root of 16 is 4 because (4)(4) is 16. The operation of finding the square root of a number is symbolized as

$$\sqrt{X}$$

Be sure that you have access to a calculator with a built-in square root function.

A final operation with which you should be familiar is summation, or the addition of the scores associated with a particular variable. When a formula requires the addition of a series of scores, this operation is usually symbolized as ΣX_i. The symbol Σ is the uppercase Greek letter sigma and stands for "the summation of." So the combination of symbols ΣX_i means "the summation of all the scores" and directs us to add the value of all the scores for that variable. If four people had family sizes of 2, 4, 5, and 7, then the summation of these four scores for this variable could be symbolized as

$$\Sigma X_i = 2 + 4 + 5 + 7 = 18$$

The symbol Σ is an operator, just like the $+$ or $\times$ signs. It directs us to add all of the scores on the variable indicated by the X symbol.

There are two other common uses of the summation sign and, unfortunately, the symbols denoting these uses are not, at first glance, sharply different from each other or from the symbol used above. A little practice and some careful attention to these various meanings should minimize the confusion. The first set of symbols is ΣX_i^2, which means "the sum of the squared scores." This quantity is found by *first* squaring each of the scores and *then* adding the squared scores together. A second common set of symbols will be $(\Sigma X_i)^2$, which means "the sum of the scores, squared." This quantity is found by *first* summing the scores and *then* squaring the total.

These distinctions might be confusing at first, so let's see if an example helps to clarify the situation. Suppose we had a set of three scores: 10, 12, and 13. So,

$$X_i = 10, 12, 13$$

The sum of these scores would be indicated as

$$\Sigma X_i = 10 + 12 + 13 = 35$$

The sum of the squared scores would be

$$\Sigma X_i^2 = (10)^2 + (12)^2 + (13)^2 = 100 + 144 + 169 = 413$$

Take careful note of the order of operations here. First, the scores are squared one at a time and then the squared scores are added. This is a completely different operation from squaring the sum of the scores:

$$\left(\Sigma X_i\right)^2 = (10 + 12 + 13)^2 = (35)^2 = 1{,}225$$

To find this quantity, first the scores are summed and then the total of all the scores is squared. The value of the sum of the scores squared (1,225) is not the same as the value of the sum of the squared scores (413). In summary, the operations associated with each set of symbols are:

Symbols	Operations
$\sum X_i$	Add the scores
$\sum X_i^2$	First square the scores and then add the squared scores
$(\sum X_i)^2$	First add the scores and then square the total

OPERATIONS WITH NEGATIVE NUMBERS

A number can be either positive (if it is preceded by a $+$ sign or by no sign at all) or negative (if it is preceded by a $-$ sign). Positive numbers are greater than zero, and negative numbers are less than zero. It is very important to keep track of signs because they will affect the outcome of virtually every mathematical operation. This section will briefly summarize the relevant rules for dealing with negative numbers. First, adding a negative number is the same as subtraction. For example,

$$3 + (-1) = 3 - 1 = 2$$

Second, subtraction changes the sign of a negative number:

$$3 - (-1) = 3 + 1 = 4$$

Note the importance of keeping track of signs here. If you neglected to change the sign of the negative number in the second expression, you would arrive at the wrong answer.

For multiplication and division, there are various combinations of negative and positive numbers you should be aware of. For purposes of this textbook, you will rarely have to multiply or divide more than two numbers at a time, and we will confine our attention to this situation. Ignoring the case of all positive numbers, this leaves several possible combinations. A negative number times a positive number results in a negative value:

$$(-3)(4) = -12$$

or

$$(3)(-4) = -12$$

A negative number times a negative number is always positive:

$$(-3)(-4) = 12$$

Division follows the same patterns. If there is a single negative number in the calculations, the answer will be negative. If both numbers are negative, the answer will be positive. So,

$$(-4)/(2) = -2$$

and

$$(4)/(-2) = -2$$

but

$$(-4)/(-2) = 2$$

Note that negative numbers do not have square roots, because multiplying a number by itself cannot result in a negative value. Squaring a negative number always results in a positive value (see the multiplication rules above).

ACCURACY AND ROUNDING OFF

A possible source of confusion in computation involves the issues of accuracy and rounding off. People work at different levels of accuracy and precision and, for this reason alone, may arrive at different answers to problems. This is important because, if you works at one level of precision and the textbook (or your instructor or your study partner) works at another, the resulting solutions will be at least slightly different. You may sometimes think you've gotten the wrong answer when all you've really done is round off at a different place in the calculations or in a different way.

There are two issues here: when to round off and how to round off. In this textbook, we have followed the convention of working in as much accuracy as our calculator or statistics package will allow and then rounding off to two places of accuracy (two places beyond the decimal point) at the very end. If a set of calculations is lengthy and requires the reporting of intermediate sums or subtotals, we will round the subtotals off to two places also.

In terms of how to round off, begin by looking at the digit immediately to the right of the last digit you want to retain. If you want to round off to 100ths (two places beyond the decimal point), look at the digit in the 1000ths place (three places beyond the decimal point). If that digit is greater than 5, round up. For example, 23.346 would round off to 23.35. If the digit to the right is less than 5, round down. So, 23.343 would become 23.34. If the digit to the right is 5, round up if the digit immediately to the left is even and round down if the digit is odd. So, 23.345 would become 23.35 and 23.355 would round to 23.35.

Let's look at some more examples of how to follow the rounding rules stated above. If you are calculating the mean value of a set of test scores and your calculator shows a final value of 83.459067, and you want to round off to two places beyond the decimal point, look at the digit three places beyond the decimal point. In this case the value is 9 (greater than 5), so we would round the second digit beyond the decimal point up and report the mean as 83.46. If the value had been 83.453067, we would have reported our final answer as 83.45. A value of 83.455067 would round to 83.45, and a value of 83.445067 would be 83.45.

FORMULAS, COMPLEX OPERATIONS, AND THE ORDER OF OPERATIONS

A mathematical formula is a set of directions, stated in general symbols, for calculating a particular statistic. To "solve a formula" means that you must replace the symbols with the proper values and then manipulate the values through a series of calculations. Even the most complex formula can be rendered manageable if it is broken down into smaller steps. Working through these steps requires some knowledge of general procedure and the rules of precedence of mathematical operations. This is because the order in which you perform calculations may affect your final answer. Consider the following expression:

$$2 + 3(4)$$

Note that if you do the addition first, you will evaluate the expression as

$$5(4) = 20$$

but if you do the multiplication first, the expression becomes

$$2 + 12 = 14$$

Obviously, it is crucial to complete the steps of a calculation in the correct order.

The basic rules of precedence are to find all squares and square roots first, then do all multiplication and division, and finally complete all addition and subtraction. So the following expression:

$$8 + 2 \times 2^2/2$$

would be evaluated as

$$8 + 2 \times 4/2 = 8 + 8/2 = 8 + 4 = 12$$

The rules of precedence may be overridden when an expression contains parentheses. Solve all expressions within parentheses before applying the rules stated above. For most of the complex formulas in this textbook, the order of calculations will be controlled by the parentheses. Consider the following expression:

$$(8 + 2) - 4(3)^2/(8 - 6)$$

Resolving the parenthetical expressions first, we would have

$$(10) - 4 \times 9/(2) = 10 - 36/2 = 10 - 18 = -8$$

Without the parentheses, the same expression would be evaluated as

$$8 + 2 - 4 \times 3^2/8 - 6$$
$$= 8 + 2 - 4 \times 9/8 - 6$$
$$= 8 + 2 - 36/8 - 6$$
$$= 8 + 2 - 4.5 - 6$$
$$= 10 - 10.5$$
$$= -.5$$

A final operation you will encounter in some formulas in this textbook involves denominators of fractions that themselves contain fractions. In this situation, solve the fraction in the denominator first and then complete the division. For example,

$$15 - 9/6/2$$

would become

$$15 - 9/3 = 6/3 = 2$$

When you are confronted with complex expressions such as these, don't be intimidated. If you're patient with yourself and work through them step by step, beginning with the parenthetical expression, even the most imposing formulas can be managed.

EXERCISES

You can use the problems below as a "self-test" on the material presented in this review. If you can handle these problems, you're ready to do all of the arithmetic in this textbook. If you have difficulty with any of these problems, please review the appropriate section of this prologue. You might also want to use this section as an opportunity to become more familiar with your calculator. Answers are given on the next page, along with some commentary and some reminders.

1. Complete each of the following:
   a. $17 \times 3 =$
   b. $17(3) =$
   c. $(17)(3) =$
   d. $17/3 =$
   e. $(42)^2 =$
   f. $\sqrt{113} =$

2. For the set of scores (X_i) of 50, 55, 60, 65, and 70, evaluate each of the expressions below:
   $\sum X_i =$
   $\sum X_i^2 =$
   $\sum (X_i)^2 =$

3. Complete each of the following:
   a. $17 + (-3) + (4) + (-2) =$
   b. $15 - 3 - (-5) + 2 =$
   c. $(-27)(54) =$
   d. $(113)(-2) =$
   e. $(-14)(-100) =$
   f. $-34/-2 =$
   g. $322/-11 =$

4. Round off each of the following to two places beyond the decimal point:
   a. 17.17532
   b. 43.119
   c. 1,076.77337
   d. 32.4651152301
   e. 32.4751152301

5. Evaluate each of the following:
   a. $(3 + 7)/10 =$
   b. $3 + 7/10 =$
   c. $((4 - 3) + (7 + 2))/((4 + 5)(10)) =$

ANSWERS TO EXERCISES

1. a. 51   **b.** 51   **c.** 51
(The obvious purpose of these first three problems is to remind you that there are several different ways of expressing multiplication.)
d. 5.67 (Note the rounding off.)   **e.** 1,764   **f.** 10.63

2. The first expression translates to "the sum of the scores," so this operation would be

$$\sum X_i = 50 + 55 + 60 + 65 + 70 = 300$$

The second expression is the "sum of the squared scores." So

$$\sum X_i^2 = (50)^2 + (55)^2 + (60)^2 + (65)^2 + (70)^2$$

$$\sum X_i^2 = 2,500 + 3,025 + 3,600 + 4,225 + 4,900$$

$$\sum X_i^2 = 18,250$$

The third expression is "the sum of the scores, squared":

$$\left(\sum X_i\right)^2 = (50 + 55 + 60 + 65 + 70)^2$$

$$\left(\sum X_i\right)^2 = (300)^2$$

$$\left(\sum X_i\right)^2 = 90,000$$

Remember that $\sum X_i^2$ and $(\sum X_i)^2$ are two completely different expressions with very different values.

3. a. 16   **b.** 19 (Remember to change the sign of -5.)   **c.** $-1,458$
   d. -226 **e.** 1,400   **f.** 17   **g.** -29.27

4. a. 17.17   **b.** 43.12   **c.** 1,076.77
   d. 32.47   **e.** 32.47

5. a. 1   **b.** 3.7 (Note again the importance of parentheses.)   **c.** 0.11

1 Introduction

1.1 WHY STUDY STATISTICS?

Students sometimes approach their first course in statistics with questions about the value of the subject matter. What, after all, do numbers and statistics have to do with understanding people and society? In a sense, this entire textbook will attempt to answer this question, and the value of statistics will become clear as we move from chapter to chapter. For now, the importance of statistics can be demonstrated, in a preliminary way, by briefly reviewing the research process as it operates in the social sciences. These disciplines are scientific in the sense that social scientists attempt to verify their ideas and theories through research. Broadly conceived, **research** is any process by which information is systematically and carefully gathered for the purpose of answering questions, examining ideas, or testing theories. Research is a disciplined inquiry that can take numerous forms. Statistical analysis is relevant only for those research projects where the information collected is represented by numbers. Numerical information is called **data**, and the sole purpose of statistics is to manipulate and analyze data. **Statistics**, then, are a set of mathematical techniques used by social scientists to organize and manipulate data for the purpose of answering questions and testing theories.

What is so important about learning how to manipulate data? On one hand, some of the most important and enlightening works in the social sciences do not utilize any statistical techniques. There is nothing magical about data and statistics. The mere presence of numbers guarantees nothing about the quality of a scientific inquiry. On the other hand, data can be the most trustworthy information available to the researcher and, consequently, deserve special attention. Data that have been carefully collected and thoughtfully analyzed are the strongest, most objective foundations for building theory and enhancing understanding. Without a firm base in data, the social sciences would lose the right to the name *science* and would be of far less value.

Thus, the social sciences rely heavily on data analysis for the advancement of knowledge. Let us be very clear about one point: it is never enough merely to gather data (or, for that matter, any kind of information). Even the most objective and carefully collected numerical information does not and cannot speak for itself. The researcher must be able to use statistics effectively to organize, evaluate, and analyze the data. Without a good understanding of the principles of statistical analysis, the researcher will be unable to make sense of the data. Without the appropriate application of statistical techniques, the data will remain mute and useless.

Statistics are an indispensable tool for the social sciences. They provide the scientist with some of the most useful techniques for evaluating ideas, testing theory, and discovering the truth. The next section describes the relationships among theory, research, and statistics in more detail.

1.2 THE ROLE OF STATISTICS IN SCIENTIFIC INQUIRY

Figure 1.1 graphically represents the role of statistics in the research process. The diagram is based on the thinking of Walter Wallace and illustrates how the knowledge base of any scientific enterprise grows and develops. One point the diagram makes is that scientific theory and research continually shape each other. Statistics are one of the most important means by which research and theory interact. Let's take a closer look at the wheel.

Because the figure is circular, it has no beginning or end, and we could begin our discussion at any point. For the sake of convenience, let's begin at the top and follow the arrows around the circle. A **theory** is an explanation of the relationships between phenomena. People naturally (and endlessly) wonder about problems in society (like prejudice, poverty, child abuse, or serial murders), and in their attempt to understand these phenomena, they develop explanations ("lack of education causes prejudice"). This kind of informal "theorizing" about society is no doubt very familiar to you. One major difference between our informal, everyday explanations of social phenomena and

FIGURE 1.1   THE WHEEL OF SCIENCE

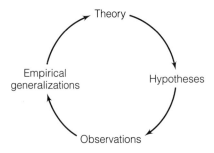

Source: Adapted from Walter Wallace, *The Logic of Science in Sociology.* Copyright © 1971 by Transactions Publishers. Reprinted by permission of the publisher.

scientific theory is that the latter is subject to a rigorous testing process. Let's take the problem of health inequality as an example to illustrate how the research process works.

Why do people differ in their health? One possible answer to this question is provided by the *materialistic theory*. This theory was stated over 25 years ago in the groundbreaking *Black Report*, named after the physician Sir Douglas Black, on health inequalities in the United Kingdom.* It has been tested on a number of occasions since that time.

According to the materialistic theory, health is affected by social class. We often think that it is the individual who chooses whether to have a healthy diet, participate in leisure-time exercise, protect one's own health and prevent illness (e.g., annual physical, flu shot), and so on. The materialist theory asserts that such "individual choices" are constrained by one's social class. Social class is linked to health by one's access to items such as nutritional foods; health care; preventative health care information and services; and safe housing, living, and working conditions that are necessary to maintain and improve health.

The materialistic theory is not a complete explanation of health inequality, but it can serve to illustrate a sociological theory. This theory offers an explanation for the relationship between two social phenomena: (1) health inequality and (2) social class. People who have lower social class will have poorer health, and those with higher social class will have better health.

Before moving on, let us examine theory in a little more detail. The materialistic theory, like most theories, is stated in terms of causal relationships between variables. A **variable** is any trait that can change values from case to case. Examples of variables would be gender, age, ethnicity, or political party affiliation. In any specific theory, some variables will be identified as causes and others will be identified as effects or results. In the language of science, the causes are called **independent variables** and the effects or result variables are called **dependent variables**. In our theory, social class is the independent variable (or the cause) and health is the dependent variable (the result or effect). In other words, we are arguing that social class is a cause of health condition or that an individual's level of health depends on his/her social class.

So far, we have a theory of health, and an independent and a dependent variable. What we do not know yet is whether the theory is true or false. To find out, we need to compare our theory with the facts—we need to do some research. The next step in the process would be to define our terms and ideas more specifically and exactly. One problem we often face in conducting research is that scientific theories are too complex and

---

*Source: Townsend, P. and Davidson, N. (eds). 1982. *Inequalities in Health: The Black Report*. Harmondsworth, UK: Penguin Books.

abstract to be fully tested in a single research project. To conduct research, one or more hypotheses must be derived from the theory. A **hypothesis** is a statement about the relationship between variables that, while logically derived from the theory, is much more specific and exact.

For example, if we wish to test the materialistic theory, we have to say exactly what we mean by social class and health. There has been a great deal of research on the effect of social class on health, and we would consult the research literature to develop and clarify our definitions of these concepts. As our definitions develop and the hypothesis takes shape, we begin the next step of the research process during which we will decide exactly how we will gather our data. We must decide how cases will be selected and tested, and how the variables will be measured. Ultimately, these plans will lead to the observation phase (the bottom of the wheel of science), where we actually measure social reality. Before we can do this, however, we must have a very clear idea of what we are looking for and a well-defined strategy for conducting the search.

To test the materialistic theory, we would begin by considering people from all sections of society (rich, poor, healthy, unhealthy, and so on). Then, we need to decide what our measures of social class and health status are. In other words, we need to operationalize the concepts of social class and health status. For example, we may decide to use those measures used in the *Black Report*: occupation and chronic illness as measures of social class and health respectively. We would then administer a survey that asked each person, "What is your current main occupation?" and "How many long-term or chronic medical conditions diagnosed by a health professional do you have?" Our goal would be to see whether people with higher occupational status have fewer chronic illnesses.

Now, finally, we come to statistics. As the observation phase of our research project comes to an end, we will be confronted with a large collection of numerical information or data. If our sample consisted of 2,000 people, we would have 2,000 completed surveys measuring social class and health. Try to imagine dealing with 2,000 completed surveys. If we had asked each respondent five questions about their health, instead of just one question, we would have a total of 10,000 separate pieces of information to deal with. What do we do? We need to have some systematic way to organize and analyze this information; at this point, statistics will be very valuable. Statistics will provide us many ideas about "what to do" with the data, and we will begin to look at some of the options in Chapter 2. For now, let us stress two points about statistics.

First, statistics are crucial. Simply put, without statistics, quantitative research is impossible. Without quantitative research, the development of the social sciences would be severely impaired. Only by the application of statistical techniques can mere data help us shape and refine our theories and understand the social world better. Second, and somewhat paradoxically, the role of statistics is rather limited. As Figure 1.1 makes clear, scientific research proceeds through several mutually interdependent stages, and statistics become directly relevant only at the end of the observation stage. Before any statistical analysis can be legitimately applied, the preceding phases of the process must have been successfully completed. If the researcher has asked poorly conceived questions or has made serious errors of design or method, then even the most sophisticated statistical analysis is valueless. As useful as they can be, statistics cannot substitute for rigorous conceptualization, detailed and careful planning, or creative use of theory. Statistics cannot salvage a poorly conceived or designed research project. They cannot make sense out of garbage.

Conversely, inappropriate statistical applications can limit the usefulness of an otherwise carefully done project. Only by successfully completing *all* phases of the process can a quantitative research project hope to contribute to understanding. A reasonable knowledge of the uses and limitations of statistics is as essential to the education of the social scientist as is training in theory and methodology.

As the statistical analysis comes to an end, we would begin to develop empirical generalizations. While we would be primarily focused on assessing our theory, we would also look for other trends in the data. Assuming that we found that social class was linked to health in general, we might go on to ask if the pattern applies to males as well as females or to older respondents as well as younger. As we probed the data, we might begin to develop some generalizations based on the empirical patterns we observe. For example, what if we found that social class was linked to health for older respondents but not for younger respondents? Could it be that material advantages and disadvantages have an accumulative effect on health, and thus the social class-health link does not emerge until old age? As we developed tentative explanations, we would begin to revise or elaborate our theory.

If we change the theory to take account of these findings, however, a new research project designed to test the revised theory is called for and the wheel of science would begin to turn again. We (or perhaps some other researchers) would go through the entire process once again with this new—and, hopefully, improved—theory. This second project might result in further revisions and elaboration that would (you guessed it) require still more research projects, and the wheel of science would continue turning as long as scientists were able to suggest additional revisions or develop new insights. Every time the wheel turned, our understandings of the phenomena under consideration would (hopefully) improve.

This description of the research process does not include white-coated, clipboard-carrying scientists who, in a blinding flash of inspiration, discover some fundamental truth about reality and shout, "Eureka!" The truth is that, in the normal course of science, it is a rare occasion when we can say with absolute certainty that a given theory or idea is definitely true or false. Rather, evidence for (or against) a theory will gradually accumulate over time, and ultimate judgments of truth will likely be the result of many years of hard work, research, and debate.

Let's briefly review our imaginary research project. We began with an idea or theory about social class and health. We imagined some of the steps we would have to take to test the theory and took a quick look at the various stages of the research project. We wound up back at the level of theory, ready to begin a new project guided by a revised theory. We saw how theory can motivate a research project and how our observations might cause us to revise the theory and, thus, motivate a new research project. Wallace's wheel of science illustrates how theory stimulates research and how research shapes theory. This constant interaction between theory and research is the lifeblood of science and the key to enhancing our understandings of the social world.

The dialogue between theory and research occurs at many levels and in multiple forms. Statistics are one of the most important links between these two realms. Statistics permit us to analyze data, to identify and probe trends and relationships, to develop generalizations, and to revise and improve our theories. As you will see throughout this textbook, statistics are limited in many ways. They are also an indispensable part of the research enterprise. Without statistics, the interaction between theory and research would become extremely difficult, and the progress of our disciplines would be severely retarded. *(For practice in describing the relationship between theory and research and the role of statistics in research, see problems 1.1 and 1.2.)*

1.3 THE GOALS OF THIS TEXTBOOK

In the preceding section, we argued that statistics are a crucial part of the process by which scientific investigations are carried out and that, therefore, some training in statistical analysis is a crucial component in the education of every social scientist. In this section, we will address the questions of how much training is necessary and what the purposes of that training are. First, this textbook takes the point of view that statistics are tools. They can be a very useful means of increasing our knowledge of the social world, but they are not ends in themselves. Thus, we will not take a "mathematical" approach to the subject. The techniques will be presented as a set of tools that can be used to answer important questions. This emphasis does not mean that we will dispense with arithmetic entirely, of course. This textbook includes enough mathematical material to help you develop a basic understanding of why statistics "do what they do." Our focus, however, will be on how these techniques are applied in the social sciences.

Second, all of you will soon become involved in advanced coursework in your major fields of study, and you will find that much of the literature used in these courses assumes at least basic statistical literacy. Furthermore, many of you, after graduation, will find yourselves in positions—either in a career or in graduate school—where some understanding of statistics will be very helpful or perhaps even required. Very few of you will become statisticians per se (and this textbook is not intended for the preprofessional statistician), but you must have a grasp of statistics in order to read and critically appreciate your own professional literature. As a student in the social sciences and in many careers related to the social sciences, you simply cannot realize your full potential without a background in statistics.

Within these constraints, this textbook is an introduction to statistics as they are utilized in the social sciences. The general goal of the textbook is to develop an appreciation—a "healthy respect"—for statistics and their place in the research process. You should emerge from this experience with the ability to use statistics intelligently and to know when other people have done so. You should be familiar with the advantages and limitations of the more commonly used statistical techniques, and you should know which techniques are appropriate for a given set of data and a given purpose. Lastly, you should develop sufficient statistical and computational skills and enough experience in the interpretation of statistics to be able to carry out some elementary forms of data analysis by yourself.

1.4 DESCRIPTIVE AND INFERENTIAL STATISTICS

As noted earlier, the general function of statistics is to manipulate data so that research questions can be answered. There are two general classes of statistical techniques that, depending on the research situation, are available to accomplish this task, and each is introduced in this section.

Descriptive Statistics.   The first class of techniques is called **descriptive statistics** and is relevant in several different situations:

1. When the researcher needs to summarize or describe the distribution of a single variable. These statistics are called *univariate* ("one variable") descriptive statistics.
2. When the researcher wishes to describe the relationship between two or more variables. These statistics are called *bivariate* ("two variable") or *multivariate* (more than two variables) descriptive statistics.

To describe a single variable, we would arrange the values or scores of that variable so that the relevant information can be quickly understood and appreciated. Many of the statistics that might be appropriate for this summarizing task are probably familiar to you. For example, percentages, graphs, and charts can all be used to describe single variables.

To illustrate the usefulness of univariate descriptive statistics, consider the following problem: Suppose you wanted to summarize the distribution of the variable "family income" for a community of 10,000 families. How would you do it? Obviously, you couldn't simply list all incomes in the community and let it go at that. Imagine trying to make sense of a list of 10,000 different incomes! Presumably, you would want to develop some summary measures of the overall income distributions—perhaps an arithmetic average or the proportions of incomes that fall in various ranges (such as low, middle, and high). Or perhaps a graph or a chart would be more useful. Whatever specific method you choose, its function is the same: to reduce these thousands of individual items of information into a few easily understood numbers. The process of allowing a few numbers to summarize many numbers is called **data reduction** and is the basic goal of univariate descriptive statistical procedures. Part I of this textbook is devoted to these statistics, which allow you to report, clearly and concisely, essential information about a variable.

The second type of descriptive statistics is designed to help the investigator understand the relationship between two or more variables. These statistics, called **measures of association**, allow the researcher to quantify the strength and direction of a relationship. These statistics are very useful because they enable us to investigate two matters of central theoretical and practical importance to any science: causation and prediction. These techniques help us disentangle and uncover the connections between variables. They help us trace the ways in which some variables might have causal influences on others; and, depending on the strength of the relationship, they enable us to predict scores on one variable from the scores on another. Note that measures of association cannot, by themselves, prove that two variables are causally related. However, these techniques can provide valuable clues about causation and are therefore extremely important for theory testing and theory construction.

For example, suppose you were interested in the relationship between "time spent studying statistics" and "final grade in statistics" and had gathered data on these two variables from a group of university students. By calculating the appropriate measure of association, you could determine the strength of the bivariate relationship and its direction. Suppose you found a strong, positive relationship. This would indicate that "study time" and "grade" were closely related (strength of the relationship) and that as one increased in value, the other also increased (direction of the relationship). You could make predictions from one variable to the other ("the longer the study time, the higher the grade").

As a result of finding this strong, positive relationship, you might be tempted to make causal inferences. That is, you might jump to such conclusions as "longer study time leads to (causes) higher grades." Such a conclusion might make a good deal of common sense and would certainly be supported by your statistical analysis. However, the causal nature of the relationship cannot be proven by the statistical analysis. Measures of association can be taken as important clues about causation, but the mere existence of a relationship can never be taken as conclusive proof of causation.

In fact, other variables might have an effect on the relationship. In the example above, we probably would not find a perfect relationship between "study time" and "final grade." That is, we will probably find some individuals who spend a great deal of time studying but receive low grades and some individuals who fit the opposite pattern. We know intuitively that other variables besides study time affect grades (such as efficiency of study techniques, amount of background in mathematics, and even random chance). Fortunately, researchers can incorporate these other variables into the analysis and measure their effects. Part III of this textbook is devoted to bivariate (two-variable) and Part IV to multivariate (more than two variables) descriptive statistics.

Inferential Statistics. This second class of statistical techniques becomes relevant when we wish to generalize our findings from a **sample** to a **population**. A population is the total collection of all cases that the researcher is interested in and wishes to understand better. Examples of possible populations would be all eligible voters in Canada, unemployed youth in the greater Toronto area, or students enrolled at the University of British Columbia.

Populations can theoretically range from inconceivable in size ("all humanity") to quite small (all professional hockey players residing in the city of Ottawa) but are usually fairly large. In fact, they are almost always too large to be measured. To put the problem another way, social scientists almost never have the resources or time to test every case in a population. Hence the need for **inferential statistics**, which involve using information from a sample (a carefully chosen subset of the population) to make inferences about a population. Because they have fewer cases, samples are much cheaper to assemble, and—if the proper techniques are followed—generalizations based on these samples can be very accurate representations of the population.

Many of the concepts and procedures involved in inferential statistics may be unfamiliar. However, most of us are experienced consumers of inferential statistics—most familiarly, perhaps, in the form of public-opinion polls and election projections. When a public-opinion poll reports that 36 percent of the Canadian electorate plans to vote for a certain political party, it is essentially reporting a generalization to a population (the "Canadian electorate," which numbers about 23 million people) from a carefully drawn sample (usually about 1,500 respondents). Matters of inferential statistics will occupy our attention in Part II of this textbook. *(For practice in describing different statistical applications, see problems 1.3 and 1.7.)*

1.5 DISCRETE AND CONTINUOUS VARIABLES

In Chapter 2, you will begin to encounter some of the broad array of statistics available to the social scientist. One aspect of using statistics that can be puzzling is deciding when to use which statistic. You will learn specific guidelines as you go along, but we will introduce some basic and general guidelines at this point. The first of these concerns discrete and continuous variables; the second, covered in the next section, concerns level of measurement.

A variable is said to be **discrete** if it has a basic unit of measurement that cannot be subdivided. For example, number of people per household is a discrete variable. The basic unit is people, a variable that will always be measured in whole numbers: you'll never find 2.7 people living in a specific household. The scores for a discrete variable will be zero, one, two, three, or some other whole integer. Other discrete variables include number of siblings, children, or cars. To measure these variables, we count the number of units for each case and record results in whole numbers.

A variable is **continuous** if the measurement of it can be subdivided infinitely—at least in a theoretical sense. One example of a continuous variable would be time, which can be measured in minutes, seconds, milliseconds (thousandths of a second), nanoseconds (billionths of a second), or even smaller units. In a sense, when we measure a continuous variable, we are always approximating and rounding off the scores. We could report somebody's time in the 100-metre dash as 10.7 seconds or 10.732451 seconds, but, because time can be infinitely subdivided (if we have the technology to make the precise measurements), we will never be able to report the exact time elapsed. Since we cannot work with infinitely long numbers, we must report the scores on continuous variables as if they were discrete.

The distinction between these two types of variables relates more to measuring and processing the information than to the appearance of the data. This distinction between discrete and continuous variables is one of the most basic in statistics and will constitute one of the criteria by which we will choose among various statistics and graphic devices. *(For practice in distinguishing between discrete and continuous variables, see problems 1.4–1.8.)*

1.6 LEVEL OF MEASUREMENT

A second basic and very important guideline for the selection of statistics is the **level of measurement** or the mathematical nature of the variables under consideration. Variables at the highest level of measurement have numerical scores and can be analyzed with a broad range of statistics. Variables at lower levels of measurement have "scores" that are really just labels, not numbers at all. Statistics that require numerical variables are inappropriate, and often completely meaningless, when used with non-numerical variables. When selecting statistics, you must be sure that the level of measurement of the variable justifies the mathematical operations required to compute the statistic.

For example, consider the variables age (measured in years) and income (measured in dollars). Both these variables have numerical scores and could be summarized with a statistic such as the mean or average (e.g., "The average income of this city is $43,000." "The average age of students on this campus is 19.7.").

However, the mean or average would be meaningless as a way of describing gender or area codes, which are variables with non-numerical scores. Your personal area code might *look* like a number but it is merely an arbitrary label that happens to be expressed in digits. These "numbers" cannot be added or divided and statistics like the average cannot be applied to this variable: the average area code of a group of people is a meaningless statistic.

Determining the level at which a variable has been measured is one of the first steps in any statistical analysis, and we will consider this matter at some length. We will make it a practice throughout this textbook to introduce level-of-measurement considerations for each statistical technique.

The three levels of measurement, in order of increasing sophistication, are nominal, ordinal, and interval-ratio. Each is discussed separately.

The Nominal Level of Measurement.   Variables measured at the nominal level have "scores" or categories that are not numerical. Examples of variables at this level include gender, area code, province of residence, religious affiliation, and place of birth. At this lowest level of measurement, the only mathematical operation permitted is comparing the relative sizes of the categories (e.g., "there are more females than males in this residence"). The categories or scores of nominal-level variables cannot be ranked with respect to each other and cannot be added, divided, or otherwise manipulated mathematically. Even when the scores or categories are expressed in digits (like area codes or street addresses), all we can do is compare relative sizes of categories (e.g., "the most common area code on this campus is 221"). The categories themselves are not a mathematical scale: they are different from each other but not more or less, or higher or lower than each other. Males and females differ in terms of gender but neither category has more or less gender than the other. In the same way, an area code of 621 is different from but not "more than" an area code of 221.

Although nominal variables are rudimentary, we need to observe certain criteria and procedures in order to assure adequate measurement. In fact, these criteria apply to variables measured at all levels, not just nominal variables. First, the categories of nominal-level variables must be mutually exclusive so that no ambiguity exists concerning classification of any given case. There must be one and only one category for each case. Second, the categories must be exhaustive: a category must exist for every possible score that might be found, even if it is only an "other" or miscellaneous category.

Third, the categories of nominal variables should be relatively homogeneous, that is, our categories should include cases that are comparable. To put it another way, we need to avoid categories that lump apples with oranges. There are no hard and fast guidelines for judging if a set of categories is appropriately homogeneous. The researcher must make that decision in terms of the specific purpose of the research. Categories that are too broad for some purposes may be perfectly adequate for others.

Table 1.1 demonstrates some errors of measurement in four different schemes for measuring the variable "religious affiliation." Scale A in the table violates the criterion of mutual exclusivity because of the overlap between the categories Catholic and Christian and Protestant and Christian. Scale B is not exhaustive because it does not provide a category for people who belong to religions other than the eight listed or for people with no religious affiliation (None). Scale C uses a category (Non-Catholic) that would be too broad for many research purposes. Scale D represents the way religious affiliation is often measured in Canada, but note that these categories may be too general for some research projects and not comprehensive enough for others. For example, an investigation of issues that have strong moral and religious content (assisted suicide, abortion, or capital punishment, for example) might need to distinguish between the various Protestant denominations (e.g., United Church, Presbyterian, Lutheran, Anglican, Baptist, Jehovah's Witnesses, Pentecostal, Mormons), and an effort to document religious diversity would need to add categories for other Eastern or Christian religions (e.g., Bahai, Greek Orthodox). Likewise, Scale D does not capture the variety within Islam, Judaism, and other non-Christian religions.

Numerical labels are often used to identify the categories of variables measured at the nominal level. This practice is especially common when the data are being prepared for computer analysis. For example, the various religions might be labelled with a 1 indicating Protestant, a 2 signifying Catholic. Remember that these numbers are merely labels or names and have no numerical quality to them. They cannot be added, subtracted,

TABLE 1.1   FOUR SCALES FOR MEASURING RELIGIOUS AFFILIATION

Scale A (not mutually exclusive)	Scale B (not exhaustive)	Scale C (not homogeneous)	Scale D (an adequate scale)
Catholic	Catholic	Catholic	Catholic
Protestant	Protestant	Non-Catholic	Protestant
Christian	Other Christian		Other Christian
Jewish	Jewish		Jewish
Muslim	Muslim		Muslim
Buddhist	Buddhist		Buddhist
Hindu	Hindu		Hindu
Sikh	Sikh		Sikh
Other religions			Other religions
None			None

multiplied, or divided. The only mathematical operation permissible with nominal variables is counting and comparing the number of cases in each category of the variable.

The Ordinal Level of Measurement.   Variables measured at the ordinal level are more sophisticated than nominal-level variables. They have scores or categories that can be ranked from high to low so that, in addition to classifying cases into categories, we can describe the categories in terms of "more or less" with respect to each other. Thus, with variables measured at this level, not only can we say that one case is different from another; we can also say that one case is higher or lower, more or less, than another.

For example, the variable socio-economic status (SES) is usually measured at the ordinal level. The categories of the variable are often ordered according to the following scheme:

4. Upper class
3. Middle class
2. Working class
1. Lower class

Individual cases can be compared in terms of the categories into which they are classified. Thus, an individual classified as a 4 (upper class) would be ranked higher than an individual classified as a 2 (working class) and a lower-class person (1) would rank lower than a middle-class person (3). Other variables that are usually measured at the ordinal level include attitude and opinion scales such as those that measure prejudice, alienation, or political conservatism.

The major limitation of the ordinal level of measurement is that a particular score represents only position with respect to some other score. We can distinguish between high and low scores, but the distance between the scores cannot be described in precise terms. Although we know that a score of 4 is more than a score of 2, we do not know if it is twice as much as 2.

Because we don't know the exact distances from score to score on an ordinal scale, our options for statistical analysis are limited. For example, addition (and most other mathematical operations) assumes that the intervals between scores are exactly equal. If the distances from score to score are not equal, 2 + 2 might equal 3 or 5 or even 15. Thus, strictly speaking, statistics such as the average or mean (which requires that the scores be added together and then divided by the number of scores) are not permitted with ordinal-level variables. The most sophisticated mathematical operation fully justified with an ordinal variable is the ranking of categories and cases (although, as we will see, it is not unusual for social scientists to take some liberties with this strict criterion).

READING STATISTICS 1: Introduction

By this point in your education you have developed an impressive array of skills for reading words. Although you may sometimes struggle with a difficult idea or stumble over an obscure meaning, you can comprehend virtually any written work that you are likely to encounter.

As you continue your education in the social sciences, you must develop an analogous set of skills for reading numbers and statistics. To help you reach a reasonable level of literacy in statistics, we have included a series of boxed inserts in this textbook labelled "Reading Statistics." These will appear in most chapters and will discuss how statistical results are typically presented in the professional literature. Each installment will include an extract or quotation from the professional literature so that we can analyze a realistic example.

As you will see, professional researchers use a reporting style that is quite different from the statistical language you will find in this textbook. Space in research journals and other media is expensive, and the typical research project requires the analysis of many variables. Thus, a large volume of information must be summarized in very few words. Researchers may express in a word or two a result or an interpretation that will take us a paragraph or more to state.

Because this is an introductory textbook, we have been careful to break down the computation and logic of each statistic and to identify, even to the point of redundancy, what we are doing when we use statistics. In this textbook we will never be concerned with more than a few variables at a time. We will have the luxury of analysis in detail and of being able to take pages or even entire chapters to develop a statistical idea or analyze a variable. Thus, a major theme of these boxed inserts will be to summarize how our comparatively long-winded (but more careful) vocabulary is translated into the concise language of the professional researcher.

When you have difficulty reading words, your tendency is (or, at least, should be) to consult reference books (especially dictionaries) to help you identify and analyze the elements (words) of the passage. When you have difficulty reading statistics, you should do exactly the same thing. We hope you will find this textbook a valuable reference book, but if you learn enough from this textbook to be able to use any source to help you read statistics, this textbook will have fulfilled one of its major goals.

The Interval-Ratio Level of Measurement.[*]   The categories of nominal-level variables have no numerical quality to them. Ordinal-level variables have categories that can be arrayed along a scale from high to low, but the exact distances between categories or scores are undefined. Variables measured at the interval-ratio level not only permit classification and ranking but also allow the distance from category to category (or score to score) to be exactly defined.

Interval-ratio variables have two characteristics. First, they are measured in units that have equal intervals. For example, asking people how old they are will produce an interval-ratio level variable (age) because the unit of

---

[*]Many statisticians distinguish between the interval level (equal intervals) and the ratio level (true zero point). We find the distinction unnecessarily cumbersome in an introductory textbook, and since most statistical analysis that is appropriate for interval variables is also appropriate for ratio variables we will treat these two levels as one.

TABLE 1.2 BASIC CHARACTERISTICS OF THE THREE LEVELS OF MEASUREMENT

Levels	Examples	Measurement Procedures	Mathematical Operations Permitted
Nominal	Sex, race, religion, marital status	Classification into categories	Counting number of cases in each category of the variable; comparing sizes of categories
Ordinal	Social class (SES), attitude and opinion scales	Classification into categories plus ranking of categories with respect to each other	All operations above plus judgments of " greater than" and "less than"
Interval Ratio	Age, number of children, income	All above plus description of distances between scores in terms of equal units	All above plus all other mathematical operations (addition, subtraction, multiplication, division, square roots, etc.)

measurement (years) has equal intervals (the distance from year to year is 365 days). Similarly, if we ask people how many siblings they have, we would produce a variable with equal intervals: two siblings are one more than one and thirteen is one more than twelve.

The second characteristic of interval-ratio variables is that they have a true zero point. That is, the score of zero for these variables is not arbitrary: it indicates the absence or complete lack of whatever is being measured. For example, the variable "number of siblings" has a true zero point because it is possible to have no siblings at all. Similarly, it is possible to have zero years of education, no income at all, a score of zero on a multiple-choice test, and to be zero years old (although not for very long). Other examples of interval-ratio variables would be number of children, life expectancy, and years married. All mathematical operations are permitted for data measured at the interval-ratio level.

Table 1.2 summarizes this discussion by presenting the basic characteristics of the three levels of measurement. Note that the number of permitted mathematical operations increases as we move from nominal to ordinal to interval-ratio levels of measurement. Ordinal-level variables are more sophisticated and flexible than nominal-level variables and interval-ratio-level variables permit the broadest range of mathematical operations.

Level of Measurement and Discrete Versus Continuous Variables. The distinction made earlier between discrete and continuous variables is a concern only for interval-ratio-level variables. Nominal- and ordinal-level variables are discrete, at least in the way they are usually measured. For example, to measure marital status, researchers usually ask people to choose one category from a list: married, living common law, widowed, and so on. What makes this variable discrete is that respondents can place themselves in a single category only; no subcategories or more refined classifications are permitted.

The distinction is usually a concern only for interval-ratio-level variables, of which some are discrete (number of times you've been divorced) and others are continuous (income or age). Remember that because we cannot work with infinitely long numbers, continuous variables have to be rounded off at some level and reported as if they were discrete. The distinction relates more to our options for appropriate statistics or graphs, not to the appearance of the variables.

Level of Measurement: A Summary.   Remember that the level of measurement of a variable is important because different statistics require different mathematical operations. The level of measurement of a variable is the key characteristic that tells us which statistics are permissible and appropriate.

Ideally, researchers would utilize only those statistics that were fully justified by the level-of-measurement criteria. In this imperfect world, however, the most powerful and useful statistics (such as the mean) require interval-ratio variables, while most of the variables of interest to the social sciences are only nominal (race, sex, marital status) or ordinal (attitude scales). Relatively few concepts of interest to the social sciences are so precisely defined that they can be measured at the interval-ratio level. This disparity creates some very real difficulties for social science research. On one hand, researchers should use the most sophisticated statistical procedures fully justified for a particular variable. Treating interval-ratio data as if they were only ordinal, for example, results in a significant loss of information and precision. Treated as an interval-ratio variable, the variable "age" can supply us with exact information regarding the differences between the cases (e.g., "Individual A is three years and two months older than Individual B"). Treated only as an ordinal variable, however, the precision of our comparisons would suffer and we could say only that "Individual A is older (or greater than) Individual B."

On the other hand, given the nature of the disparity, researchers are more likely to treat variables as if they were higher in level of measurement than they actually are. In particular, variables measured at the ordinal level, especially when they have many possible categories or scores, are often treated as if they were interval-ratio because the statistical procedures available at the higher level are more powerful, flexible, and interesting. This practice is common but researchers should be cautious in assessing statistical results and developing interpretations when the level-of-measurement criterion has been violated. Level of measurement is a very basic characteristic of a variable, and we will always consider it when presenting statistical procedures. Level of measurement is also a major organizing principle for the material that follows, and you should make sure that you are familiar with these guidelines. *(For practice in determining the level of measurement of a variable, see problems 1.4–1.8.)*

SUMMARY

1. Within the context of social research, the purpose of statistics is to organize, manipulate, and analyze data so that researchers can test their theories and answer their questions. Along with theory and methodology, statistics are a basic tool by which social scientists attempt to enhance their understanding of the social world.

2. There are two general classes of statistics. Descriptive statistics are used to summarize the distribution of a single variable and the relationships between two or more variables. Inferential statistics provide us with techniques by which we can generalize to populations from random samples.

3. Two basic guidelines for selecting statistical techniques were presented. Variables may be either discrete or continuous and may be measured at any of three different levels. At the nominal level, we can compare category sizes. At the ordinal level, categories and cases can be ranked with respect to each other. At the interval-ratio level, all mathematical operations are permitted. Interval-ratio-level variables can be either discrete or continuous. Variables at the nominal or ordinal level are almost always discrete.

GLOSSARY

Continuous variable. A variable with a unit of measurement that can be subdivided infinitely. (p. 18)

Data. Any information collected as part of a research project and expressed as numbers. (p. 9)

Data reduction. Summarizing many scores with a few statistics. A major goal of descriptive statistics. (p. 16)

Dependent variable. A variable that is identified as an effect, result, or outcome variable. The dependent variable is thought to be caused by the independent variable. (p. 11)

Descriptive statistics. The branch of statistics concerned with (1) summarizing the distribution of a single variable or (2) measuring the relationship between two or more variables. (p. 15)

Discrete variable. A variable with a basic unit of measurement that cannot be subdivided. (p. 18)

Hypothesis. A statement about the relationship between variables that is derived from a theory. Hypotheses are more specific than theories, and all terms and concepts are fully defined. (p. 12)

Independent variable. A variable that is identified as a causal variable. The independent variable is thought to cause the dependent variable. (p. 11)

Inferential statistics. The branch of statistics concerned with making generalizations from samples to populations. (p. 17)

Level of measurement. The mathematical characteristic of a variable and the major criterion for selecting statistical techniques. Variables can be measured at any of three levels, each permitting certain mathematical operations and statistical techniques. The characteristics of the three levels are summarized in Table 1.2. (p. 18)

Measures of association. Statistics that summarize the strength and direction of the relationship between variables. (p. 16)

Population. The total collection of all cases in which the researcher is interested. (p. 17)

Research. Any process of gathering information systematically and carefully to answer questions or test theories. Statistics are useful for research projects in which the information is represented in numerical form or as data. (p. 9)

Sample. A carefully chosen subset of a population. In inferential statistics, information is gathered from a sample and then generalized to a population. (p. 17)

Statistics. A set of mathematical techniques for organizing and analyzing data. (p. 9)

Theory. A generalized explanation of the relationship between two or more variables. (p. 10)

Variable. Any trait that can change values from case to case. (p. 11)

PROBLEMS

1.1 In your own words, describe the role of statistics in the research process. Using the "wheel of science" as a framework, explain how statistics link theory with research.

1.2 Find a research article in any social science journal. Choose an article on a subject of interest to you and don't worry about being able to understand all of the statistics that are reported.
   a. How much of the article is devoted to statistics per se (as distinct from theory, ideas, discussion, and so on)?
   b. Is the research based on a sample from some population? How large is the sample? How were subjects or cases selected? Can the findings be generalized to some population?
   c. What variables are used? Which are independent and which are dependent? For each variable, determine the level of measurement and whether the variable is discrete or continuous.
   d. What statistical techniques are used? Try to follow the statistical analysis and see how much you can understand. Save the article and read it again after you finish this course to see if you understand more.

1.3 Distinguish between descriptive and inferential statistics. Describe a research situation that would use both types.

1.4 Below are some items from a public-opinion survey. For each item, indicate the level of measurement and whether the variable will be discrete or continuous. *(HINT: Remember that only interval-ratio-level variables can be continuous.)*
   a. What is your occupation? _____
   b. How many years of school have you completed? _____
   c. If you were asked to use one of these four names for your social class, which would you say you belonged in?
       _____ Upper   _____ Middle
       _____ Working   _____ Lower
   d. What is your age? _____
   e. In what country were you born? _____
   f. What is your grade point average? _____
   g. What is your major? _____

   h. The only way to deal with the drug problem is to legalize all drugs.
       _____ Strongly agree
       _____ Agree
       _____ Undecided
       _____ Disagree
       _____ Strongly disagree
   i. What is your astrological sign? _____
   j. How many brothers and sisters do you have? _____

1.5 Below are brief descriptions of how researchers measured a variable. For each situation, determine the level of measurement of the variable and whether it is continuous or discrete.
   a. **Sex.** Respondents were asked to select a category from the following list:
       _____ Male   _____ Female
   b. **Honesty.** Subjects were observed as they passed by a spot on campus where an apparently lost wallet was lying. The wallet contained money and complete identification. Subjects were classified into one of the following categories:
       _____ Returned the wallet with the money.
       _____ Returned the wallet but kept the money.
       _____ Did not return the wallet.
   c. **Social class.** Subjects were asked about their family situation when they were 16 years old. Was their family:
       _____ Very well off compared to other families?
       _____ About average?
       _____ Not so well off?
   d. **Education.** Subjects were asked how many years of schooling they and each parent had completed.
   e. **Sex integration on campus.** Students were observed during lunchtime at the cafeteria for a month. The number of students sitting with students of the opposite sex was counted for each meal period.
   f. **Number of children.** Subjects were asked: "How many children have you ever had? Please include any that may have passed away."
   g. **Student seating patterns in classrooms.** On the first day of class, instructors noted where

each student sat. Seating patterns were remeasured every two weeks until the end of the semester. Each student was classified as

_____ same seat as last measurement;

_____ adjacent seat;

_____ different seat, not adjacent;

_____ absent.

h. Physicians per capita. The number of practicing physicians was counted in each of 50 cities, and the researchers used population data to compute the number of physicians per capita.

i. Physical attractiveness. A panel of 10 judges rated each of 50 photos of a sample of males and females for physical attractiveness on a scale from 0 to 20 with 20 being the highest score.

j. Number of accidents. The number of traffic accidents for each of 20 busy intersections in a city was recorded. Also, each accident was rated as

_____ minor damage, no injuries;

_____ moderate damage, personal injury requiring hospitalization;

_____ severe damage and injury.

1.6 For each of the first 20 items in the General Social Survey (see Appendix G), indicate the level of measurement and whether the variable is continuous or discrete.

1.7 For each research situation summarized below, identify the level of measurement of all variables and indicate whether they are discrete or continuous. Also, decide which statistical applications are used: descriptive statistics (single variable), descriptive statistics (two or more variables), or inferential statistics. Remember that it is quite common for a given situation to require more than one type of application.

a. The administration of your university is proposing a change in parking policy. You select a random sample of students and ask each one whether he or she favours or opposes the change.

b. You ask everyone in your social research class to tell you (1) the highest grade he or she ever received in a math course and (2) the grade on a recent statistics test. You then compare the two sets of scores to find out whether there is any relationship.

c. Your aunt is running for mayor and hires you (for a huge fee, incidentally) to question a sample of voters about their concerns in local politics. Specifically, she wants a profile of the voters that will tell her what percent belong to each political party, what percent are male or female, and what percent favour or oppose the widening of the main street in town.

d. Several years ago, a country reinstituted the death penalty for first-degree homicide. Supporters of capital punishment argued that this change would reduce the homicide rate. To investigate this claim, a researcher has gathered information on the number of homicides in the country for the two-year periods before and after the change.

e. A local automobile dealer is concerned about customer satisfaction. He wants to mail a survey form to all customers for the past year and ask them if they are satisfied, very satisfied, or not satisfied with their purchases.

1.8 For each research situation below, identify the independent and dependent variables. Classify each in terms of level of measurement and whether or not the variable is discrete or continuous.

a. A graduate student is studying sexual harassment on university campuses and asks 500 female students if they personally have experienced any such incidents. Each student is asked to estimate the frequency of these incidents as either "often, sometimes, rarely, or never." The researcher also gathers data on age and major to find out whether there is any connection between these variables and frequency of sexual harassment.

b. A supervisor in the Solid Waste Management Division of a municipal government is attempting to assess two different methods of trash collection. One area of the city is served by trucks with two-person crews who do "backyard" pickups, and the rest of the city is served by "high-tech" single-person trucks with curbside pickup. The assessment measures include the number of complaints received from the two different areas over a six-month period, the amount of time per day required to service each area, and the cost per tonne of trash collected.

c. The adult bookstore near campus has been raided and closed by the police. Your social research class has decided to poll the student body and get their reactions and opinions. The class decides to ask each student if he or she supports or opposes the closing of the store, how many times each one has visited the store, and if he or she agrees or disagrees that "pornography is a direct cause of sexual assaults on women." The class also collects information on the sex, age, religious and political philosophy, and major of each student to see if opinions are related to these characteristics.

d. For a research project in a political science course, a student has collected information about the quality of life and the degree of political democracy in 50 nations. Specifically, she used infant mortality rates to measure quality of life, and the percentage of all adults who are permitted to vote in national elections was the measure of democratization. Her hypothesis is that quality of life is higher in more democratic nations.

e. A highway engineer wonders if a planned increase in speed limit on a heavily travelled local avenue will result in any change in number of accidents. He plans to collect information on traffic volume, number of accidents, and number of fatalities for the six-month periods before and after the change.

f. Students are planning a program to promote "safe sex" and awareness of a variety of other health concerns for university students. To measure the effectiveness of the program, they plan to give a survey measuring knowledge about these matters to a random sample of the student body before and after the program.

g. Several provinces have drastically cut their budgets for mental health care. Will this increase the number of homeless people in these provinces? A researcher contacts a number of agencies serving the homeless in each province and develops an estimate of the size of the population before and after the cuts.

h. Does tolerance for diversity vary by race, ethnicity, or gender? Samples of males and females from various racial and ethnic groups have been given a survey that measures their interest in and appreciation of cultures and groups other than their own.

SPSS for Windows

Introduction to the Canadian General Social Survey, Census of Canada, and SPSS

Two types of exercises are located at the end of each chapter of this textbook. While the "Problems" exercises are based on fictitious data for the most part and designed to be solved with a simple hand calculator, the "SPSS for Windows" computer-based exercises provide a more realistic experience and use actual social science data from two Canadian social surveys, the Census of Canada (Census) and the Canadian General Social Survey (GSS).

The GSS is an annual public-opinion poll, administered by Statistics Canada, of a representative sample of Canadians. It has been conducted since 1985, and explores a broad range of social issues. Each year the survey collects information on specific aspects of society relevant to social policy. Since survey topics are often repeated every few years, GSS data can also be used to track trends and changes in these characteristics over time. The GSS has proven to be a very valuable resource for testing theory, for learning more about Canadian society, and for informing public debates.

The 2009 GSS is supplied and used in this textbook. It collected information on the nature and extent of criminal victimization in Canada and perceptions of crime and the criminal justice system, including the police, criminal courts, and prisons.

Using the 2009 GSS data, students can describe how Canadians feel about crime or their personal safety, as well as their satisfaction with the criminal justice system. Students can further examine if variables such as gender, age, province of residence, and so on are associated with opinions and assessments of crime and justice in Canada.

Two versions of the 2009 GSS are supplied with this textbook. The first version, named *GSSFull.sav*, contains the original random sample. The second (*GSS.sav*) is a shortened version with 1,500 cases randomly selected from the original random sample.

The Census provides information on the demographic, social, and economic characteristics of a random sample of Canadians. The Census is conducted by Statistics Canada every five years. The 2006 Census is provided here. Using Census data, students can describe and explain many aspects of Canadian society, including family composition, labour force activity, income, and poverty.

The 2006 Census contains dozens of variables for a sample of hundreds of thousands of Canadians. As with the GSS, we provide both the complete version of the Census (*CensusFull.sav*) containing the original random sample and a shortened version (*Census.sav*) with 1,500 randomly selected cases.

The four databases (*GSS.sav*, *Census.sav*, *GSSFull.sav*, and *CensusFull.sav*) and the user's guide for the 2009 GSS (*GSS_guide.pdf*) and 2006 Census (*Census_guide.pdf*) can be downloaded from our website at http://www.healeystatistics.nelson.com. The user's guides provide a detailed description of each survey; however, for quick reference, a list of the variables in each database is shown in Appendix G.

One of the problems with using "real-life" data such as the GSS and Census is that they very often contain too many cases to be solved with just a simple hand calculator. Instead, computers and statistical packages are almost always needed to analyze the data. A statistical package is a set of computer programs for data analysis. The advantage of these packages is that, since the programs are already written, you can capitalize on the power of the computer with minimal computer literacy and virtually no programming experience.

This textbook utilizes SPSS (Statistical Package for the Social Sciences) for Windows. Version 20 of SPSS for Windows is used, though Versions 10 through 19 of SPSS for Windows are completely compatible with the textbook. In the SPSS for Windows exercise sections at the end of each chapter, we will explain how to use this package in various ways to manipulate and analyze the GSS or Census data, and we will illustrate and interpret the results. Also be sure to read Appendix F, which gives a general introduction to SPSS, before attempting any data analysis.

As a final note, there are two versions of SPSS: a full version and a student version. The student version, created for classroom instruction, is, in essence, the full version of the SPSS base software package but is limited to a maximum of 50 variables and 1,500 cases. Hence, the student version is compatible with the *GSS.sav* and *Census.sav* data files.

PART 1

Descriptive Statistics

Part I consists of three chapters, each devoted to a different application of univariate descriptive statistics. Chapter 2 covers "basic" descriptive statistics, including percentages, ratios, rates, frequency distributions, and graphs. It is a lengthy chapter, but the material is relatively elementary and at least vaguely familiar to most people. Although the statistics covered in this chapter are "basic," they are not necessarily simple or obvious and the explanations and examples should be considered carefully before attempting the end-of-chapter problems or using them in actual research.

Chapter 3 covers measures of central tendency and dispersion. Measures of central tendency describe the typical case or average score (e.g., the mean), while measures of dispersion describe the amount of variety or diversity among the scores (e.g., the range or the distance from the high score to the low score). These two types of statistics are presented in a single chapter to stress the point that centrality and dispersion depend on each other to describe the characteristics of a variable. You will come to realize that both measures are necessary and commonly reported together. To reinforce the idea that measures of centrality and dispersion are complementary descriptive statistics, many of the problems at the end of Chapter 3 require the simultaneous computation of a measure of central tendency and dispersion.

Chapter 4 is a pivotal chapter in the flow of the textbook. It takes some of the statistics from Chapters 2 and 3 and applies them to the normal curve, a concept of great importance in statistics. The normal curve is a type of frequency polygon (Chapter 2), which can be used to describe the position of scores using means and standard deviations (Chapter 3). Chapter 4 also uses proportions and percentages (Chapter 2).

In addition to its role in descriptive statistics, the normal curve is a central concept in inferential statistics, the topic of Part II of this textbook. Thus, Chapter 4 serves a dual purpose: it ends the presentation of univariate descriptive statistics and lays essential groundwork for the material to come.

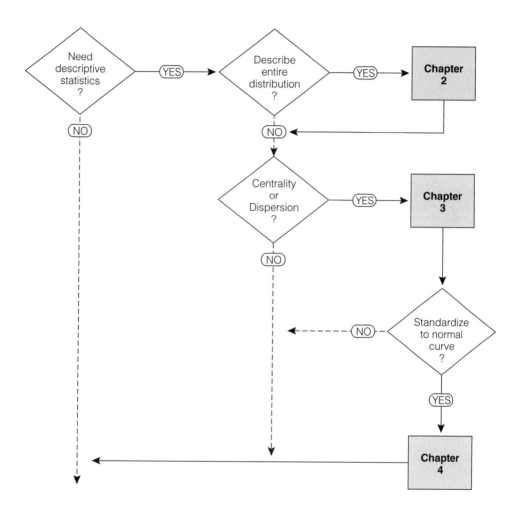

2

Basic Descriptive Statistics
Percentages, Ratios and Rates, Tables, Charts, and Graphs

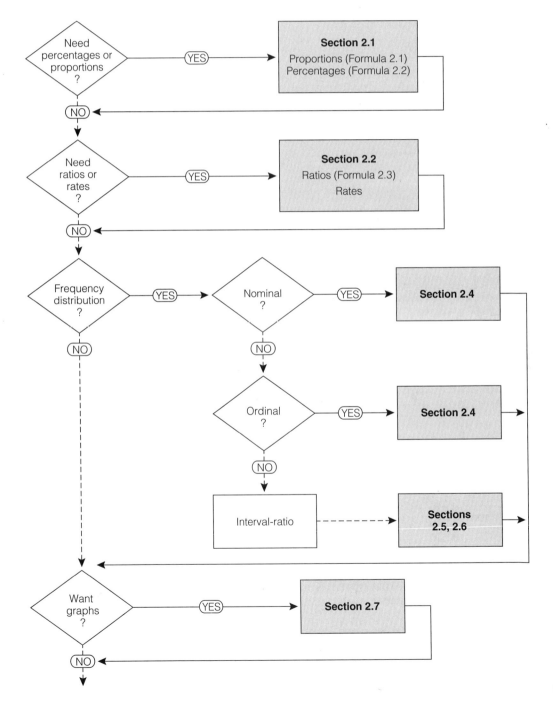

LEARNING OBJECTIVES

By the end of this chapter, you will be able to

1. Explain the purpose of descriptive statistics in making data comprehensible.
2. Compute and interpret percentages, proportions, ratios, and rates.
3. Construct and analyze frequency distributions for variables at each of the three levels of measurement.
4. Construct and analyze bar and pie charts, histograms, and frequency polygons.

Research results do not speak for themselves. They must be organized and manipulated so that whatever meaning they have can be quickly and easily understood by the researcher and by his or her readers. Researchers use statistics to clarify their results and communicate effectively. In this chapter, we will consider some commonly used techniques for presenting research results: percentages and proportions, ratios and rates, tables, charts, and graphs. Mathematically speaking, these univariate descriptive statistics are not very complex (although they may not be as simple as they appear at first glance), but, as you will see, they are extremely useful for presenting research results clearly and concisely.

2.1 PERCENTAGES AND PROPORTIONS

Consider the following statement: "Of the 781 survey respondents who plan to celebrate St. Valentine's Day, 312 will go out to a restaurant." While there is nothing wrong with this statement, the same fact could have been more clearly conveyed if it had been reported as a percentage: "Of those who plan to celebrate St. Valentine's Day, almost 40% will go out to a restaurant."

Percentages and proportions supply a frame of reference for reporting research results in the sense that they standardize the raw data: percentages to the base 100 and proportions to the base 1.00. The mathematical definitions of **proportions** and **percentages** are

FORMULA 2.1
$$\text{Proportion } (p) = \frac{f}{n}$$

FORMULA 2.2
$$\text{Percentage } (\%) = \left(\frac{f}{n}\right) \times 100$$

where f = frequency, or the number of cases in any category
n = the number of cases in all categories

To illustrate the computation of percentages, consider the data presented in Table 2.1. How can we find the percentage of cases in the first

TABLE 2.1   MOST POPULAR WAYS FOR CANADIANS TO CELEBRATE ST. VALENTINE'S DAY

Ways to Celebrate	Frequency (f)	Proportion (p)	Percentage (%)
Going to a restaurant	312	0.3995	39.95
Romantic evening at home	110	0.1408	14.08
Giving a gift/card/flowers/chocolate	92	0.1178	11.78
Going on a trip	22	0.0282	2.82
Going out dancing	7	0.0090	0.90
Other	74	0.0947	9.47
Don't know	164	0.2100	21.00
	$n = 781$	1.0000	100.00

Source: Adapted from "Canadians and St. Valentine's Day," Leger Marketing (2007). www.legermarketing. com/documents/SPCLM/070212ENG.pdf

category (going to a restaurant)? Note that there are 312 cases in the category ($f = 312$) and a total of 781 cases in all ($n = 781$). So,

$$\text{Percentage (\%)} = \left(\frac{f}{n}\right) \times 100 = \left(\frac{312}{781}\right) \times 100 = (0.3995) \times 100 = 39.95\%$$

Using the same procedures, we can also find the percentage of cases in the second category:

$$\text{Percentage (\%)} = \left(\frac{f}{n}\right) \times 100 = \left(\frac{110}{781}\right) \times 100 = (0.1408) \times 100 = 14.08\%$$

Both results could have been expressed as proportions. For example, the proportion of cases in the third category is 0.1178.

$$\text{Proportion } (p) = \frac{f}{n} = \frac{92}{781} = 0.1178$$

Percentages and proportions are easier to read and comprehend than frequencies. This advantage is particularly obvious when attempting to compare groups of different sizes. For example, Table 2.2 provides actual

TABLE 2.2   DECLARED MAJOR FIELDS OF STUDY FOR MALE AND FEMALE UNDERGRADUATE UNIVERSITY STUDENTS

Major	Male	Female
Business	101	112
Natural sciences*	156	192
Social sciences†	156	246
Engineering	69	26
Other	106	122
	$n = 588$	$n = 698$

*Includes computer science, health, and medicine.
†Includes fine arts, education, humanities, and law.

Source: Data from *Making Ends Meet, 2001–2002 Student Financial Survey*, Canada Millennium Scholarship Foundation. March 2003.

Application 2.1

Not long ago, in a large social service agency, the following conversation took place between the executive director of the agency and a supervisor of one of the divisions.

> *Executive director:* Well, I don't want to seem abrupt, but I've only got a few minutes. Tell me, as briefly as you can, about this staffing problem you claim to be having.
>
> *Supervisor:* Ma'am, we just don't have enough people to handle our workload. Of the 177 full-time employees of the agency, only 50 are in my division. Yet, 6,231 of the 16,722 cases handled by the agency last year were handled by my division.
>
> *Executive director (smothering a yawn):* Very interesting. I'll certainly get back to you on this matter.

How could the supervisor have presented his case more effectively? Because he wants to compare two sets of numbers (his staff versus the total staff and the workload of his division versus the total workload of the agency), proportions or percentages would be a more forceful way of presenting results. What if the supervisor had said, "Only 28.25% of the staff is assigned to my division, but we handle 37.26% of the total workload of the agency"? Is this a clearer message?

The first percentage is found by

$$\% = \left(\frac{f}{n}\right) \times 100 = \frac{50}{177} \times 100$$

$$= (0.2825) \times 100 = 28.25\%$$

and the second percentage is found by

$$\% = \left(\frac{f}{n}\right) \times 100 = \left(\frac{6231}{16{,}722}\right) \times 100$$

$$= (0.3726) \times 100 = 37.26\%$$

---

data collected by the Student Financial Survey (a survey sponsored by the Canada Millennium Scholarship Foundation) on program-of-study of post-secondary students from across Canada during the 2001–2002 academic year. Based on the program-of-study information presented in the table, which sex has the higher relative number of business majors? Because the total enrollments are much different, comparisons are difficult to make from the raw frequencies. Computing percentages eliminates the difference in size of the two groups by standardizing both distributions to the base of 100. The same data are presented in percentages in Table 2.3.

The percentages in Table 2.3 make it easier to identify both differences and similarities between the sexes. We now see that a greater percentage of males than females study business at Canadian universities, even though the absolute number of female business majors is more than that of male business majors. How would you describe the differences in the other major fields? *(For practice in computing and interpreting percentages and proportions, see problems 2.1 and 2.2.)*

Some further guidelines on the use of percentages and proportions:

TABLE 2.3   DECLARED MAJOR FIELDS OF STUDY FOR MALE AND FEMALE
UNDERGRADUATE UNIVERSITY STUDENTS

Major	Male	Female
Business	17.18	16.05
Natural sciences*	26.53	27.51
Social sciences†	26.53	35.24
Engineering	11.73	3.73
Other	18.03	17.47
	100.00%	100.00%
	(588)	(698)

*Includes computer science, health, and medicine.
†Includes fine arts, education, humanities, and law.

Source: Based on data from *Making Ends Meet, 2001–2002 Student Financial Survey*, Canada Millennium
Scholarship Foundation. March 2003.

1. When working with a small number of cases (say, fewer than 20), it is usually preferable to report the actual frequencies rather than percentages or
proportions. With a small number of cases, the percentages can change
drastically with relatively minor changes in the data. For example, if you
begin with a data set that includes 10 males and 10 females (i.e., 50% of
each gender) and then add another female, the percentage distributions
will change noticeably to 52.38% female and 47.62% male. Of course, as
the number of observations increases, each additional case will have a
smaller impact. If we started with 500 males and females and then added
one more female, the percentage of females would change by only a
tenth of a percent (from 50% to 50.10%).

2. Always report the number of observations along with proportions and
percentages. This permits the reader to judge the adequacy of the sample
size and, conversely, helps to prevent the researcher from lying with
statistics. Statements like "two out of three people questioned prefer
courses in statistics to any other course" might impress you, but the claim
would lose its gloss if you learned that only three people were tested.
*You should be extremely suspicious of reports that fail to state the number
of cases that were tested.*

Application 2.2

In Table 2.2, how many male social science majors
are there compared to male business majors? This
question could be answered with frequencies, but
a more easily understood way of expressing the
answer would be with a ratio. The ratio of male
social science to business majors would be

$$\text{Ratio} = \frac{f_1}{f_2} = \frac{156}{101} = 1.54$$

For every male business major, there are 1.54 male
social science majors.

3. Percentages and proportions can be calculated for variables at the ordinal and nominal levels of measurement, even though they require division. This is not a violation of the level-of-measurement guideline (see Table 1.2). Percentages and proportions do not require the division of the *scores* of the variable (as would be the case in computing the average score on a test, for example) but rather the *number of cases* in a particular category (*f*) of the variable by the total number of cases in the sample (*n*). When we make a statement like "43% of the sample is female," we are merely expressing the relative size of a category (female) of the variable (gender) in a convenient way.

2.2 RATIOS AND RATES

Ratios and rates provide some additional ways of summarizing results simply and clearly. Although they are similar to each other, each statistic has a specific application and purpose.

Ratios.   **Ratios** are especially useful for comparing categories of a variable in terms of relative frequency. Instead of standardizing the distribution of the variable to the base 100 or 1.00, as we did in computing percentages and proportions, we determine ratios by dividing the frequency of one category by the frequency in another. Mathematically, a ratio can be defined as

FORMULA 2.3

$$\text{Ratio} = \frac{f_1}{f_2}$$

where f_1 = the number of cases in the first category
f_2 = the number of cases in the second category

To illustrate the use of ratios, we will use actual information from the 2006 Canadian Election Study, which is an interuniversity project that regularly conducts a survey of Canadian voters on a variety of political issues. Canadians were asked about their feelings toward the federal sponsorship scandal that involved the misappropriation and misdirection of government funds. Of those polled, 3,351 people said that they were angry about the sponsorship scandal, while 630 said that they were not angry.* What is the relative size of these two groups? To find the ratio of "angry" Canadians (f_1) to "not angry" Canadians (f_2), divide 3,351 by 630:

$$\text{Ratio} = \frac{f_1}{f_2} = \frac{3,351}{630} = 5.32$$

The resultant ratio is 5.32, which means that for every Canadian who is not angry about the sponsorship scandal, there are 5.32 Canadians who are angry about the scandal.

*Source: 2006 Canadian Election Study.

Application 2.3

In 2007, there were 367,864 births in Canada, within a population of 32,929,700 persons. In 1972, when the population of Canada was only 22,218,475, there were 351,256 births. Is the birth rate rising or falling? Although this question can be answered from the preceding information, the trend in birth rates will be much more obvious if we compute birth rates for both years. Like crude death rates, crude birth rates are usually multiplied by 1,000 to eliminate decimal points. For 1972:

$$\text{Crude birth rate} = \frac{351,256}{22,218,475} \times 1,000 = 15.81$$

In 1972, there were 15.81 births for every 1,000 people in Canada. For 2007:

$$\text{Crude birth rate} = \frac{367,864}{32,929,700} \times 1,000 = 11.17$$

In 2007, there were 11.17 births for every 1,000 people in Canada. With the help of these statistics, the decline in the birth rate is clearly expressed.

Source: Data from Statistics Canada, CANSIM, Tables 051-0001 and 051-0051.

Ratios can be very economical ways of expressing the relative predominance of two categories. That "angry" Canadians outnumber "not angry" Canadians in our example is obvious from the raw data. Percentages or proportions could have been used to summarize the overall distribution (e.g., "84.17% of Canadians were angry about the sponsorship scandal, and 15.83% were not"). In contrast to these other methods, ratios express the relative size of the categories: they tell us exactly how much one category outnumbers the other.

Ratios are often multiplied by some power of 10 to eliminate decimal points. For example, the ratio computed above might be multiplied by 100 and reported as 532 instead of 5.32. This would mean that, for every 100 Canadians who are not angry about the sponsorship scandal, there are 532 Canadians who are angry about it. To ensure clarity, the comparison units for the ratio are often expressed as well. Based on a unit of ones, the ratio of "angry" Canadians to "not angry" Canadians would be expressed as 5.32:1. Based on hundreds, the same statistic might be expressed as 532:100. *(For practice in computing and interpreting ratios, see problems 2.1 and 2.2.)*

Rates.   **Rates** provide still another way of summarizing the distribution of a single variable. Rates are defined as the number of actual occurrences of some phenomenon divided by the number of possible occurrences per some unit of time. Rates are usually multiplied by some power of 10 to eliminate decimal points. For example, the crude death rate for a population is defined as the number of deaths in that population (actual occurrences) divided by the number of people in the population (possible occurrences) per year. This quantity is then multiplied by 1,000. The formula for the crude death rate can be expressed as

$$\text{Crude death rate} = \frac{\text{Number of deaths}}{\text{Total population}} \times 1{,}000$$

In 2007, a total of 235,217 deaths were registered in Canada. With a population of 32,929,700, Canada's crude death rate for that year was*

$$\text{Crude death rate} = \frac{235{,}217}{32{,}929{,}700} \times 1{,}000 = (0.00714) \times 1{,}000 = 7.14$$

Or, for every 1,000 Canadians, there were 7.14 deaths in 2007.

Rates are often multiplied by 100,000 when the number of actual occurrences of some phenomenon is extremely small relative to the size of the population, such as homicides in Canada. Canadian police reported 594 homicides in 2007, hence the homicide rate was**

$$\text{Homicide rate} = \frac{594}{32{,}929{,}700} \times 100{,}000 = (0.000018) \times 100{,}000 = 1.8$$

Or, for every 100,000 Canadians, there were 1.8 homicides in 2007. *(For practice in computing and interpreting rates, see problems 2.3 and 2.4.)*

2.3 FREQUENCY DISTRIBUTIONS INTRODUCTION

Table 2.1 above is an example of what is formally called a **frequency distribution**. A frequency distribution is a table that summarizes the distribution of a variable by reporting the number of cases contained in each category of the variable. It is a very helpful and commonly used way of organizing and working with data. In fact, the construction of a frequency distribution is almost always the first step in any statistical analysis.

To illustrate the construction of frequency distributions and to provide some data for examples, let's assume a hypothetical situation in which students who recently visited the health and counselling services centre at a university were sent an email asking them to complete a brief patient-satisfaction survey. Any realistic evaluation research would collect a variety of information from a large group of students, but for the sake of this example, we will confine our attention to just four variables and 20 students. The data are reported in Table 2.4.

Note that even though the data in Table 2.4 represent an unrealistically low number of cases, it is difficult to discern any patterns or trends. For example,

---

*Source: Data from Statistics Canada, CANSIM, Tables 051-0001 (population) and 102-0503 (deaths).
**Source: Data from Statistics Canada, CANSIM, Tables 051-0001 (population) and 253-0001 (homicides).

TABLE 2.4   DATA FROM HEALTH AND COUNSELLING SERVICES SURVEY

Student	Sex	Type of Health Professional Seen[1]	Satisfaction with Services[2]	Age
A	Male	Medical Doctor	1	18
B	Male	Counsellor	2	19
C	Female	Medical Doctor	4	18
D	Female	Medical Doctor	2	19
E	Male	Counsellor	1	20
F	Male	Medical Doctor	1	20
G	Female	Counsellor	4	18
H	Female	Medical Doctor	3	21
I	Male	Medical Doctor	2	19
J	Female	Other	3	23
K	Female	Medical Doctor	3	24
L	Male	Counsellor	3	18
M	Female	Medical Doctor	1	22
N	Female	Counsellor	4	26
O	Male	Medical Doctor	3	18
P	Male	Counsellor	4	19
Q	Female	Counsellor	2	19
R	Male	Other	1	19
S	Female	Other	4	21
T	Male	Medical Doctor	2	20

[1]Based on the question, "What type of health professional did you see or talk to during your visit?"
[2]Measured on a scale from 1 (very dissatisfied) to 4 (very satisfied).

try to ascertain the general level of satisfaction of the students from Table 2.4. You may be able to do so with just 20 cases, but it will take some time and effort. Imagine the difficulty with 50 cases or 100 cases presented in this fashion. Clearly the data need to be organized in a format that allows the researcher (and his or her audience) to understand easily the distribution of the variables.

One general rule that applies to all frequency distributions is that the categories of the frequency distribution must be exhaustive and mutually exclusive. In other words, the categories must be stated in a way that permits each case to be counted in one and only one category. This basic principle applies to the construction of frequency distributions for variables measured at all three levels of measurement.

Beyond this rule, there are only guidelines to help you construct useful frequency distributions. As you will see, the researcher has a fair amount of discretion in stating the categories of the frequency distribution (especially with variables measured at the interval-ratio level). We will identify the issues to consider as you make decisions about the nature of any particular frequency distribution. Ultimately, however, the guidelines we state are aids for decision making, nothing more than helpful suggestions. As always, the researcher has the final responsibility for making sensible decisions and presenting his or her data in a meaningful way.

2.4 FREQUENCY DISTRIBUTIONS FOR VARIABLES MEASURED AT THE NOMINAL AND ORDINAL LEVELS

Nominal-Level Variables.   For nominal-level variables, construction of the frequency distribution is typically very straightforward. For each category of the variable being displayed, the occurrences are counted and the subtotals, along with the total number of cases (n), are reported. Table 2.5 displays a frequency distribution for the variable "sex" from the health and counselling services survey. For purposes of illustration, a column for tallies has been included in this table to illustrate how the cases would be sorted into categories. (This column would not be included in the final form of the frequency distribution.) Take a moment to notice several other features of the table. Specifically, the table has a descriptive title, clearly labelled categories (male and female), and a report of the total number of cases at the bottom of the frequency column. These items must be included in all tables regardless of the variable or level of measurement.

The meaning of the table is quite clear. There are 10 males and 10 females in the sample, a fact that is much easier to comprehend from the frequency distribution than from the unorganized data presented in Table 2.4.

For some nominal variables, the researcher might have to make some choices about the number of categories he or she wishes to report. For example, the distribution of the variable "type of health professional seen" could be reported using the categories listed in Table 2.4. The resultant frequency distribution is presented in Table 2.6. Although this is a perfectly fine frequency distribution, it may be too detailed for some purposes. For example, the researcher might want to focus solely on "non-medical doctor" as distinct from "medical doctor" as the type of health professional seen by respondents during their visit to the health and counselling services centre. That is, the researcher might not be concerned with the difference between respondents who saw a "counsellor" and respondents who saw any "other" type of health professional but may want to treat both as simply "non-medical doctor." In that case, these categories could be grouped together and treated as a single entity, as in Table 2.7. Notice that, when categories are collapsed like this, information and detail will be lost. This latter version of the table would not allow the researcher to discriminate between the two types of non-medical doctor health professionals.

Ordinal-Level Variables.   Frequency distributions for ordinal-level variables are constructed following the same routines used for nominal-level variables. Table 2.8 reports the frequency distribution of the "satisfaction" variable from the health and counselling services survey. Note that a column

TABLE 2.5   SEX OF RESPONDENTS, HEALTH AND COUNSELLING SERVICES SURVEY

Sex	Tallies	Frequency (f)
Male	LHT LHT	10
Female	LHT LHT	10
		$n = 20$

TABLE 2.6 TYPE OF HEALTH PROFESSIONAL SEEN BY RESPONDENTS, HEALTH AND COUNSELLING SERVICES SURVEY

Health Professional	Frequency (f)
Medical Doctor	10
Counsellor	7
Other	3
	$n = 20$

TABLE 2.7 TYPE OF HEALTH PROFESSIONAL SEEN BY RESPONDENTS, HEALTH AND COUNSELLING SERVICES SURVEY

Health Professional	Frequency (f)
Medical Doctor	10
Non-medical Doctor	10
	$n = 20$

TABLE 2.8 SATISFACTION WITH SERVICES, HEALTH AND COUNSELLING SERVICES SURVEY

Satisfaction	Frequency (f)	Percentage (%)
(4) Very satisfied	5	25
(3) Satisfied	5	25
(2) Dissatisfied	5	25
(1) Very dissatisfied	5	25
	$n = 20$	100

of percentages by category has been added to this table. Such columns heighten the clarity of the table (especially with larger samples) and are common adjuncts to the basic frequency distribution for variables measured at all levels.

This table reports that students were neither satisfied nor dissatisfied with health and counselling services. Students were just as likely to be "satisfied" as "dissatisfied." *(For practice in constructing and interpreting frequency distributions for nominal- and ordinal-level variables, see problem 2.5.)*

2.5 FREQUENCY DISTRIBUTIONS FOR VARIABLES MEASURED AT THE INTERVAL-RATIO LEVEL

Basic Considerations. In general, the construction of frequency distributions for variables measured at the interval-ratio level is more complex than for nominal and ordinal variables. Interval-ratio variables usually have a large number of possible scores (i.e., a wide range from the lowest to the highest score). The large number of scores requires some collapsing or grouping of categories to produce reasonably compact frequency distributions. To construct frequency distributions for interval-ratio-level variables, you must decide how many categories to use and how wide these categories should be.

For example, suppose you wished to report the distribution of the variable "age" for a sample drawn from a community. Unlike the university data reported in Table 2.4, a community sample would have a very broad range of ages. If you simply reported the number of times that each year of age (or score) occurred, you could easily wind up with a frequency distribution that contained 70, 80, or even more categories. Such a large frequency distribution would not present a concise picture. The scores (years) must be grouped into larger categories to heighten clarity and ease of comprehension. How large should these categories be? How many categories should be included in the table? Although there are no hard-and-fast rules for making these decisions, they always involve a trade-off between more detail (a greater number of narrow categories) or more compactness (a smaller number of wide categories).

Constructing the Frequency Distribution.   To introduce the mechanics and decision-making processes involved, we will construct a frequency distribution to display the ages of the students in the health and counselling services centre survey. Because of the narrow age range of a group of university students, we can use categories of only one year (these categories are often called **intervals** when working with interval-ratio data). The frequency distribution is constructed by listing the ages from youngest to oldest, counting the number of times each score (year of age) occurs, and then totalling the number of scores for each category. Table 2.9 presents the information and reveals a concentration or clustering of scores in the 18 and 19 intervals.

Even though the picture presented in this table is fairly clear, assume for the sake of illustration that you desire a more compact (less detailed) summary. To do this, you will have to group scores into wider intervals. By increasing the interval width (say to two years), you can reduce the number of intervals and achieve a more compact expression. The grouping of scores in Table 2.10 clearly emphasizes the relative predominance of younger respondents. This trend in the data can be stressed even more by the addition of a column displaying the percentage of cases in each category.

Note that the intervals in Table 2.10 have been stated with an apparent gap between them (i.e., the intervals are separated by a distance of one unit). At first glance, these gaps may appear to violate the principle of

TABLE 2.9   AGE OF RESPONDENTS, HEALTH AND COUNSELLING SERVICES SURVEY (interval width = one year of age)

Interval	Frequency (f)
18	5
19	6
20	3
21	2
22	1
23	1
24	1
25	0
26	1
	$n = 20$

TABLE 2.10 AGE OF RESPONDENTS, HEALTH AND COUNSELLING
SERVICES SURVEY (interval width = two years of age)

Interval	Frequency (f)	Percentage (%)
18–19	11	55
20–21	5	25
22–23	2	10
24–25	1	5
26–27	1	5
	$n = 20$	100

exhaustiveness; but because age has been measured in whole numbers, the gaps actually pose no problem. Given the level of precision of the measurement (in years, as opposed to 10ths or 100ths of a year), no case could have a score falling between these intervals. In fact, for these data, the set of intervals contained in Table 2.10 constitutes a scale that is exhaustive and mutually exclusive. Each of the 20 respondents in the sample can be sorted into one and only one age category.

However, consider the difficulties that might have been encountered if age had been measured with greater precision. If age had been measured in 10ths of a year, into which interval in Table 2.10 would a 19.4-year-old subject be placed? You can avoid this ambiguity by always stating the limits of the intervals at the same level of precision as the data. Thus, if age were being measured in 10ths of a year, the limits of the intervals in Table 2.10 would be stated in 10ths of a year. For example:

17.0–18.9
19.0–20.9
21.0–22.9
23.0–24.9
25.0–26.9

To maintain mutual exclusivity between categories, do not overlap the intervals. If you state the limits of the intervals at the same level of precision as the data (which might be in whole numbers, tenths, hundredths, etc.) and maintain a "gap" between intervals, you will always produce a frequency distribution with which each case can be assigned to one and only one category.

Midpoints.   On occasion, you will need to work with the **midpoints** of the intervals, for example, when constructing or interpreting certain graphs like the frequency polygon (see Section 2.7). Midpoints are defined as the points exactly halfway between the upper and lower limits and can be found for any interval by dividing the sum of the upper and lower limits by two. Table 2.11 displays midpoints for two different sets of intervals. *(For practice in finding midpoints, see problems 2.8b and 2.9b.)*

TABLE 2.11   MIDPOINTS

Interval Width = Three	
Interval	Midpoints
0–2	1
3–5	4
6–8	7
9–11	10

Interval Width = Six	
Interval	Midpoints
100–105	102.5
106–111	108.5
112–117	114.5
118–123	120.5

Real Limits.   For certain purposes, you must eliminate the "gap" between intervals and treat a distribution as a continuous series of categories that border each other. This is necessary, for example, in constructing some graphs, such as the histogram (see Section 2.7).

To illustrate, let's begin with Table 2.10. Note the "gap" of one year between intervals. As we saw before, the gap is only apparent: scores are measured in whole years (i.e., 19, 21 vs. 19.5 or 21.3) and cannot fall between intervals. These types of intervals are called **stated limits** and they organize the scores of the variable into a series of discrete, non-overlapping intervals.

To treat the variable as continuous, we must use the **real limits**. To find the real limits of any interval, divide the distance between the stated limits (the "gap") in half and add the result to all upper stated limits and subtract it from all lower stated limits. This process is illustrated below with the intervals stated in Table 2.10. The distance between intervals is one, so the real limits can be found by adding 0.5 to all upper limits and subtracting 0.5 from all lower limits.

Stated Limits	Real Limits
18–19	17.5–19.5
20–21	19.5–21.5
22–23	21.5–23.5
24–25	23.5–25.5
26–27	25.5–27.5

Note that when conceptualized with real limits, the intervals overlap with each other and the distribution can be seen as continuous. Table 2.12 presents additional illustrations of real limits for two different sets of intervals. In both cases, the "gap" between the stated limits is one. *(For practice in finding real limits, see problem 2.7c and problem 2.8d.)*

TABLE 2.12   REAL LIMITS

Stated Limits	Real Limits
3–5	2.5–5.5
6–8	5.5–8.5
9–11	8.5–11.5
Stated Limits	**Real Limits**
100–105	99.5–105.5
106–111	105.5–111.5
112–117	111.5–117.5
118–123	117.5–123.5

Cumulative Frequency and Cumulative Percentage.   Two commonly used adjuncts to the basic frequency distribution for interval-ratio data are the **cumulative frequency** and **cumulative percentage** columns. Their primary purpose is to allow the researcher (and his or her audience) to tell at a glance how many cases fall below a given score or interval in the distribution.

To construct a cumulative frequency column, begin with the lowest interval (i.e., the interval with the lowest scores) in the distribution. The entry in the cumulative frequency columns for that interval will be the same as the number of cases in the interval. For the next higher interval, the cumulative frequency will be all cases in the interval plus all the cases in the first interval. For the third interval, the cumulative frequency will be all cases in the interval plus all cases in the first two intervals. Continue adding (or accumulating) cases until you reach the highest interval, which will have a cumulative frequency of all the cases in the interval plus all cases in all other intervals. For the highest interval, cumulative frequency equals the total number of cases. Table 2.13 shows a cumulative frequency column added to Table 2.10.

The cumulative percentage column is quite similar to the cumulative frequency column. Begin by adding a column to the basic frequency distribution

TABLE 2.13   AGE OF RESPONDENTS, HEALTH AND COUNSELLING SERVICES SURVEY

Interval	Frequency (f)	Cumulative Frequency
18–19	11	11
20–21	5	16
22–23	2	18
24–25	1	19
26–27	1	20
	$n = 20$	

TABLE 2.14   AGE OF RESPONDENTS, HEALTH AND COUNSELLING SERVICES SURVEY

Interval	Frequency (f)	Cumulative Frequency	Percentage (%)	Cumulative Percentage (%)
18–19	11	11	55	55
20–21	5	16	25	80
22–23	2	18	10	90
24–25	1	19	5	95
26–27	1	20	5	100
	$n = 20$		100	

for percentages as in Table 2.10. This column shows the percentage of all cases in each interval. To find cumulative percentages, follow the same addition pattern explained above for cumulative frequency. That is, the cumulative percentage for the lowest interval will be the same as the percentage of cases in the interval. For the next higher interval, the cumulative percentage is the percentage of cases in the interval plus the percentage of cases in the first interval, and so on. Table 2.14 shows the age data with a cumulative percentage column added.

These cumulative columns are quite useful in situations where the researcher wants to make a point about how cases are spread across the range of scores. For example, Tables 2.13 and 2.14 show quite clearly that most students in the health and counselling services survey are 21 years of age or younger. If the researcher wishes to impress this feature of the age distribution on his or her audience, then these cumulative columns are quite handy. Most realistic research situations will be concerned with many more than 20 cases and/or many more categories than our tables have. Because the cumulative percentage column is clearer and easier to interpret in such cases, it is normally preferred to the cumulative frequencies column.

Procedures for Constructing Frequency Distributions for Interval-Ratio Variables.   Guidelines for dealing with interval-ratio variables with many scores (wide ranges) can now be stated:

1. Decide how many intervals you wish to use. One reasonable convention suggests that the number of intervals should be about 10. Many research situations may require fewer than 10 intervals, and it is common to find frequency distributions with as many as 15 intervals. Only rarely will more than 15 intervals be used, as the resultant frequency distribution would not be very concise.
2. Find the size of the interval. Once you have decided how many intervals you will use, interval size can be found by dividing the range of the scores by the number of intervals and rounding to a convenient whole number.

3. State the lowest interval so that its lower limit is equal to or below the lowest score. By the same token, your highest interval will be the one that contains the highest score. All intervals must be equal in size.
4. State the limits of the intervals at the same level of precision as you have used to measure the data. Do not overlap intervals. You will thereby define the intervals so that each case can be sorted into one and only one category.
5. Count the number of cases in each interval and report these subtotals in a column labelled "frequency." Report the total number of cases (n) at the bottom of this column. The table may also include a column for percentages, cumulative frequencies, and cumulative percentages.
6. Inspect the frequency distribution carefully. Has too much detail been lost? If so, reconstruct the table with a greater number of intervals (or smaller interval size). Is the table too detailed? If so, reconstruct the table with fewer intervals (or use wider intervals). Remember that the frequency distribution results from a number of decisions you make in a rather arbitrary manner. If the appearance of the table seems less than optimal given the purpose of the research, redo the table until you are satisfied that you have struck the best balance between detail and conciseness.
7. Remember to give your table a clear, concise title, and number the table if your report contains more than one. All categories and columns must also be clearly labelled. *(For practice in constructing and interpreting frequency distributions for interval-ratio-level variables, see problems 2.5 to 2.9.)*

2.6 CONSTRUCTING FREQUENCY DISTRIBUTIONS FOR INTERVAL-RATIO VARIABLES: A REVIEW

We covered a lot of ground in the preceding section, so let's pause and review these principles by considering a specific research situation. Below are hypothetical data on the number of hours each student in an introduction to sociology course spent studying for the final exam ($n = 105$).

17	20	21	26	35	10	12	12	15	22
20	15	18	15	12	21	20	11	12	12
14	35	5	7	27	18	2	12	35	12
20	21	20	18	35	10	16	10	35	36
32	23	7	14	15	35	10	35	16	35
20	14	18	27	10	35	19	27	7	15
30	25	14	28	35	20	25	29	18	14
3	30	23	20	17	35	25	3	7	12
18	35	9	14	24	10	12	3	15	20
15	18	10	6	25	20	34	18	3	15
20	33	14	7	30					

Listed in this format, the data are a hopeless jumble from which no one could derive much meaning. The function of the frequency distribution is to arrange and organize these data so that their meanings will be made obvious.

First, we must decide how many intervals to use in the frequency distribution. Following the guidelines established in the previous section, let's use about 10 intervals. By inspecting the data, we can see that the lowest score is 2 and the highest is 36. The range of these scores is 36 − 2, or 34. To find the approximate interval size, divide the range (34) by the number of intervals (10). Since 34/10 = 3.4, we can set the interval size at 3.

The lowest score is 2, so the lowest interval will be 2–4. The highest interval will be 35–37, which will include the high score of 36. All that remains is to state the intervals in table format, count the number of scores that fall into each interval, and report the totals in a frequency column. These steps have been taken in Table 2.15, which also includes columns for the percentages and cumulative percentages. Note that this table is the product of several relatively arbitrary decisions. The researcher should remain aware of this fact and inspect the frequency distribution carefully. If the table is unsatisfactory for any reason, it can be reconstructed with a different number of categories and interval sizes.

Now, with the aid of the frequency distribution, some patterns in the data can be discerned. There are three distinct clusterings of scores in the table. The single largest interval, with 17 cases, is 14–16. Nearly as many students, 15 cases, spent between 20 and 22 hours studying for the final exam. Combined with the interval between them (17–19 hours), this represents quite a sizable grouping of cases (43 out of 105, or 40.95% of all cases). The third grouping is in the 35–37 interval with 13 cases, showing that a rather large

TABLE 2.15   NUMBER OF HOURS STUDIED FOR FINAL EXAM IN INTRODUCTION
TO SOCIOLOGY COURSE

Interval	Frequency (f)	Cumulative Frequency	Percentage (%)	Cumulative Percentage (%)
2–4	5	5	4.76	4.76
5–7	7	12	6.67	11.43
8–10	8	20	7.62	19.05
11–13	10	30	9.52	28.57
14–16	17	47	16.19	44.76
17–19	11	58	10.48	55.24
20–22	15	73	14.29	69.53
23–25	7	80	6.67	76.20
26–28	5	85	4.76	80.96
29–31	4	89	3.81	84.77
32–34	3	92	2.86	87.63
35–37	13	105	12.38	100.01
	$n = 105$		100.01*	

*Percentage columns will occasionally fail to total to 100% because of rounding error. If the total is between 99.90% and 100.10%, ignore the discrepancy. Discrepancies greater than ± 0.10% may indicate mathematical errors, and the entire column should be computed again.

percentage of students (12.38%) spent relatively many hours studying for the final exam. The cumulative percentage column indicates that the majority of the students (55.24%) spent less than 20 hours studying for the exam.

2.7 CHARTS AND GRAPHS

Researchers frequently use charts and graphs to present their data in ways that are visually more dramatic than frequency distributions. These devices are particularly useful for conveying an impression of the overall shape of a distribution and for highlighting any clustering of cases in a particular range of scores. Many graphing techniques are available, but we will examine just four. The first two, pie and bar charts, are appropriate for discrete variables at any level of measurement. The last two, histograms and frequency polygons, are used with both discrete and continuous interval-ratio variables but are particularly appropriate for the latter.

The sections that follow explain how to construct graphs and charts "by hand." These days, however, computer programs are almost always used to produce graphic displays. Graphing software is sophisticated and flexible but also relatively easy to use and, if such programs are available to you, you should familiarize yourself with them. The effort required to learn these programs will be repaid in the quality of the final product. The section on computer applications at the end of this chapter includes a demonstration of how to produce bar charts.

Pie Charts. To construct a **pie chart**, begin by computing the percentage of all cases that fall into each category of the variable. Then divide a circle (the pie) into segments (slices) proportional to the percentage distribution. Be sure that the chart and all segments are clearly labelled.

Figure 2.1 is a pie chart that displays the distribution of the "type of health professional seen" variable from the health and counselling services survey. The frequency distribution (see Table 2.6) is reproduced as Table 2.16, with a column added for the percentage distribution. Because a circle's circumference

FIGURE 2.1 PIE CHART: TYPE OF HEALTH PROFESSIONAL SEEN BY RESPONDENTS, HEALTH AND COUNSELLING SERVICES SURVEY ($n = 20$)

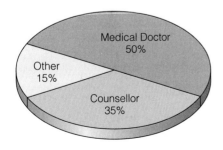

TABLE 2.16 TYPE OF HEALTH PROFESSIONAL SEEN BY RESPONDENTS, HEALTH AND COUNSELLING SERVICES SURVEY

Status	Frequency (f)	Percentage (%)
Medical Doctor	10	50
Counsellor	7	35
Other	3	15
	$n = 20$	100

is 360°, we will apportion 180° (or 50%) for the first category, 126° (35%) for the second, and 54° (15%) for the last category. The pie chart visually reinforces the relative preponderance of respondents who saw a medical doctor and the relative absence of respondents who saw other types of health professionals in the health and counselling services survey.

Bar Charts. Like pie charts, **bar charts** are relatively straightforward. Conventionally, the categories of the variable are arrayed along the horizontal axis (or abscissa) and frequencies, or percentages if you prefer, along the vertical axis (or ordinate). For each category of the variable, construct (or draw) a rectangle of constant width and with a height that corresponds to the number of cases in the category. The bar chart in Figure 2.2 reproduces the data for the "type of health professional seen" variable from Figure 2.1 and Table 2.16.

This chart would be interpreted in exactly the same way as the pie chart in Figure 2.1, and researchers are free to choose between these two methods of displaying data. However, if a variable has more than four or five categories, the bar chart would be preferred. With too many categories, the pie chart gets very crowded and loses its visual clarity.

Bar charts are also particularly effective ways to display the relative frequencies for two or more categories of a variable when you want to emphasize some comparisons. Suppose, for example, that you wished to compare males and females on satisfaction with health and counselling services. Figure 2.3 displays these data, derived from Table 2.4, in an easily comprehensible way. The bar chart shows that satisfaction with services steadily increases for females, while it steadily decreases for males. *(For practice in constructing and interpreting pie and bar charts, see problems 2.5b and 2.10.)*

Histograms. **Histograms** look a lot like bar charts and, in fact, are constructed in much the same way. However, histograms use real limits rather than stated limits and the categories or scores of the variable border each other, as if they merged into each other in a continuous series. Therefore,

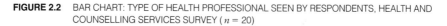

FIGURE 2.2 BAR CHART: TYPE OF HEALTH PROFESSIONAL SEEN BY RESPONDENTS, HEALTH AND COUNSELLING SERVICES SURVEY ($n = 20$)

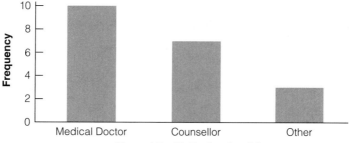

FIGURE 2.3 SATISFACTION WITH SERVICES BY SEX, HEALTH AND COUNSELLING SERVICES SURVEY ($n = 20$)

these graphs are most appropriate for continuous interval-ratio-level variables, but they are commonly used for discrete interval-ratio-level variables as well. To construct a histogram from a frequency distribution, follow these steps:

1. Array the real limits of the intervals or scores along the horizontal axis (abscissa).
2. Array frequencies along the vertical axis (ordinate).
3. For each category in the frequency distribution, construct a bar with height corresponding to the number of cases in the category and with width corresponding to the real limits of the intervals.
4. Label each axis of the graph.
5. Title the graph.

As an example, Table 2.17 presents the real limits, along with midpoints, of the intervals for the frequency distribution shown in Table 2.15.

TABLE 2.17 REAL LIMITS AND MIDPOINTS OF INTERVALS FOR FREQUENCY DISTRIBUTION SHOWN IN TABLE 2.15

Interval (Stated Limits)	Real Limits	Midpoints	Frequency (f)
2–4	1.5–4.5	3	5
5–7	4.5–7.5	6	7
8–10	7.5–10.5	9	8
11–13	10.5–13.5	12	10
14–16	13.5–16.5	15	17
17–19	16.5–19.5	18	11
20–22	19.5–22.5	21	15
23–25	22.5–25.5	24	7
26–28	25.5–28.5	27	5
29–31	28.5–31.5	30	4
32–34	31.5–34.5	33	3
35–37	34.5–37.5	36	13
			$n = 105$

FIGURE 2.4   HISTOGRAM OF STUDY HOURS FOR FINAL EXAM IN INTRODUCTION TO SOCIOLOGY COURSE ($n = 105$)

This information was used to construct a histogram of the distribution of study hours, as presented in Figure 2.4. Note that the edges of each bar correspond to the real limits, and that the middle of each bar is directly over the midpoint of the interval. Overall, the histogram visually reinforces the relative concentration of students in the middle of the distribution, as well as the relatively large grouping of students who spent between 35 to 37 hours studying for the final exam in the introduction to sociology course.

Frequency Polygons.   Construction of a **frequency polygon** is similar to construction of a histogram. Instead of using bars to represent the frequencies, however, it uses dots at the midpoint of each interval. A straight line then connects the dots. Finally, to form a polygon, the line is dropped to the horizontal axis at the midpoint of the adjacent interval at ends. Because the line is continuous from highest to lowest score, these graphs are especially appropriate for continuous interval-ratio-level variables but are frequently used with discrete interval-ratio-level variables. Figure 2.5 displays a frequency polygon for the study hours data previously displayed in the histogram in Figure 2.4.

Histograms and frequency polygons are alternative ways of displaying essentially the same message. Thus, the choice between the two techniques is left to the aesthetic pleasures of the researcher. *(For practice in constructing and interpreting histograms and frequency polygons, see problems 2.7b, 2.8e, and 2.9d.)*

FIGURE 2.5 FREQUENCY POLYGON OF STUDY HOURS FOR FINAL EXAM IN INTRODUCTION TO SOCIOLOGY COURSE ($n = 105$)

SUMMARY

1. We considered several different ways of summarizing the distribution of a single variable and, more generally, reporting the results of our research. Our emphasis throughout was on the need to communicate our results clearly and concisely. You will often find that, as you strive to communicate statistical information to others, the meanings of the information will become clearer to you as well.

2. Percentages and proportions, ratios and rates, represent several different techniques for enhancing clarity by expressing our results in terms of relative frequency. Percentages and proportions report the relative occurrence of some category of a variable compared with the distribution as a whole. Ratios compare two categories with each

other, and rates report the actual occurrences of some phenomenon compared with the number of possible occurrences per some unit of time.

3. Frequency distributions are tables that summarize the entire distribution of some variable. It is very common to construct these tables for each variable of interest as the first step in a statistical analysis. Columns for percentages, cumulative frequency, and/or cumulative percentages often enhance the readability of frequency distributions.

4. Pie and bar charts, histograms, and frequency polygons are graphic devices used to express the basic information contained in the frequency distribution in a compact and visually dramatic way.

SUMMARY OF FORMULAS

Proportions	2.1	$p = \dfrac{f}{n}$
Percentage	2.2	$\% = \left(\dfrac{f}{n}\right) \times 100$
Ratios	2.3	$\text{Ratio} = \dfrac{f_1}{f_2}$

GLOSSARY

Bar chart. A graphic display device for discrete variables. Categories are represented by bars of equal width, the height of each corresponding to the number (or percentage) of cases in the category. (p. 51)

Cumulative frequency. An optional column in a frequency distribution that displays the number of cases within an interval and all preceding intervals. (p. 46)

Cumulative percentage. An optional column in a frequency distribution that displays the percentage of cases within an interval and all preceding intervals. (p. 46)

Frequency distribution. A table that displays the number of cases in each category of a variable. (p. 39)

Frequency polygon. A graphic display device for interval-ratio variables. Intervals are represented by dots placed over the midpoints, the height of each corresponding to the number (or percentage) of cases in the interval. All dots are connected by straight lines. (p. 53)

Histogram. A graphic display device for interval-ratio variables. Intervals are represented by contiguous bars of equal width (equal to the real limits), the height of each corresponding to the number (or percentage) of cases in the interval. (p. 51)

Intervals. The categories used in the frequency distributions for interval-ratio variables. (p. 43)

Midpoint. The point exactly halfway between the upper and lower limits of an interval. (p. 44)

Percentage. The number of cases in a category of a variable divided by the number of cases in all categories of the variable, the entire quantity multiplied by 100. (p. 33)

Pie chart. A graphic display device especially for discrete variables with only a few categories. A circle (the pie) is divided into segments proportional in size to the percentage of cases in each category of the variable. (p. 50)

Proportion. The number of cases in one category of a variable divided by the number of cases in all categories of the variable. (p. 33)

Rate. The number of actual occurrences of some phenomenon or trait divided by the number of possible occurrences per some unit of time. (p. 38)

Ratio. The number of cases in one category divided by the number of cases in some other category. (p. 37)

Real limits. The intervals of a frequency distribution when stated as continuous categories. (p. 45)

Stated limits. The intervals of a frequency distribution when stated as discrete categories. (p. 45)

MULTIMEDIA RESOURCES

 http://www.healeystatistics.nelson.com

Visit the companion website for the second Canadian edition of *Statistics: A Tool for Social Research* to access a wide range of student resources. Begin by clicking on the Student Resources section of the book's website to access review quizzes, flashcards, and other study tools.

PROBLEMS

2.1 | SOC | The tables that follow report the marital status of 20 respondents in two different apartment complexes. *(HINT: Make sure that you have the correct numbers in the numerator and denominator before solving the following problems. For example, problem 2.1a asks for "the percentage of respondents who are married in each complex," and the denominators will be 20 for these two fractions.*

Problem 2.1d, however, asks for the "percentage of the single respondents who live in Complex B," and the denominator for this fraction will be 4 + 6, or 10.)

Status	Complex A	Complex B
Married	5	10
Unmarried ("living together")	8	2
Single	4	6
Separated	2	1
Widowed	0	1
Divorced	1	0
	20	20

a. What percentage of the respondents in each complex are married?

b. What is the ratio of single to married respondents at each complex?

c. What proportion of each sample are widowed?

d. What percentage of the single respondents live in Complex B?

e. What is the ratio of the "unmarried/living together" to the married at each complex?

2.2 At Algebra University, the numbers of males and females in the various major fields of study are as follows:

Major	Males	Females	Totals
Humanities	117	83	200
Social sciences	97	132	229
Natural sciences	72	20	92
Business	156	139	295
Nursing	3	35	38
Education	30	15	45
Totals	475	424	899

Read each of the following problems carefully before constructing the fraction and solving for the answer. *(HINT: Be sure you place the proper number in the denominator of the fractions. For example, some problems use the total number of males or females as the denominator but others use the total number of majors.)*

a. What percentage of social science majors are male?

b. What proportion of business majors are female?

c. For the humanities, what is the ratio of males to females?

d. What percentage of the total student body are males?

e. What is the ratio of males to females for the entire sample?

f. What proportion of the nursing majors are male?

g. What percentage of the sample are social science majors?

h. What is the ratio of humanities majors to business majors?

i. What is the ratio of female business majors to female nursing majors?

j. What proportion of the males are education majors?

2.3 CJ The city of Pearson, Ontario, has a population of 211,732 and experienced 47 bank robberies, 13 murders, and 23 auto thefts during the past year. Compute a rate for each type of crime per 100,000 population. *(HINT: Make sure that you set up the fraction with size of population in the denominator.)*

2.4 CJ The numbers of homicides in five states and five Canadian provinces for the years 1997 and 2001 are as follows:

State	1997		2001	
	Homicides	Population	Homicides	Population
New Jersey	338	8,053,000	336	8,484,431
Iowa	52	2,852,000	50	2,923,179
Alabama	426	4,139,000	379	4,464,356
Texas	1,327	19,439,000	1,332	21,325,018
California	2,579	32,268,000	2,206	34,501,130
Nova Scotia	24	936,100	9	942,900
Quebec	32	7,323,600	149	7,417,700

(continued next page)

(continued)

Province	1997		2001	
	Homicides	Population	Homicides	Population
Ontario	178	11,387,400	170	12,068,300
Manitoba	31	1,137,900	34	1,150,800
British Columbia	116	3,997,100	85	4,141,300

Sources: US Census Bureau; Adapted from "Number of homicides, by province/territory, 1961 to 2005," *Juristat*, Catalogue 85-002-XIE, Volume 26, no. 6, Table 1. http://www.statcan.ca/english/freepub/85-002-XIE/85-002-XIE2006006.pdf. "Annual population estimates for July 1, 1971 to 2005, Canada, provinces and territories," *Annual Demographic Statistics, 2005*, Catalogue 91-213-XIB, Table 1.1. http://www.statcan.ca/english/freepub/91-213-XIB/0000591-213-XIB.pdf.

Calculate the homicide rate per 100,000 population for each state and each province for each year. Relatively speaking, which state and which province had the highest homicide rates in each year? Which country seems to have the higher homicide rate? Write a paragraph describing these results.

2.5 SOC The scores of 15 respondents on four variables are reported below. The numerical codes for the variables are as follows:

Sex	Support for Legalization of Marijuana	Level of Education	Age
1 = Male	1 = In favour	0 = Less than high school	Actual years
2 = Female	2 = Opposed	1 = High school	
		2 = Community college	
		3 = Bachelor's	
		4 = Graduate	

Case Number	Sex	Support for Legalization of Marijuana	Level of Education	Age
1	2	1	1	45
2	1	2	1	48
3	2	1	3	55
4	1	1	2	32
5	2	1	3	33
6	1	1	1	28
7	2	2	0	77
8	1	1	1	50
9	1	2	0	43
10	2	1	1	48
11	1	1	4	33

(continued next column)

(continued)

Case Number	Sex	Support for Legalization of Marijuana	Level of Education	Age
12	1	1	4	35
13	1	1	0	39
14	2	1	1	25
15	1	1	1	23

a. Construct a frequency distribution for each variable. Include a column for percentages.
b. Construct pie and bar charts to display the distributions of sex, support for legalization of marijuana, and level of education.

2.6 SW A local youth service agency has begun a sex education program for teenage girls who have been referred by the youth courts. The girls were given a 20-item test for general knowledge about sex, contraception, and anatomy and physiology upon admission to the program and again after completing the program. The scores of the first 15 girls to complete the program are listed below.

Case	Pretest	Post-test	Case	Pretest	Post-test
A	8	12	I	5	7
B	7	13	J	15	12
C	10	12	K	13	20
D	15	19	L	4	5
E	10	8	M	10	15
F	10	17	N	8	11
G	3	12	O	12	20
H	10	11			

Construct frequency distributions for the pretest and post-test scores. Include a column for percentages. (*HINT: There were 20 items on the test, so the maximum range for these scores is 20. If you use 10 intervals to display these scores, the interval size will be 2. Because there are no scores of 0 or 1 for either test, you may state the first interval as 2–3. To make comparisons easier, both frequency distributions should have the same intervals.)*

2.7 | SOC | Sixteen students in their final year of undergraduate studies completed a class to prepare them for the GRE (Graduate Record Examination). Their scores are reported below.

420	345	560	650
459	499	500	657
467	480	505	555
480	520	530	589

These same 16 students were given a test of math and verbal ability to measure their readiness for graduate-level work. Scores are reported below in terms of the percentage of correct answers for each test.

Math Test

67	45	68	70
72	85	90	99
50	73	77	78
52	66	89	75

Verbal Test

89	90	78	77
75	70	56	60
77	78	80	92
98	72	77	82

a. Display each of these variables in a frequency distribution with columns for percentages and cumulative percentages.
b. Construct a histogram and a frequency polygon for these data.
c. Find the upper and lower real limits for the intervals you established.

2.8 | GER | Following are reported the number of times 25 residents of a community for senior citizens left their homes for any reason during the past week.

0	2	1	7	3
7	0	2	3	17
14	15	5	0	7
5	21	4	7	6
2	0	10	5	7

a. Construct a frequency distribution to display these data.
b. What are the midpoints of the intervals?
c. Add columns to the table to display the percentage distribution, cumulative frequency, and cumulative percentages.

d. Find the real limits for the intervals you selected.
e. Construct a histogram and a frequency polygon to display these data.
f. Write a paragraph summarizing this distribution of scores.

2.9 | SOC | Twenty-five students completed a questionnaire that measured their attitudes toward interpersonal violence. Respondents who scored high believed that in many situations a person could legitimately use physical force against another person. Respondents who scored low believed that in no situation (or very few situations) could the use of violence be justified.

52	47	17	8	92
53	23	28	9	90
17	63	17	17	23
19	66	10	20	47
20	66	5	25	17

a. Construct a frequency distribution to display these data.
b. What are the midpoints of the intervals?
c. Add columns to the table to display the percentage distribution, cumulative frequency, and cumulative percentage.
d. Construct a histogram and a frequency polygon to display these data.
e. Write a paragraph summarizing this distribution of scores.

2.10 | PA/CJ | As part of an evaluation of the efficiency of your local police force, you have gathered the following data on police response time to calls for assistance during two different years. (Response times were rounded off to whole minutes.) Convert both frequency distributions into percentages and construct pie charts and bar charts to display the data. Write a paragraph comparing the changes in response time between the two years.

Response Time, 2000	f	Response Time, 2010	f
21 minutes or more	35	21 minutes or more	45
16–20 minutes	75	16–20 minutes	95
11–15 minutes	180	11–15 minutes	155
6–10 minutes	375	6–10 minutes	350
Less than 6 minutes	275	Less than 6 minutes	250
	875		895

Using SPSS for Windows to Produce Frequency Distributions and Graphs with the 2009 GSS

The demonstrations and exercises below use the shortened version of the 2009 GSS data set supplied with this textbook. Click the SPSS icon on your monitor screen to start SPSS for Windows. Load the 2009 GSS by clicking the file name (*GSS.sav*) on the first screen, or by clicking **File**, **Open**, and **Data** on the **SPSS Data Editor** window. In the **Open Data** dialog box, you may have to change the drive specification to locate the 2009 GSS data. Double-click the file name (*GSS.sav*) to open the data set. You are ready to proceed when you see the message "IBM SPSS Statistics Processor is ready" on the status bar at the bottom of the **SPSS Data Editor** window as shown in Figure 2.6.

The **SPSS Data Editor** window can actually be viewed in one of two unique modes. The **Data View** mode (Figure 2.6), which is the default mode when you start SPSS, displays the data in the data set. Each row represents a particular case and each column a particular variable. By contrast, the **Variable View** mode (Figure 2.7) shows the variables in that data set, where each row represents a particular variable and each column a particular piece of information (e.g., name, label) about the variable. To change from one mode to the other, click the appropriate tab located at the bottom of the **SPSS Data Editor** window.

FIGURE 2.6 SPSS DATA EDITOR WINDOW: DATA VIEW

FIGURE 2.7   SPSS DATA EDITOR WINDOW: VARIABLE VIEW

Before we begin our demonstrations, it is important to note that SPSS provides the user with a variety of options for displaying information about the data file and output on the screen. We highly recommend that you tell SPSS to display lists of variables by name (e.g., *acmyr*) rather than labels (e.g., main activity of the respondent in the last 12 months). Lists displayed this way will be easier to read and to compare to the GSS and Census codebooks in Appendix G. To do this, click **Edit** on the main menu bar at the top of the **SPSS Data Editor** window, and then click **Options** from the drop-down submenu. A dialog box labelled **Options** will appear with a series of tabs along the top. The **General** options should be displayed but, if not, click on the **General** tab. On the **General** screen, find the box labelled **Variable Lists** and, if they are not already selected, click **Display names** and then **Alphabetical** and then click **OK**. If you make changes, a message may appear on the screen that tells you that changes will take effect the next time a data file is opened. Click **OK**.

SPSS DEMONSTRATION 2.1 Frequency Distributions

In this demonstration, we will use the **Frequencies** procedure to produce a frequency distribution for the variable *marstat* (marital status).

From the menu bar on the **SPSS Data Editor** window, click **Analyze**. From the menu that drops down, click **Descriptive Statistics** and then **Frequencies**. The **Frequencies** dialog box appears with the variables listed in alphabetical order in the left-hand box. Find *marstat* in the left-hand box by using the slider button or the arrow keys on the right-hand border to scroll through the variable list. As an alternative, type "m," and the cursor will move to the first variable name in the list that begins with the letter "m." In this case, the variable is *marstat,* the variable in which we are interested. Once *marstat* is highlighted, click the arrow button in the centre of the screen to move the variable name to the **Variable(s)** box. The variable name *marstat* should now appear in the box. Click the **OK** button at the bottom of the dialog box, and SPSS will rush off to create the frequency distributions you requested.

The output table (frequency distribution) will be in the **SPSS Output**, or **Viewer**, window that will now be "closest" to you on the screen. As illustrated in Figure 2.8, the output table, along with other information, is in the right-hand box of the window, while the left-hand box contains an "outline" of the entire output. To change the size of the **SPSS Output** window, click on the **Maximize** button, the middle symbol (shaped like either a square or two intersecting squares) in the upper-right-hand corner of the window. The actual output can also be edited by double-clicking on any part of the table. (See Appendix F.6 for more information on editing output.)

Let's briefly examine the elements of the output table in Figure 2.8. The variable description, or label, is printed at the top of the output ("Marital status"). The various categories are printed on the left. Moving one column to the right, we find the actual frequencies, or the number of times each score of the variable occurred. We see that 745 of the respondents were married, 176 had common-law status, and so forth.

Next are two columns that report percentages. The entries in the "Percent" column are based on all respondents in the sample. In this case, the denominator would include any respondents, even the ones coded as missing. The "Valid

FIGURE 2.8   SPSS VIEWER (OUTPUT) WINDOW

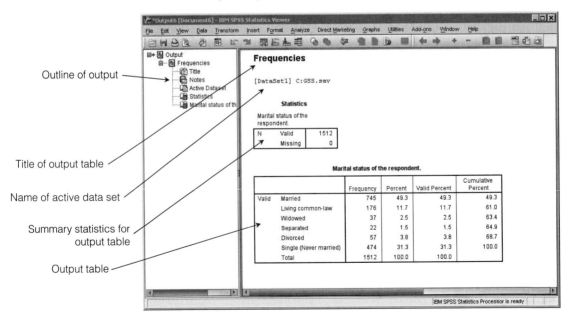

Outline of output

Title of output table

Name of active data set

Summary statistics for output table

Output table

Percent" column eliminates all cases with missing values. Because we almost always ignore missing values, we will pay attention only to the "Valid Percent" column. (Note that because all respondents supplied information on marital status, there is no difference between the two columns.) The final column is a cumulative percentage column (see Table 2.14). For nominal-level variables like *marstat,* this information is not meaningful because the order in which the categories are stated is arbitrary.

The output table in the **SPSS Output** window can be printed or saved by selecting the appropriate command from the **File** menu. You can also transfer the table to a word processor document: right-click on any part of the table, choose **Copy**, right-click on the spot in the word processor document where you want to place the table, and choose **Paste**. Appendix F.7 provides more information on these topics.

As a final note, the total number of cases in the GSS data set is 1,500. This can be verified by scrolling to the bottom of the **SPSS Data Editor** window, where you will find a total of 1,500 rows. However, the "total" number of cases in the output table above is 1,512. The reason for the difference is that the GSS data set is weighted to correct for sampling bias. Like many social surveys, the GSS under- and over-samples various groups of individuals. Some individuals are therefore more likely than others to be included in the GSS sample. The weight variable included with the GSS, *wght_per,* corrects for this bias. Once you open the *GSS.sav* file, the weight variable is automatically "turned on." So, you are really analyzing 1,512, not 1,500, individuals when using this data file. (See Appendix G.4 for more information on this topic.)

SPSS DEMONSTRATION 2.2 Graphs and Charts

SPSS for Windows can produce a variety of graphs and charts, and we will use the program to produce a bar chart in this demonstration. To conserve space, we will keep the choices as simple as possible, but you should explore the options for yourself. For any questions you might have that are not answered in this demonstration, click **Help** on the main menu bar.

To produce a bar chart, first click **Graphs** on the main menu bar and then click **Legacy Dialogs** and then **Bar**. The **Bar Charts** dialog box appears with three choices for the type of graph we want. The **Simple** option is already highlighted, and this is the one we want. Make sure that **Summaries for groups of cases** in the **Data in Chart Are** box is selected and then click **Define** at the bottom of the dialog box. The **Define Simple Bar** dialog box appears with variable names listed on the left. Choose *edu10* (highest level of education) from the variable list by moving the cursor to highlight this variable name. Click the arrow button in the middle of the screen to move *edu10* to the **Category Axis** text box.

Note the **Bars Represent** box is above the **Category Axis** box. The options in this box give you control over the vertical axis of the graph, which can be calibrated in frequencies, percentages, or cumulative frequencies or percentages. Let's choose **N of cases** (frequencies), the option that is already selected. Click **OK** in the **Define Simple Bar** dialog box, and the following bar chart will be produced. (Note, to save space only the output graph, and not the whole **SPSS**

Output window, is shown. Also, this output has been slightly edited for clarity, and will not exactly match the output on your screen.)

FIGURE 2.9

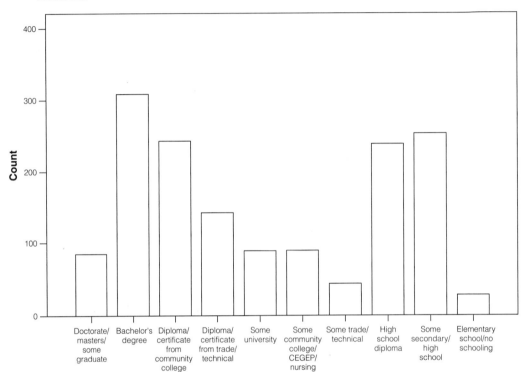

Highest Level of Education Obtained by the Respondent

Figure 2.9 reveals that the most common levels of education for this sample are "Bachelor's degree" and "Some secondary/high school." The least common level is "Elementary school/no schooling." Don't forget to **Save** or **Print** the chart if you wish.

Exercises (using *GSS.sav*)

2.1 Get frequency distributions for five nominal or ordinal variables in the GSS data set. Write a sentence or two summarizing each frequency distribution. Your description should clearly identify the most and least common scores and any other noteworthy patterns you observe.

2.2 Get a bar chart for *srh_q110* (state of health of the respondent) and *hsdsizec* (household size). Write a sentence or two of interpretation for each chart.

3

Measures of Central Tendency and Dispersion

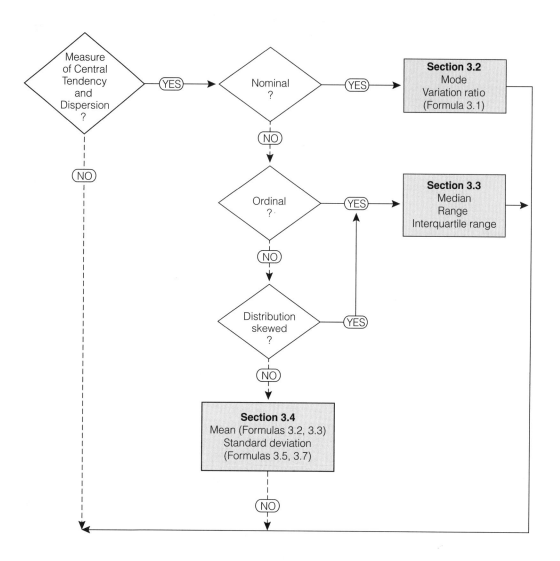

LEARNING OBJECTIVES

By the end of this chapter, you will be able to

1. Explain the purposes of measures of central tendency and dispersion, and interpret the information they convey.

2. Calculate and explain the mode, median, and mean.

3. Calculate and explain the variation ratio, the range, the interquartile range, and the standard deviation.

4. Describe and explain the mathematical characteristics of the mean and the standard deviation.

5. Select an appropriate measure of central tendency and dispersion according to level of measurement and skew.

3.1 INTRODUCTION

One clear benefit of frequency distributions, graphs, and charts is that they summarize the overall shape of a distribution of scores in a way that can be quickly comprehended. Often, however, you will need to report more detailed information about the distribution. Specifically, two additional kinds of statistics are almost always useful: some idea of the typical or average case in the distribution (e.g., "the average starting salary for social workers is $49,000 per year") and some idea of how much variety or heterogeneity there is in the distribution ("In this province, starting salaries for social workers range from $43,000 per year to $55,000 per year"). These two kinds of statistics, the subjects of this chapter, are referred to as **measures of central tendency** and **measures of dispersion** respectively.

The three commonly used measures of central tendency—the mode, median, and mean—are all probably familiar to you. All three summarize an entire distribution of scores by describing the most common score (the mode), the middle case (the median), or the average of the scores of the cases (the mean) of that distribution. These statistics are powerful because they can reduce huge arrays of data to a single, easily understood number. Remember that the central purpose of descriptive statistics is to summarize or "reduce" data.

Nonetheless, measures of central tendency by themselves cannot summarize data completely. For a full description of a distribution of scores, measures of central tendency must be paired with measures of dispersion. While measures of central tendency are designed to locate the typical and/or central scores, measures of dispersion provide information about the amount of variety, diversity, or heterogeneity within a distribution of scores.

The importance of the concept of **dispersion** might be easier to grasp if we consider an example. Suppose that a sociology professor wants to evaluate the different styles of final exams that she administered last semester to students in the two sections of her introduction to sociology course. Students in Section A of the course received an essay-style final exam, while students in Section B received a multiple-choice final exam. As a part of her investigation, she calculated that the mean exam score was 65% for students who wrote the essay-style exam and 65% for those who wrote the multiple-choice exam. The average exam score is the same which provides no basis for judging if scores for one exam style are less or more diverse than scores for the other exam style. Measures of dispersion, however, can reveal substantial differences in the underlying distributions even when the measures of central tendency are equivalent. For example, consider Figure 3.1, which displays the distribution of exam scores for students in each section of the course in the form of frequency polygons (see Chapter 2).

Compare the shapes of these two figures. Note that the frequency polygon of exam scores for students who wrote the multiple-choice exam (Section B) is much flatter than the frequency polygon of exam scores for students who wrote the essay exam (Section A). This is because the scores for students who wrote the multiple-choice exam are more spread out or more diverse than the scores for students who wrote the essay exam. In other words, the scores for the multiple-choice exam are much more

FIGURE 3.1   EXAMS SCORES FOR TWO STYLES OF EXAMS

variable and there are more scores in the high and low ranges and fewer in the middle, than there are on the essay exam. The essay exam scores are more similar to each other and clustered around the mean. Both distributions have the same "average" score but there is considerably more "variation" or dispersion in the scores for the multiple-choice exam. If you were the professor, would you be more likely to select an exam style for which students receive similar exam results (essay exam) or one for which some students receive very low scores and some other students very high scores (multiple-choice exam)? Note that if we had not considered dispersion, a possibly important difference in the performance of students writing the two different types of exams might have gone unnoticed.

Keep the two shapes in Figure 3.1 in mind as visual representations of the concept of dispersion. The greater clustering of scores around the mean in the distribution in the upper part of the figure (essay exam distribution) indicates *less* dispersion and the flatter curve of the distribution in the lower part of the figure (multiple-choice exam distribution) indicates *more* variety or dispersion. Each of the measures of dispersion discussed in this chapter—variation ratio, range, interquartile range, variance, and standard deviation—will increase in value as distributions become flatter (as the scores become more dispersed). However, as with the three measures of central tendency, choosing which of the measures of dispersion to use depends on how the variables are measured. The mode and variation ratio are most appropriate for nominal-level variables. The median and range and interquartile range can be used with variables measured at either the ordinal- or interval-ratio level, however the mean, variance, and standard deviation are more appropriate for interval-ratio-level variables.

3.2 NOMINAL-LEVEL MEASURES

Mode. We begin our consideration of measures of central tendency with the **mode**. The mode of any distribution is the value that occurs most frequently. For example, in the set of scores 58, 82, 82, 90, 98, the mode is 82 because it occurs twice and the other scores occur only once.

The mode is, relatively speaking, a rather simple statistic, most useful when you want a "quick and easy" indicator of central tendency or when you are working with nominal-level variables. In fact, the mode is the only measure of central tendency that can be used with nominal-level variables. Such variables do not, of course, have numerical "scores" per se, and the mode of a nominally measured variable would be its largest category. For example, Table 3.1 reports the method of travel to work for a hypothetical sample of 100 workers. The mode of this distribution, the single largest category, is "Automobile."

If a researcher desires to report only the most popular or common value of a distribution, or if the variable under consideration is nominal, then the mode is the appropriate measure of central tendency. However, keep in mind that the mode does have limitations. First, some distributions have no mode at all (see Table 2.5) or so many modes that the statistic loses all meaning.

TABLE 3.1   METHOD OF TRAVEL TO WORK

Method	Frequency
Automobile	50
Public transportation	30
Walk	10
Bicycle	5
Other	5
	$n = 100$

Second, with ordinal and interval-ratio data, the modal score may not be central to the distribution as a whole. That is, *most common* does not necessarily mean "typical" in the sense of identifying the centre of the distribution. For example, consider the rather unusual (but not impossible) distribution of scores on an exam as illustrated in Table 3.2. The mode of the distribution is 93. Is this score very close to the majority of the scores? If the instructor summarized this distribution by reporting only the modal score, would he or she be conveying an accurate picture of the distribution as a whole?

Variation Ratio.   To conveniently measure dispersion of a variable we can use a statistic based on the mode called the **variation ratio (v)**. The underlying logic of the variation ratio is that the larger the proportion of cases in the mode of a variable (i.e., the more concentrated and similar the data), the less the dispersion among cases of that variable. The ratio has a lower limit of 0.00, indicating no variation (i.e., all cases fall into one category of a variable), and increases to a maximum value of 1.00 as the proportion of cases in the modal category of a variable decreases. The formula for the v is:

FORMULA 3.1
$$v = 1 - \left(\frac{f_m}{n}\right)$$

where f_m = the number of cases in the mode
n = the total number of cases

TABLE 3.2   A DISTRIBUTION OF EXAM SCORES

Scores	Frequency
58	2
60	2
62	3
64	2
66	3
67	4
68	1
69	1
70	2
93	5
	$n = 25$

To illustrate the logic of this statistic, consider the idea that Canada will grow more ethnoculturally diverse in the future. Over the past few decades Canada has experienced an increase in immigration from non-European countries. This has led to a change in the ethnocultural makeup of Canada. Will Canada continue to grow more diverse in the years to come?

Table 3.3 presents data on the size of visible and non-visible minority groups for 1996 and projections for 2006 and 2017. (Note that the values in the table are per 100 people in the population, since this will greatly simplify computations.) By inspection, you can see that Canada is becoming more ethnoculturally diverse over time. For every 100 Canadians, about 11 were visible minorities in 1996. By 2017 this rate is projected to increase to approximately 21 per 100 people. Let's see how the v substantiates these observations.

For the year 1996, the number of cases in the mode (i.e., the non-visible minority category) is 89. The total number of cases in that year is 100. Substituting these values into Formula 3.1, we have a v of 0.11 for the year 1996:

$$v = 1 - \left(\frac{89}{100} \right) = 1 - 0.89 = 0.11$$

For 2006,

$$v = 1 - \left(\frac{84}{100} \right) = 1 - 0.84 = 0.16$$

and for 2017,

$$v = 1 - \left(\frac{79}{100} \right) = 1 - 0.79 = 0.21$$

Thus, the v, in a quantitative and precise way, substantiates our earlier impressions. Canada is growing more ethnoculturally diverse.

The v of 0.11 for the year 1996 means that the distribution of frequencies shows 11% of the maximum variation possible. By 2017, the variation

TABLE 3.3 VISIBLE MINORITY STATUS IN CANADA, 1996, 2006, 2017 (per 100 people in the population)

Status*	Year		
	1996	2006	2017
Visible minority	11	16	21
Non-visible minority	89	84	79
Total	100	100	100

*In Canada, visible minorities, as defined by the Employment Equity Act, are persons, other than Aboriginal peoples, who are non-Caucasian in race or non-white in colour.

Source: Statistics Canada. 2005. *Population Projections of Visible Minority Groups, Canada, Provinces and Regions, 2001–2017.* Catalogue no. 91-541-XIE.

will increase to 21% of the maximum variation possible. Canadian society has grown increasingly diverse in its ethnocultural composition, and will be quite heterogeneous by 2017.

In summary, the variation ratio provides a quick and easy method of calculating measure of dispersion. The larger the variation ratio, the more dispersed the data are for that variable; the smaller the variation ratio, the more similar the data. Although the variation ratio can be used with any variable, it is most appropriate for nominal-level variables. (*For practice in calculating and interpreting the mode and the variation ratio, see problems 3.1 to 3.6.*)

3.3 ORDINAL-LEVEL MEASURES

Median. The **median (Md)** is a measure of central tendency that represents the exact centre of a distribution of scores. The median is the score of the case that is in the exact middle of a distribution: half the cases have scores higher and half the cases have scores lower than the case with the median score. Thus, if the median family income for a community is $35,000, half the families earn more than $35,000 and half earn less.

Before finding the median, the cases must be placed in order from the highest to the lowest score—or from the lowest to the highest. Once this is done, find the central or middle case. The median is the score associated with that case.

When the number of cases (n) is odd, the value of the median is unambiguous because there will always be a middle case. With an even number of cases, however, there will be two middle cases; in this situation, the median is defined as the score exactly halfway between the scores of the two middle cases.

To illustrate, assume that seven students were asked to indicate their level of support for the interuniversity athletic program at their universities on a scale ranging from 10 (indicating great support) to 0 (no support). After arranging their responses from high to low, you can find the median by locating the case that divides the distribution into two equal halves. With a total of seven cases, the middle case would be the fourth case, as there will be three cases above and three cases below the fourth case. If the seven scores were 10, 10, 8, 7, 5, 4, and 2, then the median is 7, the score of the fourth case.

To summarize: when n is odd, find the middle case by adding 1 to n and then dividing that sum by 2. With an n of 7, the median is the score associated with the $(7 + 1)/2$, or fourth, case. If n had been 21, the median would be the score associated with the $(21 + 1)/2$, or 11th, case.

Now, if we make n an even number (8) by adding a student to the sample whose support for athletics was measured as a 1, we would no longer have a single middle case. The ordered distribution of scores would now be 10, 10, 8, 7, 5, 4, 2, 1; any value between 7 and 5 would technically satisfy the definition of a median (that is, would split the distribution into two equal halves of four cases each). This ambiguity is resolved by defining the median as the average of the scores of the two middle cases. In the example above, the median would be defined as $(7 + 5)/2$, or 6.

To summarize: to identify the two middle cases when n is an even number, divide n by 2 to find the first middle case and then increase that number by 1 to find the second middle case. In the example above with eight cases, the first middle case would be the fourth case ($n/2 = 4$) and the second middle case would be the ($n/2$) + 1, or fifth, case. If n had been 142, the first middle case would have been the 71st case and the second middle case would have been the 72nd case. Remember that the median is defined as the average of the scores associated with the two middle cases.*

Table 3.4 summarizes the procedures for finding the median. It is important to emphasize that since the median requires that scores be ranked from high to low, it cannot be calculated for variables measured at the nominal level. Remember that the scores of nominal-level variables cannot be ordered or ranked: the scores are different from each other but do not form a mathematical scale of any sort. The median can be found for either ordinal- or interval-ratio data but it is generally more appropriate for ordinal level data.

Range and Interquartile Range. The **range (R)**, defined as the difference or interval between the highest score (H) and lowest score (L) in a distribution, provides a quick and general notion of variability for variables

TABLE 3.4   FINDING THE MEDIAN

Situation	Location of Md	Procedure to Find Md	Examples
n is odd	The Md is the score of the middle case.	Add 1 to n and divide by 2. This is the number of the middle case. The Md is the score of this case.	If n is 13, the Md is the score of the $(13 + 1)/2$, or seventh, case. If n is 365, the Md would be the score of the $(365 + 1)/2$, or 183rd case.
n is even	The Md is halfway between the scores of the two middle cases.	Divide n by 2 to find the first middle case and then increase that number by 1 to find the second middle case. The Md is the average of the scores of the two middle cases.	If n is 14, the Md is the score halfway between the scores of the seventh and eighth cases. If n is 366, the Md is the score halfway between the scores of the 183rd and 184th cases.

*If the middle cases have the same score, that score is defined as the median. In the distribution 10, 10, 8, 6, 6, 4, 2, and 1, the middle cases both have scores of 6 and, thus, the median would be defined as 6.

measured at either the ordinal- or interval-ratio level. Unfortunately, since it is based on only the two most extreme scores in a distribution, R will be misleading as a measure of dispersion if just one of these scores is either exceptionally high or low. Such scores are often referred to as **outliers**.

The **interquartile range (Q)** is a type of range that avoids this problem. The interquartile range is the distance from the third quartile (Q_3) to the first quartile (Q_1) of a distribution of scores, or symbolically $Q = Q_3 - Q_1$.* The first quartile, Q_1, is the point below which 25% of the cases fall and above which 75% of the cases fall. The third quartile, Q_3, is the point below which 75% of the cases fall and above which 25% of the cases fall. If line LH represents a distribution of scores, the first and third quartiles and the interquartile range are located as shown:

Thus, Q is the range of the middle 50% of the cases in a distribution. Since it uses only the middle 50%, Q is not influenced by outliers.

To illustrate the computation of the range and the interquartile range, let's consider the following set of eleven scores: 5, 8, 10, 12, 15, 18, 21, 22, 24, 26, and 99. These scores are ordered from low to high, though placing them in order from high to low will produce identical results. Either way, an ordered distribution of scores makes the range easy to calculate and is necessary for finding the interquartile range.

To find the range, R, for this set of scores, the lowest score (L) is subtracted from the highest score (H). Therefore:

$$R = H - L$$
$$= 99 - 5$$
$$= 94$$

---

*A quartile is a member of a class of statistics called percentiles. A percentile identifies the point below which a specific percentage of cases fall. For example, if a score of 476 is reported as the 95th percentile, this means that 95% of the cases had scores lower than 476. Hence, the first quartile, Q_1, is simply the 25th percentile, second quartile, Q_2, the 50th percentile, which is the same as (you guessed it) the median, and third quartile, Q_3, the 75th percentile. Other commonly used percentiles are the decile and quintile. Deciles divide the distribution of scores into tenths. So, the first decile is the point below which 10% of the cases fall and is equivalent to the 10th percentile; the second decile is the same as the 20th percentile; and so on. Quintiles divide the distribution into fifths. The first quintile is the point below which 20% of the cases fall and is the same as the 20th percentile, the second quintile is the 40th percentile, etc.

To calculate Q, we must locate the first and third quartiles (Q_1 and Q_3). To find the quartiles, first find the median for the ordered data (see Table 3.4). Next, divide the data so that there are an equal number of cases above and below the median. Finally, find the median of the lower and upper parts of the data (again see Table 3.4). Q_1 is equal to the median of the lower half of the data and Q_3 to the median of the upper half. Q equals the difference between Q_3 and Q_1. Table 3.5 provides a step-by-step guide for finding the interquartile range.

Continuing with the example above, we first divide the ordered data into two equal parts at the median (Md = 18). The scores in the lower half are 5, 8, 10, 12, and 15 and the scores in the upper half are 21, 22, 24, 26, and 99. We then find the median of the lower half of the data, or Q_1, which equals 10, and the median of the upper half of the data, or Q_3, which equals 24. We subtract Q_1 from Q_3 to find the interquartile range. Therefore:

$$Q = Q_3 - Q_1$$
$$= 24 - 10$$
$$= 14$$

Clearly, the interquartile range ($Q = 14$) is preferred to the range ($R = 94$) as a measure of dispersion for this example, because it eliminates the influence of outliers and provides more accurate information about the amount of diversity within the distribution.

As another example consider the following set of four scores: 2, 3, 8, and 9. R for this data set is $9 - 2$, or 7. To calculate Q, the data set is divided into two equal parts at the median (Md = 5.5 or [3 + 8]/2), so scores 2 and 3 make-up the lower half of the data set and scores 8 and 9 the upper half. The median of the lower half, Q_1, is 2.5, or (2 + 3)/2 and the

TABLE 3.5   STEPS IN FINDING THE INTERQUARTILE RANGE

Step	Example
1. Array the scores in order from low to high score.*	2, 4, 6, 8, 10, 12, 14, 16, 18, 20, 22, 24
2. Find the median of the data. (See Table 3.4).	Md = (12 + 14)/2 = 13
3. Divide the ordered data into two equal parts at the median.	Lower half = 2, 4, 6, 8, 10, 12 Upper half = 14, 16, 18, 20, 22, 24
4. Find the median of the lower half of the data. (This value is equal to Q_1.)	Md of 2, 4, 6, 8, 10, 12 = (6 + 8)/2 = 7
5. Find the median of the upper half of the data. (This value is equal to Q_3.)	Md of 14, 16, 18, 20, 22, 24 = (18 + 20)/2 = 19
6. Subtract Q_1 from Q_3. (This value is equal to Q.)	$Q = 19 - 7 = 12$

*The same steps are to be followed, and the same result (Q) will ensue, if scores are ordered from high to low.

median of the upper half, Q_3, is 8.5, or (8 + 9)/2. Hence, Q_1 equals 8.5 − 2.5, or 6.

In conclusion, the range and interquartile range provide a measure of dispersion based on just two scores from a set of data. These statistics require that scores be ranked from low to high—or from high to low—, so they can be calculated for variables measured at either the ordinal or interval-ratio, but not nominal, level. Since almost any sizable distribution will contain some atypically high and low scores, the interquartile range is a more useful measure of dispersion than the range because it is not affected by extremes scores or outliers. (*For practice in finding and interpreting the median, R, and Q, see any problem at the end of this chapter.*)

3.4 INTERVAL-RATIO-LEVEL MEASURES

Mean. The **mean** ($\overline{X}$, read this as "ex-bar"), or arithmetic average, is by far the most commonly used measure of central tendency. It reports the average score of a distribution, and its calculation is straightforward: to compute the mean, add the scores and then divide by the number of scores (n). To illustrate: a family-planning clinic administered a 20-item test of general knowledge about contraception to 10 clients. The number of correct responses (the scores of the 10 clients) was 2, 10, 15, 11, 9, 16, 18, 10, 11, and 7. To find the mean of this distribution, add the scores (total = 109) and divide by the number of scores (10). The result (10.9) is the average number of correct responses on the test.

The mathematical formula for the mean is:

FORMULA 3.2

$$\overline{X} = \frac{\Sigma(X_i)}{n}$$

where
$$\overline{X} = \text{the mean}$$
$$\Sigma(X_i) = \text{the summation of the scores}$$
$$n = \text{the number of cases}$$

Since this formula introduces some new symbols, let us take a moment to consider it. First, the symbol Σ is a mathematical operator just like the plus sign (+) or divide sign (÷). It stands for "the summation of" and directs us to add whatever quantities are stated immediately following it.* The second new symbol is X_i ("X sub i"), which refers to any single score—the "ith" score. If we wished to refer to a particular score in the distribution, the specific number of the score could replace the subscript. Thus, X_1 would refer to the first score, X_2 to the second, X_{26} to the 26th, and so forth. The operation of adding all the scores is symbolized as $\Sigma(X_i)$.

---

*See the Prologue (Basic Mathematics Review) for further information on the summation sign and on summation operations.

This combination of symbols directs us to sum the scores, beginning with the first score and ending with the last score in the distribution. Thus, Formula 3.2 states in symbols what has already been stated in words (to calculate the mean, add the scores and divide by the number of scores), but in a very succinct and precise way.

Strictly speaking, the formula expressed in Formula 3.2 is for the mean of a sample. The mean of a population is calculated using exactly the same method as for calculating the sample mean, however it is symbolized with the Greek letter mu, μ, (pronounced "mew") as shown in Formula 3.3.

FORMULA 3.3

$$\mu = \frac{\Sigma(X_i)}{N}$$

where $\Sigma(X_i)$ = the summation of the scores
N = the number of cases in the population

Note that to differentiate between population measures, technically called population parameters, and sample measures, called sample statistics, it is common practice to use Greek letters for parameters and Roman letters for statistics. So, for example, the Greek letter, μ, represents the population mean and the Roman letter, $\overline{X}$, represents the sample mean. Also note that it is customary to symbolize "number of cases" with the uppercase letter, N, in formulas for population parameters (e.g., Formula 3.3) and the lowercase letter, n, in formulas for sample statistics (e.g., Formula 3.2). These practices are followed throughout this textbook.

Some Characteristics of the Mean. The mean is the most commonly used measure of central tendency, and we will consider its mathematical and statistical characteristics in some detail. First, the mean is always the centre of any distribution of scores in the sense that it is the point around which all of the scores cancel out. Symbolically:*

$$\Sigma(X_i - \overline{X}) = 0$$

Or, if we take each score in a distribution, subtract the mean from it, and add all of the differences, the resultant sum will always be 0. To illustrate, consider the following sample of scores: 10, 20, 30, 40, and 50. The mean of these five scores is 150/5, or 30, and the sum of the differences is presented in Table 3.6.

The total of the negative differences (-30) is exactly equal to the total of the positive differences ($+30$), and this will always be the case. This algebraic relationship between the scores and the mean indicates that the mean is a good descriptive measure of the centrality of scores. You may think of the mean as a fulcrum that exactly balances all of the scores.

---

*For the population, this characteristic is expressed symbolically as: $\Sigma(X_i - \mu) = 0$

TABLE 3.6   A DEMONSTRATION SHOWING THAT ALL
SCORES CANCEL OUT AROUND THE MEAN

X_i	$(X_i - \overline{X})$
10	$10 - 30 = -20$
20	$20 - 30 = -10$
30	$30 - 30 = \quad 0$
40	$40 - 30 = \quad 10$
50	$50 - 30 = \quad 20$
$\Sigma(X_i) = 150$	$\Sigma(X_i - \overline{X}) = \quad 0$

$$\overline{X} = \frac{\Sigma(X_i)}{n} = \frac{150}{5} = 30$$

A second characteristic of the mean is called the "least squares" principle, a characteristic that is expressed in the statement:*

$$\sum(X_i - \overline{X})^2 = \text{minimum}$$

or the mean is the point in a distribution around which the variation of the scores (as indicated by the squared differences) is minimized. If the differences between the scores and the mean are squared and then added, the resultant sum will be less than the sum of the squared differences between the scores and any other point in the distribution.

To illustrate this principle, consider the distribution of the five sample scores mentioned above: 10, 20, 30, 40, and 50. The differences between the scores and the mean have already been found. As illustrated in Table 3.7, if we square and sum these differences, we would get a total of 1,000. If we performed that same mathematical operation with any number other than the mean—say the value 31—the resultant sum would be greater than 1,000. Table 3.7 illustrates this point by showing that the sum of the squared differences around 31 is 1,005, a value greater than 1,000.

In a sense, the least-squares principle merely underlines the fact that the mean is closer to all of the scores than the other measures of central tendency.

TABLE 3.7   A DEMONSTRATION SHOWING THAT THE MEAN IS THE POINT OF MINIMIZED VARIATION

X_i	$(X_i - \overline{X})$	$(X_i - \overline{X})^2$	$(X_i - 31)^2$
10	$10 - 30 = -20$	$(-20)^2 = 400$	$(10 - 31)^2 = (-21)^2 = 441$
20	$20 - 30 = -10$	$(-10)^2 = 100$	$(20 - 31)^2 = (-11)^2 = 121$
30	$30 - 30 = \quad 0$	$(0)^2 = \quad 0$	$(30 - 31)^2 = \ (-1)^2 = \quad 1$
40	$40 - 30 = \quad 10$	$(10)^2 = 100$	$(40 - 31)^2 = \quad (9)^2 = \quad 81$
50	$50 - 30 = \quad 20$	$(20)^2 = 400$	$(50 - 31)^2 = \quad (19)^2 = 361$
$\Sigma(X_i) = 150$	$\Sigma(X_i - \overline{X}) = \quad 0$	$\Sigma(X_i - \overline{X})^2 = 1,000$	$\Sigma(X_i - 31)^2 = 1,005$

*For the population, this characteristic is expressed symbolically as: $\sum(X_i - \mu)^2 = \text{minimum}$

However, this characteristic of the mean is also the foundation of some of the most important techniques in statistics, including the variance and standard deviation.

The final important characteristic of the mean is that every score in the distribution affects it. The mode (which is only the most common score) and the median (which deals only with the score of the middle case or cases) are not so affected. This quality is both an advantage and a disadvantage. On one hand, the mean utilizes all the available information—every score in the distribution affects the mean. On the other hand, when a distribution has a few very high or very low scores (as noted in the previous section, these extreme scores are often referred to as outliers), the mean may become a very misleading measure of centrality.

To illustrate, consider again the sample of five scores mentioned above: 10, 20, 30, 40, and 50. Both the mean and the median of this distribution are 30. ($\overline{X} = 150/5 = 30$. Md = score of third case = 30.) What will happen if we change the last score from 50 to 500? This change would not affect the median at all; it would remain at exactly 30. This is because the median is based only on the score of the middle case and is not affected by changes in the scores of other cases in the distribution.

The mean, in contrast, would be very much affected because it takes *all* scores into account. The mean would become 600/5, or 120. Clearly, the one extreme score in the data set disproportionately affects the mean. For a distribution that has a few scores much higher or lower than the other scores, the mean may present a very misleading picture of the typical or central score.

The general principle to remember is that, relative to the median, the mean is always pulled in the direction of extreme scores. The mean and median will have the same value when and only when a distribution is symmetrical. When a distribution has some extremely high scores (this is called a positive **skew**), the mean will always have a greater numerical value than the median. If the distribution has some very low scores (a negative skew), the mean will be lower in value than the median. So, a quick comparison of the median and mean will always tell you if a distribution is skewed and the direction of the skew. If the mean is less than the median, the distribution has a negative skew. If the mean is greater than the median, the distribution has a positive skew. Figures 3.2 to 3.4 depict three different frequency polygons that demonstrate these relationships.

So, which measure is most appropriate for each distribution? If the distribution is highly skewed (as depicted in Figures 3.2 and 3.3), the mean no longer describes the typical or central score. Hence, the median should be used. If the distribution is unskewed, as shown in Figure 3.4, either measure can be used.

As a final note regarding the mean, since its computation requires addition and division, it should be used with variables measured at the interval-ratio level.

FIGURE 3.2   A POSITIVELY SKEWED DISTRIBUTION (The mean is greater in value than the median.)

FIGURE 3.3   A NEGATIVELY SKEWED DISTRIBUTION (The mean is less than the median.)

FIGURE 3.4   AN UNSKEWED, SYMMETRICAL DISTRIBUTION (The mean and median are equal.)

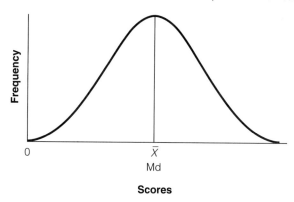

Variance and Standard Deviation.   In the previous section we explored the range and interquartile range as measures of dispersion. A basic limitation of both statistics, however, is that they are based on only two scores. They do not use all the scores in the distribution, and, in this sense, they do not capitalize on all the available information. Also, neither statistic provides any information on how far the scores are from each other or from some central point such as the mean. How can we design a measure of dispersion that would correct these faults? We can begin with some specifications: a good measure of dispersion should

1. Use all the scores in the distribution. The statistic should use all the information available.
2. Describe the average or typical deviation of the scores. The statistic should give us an idea of how far the scores are from each other or from the centre of the distribution.
3. Increase in value as the distribution of scores becomes more diverse. This would be a very handy feature because it would permit us to tell at a glance which distribution was more variable: the higher the numerical value of the statistic, the greater the dispersion.

One way to develop a statistic to meet these criteria would be to start with the distances between each score and the mean. The distances between the scores and the mean are technically called **deviations** and this quantity will increase in value as the scores increase in their variety or heterogeneity. If the scores are more clustered around the mean (remember the graph for essay-style exam scores (Section A) in Figure 3.1), the deviations would be small. If the scores are more spread out or more varied (like the scores for multiple-choice exams (Section B) in Figure 3.1), the deviations would be greater in value. How can we use the deviations of the scores around the mean to develop a useful statistic?

One course of action would be to use the sum of the deviations as the basis for a statistic, but, as we saw earlier in this section (see Table 3.6) the sum of deviations will always be zero. Still, the sum of the deviations is a logical basis for a statistic that measures the amount of variety in a set of scores, and statisticians have developed two ways around the fact that the positive deviations always equal the negative deviations. Both solutions eliminate the negative signs. The first does so by using the absolute values or by ignoring signs when summing the deviations. This is the basis for a statistic called the **average deviation**, a measure of dispersion that is rarely used and will not be mentioned further.

The second solution squares each of the deviations. This makes all values positive because a negative number multiplied by a negative number becomes positive. For example, Table 3.8 lists the sample of five scores from Table 3.6, along with the deviations and the squared deviations. The sum of the squared deviations (400 + 100 + 0 + 100 + 400) equals 1,000. Thus, a statistic based on the sum of the squared deviations will have many of the properties we want in a good measure of dispersion.

Before we finish designing our measure of dispersion, we must deal with another problem. The sum of the squared deviations will increase with the number of cases: the larger the number of cases, the greater the value of the measure. This would make it very difficult to compare the relative variability of distributions with different numbers of cases. We can solve this problem by dividing the sum of the squared deviations by the number of cases and thus standardizing for distributions of different sizes.

TABLE 3.8   COMPUTING THE STANDARD DEVIATION

Scores (X_i)	Deviations $(X_i - \overline{X})$	Deviations Squared $(X_i - \overline{X})^2$
10	$(10 - 30) = -20$	$(-20)^2 = 400$
20	$(20 - 30) = -10$	$(-10)^2 = 100$
30	$(30 - 30) = 0$	$(0)^2 = 0$
40	$(40 - 30) = 10$	$(10)^2 = 100$
50	$(50 - 30) = 20$	$(20)^2 = 400$
$\Sigma(X_i) = 150$	$\Sigma(X_i - \overline{X}) = 0$	$\Sigma(X_i - \overline{X})^2 = 1,000$

$$\overline{X} = \frac{\Sigma(X_i)}{n} = \frac{150}{5} = 30$$

These procedures yield a statistic known as the **variance**, which is symbolized as s^2 for a sample and σ^2 for a population. The variance is used primarily in inferential statistics, although it is a central concept in the design of some measures of association. For purposes of describing the dispersion of a distribution, a closely related statistic called the **standard deviation** (symbolized as s for a sample and σ for a population) is typically used, and this statistic will be our focus for the remainder of this section.

Let's first look at the formulas for the sample variance and standard deviation. They are:

FORMULA 3.4

$$s^2 = \frac{\Sigma(X_i - \overline{X})^2}{n}$$

FORMULA 3.5

$$s = \sqrt{\frac{\Sigma(X_i - \overline{X})^2}{n}}$$

where X_i = the score
$\overline{X}$ = the sample mean
n = the number of cases in the sample

To compute the standard deviation, it is advisable to construct a table such as Table 3.8 to organize computations. The five scores are listed in the left-hand column, the deviations are in the middle column, and the squared deviations are in the right-hand column.

The sum of the last column in Table 3.8 is the sum of the squared deviations and can be substituted into the numerator of the formula:

$$s = \sqrt{\frac{\Sigma(X_i - \overline{X})^2}{n}}$$
$$= \sqrt{\frac{1,000}{5}}$$
$$= \sqrt{200}$$
$$= 14.14$$

The percent of persons in the labour force that work part-time in five cities in Western Canada and five cities in Eastern Canada is compared using data from the 2001 Census of Canada. Part-time workers are defined in the census as persons who work mainly part-time weeks (29 hours or less per week) on the basis of all jobs held during the year 2000. Columns for the computation of the standard deviation have already been added to the tables below. Which group of cities tends to have a higher percentage of part-time workers? Which group varies the most in terms of this variable? Computations for both the mean and standard deviation are shown below.

PERCENT OF LABOUR FORCE WITH PART-TIME JOBS, 2000, EASTERN CITIES

City	Part-timers (X_i)	Deviations ($X_i - \overline{X}$)	Deviations Squared ($X_i - \overline{X})^2$
Halifax	21.3	$21.3 - 20.22 = 1.08$	1.1664
Quebec	20.6	$20.6 - 20.22 = 0.38$	0.1444
Ottawa-Hull	20.1	$20.1 - 20.22 = -.12$	0.0144
Toronto	19.6	$19.6 - 20.22 = -.62$	0.3844
Montreal	19.5	$19.5 - 20.22 = -.72$	0.5184
	$\Sigma(X_i) = 101.1$	$\Sigma(X_i - \overline{X}) = 0$	$\Sigma(X_i - \overline{X})^2 = 2.2280$

Source: Data from Statistics Canada, *2001 Canadian Census*, individual PUMF.

$$\overline{X} = \frac{\Sigma(X_i)}{n} = \frac{101.1}{5} = 20.22$$

$$s = \sqrt{\frac{\Sigma(X_i - \overline{X})^2}{n}} = \sqrt{\frac{2.228}{5}}$$
$$= \sqrt{0.4456} = 0.6675$$

PERCENT OF LABOUR FORCE WITH PART-TIME JOBS, 2000, WESTERN CITIES

City	Part-timers (X_i)	Deviations ($X_i - \overline{X}$)	Deviations Squared ($X_i - \overline{X})^2$
Victoria	27.4	$27.4 - 23.96 = 3.44$	11.8336
Regina/Saskatoon	24.7	$24.7 - 23.96 = 0.74$	0.5476
Vancouver	23.9	$23.9 - 23.96 = -.06$	0.0036
Winnipeg	22.8	$22.8 - 23.96 = -1.16$	1.3456
Calgary	21.0	$21.0 - 23.96 = -2.96$	8.7616
	$\Sigma(X_i) = 119.8$	$\Sigma(X_i - \overline{X}) = 0$	$\Sigma(X_i - \overline{X})^2 = 22.492$

Source: Data from Statistics Canada, *2001 Canadian Census*, individual PUMF.

$$\overline{X} = \frac{\Sigma(X_i)}{n} = \frac{119.8}{5} = 23.96$$

$$s = \sqrt{\frac{\Sigma(X_i - \overline{X})^2}{n}} = \sqrt{\frac{22.492}{5}}$$
$$= \sqrt{4.4984} = 2.1209$$

With such small groups, you can tell by simply inspecting the scores that the western cities have higher percentages of part-time workers in their labour forces. This impression is confirmed by both the median, which is 20.1 for the eastern cities (Ottawa-Hull is the middle case) and 23.9 for the western cities (Vancouver is the middle case), and the mean (20.22 for the eastern cities and 23.96 for the western cities). For both groups, the mean is very similar to the median, indicating an unskewed distribution of scores. The five western cities are also much more variable and diverse than the eastern cities. The range for the western cities is 6.4 ($R = 27.4 - 21.0 = 6.4$), much higher than the range for the eastern cities of 1.8 ($R = 21.3 - 19.5 = 1.8$). Similarly, the standard deviation for the western cities (2.12) is about three times greater in value than the standard deviation for the eastern cities (0.67). In summary, the five western cities average higher rates of part-time work and are also more variable than the five eastern cities.

To finish solving the formula, divide the sum of the squared deviations by n and take the square root of the result. To find the variance, square the standard deviation. For this problem, the variance is $s^2 = (14.14)^2 = 200$.

It is important to point out that some electronic calculators and statistical software packages (including SPSS) use slightly different formulas, with "$n - 1$" instead of "n" in the denominator to calculate the sample variance and standard deviation. Thus, they will produce results that are at least slightly different from results produced using Formulas 3.4 and 3.5. The size of the difference will decrease as sample size increases, but the problems and examples in this chapter use small samples so the difference between using n and $n - 1$ in the denominator can be considerable. Some calculators offer the choice of "$n - 1$" or "n" in the denominator. If you use "n", the values calculated for the sample standard deviation will match the values in this textbook.

As a final point, like the mean, the variance and standard deviation for populations are calculated using exactly the same method as for samples, but population and sample measures are distinguished from each other using different symbols. The variance and standard deviation formulas for populations are shown in Formulas 3.6 and 3.7 respectively.

FORMULA 3.6
$$\sigma^2 = \frac{\Sigma(X_i - \mu)^2}{N}$$

FORMULA 3.7
$$\sigma = \sqrt{\frac{\Sigma(X_i - \mu)^2}{N}}$$

where X_i = the score
μ = the population mean
N = the number of cases in the population

Interpreting the Standard Deviation. It is very possible that the meaning of the standard deviation (i.e., why we calculate it) is not completely obvious to you at this point. You might be asking: "Once I've gone to the trouble of calculating the standard deviation, what do I have?" The meaning of this measure of dispersion can be expressed in three ways. The first and most important involves the normal curve, and we will defer this interpretation until the next chapter.

A second way of thinking about the standard deviation is as an index of variability that increases in value as the distribution becomes more variable. In other words, the standard deviation is higher for more diverse distributions and lower for less diverse distributions. The lowest value the standard deviation can have is 0, and this would occur for distributions with no dispersion (i.e., if every single case in the distribution had exactly the same score). Thus, 0 is the lowest value possible for the standard deviation (although there is no upper limit).

A third way to get a feel for the meaning of the standard deviation is by comparing one distribution with another. You might do this when comparing one group against another (e.g., men vs. women) or the same variable at two different times or places. For example, according to data collected by Environment Canada, Montreal and Calgary have the same mean daily temperature in the month of January: −8.9°C.

Montreal	Calgary
$\bar{X} = -8.9$	$\bar{X} = -8.9$
$s = 2.8$	$s = 5.0$

Source: Environment Canada.
National Climate Data and Information
Archive. www.climate.weatheroffice.gc.ca

While the cities have identical average daily temperatures, the standard deviation reveals that temperatures fluctuate much more during the month of January in Calgary. (This may partly reflect strong "chinook" winds, common to southern Alberta, that can dramatically raise the temperature for a few hours or days before it falls back to a normal level.) The higher standard deviation for Calgary (5.0°C) indicates a distribution of daily temperatures that is flatter and more spread out around the mean (remember the distribution for Section B in Figure 3.1), while the lower standard deviation for Montreal (2.8°C) reflects a distribution that is more clustered around the mean (like the distribution for Section A in Figure 3.1). So, compared to Calgary, daily temperatures in January in Montreal are more similar to each other and more clustered in a narrower range of temperatures. The standard deviation is extremely useful for making comparisons of this sort between distributions of scores or in this example, temperatures.

In conclusion, the standard deviation is the most important measure of dispersion because of its central role in many more advanced statistical applications. Since it is based on the mean, it should be used with variables measured at the interval-ratio level. Also, like the mean, the standard deviation uses all the scores in the distribution, and thus is disproportionately influenced by outliers/extreme scores. When a distribution has outliers/extreme scores (a highly skewed distribution), the interquartile range should be used as the measure of dispersion. As noted in the previous section, the interquartile range uses only the middle 50% of the data in the distribution, and thus is resistant to extreme scores. (*For practice in computing and interpreting the mean and standard deviation, see any of the problems at the end of this chapter.*)

3.5 CHOOSING A MEASURE OF CENTRAL TENDENCY AND DISPERSION

Throughout this chapter, we have emphasized that the selection of a measure of central tendency or dispersion should, in general, be based on the level of measurement, meaning whether you are working with a nominal-, ordinal-, or interval-ratio variable. Table 3.9 summarizes the relationship between the levels of measurement and the measures of central tendency and dispersion. The most appropriate measure of central tendency and dispersion for each level of measurement is in italic.

TABLE 3.9 THE RELATIONSHIP BETWEEN LEVEL OF MEASUREMENT AND MEASURE OF CENTRAL TENDENCY AND DISPERSION*

Level of Measurement	Measure(s) of Central Tendency	Measure(s) of Dispersion
Nominal	*Mode*	*Variation Ratio*
Ordinal	Mode, *Median*	Variation Ratio, Range, *Interquartile Range*
Interval-ratio**	Mode, Median, *Mean*	Variation Ratio, Range, Interquartile Range, Variance, *Standard Deviation*

*The most appropriate measure of central tendency and dispersion for each level of measurement is in italic.
**The median and interquartile range should be used for interval-ratio variables with highly skewed distributions.

We have to keep in mind, however, that each measure of central tendency and dispersion is defined in a unique way. For example, even though they share a common purpose, the three measures of central tendency are quite different from each other and will have the same value only under certain, specific conditions (i.e., for symmetrical distributions). So, while your choice of an appropriate measure of central tendency or dispersion will generally depend on the way you measure the variable, you must also consider how the variable is distributed. The mean and standard deviation would be the most appropriate measures for a variable measured at the interval-ratio level, however the median and interquartile range should alternatively be used if an interval-ratio variable has outliers/extreme scores (i.e., is highly skewed).

3.6 INTERPRETING STATISTICS: THE CENTRAL TENDENCY AND DISPERSION OF INCOME IN CANADA

A sizable volume of statistical material has been introduced in this chapter, so we will conclude by focusing on meaning and interpretation. What can you say after you have calculated, for example, means and standard deviations? Remember that statistics are tools to help us analyze information and answer questions. They never speak for themselves and they always have to be understood within the context of some research question or test of a hypothesis. This section will provide an example of interpretation by posing and answering some questions about the changing distribution of income in Canada: "Is average income rising or falling?" "Does the average Canadian receive more or less income today than in the past?" "Is the distribution of income becoming more unequal (i.e., are the rich getting richer)?" The interpretation (words) will be explicitly linked to the statistics (numbers) so that you will be able to see how and why conclusions are developed.

We can answer these questions by looking at changes in measures of central tendency and dispersion. Changes in the mean and median will tell us, respectively, about changes in the average income for all Canadians (mean income) and income for the average Canadian (median income). The standard deviation would be the preferred measure of dispersion for an interval-ratio level variable like income, but unfortunately, Statistics

Canada does not provide this information. We will instead measure dispersion with a statistic called the Gini coefficient that is calculated by Statistics Canada.

The Gini coefficient measures the level of dispersion, or more specifically the level of inequality, in a given distribution. So, if everyone in Canada had the same income (i.e., no dispersion or inequality), the Gini coefficient would be 0; conversely, if just one individual held all income in Canada, it would be 1. Thus, the Gini coefficient ranges from 0 to 1. A decrease in the value of the Gini coefficient means a decrease in income inequality (less dispersion), and vice versa.

Before considering the data, we should keep in mind that virtually any distribution of income will be positively skewed (see Figure 3.2). That is, in any group, locality, province, or nation, the incomes of most people will be grouped around the mean or median, but some people—the wealthiest members of the group—will have incomes far higher than the average. Because the mean uses *all* the scores, it will be pulled in the direction of the extreme scores relative to the median. In a positively skewed distribution, the mean will be greater than the median.

Also, be aware that the values in Figure 3.5 are expressed in 2004 dollars. This eliminates any changes in the mean and median caused by inflation over the years. Without this adjustment, recent incomes would appear to be much higher than older incomes, not because of increased purchasing power and well-being, but rather because of the changing value of the dollar. Finally, Figure 3.5 is based on total income of Canadian households, not individual income.

FIGURE 3.5 MEAN AND MEDIAN INCOME OF HOUSEHOLDS, 1980–2004, CANADA

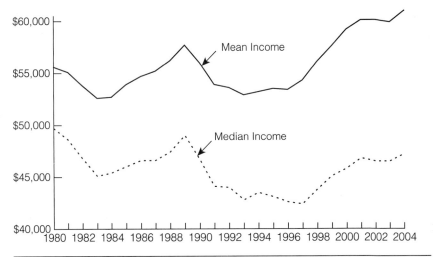

Source: Data from Statistics Canada, CANSIM, Table 202–0403 (Mean Income) and Table 202–0411 (Median Income).

Figure 3.5 shows that, expressed in 2004 dollars, the average Canadian household earned about $50,000 in 1980 (median = $49,700). By 2004, median income for the average Canadian household was $47,200, or $2,500 less than in 1980, indicating a marked decrease in standard of living. This trend downward has some noticeable declines in both the early 1980s and 1990s, both periods of recession. However, we also see periods of incline during the "boom economies" of the late 1980s and the late 1990s to early 2000s.

The overall pattern of the mean income is almost identical to that of the median. It rises and falls in almost exactly the same ways and at the same times. Notice, however, that the mean is always higher than the median, a reflection of the characteristic positive skew of income data. In 1980, the mean income was $55,600, almost $6,000 higher than the median. By 2004, the mean was $61,000, almost $14,000 higher. What is this telling us? This increasingly positive skew means that the households with the highest incomes are becoming even more affluent relative to the bulk of the population. In other words, the growing distance between the mean and median suggests that, in recent years, the wealthiest Canadians are growing even wealthier relative to the rest of the population.

An increasing positive skew will be reflected by increases in the value of virtually any measure of dispersion. Although it does not supply information about the standard deviation, Statistics Canada calculates the Gini coefficient, reproduced in Figure 3.6. You can see by inspecting Figure 3.6 that the Gini coefficient is increasing, which indicates that incomes are growing in dispersion or variety. (Recall that the higher the Gini coefficient, the more dispersion or inequality that exists.) In 1980, the Gini coefficient was at 0.379. It rises to 0.43 by 2004, with most of the increase occurring in the 1990s. (To put this increase

FIGURE 3.6   DISPERSION OF HOUSEHOLD INCOME MEASURED BY THE GINI COEFFECIENT, 1980–2004, CANADA

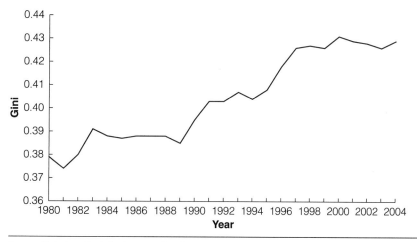

Source: Data from Statistics Canada, CANSIM, Table 202-0705.

READING STATISTICS 2: Measures of Central Tendency and Dispersion

As was the case with frequency distributions, measures of central tendency and dispersion may not be presented in research reports in the professional literature. Given the large number of variables included in a typical research project and the space limitations in journals and other media, there may not be room for the researcher to describe each variable fully. Furthermore, the great majority of research reports focus on relationships between variables rather than the distribution of single variables. In this sense, univariate descriptive statistics will be irrelevant to the main focus of the report.

This does not mean, of course, that univariate descriptive statistics are irrelevant to the research project. Nor do we mean to imply that researchers do not calculate and interpret these statistics. In fact, measures of central tendency and dispersion will be calculated and interpreted for virtually every variable, in virtually every research project. However, these statistics are less likely to be included in final research reports than the more analytical statistical techniques presented in the remainder of this textbook. Furthermore, some of these statistics (for example, the mean and standard deviation) serve a dual function. They not only are valuable descriptive statistics but also form the basis for many analytical techniques. Thus, they may be reported in the latter role if not in the former.

When included in research reports, measures of central tendency and dispersion will most often be presented in some summary form for all relevant variables—often in the form of a table. Means and standard deviations for many variables might, for example, be presented in the following table format.

Variable	$\overline{X}$	s	n
Age	33.2	1.3	1078
Number of children	2.3	0.7	1078
Years married	7.8	1.5	1052
Income	55,786	1500	987
.	.	.	.
.	.	.	.
.	.	.	.
.	.	.	.

These tables describe the overall characteristics of the sample succinctly and clearly. If you inspect the table carefully, you will have a good sense of the nature of the sample on the traits relevant to the project. Note that the number of cases varies from variable to variable in the preceding table. This is normal and is caused by missing data or incomplete information on some of the cases.

Statistics in the Professional Literature

The Program for International Student Assessment, or PISA, is an international study of youth literacy skills in reading, mathematics, and science. It is sponsored by the Organization for Economic Cooperation and Development (OECD). It started in 2000 with 32 countries, including 28 OECD countries and 4 non-OECD countries, and is conducted every three years.

The PISA study involves testing 15-year-olds in their reading, mathematics, and science literacy skills. It also administers questionnaires to these students and their school administrators to collect information on family- and school-related variables relevant to the development of literacy skills. Students 15 years of age are the focus of the PISA study because they are near the end of compulsory schooling. PISA assumes that by this age, students have accumulated the necessary learning experiences crucial for adulthood. More than 250,000 15-year-old students participated in the 2000 PISA, representing some 17 million 15-year-old students in the 32 countries.

The findings from the 2000 PISA are reported in the OECD paper *Knowledge and Skills for Life: First Results from the OECD Programme for International Student Assessment (PISA) 2000.* Below are the some of the key findings of the 2000 study: the average and standard deviation of PISA test scores for reading, mathematics, and science literacy for each of the 32 countries. The scores are reported on a scale of 0 to 1,000, with higher scores indicating higher literacy skills.

(continued next page)

READING STATISTICS 2: *(continued)*

The second column of Table 1, labelled "Mean," shows the average test scores in reading literacy for 15-year-olds by country, ranked from highest to lowest score. In Canada, for instance, 15-year-olds performed exceeding well on the PISA reading literacy scale. Only students in Finland (mean = 546) outperformed Canadian students (mean = 534). Canadian 15-year-olds also did much better than their U.S. counterparts (mean = 504). To put

this in context, it has been shown that a difference in PISA test scores in the range of 30 to 40 points (such as the Canada–U.S. difference, where there is a 30-point gap, or 534 to 504) is equal to about one full year of schooling.

The third column of Table 1 (labelled "SD," or standard deviation) shows the amount of variation in reading literacy test scores for 15-year-olds in each country. For example, there is less variation in reading scores in Canada compared to the United States. Canada has a standard deviation of 95, or 10 points lower than the standard deviation for the United States (SD = 105). That is, Canadian students are more alike in reading performance compared to students in the United States.

Table 2 shows the average test score (mean) and variation (SD) in mathematical literacy. Table 3 shows the scores for scientific literacy. Overall, Canada outscores most countries in mathematics literacy and science literacy, with mean test scores of 533 and 529, respectively. Further, the standard deviations for Canada tell us that both mathematics test scores (SD = 85) and science test scores (SD = 89) are less dispersed than most other countries, including the United States. Overall, mathematics and science performance is above average in Canada with less-than-average variation in students' performance.

Together, the mean and standard deviation provide a robust numerical description of literacy within and between countries. Compared to students in other countries, Canadian students on average perform better with less variation on all three measures of literacy. Do you want to find out more? The reference is given below.

TABLE 1 TEST SCORES FOR READING LITERACY, BY COUNTRY

Country	Mean	SD
Finland	546	89
Canada	534	95
New Zealand	529	108
Australia	528	102
Ireland	527	94
South Korea	525	70
United Kingdom	523	100
Japan	522	86
Sweden	516	92
Austria	507	93
Belgium	507	107
Iceland	507	92
France	505	92
Norway	505	104
United States	504	105
Denmark	497	98
Switzerland	494	102
Spain	493	85
Czech Republic	492	96
Italy	487	91
Germany	484	111
Liechtenstein	483	96
Hungary	480	94
Poland	479	100
Greece	474	97
Portugal	470	97
Russia	462	92
Latvia	458	102
Luxembourg	441	100
Mexico	422	86
Brazil	396	86

Source: Based on data from OECD (2001), *Knowledge and Skills for Life: First Results from PISA 2000*, PISA, OECD Publishing, http://dx.doi.org/10.1787/9789264195905-en

Source: OECD, 2001. *Knowledge and Skills for Life: First Results from the OECD Programme for International Student Assessment (PISA) 2000.* Paris: OECD Publications.

(continued)

READING STATISTICS 2: *(continued)*

TABLE 2 TEST SCORES FOR MATHEMATICAL LITERACY, BY COUNTRY

Country	Mean	SD
Japan	557	87
South Korea	547	84
New Zealand	537	99
Finland	536	80
Australia	533	90
Canada	533	85
Switzerland	529	100
United Kingdom	529	92
Belgium	520	106
France	517	89
Austria	515	92
Denmark	514	87
Iceland	514	85
Liechtenstein	514	96
Sweden	510	93
Ireland	503	84
Norway	499	92
Czech Republic	498	96
United States	493	98
Germany	490	103
Hungary	488	98
Russia	478	104
Spain	476	91
Poland	470	103
Latvia	463	103
Italy	457	90
Portugal	454	91
Greece	447	108
Luxembourg	446	93
Mexico	387	83
Brazil	334	97

Source: Based on data from OECD (2001), *Knowledge and Skills for Life: First Results from PISA 2000*, PISA, OECD Publishing, http://dx.doi.org/10.1787/9789264195905-en

TABLE 3 TEST SCORES FOR SCIENTIFIC LITERACY, BY COUNTRY

Country	Mean	SD
South Korea	552	81
Japan	550	90
Finland	538	86
United Kingdom	532	98
Canada	529	89
Australia	528	94
New Zealand	528	101
Austria	519	91
Ireland	513	92
Sweden	512	93
Czech Republic	511	94
France	500	102
Norway	500	96
United States	499	101
Belgium	496	111
Hungary	496	103
Iceland	496	88
Switzerland	496	100
Spain	491	95
Germany	487	102
Poland	483	97
Denmark	481	103
Italy	478	98
Liechtenstein	476	94
Greece	461	97
Latvia	460	98
Russia	460	99
Portugal	459	89
Luxembourg	443	96
Mexico	422	77
Brazil	375	90

Source: Based on data from OECD (2001), *Knowledge and Skills for Life: First Results from PISA 2000*, PISA, OECD Publishing, http://dx.doi.org/10.1787/9789264195905-en

of 0.051, from 0.379 to 0.43, in the Gini coefficient in context, a difference of just 0.01 or more between two Gini coefficients is often considered to be meaningful and of consequence.) This trend would seem to indicate a growing income gap between less and more affluent Canadians over the time period, and is very consistent with the increasing positive skew in Figure 3.5.

In the end, the data show no increase in the income of the average Canadian (median) but an increase in the average income for all Canadians (mean). The increasing Gini coefficient indicates that incomes are growing in dispersion. Taken together, these findings would suggest that people with modest incomes continue to have modest incomes and, consistent with the ancient folk wisdom, the rich are getting richer.

SUMMARY

1. The three measures of central tendency presented in this chapter (mode, median, and mean) share a common purpose. Each reports some information about the most typical or representative value in a distribution. Appropriate use of these statistics permits the researcher to report important information about a distribution of scores in a single, easily understood number.

2. To provide a full description of a distribution of scores, measures of central tendency must be paired with measures of dispersion. Measures of dispersion, such as the variation ratio, range and interquartile range, variance, and standard deviation, summarize information about the heterogeneity or variety in a distribution.

3. The mode reports the most common score and is used most appropriately with nominally measured variables. The median reports the score that is at the exact centre of the distribution, and is most appropriately used with variables measured at the ordinal level and with highly skewed interval-ratio-level variables. The mean, the most frequently used

of the three measures of central tendency, reports the most typical score. It is used most appropriately with variables measured at the interval-ratio level (except when the distribution is highly skewed).

4. The variation ratio is defined as the proportion of cases that are not in the mode of a variable, and is most appropriate for variables measured at the nominal level. The range is the distance from the highest to the lowest score in the distribution. The interquartile range is the distance from the third to the first quartile. These two ranges are most appropriate for variables measured at the ordinal level. The standard deviation has a minimum value of zero (no variation) and increases in value as the variability of the distribution increases. It is used most appropriately with variables measured at the interval-ratio level, however the interquartile range should be used if variables are highly skewed. The variance is used primarily in inferential statistics and in the design of some measures of association.

SUMMARY OF FORMULAS

Variation Ratio	3.1	$v = 1 - \left(\dfrac{f_m}{n}\right)$
Mean (sample)	3.2	$\bar{X} = \dfrac{\Sigma(X_i)}{n}$
Mean (population)	3.3	$\mu = \dfrac{\Sigma(X_i)}{N}$
Variance (sample)	3.4	$s^2 = \dfrac{\Sigma(X_i - \bar{X})^2}{n}$
Standard Deviation (sample)	3.5	$s = \sqrt{\dfrac{\Sigma(X_i - \bar{X})^2}{n}}$
Variance (population)	3.6	$\sigma^2 = \dfrac{\Sigma(X_i - \mu)^2}{N}$
Standard Deviation (population)	3.7	$\sigma = \sqrt{\dfrac{\Sigma(X_i - \mu)^2}{N}}$

GLOSSARY

Average deviation. The average of the absolute deviations of the scores around the mean. (p. 80)

Deviations. The distances between the scores and the mean. (p. 80)

Dispersion. The amount of variety or heterogeneity in a distribution of scores. (p. 66)

Interquartile range. The distance from the third quartile to the first quartile. (p. 73)

Mean. The arithmetic average of the scores. $\bar{X}$ represents the mean of a sample, and μ, the mean of a population. (p. 75)

Measures of central tendency. Statistics that summarize a distribution of scores by reporting the most typical or representative value of the distribution. (p. 66)

Measures of dispersion. Statistics that indicate the amount of variety or heterogeneity in a distribution of scores. (p. 66)

Median. The point in a distribution of scores above and below which exactly half of the cases fall. (p. 71)

Mode. The most common value in a distribution or the largest category of a variable. (p. 68)

Outliers. Extreme high or low scores in a distribution. (p. 73).

Range. The highest score minus the lowest score. (p. 72)

Skew. The extent to which a distribution of scores has a few scores that are extremely high (positive skew) or extremely low (negative skew). (p. 78)

Standard deviation. The square root of the squared deviations of the scores around the mean, divided by the number of cases. The most important and useful descriptive measure of dispersion; s represents the standard deviation of a sample; σ, the standard deviation of a population. (p. 81)

Variance. The squared deviations of the scores around the mean divided by the number of cases. A measure of dispersion used primarily in inferential statistics and also in correlation and regression techniques; s^2 represents the variance of a sample; σ^2, the variance of a population. (p. 81)

Variation ratio. The proportion of cases that are not in the modal category (mode) of a variable. (p. 69)

MULTIMEDIA RESOURCES

  http://www.healeystatistics.nelson.com

Visit the companion website for the second Canadian edition of *Statistics: A Tool for Social Research* to access a wide range of student resources. Begin by clicking on the Student Resources section of the book's website to access review quizzes, flashcards, and other study tools.

PROBLEMS

3.1 SOC A variety of information has been gathered from a sample of lower- and upper-year students living in residence at a large university, including their region of birth; the extent to which they support legalization of marijuana (measured on a scale on which 7 = strong support, 4 = neutral, and 1 = strong opposition); the amount of money they spend each week out-of-pocket for food, drinks, and entertainment; how many movies they watched in their residence rooms last week, and their opinion of cafeteria food (10 = excellent, 0 = very bad). Some results are presented below. Find the *most appropriate* measure of central tendency for each variable for lower-year students and then for upper-year students. Report both the measure you selected as well as its value for each variable (e.g., "Mode = 3" or "Median = 3.5"). *(HINT: Determine the level of measurement for each variable first. In general, this will tell you which measure of central tendency is appropriate. See Section 3.5 to review the relationship between measure of central tendency and level of measurement. Also, remember that the mode is the most common score and, especially, remember to array scores from high to low before finding the median.)*

LOWER-YEAR STUDENTS

Student	Region of Birth	Legali- zation	Out-of- pocket Expenses	Movies	Cafeteria Food
A	Atlantic	7	33	0	10
B	Atlantic	4	39	14	7
C	Ontario	3	45	10	2
D	Prairies/West	2	47	7	1
E	Atlantic	3	62	5	8
F	Atlantic	5	48	1	6
G	Ontario	1	52	0	10
H	Ontario	4	65	14	0
I	Prairies/West	1	51	3	5
J	Quebec	2	43	4	6

UPPER-YEAR STUDENTS

K	Atlantic	7	65	0	1
L	Prairies/West	6	62	5	2
M	Atlantic	7	60	11	8
N	Atlantic	5	90	3	4
O	Ontario	1	62	4	3
P	Ontario	5	57	14	6
Q	Quebec	6	40	0	2
R	Quebec	7	49	7	9
S	Atlantic	3	45	5	4
T	Quebec	5	85	3	7
U	Atlantic	4	78	5	4

3.2 The marital status of residents of four apartment complexes is reported below. Compute the variation ratio (v) for each neighbourhood. Which is the most heterogeneous of the four? Which is the least heterogeneous?

Complex A	
Marital Status	Frequency
Single	26
Married	31
Divorced	12
Widowed	5
	$n = 74$

Complex B	
Marital Status	Frequency
Single	10
Married	12
Divorced	8
Widowed	7
	$n = 37$

Complex C	
Marital Status	Frequency
Single	20
Married	30
Divorced	2
Widowed	1
	$n = 53$

Complex D	
Marital Status	Frequency
Single	52
Married	3
Divorced	20
Widowed	10
	$n = 85$

3.3 PS You have been observing the local Liberal Party in a large city and have compiled some information about a small sample of party regulars. Find the appropriate measure of central tendency for each variable.

Respondent	Sex	Social Class	Number of Years in Party	Education	Marital Status	Number of Children
A	M	High	32	High school	Married	5
B	M	Medium	17	High school	Married	0
C	M	Low	32	High school	Single	0
D	M	Low	50	Grade 8	Widowed	7
E	M	Low	25	Grade 4	Married	4
F	M	Medium	25	High school	Divorced	3
G	F	High	12	College/University	Divorced	3
H	F	High	10	College/University	Separated	2
I	F	Medium	21	College/University	Married	1
J	F	Medium	33	College/University	Married	5
K	M	Low	37	High school	Single	0
L	F	Low	15	High school	Divorced	0
M	F	Low	31	Grade 8	Widowed	1

3.4 SOC You have compiled the information below on each of the graduates voted "most likely to succeed" by a local high school for a 10-year period. For each variable, find the appropriate measure of dispersion. (*HINT: See Section 3.5 to review the relationship between measure of dispersion and level of measurement.*)

Case	Present Income	Marital Status	Owns a BMW?	Years of Education Post–High School
A	24,000	Single	No	8
B	48,000	Divorced	No	4
C	54,000	Married	Yes	4
D	45,000	Married	No	4
E	30,000	Single	No	4
F	35,000	Separated	Yes	8
G	30,000	Married	No	3
H	17,000	Married	No	1
I	33,000	Married	Yes	6
J	48,000	Single	Yes	4

3.5 SOC For 15 respondents, data have been gathered on four variables. Find and report the appropriate measure of central tendency for each variable.

Respondent	Marital Status	Sex	Age	Attitude on Legalization of Marijuana Scale*
A	Single	Female	18	10
B	Single	Male	20	9
C	Widowed	Female	21	8

(continued next column)

(continued)

Respondent	Marital Status	Sex	Age	Attitude on Legalization of Marijuana Scale*
D	Married	Female	30	10
E	Married	Male	25	7
F	Married	Female	26	7
G	Divorced	Male	19	9
H	Widowed	Female	29	6
I	Divorced	Female	31	10
J	Married	Male	55	5
K	Widowed	Male	32	4
L	Married	Male	28	3
M	Divorced	Female	23	2
N	Married	Female	24	1
O	Divorced	Male	32	9

*This scale is constructed so that a high score indicates strong opposition to legalization of marijuana.

3.6 SOC Below are four variables for 30 cases taken from a national survey. Age is reported in years. The variable "happiness" consists of answers to the question "Taken all together, would you say that you are (1) very happy, (2) pretty happy, or (3) not too happy?" Respondents were asked how many sex partners they had over the past five years. Responses were measured on the following scale: 0–4 = actual numbers; 5 = 5–10 partners; 6 = 11–20 partners; 7 = 21–100 partners; and 8 = more than 100. For each variable, find the appropriate measure of dispersion.

Respondent	Age	Happi-ness	Number of Partners	Sex
1	20	1	2	Male
2	32	1	1	Male
3	31	1	1	Female
4	34	2	5	Male
5	34	2	3	Male
6	31	3	0	Female
7	35	1	4	Male
8	42	1	3	Male
9	48	1	1	Female
10	27	2	1	Male
11	41	1	1	Male
12	42	2	0	Female
13	29	1	8	Male
14	28	1	1	Female
15	47	2	1	Male
16	69	2	2	Female
17	44	1	4	Female
18	21	3	1	Male
19	33	2	1	Male
20	56	1	2	Male
21	73	2	0	Female
22	31	1	1	Female
23	53	2	3	Male
24	78	1	0	Male
25	47	2	3	Male
26	88	3	0	Female
27	43	1	2	Male
28	24	1	1	Male
29	24	2	3	Male
30	60	1	1	Male

3.7 Compute the median, interquartile range, mean, and standard deviation of the 10 scores reported below.

10, 12, 15, 20, 25, 30, 32, 35, 40, 50

3.8 SOC The table below lists the average weekly earnings for the 10 provinces in 2000 and 2005 (fictitious data). Compute the mean and median for each year and compare the two measures of central tendency. Which measure of central tendency is greater for each year? Are the distributions skewed? In which direction?

Province	2000	2005
Newfoundland and Labrador	712	734
Prince Edward Island	667	709
Nova Scotia	570	697
New Brunswick	660	662
Quebec	648	745
Ontario	682	700
Manitoba	633	656
Saskatchewan	645	706
Alberta	617	680
British Columbia	712	741

3.9 SOC In problem 3.8, you computed the mean and median weekly earnings for 10 Canadian provinces in two separate years. Now compute the standard deviation for each year. Did the average weekly earnings for the provinces become more or less variable over the period?

3.10 SW As the head of a social services agency, you believe that your staff of 20 social workers is very much overworked compared to 10 years ago. The case loads for each worker are reported below for each of the two years in question. Has the average case load increased? What measure of central tendency is most appropriate to answer this question? Why?

2000		2010	
52	55	42	82
50	49	75	50
57	50	69	52
49	52	65	50
45	59	58	55
65	60	64	65
60	65	69	60
55	68	60	60
42	60	50	60
50	42	60	60

3.11 SOC The table below lists the approximate number of cars per 100 population for eight nations. Compute the mean and median for this data. Which is greater in value? Is there a positive skew in this data? How do you know?

Nation	Number of Cars per 100 Population
United States	50
Canada	45
France	46
Germany	51
Japan	39
Mexico	10
Sweden	44
United Kingdom	37

3.12 SW For the test scores first presented in problem 2.6 and reproduced below, compute a mean and standard deviation for both the pretest and post-test. Based on these statistics, write a paragraph describing how the sample changed from test to test.

Case	Pretest	Post-test
A	8	12
B	7	13
C	10	12
D	15	19
E	10	8
F	10	17
G	3	12
H	10	11
I	5	7
J	15	12
K	13	20
L	4	5
M	10	15
N	8	11
O	12	20

3.13 SOC A sample of 25 first-year students at a university wrote a test that measured their literacy skills in reading and writing (their test scores were the number of incorrect answers, so the higher the score, the poorer the skills).
  a. Compute the median and mean scores for these data.

10	43	30	30	45
40	12	40	42	35
45	25	10	33	50
42	32	38	11	47
22	26	37	38	10

  b. These same 25 students wrote the same test during their final year. Compute the median and mean for this second set of scores and compare them to the earlier set. What happened?

10	45	35	27	50
35	10	50	40	30
40	10	10	37	10
40	15	30	20	43
23	25	30	40	10

3.14 PA The data below represent the percentage of workers living in each city who used public transportation to commute to work in 2010 (fictitious data).

City	Percent
Abbotsford	20
Barrie	32
Calgary	26
Dawson	6
Fredericton	9
Edmonton	6
Hamilton	10
Halifax	11
Kelowna	15
Mississauga	14
Montreal	53
Quebec	25
Saskatoon	3
St. John's	4
Thunder Bay	4
Toronto	31
Vancouver	18
Winnipeg	33

  a. Calculate and compare the mean and median of this distribution. Summarize the results in a paragraph.
  b. Compute and compare the standard deviation and interquartile range. Summarize the results in a paragraph.
  c. If you removed Montreal from this distribution and recalculated, what would happen to the mean? To the median? Why?
  d. What would happen to the value of the standard deviation if you removed Montreal from this distribution and recalculated? To the interquartile range? Why?

3.15 At Algebra University the math department ran some special sections of the introductory math course using a variety of innovative teaching techniques. Students were randomly assigned to either the traditional sections or the experimental sections, and all students were given the same final exam. The results of the final are summarized below. What was the effect of the experimental course?

Traditional	Experimental
$\overline{X} = 77.8$	$\overline{X} = 76.8$
$s = 12.3$	$s = 6.2$
$n = 478$	$n = 465$

SPSS for Windows

Using SPSS for Windows to Compute Measures of Central Tendency and Dispersion with the 2006 Census

The demonstrations and exercises below use the shortened version of the 2006 Census data set (*Census.sav*) supplied with this textbook. Start SPSS for Windows by clicking the SPSS icon on your monitor screen. Load the 2006 Census, and when you see the message "IBM SPSS Statistics Processor is ready" on the bottom of the "closest" screen, you are ready to proceed.

It is again important to note that SPSS displays information on variables by name (e.g., *agegrp*) or by label (e.g., age groups). If labels are displayed, we highly recommend that you switch to variable names by clicking **Edit**, **Options**, and then, on the **General** tab, select **Display names** and **Alphabetical** and then click **OK**. These changes may not take effect until you load a new data set or restart SPSS.

SPSS DEMONSTRATION 3.1 Producing Measures of Central Tendency and Dispersion

Most of the statistics discussed in this chapter are available from either the **Frequencies** or **Descriptives** procedures. Here we will use **Frequencies**, which we used to produce a frequency distribution in Demonstration 2.1, to calculate measures of central tendency and dispersion for three variables: *pr* (province), *uphwrk* (unpaid housework), and *grosrt* (monthly gross rent).

The three variables vary in level of measurement, and we could request only the appropriate measure of central tendency and dispersion for each variable. For example, we could request the mode for *pr* (nominal), the median for *uphwrk* (ordinal), and the mean for *grosrt* (interval-ratio). While this would be reasonable, it's actually more convenient to get all measures of central tendency and dispersion for each variable and ignore the irrelevant output. Statistical packages typically generate more information than necessary, and it is common to disregard some of the output.

To produce measures of central tendency and dispersion begin by clicking **Analyze** from the menu bar and then click **Descriptive Statistics** and **Frequencies.** In the **Frequencies** dialog box, find the variable names in the list on the left and click the arrow button in the middle of the screen to move the names (*pr*, *uphwrk*, and *grosrt*) to the **Variable(s)** box on the right.

To request specific statistics, click the **Statistics** button in the upper-right-hand corner of the **Frequencies** dialog box, and the **Frequencies: Statistics** dialog box opens. Find the **Central Tendency** box on the right and click **Mean**, **Median**, and **Mode**. Next, find the **Dispersion** box on the left and click **Std. Deviation**, **Variance**, and **Range**. Then, in the **Percentile Values** section, click the checkbox next to **Quartiles**. Click **Continue**, and you will be returned to the **Frequencies** dialog box, where you might want to click the **Display Frequency Tables** box. When this box is *not* checked, SPSS will not produce frequency distribution tables, and only the statistics we request will appear in the **Output** window. Click **OK**, and SPSS will produce the following output:

Statistics

		Province	Hours spent doing unpaid houseword	Gross rent
N	Valid	1500	1500	401
	Missing	0	0	1099
Mean		35.85	3.00	769.94
Median		35.00	3.00	700.00
Mode		35	3	700
Std. Deviation		13.043	1.229	366.141
Variance		170.125	1.510	134058.899
Range		49	5	2052
Percentiles	25	24.00	2.00	500.00
	50	35.00	3.00	700.00
	75	47.00	4.00	950.00

Looking only at the most appropriate measure of central tendency and dispersion for each variable, the mode for *pr* (province) is "35". You can find out about the meaning or label of this value by consulting either the code book in Appendix G of the textbook or the online code book. To use the latter, click **Utilities** and then click **Variables** and find *pr* in the variable list on the left. Either way, you will find that a score of 1 indicates "Ontario." This was the most common province of residence for persons in the sample and, thus, is the mode. (Note, the variation ratio statistic is not available in the **Frequencies** command, however it can easily be computed by producing a frequency distribution table, as illustrated in Demonstration 2.1, then inputting the appropriate information into Formula 3.1.)

The median for *uphwrk* (unpaid housework) is a value of "3.00." Again, use either Appendix G or the online code book, and you will see that the category associated with this score is "5–14 hours." This means that the middle case in this distribution of 1,500 cases has a score of 3 (or that the middle case is in the interval "5–14 hours").

As for dispersion, the range for *uphwrk* is equal to 5. In other words, scores range from 1 ("No" hours persons spent doing unpaid work) to 6 ("60 hours or more"). The interquartile range is the difference between the third quartile (labelled as "75" in the "Percentiles" row, meaning the 75th percentile) and the first quartile (labelled "25," or the 25th percentile). The score associated with the 75th percentile is 4, which indicates that 75% of the sample has a score below 4. Similarly, 25% has a score below 2. Hence the interquartile range is equal to 4 – 2 or 2. (Note that the second quartile is labelled "50," or the 50th percentile, which is the same as the median.)

The output for *grosrt* (rent) indicates that for the 401 tenants in the sample, the average monthly rent is $769.94. Since rent is an interval-ratio variable that has been measured in a defined unit (dollars), the value of the mean is numerically meaningful, and we do not need to consult the code book to interpret its meaning. The standard deviation, reported in the row labelled "Std. Deviation," for *grosrt* is about $366.14, suggesting that Canadians are quite diverse in what they pay in monthly rent. Remember, a standard deviation of zero indicates that every person has exactly the same score. So, with a standard deviation of almost $370, there is plenty of diversity or heterogeneity in the distribution of rent in Canada.

Note that SPSS used "N" in the output to refer to sample size (e.g., the "valid" number of cases in the sample for the variable *pr* is 1,500), rather than the standard notation of "*n*" used in the text of this textbook. Also note that SPSS did not hesitate to compute means and standard deviations for the two variables that were not interval-ratio. The program cannot distinguish between numerical codes (such as the scores for *pr*) and actual numbers—to SPSS, all numbers are the same. Also, SPSS cannot screen your commands to see if they are statistically appropriate. If you request nonsensical statistics (e.g., average sex or median province), SPSS will carry out your instructions without hesitation. The blind willingness of SPSS to simply obey commands makes it easy for you, the user, to request statistics that are completely meaningless. Computers don't care about meaning; they just crunch the numbers.

In this case, it was more convenient for us to produce statistics indiscriminately and then ignore the ones that are nonsensical. This will not always be the case, and the point of all this, of course, is to caution you to use SPSS wisely. As the manager of your local computer centre will be quick to remind you, computer resources (including paper) are not unlimited.

SPSS DEMONSTRATION 3.2 The Descriptives Command

The **Descriptives** command in SPSS for Windows is designed to provide summary statistics for continuous interval-ratio-level variables. By default (i.e., unless you tell it otherwise), **Descriptives** produces the mean, the minimum and maximum scores (i.e., the lowest and highest scores), and the standard deviation. Unlike **Frequencies**, this procedure will not produce frequency distributions.

To illustrate the use of **Descriptives**, let's run the procedure for *value* (value of dwelling), *totinc* (total income of individual), and *grosrt* (monthly gross rent). Click **Analyze**, **Descriptive Statistics**, and **Descriptives**. The **Descriptives** dialog box will open. This dialog box looks just like the **Frequencies** dialog box and works in the same way. Find the variable names in the list on the left and, once they are highlighted, click the arrow button in the middle of the screen to transfer them to the **Variable(s)** box on the right. Click **OK**, and the following output will be produced:

Descriptive Statistics

	N	Minimum	Maximum	Mean	Std. Deviation
Gross rent	401	0	2052	769.94	366.141
Value of dwelling	1090	0	1388169	292755.87	241424.267
Total income of individual	1500	0	866341	33767.06	48987.577
Valid N (listwise)	0				

The sample, on the average, pays $769.94 in rent with a standard deviation (reported in the column labelled "Std. Deviation") of $366.14 (this duplicates the frequencies output in Demonstration 3.1). The output also shows that people in the sample have, on average, an annual income of $33,767.06 with a standard deviation of about $48,987.58. Finally, it reveals that for the 1,090 home owners in the sample, the average home is worth $292,755.87 with a standard deviation of $241,424.27.

Exercises (using *Census.sav*)

3.1 Use the **Frequencies** command to get the most appropriate measure of central tendency for any three nominal or ordinal variables of your own choosing. (*Hint: Use the level of measurement of the variable as your criteria for selecting the appropriate measure of central tendency.*) Write a sentence or two reporting each measure.

3.2 Use the **Descriptives** command to get means and standard deviations for any two interval-ratio variables. Write a sentence or two reporting and explaining the mean and standard deviation of each variable.

3.3 Use the **Frequencies** command to find the interquartile range for each variable in Exercise 3.2. Write a few sentences summarizing these results.

4 The Normal Curve

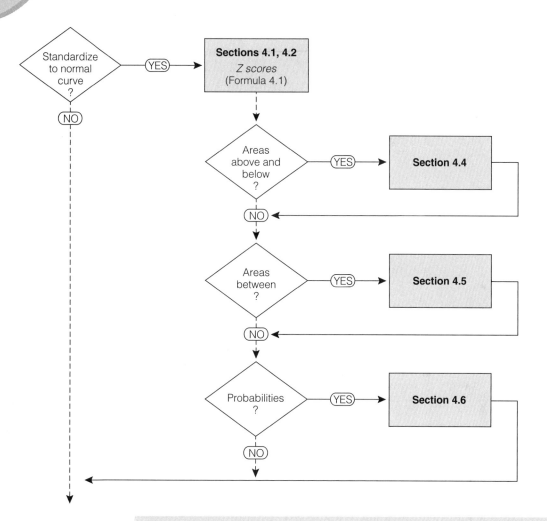

4.1 INTRODUCTION

The **normal curve** is a concept of great importance in statistics. In combination with the mean and standard deviation, the normal curve can be used to construct precise descriptive statements about empirical distributions. In addition, as we shall see in Part II, it is also central to the theory that underlies inferential statistics. This chapter will conclude our treatment of descriptive statistics in Part I and lay important groundwork for Part II.

The normal curve is a theoretical model, a kind of frequency polygon that is unimodal (i.e., it has a single mode or peak), perfectly smooth and symmetrical (unskewed) so that its mean, median, and mode are all exactly the same value. It is bell shaped and its tails extend infinitely in both directions. Of course, no empirical distribution has a shape that perfectly matches this ideal model, but many variables (e.g., test results from large classes, test scores such as the GRE, people's height and weight) are close enough to permit the assumption of normality. In turn, this assumption makes possible one of the most important uses of the normal curve—the description of empirical distributions based on our knowledge of the theoretical normal curve.

The crucial point about the normal curve is that distances along the abscissa (horizontal axis) of the distribution, when measured in standard deviations from the mean, always encompass the *same* proportion of the total area under the curve. In other words, on any normal curve, the distance from any given point to the mean (when measured in standard deviations) will cut off exactly the *same* proportion of the total area.

To illustrate, Figures 4.1 and 4.2 present two hypothetical distributions of IQ scores, one for a sample of males and one for a sample of females, both normally distributed (or nearly so), such that:

Males	Females
$\overline{X} = 100$	$\overline{X} = 100$
$s = 20$	$s = 10$
$n = 1,000$	$n = 1,000$

Figures 4.1 and 4.2 are drawn with two scales on the horizontal axis or abscissa of the graph. The upper scale is stated in "IQ units" and the lower scale in standard deviations from the mean. These scales are interchangeable, and we can easily shift from one to the other. For example, for the males, an IQ score of 120 is one standard deviation (remember that, for the male group, $s = 20$) above the mean and an IQ of 140 is two standard deviations above (to the right of) the mean. Scores to the left of the mean are marked as negative values because they are less than the mean. An IQ of 80 is one standard deviation below the mean, an IQ score of 60 is two standard deviations less than the mean, and so forth. Figure 4.2 is marked in a similar way except that, because its standard deviation is a different value ($s = 10$), the markings occur at different points. For the female sample, one standard deviation above the mean is an IQ of 110, one standard deviation below the mean is an IQ of 90, and so forth.

FIGURE 4.1   IQ SCORES FOR A SAMPLE OF MALES

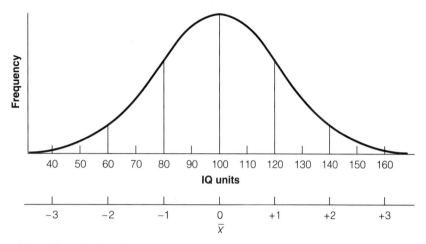

FIGURE 4.2   IQ SCORES FOR A SAMPLE OF FEMALES

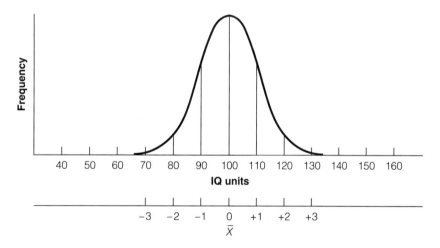

Recall that, on any normal curve, distances along the horizontal axis (or abscissa), when measured in standard deviations, always encompass exactly the same proportion of the total area under the curve. Specifically, the distance between one standard deviation above the mean and one standard deviation below the mean (or ±1 standard deviation) encompasses exactly 68.26% of the total area under the curve. This means that in Figure 4.1, 68.26% of the total area lies between the score of 80 (−1 standard deviation) and 120 (+1 standard deviation). The standard deviation for females is 10, so the same percentage of the area (68.26%) lies between the scores of 90 and 110. As long as an empirical distribution is normal, 68.26% of the total area will always be encompassed between ±1 standard deviation—regardless of the trait being measured and the number values of the mean and standard deviation.

FIGURE 4.3   AREAS UNDER THE THEORETICAL NORMAL CURVE

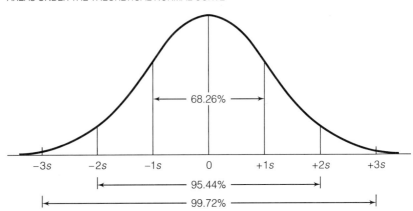

It will be useful to familiarize yourself with the following relationships between distances from the mean and areas under the curve:

Between	Lies
±1 standard deviation	68.26% of the area
±2 standard deviations	95.44% of the area
±3 standard deviations	99.72% of the area

These relationships are displayed graphically in Figure 4.3. Note that the relationships apply equally to normally distributed data in the population, but instead Greek letters are used to represent the mean, μ, and standard deviation, σ (see Section 3.4). So, 68.26% of all cases in a normally distributed population are contained within $\pm 1\sigma$ of μ; 95.44% of all cases in normally distributed population are contained within $\pm 2\sigma$ of μ; and 99.72% of all cases in normally distributed population are contained within $\pm 3\sigma$ of μ. For sake of brevity, we will refer to only sample data and symbols ($\overline{X}$ and s) for the remainder of this chapter.

The relationship between distance from the mean and area allows us to describe an empirical distribution of a variable in the sample (or population), provided that it is at least approximately normal. The position of individual scores can be described with respect to the mean, the distribution as a whole, or any other score in the distribution.

The areas between scores can also be expressed, if desired, in numbers of cases rather than percentage of total area. For example, a normal distribution of 1,000 cases will contain about 683 cases (68.26% of 1,000 cases) between ±1 standard deviation of the mean, about 954 cases between ±2 standard deviations, and about 997 cases between ±3 standard deviations. Thus, for any normal distribution, only a few cases will be farther away from the mean than ±3 standard deviations.

4.2 COMPUTING Z SCORES

To find the percentage of the total area (or number of cases) above, below, or between scores in an empirical distribution, the original scores must first be expressed in units of the standard deviation or converted into **Z scores**. The original scores could be in any unit of measurement (metres, IQ, dollars), but Z scores always have the same values for their mean (0) and standard deviation (1).

Think of converting the original scores into Z scores as a process of changing value scales—similar to changing from metres to yards, kilometres to miles, or gallons to litres. These units are different but equally valid ways of expressing distance, length, or volume. For example, a mile is equal to 1.61 kilometres, so two towns that are 10 miles apart are also 16.1 kilometres apart and a "5k" race covers about 3.10 miles. Although you may be more familiar with kilometres than miles, either unit works perfectly well as a way of expressing distance.

In the same way, the original (or "raw") scores and Z scores are two equally valid but different ways of measuring distances under the normal curve. In Figure 4.1, for example, we could describe a particular score in terms of IQ units ("Amal's score was 120") or standard deviations ("Amal scored one standard deviation above the mean").

When we compute Z scores, we convert the original units of measurement (IQ units, centimetres, dollars, etc.) to Z scores and, thus, "standardize" the normal curve to a distribution that has a mean of 0 and a standard deviation of 1. The mean of the empirical normal distribution will be converted to 0, its standard deviation to 1, and all values will be expressed in Z-score form. The formula for converting original scores in a sample to Z scores is:*

FORMULA 4.1

$$Z = \frac{X_i - \overline{X}}{s}$$

Formula 4.1 will convert any score (X_i) from an empirical distribution into the equivalent Z score. To illustrate, consider the following sample of scores from Table 3.8: 10, 20, 30, 40, and 50. Their Z-score equivalents are presented in Table 4.1.

A Z score of positive 1.00 indicates that the original score lies one standard deviation unit above (to the right of) the mean. A negative Z score of 1.00 would fall one standard deviation unit below (to the left of) the mean. Thus in the above example, the Z score of 1.414 indicates that the original score of 50 lies 1.414 standard deviation units above the mean, while −1.414 indicates that the original score of 10 lies 1.414 standard deviation units below the mean.

By inspection, you can see that the distribution of Z scores in Table 4.1 has a mean of 0 and a standard deviation of 1. To substantiate these observations,

---

*When converting original scores in a population, this formula is written as: $Z = \dfrac{X_i - \mu}{\sigma}$

TABLE 4.1   COMPUTING Z SCORES FOR A DISTRIBUTION OF ORIGINAL SCORES

Score (X_i)	Z Score $= \dfrac{X_i - \overline{X}}{s}$
10	$\dfrac{10 - 30}{14.14} = -1.414$
20	$\dfrac{20 - 30}{14.14} = -0.707$
30	$\dfrac{30 - 30}{14.14} = 0.000$
40	$\dfrac{40 - 30}{14.14} = 0.707$
50	$\dfrac{50 - 30}{14.14} = 1.414$

Recall from Table 3.8: $\overline{X} = 30$, $s = 14.14$

the mean and standard deviation of the Z distribution are computed using Formulas 3.2 and 3.5. The results are shown in Table 4.2. *(For practice in computing Z scores, see any of the problems at the end of this chapter.)*

4.3 THE NORMAL CURVE TABLE

The theoretical normal curve has been very thoroughly analyzed and described by statisticians. The areas related to any Z score have been precisely determined and organized into a table format. This **normal curve table** or Z-score table is presented as Appendix A in this textbook and a small portion of it is reproduced here for purposes of illustration as Table 4.3.

The normal curve table consists of three columns, with Z scores in the left-hand column "a," areas between the Z score and the mean of the curve

TABLE 4.2   COMPUTING THE MEAN AND STANDARD DEVIATION FOR A DISTRIBUTION OF Z SCORES

Scores (X_i)	Deviations $(X_i - \overline{X})$	Deviations Squared $(X_i - \overline{X})^2$
−1.414	−1.414	2.0
−0.707	−0.707	0.5
0.000	0.000	0.0
0.707	0.707	0.5
1.414	1.414	2.0
$\sum (X_i) = 0.000$		$\sum (X_i - \overline{X})^2 = 5.0$

$$\overline{X} = \frac{\sum (X_i)}{n} = \frac{0}{5} = 0 \quad \text{(Formula 3.2)}$$

$$s = \sqrt{\frac{\sum (X_i - \overline{X})^2}{n}} = \sqrt{\frac{5}{5}} = \sqrt{1} = 1 \quad \text{(Formula 3.5)}$$

TABLE 4.3 AN ILLUSTRATION OF HOW TO FIND AREAS UNDER THE
NORMAL CURVE USING APPENDIX A

(a) Z	(b) Area between Mean and Z	(c) Area beyond Z
0.00	0.0000	0.5000
0.01	0.0040	0.4960
0.02	0.0080	0.4920
0.03	0.0120	0.4880
⋮	⋮	⋮
1.00	0.3413	0.1587
1.01	0.3438	0.1562
1.02	0.3461	0.1539
1.03	0.3485	0.1515
⋮	⋮	⋮
1.50	0.4332	0.0668
1.51	0.4345	0.0655
1.52	0.4357	0.0643
1.53	0.4370	0.0630
⋮	⋮	⋮

in the middle column "b," and areas beyond the Z score in the right-hand column "c." To find the area between any Z score and the mean, go down the column labelled "Z" until you find the Z score. For example, go down column "a" either in Appendix A or in Table 4.3 until you find a Z score of +1.00. The entry in column "b" ("Area between Mean and Z") is 0.3413. The table presents all areas in the form of proportions, but we can easily translate these into percentages by multiplying them by 100 (see Chapter 2). We could say either "a proportion of 0.3413 of the total area under the curve lies between a Z score of 1.00 and the mean," or "34.13% of the total area lies between a score of 1.00 and the mean."

To illustrate further, find the Z score of 1.50 either in column "a" of Appendix A or the abbreviated table presented in Table 4.3. This score is 1½ standard deviations to the right of the mean and corresponds to an IQ of 130 for the men's IQ data. The area in column "b" for this score is 0.4332. This means that a proportion of 0.4332—or a percentage of 43.32%—of all the area under the curve lies between this score and the mean.

The third column in the table, column c, presents "Area beyond Z." These are areas above positive scores or below negative scores. This column will be used when we want to find an area above or below certain Z scores, an application that will be explained in Section 4.4.

To conserve space, the normal curve table in Appendix A includes only positive Z scores. Because the normal curve is perfectly symmetrical, however, the area between the score and the mean (column b) for a negative score will be exactly the same as those for a positive score of the same numerical value. For example, the area between a Z score of −1.00 and the mean will also be 34.13%, exactly the same as the area we found previously for a score of $+1.00$. As will be repeatedly demonstrated below, however, the sign of the Z score is extremely important and should be carefully noted.

For practice in using Appendix A to describe areas under an empirical normal curve, verify that the Z scores and areas given below are correct for the sample distribution of men's IQ. For each IQ score, the equivalent Z score is computed using Formula 4.1, and then Appendix A is used to find areas between the score and the mean. ($\overline{X} = 100$, $s = 20$ throughout.)

IQ Score	Z Score	Area between Z and the Mean
110	+0.50	19.15%
125	+1.25	39.44%
133	+1.65	45.05%
138	+1.90	47.13%

The same procedures apply when the Z-score equivalent of an actual score happens to be a minus value (i.e., when the raw score lies below the mean).

IQ Score	Z Score	Area between Z and the Mean
93	−0.35	13.68%
85	−0.75	27.34%
67	−1.65	45.05%
62	−1.90	47.13%

Remember that the areas in Appendix A will be the same for Z scores of the same numerical value regardless of sign. The area between the score of 138 ($+1.90$) and the mean is the same as the area between 62 (-1.90) and the mean. *(For practice in using the normal curve table, see any of the problems at the end of this chapter.)*

4.4 FINDING TOTAL AREA ABOVE AND BELOW A SCORE

To this point, we have seen how the normal curve table can be used to find areas between a Z score and the mean. The information presented in the table can also be used to find other kinds of areas in an empirical distribution of a variable in the sample (or population), provided that it is at least approximately normal in shape. For example, suppose you need to determine the total area below the scores of two male subjects in the sample distribution described in Figure 4.1. The first subject has a score of 117 ($X_1 = 117$), which is equivalent to a Z score of $+0.85$:

$$Z_1 = \frac{X_1 - \overline{X}}{s} = \frac{117 - 100}{20} = \frac{17}{20} = +0.85$$

The plus sign of the Z score indicates that the score should be placed above (to the right of) the mean. To find the area below a positive Z score, the area between the score and the mean (given in column b) must be added to the area below the mean. As we noted earlier, the normal curve is

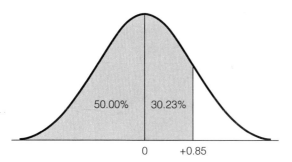

FIGURE 4.4   FINDING THE AREA BELOW A POSITIVE *Z* SCORE

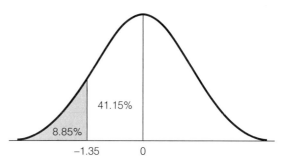

FIGURE 4.5   FINDING THE AREA BELOW A NEGATIVE *Z* SCORE

symmetrical (unskewed) and its mean will be equal to its median. Therefore, the area below the mean (just like the median) will be 50%. Study Figure 4.4 carefully. We are interested in the shaded area.

By consulting the normal curve table, we find that the area between the score and the mean (see column b) is 30.23% of the total area. The area below a *Z* score of +0.85 is therefore 80.23% (50.00% + 30.23%). This subject scored higher than 80.23% of the persons tested.

The second subject has an IQ score of 73 ($X_2 = 73$), which is equivalent to a *Z* score of −1.35:

$$Z_2 = \frac{X_2 - \overline{X}}{s} = \frac{73 - 100}{20} = -\frac{27}{20} = -1.35$$

To find the area below a negative score, we use the column labelled "Area beyond *Z*." The area of interest is depicted in Figure 4.5, and we must determine the size of the shaded area. The area beyond a score of −1.35 is given as 0.0885, which we can express as 8.85%. The second subject ($X_2 = 73$) scored higher than 8.85% of the tested group.

In the examples above, we use the techniques for finding the area below a score. Essentially the same techniques are used to find the area above a

FIGURE 4.6   FINDING THE AREA ABOVE A POSITIVE *Z* SCORE

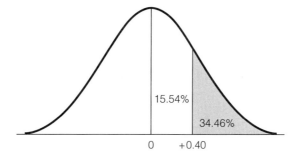

TABLE 4.4 FINDING AREAS ABOVE AND BELOW POSITIVE AND NEGATIVE Z SCORES

	When the Z Score Is	
To Find Area:	Positive	Negative
Above Z	Look in column c	Add column b area to 0.5000 or 50.00%
Below Z	Add column b area to 0.5000 or 50.00%	Look in column c

score. If we need to determine the area above an IQ score of 108, for example, we would first convert to a Z score,

$$Z = \frac{X_i - \overline{X}}{s} = \frac{108 - 100}{20} = \frac{8}{20} = +0.40$$

and then proceed to Appendix A. The shaded area in Figure 4.6 represents the area in which we are interested. The area above a positive score is found in the "Area beyond Z" column, and, in this case, the area is 0.3446, or 34.46%.

These procedures are summarized in Table 4.4. To find the total area above a positive Z score or below a negative Z score, go down the "Z" column of Appendix A until you find the score. The area you are seeking will be in the "Area beyond Z" column (column c). To find the total area below a positive Z score or above a negative score, locate the score and then add the area in the "Area between Mean and Z" (column b) to either 0.5000 (for proportions) or 50.00 (for percentages). These techniques might be confusing at first, and you will find it helpful to draw the curve and shade in the areas in which you are interested. *(For practice in finding areas above or below Z scores, see problems 4.1 to 4.7.)*

4.5 FINDING AREAS BETWEEN TWO SCORES

On occasion, you will need to determine the area between two scores rather than the total area above or below one score. In the case where the scores are on opposite sides of the mean, the area between the scores can be found by adding the areas between each score and the mean. Using the sample data of men's IQ as an example, if we wished to know the area between the IQ scores of 93 and 112, we would convert both scores to Z scores, find the area between each score and the mean from Appendix A, and add these two areas together. The first IQ score of 93 converts to a Z score of -0.35:

$$Z_1 = \frac{X_1 - \overline{X}}{s} = \frac{93 - 100}{20} = -\frac{7}{20} = -0.35$$

The second IQ score (112) converts to $+0.60$:

$$Z_2 = \frac{X_2 - \overline{X}}{s} = \frac{112 - 100}{20} = \frac{12}{20} = 0.60$$

FIGURE 4.7   FINDING THE AREA BETWEEN TWO SCORES

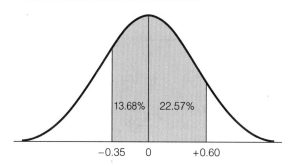

Both scores are placed on Figure 4.7. We are interested in the total shaded area. The total area between these two scores is 13.68% + 22.57%, or 36.25%. Therefore, 36.25% of the total area (or about 363 of the 1,000 cases) lies between the IQ scores of 93 and 112.

When the scores of interest are on the same side of the mean, a different procedure must be followed to determine the area between them. For example, if we were interested in the area between the scores of 113 and 121, we would begin by converting these scores into Z scores:

$$Z_1 = \frac{X_1 - \overline{X}}{s} = \frac{113 - 100}{20} = \frac{13}{20} = +0.65$$

$$Z_2 = \frac{X_2 - \overline{X}}{s} = \frac{121 - 100}{20} = \frac{21}{20} = +1.05$$

The scores are noted in Figure 4.8; we are interested in the shaded area. To find the area between two scores on the same side of the mean, find the area between each score and the mean (given in column b of Appendix A) and then subtract the smaller area from the larger. Between the Z score of +0.65 and the mean lies 24.22% of the total area. Between +1.05 and the mean lies 35.31% of the total area. Therefore, the area between these two scores is

FIGURE 4.8   FINDING THE AREA BETWEEN TWO SCORES

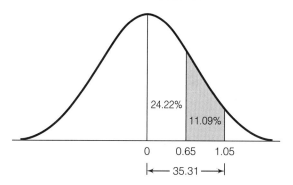

Application 4.1

There has been a sharp increase in the number of overweight and obese Canadians over the last 30 years—a trend that has been observed in several developed countries. The rise in obesity is due to a variety of factors, notably changes in the general dietary and lifestyle habits of Canadians, including increased levels of sedentary living and increased consumption of processed and "junk" food. Social scientists also have shown that present social, economic, and political factors create an environment in which it is challenging to maintain a healthy diet and weight. Sociologists, for example, contend that time and cost pressures on families have led to an increase in families' consumption of fast food, which is high in calories and fats and is readily available to consumers. Also, many children and youth spent their leisure time doing sedentary activities such as watching television and playing video games instead of participating in physical outdoor activities.

Trends in overweight and obesity are observed using the body mass index (BMI), which is a measure of body fat for men and women. BMI is a number calculated from an individual's body weight and height. The BMI is not a direct measure of body fat (e.g., it can overestimate body fatness in muscular and athletic persons, such as many professional football players), but studies show that it is correlated with direct measures of body fat (e.g., skinfold thickness) as well as several overweight- and obesity-related diseases (e.g., Type II diabetes and heart disease). BMI is also easy to calculate. The BMI formula is

$$\text{in standard units: } \left(\frac{\text{weight in pounds}}{\text{height in inches}^2} \right) \times 703$$

$$\text{in metric units: } \left(\frac{\text{weight in kilograms}}{\text{height in metres}^2} \right)$$

The BMI is interpreted using a weight classification system that is the same for adult men and women (but not for children because their body fat changes with age) as follows:

BMI Score	Weight Status
Less than 18.5	Underweight
18.5–24.9	Normal
25.0–29.9	Overweight
30.0 and over	Obese

Note that health care professionals and researchers often further divide the obese category, for example, into obese (BMI of 30.0–34.9), severely obese (BMI of 35.0–39.9), and morbidly obese (BMI of 40.0 and over).

Using this system, an adult with a height of 5'9" and weight of 200 pounds has a BMI score of 29.5 and is classified as overweight. However, how does this score compare with the distribution of all BMI scores? To answer this question we can compute a Z score and find the area below or above the score.

According to the 2005 Canadian Community Health Survey, Statistics Canada's main health survey, the distribution of BMI scores of adult Canadians is normal with a mean of 26.1 and a standard deviation of 4.9 (see the frequency polygon on the next page):

Hence, the Z-score equivalent of the original raw BMI score of 29.5 would be

$$Z = \frac{X_i - \overline{X}}{s} = \frac{29.5 - 26.1}{4.9} = \frac{3.4}{4.9} = 0.69$$

Turning to Appendix A, we find that the "Area between Mean and Z" for a Z score of $+0.69$ is 0.2549, which could also be expressed as 25.49%. Because this is a positive Z score, we need to add this area to 50.00% to find the total area below. A BMI score of 29.5 is higher than 75.49% (or 25.49 + 50.00) of all adult BMI scores in Canada.

(continued next page)

Application 4.1: *(continued)*

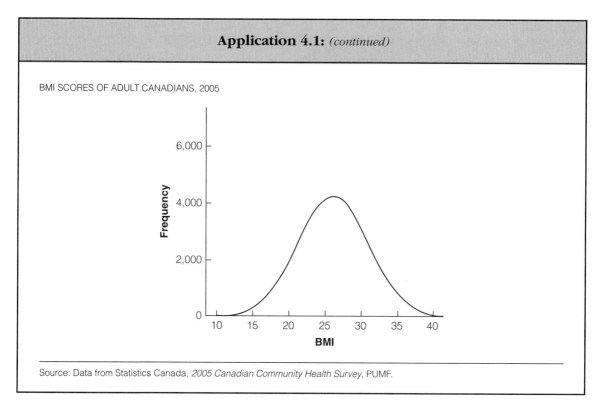

BMI SCORES OF ADULT CANADIANS, 2005

Source: Data from Statistics Canada, *2005 Canadian Community Health Survey*, PUMF.

TABLE 4.5   FINDING AREAS BETWEEN SCORES

Situation	Procedure
Scores are on the SAME side of the mean	Find areas between each score and the mean in column b. Subtract the smaller area from the larger area.
Scores are on OPPOSITE sides of the mean	Find areas between each score and the mean in column b. Add the two areas together.

35.31% − 24.22%, or 11.09% of the total area. The same technique would be followed if both scores had been below the mean. The procedures for finding areas between two scores are summarized in Table 4.5. *(For practice in finding areas between two scores, see problems 4.3, 4.4, and 4.6 to 4.9.)*

4.6 USING THE NORMAL CURVE TO ESTIMATE PROBABILITIES

To this point, we have thought of the theoretical normal curve as a way of describing the percentage of total area above, below, and between scores in an empirical distribution. We have also seen that these areas can be converted into the number of cases above, below, and between scores. In this section, we

---

Application 4.2

In Application 4.1 we used a Z score and the normal curve table to find the total area below a BMI (a measure of body fat) score of 29.5 in the distribution of BMI scores. In this application we will determine the area between two BMI scores rather than the total area below one BMI score. We should recall that according to the Canadian Community Health Survey, BMI scores among adults in Canada are distributed normally with a mean of 26.1 and a standard deviation of 4.9.

What percentage of adults in Canada is normal weight and what percentage is overweight? That is, what percentage has a BMI score between 18.5 and 24.9 (normal) and what percentage has a score between 25.0 and 29.9 (overweight)?

The first two scores are both below the mean. Using Table 4.5 as a guide, we must first compute Z scores, find areas between each score and the mean, and then subtract the smaller area from the larger.

$$Z_1 = \frac{X_1 - \overline{X}}{s} = \frac{18.5 - 26.1}{4.9} = -\frac{7.6}{4.9} = -1.55$$

$$Z_2 = \frac{X_2 - \overline{X}}{s} = \frac{24.9 - 26.1}{4.9} = -\frac{1.2}{4.9} = -0.25$$

Using column b, we see that the area between $Z = -1.55$ and the mean is 0.4394 and the area between $Z = -0.25$ and the mean is 0.0987. Subtracting the smaller from the larger (0.4394 − 0.0987) gives 0.3407. Changing to percentage format, we can say that 34.07% of adults in Canada have normal body weight.

To find the percentage of Canadians who are overweight, we must add column b areas together since the scores (25.0 and 29.9) are on opposite sides of the mean (see Table 4.5).

$$Z_1 = \frac{X_1 - \overline{X}}{s} = \frac{25.0 - 26.1}{4.9} = -\frac{1.1}{4.9} = -0.23$$

$$Z_2 = \frac{X_2 - \overline{X}}{s} = \frac{29.9 - 26.1}{4.9} = \frac{3.8}{4.9} = 0.78$$

Using column b, we see that the area between $Z = -0.23$ and the mean is 0.0910 and the area between $Z = +0.78$ and the mean is 0.2823. Therefore, the total area between these two scores is (0.0910 + 0.2823) or 0.3733. Translating to percentages again, we can say that 37.33% of Canadian adults are overweight. In fact, more adults in Canada are overweight than normal weight: 37.33% vs. 34.07%.

---

introduce the idea that the theoretical normal curve may also be thought of as a distribution of probabilities. Specifically, we may use the properties of the theoretical normal curve (Appendix A) to estimate the probability that a case randomly selected from an empirical normal distribution will have a score that falls in a certain range. In terms of techniques, these probabilities will be found in exactly the same way as areas were found. Before we consider these mechanics, however, let us examine what is meant by the concept of probability.

Although we are rarely systematic or rigorous about it, we all attempt to deal with probabilities every day and, indeed, we base our behaviour on our estimates of the likelihood that certain events will occur. We constantly ask (and answer) questions such as: "What is the probability of rain?" "Of drawing to an inside straight in poker?" "Of the worn-out tires on my car going flat?" "Of passing a test if I don't study?"

To estimate the probability of an event, we must first be able to define what would constitute a "success." The examples above contain several

Application 4.3

We know that the BMI scores of adult Canadians are normally distributed with a mean of 26.1 and a standard deviation of 4.9 (see Applications 4.1 and 4.2). What is the probability that a Canadian adult selected at random will have a BMI score of less than 20.0? More than 31? Less than 40? To answer these questions, we must first calculate Z scores and then consult Appendix A. We are looking for probabilities, so we will leave the areas in proportion form. The Z score for a score of 20 is

$$Z = \frac{X_i - \overline{X}}{s} = \frac{20.0 - 26.1}{4.9} = -\frac{6.1}{4.9} = -1.25$$

This score is a negative value (below or to the left of the mean) and we are looking for the area below. Using Table 4.4 as a guide, we see that we must use column c to find the area below a negative score. This area is 0.1056. Rounding off, we can say that the odds of selecting a Canadian adult with a BMI score of less than 20 are only 1 out of 10. This low value tells us that this would be an unlikely event.

The Z score for the score of 31 is

$$Z = \frac{X_i - \overline{X}}{s} = \frac{31.0 - 26.1}{4.9} = \frac{4.9}{4.9} = 1.00$$

The Z score is positive and to find the area above (greater than) 31, we look in column c (see Table 4.4). This value is 0.1587. The odds of selecting a Canadian with a BMI score of greater than 31 is roughly 16 out of 100, slightly more likely than selecting a Canadian with a BMI score of less than 20.

The Z score for the score of 40 is

$$Z = \frac{X_i - \overline{X}}{s} = \frac{40.0 - 26.1}{4.9} = \frac{13.9}{4.9} = 2.84$$

To find the area below a positive Z score, we add the area between the score and the mean (column b) to 0.5000 (see Table 4.4). This value is (0.4977 + 0.5000) or 0.9977. It is extremely likely that a randomly selected Canadian adult will have a BMI score of less than 40.

different definitions of a success (i.e., rain, drawing a certain card, flat tires, and passing grades). To determine a probability, a fraction must be established, with the numerator equalling the number of events that would constitute a success and the denominator equalling the total number of possible events where a success could theoretically occur:

$$\text{Probability} = \frac{\#\ \text{successes}}{\#\ \text{events}}$$

To illustrate, assume that we wish to know the probability of selecting a specific card—say, the king of hearts—in one draw from a well-shuffled deck of cards. Our definition of a success is quite specific (drawing the king of hearts); and with the information given, we can establish a fraction. Only one card satisfies our definition of success, so the number of events that would constitute a success is 1; this value will be the numerator of the fraction. There are 52 possible events (i.e., 52 cards in the deck), so the denominator will be 52. The fraction is thus 1/52, which represents the probability of selecting the king of hearts on one draw from a well-shuffled deck of cards. Our probability of success is 1 out of 52.

We can leave the fraction established above as it is, or we can express it in several other ways. For example, we can express it as an odds ratio by inverting the fraction, showing that the odds of selecting the king of hearts on a single draw are 52:1 (or fifty-two to one). We can express the fraction as a proportion by dividing the numerator by the denominator. For our example above, the corresponding proportion is 0.0192, which is the proportion of all possible events that would satisfy our definition of a success. In the social sciences, probabilities are usually expressed as proportions, and we will follow this convention throughout the remainder of this section. Using p to represent "probability," the probability of drawing the king of hearts (or any specific card) can be expressed as

$$p\,(\text{king of hearts}) = \frac{\text{\# successes}}{\text{\# events}} = \frac{1}{52} = 0.0192$$

As conceptualized here, probabilities have an exact meaning: over the long run, the events that we define as successes will bear a certain proportional relationship to the total number of events. The probability of 0.0192 for selecting the king of hearts in a single draw really means that, over an infinite number of draws of one card at a time from a full deck of 52 cards, the proportion of successful draws would be 0.0192. Or, for every 10,000 draws, 192 would be the king of hearts, and the remaining 9,808 selections would be other cards. Thus, when we say that the probability of drawing the king of hearts in one draw is 0.0192, we are essentially applying our knowledge of what would happen over an infinite number of draws to a single draw.

Like proportions, probabilities range from 0.00 (meaning that the event has absolutely no chance of occurrence) to 1.00 (a certainty). As the value of the probability increases, the likelihood that the defined event will occur also increases. A probability of 0.0192 is close to zero, and this means that the event (drawing the king of hearts) is unlikely or improbable.

These techniques can be used to establish simple probabilities in any situation in which we can specify the number of successes and the total number of events. For example, a single die has six sides or faces, each with a different value ranging from 1 to 6. The probability of getting any specific number (say, a 4) in a single roll of a die is therefore

$$p\,(\text{rolling a four}) = \frac{1}{6} = 0.1667$$

Combining this way of thinking about probability with our knowledge of the theoretical normal curve allows us to estimate the likelihood of selecting a case that has a score within a certain range. For example, suppose we wished to estimate the probability that a randomly chosen subject from the distribution of men's IQ scores would have an IQ score between 95 and the mean score of 100. Our definition of a success would be the selection of any subject with a score in the specified range. Normally, we would next establish a fraction with the numerator equal to the number of subjects with scores in the defined range and the denominator equal to the total number of subjects. However, if the empirical distribution is normal in form, we can skip this step since the probabilities, in proportion form, are already stated in Appendix A. That is, the areas in Appendix A can be interpreted as probabilities.

To determine the probability that a randomly selected case will have a score between 95 and the mean, we would convert the original score to a Z score:

$$Z = \frac{X_i - \overline{X}}{s} = \frac{95 - 100}{20} = -\frac{5}{20} = -0.25$$

Using Appendix A, we see that the area between this score and the mean is 0.0987. This is the probability we are seeking. The probability that a randomly selected case will have a score between 95 and 100 is 0.0987 (or, rounded off, 0.1, or one out of 10). In the same fashion, the probability of selecting a subject from any range of scores can be estimated. Note that the techniques for estimating probabilities are exactly the same as those for finding areas. The only new information introduced in this section is the idea that the areas in the normal curve table can also be thought of as probabilities.

To consider an additional example, what is the probability that a randomly selected male will have an IQ less than 123? We will find probabilities in exactly the same way we found areas. The score (X_i) is above the mean and, following the directions in Table 4.4, we will find the probability we are seeking by adding the area in column b to 0.5000. First, we find the Z score:

$$Z = \frac{X_i - \overline{X}}{s} = \frac{123 - 100}{20} = \frac{23}{20} = +1.15$$

Next, look in column b of Appendix A to find the area between this score and the mean. Then, add the area (0.3749) to 0.5000. The probability of selecting a male with an IQ of less than 123 is 0.3749 + 0.5000 or 0.8749. Rounding this value to 0.88, we can say that the odds are 0.88 (very high) that we will select a male with an IQ score in this range. Technically, remember that this probability expresses what would happen over the long run: for every 100 males selected from this group over an infinite number of trials, 88 would have IQ scores less than 123 and 12 would not.

Let us close by stressing a very important point about probabilities and the normal curve. The probability is very high that any case randomly selected from a normal distribution will have a score close in value to that of the mean. The shape of the normal curve is such that most cases are clustered around the mean and decline in frequency as we move farther away—either to the right or to the left—from the mean value. In fact, given what we know about the normal curve, the probability that a randomly selected case will have a score within ±1 standard deviation of the mean is 0.6826.

Rounding off, we can say that 68 out of 100 cases—or about two-thirds of all cases—selected over the long run will have a score between ±1 standard deviation or Z score of the mean. The probabilities are that any randomly selected case will have a score close in value to the mean.

In contrast, the probability of the case having a score beyond 3 standard deviations from the mean is very small. Look in column c ("Area beyond Z") for a Z score of 3.00 and you will find the value 0.0014. Adding the areas in the upper tail (beyond +3.00) to the area in the lower tail (beyond −3.00), gives us 0.0014 + 0.0014 for a total of 0.0028. The probability of selecting a case with a very high score or a very low score is 0.0028. If we randomly select cases from a normally distributed variable, we would select cases with Z scores beyond ±3.00 only 28 times out of every 10,000 trials.

The general point to remember is that cases with scores close to the mean are common and cases with scores far above or below the mean are rare. This relationship is central for an understanding of inferential statistics in Part II. As a final note, a supplement containing a more detailed and methodical discussion of probability has been added to our website. The supplement should be read in conjunction with Section 4.6, and not as a replacement for it. *(For practice in using the normal curve table to find probabilities, see problems 4.8 to 4.10 and 4.13.)*

SUMMARY

1. The normal curve, in combination with the mean and standard deviation, can be used to construct precise descriptive statements about empirical distributions that are normally distributed. This chapter also lays some important groundwork for Part II.

2. To work with the theoretical normal curve, raw scores must be transformed into their equivalent Z scores. Z scores allow us to find areas under the theoretical normal curve (Appendix A).

3. We considered three uses of the theoretical normal curve: finding total areas above and below a score, finding areas between two scores, and expressing these areas as probabilities. This last use of the normal curve is especially germane because inferential statistics are centrally concerned with estimating the probabilities of defined events in a fashion very similar to the process introduced in Section 4.6.

SUMMARY OF FORMULAS

Z scores	4.1	$Z = \dfrac{X_i - \overline{X}}{s}$

GLOSSARY

Normal curve. A theoretical distribution of scores that is symmetrical, unimodal, and bell shaped. The standard normal curve always has a mean of 0 and a standard deviation of 1. (p. 102)

Normal curve table. Appendix A; a detailed description of the area between a Z score and the mean of any standardized normal distribution. (p. 106)

Z scores. Standard scores; the way scores are expressed after they have been standardized to the theoretical normal curve. (p. 105)

MULTIMEDIA RESOURCES

 http://www.healeystatistics.nelson.com

Visit the companion website for the second Canadian edition of *Statistics: A Tool for Social Research* to access a wide range of student resources. Begin by clicking on the Student Resources section of the textbook's website to access review quizzes, flashcards, and other study tools.

PROBLEMS

4.1 Scores on a quiz were normally distributed and had a mean of 10 and a standard deviation of 3. For each score below, find the Z score and the percentage of area above and below the score.

X_i	Z Score	% Area Above	% Area Below
5			
6			
7			
8			
9			
11			
12			
14			
15			
16			
18			

4.2 Assume that the distribution of a graduate-school entrance exam is normal with a mean of 500 and a standard deviation of 100. For each score below, find the equivalent Z score, the percentage of the area above the score, and the percentage of the area below the score.

X_i	Z Score	% Area Above	% Area Below
650			
400			
375			
586			
437			
526			
621			
498			
517			
398			

4.3 A class of final-year students at a university has been given a comprehensive examination to assess their educational experience. The mean on the test was 74 and the standard deviation was 10. What percentage of the students had scores
  a. between 75 and 85? _____
  b. between 80 and 85? _____
  c. above 80? _____
  d. above 83? _____
  e. between 80 and 70? _____
  f. between 75 and 70? _____
  g. below 75? _____

h. below 77? _____
i. below 80? _____
j. below 85? _____

4.4 For a normal distribution where the mean is 50 and the standard deviation is 10, what percentage of the area is
  a. between the scores of 40 and 47? _____
  b. above a score of 47? _____
  c. below a score of 53? _____
  d. between the scores of 35 and 65? _____
  e. above a score of 72? _____
  f. below a score of 31 and above a score of 69? _____
  g. between the scores of 55 and 62? _____
  h. between the scores of 32 and 47? _____

4.5 At Algebra University the 200 students enrolled in Introductory Biology took a final exam on which their mean score was 72 and their standard deviation was 6. The table below presents the grades of 10 students. Convert each into a Z score and determine the *number of people* who scored higher or lower than each of the 10 students. *(HINT: Multiply the appropriate proportion by n and round the result.)*

X_i	Z Score	Number of Students Above	Number of Students Below
60			
57			
55			
67			
70			
72			
78			
82			
90			
95			

4.6 If a distribution of test scores is normal with a mean of 78 and a standard deviation of 11, what percentage of the area lies
  a. below 60? _____
  b. below 70? _____
  c. below 80? _____
  d. below 90? _____
  e. between 60 and 65? _____
  f. between 65 and 79? _____
  g. between 70 and 95? _____
  h. between 80 and 90? _____

i. above 99? _____
j. above 89? _____
k. above 75? _____
l. above 65? _____

4.7 A scale measuring ageism (age discrimination) has been administered to a large sample of human resources managers at major corporations. The distribution of scores is approximately normal with a mean of 31 and a standard deviation of 5. What percentage of the sample had scores
  a. below 20? _____
  b. below 40? _____
  c. between 30 and 40? _____
  d. between 35 and 45? _____
  e. above 25? _____
  f. above 35? _____

4.8 The average burglary rate for a jurisdiction has been 311 per year with a standard deviation of 50. What is the probability that next year the number of burglaries will be
  a. less than 250? _____
  b. less than 300? _____
  c. more than 350? _____
  d. more than 400? _____
  e. between 250 and 350? _____
  f. between 300 and 350? _____
  g. between 350 and 375? _____

4.9 For a math test on which the mean was 59 and the standard deviation was 4, what is the probability that a student randomly selected from this class will have a score
  a. between 55 and 65? _____
  b. between 60 and 65? _____
  c. above 65? _____
  d. between 60 and 50? _____
  e. between 55 and 50? _____
  f. below 55? _____

4.10 SOC On the scale mentioned in problem 4.7, if a score of 40 or more is considered "highly discriminatory" what is the probability that a human resources manager selected at random will have a score in that range?

4.11 The local police force gives all applicants an entrance exam and accepts only those applicants who score in the top 15% on the exam. If the mean score this year is 87 and the standard deviation is 8, would an individual with a score of 110 be accepted?

4.12 After taking a city's merit examinations for the positions of social worker and employment counsellor you receive the following information on the tests and on your performance. On which of the tests did you do better?

Social Worker	Employment Counsellor
$\overline{X} = 118$	$\overline{X} = 27$
$s = 17$	$s = 3$
Your score = 127	Your score = 29

4.13 In a distribution of scores with a mean of 35 and a standard deviation of 4, which event is more likely: that a randomly selected score will be between 29 and 31 or that a randomly selected score will be between 40 and 42?

4.14 To be accepted into a university's co-op education program students must have GPAs in the top 10% of the school. If the mean GPA is 2.78 and the standard deviation is 0.33, which of the following GPAs would qualify?
3.20, 3.21, 3.25, 3.30, 3.35

SPSS for Windows

Using SPSS for Windows to Produce Histograms and Compute *Z* Scores with the 2006 Census

The demonstrations and exercises below use the shortened version of the 2006 Census data set supplied with this textbook. Start SPSS for Windows and open the *Census.sav* file.

SPSS DEMONSTRATION 4.1 The Histogram

Before we can compute and use Z scores and the normal curve table (Appendix A), we need to find out if a variable has a normal, bell-shaped curve. The histogram, discussed in Chapter 2, provides a convenient method to display the distribution of a variable. Here we will use the **Histogram** command to show the distribution of *grosrt* (monthly gross rent).

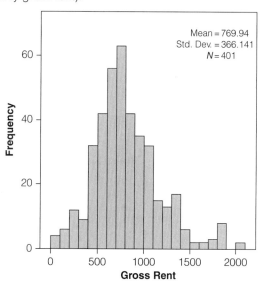

The SPSS procedure for producing a histogram is very similar to that of the bar chart illustrated in Demonstration 2.2. Click **Graphs**, **Legacy Dialogs**, and then **Histogram**. The **Histogram** dialog box will appear. Select *grosrt* from the variable list on the left and click the arrow button at the top of the screen to move *grosrt* to the **Variable** box. Click **OK** in the **Histogram** dialog box, and the histogram for *grosrt* will be produced.

The distribution of *grosrt* is approximately normal in shape. No empirical distribution is perfectly normal, but *grosrt* is close enough to permit the assumption of normality. We can proceed to use the normal curve to convert the original scores of *grosrt* into Z scores.

SPSS DEMONSTRATION 4.2 Computing *Z* Scores

The **Descriptives** command introduced in Demonstration 3.2 can also be used to compute *Z* scores for any variable. These *Z* scores are then available for further operations and may be used in other tasks. SPSS will create a new variable consisting of the transformed scores of the original variable. The program uses the letter *Z* with the letters of the variable name to designate the standardized scores of a variable.

In this demonstration, we will have SPSS compute *Z* scores for *grosrt*. First, click **Analyze**, **Descriptive Statistics**, and **Descriptives**. Find *grosrt* in the variable list and click the arrow to move the variable to the **Variable(s)** box. Find the "**Save standardized values as variables**" option below the variable list and click the checkbox next to it. With this option selected for **Descriptives**, SPSS will compute *Z* scores for all variables listed in the **Variable(s)** box. Click **OK**, and SPSS will produce the usual set of descriptive statistics for *grosrt*. It will also add the new variable (called *Zgrosrt*), which contains the standardized scores for *grosrt,* to the data set. To verify this, run the **Descriptives** command again, and you will find *Zgrosrt* in the variable list. Transfer *Zgrosrt* to the **Variable(s)** box with *grosrt,* then unclick the checkbox next to "**Save standardized values as variables**" and finally click **OK**. The following output will be produced:

Descriptive Statistics

	N	Minimum	Maximum	Mean	Std. Deviation
Gross rent	401	0	2052	769.94	366.141
Z score: Gross rent	401	−2.1029	3.5015	.000000	1.0000000
Valid N (listwise)	401				

Like any set of *Z* scores, *Zgrosrt* has a mean of 0 and a standard deviation of 1. The new variable *Zgrosrt* can be treated just like any other variable and used in any SPSS procedure.

If you would like to inspect the scores of *Zgrosrt,* use the **Case Summaries** procedure. Click **Analyze**, **Reports**, and then **Case Summaries**. Move both *grosrt* and *Zgrosrt* to the **Variable(s)** box. Be sure that the "**Display cases**" checkbox at the bottom of the window is selected. Find the "**Limit cases to first**" option. This option can be used to set the number of cases included in the output. By default, the system lists only the first 100 cases in your file. You can raise or lower the value for "**Limit cases to first**" *n* cases in your file or deselect this option to list all cases. For this exercise, let's set a limit of 20 cases. Make sure the checkbox to the left of the option is checked and type 20 in the textbox to the right. Click **OK**, and the following output will be produced (note, because some cases are missing, that is those who do not rent, only valid cases are shown in the output: of the first 20 cases, just 10 cases are renters):

Case Summaries[a]

	Gross rent	Z Score: Gross rent
1	1100	.90145
2	1000	.62833
3	600	−.46415
4	1200	1.17457
5	1319	1.49958
6	600	−.46415
7	900	.35521
8	1751	2.67946
9	500	−.73727
10	600	−.46415
Total *N*	10	10

a. Limited to first 20 cases.

Scan the list of scores and note that the scores that are close in value to the mean of *grosrt* ($769.94), are very close to the mean of *Zgrosrt* (.00), and the further away the score is from $769.94, the greater the numerical value of the *Z* score. Also note that, of course, scores below the mean (less than $769.94) have negative signs and scores above the mean (greater than $769.94) have positive signs.

Exercises (using *Census.sav*)

4.1 Use the **Histogram** command to get a histogram of *hhsize*. How close is this curve to a smooth, bell-shaped normal curve? Write a sentence or two of interpretation for the graph.

4.2 Using Demonstration 4.2 as a guide, compute *Z* scores for *hhsize*. Use the **Case Summaries** procedure to display the normalized and raw scores for each variable for 20 cases. Write a sentence or two summarizing these results.

PART I CUMULATIVE EXERCISES

1. To what extent do people apply religion to the problems of everyday living? Fifteen people have responded to a series of questions including the following:

   1. What is your religious preference?
      1. Protestant
      2. Catholic
      3. Jewish
      4. Muslim
      5. Other
      6. None
   2. On a scale of 1 to 10 (with 10 being the highest), how strong would you say your faith is?
   3. How many times a day do you pray?
   4. When things aren't going well, my religion is my major source of comfort.
      1. Strongly agree
      2. Slightly agree
      3. Neither agree nor disagree
      4. Slightly disagree
      5. Strongly disagree
   5. How old are you?

Case	Religion	Strength	Pray	Comfort	Age
1	1	2	0	2	30
2	4	8	1	1	67
3	1	8	3	1	45
4	5	6	0	1	43
5	3	9	3	1	32
6	3	3	0	3	18
7	6	0	0	5	52
8	5	9	6	1	37
9	1	5	0	2	54
10	2	8	2	1	55
11	2	3	0	5	33
12	1	6	1	3	45
13	1	8	2	2	37
14	4	7	2	1	50
15	5	9	1	1	25

   For each variable, construct a frequency distribution and calculate appropriate measures of central tendency and dispersion. Write a sentence summarizing each variable.

2. A survey measuring attitudes toward same-sex marriage was administered to 1,000 people. The survey asked the following questions:

   1. What is your age?
   2. What is your sex?
      1. Male
      2. Female

3. Marriages between people of the same sex do not work out and should be banned by law.
    1. Strongly agree
    2. Agree
    3. Undecided
    4. Disagree
    5. Strongly disagree
4. How many years of schooling have you completed?
5. Which category below best describes the place where you grew up?
    1. Large city
    2. Medium-size city
    3. Suburbs of a city
    4. Small town
    5. Rural area
6. What is your marital status?
    1. Married
    2. Separated or divorced
    3. Widowed
    4. Never married

The scores of 20 respondents are reproduced below.

Case	Age	Sex	Attitude on Same-sex Marriage	Years of School	Area	Marital Status
1	17	1	5	12	1	4
2	25	2	3	12	2	1
3	55	2	3	14	2	1
4	45	1	4	12	3	1
5	38	2	1	10	3	1
6	21	1	5	16	5	1
7	29	2	2	16	2	2
8	30	2	1	12	4	1
9	37	1	1	12	2	1
10	42	2	4	18	5	4
11	57	2	4	12	2	3
12	24	2	2	12	4	1
13	27	1	5	18	3	2
14	44	1	5	15	1	1
15	37	1	1	10	5	4
16	35	1	4	12	4	1
17	41	2	2	15	3	1
18	42	2	1	10	2	4
19	20	2	4	16	1	4
20	21	2	5	16	1	4

a. For each variable, construct a frequency distribution and select and calculate an appropriate measure of central tendency and a measure of dispersion. Summarize each variable in a sentence.

b. For all 1,000 respondents, the mean age was 34.70 with a standard deviation of 3.4 years. Assuming the distribution of age is approximately normal, compute Z scores for each of the first 10 respondents above and determine the percentage of the area below (younger than) each respondent.

3. The data from 25 respondents shown below are taken from a social survey administered to adults. Abbreviated versions of the survey questions, along with the meanings of the codes, are also presented. For each variable, construct a frequency distribution, then select and calculate an appropriate measure of central tendency and a measure of dispersion. Summarize each variable in a sentence.

1. How many children have you ever had? (Values are actual numbers.)
2. Respondent's educational level:
   0. Less than high school
   1. High school diploma
   2. Diploma/certificate from community college or trade school
   3. Bachelor's degree
   4. Graduate degree
3. Sex
   1. Male
   2. Female
4. It is sometimes necessary to discipline a child with a good, hard spanking.
   1. Strongly agree
   2. Agree
   3. Disagree
   4. Strongly disagree
5. Number of hours of TV watched per day. (Values are actual numbers of hours.)
6. What is your age?
   1. Less than 35 years
   2. 35 to 54 years
   3. 55 or more years

Case	Number of Children	Years of School	Sex	Attitude on Spanking	TV Hours	Age
1	3	1	1	3	3	1
2	2	0	1	4	1	1
3	4	2	1	2	3	1
4	0	3	1	1	2	1
5	5	1	1	3	2	1
6	1	1	1	3	3	1
7	9	0	1	1	6	1
8	6	1	2	3	4	1
9	4	3	1	1	2	3
10	2	1	2	1	1	1
11	2	0	1	2	4	1
12	4	1	2	1	5	2
13	0	1	1	3	2	2

(continued next page)

(continued)

Case	Number of Children	Years of School	Sex	Attitude on Spanking	TV Hours	Age
14	2	1	1	4	2	1
15	3	1	2	3	4	1
16	2	0	1	2	2	1
17	2	1	1	2	2	1
18	0	3	1	3	2	1
19	3	0	1	3	5	2
20	2	1	2	1	10	1
21	2	1	1	3	4	1
22	1	0	1	3	5	1
23	0	2	1	1	2	2
24	0	1	1	2	0	3
25	2	4	1	1	1	2

Inferential Statistics

The six chapters in this part cover the techniques and concepts of inferential or inductive statistics. Generally speaking, these applications allow us to learn about large groups (populations) from small, carefully selected subgroups (samples). These statistical techniques are powerful and extremely useful. They are used to poll public opinion, research the potential market for new products, project the winners of elections, test the effects of new drugs, and in hundreds of other ways both inside and outside of the social sciences.

Chapter 5 includes a brief description of the sampling technology used to select subgroups so as to justify making inferences to populations. This section is intended to give you a general overview of the process, not as a comprehensive or detailed treatment of the subject. The most important part of this chapter, however, concerns the sampling distribution, the single most important concept in inferential statistics. The sampling distribution is normal in shape and is the key link between populations and samples.

There are two main applications in inferential statistics and Chapter 6 covers the first: using statistical information from a sample (e.g., a mean or a proportion) to estimate the characteristics of a population. The technique is called "estimation," and it is most commonly used in public-opinion polling and election projection.

Chapters 7 through 10 cover the second application of inferential statistics: hypothesis testing. Most of the relevant concepts for this material are introduced in Chapter 7, and each chapter covers a different situation in which hypothesis testing is done. For example, Chapter 8 presents the techniques that are used when we are comparing information from two different samples or groups (e.g., men vs. women), while Chapter 9 covers applications involving more than two groups or samples (e.g., married/common-law, single, widowed, separated, and divorced).

Because hypothesis testing is one of the more challenging aspects of statistics for beginning students, we have included an abundance of learning aids to ease the chore of assimilating this material. Hypothesis testing is also one of the most common and important statistical applications to be found in social science research, and mastery of this material is essential for developing the ability to read the professional literature.

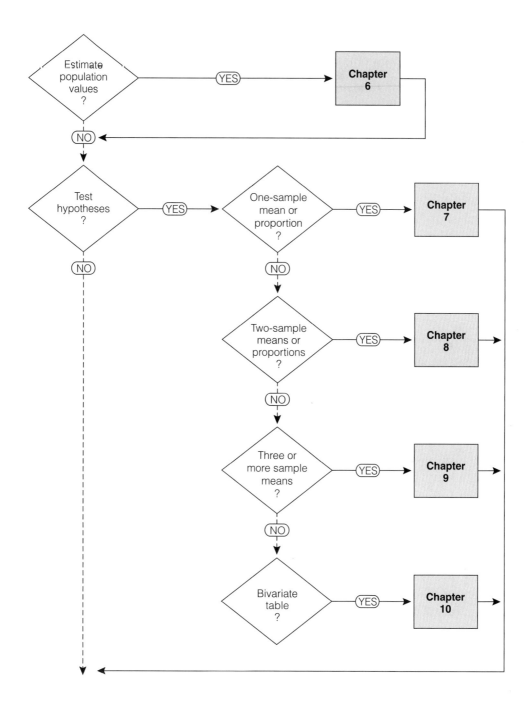

5

Introduction to Inferential Statistics
Sampling and the Sampling Distribution

LEARNING OBJECTIVES

By the end of this chapter, you will be able to

1. Explain the purpose of inferential statistics in terms of generalizing from a sample to a population.
2. Explain the principle of random sampling and these key terms: population, sample, parameter, statistic, representative, and EPSEM.
3. Differentiate between the sampling distribution, the sample, and the population.
4. Explain the two theorems presented.

5.1 INTRODUCTION

One of the goals of social science research is to test our theories and hypotheses using many different populations of people, groups, societies, and historical eras. Obviously, we can have the greatest confidence in theories that have stood up to testing against the greatest variety of populations and social settings. A major problem we often face in social science research, however, is that the populations in which we are interested are too large to test. For example, a theory concerning political party preference among Canadian voters would be most suitably tested using the entire electorate, but it is impossible to interview every member of this group (about 23 million people). Indeed, even for theories that could be reasonably tested with smaller populations—such as a local community or the student body at a university—the logistics of gathering data from every single case (entire populations) are staggering to contemplate.

If it is too difficult or expensive to do research with entire populations, how can we reasonably test our theories? To deal with this problem, social scientists select samples, or subsets of cases, from the populations of interest. Our goal in inferential statistics is to learn about the characteristics of a population (often called **parameters**), based on what we can learn from our samples. Two applications of inferential statistics are covered in this textbook. In estimation procedures, covered in Chapter 6, a "guess" of the population parameter is made, based on what is known about the sample. In hypothesis testing, covered in Chapters 7 through 10, the validity of a hypothesis about the population is tested against sample outcomes. In this chapter, we will look briefly at sampling (the techniques for selecting cases for a sample) and then introduce a key concept in inferential statistics: the sampling distribution.

5.2 PROBABILITY SAMPLING

In this chapter, we will review the basic procedures for selecting probability samples, the only type of sample that fully supports the use of inferential statistical techniques to generalize to populations. These types of samples are often described as "random," and you may be more familiar with this terminology. Because of its greater familiarity, we will often use the phrase "random sample" in the following chapters. The term "probability sample" is preferred, however, because, in everyday language, "random" is often used to mean "by coincidence" or to give a connotation of unpredictability. As you will see, probability samples are selected by techniques that are careful and methodical and leave no room for haphazardness. Interviewing the people you happen to meet in a mall one afternoon may be "random" in some sense, but this technique will not result in a sample that could support inferential statistics.

Before considering probability sampling, let us point out that social scientists often use nonprobability samples. For example, social scientists studying small group dynamics or the structure of attitudes or personal values might use the students enrolled in their classes as subjects. Such "convenience" samples are very useful for a number of purposes (e.g., exploring ideas or pretesting survey forms before embarking on a more ambitious project) and are typically less costly and easier to assemble. The major limitation of these samples is that results cannot be generalized beyond the group being tested. If a theory of ageism (prejudice, discrimination, and stereotyping of older people and old age), for example, has been tested only on the students who happen to have been enrolled in a particular section of an Introduction to Gerontology course (i.e., a course on the aging process from a multidisciplinary perspective) at a particular university, we cannot conclude that the theory would be true for other types of people. Therefore, even when the evidence is very strong, we cannot place a lot of confidence in theories tested on nonprobability samples only.

The goal of probability sampling is to select cases so that the final sample is **representative** of the population from which it was drawn. A sample is representative if it reproduces the important characteristics of the population. For example, if the population consists of 60% females and 40% males, the sample should contain essentially the same proportions. In other words, a representative sample is very much like the population—only smaller. It is crucial for inferential statistics that samples be representative; if they are not, generalizing to the population becomes, at best, extremely hazardous.

How can we assure ourselves that our samples are representative? Unfortunately, it is not possible to guarantee that our samples will meet this crucial criterion. However, we can maximize the chances of a representative sample by following the principle of **EPSEM** (the "**E**qual **P**robability of **SE**lection **M**ethod"), the fundamental principle of probability sampling. To follow the EPSEM principle, we select the sample so that every element or case in the population has an equal probability of being selected. Our goal is to select a representative sample, and the technique we use to achieve that goal is to follow the rule of EPSEM.

The most basic EPSEM sampling technique produces a **simple random sample**. There are numerous variations and refinements on this technique but, in this textbook, we will consider only the most straightforward application. To draw a simple random sample, we need a list of all elements or cases in the population and a system for selecting cases from the list that will guarantee that every case has an equal chance of being selected for the sample. The selection process could be based on a number of different kinds of operations such as drawing cards from a well-shuffled deck, flipping coins, throwing dice, drawing numbers from a hat, however, cases are often selected by using tables of random numbers. These tables are lists of numbers that have no pattern to them (i.e., they are random), and an example of such a table is available on the website for this textbook.

To use the table of random numbers, first assign each case on the population list a unique identification number. Then, select cases for the sample when their identification number corresponds to the number chosen from the table. This procedure will produce an EPSEM sample because the numbers in the table are in random order and any number is just as likely to be chosen any other number. Stop selecting cases when you have reached your desired sample size and, if an identification number is selected more than once, ignore the repeats.*

Remember that the EPSEM selection technique and the representativeness of the final sample are two different things. In other words, the fact that a sample is selected according to EPSEM does not guarantee that the sample will be an exact representation or microcosm of the population. The probability is very high that an EPSEM sample will be representative but, just as a perfectly honest coin will sometimes show 10 heads in a row when flipped, an EPSEM sample will occasionally present an inaccurate picture of the population. One of the great strengths of inferential statistics is that they allow the researcher to estimate the probability of this type of error and interpret results accordingly.

To summarize, the purpose of inferential statistics is to acquire knowledge about populations, based on information derived from samples of that population. Each of the statistics to be presented in the following chapters requires that samples be selected according to EPSEM. While EPSEM sampling techniques, of which simple random sampling is the most basic form, do not guarantee representativeness, the probability is high that EPSEM samples will be representative of the populations from which they are selected.

---

*Ignoring identification numbers when they are repeated is called "sampling without replacement." Technically, this practice compromises the randomness of the selection process. However, if the sample is a small fraction of the total population, we will be unlikely to select the same case twice and ignoring repeats will not bias our conclusions.

5.3 THE SAMPLING DISTRIBUTION

Once we have selected a probability sample, what do we know? On one hand, we can gather a great deal of information from the cases in the sample. On the other hand, we know nothing about the population. Indeed, if we had information about the population, we probably wouldn't need the sample. Remember that we use inferential statistics to learn more about populations, and information from the sample is important primarily insofar as it allows us to generalize to the population.

When we use inferential statistics, we generally measure some variable (e.g., age, political party preference, or opinions about global warming) in the sample and then use the information from the sample to learn more about that variable in the population. In Part I of this textbook, you learned that three types of information are generally necessary to adequately characterize a variable: (1) the shape of its distribution, (2) some measure of central tendency, and (3) some measure of dispersion. Clearly, all three kinds of information can be gathered (or computed) on a variable from the cases in the sample. Just as clearly, none of the information is available for the population. Except in rare situations (e.g., IQ and height are thought to be approximately normal in distribution), nothing can be known about the exact shape of the distribution of a variable in the population. The means and standard deviations of variables in the population are also unknown. Let us remind you that if we had this information for the population, inferential statistics would be unnecessary.

In statistics, we link information from the sample to the population with a device known as the **sampling distribution**, the theoretical, probabilistic distribution of a statistic for all possible samples of a certain sample size (n). That is, the sampling distribution includes statistics that represent every conceivable combination of cases (i.e., every possible sample) from the population. A crucial point about the sampling distribution is that its characteristics are based on the laws of probability, not on empirical information, and are very well known. In fact, the sampling distribution is the central concept in inferential statistics, and a prolonged examination of its characteristics is certainly in order.

As illustrated by Figure 5.1, the general strategy of all applications of inferential statistics is to move between the sample and the population via the sampling distribution. Thus, three separate and distinct distributions are involved in every application of inferential statistics:

FIGURE 5.1 THE RELATIONSHIPS BETWEEN THE SAMPLE, SAMPLING DISTRIBUTION, AND POPULATION

1. The sample distribution, which is empirical (i.e., it exists in reality) and known in the sense that the shape, central tendency, and dispersion of any variable can be ascertained for the sample. Remember that the information from the sample is important primarily insofar as it allows the researcher to learn about the population.
2. The population distribution, which, while empirical, is unknown. Amassing information about or making inferences to the population is the sole purpose of inferential statistics.

3. The sampling distribution, which is nonempirical or theoretical. Because of the laws of probability, a great deal is known about this distribution. Specifically, the shape, central tendency, and dispersion of the distribution can be deduced and, therefore, the distribution can be adequately characterized.

The utility of the sampling distribution is implied by its definition. Because it encompasses all possible sample outcomes, the sampling distribution enables us to estimate the probability of any particular sample outcome, a process that will occupy our attention for the next five chapters.

The sampling distribution is theoretical, which means that it is obtained hypothetically, but not in practice. However, to understand better the structure and function of the distribution, let's consider an example of how one might be constructed. Suppose that we wanted to gather some information about the age of a particular community of 10,000 individuals. We draw an EPSEM sample of 100 residents, ask all 100 respondents their age, and use those individual scores to compute a mean age of 27. This score is noted on the graph in Figure 5.2. Note that this sample is one of countless possible combinations of 100 people taken from this population of 10,000, and the mean of 27 is one of millions of possible sample outcomes.

Now, replace the 100 respondents in the first sample and draw another sample of the same size ($n = 100$) and again compute the average age. Assume that the mean for the second sample is 30 and note this sample outcome on Figure 5.2. This second sample is another of the countless possible combinations of 100 people taken from this population of 10,000, and the sample mean of 30 is another of the millions of possible sample outcomes. Replace the respondents from the second sample and draw still another sample, calculate and note the mean, replace this third sample, and draw a fourth sample, continuing these operations an infinite number of times, calculating and noting the mean of each sample. Now, try to imagine what Figure 5.2 would look like after tens of thousands of individual samples had been collected and the mean had been computed for each sample. What shape, mean, and standard deviation would this distribution of sample means have after we had collected all possible combinations of 100 respondents from the population of 10,000?

For one thing, we know that each sample will be at least slightly different from every other sample, because it is very unlikely that we will sample exactly the same 100 people twice. Because each sample will almost certainly

FIGURE 5.2   CONSTRUCTING A SAMPLING DISTRIBUTION

be a unique combination of individuals, each sample mean will be at least slightly different in value. We also know that even though the samples are chosen according to EPSEM, they will not be representative of the population in every single case. For example, if we continue taking samples of 100 people long enough, we will eventually choose a sample that includes only the very youngest residents. Such a sample would have a mean much lower than the true population mean. Likewise, some of our samples will include only senior citizens and will have means that are much higher than the population mean. Common sense suggests, however, that such non-representative samples will be rare and that most sample means will cluster around the true population value.

To illustrate further, assume that we somehow come to know that the true mean age of the population is 30. As we have seen above, most of the sample means will also be approximately 30 and the sampling distribution of these sample means should peak at 30. Some of the sample means will "miss the mark," but the frequency of such misses should decline as we get farther away from 30. That is, the distribution should slope to the base as we get farther away from the population value—sample means of 29 or 31 should be common; means of 20 or 40 should be rare. Because the samples are random, the means should miss an equal number of times on either side of the population value, and the distribution itself should therefore be roughly symmetrical. In other words, the sampling distribution of all possible sample means should be approximately normal and will resemble the distribution presented in Figure 5.3. Recall from Chapter 4 that, on any normal curve, cases close to the mean (say, within ±1 standard deviation) are common and cases far away from the mean (say, beyond ±3 standard deviations) are rare.

These common-sense notions about the shape of the sampling distribution and other very important information about central tendency and dispersion are stated in two theorems. The first of these theorems states that

If repeated random samples of size n are drawn from a normal population with mean μ and standard deviation σ, then the sampling distribution of sample means will be normal with a mean μ and a standard deviation of $\sigma/\sqrt{n}$.

FIGURE 5.3   A SAMPLING DISTRIBUTION OF SAMPLE MEANS

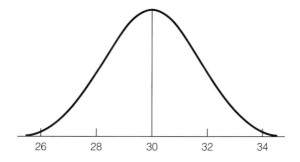

| 26 | 28 | 30 | 32 | 34 |

To translate: if we begin with a trait that is normally distributed across a population (IQ, height, or weight, for example) and take an infinite number of equally sized random samples from that population, then the sampling distribution of sample means will be normal. If it is known that the variable is distributed normally in the population, it can be assumed that the sampling distribution will be normal.

The theorem tells us more than the shape of the sampling distribution of all possible sample means, however. It also defines its mean and standard deviation. In fact, it says that the mean of the sampling distribution will be exactly the same value as the mean of the population. That is, if we know that the mean IQ of the entire population is 100, then we know that the mean of any sampling distribution of sample mean IQs will also be 100. Exactly why this should be so is explained and demonstrated in Section 5.4. Recall for now, however, that most sample means will cluster around the population value over the long run. Thus, the fact that these two values are equal should have intuitive appeal. As for dispersion, the theorem says that the standard deviation of the sampling distribution, also called the **standard error**, will be equal to the standard deviation of the population divided by the square root of n (symbolically: $\sigma/\sqrt{n}$).

If the mean and standard deviation of a normally distributed population are known, the theorem allows us to compute the mean and standard deviation of the sampling distribution.* Thus, we will know exactly as much about the sampling distribution (shape, central tendency, and dispersion) as we ever knew about any empirical distribution.

The first theorem requires a normal population distribution. What happens when the distribution of the variable in question is unknown or is known to not be normal in shape (like income, which always has a positive skew)? These eventualities (very common, in fact) are covered by a second theorem, called the **Central Limit Theorem**:

> If repeated random samples of size n are drawn from any population, with mean μ and standard deviation σ, then, as n becomes large, the sampling distribution of sample means will approach normality, with mean μ and standard deviation $\sigma/\sqrt{n}$.

To translate: for *any* trait or variable, even those that are not normally distributed in the population, as sample size grows larger, the sampling distribution of sample means will become normal in shape.

The importance of the Central Limit Theorem is that it removes the constraint of normality in the population. Whenever sample size is large, we can assume that the sampling distribution is normal, with a mean equal to the

---

*In the typical research situation, the values of the population mean and standard deviation are, of course, unknown. However, these values can be estimated from sample statistics, as we shall see in the chapters that follow.

population mean and a standard deviation equal to $\sigma/\sqrt{n}$ regardless of the shape of the variable in the population. Thus, even if we are working with a variable that is known to have a skewed distribution (like income), we can still assume a normal sampling distribution.

The issue remaining, of course, is to define what is meant by a large sample. A good rule of thumb is that if sample size (n) is 100 or more, the Central Limit Theorem applies, and you can assume that the sampling distribution is normal in shape. When n is less than 100, you must have good evidence of a normal population distribution before you can assume that the sampling distribution is normal. Thus, a normal sampling distribution can be ensured by the expedient of using fairly large samples.

5.4 CONSTRUCTING THE SAMPLING DISTRIBUTION

Developing an understanding of the sampling distribution—what it is and why it's important—is often one of the more challenging tasks for beginning students of statistics. It may be helpful to briefly list the most important points about the sampling distribution:

1. Its definition: *the sampling distribution is the distribution of a statistic (like means or proportions) for all possible sample outcomes of a certain size.*
2. Its shape: *normal* (see Appendix A).
3. Its central tendency and dispersion: *the mean of the sampling distribution is the same value as the mean of the population. The standard deviation of the sampling distribution—or the standard error—is equal to the population standard deviation divided by the square root of n.* (See the theorems above.)

To reinforce these points, we will construct a sampling distribution from hypothetical data. Suppose we have a population of four people and are interested in the amount of money each person has in his/her possession. (The number of cases in this problem is kept very small to simplify the computations.) We find that the first person in our population has $2, the second person has $4, the third person has $6, and the fourth person has $8. So this population has a mean, μ, of $5 and a standard deviation, σ, of $2.236, as calculated in Table 5.1.

Recall that the sampling distribution of sample means is the theoretical distribution of the mean for all possible samples of a certain sample size (n), with a mean, μ, and a standard deviation of $\sigma/\sqrt{n}$. So let us derive the sampling distribution of sample means for $n = 2$; that is, draw every conceivable combination (every possible sample) of two people from our population of four people. In order to draw every possible sample, sampling with replacement must be used; we randomly select a person from the

TABLE 5.1 CALCULATING THE MEAN AND STANDARD DEVIATION OF THE POPULATION

Case	(X_i)	Deviations $(X_i - \mu)$	Deviations Squared $(X_i - \mu)^2$
1	2	$2 - 5 = -3.0$	9
2	4	$4 - 5 = -1.0$	1
3	6	$6 - 5 = 1.0$	1
4	8	$8 - 5 = 3.0$	9
	$\Sigma(X_i) = 20$	$\Sigma(X_i - \mu) = 0.0$	$\Sigma(X_i - \mu)^2 = 20$

$$\mu = \frac{\Sigma(X_i)}{N} = \frac{20}{4} = 5 \text{ (Formula 3.3)}$$

$$\sigma = \sqrt{\frac{\Sigma(X_i - \mu)^2}{N}} = \sqrt{\frac{20}{4}} = \sqrt{5} = 2.236 \text{ (Formula 3.7)}$$

population, replace that person back in the population, and then again randomly select a person from the population. Hence, we end up drawing several "odd" looking samples as the same person can be selected twice into the same sample.

In a population of four people, there will be 16 theoretical samples of two people (i.e., when $n = 2$, there are only 4×4, or 16, possible samples). With 16 samples, there will be 16 sample means. Table 5.2 presents every possible sample of two people from our population of four people.

TABLE 5.2 CALCULATING THE SAMPLING DISTRIBUTION
OF SAMPLE MEANS ($n = 2$)

	Sample Scores	Sample Mean
1	($2, $2)	$2
2	($2, $4)	$3
3	($2, $6)	$4
4	($2, $8)	$5
5	($4, $2)	$3
6	($4, $4)	$4
7	($4, $6)	$5
8	($4, $8)	$6
9	($6, $2)	$4
10	($6, $4)	$5
11	($6, $6)	$6
12	($6, $8)	$7
13	($8, $2)	$5
14	($8, $4)	$6
15	($8, $6)	$7
16	($8, $8)	$8

In the first sample, the person in our population with $2 in his/her possession was randomly selected twice—this is one of those "odd" looking samples. The mean for this sample is $2, or $(2 + 2)/2 = 2$. In the second theoretical sample, the first person randomly selected from the population was again the person with $2. This person was replaced back in the population. Next a second person was then randomly selected from the population, which was the person with $4. The mean for this sample is $3, or $(2 + 4)/2 = 3$. This process continues until every possible sample of two people from our population of four people has been drawn, as shown in Table 5.2.

With all possible combinations of samples in hand (16 in total), we can build the sampling distribution of sample means. The histogram in Figure 5.4 displays this information. The histogram shows that the sample mean of 5 occurs four times, more than any other mean. We can confirm this by counting the number of times the mean of 5 occurs in Table 5.2. The means of 4 and 6 occur three times each, while the means of 3 and 7 occur twice, and the means of 2 and 8 occur once each. As per the theorems stated in the previous section, Figure 5.4 demonstrates that our sampling distribution of means is symmetrical and approximately normal in shape.

The theorems also tell us that the mean of the sampling distribution will be exactly the same value as the mean of the population and that the standard deviation of the sampling distribution will be equal to the standard deviation of the population divided by the square root of n ($\sigma/\sqrt{n}$). This is proved in Table 5.3.

Comparing Table 5.3 and Table 5.1 we see that the mean of the sampling distribution, 5, is exactly the same as the mean of the population, 5. We also see that the standard deviation of the sampling distribution, 1.581, is equal to the standard deviation of the population divided by the square root of n. That is, the population standard deviation, 2.236, divided by the

FIGURE 5.4   SAMPLING DISTRIBUTION OF SAMPLE MEANS ($n = 2$) (*BASED ON TABLE 5.2.*)

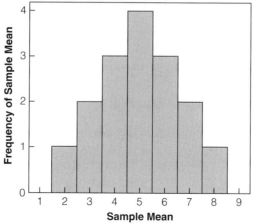

TABLE 5.3 CALCULATING THE MEAN AND STANDARD DEVIATION OF THE SAMPLING DISTRIBUTION OF SAMPLE MEANS ($n = 2$)

	Sample Mean (X_i)	Deviations $(X_i - \mu)$	Deviations Squared $(X_i - \mu)^2$
1	2	$2 - 5 = -3.0$	9
2	3	$3 - 5 = -2.0$	4
3	4	$4 - 5 = -1.0$	1
4	5	$5 - 5 = \ \ \ 0.0$	0
5	3	$3 - 5 = -2.0$	4
6	4	$4 - 5 = -1.0$	1
7	5	$5 - 5 = \ \ \ 0.0$	0
8	6	$6 - 5 = \ \ \ 1.0$	1
9	4	$4 - 5 = -1.0$	1
10	5	$5 - 5 = \ \ \ 0.0$	0
11	6	$6 - 5 = \ \ \ 1.0$	1
12	7	$7 - 5 = \ \ \ 2.0$	4
13	5	$5 - 5 = \ \ \ 0.0$	0
14	6	$6 - 5 = \ \ \ 1.0$	1
15	7	$7 - 5 = \ \ \ 2.0$	4
16	8	$8 - 5 = \ \ \ 3.0$	9
	$\Sigma(X_i) = 80$	$\Sigma(X_i - \mu) = \ \ \ 0.0$	$\Sigma(X_i - \mu)^2 = 40$

$$\mu = \frac{\Sigma(X_i)}{N} = \frac{80}{16} = 5 \text{ (Formula 3.3)}$$

$$\sigma = \sqrt{\frac{\Sigma(X_i - \mu)^2}{N}} = \sqrt{\frac{40}{16}} = \sqrt{2.5} = 1.581 \text{ (Formula 3.7)}$$

square root of 2, or $2.236/\sqrt{2}$, is 1.581, which is identical to the standard deviation of the sampling distribution.

As further proof, Figure 5.5 shows the sampling distribution of sample means for $n = 3$. (Note, in a population of four people, when sample size equals three, there are $4 \times 4 \times 4$, or 64, possible samples.) We see that the mean of this sampling distribution is also 5, and that it is approximately normal in shape. However, in comparison to Figure 5.4, we see that the sampling distribution for $n = 3$ is less variable or spread out. That is, the standard deviation of this sampling distribution is equal to 1.291, or $2.236/\sqrt{3}$.

In conclusion, we have confirmed the three fundamental components of the theorems in Section 5.3. First, the sampling distribution is normal if either the sample size is large ($n = 100$ or more) or the shape of the distribution of the variable in the population is normal. We have seen that a sampling distribution will be approximately normal in shape even with a small sample size of $n = 2$ or 3 and a population of just four cases. Second, the sampling distribution has a mean, $\mu = 5$, which is identical to the mean of the population. Third, the standard deviation of the sampling distribution of sample means is equal to the standard deviation of the population divided by the square root of n.

FIGURE 5.5   SAMPLING DISTRIBUTION OF SAMPLE MEANS ($n = 3$)

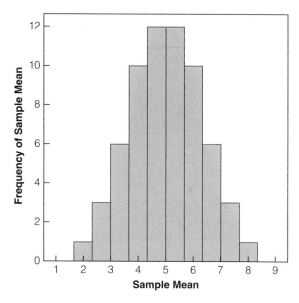

5.5 LINKING THE POPULATION, SAMPLING DISTRIBUTION, AND SAMPLE

The role of the sampling distribution in inferential statistics is to link the sample with the population. In this section we look at how the sampling distribution works together with the sample and the population using the General Social Survey (GSS), the database used for SPSS exercises in this textbook.

We will start with the "population," or the group we are actually interested in and want to learn more about. In the case of the GSS, the population consists of all Canadians (aged 15 and older) living in private households in the 10 provinces. This includes about 27 million people. Clearly, we can never interview all of these people and learn what they are like or their views on various social issues.

What can be done to learn more about this huge population? This brings us to the concept of "sample," a carefully chosen subset of the population. The GSS is administered to about 25,000 people, each of whom is chosen by a sophisticated technique that is ultimately based on the principle of EPSEM. The respondents are contacted at home and asked for background information (e.g., age, gender, years of education) as well as their behaviours, opinions, or attitudes regarding selected social issues. When all of this information is collated, the GSS database includes information on hundreds of variables for the people in the sample.

So we have a lot of information about the variables for the sample (the 25,000 or so people who actually respond to the survey), but no information about these variables for the population (the 27 million Canadians aged 15 and older). How do we go from the known characteristics of the sample to the unknown population?

This is the central question of inferential statistics, and the answer is "by using the sampling distribution." Remember that, unlike the sample and the population, the sampling distribution is a theoretical device. However, we can work with the sampling distribution because its shape, central tendency, and dispersion are defined by the theorems presented earlier in this chapter. First, for any variable from the GSS, we know that the sampling distribution will be normal in shape because the sample is "large" (n is much greater than 100). Second, the theorems tell us that the mean of the sampling distribution will be the same value as the mean of the population. If all Canadians aged 15 and older spend on average 7.5 hours using the Internet at home per week ($\mu = 7.5$), the mean of the sampling distribution will also be 7.5. Third, the theorems tell us that the standard deviation (or standard error) of the sampling distribution is equal to the population standard deviation (σ) divided by the square root of n. Therefore, the theorems tell us the statistical characteristics of this distribution (shape, central tendency, and dispersion), and this information allows us to link the sample to the population.

How does the sampling distribution link the sample to the population? It is crucial to know that the sampling distribution will be normal when n is large. This means that more than two-thirds (68%) of all samples will be within ± 1 standard deviation (i.e., standard error) of the mean (which is the same value as the population parameter), about 95% are within ± 2 standard deviations, and so forth. We do not (and cannot) know the actual value of the mean of the sampling distribution because it is impractical to draw every conceivable combination (i.e., every possible sample) of 25,000 Canadians from the population of 27 million Canadians. However, there is no need to draw all possible samples because the theorems give us crucial information about the mean and standard error of the sampling distribution that we can use to link the sample to the population. In practice, as you will see in the following chapters, we draw just one sample and use this information (i.e., the sampling distribution of all possible sample means will be normal with a mean equal to the population mean and a standard deviation equal to the population standard deviation divided by the square root of n) to link the sample to the population.

To summarize, we have focused on the GSS to see the roles played by the population, sample, and sampling distribution. Our goal is to infer information about the population (all Canadians aged 15 and older). When populations are too large to test (and contacting 27 million Canadians is far beyond the capacity of even the most energetic pollster), we use information from carefully drawn probability samples to estimate the characteristics of the population—the full sample of the GSS consists of about 25,000 Canadians aged 15 and older. The sampling distribution, the theoretical distribution whose characteristics are defined by the theorems, links the known sample to the unknown population.

TABLE 5.4   SYMBOLS FOR MEANS AND STANDARD DEVIATIONS OF THREE DISTRIBUTIONS

	Mean	Standard Deviation	Proportion
1. Samples	$\overline{X}$	s	P_s
2. Populations	μ	σ	P_u
3. Sampling distributions			
of means	$\mu_{\overline{X}}$	$\sigma_{\overline{X}}$	
of proportions	μ_p	σ_p	

5.6 SYMBOLS AND TERMINOLOGY

In the following chapters, we will be working with three entirely different distributions. The purpose of inferential statistics is to acquire knowledge of the population from information gathered from a sample by means of the sampling distribution. Further, while we have focused on the sampling distribution of sample means, other statistics like the sample proportion, which the Central Limit Theorem applies to, have a sampling distribution.

To distinguish clearly among these various distributions, we will often use symbols. The symbols used for the means and standard deviations of samples and populations have already been introduced in Chapter 3. In this chapter, we have also used these population symbols for the sampling distribution for convenience. However, Table 5.4 provides new symbols for this distribution, denoted with Greek letter symbols that are subscripted according to the sample statistic of interest.

To read this table, note that the mean and standard deviation of a sample are denoted with Roman letters ($\overline{X}$ and s) while the mean and standard deviation of a population are denoted with the Greek letter equivalents (μ and σ). Proportions calculated on samples are symbolized as P-sub-s (s for sample) while population proportions are denoted as P-sub-u (u for population). The symbols for the sampling distribution are Greek letters with Roman letter subscripts. The mean and standard deviation of a sampling distribution of sample means are "mu-sub-x-bar" and "sigma-sub-x-bar." The mean and standard deviation of a sampling distribution of sample proportions are "mu-sub-p" and "sigma-sub-p."

SUMMARY

1. Because populations are almost always too large to test, a fundamental strategy of social science research is to select a sample from the defined population and then use information from the sample to generalize to the population. This is done either by estimation or by hypothesis testing.

2. Researchers choose simple random samples by selecting cases from a list of the population following the rule of EPSEM (each case has an equal probability of being selected). Samples selected by the rule of EPSEM have a very high probability of being representative.

3. The sampling distribution, the central concept in inferential statistics, is a theoretical distribution of all possible sample outcomes. Because its overall shape, mean, and standard deviation are known (under the conditions specified in the two theorems), the sampling distribution can be adequately characterized and utilized by researchers.

4. The two theorems that were introduced in this chapter state that when the variable of interest is normally distributed in the population or when sample size is large, the sampling distribution will be normal in shape, with its mean equal to the population mean and its standard deviation (or standard error) equal to the population standard deviation divided by the square root of n.

5. All applications of inferential statistics involve generalizing from the sample to the population by means of the sampling distribution. Both estimation procedures and hypothesis testing incorporate the three distributions, and it is crucial that you develop a clear understanding of each distribution and its role in inferential statistics.

GLOSSARY

Central Limit Theorem. A theorem that specifies the mean, standard deviation, and shape of the sampling distribution, given that the sample is large. (p. 136)

EPSEM. The **E**qual **P**robability of **SE**lection **M**ethod for selecting samples. Every element or case in the population must have an equal probability of selection for the sample. (p. 131)

Parameter. A characteristic of a population. (p. 130)

Representative. The quality a sample is said to have if it reproduces the major characteristics of the population from which it was drawn. (p. 131)

Sampling distribution. The distribution of a statistic for all possible sample outcomes of a certain size. Under conditions specified in two theorems, the sampling distribution will be normal in shape with a mean equal to the population value and a standard deviation equal to the population standard deviation divided by the square root of n. (p. 133)

Simple random sample. A method for choosing cases from a population by which every case has an equal chance of being included. (p. 132)

Standard error. The standard deviation of a sampling distribution. (p. 136)

MULTIMEDIA RESOURCES

 http://www.healeystatistics.nelson.com

Visit the companion website for the second Canadian edition of *Statistics: A Tool for Social Research* to access a wide range of student resources. Begin by clicking on the Student Resources section of the textbook's website to access review quizzes, flashcards, and other study tools.

PROBLEMS

5.1 This exercise is extremely tedious and hardly ever works out the way it ought to (mostly because not many people have the patience to draw an "infinite" number of even very small samples). However, if you want a more concrete and tangible understanding of sampling distributions and the two theorems presented in this chapter, then this exercise may have a significant payoff. Below are listed the ages of a population of students at a very small community college ($N = 50$). By a random method (such as a table of random numbers), draw at least 50 samples of size 2 (i.e.,

50 pairs of cases), compute a mean for each sample, and plot the means on a frequency polygon. (Incidentally, this exercise will work better if you draw 100 or 200 samples and/or use larger samples than $n = 2$.)

a. The curve you've just produced is a sampling distribution. Observe its shape; after 50 samples, it should be approaching normality. What is your estimate of the population mean (μ) based on the shape of the curve?

b. Calculate the mean of the sampling distribution ($\mu_{\bar{X}}$). Be careful to do this by summing the sample means (not the scores) and dividing by the number of samples you've drawn. Now compute the population mean (μ). These two means should be very close in value because $\mu_{\bar{X}} = \mu$ by the Central Limit Theorem.

c. Calculate the standard deviation of the sampling distribution (use the means as scores) and the standard deviation of the population. Compare these two values. You should find that the two standard deviations are very close in value because $\sigma_{\bar{X}} = \sigma/\sqrt{n}$.

d. If none of the above exercises turned out as they should have, it is for one or more of the following reasons:

1. You didn't take enough samples. You may need as many as 100 or 200 (or more) samples to see the curve begin to look "normal."
2. Sample size (2) is too small. An n of 5 or 10 would work much better.
3. Your sampling method is not truly random and/or the population is not arranged in random fashion.

17	20	20	19	20
18	21	19	20	19
19	22	19	23	19
20	23	18	20	20
22	19	19	20	20
23	17	18	21	20
20	18	20	19	20
22	17	21	21	21
21	20	20	20	22
18	21	20	22	21

SPSS for Windows

Using SPSS for Windows to Draw Random Samples with the 2006 Census

The demonstration and exercise below use the shortened version of the 2006 Census data. Start SPSS for Windows and open the *Census.sav* file.

SPSS DEMONSTRATION 5.1 Estimating Average Income

SPSS for Windows includes a procedure for drawing random samples from a database. We can use this procedure to illustrate some points about sampling and to convince the skeptics in the crowd that properly selected samples will produce statistics that are close approximations of the corresponding population values or parameters. For purposes of this demonstration, the Census sample will be treated as a population and its characteristics will be treated as parameters.

The instructions below will calculate a mean for *totinc* (total income of individual) for three random samples of different sizes drawn from the Census sample. The actual average income of the sample (which will be the parameter or μ) is $33,767.06 (see Demonstration 3.2). The samples are roughly 10%, 25%, and 50% of the population size, and the program selects them by a process that is quite similar to a table of random numbers. Therefore, these samples may be considered "simple random samples."

As a part of this procedure we also request the "standard error of the mean" or S.E. MEAN. This is the standard deviation of the sampling distribution of means $(\sigma_{\bar{x}})$ for a sample of this size. This statistic will be of interest because we can expect our sample means to be within this distance of the population value or parameter.

With the *Census.sav* file loaded, click **Data** from the menu bar of the **Data Editor** window and then click **Select Cases**. The **Select Cases** window appears and presents a number of different options. To select random samples, check the circle next to "**Random sample of cases**" and then click on the **Sample** button. The **Select Cases: Random Sample** dialog box will open. We can specify the size of the sample in two different ways. If we use the first option, we can specify that the sample will include a certain percentage of cases in the database. The second option allows us to specify the exact number of cases in the sample. Let's use the first option and request a 10% sample by typing 10 into the box on the first line. Click **Continue**, and then click **OK** on the **Select Cases** window. The sample will be selected and can now be processed.

To find the mean income for the 10% sample, click **Analyze, Descriptive Statistics**, and then **Descriptives**. The **Descriptives** dialog box will be open. Find *totinc* in the variable list and transfer it to the **Variable(s)** box. On the **Descriptives** dialog box, click the **Options** button and select **S.E. mean** in addition to the usual statistics. Click **Continue** and then **OK**, and the requested statistics will appear in the output window.

Now, to produce a 25% sample, return to the **Select Cases** window by clicking **Data** and **Select Cases**. Click the **Reset** button at the bottom of the window and then click **OK** and the full data set ($N = 1,500$) will be restored. Repeat the procedure we followed for selecting the 10% sample. Click the button next to "**Random sample of cases**" and then click on the **Sample** button. The **Select Cases: Random Sample** window will open. Request a 25% sample by typing 25 in the box, click **Continue** and **OK**, and the new sample will be selected.

Run the **Descriptives** procedure for the 25% sample (don't forget **S.E. mean**) and note the results. Finally, repeat these steps for a 50% sample. The results are summarized below:

Sample %	Sample Size	Sample Mean	Standard Error	Sample Mean ± Standard Error
10%	154	28,688.34	2,087.29	26,601.05 – 30,775.63
25%	364	32,731.12	1,884.15	30,846.97 – 34,615.27
50%	755	33,489.51	1,498.26	31,991.25 – 34,987.77

Notice that standard error of the mean (i.e., the standard deviation of the sampling distribution of sample means) decreases as sample size increases. This should reinforce the common-sense notion that larger samples will provide more accurate estimates of population values. All three samples produced estimates (sample means) that are quite close in value to the population value of $33,767.06. However, the largest sample is the most accurate or closest to the true population value of $33,767.06, only 277.55 dollars too low.

This demonstration should reinforce one of the main points of this chapter: statistics calculated on samples that have been selected according to the principle of EPSEM will (almost always) be reasonable approximations of their population counterparts.

Exercise (using *Census.sav*)

5.1 Following the procedures in Demonstration 5.1, select three samples from the 2006 Census database (*Census.sav*): 15%, 30%, and 60%. Get descriptive statistics for *totinc* (don't forget to get the standard error), and use the results to complete the following table:

Sample %	Sample Size	Sample Mean	Standard Error	Sample Mean ± Standard Error
15%	_____	_____	_____	_____
30%	_____	_____	_____	_____
60%	_____	_____	_____	_____

Summarize these results. What happens to standard error as sample size increases? Why? How accurate are the estimates (sample means)? Are all sample means within a standard error of $33,767.06? How does the accuracy of the estimates change as sample size changes?

6 Estimation Procedures

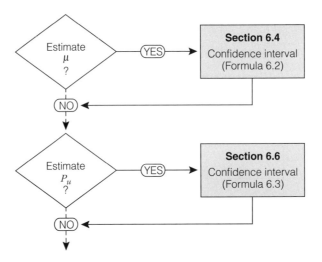

6.1 INTRODUCTION

The object of this branch of inferential statistics is to estimate population values or parameters from statistics computed from samples. Although the techniques presented in this chapter may be new to you, you are certainly familiar with their most common applications: public-opinion polls and election projections. Polls and surveys on every conceivable issue—from the sublime to the trivial—have become a staple of the mass media and popular culture. The techniques you will learn in this chapter are essentially the same as those used by the most reputable, sophisticated, and scientific pollsters.

There are two kinds of estimation procedures. First, a **point estimate** is a sample statistic that is used to estimate a population value. For example, a newspaper story that reports that 50% of a sample of randomly selected

Canadian drivers are driving less than usual due to high gas prices is reporting a point estimate. The second kind of estimation procedure involves **confidence intervals**, which consist of a range of values (an interval) instead of a single point. Rather than estimating a specific figure as in a point estimate, an interval estimate might be phrased as "between 47% and 53% of Canadian drivers report driving less than usual due to high gas prices." In this latter estimate, we are estimating that the population value falls between 47% and 53%, but we do not specify its exact value. The size of the confidence interval, which in this example is 6%, or the percentage-point difference between 47% and 53%, is called the **margin of error**, or sampling error.

6.2 BIAS AND EFFICIENCY

Both point and interval estimation procedures are based on sample statistics. Which of the many available sample statistics should be used? Estimators can be selected according to two criteria: **bias** and **efficiency**. Estimates should be based on sample statistics that are unbiased and relatively efficient. We will cover each of these criteria separately.

Bias.   An estimator is unbiased if, and only if, the mean of its sampling distribution is equal to the population value of interest. We know from the theorems presented in Chapter 5 that sample means conform to this criterion. The mean of the sampling distribution of sample means (which we note symbolically as $\mu_{\bar{X}}$) is the same as the population mean (μ).

Sample proportions (P_s) are also unbiased. That is, if we calculate sample proportions from repeated random samples of size n and then array them in a frequency polygon, the sampling distribution of sample proportions will have a mean (μ_p) equal to the population proportion (P_u). Thus, if we are concerned with coin flips and sample honest coins 10 at a time ($n = 10$), the sampling distribution will have a mean equal to 0.5, which is the probability that an honest coin will be heads (or tails) when flipped. However, other statistics are biased (i.e., have sampling distributions with means not equal to the population value).*

Knowing that sample means and proportions are unbiased allows us to determine the probability that they lie within a given distance of the population values we are trying to estimate. To illustrate, consider a specific problem. Assume that we wish to estimate the average income of a community. A random sample of 500 households is taken ($n = 500$), and a sample mean of $35,000 is computed. In this example, the population mean is the average income of *all* households in the community and the sample mean is the

---

*In particular, the sample standard deviation (s) is a biased estimator of the population standard deviation (σ). As you might expect, there is less dispersion in a sample than in a population and, as a consequence, s will underestimate σ. As we shall see, however, sample standard deviation can be corrected for this bias and still serve as an estimate of the population standard deviation for large samples.

FIGURE 6.1   AREAS UNDER THE SAMPLING DISTRIBUTION OF SAMPLE MEANS

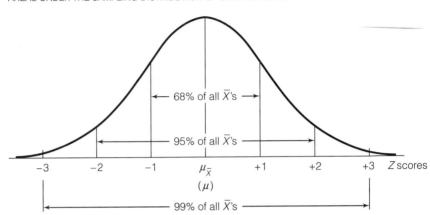

average income for the 500 households that happened to be selected for our sample. Note that we do not know the value of the population mean (μ)—if we did, we wouldn't need the sample—but it is μ that we are interested in. The sample mean of \$35,000 is important and interesting primarily insofar as it can give us information about the population mean.

The two theorems presented in Chapter 5 give us a great deal of information about the sampling distribution of all possible sample means. Because n is large, we know that the sampling distribution is normal and that its mean is equal to the population mean. We also know that all normal curves contain about 68% of the cases (the cases here are sample means) within $\pm 1Z$ (i.e., ± 1 standard deviation), 95% of the cases within $\pm 2Z$'s (± 2 standard deviations), and more than 99% of the cases within $\pm 3Z$'s (± 3 standard deviations) of the mean. Remember that we are discussing the sampling distribution here—the distribution of all possible sample outcomes or, in this instance, sample means. Thus, the probabilities are very good (approximately 68 out of 100 chances) that our sample mean of \$35,000 is within $\pm 1Z$, excellent (95 out of 100) that it is within $\pm 2Z$'s, and overwhelming (99 out of 100) that it is within $\pm 3Z$'s of the mean of the sampling distribution (which is the same value as the population mean). These relationships are graphically depicted in Figure 6.1.

If an estimator is unbiased, it is probably an accurate estimate of the population parameter (μ in this case). However, in less than 1% of the cases, a sample mean will be more than $\pm 3Z$'s away from the mean of the sampling distribution (very inaccurate) by random chance alone. We literally have no idea if our particular sample mean of \$35,000 is in this small minority. We do know, however, that the odds are high that our sample mean is considerably closer than $\pm 3Z$'s to the mean of the sampling distribution and, thus, to the population mean.

Efficiency.   The second desirable characteristic of an estimator is efficiency, which is the extent to which the sampling distribution is clustered about its mean. Efficiency or clustering is essentially a matter of dispersion, as we saw

FIGURE 6.2 A SAMPLING DISTRIBUTION WITH n = 100 AND $\sigma_{\bar{x}}$ = $50.00

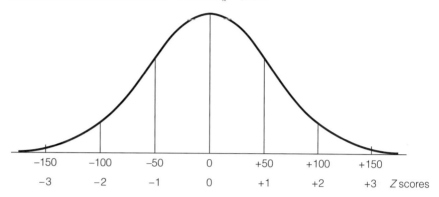

in Chapter 3 (see Figure 3.1). The smaller the standard deviation of a sampling distribution, the greater the clustering and the higher the efficiency. Remember that the standard deviation of the sampling distribution of sample means, or the standard error of the mean, is equal to the population standard deviation divided by the square root of n. Therefore, the standard deviation of the sampling distribution is an inverse function of n $(\sigma_{\bar{X}} = \sigma/\sqrt{n})$. As sample size increases, $\sigma_{\bar{X}}$ will decrease. We can improve the efficiency (or decrease the standard deviation of the sampling distribution) for any estimator by increasing sample size.

An example should make this clearer. Consider two samples of different sizes:

Sample 1	Sample 2
$\overline{X}_1$ = $35,000	$\overline{X}_2$ = $35,000
n_1 = 100	n_2 = 1,000

Both sample means are unbiased, but which is the more efficient estimator? Consider sample 1 and assume, for the sake of illustration, that the population standard deviation (σ) is $500.* In this case, the standard deviation of the sampling distribution of all possible sample means with an n of 100 would be or $\sigma/\sqrt{n}$ or $500/\sqrt{100}$ or $50.00. For sample 2, the standard deviation of all possible sample means with an n of 1,000 would be much smaller. Specifically, it would be equal to $500/\sqrt{1,000}$ or $15.81.

Sampling distribution 2 is much more clustered than sampling distribution 1. In fact, distribution 2 contains 68% of all possible sample means within ±15.81 of μ while distribution 1 requires a much broader interval of ±50.00 to do the same. The estimate based on a sample with 1,000 cases is much more likely to be close in value to the population parameter than is

---

*In reality, of course, the value of σ would be unknown.

FIGURE 6.3   A SAMPLING DISTRIBUTION WITH $n = 1,000$ AND $\sigma_{\bar{x}} = \$15.81$

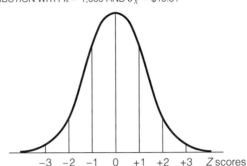

an estimate based on a sample of 100 cases. Figures 6.2 and 6.3 illustrate these relationships graphically.

To summarize: the standard deviation of all sampling distributions is an inverse function of n. Therefore, the larger the sample, the greater the clustering and the higher the efficiency. In part, these relationships between sample size and the standard deviation of the sampling distribution do nothing more than underscore our common-sense notion that much more confidence can be placed in large samples than in small (as long as both have been randomly selected).

6.3 ESTIMATION PROCEDURES: INTRODUCTION

The procedure for constructing a point estimate is straightforward. Draw an EPSEM sample, calculate either a proportion or a mean, and estimate that the population parameter is the same as the sample statistic. Remember that the larger the sample, the greater the efficiency and the more likely that the estimator is approximately the same as the population value. Also remember that, no matter how rigid the sampling procedure or how large the sample, there is always some chance that the estimator is very inaccurate.

Compared to point estimates, interval estimates are more complicated but safer because when we guess a range of values, we are more likely to include the population parameter. The first step in constructing an interval estimate is to decide on the risk that you are willing to take of being wrong. An interval estimate is wrong if it does not include the population parameter. This probability of error is called **alpha** (symbolized α). The exact value of alpha will depend on the nature of the research situation, but a 0.05 probability is commonly used. Setting alpha equal to 0.05, also called using the 95% **confidence level**, means that over the long run the researcher is willing to be wrong only 5% of the time. Or, to put it another way, if an infinite number of intervals were constructed at this alpha level (and with all other things being equal), 95% of them would contain the population value and 5% would not. In reality, of course, only one interval is constructed and, by setting the probability of error very low, we are setting the odds in our favour that the interval will include the population value.

FIGURE 6.4   THE SAMPLING DISTRIBUTION WITH ALPHA (α) EQUAL TO 0.05

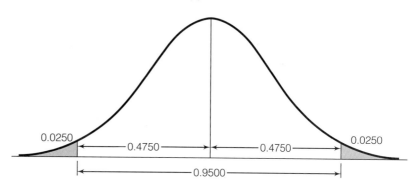

The second step is to picture the sampling distribution, divide the probability of error equally into the upper and lower tails of the distribution, and then find the corresponding Z score. For example, if we decided to set alpha equal to 0.05, we would place half (0.025) of this probability in the lower tail and half in the upper tail of the distribution. The sampling distribution would thus be divided as illustrated in Figure 6.4.

We need to find the Z score that marks the beginnings of the shaded areas. In Chapter 4, we learned how to calculate Z scores and find areas under the normal curve. Here, we will reverse that process. We need to find the Z score beyond which lies a proportion of 0.0250 of the total area. To do this, go down column c of Appendix A until you find this proportion (0.0250). The associated Z score is 1.96. Because the curve is symmetrical and we are interested in both the upper and lower tails, we designate the Z score that corresponds to an alpha of 0.05 as ± 1.96 (see Figure 6.5).

We now know that 95% of all possible sample outcomes fall within ± 1.96 Z-score units of the population value. In reality, of course, there is only one sample outcome but, if we construct an interval estimate based on $\pm 1.96 Z$'s, the probabilities are that 95% of all such intervals will trap the population value. Thus, we can be 95% confident that our interval contains the population value.

FIGURE 6.5   FINDING THE Z SCORE THAT CORRESPONDS TO AN ALPHA (α) OF 0.05

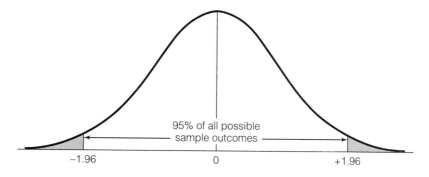

TABLE 6.1 Z SCORES FOR VARIOUS LEVELS OF ALPHA (α)

Confidence Level (%)	Alpha	$\alpha/2$	Z Score
90	0.10	0.0500	± 1.65
95	0.05	0.0250	± 1.96
99	0.01	0.0050	± 2.58
99.9	0.001	0.0005	± 3.29

Besides the 95% level, there are three other commonly used confidence levels: the 90% level ($\alpha = 0.10$), the 99% level ($\alpha = 0.01$), and the 99.9% level ($\alpha = 0.001$). To find the corresponding Z scores for these levels, follow the procedures outlined above for an alpha of 0.05. Table 6.1 summarizes all the information you will need.

You should turn to Appendix A and confirm for yourself that the Z scores in Table 6.1 do indeed correspond to these alpha levels. As you do, note that, in the cases where alpha is set at 0.10 and 0.01, the precise areas we seek do not appear in the table. For example, with an alpha of 0.10, we would look in column c ("Area beyond") for the area 0.0500. Instead we find an area of 0.0505 ($Z = \pm 1.64$) and an area of 0.0495 ($Z = \pm 1.65$). The Z score we are seeking is somewhere between these two other scores. When this condition occurs, take the larger of the two scores as Z. This will make the interval as wide as possible under the circumstances and is thus the most conservative course of action. In the case of an alpha of 0.01, we encounter the same problem (the exact area 0.0050 is not in the table), resolve it the same way, and take the larger score as Z. Finally, note that in the case where alpha is set at 0.001, we can choose from several Z scores. Although our table is not detailed enough to show it, the closest Z score to the exact area we want is ± 3.291, which we can round off to ± 3.29. *(For practice in finding Z scores for various levels of confidence, see problem 6.3.)*

The third step is to actually construct the confidence interval. In the following section, we illustrate how to construct an interval estimate with sample means; in Section 6.6, we show how to construct an interval estimate with sample proportions.

6.4 INTERVAL ESTIMATION PROCEDURES FOR SAMPLE MEANS (LARGE SAMPLES)

The formula for constructing a confidence interval based on sample means is given in Formula 6.1:

FORMULA 6.1

$$\text{c.i.} = \overline{X} \pm Z\left(\frac{\sigma}{\sqrt{n}}\right)$$

where c.i. = confidence interval
$\overline{X}$ = the sample mean
Z = the Z score as determined by the alpha level
$\dfrac{\sigma}{\sqrt{n}}$ = the standard deviation of the sampling distribution or the standard error of the mean

As an example, suppose you wanted to estimate the average IQ of a community and had randomly selected a sample of 200 residents, with a sample mean IQ of 105. Assume that the population standard deviation for IQ scores is about 15, so we can set σ equal to 15. If we are willing to run a 5% chance of being wrong and set alpha at 0.05, the corresponding Z score will be 1.96. These values can be directly substituted into Formula 6.1, and an interval can be constructed

$$\text{c.i.} = \overline{X} \pm Z\left(\frac{\sigma}{\sqrt{n}}\right)$$

$$\text{c.i.} = 105 \pm 1.96\left(\frac{15}{\sqrt{200}}\right)$$

$$\text{c.i.} = 105 \pm 1.96\left(\frac{15}{14.14}\right)$$

$$\text{c.i.} = 105 \pm (1.96)(1.06)$$

$$\text{c.i.} = 105 \pm 2.08$$

That is, our estimate is that the average IQ for the population in question is somewhere between 102.92 (105 − 2.08) and 107.08 (105 + 2.08). Since 95% of all possible sample means are within ±1.96Z's (or 2.08 IQ units in this case) of the mean of the sampling distribution, the odds are very high that our interval will contain the population mean. In fact, even if the sample mean is as far off as ±1.96Z's (which is unlikely), our interval will still contain $\mu_{\overline{X}}$ and, thus, μ. Only if our sample mean is one of the few that is more than ±1.96Z's from the mean of the sampling distribution will we have failed to include the population mean.

Note that in the example above, the value of the population standard deviation was supplied. Needless to say, it is unusual to have such information about a population. In the great majority of cases, we will have no knowledge of σ. In such cases, however, we can estimate σ with s, the sample standard deviation. Unfortunately, s is a biased estimator of σ, and the formula must be changed slightly to correct for the bias. For larger samples, the bias of s will not affect the interval very much. The revised formula for cases in which σ is unknown is

FORMULA 6.2

$$\text{c.i.} = \overline{X} \pm Z\left(\frac{s}{\sqrt{n-1}}\right)$$

In comparing this formula with Formula 6.1, note that there are two changes. First, σ is replaced by s, and, second, the denominator of the last term is the square root of $n - 1$ rather than the square root of n. The latter change is the correction for the fact that s is biased.

It is important to stress here that the substitution of s for σ is permitted only for large samples (i.e., samples with 100 or more cases). For smaller samples, when the value of the population standard deviation is unknown, the standardized normal distribution summarized in Appendix A cannot be

Application 6.1

Based on a random sample of 15,222 households, the Survey of Household Spending (SHS; a survey conducted by Statistics Canada to collect detailed information on the spending patterns of Canadian households) reveals that the average Canadian household spends a total of $65,535 annually. Total expenditure includes consumption of food, shelter, clothing, transportation, recreation, education, tobacco and alcohol products, and so on, as well as personal taxes, personal insurance payments, and pension and other contributions. Given the SHS sample reported a mean annual expenditure of $65,535, what is the estimate of the population mean? The information from the sample is

$$\overline{X} = 65,535$$
$$s = 51,246$$
$$n = 15,222$$

If we set alpha at 0.05, the corresponding Z score will be ±1.96, and the 95% confidence interval will be

$$\text{c.i.} = \overline{X} \pm Z\left(\frac{s}{\sqrt{n-1}}\right)$$

$$\text{c.i.} = 65,535 \pm 1.96\left(\frac{51,246}{\sqrt{15,222-1}}\right)$$
$$\text{c.i.} = 65,535 \pm 1.96\left(\frac{51,246}{123}\right)$$
$$\text{c.i.} = 65,535 \pm (1.96)(417)$$
$$\text{c.i.} = 65,535 \pm 817$$

Based on this result, we would estimate the population spends an average of $65,535 ± $817 per year. The lower limit of our interval estimate (65,535 − 817) is 64,718, and the upper limit (65,535 + 817) is 66,352. Thus, another way to state the interval would be

$$64,718 \leq \mu \leq 66,352$$

The population mean is greater than or equal to $64,718 and less than or equal to $66,352. Because alpha was set at the 0.05 level, this estimate has a 5% chance of being wrong (i.e., of not containing the population mean).

Source: Data from Statistics Canada, *Survey of Household Spending*, 2005, PUMF.

used in the estimation process. To construct confidence intervals from sample means with samples smaller than 100, we must use a different theoretical distribution, called the Student's *t* distribution, to find areas under the sampling distribution. We will defer the presentation of the *t* distribution until Chapter 7 and confine our attention here to estimation procedures for large samples only.

Let us close this section by working through a sample problem with Formula 6.2. Average income for a random sample of a particular community is $35,000, with a standard deviation of $200. What is the 95% interval estimate of the population mean, μ?

Given that

$$\overline{X} = \$35,000$$
$$s = \$200$$
$$n = 500$$

and using an alpha of 0.05, the interval can be constructed:

$$\text{c.i.} = \overline{X} \pm Z\left(\frac{s}{\sqrt{n-1}}\right)$$

$$\text{c.i.} = 35{,}000 \pm 1.96\left(\frac{200}{\sqrt{499}}\right)$$

$$\text{c.i.} = 35{,}000 \pm 17.55$$

The average income for the community as a whole is between \$34,982.45 (35,000 − 17.55) and \$35,017.55 (35,000 + 17.55). Remember that this interval has only a 5% chance of being wrong (i.e., of not containing the population mean). *(For practice with confidence intervals for sample means, see problems 6.1, 6.4–6.7, 6.18, and 6.19a–6.19c.)*

6.5 GRAPHING A CONFIDENCE INTERVAL OF A SAMPLE MEAN

A confidence interval of a sample mean can be depicted using a graph called the **error bar**. The error bar graph is based on the lower and upper limits of the confidence interval of a sample mean. The construction of an error bar requires a couple of steps. First, the sample mean is plotted with a symbol, such as a dot, at the centre of a graph. Second, a vertical line or "error bar" is drawn from the sample mean to the lower limit of its confidence interval, marked by a small horizontal line. The same is done between the sample mean and the upper limit of the confidence interval. The area bounded by the two error bars is equal to the width of the confidence interval of the sample mean.

Figure 6.6 displays the error bar graph for the 95% confidence interval of the mean income of the community described in Section 6.4. Recall

FIGURE 6.6   ERROR BAR GRAPH FOR THE 95% CONFIDENCE INTERVAL OF THE MEAN INCOME OF A COMMUNITY

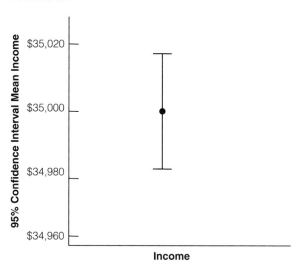

that the average income for the random sample of 500 households in that community is \$35,000, with a standard deviation of \$200. At the 95% confidence level, the average income for the community as a whole is between \$34,982.45 (35,000 − 17.55) and \$35,017.55 (35,000 + 17.55). Graphically, the dot in the middle of the error bar graph represents the sample mean and the vertical line above and below the sample mean represents the upper and lower limits of the confidence interval. *(For practice in constructing and interpreting error bars, see problems 6.4 and 6.6.)*

6.6 INTERVAL ESTIMATION PROCEDURES FOR SAMPLE PROPORTIONS (LARGE SAMPLES)

Estimation procedures for sample proportions are essentially the same as those for sample means. The major difference is that, because proportions are different statistics, we must use a different sampling distribution. In fact, again based on the Central Limit Theorem, we know that sample proportions have sampling distributions that are normal in shape with means (μ_p) equal to the population value (P_u) and standard deviations (σ_p) equal to $\sqrt{P_u(1 - P_u)/n}$. The formula for constructing confidence intervals based on sample proportions is

FORMULA 6.3

$$\text{c.i.} = P_s \pm Z\sqrt{\frac{P_u(1 - P_u)}{n}}$$

The values for P_s and n come directly from the sample, and the value of Z is determined by the confidence level, as was the case with sample means. This leaves one unknown in the formula, P_u—the same value we are trying to estimate. This dilemma can be resolved by setting the value of P_u at 0.5. Because the second term in the numerator under the radical $(1 - P_u)$ is the reciprocal of P_u, the entire expression will always have a value of 0.5 × 0.5, or 0.25, which is the maximum value this expression can attain. That is, if we set P_u at any value other than 0.5, the expression $P_u(1 - P_u)$ will decrease in value. If we set P_u at 0.4, for example, the second term $(1 - P_u)$ would be 0.6, and the value of the entire expression would decrease to 0.24. Setting P_u at 0.5 ensures that the expression $P_u(1 - P_u)$ will be at its maximum possible value and, consequently, the interval will be at maximum width. This is the most conservative possible solution to the dilemma posed by having to assign a value to P_u in the estimation equation.

To illustrate these procedures, assume that you wish to estimate the proportion of students at your university who missed at least one day of classes because of illness last semester. Out of a random sample of 200 students, 60 reported that they had been sick enough to miss classes at least one day during the previous semester. The sample proportion upon which

Application 6.2

Canadians overwhelmingly believe that global warming, produced by greenhouse gases, is a real and major threat to future generations. According to a Leger Marketing survey, 81% of a random sample of 1,500 Canadians said "yes" to the question, "In your view, should the Government of Canada be tougher on Canadian citizens and corporations to ensure that collectively Canadians reduce greenhouse gas emissions?" Based on this finding, what is the estimate of the population value? The sample information is

$$P_s = 0.81$$
$$n = 1,500$$

Note that the percentage of those who said "yes" to the question has been stated as a proportion. If we set alpha at 0.05, the corresponding Z score will be ± 1.96, and the interval estimate of the population proportion will be

$$\text{c.i.} = P_s \pm Z\sqrt{\frac{P_u(1 - P_u)}{n}}$$

$$\text{c.i.} = 0.81 \pm 1.96\sqrt{\frac{(0.5)(0.5)}{1,500}}$$
$$\text{c.i.} = 0.81 \pm 1.96\sqrt{0.00017}$$
$$\text{c.i.} = 0.81 \pm (1.96)(0.013)$$
$$\text{c.i.} = 0.81 \pm 0.03$$

We can now estimate that the proportion of the population that believes the federal government needs to get tough on citizens and corporations to reduce greenhouse gas emissions is between 0.78 and 0.84. That is, the lower limit of the interval estimate is $(0.81 - 0.03)$ or 0.78, and the upper limit is $(0.81 + 0.03)$ or 0.84. We may also express this result in percentages and say that between 78% and 84% of the population is of the opinion that the government should be tougher on citizens and corporations in order to reduce greenhouse gas emissions. This interval has a 5% chance of not containing the population value.

Source: Data from Leger Marketing, *Canadians and the Environmental Policies of Canada* (2005).

we will base our estimate is thus 60/200, or 0.30. At the 95% level, the interval estimate will be

$$\text{c.i.} = P_s \pm Z\sqrt{\frac{P_u(1 - P_u)}{n}}$$

$$\text{c.i.} = 0.30 \pm 1.96\sqrt{\frac{(0.5)(0.5)}{200}}$$

$$\text{c.i.} = 0.30 \pm 1.96\sqrt{\frac{0.25}{200}}$$
$$\text{c.i.} = 0.30 \pm (1.96)(0.035)$$
$$\text{c.i.} = 0.30 \pm 0.07$$

Based on this sample proportion of 0.30, you would estimate that the proportion of students who missed at least one day of classes because of illness was between 0.23 and 0.37. The estimate could, of course, also be phrased in percentages by reporting that between 23% and 37% of the student body was affected by illness at least once during the past semester. Additionally, as with the sample mean, the error bar can be used to graph the confidence interval of a sample proportion. *(For practice with confidence intervals for sample proportions, see problems 6.2, 6.8–6.12, 6.14–6.17, and 6.19d–6.19g.)*

TABLE 6.2 CHOOSING FORMULAS FOR CONFIDENCE INTERVALS

If the Sample Statistic Is a	and	Use Formula
mean	the population standard deviation is known	6.1 c.i. $= \overline{X} \pm Z\left(\dfrac{\sigma}{\sqrt{n}}\right)$
mean	the population standard deviation is unknown	6.2 c.i. $= \overline{X} \pm Z\left(\dfrac{s}{\sqrt{n-1}}\right)$
proportion		6.3 c.i. $= P_s \pm Z\sqrt{\dfrac{P_u(1-P_u)}{n}}$

6.7 A SUMMARY OF THE COMPUTATION OF CONFIDENCE INTERVALS

To this point, we have covered the construction of confidence intervals for sample means and sample proportions. In both cases, the procedures assume large samples ($n = 100$ or more). The procedures for constructing confidence intervals for small samples are not covered in this textbook. Table 6.2 presents the three formulas for confidence intervals organized by the situations in which they are used. For sample means, when the population standard deviation is known, use Formula 6.1. When the population standard deviation is unknown (which is the usual case), use Formula 6.2. For sample proportions, always use Formula 6.3.

6.8 CONTROLLING THE WIDTH OF INTERVAL ESTIMATES

The width of a confidence interval for either sample means or sample proportions can be partly controlled by manipulating two terms in the equation. First, the confidence level can be raised or lowered and, second, the interval can be widened or narrowed by gathering samples of different size. The researcher alone determines the risk he or she is willing to take of being wrong (i.e., of not including the population value in the interval estimate). The exact confidence level (or alpha level) will depend, in part, on the purpose of the research. For example, if potentially harmful drugs were being tested, the researcher would naturally demand very high levels of confidence (99.99% or even 99.999%). On the other hand, if intervals are being constructed only for loose "guesstimates," then much lower confidence levels can be tolerated (such as 90%).

The relationship between interval size and confidence level is that intervals widen as confidence levels increase. This should make intuitive sense. Wider intervals are more likely to trap the population value; hence, more confidence can be placed in them.

To illustrate this relationship, let us return to the example where we estimated the average income for a community. In this problem, we were working with a sample of 500 residents, and the average income for this sample was $35,000, with a standard deviation of $200. We constructed the 95% confidence interval and found that it extended 17.55 around the sample mean (i.e., the interval was $35,000 ± $17.55).

If we had constructed the 90% confidence interval for these sample data (a lower confidence level), the Z score in the formula would have decreased to ±1.65, and the interval would have been narrower:

$$\text{c.i.} = \overline{X} \pm Z\left(\frac{s}{\sqrt{n-1}}\right)$$

$$\text{c.i.} = 35,000 \pm 1.65\left(\frac{200}{\sqrt{499}}\right)$$

$$\text{c.i.} = 35,000 \pm (1.65)(8.95)$$

$$\text{c.i.} = 35,000 \pm 14.77$$

On the other hand, if we had constructed the 99% confidence interval, the Z score would have increased to ±2.58, and the interval would have been wider:

$$\text{c.i.} = \overline{X} \pm Z\left(\frac{s}{\sqrt{n-1}}\right)$$

$$\text{c.i.} = 35,000 \pm 2.58\left(\frac{200}{\sqrt{499}}\right)$$

$$\text{c.i.} = 35,000 \pm (2.58)(8.95)$$

$$\text{c.i.} = 35,000 \pm 23.09$$

At the 99.9% confidence level, the Z score would be ±3.29, and the interval would be wider still:

$$\text{c.i.} = \overline{X} \pm Z\left(\frac{s}{\sqrt{n-1}}\right)$$

$$\text{c.i.} = 35,000 \pm 3.29\left(\frac{200}{\sqrt{499}}\right)$$

$$\text{c.i.} = 35,000 \pm (3.29)(8.95)$$

$$\text{c.i.} = 35,000 \pm 29.45$$

These four intervals are grouped together in Table 6.3, and the increase in interval size can be readily observed. Although sample means have been used to illustrate the relationship between interval width and confidence level, exactly the same relationships apply to sample proportions. *(To further explore the relationship between alpha and interval width, see problem 6.13.)*

Sample size bears the opposite relationship to interval width. As sample size increases, interval width decreases. Larger samples give more precise (narrower) estimates. Again, an example should make this clearer. In Table 6.4,

TABLE 6.3   INTERVAL ESTIMATES FOR FOUR CONFIDENCE LEVELS ($\overline{X}$ = $35,000, s = $200, n = 500 throughout)

Alpha	Confidence Level (%)	Interval	Interval Width
0.10	90	$35,000 ± 14.77	$29.54
0.05	95	$35,000 ± 17.55	$35.10
0.01	99	$35,000 ± 23.09	$46.18
0.001	99.9	$35,000 ± 29.45	$58.90

TABLE 6.4   INTERVAL ESTIMATES FOR FOUR DIFFERENT SAMPLES
($\overline{X}$ = $35,000, s = $200, alpha = 0.05 throughout)

Sample 1 (n = 100)		Sample 2 (n = 500)
c.i. = $35,000 ± 1.96(200/$\sqrt{99}$)		c.i. = $35,000 ± 1.96(200/$\sqrt{499}$)
c.i. = $35,000 ± 39.40		c.i. = $35,000 ± 17.55

Sample 3 (n = 1,000)		Sample 4 (n = 10,000)
c.i. = $35,000 ± 1.96(200/$\sqrt{999}$)		c.i. = $35,000 ± 1.96(200/$\sqrt{9,999}$)
c.i. = $35,000 ± 12.40		c.i. = $35,000 ± 3.92

Sample	n	Interval Width
1	100	$78.80
2	500	$35.10
3	1,000	$24.80
4	10,000	$ 7.84

confidence intervals for four samples of various sizes are constructed and then grouped together for purposes of comparison. The sample data are the same as in Table 6.3, and the confidence level is 95% throughout. The relationships illustrated in Table 6.4 also hold true, of course, for sample proportions. *(To further explore the relationship between sample size and interval width, see problem 6.14.)*

Notice that the decrease in interval width (or, increase in precision) does not bear a constant or linear relationship with sample size. With sample 2 as compared to sample 1, the sample size was increased by a factor of 5, but the interval is not five times as narrow. This is an important relationship because it means that n might have to be increased many times to appreciably improve the accuracy of an estimate. Because the cost of a research project is a direct function of sample size, this relationship implies a point of diminishing returns in estimation procedures. A sample of 10,000 will cost about twice as much as a sample of 5,000, but estimates based on the larger sample will not be twice as precise.

6.9 DETERMINING SAMPLE SIZE

Have you ever wondered how researchers or pollsters decide how many people to include in a random sample when conducting a survey or poll? Well, they use a process similar to "reverse engineering." That is, they determine how many people are needed in a random sample to obtain a desired confidence interval. For instance, a gerontologist wants to estimate the mean income of senior citizens in Canada. How many seniors would she have to sample to be 99% confident that the sample mean is within plus or minus $1,000 (margin of error) of the population mean, where previous research showed that the population standard deviation is $5,000 (lacking knowledge of σ, she can replace it with s, the sample standard deviation, if available). Or, what sample size would a public opinion pollster need if she wanted to know what proportion of Canadians support reinstating the death penalty for murder within plus or minus 3% with a 95% certainty? We can solve these problems by simply rearranging the formulas for constructing a confidence interval.

For the mean, Formula 6.4 finds the minimum sample size needed in a simple random sample to get results with the desired level of precision:

FORMULA 6.4

$$n = \frac{Z^2 \times \sigma^2}{ME^2}$$

where n = required sample size
Z = Z score as determined by the alpha level
σ = population standard deviation
ME = margin of error

Using this formula the gerontologist can calculate the n she needs for a 99% confidence interval, where Z equals 2.58 and the margin of error is 1,000:

$$n = \frac{Z^2 \times \sigma^2}{ME^2}$$

$$n = \frac{2.58^2 \times 5,000^2}{1,000^2}$$

$$n = \frac{6.6564 \times 25,000,000}{1,000,000}$$

$$n = \frac{166,410,000}{1,000,000}$$

$$n = 166.41$$

The gerontologist needs to randomly sample, rounding up, at least 167 senior citizens to be 99% confident that the sample mean will be within plus or minus \$1,000 of the population mean, that is, the mean income of all senior citizens in Canada.

For the proportion, Formula 6.5 finds the smallest sample size required to get the desired results in a simple random sample:

FORMULA 6.5

$$n = \frac{(Z^2 \times P_u \times (1 - P_u)) + ME^2}{ME^2}$$

where n = required sample size
Z = Z score as determined by the alpha level
P_u = population proportion
ME = margin of error

With this formula, the public opinion pollster can calculate the n she needs for a 95% confidence interval, where Z equals 1.96 and (expressed as proportions) a margin of error of 0.03 and P_u set to 0.5:

$$n = \frac{(Z^2 \times P_u \times (1 - P_u)) + ME^2}{ME^2}$$

$$n = \frac{(1.96^2 \times 0.5 \times (0.5)) + 0.03^2}{0.03^2}$$

$$n = \frac{0.9604 + 0.0009}{0.0009}$$

$$n = \frac{0.9613}{0.0009}$$

$$n = 1,068.11$$

So, at least 1,069 Canadians need to be randomly sampled for the pollster to be 95% confident that the sample proportion will be within plus or minus 0.03 of the population proportion.

The information in this example might sound familiar. Pollsters typically report their findings to the media with this information in a footnote, telling us that their estimate is "accurate within ±3%, 19 times out of 20" or that the "margin of error for a sample of 1,069 is ±3%, 19 times out of 20."

This example also reveals why political polls tend to randomly sample only 1,000 or so people—it is not necessary to have a sample much larger than around 1,000 because we are already 95% confident that our sample results will have a high level of precision, with a margin of error of just plus or minus 3%. Further, and as noted in the previous section, the relationship between sample size and level of precision is not linear. That is to say that doubling the sample size, for instance, will not cut in half the margin of error. Doubling the sample size from 1,069 to 2,138 cuts the margin of error from ±3% to just ±2.1%. A relatively small increase in precision may not justify the cost associated with doubling sample size.

As a final note, Formulas 6.4 and 6.5 are used to determine sample size of a simple random sample when the population of interest is very large, typically a population size of 100,000 or more. Otherwise these formulas need to be slightly modified to correct for sampling design (when a simple random sample is not used) and/or population size (when the population size is less than 100,000).

6.10 INTERPRETING STATISTICS: PREDICTING THE ELECTION OF THE GOVERNMENT OF CANADA AND JUDGING ITS PERFORMANCE

The statistical techniques covered in this chapter have become a part of everyday life in Canada and elsewhere. In politics, for example, estimation techniques are used to track public sentiment, measure how citizens perceive the performance of political leaders, and project the likely winners of upcoming elections. We should acknowledge, nonetheless, that these applications of estimation techniques are also controversial. Many wonder if the easy availability of polls makes politicians overly sensitive to the whims of public sentiment. Others are concerned that election projections might work against people's readiness to participate fully in the democratic process and, in particular, cast their votes on election day. These are serious concerns but, in this textbook, we can do little more than acknowledge them and hope that you have the opportunity to pursue them in other, more appropriate settings.

In this installment of Interpreting Statistics, we will examine the role of statistical estimation of voting intentions in the 2006 campaign for the federal election (election projections) that culminated in the election of Stephen Harper and the Conservative Party. We will also examine trends in post-election polls on political party support. Both kinds of polls use the same formulas introduced in this chapter to construct confidence intervals (although the random samples were assembled according to a more complex technique that is beyond the scope of this textbook).

A Shift in Popularity.   The federal election of 2006 among Liberals, Conservatives, New Democratic Party (NDP), Bloc Québécois (BQ), and the Green Party was one of the most interesting elections in recent Canadian history. Although the next election was not legally required until 2009, the dissolution of Parliament and a motion of "no confidence" passed by the opposition in the House of Commons in November 2005 contributed to the early election. In this section we will use our newly acquired knowledge of confidence intervals to explore how the popularity of the parties changed before and during the election campaign.

Table 6.5 presents the results of the last eight surveys conducted before the 2006 federal election by Nanos Research (formerly SES Research), a Canadian public-opinion research firm. The two left-hand columns show the dates of the polls and the sample size (n) for each poll. The five right-hand columns list the percentage of the sample that said, at the time the poll was conducted, that they intended to vote for each party. These are point estimates of the population parameters (which would be the actual percentage of the entire national electorate that would vote for the Liberals, Conservatives, NDP, BQ, or Green Party at that specific time). Table 6.5 expresses results in percentages for ease of communication, but actual estimates would be computed using sample proportions.

TABLE 6.5   NANOS RESEARCH POLLING RESULTS, OCTOBER 2005 TO JANUARY 2006

Poll Date	Sample Size	Percentage of Sample for				
		Liberal	Conservative	NDP	BQ	Green
Oct. 27, 2005	854	40	28	15	12	4
Nov. 13, 2005	865	34	28	20	14	4
Dec. 1, 2005	1,008	37	29	15	14	5
Dec. 15, 2005	1,012	39	33	12	12	5
Dec. 30, 2005	1,028	35	35	14	13	4
Jan. 8, 2006	987	31	34	17	11	6
Jan. 15, 2006	1,038	29	37	18	11	5
Jan. 22, 2006	1,051	30	36	17	11	6

Source: Nanos Research.

It can be seen from Table 6.5 that the Liberal Party had the lead for the first part of the campaign, up to the end of December 2005. Electoral support shifted to the Conservative Party, however, in the last few weeks of the campaign.

Let us assume that one wanted to predict the election results based on the January 8, 2006, poll, when the Conservative Party has a lead of about 3 percentage points over the Liberal Party. Does this mean that the Conservatives were actually ahead of the Liberals in the popular vote? The percentages in Table 6.5 are point estimates, and these types of estimates are unlikely to match their respective parameters exactly. In other words, it is unlikely that the sample values in the table were exactly equal to the percentage of the electorate who were going to vote for each of the parties on that particular date. For this reason, confidence intervals would be safer to utilize because they use ranges of values, not single points, to estimate population values.

Table 6.6 displays the 95% confidence intervals for each party for these eight polls, with the results again expressed as percentages rather than proportions. The dates and sample size of each poll are displayed in the left-most columns, followed by the 95% confidence intervals for each estimate and the width of the interval estimates. (Note that Table 6.6 underscores a very important point about estimation: As sample size increases, the width of the interval becomes narrower. The first two polls were based on smaller samples, 854 and 865, and were each 6.8 percentage points wide, while the polls taken in December and January were based on larger samples and, as a result, the intervals are narrower, at 6.2% wide.)

The most important information in Table 6.6 is, of course, the intervals themselves, and it is the overlap in some of these intervals that

TABLE 6.6 SAMPLE SIZE, CONFIDENCE INTERVALS, AND LIKELY WINNERS

Poll Date	Sample Size	95% Confidence Interval					Interval Width
		Liberal	Conservative	NDP	BQ	Green	
Oct. 27, 2005	854	40 ± 3.4	28 ± 3.4	15 ± 3.4	12 ± 3.4	4 ± 3.4	6.8
Nov. 13, 2005	865	34 ± 3.4	28 ± 3.4	20 ± 3.4	14 ± 3.4	4 ± 3.4	6.8
Dec. 1, 2005	1,008	37 ± 3.1	29 ± 3.1	15 ± 3.1	14 ± 3.1	5 ± 3.1	6.2
Dec. 15, 2005	1,012	39 ± 3.1	33 ± 3.1	12 ± 3.1	12 ± 3.1	5 ± 3.1	6.2
Dec. 30, 2005	1,028	35 ± 3.1	35 ± 3.1	14 ± 3.1	13 ± 3.1	4 ± 3.1	6.2
Jan. 8, 2006	987	31 ± 3.1	34 ± 3.1	17 ± 3.1	11 ± 3.1	6 ± 3.1	6.2
Jan. 15, 2006	1,038	29 ± 3.1	37 ± 3.1	18 ± 3.1	11 ± 3.1	5 ± 3.1	6.2
Jan. 22, 2006	1,051	30 ± 3.1	36 ± 3.1	17 ± 3.1	11 ± 3.1	6 ± 3.1	6.2

Source: Nanos Research.

READING STATISTICS 3: Public-Opinion Polls

You are most likely to encounter the estimation techniques covered in this chapter in the mass media in the form of public-opinion polls, election projections, and the like. Professional polling firms use interval estimates, and responsible reporting by the media will usually emphasize the estimate itself (e.g., "In a survey of the Canadian public, 57% of the respondents said that they approve of the prime minister's performance") but also will report the width of the interval ("This estimate is accurate to within ±3%," or "Figures from this poll are subject to a margin of error of ±3%"), the alpha level (usually as the confidence level of 95%), and the size of the sample ("1,458 households were surveyed").

Election projections and voter analyses have been common since the middle of the 20th century and are discussed further in Section 6.10. More recently, public-opinion polling has been increasingly used to gauge reactions to everything from the newest movies to the hottest gossip to the prime minister's conduct during the latest crisis. News magazines routinely report poll results as an adjunct to news stories, and similar stories are regular features of TV news and newspapers. We would include an example or two of these applications here, but polls have become so pervasive that you can choose your own example. Just pick up a newsmagazine or newspaper, leaf through it casually, and we bet that you'll find at least one poll. Read the story and try to identify the population, the confidence interval width, the sample size, and the confidence level. Bring the news item to class and dazzle your instructor.

As a citizen, as well as a social scientist, you should be extremely suspicious of polls that do not include such vital information as sample size or interval width. You should also check to find out how the sample was assembled. Samples

selected in a non-random fashion cannot be regarded as representative of the Canadian public or, for that matter, of any population larger than the sample itself. Such non-scientific polls can be found when local TV news or sports programs ask viewers to call in and register their opinions about some current controversy. These polls are for entertainment only and must not be taken seriously. You should, of course, read all polls and surveys critically and analytically, but you should place confidence only in polls that are based on samples selected according to the rule of EPSEM (see Chapter 5) from some defined population.

In addition, ads, commercials, and reports published by partisan groups sometimes report statistics that seem to be estimates to the population. Often, such estimates are based on woefully inadequate sampling sizes and biased sampling procedures, and the data are collected under circumstances that evoke a desired response. "Person in the street" (or shopper in the grocery store) interviews have a certain folksy appeal but must not be accorded the same credibility as surveys conducted by reputable polling firms.

The social research industry in Canada, however, is regulated to some extent. By and large, the industry is self-regulated. The Marketing Research and Intelligence Association, representing most of the industry, has adopted codes of ethics and established standards for reporting and interpreting survey research results. Further, the reporting of election survey results during federal election campaigns is formally regulated by the *Canada Elections Act*. For instance, Federal electoral legislation requires that published election-period poll results contain basic methodological information such as margin of error and date on which the poll was conducted.

(continued next page)

READING STATISTICS 3: *(continued)*

Public-Opinion Surveys in the Professional Literature

Thousands of political, social, and market research polls are conducted each year in Canada. For the social sciences, probably the single most important consequence of the growth in opinion polling is that many nationally representative databases are now available for research purposes. These high-quality databases are often available for free or a nominal fee and they make it possible to conduct "state-of-the-art" research without the expense and difficulty of collecting data yourself. This is an important development because we can now easily test our theories against very high-quality data, and our conclusions will thus have a stronger empirical basis. Our research efforts will have greater credibility with our colleagues, with policy-makers, and with the public at large.

One of the more important and widely used databases of this sort is the General Social Survey (GSS). Since 1985, Statistics Canada has annually questioned a nationally representative sample of Canadians about a wide variety of issues and concerns. Because many of the questions are asked every five years or so, the GSS offers a longitudinal record of Canadian sentiment and opinion about a large variety of topics (e.g., see Reading Statistics 4). Each year, new topics of current concern are added and explored, and the variety of information available thus continues to expand. Like other nationally representative samples, the GSS sample is chosen by a probability design based on the principle of EPSEM (see Chapter 5). With a sample size of about 25,000, GSS estimates will be highly precise (see Table 6.4 and Section 6.8 for the discussion on the relationship between sample size and precision of estimates). The computer exercises in this textbook are based on the 2009 GSS, and this database is described more fully in Appendix G.

caused the pollsters to declare the race "too close to call." So for example, the poll on January 8, 2006, showed that support for the Liberal Party was between 27.9% (31% − 3.1%) and 34.1% (31% + 3.1%), a width of 6.2 percentage points. Support for the Conservative Party in this poll was between 30.9% and 37.1%, again a width of 6.2 percentage points. (Note that the confidence intervals for each date have the same width because they are computed using the same sample size, or *n,* and the same confidence level, or 95%.)

Remember that while we can be 95% sure that the parameter is in the interval, it may be *anywhere* between the upper and lower limits. Thus, this poll tells us that it was just as likely that the Liberals would win (e.g., support for the Liberals could have been as high as 34.1%, and support for the Conservatives could have been as low as 30.9%) as it is that the Conservatives would be the victor (e.g., support for the Liberals could have been as low as 27.9%, and support for the Conservatives could

TABLE 6.7 COMPARISON OF THE LAST NANOS RESEARCH POLL (JANUARY 22) PRIOR TO THE FEDERAL ELECTION AND THE FEDERAL ELECTION RESULTS (JANUARY 23)

Party	Last Poll Prior to Federal Election (Jan. 22, 2006; sample size 1,051)	Federal Election (Jan. 23, 2006)	Difference from Nanos Research Poll
Liberal	30.1	30.2	0.1
Conservative	36.4	36.3	0.1
NDP	17.4	17.5	0.1
BQ	10.6	10.5	0.1
Green	5.6	4.5	1.1
Other	–	1.0	1.0

Source: Nanos Research.

have been as high as 37.1%). If the confidence intervals overlap, it is possible that the apparent losing party is actually ahead. In the end, when the intervals overlap—when the race is so close—the polls cannot identify a winner.

This was not the case, however, for the poll conducted on January 15, 2006. It predicted that the Conservative Party would win the federal election with 95% confidence. Indeed when the ballots were finally counted in the 2006 federal election, the parties wound up with percentages similar to the January 15 and January 22 polls. Table 6.7 provides a comparison of the last Nanos poll (January 22) prior to the election and the actual election results on January 23. Percentages are shown to the first decimal place to illustrate the accuracy of sample polls.

Liberals and Conservatives received 30.2% and 36.3% of the popular vote respectively, very close to the point estimates of 30.1% and 36.4% made in the January 22 poll. The difference between the poll and actual election results for both the Liberals and Conservatives was just 0.1%. The NDP, Bloc Québécois, and Green Party garnered 17.5%, 10.5%, and 4.5% of the vote, parameters that were within the range of the interval estimates for the last poll.

Stability in Popular Support. Once elected, a political party is not free of polls and confidence intervals. Since the federal election in January 2006, pollsters have tracked the parties' popularity by asking randomly selected samples of adult Canadians to choose their voting preferences, as illustrated in Figure 6.7. For purposes of clarity, only point estimates are shown, but you should remember that confidence interval estimates around these points would range about ±3% at the 95% confidence level (see Table 6.6).

FIGURE 6.7 2006 CANADIAN FEDERAL ELECTION RESULTS AND NANOS RESEARCH POLLING DATA AFTER THE ELECTION

Source: Nanos Research.

As observed by Nanos Research, public opinion was rather stable after the 2006 federal election (Figure 6.7). There were minor shifts in point estimates over the four polling dates, such as a decrease in popularity of the Conservative Party and an increase for the Liberal Party. However, if the 95% confidence intervals around the point estimates were considered, we would see an overlap in the intervals for the Conservative and Liberal Parties at each of the polling dates. Thus, statistically speaking, there would have been no significant shift in popular support for the two leading parties from November 2006 to May 2007.

Returning to the many controversies surrounding public-opinion polls, critics would argue that it is not a good thing to judge the government and its leader so continuously. To some extent, these approval ratings expose the prime minister and the governing party (and other political parties and leaders whose performance is similarly measured) to the whims of public sentiment and, at some level, could pressure them to cater to popular opinion and shape ("spin") their image to maintain support. However, information like that presented in Figure 6.7 supplies some interesting insights into the affairs not only of political institutions but also of society as a whole.

READING STATISTICS 4: Using Representative Samples to Track National Trends

Among other uses, the GSS can be used to track national trends and shifts in public opinion over time because many of the same questions are asked every few years. We demonstrate here how to assess trends in criminal victimization using the 1993, 1999, 2004, and 2009 General Social Surveys (GSS).

We considered two questions that measure perception of crime. Each question, asked in the 1993, 1999, 2004, and 2009 GSS, is as follows:

Q1.   Compared to other areas in Canada, do you think your neighbourhood has a higher amount of crime, about the same, or a lower amount of crime?

Q2.   Do you feel very safe, reasonably safe, somewhat unsafe, or very unsafe from crime walking alone in your area after dark?

Over this period, respondents were less likely to say that their neighbourhood had above-average crime and that they feel unsafe from crime after dark. Figure 1 shows that the point estimate for the proportion of those who think their neighbourhood has higher-than-average crime fell from 0.116 (or 11.6%) in 1993 to 0.076 (7.6%) in 2009, as did the proportion who felt unsafe from crime while walking after dark: 0.273 in 1993 to 0.129 in 2009.

To estimate the population parameters or the proportions for all Canadians, interval estimates were calculated using Formula 6.3. The results,

FIGURE 1   PROPORTION OF RESPONDENTS WHO SAID THEIR NEIGHBOURHOOD HAS HIGHER CRIME AND THEY FEEL UNSAFE WALKING ALONE AFTER DARK, 1993 TO 2009

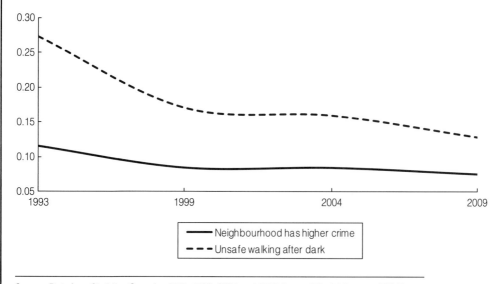

Source: Data from Statistics Canada, 1993, 1999, 2004 and 2009 General Social Surveys, PUMFs.

(continued next page)

READING STATISTICS 4: *(continued)*

expressed this time in percentages, are shown in Table 1. For example, we can conclude that at the 95% confidence level, between 12.2% and 13.6% (12.9 ± 0.7) of Canadians felt unsafe walking alone after dark in 2009. In conclusion, the trends in these data suggest that Canadians' perception of crime has generally declined over the last 16 years.

TABLE 1 95% CONFIDENCE INTERVAL OF PERCENTAGE WHO SAID NEIGHBOURHOOD HAS HIGHER CRIME AND THEY FEEL UNSAFE WALKING ALONE AFTER DARK, 1993, 1999, 2004, AND 2009

Year	Sample Size	Neighbourhood Has Higher Crime	Unsafe Walking after Dark
1993	11,960	11.6 ± 0.9	27.3 ± 0.9
1999	25,876	8.5 ± 0.6	17.1 ± 0.6
2004	23,766	8.5 ± 0.6	16.0 ± 0.6
2009	19,422	7.6 ± 0.7	12.9 ± 0.7

Source: Statistics Canada, 1993, 1999, 2004, and 2009 General Social Surveys, PUMFs.

SUMMARY

1. Population values can be estimated with sample values. With point estimates, a single sample statistic is used to estimate the corresponding population value. With confidence intervals, we estimate that the population value falls within a certain range of values.

2. Estimates based on sample statistics must be unbiased and relatively efficient. Of all the sample statistics, only means and proportions are unbiased. The means of the sampling distributions of these statistics are equal to the respective population values. Efficiency is largely a matter of sample size. The greater the sample size, the lower the value of the standard deviation of the sampling distribution, the more tightly clustered the sample outcomes will be around the mean of the sampling distribution, and the more efficient the estimate.

3. With point estimates, we estimate that the population value is the same as the sample statistic (either a mean or a proportion). With interval estimates, we construct a confidence interval, a range of values into which we estimate that the population value falls. The width of the interval is a function of the risk we are willing to take of being wrong (the alpha level) and the sample size. The interval widens as our probability of being wrong decreases and as sample size decreases.

4. A confidence interval can be depicted using an error bar graph. The middle of an error bar graph represents the sample statistic, and a vertical line above and below the sample statistic represents the upper and lower limits of the confidence interval.

5. The sample size needed to obtain a desired confidence interval can be determined prior to conducting a study. Sample size is determined by "rearranging" the formulas for confidence intervals.

SUMMARY OF FORMULAS

Confidence interval for a sample mean, large samples, population standard deviation known:

$$6.1 \quad c.i. = \overline{X} \pm Z\left(\frac{\sigma}{\sqrt{n}}\right)$$

Confidence interval for a sample mean, large samples, population standard deviation unknown:

$$6.2 \quad c.i. = \overline{X} \pm Z\left(\frac{s}{\sqrt{n-1}}\right)$$

Confidence interval for a sample proportion, large samples:

$$6.3 \quad c.i. = P_s \pm Z\sqrt{\frac{P_u(1 - P_u)}{n}}$$

Required sample size, for a mean

$$6.4 \quad n = \frac{Z^2 \times \sigma^2}{ME^2}$$

Required sample size, for a proportion

$$6.5 \quad n = \frac{\left(Z^2 \times P_u \times (1 - P_u)\right) + ME^2}{ME^2}$$

GLOSSARY

Alpha (α). The probability of error or the probability that a confidence interval does not contain the population value. Alpha levels are usually set at 0.10, 0.05, 0.01, or 0.001. (p. 152)

Bias. A criterion used to select sample statistics as estimators. A statistic is unbiased if the mean of its sampling distribution is equal to the population value of interest. (p. 149)

Confidence interval. An estimate of a population value in which a range of values is specified. (p. 149)

Confidence level. A frequently used alternative way of expressing alpha, the probability that an interval estimate will not contain the population value. Confidence levels of 90%, 95%, 99%, and 99.9%

correspond to alphas of 0.10, 0.05, 0.01, and 0.001, respectively. (p. 152)

Efficiency. The extent to which the sample outcomes are clustered around the mean of the sampling distribution. (p. 149)

Error bar. A graphic display device used to illustrate the confidence interval of a sample statistic. (p. 157)

Margin of error. The size of a confidence interval for a sample mean or sample proportion. It is also called the margin of sampling error, or just sampling error. (p. 149)

Point estimate. An estimate of a population value where a single value is specified. (p. 148)

MULTIMEDIA RESOURCES

 http://www.healeystatistics.nelson.com

Visit the companion website for the second Canadian edition of *Statistics: A Tool for Social Research* to access a wide range of student resources. Begin by clicking on the Student Resources section of the textbook's website to access review quizzes, flashcards, and other study tools.

PROBLEMS

6.1 For each set of sample outcomes below, construct the 95% confidence interval for estimating μ, the population mean.

a. $\overline{X} = 5.2$ **b.** $\overline{X} = 100$ **c.** $\overline{X} = 20$
   $s = 0.7$ $s = 9$ $s = 3$
   $n = 157$ $n = 620$ $n = 220$

d. $\overline{X} = 1{,}020$ **e.** $\overline{X} = 7.3$ **f.** $\overline{X} = 33$
   $s = 50$ $s = 1.2$ $s = 6$
   $n = 329$ $n = 105$ $n = 220$

6.2 For each set of sample outcomes below, construct the 99% confidence interval for estimating P_u.

a. $P_s = 0.14$ **b.** $P_s = 0.37$ **c.** $P_s = 0.79$
   $n = 100$ $n = 522$ $n = 121$

d. $P_s = 0.43$ **e.** $P_s = 0.40$ **f.** $P_s = 0.63$
   $n = 1049$ $n = 548$ $n = 300$

6.3 For each confidence level below, determine the corresponding Z score.

Confidence Level (%)	Alpha	Area beyond Z	Z score
95	0.05	0.0250	±1.96
94			
92			
97			
98			
99.9			

6.4 SW You have developed a series of questions to measure "burnout" in social workers. A random sample of 100 social workers working in the greater metropolitan area of Pearson, Ontario, has an average score of 10.3, with a standard deviation of 2.7. At the 95% level, what is your estimate of the average burnout score for the population as a whole? Construct an error bar to display your results.

6.5 SOC A researcher has gathered information from a random sample of 178 households. For each variable below, construct confidence intervals to estimate the population mean. Use the 90% level.

a. An average of 2.3 people resides in each household. Standard deviation is 0.35.

b. There was an average of 2.1 television sets ($s = 0.10$) and 0.78 telephones ($s = 0.55$) per household.

c. The households averaged 6.0 hours of television viewing per day ($s = 3.0$).

6.6 SOC A random sample of 100 television programs contained an average of 2.37 acts of physical violence per program. At the 99% level, what is your estimate of the population value? Construct an error bar to display your results.

$$\overline{X} = 2.37$$
$$s = 0.30$$
$$n = 100$$

6.7 SOC A random sample of 429 university students was interviewed about a number of matters.

a. They reported that they had spent an average of $178.23 on textbooks during the previous semester. If the sample standard deviation for these data is $15.78, construct an estimate of the population mean at the 99% level.

b. They also reported that they had visited the health services clinic an average of 1.5 times a semester. If the sample standard deviation is 0.3, construct an estimate of the population mean at the 99% level.

c. On the average, the sample had missed 2.8 days of classes per semester because of illness. If the sample standard deviation is 1.0, construct an estimate of the population mean at the 99% level.

d. On the average, the sample had missed 3.5 days of classes per semester for reasons other than illness. If the sample standard deviation is 1.5, construct an estimate of the population mean at the 99% level.

6.8 CJ A random sample of 500 residents of Pearson, Ontario, shows that exactly 50 of the respondents had been the victims of violent crime over the past year. Estimate the proportion of victims for the population as a whole, using the 90% confidence level. (*HINT: Calculate the sample proportion P_s before using Formula 6.3.*

Remember that proportions are equal to frequency divided by n.)

6.9 SOC The survey mentioned in problem 6.5 found that 25 of the 178 households consisted of unmarried couples who were living together. What is your estimate of the population proportion? Use the 95% level.

6.10 PA A random sample of 324 residents of a community revealed that 30% were very satisfied with the quality of trash collection. At the 99% level, what is your estimate of the population value?

6.11 SOC A random sample of 1,496 respondents of a major metropolitan area was questioned about a number of issues. Construct estimates for the population at the 90% level for each of the results reported below. Express the final confidence interval in percentages (e.g., "between 40 and 45% agreed that premarital sex was always wrong").

  a. When asked to agree or disagree with the statement "Explicit sexual books and magazines lead to rape and other sex crimes," 823 agreed.

  b. When asked to agree or disagree with the statement "Guns should be outlawed," 650 agreed.

  c. 375 of the sample agreed that marijuana should be legalized.

  d. 1,023 of the sample said that they had attended a religious service at least once within the past month.

  e. 800 agreed that public elementary schools should have sex education programs starting in grade 5.

6.12 SW A random sample of 100 patients treated in a program for alcoholism and drug dependency over the past 10 years was selected. It was determined that 53 of the patients had been readmitted to the program at least once. At the 95% level, construct an estimate for the population proportion.

6.13 For the sample data below, construct four different interval estimates of the population mean, one each for the 90%, 95%, 99%, and 99.9% level. What happens to the interval width as confidence level increases? Why?

$$\overline{X} = 100$$
$$s = 10$$
$$n = 500$$

6.14 For each of the three sample sizes below, construct the 95% confidence interval. Use a sample proportion of 0.40 throughout. What happens to interval width as sample size increases? Why?

$$P_s = 0.40$$
Sample A: $n = 100$
Sample B: $n = 1,000$
Sample C: $n = 10,000$

6.15 PS Two individuals are running for mayor of Pearson, Ontario. You conduct an election survey a week before the election and find that 51% of the respondents prefer candidate A. Can you predict a winner? Use the 99% level. *(HINT: In a two-candidate race, what percentage of the vote would the winner need? Does the confidence interval indicate that candidate A has a sure margin of victory? Remember that while the population parameter is probably ($\alpha = 0.01$) in the confidence interval, it may be anywhere in the interval.)*

$$P_s = 0.51$$
$$n = 578$$

6.16 SOC The World Values Survey is administered periodically to random samples from societies around the globe. Below are listed the number of respondents in each nation who said that they are "very happy." Compute sample proportions and construct confidence interval estimates for each nation at the 95% level.

Nation	Number "very happy"	Sample Size	Confidence Interval
Great Britain	496	1,495	
Japan	505	1,476	
Brazil	329	1,492	
Nigeria	695	1,471	
China	338	1,493	

Source: Data from EUROPEAN AND WORLD VALUES SURVEYS FOUR-WAVE INTEGRATED DATA FILE, 1981–2004, v.20060423, 2006. The European Values Study Foundation and World Values Survey Association. Aggregate File Producers: ASEP/JDS, Madrid, Spain/ Tilburg University, Tilburg, the Netherlands. Aggregate File Distributors: ASEP/JDS and ZA, Cologne, Germany.

6.17 | SOC | The fraternities and sororities at Algebra University have been plagued by declining membership over the past several years and want to know if the incoming first-year students will be a fertile recruiting ground. Not having enough money to survey all 1,600 first-year students they commission you to survey the interests of a random sample. You find that 35 of your 150 respondents are "extremely" interested in social clubs. At the 95% level, what is your estimate of the number of first-year students who would be extremely interested? (*HINT: The high and low values of your final confidence interval are proportions. How can proportions also be expressed as numbers?*)

6.18 | SOC | You are the consumer-affairs reporter for a daily newspaper. Part of your job is to investigate the claims of manufacturers, and you are particularly suspicious of a new economy car that the manufacturer claims will get 3.0 L/100 km. After checking the mileage figures for a random sample of 120 owners of this car, you find an average L/100 km of 3.1 with a standard deviation of 3.7. At the 99% level, do your results tend to confirm or refute the manufacturer's claims?

6.19 | SOC | The results listed below are from a survey given to a random sample of the Canadian public. For each sample statistic, construct a confidence interval estimate of the population parameter at the 95% confidence level. Sample size (n) is 2,987 throughout.

a. The average occupational prestige score was 43.87, with a standard deviation of 13.52.

b. The respondents reported watching an average of 2.86 hours of TV per day with a standard deviation of 2.20.

c. The average number of children was 1.81, with a standard deviation of 1.67.

d. Of the 2,987 respondents, 876 identified themselves as Catholic.

e. Five hundred thirty-five of the respondents said that they had never married.

f. The proportion of respondents who said they voted for the Conservative Party of Canada in the 2006 federal election was 0.36.

g. When asked about capital punishment, 2,425 of the respondents said that they opposed the death penalty for murder.

SPSS for Windows

Using SPSS for Windows to Produce Confidence Intervals with the 2006 Census

The demonstrations and exercises below use the shortened version of the 2006 Census data. Start SPSS for Windows and open the *Census.sav* file.

SPSS DEMONSTRATION 6.1 Using the Explore Command for Constructing Confidence Intervals for Sample Means

The **Explore** procedure can be used to construct confidence intervals for the sample mean. The **Explore** command produces many of the same summary statistics and graphical displays produced by the **Frequencies** and **Descriptives** procedures, but offers additional features. Here we will use **Explore** to compute the confidence interval for the mean of *totinc* (total income).

From the main menu, click **Analyze**, **Descriptive Statistics**, and **Explore**. The **Explore** dialog box will open. Use the cursor to find *totinc* in the list on the left and click the right-arrow button to transfer the variable to the **Dependent List** box.

SPSS by default uses the 95% confidence level, which in fact we want to use for this demonstration. To request another level, you can click on the **Statistics** button at the top of the **Explore** dialog box, and the **Explore: Statistics** dialog box will open. Type the desired level (e.g., 90%, 95%, or 99%) in the textbox next to "**Confidence Interval for Mean**," and click **Continue**. You will return to the **Explore** dialog box, where you might want to click the **Statistics** radio button within the **Display** section. Otherwise, SPSS will produce both summary statistics and plots (i.e., graphical displays).

Finally, click **OK,** and the output below will be produced:

Descriptives

			Statistic	Std. Error
Total income of individual	Mean		33767.06	1264.854
	95% Confidence Interval for Mean	Lower Bound	31285.99	
		Upper Bound	36248.13	
	5% Trimmed Mean		28057.06	
	Median		24000.00	
	Variance		2399782692	
	Std. Deviation		48987.577	
	Minimum		0	
	Maximum		866341	
	Range		866341	
	Interquartile Range		33000	
	Skewness		8.988	.063
	Kurtosis		128.318	.126

The "Descriptives" output table contains a variety of statistics used to measure central tendency and dispersion. Some of these statistics are not covered in this textbook. If you wish to explore them, please use SPSS's online Help facility. In this section, we focus on parts of the table related to confidence intervals for the sample mean: the values for the "Lower Bound" and "Upper Bound" of the "95% Confidence Interval for Mean." The lower limit of our interval estimate is 31,285.99 and the upper limit is 36,248.13. Another way to state the interval would be

$$31{,}285.99 \le \mu \le 36{,}248.13$$

We estimate that Canadians, on average, have a total income between $31,285.99 and $36,248.13. Because alpha was set at the 0.05 level, this estimate has a 5% chance of being wrong (i.e., of not containing the population mean for total income).

We should point out that the values in your output may contain numbers with the letter "E" (sometimes expressed as lower case "e"). This stands for "exponent," or the number of tens you multiply a number by. SPSS will use the exponent to represent a number with too many digits to show in the output.

For example, the value 33,767.06 can be written in exponent form as 3.4E4. In other words, 3.4 multiplied by 10 four times (or 10 raised to the fourth power) is 34,000. The exact value of 33,767.06 is not returned because the exponent is rounded off to one decimal place (i.e., 3.4). A convenient way to do this calculation is to just move the decimal point to the right four places (3.4 to the right four places equals 34,000). A negative exponent means you have to move the decimal point to the left (e.g., 3.4-E4 means 3.4 to the left four places or 0.00034).

If the exponent is shown in your output, and you wish to instead view the regular value (e.g., 33,767.06), right-click on any part of the table in the **Output** window, and click **Edit Content**. There are two options: editing "**In Viewer**" (**Output** window) and "**In Separate Window**" (SPSS **Chart Editor** window). Let's select **In Separate Window** option; the SPSS **Chart Editor** window, titled **SPSS Pivot Table Descriptives**, will appear. This window gives you a wide array of options for the final appearance of the table. Next, use your mouse to increase the width of the **Statistics** column by dragging the table line that separates the **Statistics** and **Std. Error** columns to the right, until the exponent (e.g., 3.4E4) changes to regular form (33,767.06). After you finish editing, close the **SPSS Pivot Table Descriptives** window to return to the **Output** window, where you can see the changes.

SPSS DEMONSTRATION 6.2 The Error Bar Graph

Here we'll produce an error bar graph for the confidence interval for the mean of total income (*totinc*). Click **Graphs**, **Legacy Dialogs**, and then **Error Bar**. The **Error Bars** dialog box appears with two choices for the type of graph we want. The **Simple** option is already highlighted, and this is the one we want. At the bottom of the **Error Bars** dialog box, click the "**Summaries of separate variables**" radio button within the **Data in Chart Are** box, and then click **Define**.

The **Define Simple Error Bar** dialog box appears with variable names listed on the left. Use the cursor to find *totinc* in the list on the left and click the right-arrow button to transfer the variable to the **Error Bars** box. In the **Bars Represent** box, you have the option to select whether the error bar represents the confidence interval of the mean, the standard error of mean, or the standard deviation. Let's choose "**Confidence interval for mean**," the option that is already selected. You can also enter the desired confidence level into the **Level** box. We'll use 95% level, which is the default setting. Click **OK**, and the following error bar graph will be produced:

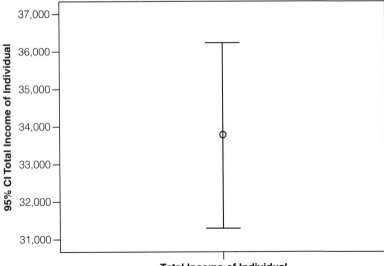

The error bar provides an illustration of the exact information given in the "Descriptives" output in Demonstration 6.1. The mean income of sample respondents is about $34,000 (marked by the small circle on the bar), and we estimate, at the 95% level of confidence (indicated by the length of the bar), that the mean income of all Canadians is somewhere between approximately $31,300 (the small horizontal line at the bottom of the bar) and $36,200 (the small horizontal line at the top of the bar).

DEMONSTRATION 6.3 Generating Statistical Information for Use in Constructing Confidence Intervals for Sample Proportions

Unlike the **Explore** procedure for constructing confidence intervals for the sample mean, SPSS does not provide a program specifically for constructing intervals for the sample proportion. However, we can use SPSS to calculate the sample statistics, namely proportions, on which the interval estimates are based. Once you know these sample statistics, the confidence interval for the sample proportion is easily computed.

To illustrate this process we'll construct a confidence interval for *marst* (legal marital status). While we can estimate the population parameter for any or all of the categories of this variable, let's estimate the proportion of the population that is married.

First, calculate the sample proportion using the **Frequencies** command. From the menu bar, click **Analyze, Descriptive Statistics**, and **Frequencies**. Find *marst* in the left-hand box and move it to **Variable(s)** box. Click **OK**. The output for *marst* will look like this:

Legal marital status

		Frequency	Percent	Valid Percent	Cumulative Percent
Valid	Divorced	116	7.7	7.7	7.7
	Legally married (and not separated)	671	44.7	44.7	52.5
	Separated, but still legally married	41	2.7	2.7	55.2
	Never legally married (single)	593	39.5	39.5	94.7
	Widowed	79	5.3	5.3	100.0
	Total	1500	100.0	100.0	

Second, substitute the values into Formula 6.3, not forgetting to change the percentages to proportions. Thus, using the 95% confidence level, we would have:

$$\text{c.i.} = P_s \pm Z \sqrt{\frac{P_u \left(1 - P_u\right)}{n}}$$

$$\text{c.i.} = 0.45 \pm 1.96 \sqrt{\frac{(0.5)(.05)}{1,500}}$$

$$\text{c.i.} = 0.45 \pm (1.96)(0.013)$$

$$\text{c.i.} = 0.45 \pm 0.03$$

Changing back to percentages, we can estimate that between 42% (45% − 3%) and 48% (45% + 3%) of Canadians are married.

Exercises (using *Census.sav*)

6.1 Use the **Explore** command to get the 95% confidence interval for *hrswrk* and *wkswrk*. Express the confidence intervals in words, as if you were reporting results in a newspaper story.

6.2 Use the **Error Bar** command to get an error bar graph for each variable in Exercise 6.1. Write a sentence or two of interpretation for each graph.

6.3 Use the **Frequencies** command to get sample proportions (convert the percentages in the frequency distributions) to estimate the population parameter for each of the following: proportion that is "First generation" immigrant (*genstat*) as well as proportion with a "Bachelor's degree " (*hdgree*). Use the 95% confidence level. Express the confidence intervals in words, as if you were reporting results in a newspaper story.

Hypothesis Testing I
The One-Sample Case

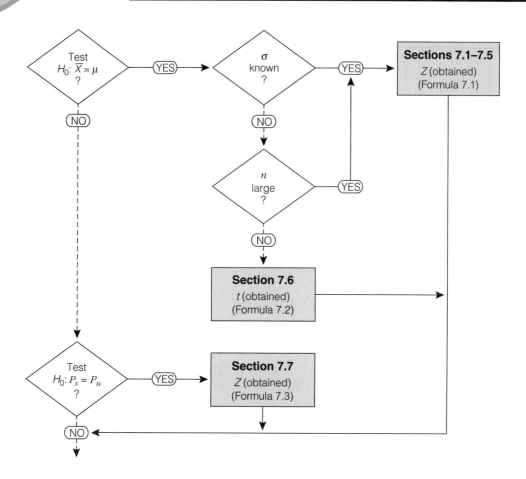

5. Test the significance of single-sample means and proportions using the five-step model and correctly interpret the results.

6. Explain the difference between one- and two-tailed tests and specify when each is appropriate.

7. Define and explain Type I and Type II errors and relate each to the selection of an alpha level.

8. Conduct a single-sample hypothesis test using a confidence interval.

7.1 INTRODUCTION

Chapter 6 introduced the techniques for estimating population parameters from sample statistics. In Chapters 7 through 10, we will investigate a second application of inferential statistics called **hypothesis testing** or **significance testing**. In this chapter, the techniques for hypothesis testing in the one-sample case will be introduced. These procedures could be used in situations such as the following:

1. A researcher has selected a sample of 789 senior citizens who live in a particular province and also has information on the percentage of the entire population of the province that was victimized by crime during the past year. Are older citizens, as represented by this sample, more or less likely to be victimized than the population in general?

2. Are the GPAs of university varsity athletes different from the GPAs of the student body as a whole? To investigate, the academic records of a random sample of 105 student athletes from a large university are compared with the overall GPA of all students.

3. The Law School Admission Test (LSAT) is a standardized test required for admission to most Canadian and U.S. law schools. The LSAT assesses reading and verbal reasoning skills and, along with GPA, is considered a critical factor in determining admission to law school. Companies offer an LSAT preparation (i.e., training) course, for a fee, with the claim that graduates of their course on average obtain higher scores on the LSAT than the general population of LSAT test takers. To test this claim, you randomly sample 100 graduates of LSAT training courses and find that, on average, those in the sample have higher LSAT scores than the population of LSAT writers as a whole. Do training-course graduates score higher than LSAT writers in general?

In each of these situations, we have randomly selected samples (of senior citizens, athletes, or graduates of the LSAT training course) that we want to compare to a population (the entire province, student body, or community of LSAT writers). Note that we are not interested in the sample per se but in the larger group from which it was selected (*all* senior citizens in the province, *all* athletes on this campus, or *all* graduates of the LSAT training course). Specifically, we want to know if the groups represented by the samples are different from the populations on a specific trait or variable (victimization rates, GPAs, or LSAT scores).

Of course, it would be better if we could include all senior citizens, athletes, or graduates of the LSAT training course rather than these smaller samples. However, as we have seen, researchers usually do not have the resources necessary to test everyone in a large group and must use random samples instead. In these situations, conclusions will be based on a comparison of the sample (which substitutes for the larger group) and the population. For example, if we found that the rate of victimization for the *sample* of senior citizens was higher than the provincial rate, we might conclude that *all* senior citizens are significantly more likely to be crime victims than the general population. The word "significantly" is a key word: It means that the difference between the sample's rate of victimization and the population's rate is very unlikely to be caused by random chance alone. In other words, if this difference is "significant," *all* senior citizens (not just the 789 people in the sample) have a higher victimization rate than the province as a whole. Alternatively, if we found little difference between the victimization rates of the sample and the population, we would conclude that senior citizens (*all* senior citizens) are essentially the same as other citizens in terms of their vulnerability to crime.

Thus, we can use samples to represent larger groups (senior citizens, athletes, or graduates of the LSAT training course) and compare and contrast the characteristics of the sample with the population and be extremely confident in our conclusions. Remember, however, that the EPSEM procedure for drawing random samples does not guarantee representativeness and, thus, there will always be a small amount of uncertainty in our conclusions. One of the great advantages of inferential statistics, however, is that we will be able to estimate the probability of error and evaluate our decisions accordingly.

7.2 AN OVERVIEW OF HYPOTHESIS TESTING

We will begin with a general overview of hypothesis testing, using our third research situation above as an example. Then, we will introduce more technical considerations and proper terminology throughout the remainder of the chapter. Let us examine this situation in detail. The main question here is, "Do graduates of the LSAT preparation course in Canada have an average LSAT score that is higher than other Canadians who write the LSAT?" In other words, the researcher wants to compare the LSAT scores of *all* graduates (the Canadian graduates of the LSAT training course) with the LSAT scores of all test takers (the entire Canadian population of LSAT test takers). If she had complete information for both of these groups (all graduates of the LSAT preparation course and all LSAT writers), she could answer the question easily and completely.

The problem is that the researcher does not have the time and/or money to gather information on the thousands of people who have graduated from the LSAT preparation course in Canada. Instead, she has drawn a random sample, following the rule of EPSEM, of 100 graduates from records provided by the companies offering the LSAT training course in Canada. Information on LSAT scores for the sample of LSAT preparation-course graduates and the entire population of LSAT test takers is as follows:

Entire Canadian Population of LSAT Test Takers*	Sample of Canadian Graduates from LSAT Preparation Course
$\mu = 151$	$\overline{X} = 154$
$\sigma = 9$	$n = 100$

*Source: Susan P. Dalessandro, Laura A. Marcus, Lynda M. Reese, *LSAT Performance with Regional, Gender, and Racial/Ethnic Breakdowns*, (2006). http://www.lsac.org/lsacresources/Research/TR/TR-10-03.pdf.

Information from the Law School Admission Council, the organization that administers the LSAT, shows that the population of test takers in Canada has a mean LSAT score of 151. At 154, the average LSAT score for the sample is higher than the average score for the entire population. (To put this information in context, there are 101 multiple-choice questions on the LSAT. One point is given for each question answered correctly. Total test scores, ranging from 0 to 101, are converted into an LSAT score ranging from 120, the lowest possible score, to 180, the highest possible score). Although it is tempting, we cannot make any conclusions yet because we are working with a random sample of the population in which we are interested, not the population itself (all graduates of the LSAT preparation course).

Figure 7.1 should clarify these relationships. The entire Canadian population of LSAT test takers is symbolized by the largest circle because it is the largest group. The Canadian population of graduates of the LSAT training

FIGURE 7.1 A TEST OF HYPOTHESIS FOR SINGLE SAMPLE MEANS

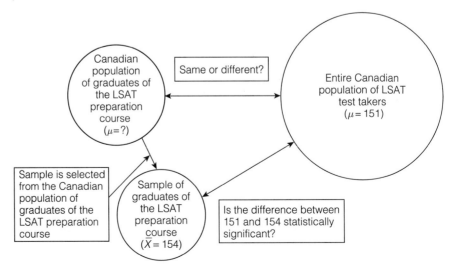

course is also symbolized by a large circle because it is a sizable group, although only a fraction of the population of LSAT writers as a whole. The random sample of 100 Canadian graduates of the LSAT training course, the smallest of the three groups, is symbolized by the smallest circle.

The arrows between the circles show how they are connected in this research situation. The researcher wants to know if the average LSAT score of all graduates of the preparation course is the "same or different" from the average LSAT score of the entire population of LSAT writers. Instead of comparing all graduates (a group that is too large to gather information on) with the entire population of LSAT writers, the researcher compares the LSAT scores of a random sample of graduates with the entire population.

We observe that the mean of the sample is higher than the mean of the population (154 vs. 151). This suggests that graduates of the preparation course do better on the LSAT. However, the graduates are represented by a random sample and we know that even the most carefully chosen sample may, on rare occasion, be unrepresentative. Does the difference between the *sample mean* and the *population mean* reflect a real difference between *all* graduates of the preparation course and the entire population of LSAT writers? Or was this difference caused by mere random chance? This is the question that a test of hypothesis is designed to answer. In other words, there are two possible explanations for the difference, and we will consider them one at a time.

The first explanation, which we will label explanation A, is that the difference between the population mean of 151 and the sample mean of 154 reflects a real difference in LSAT scores between all graduates and the entire population. The difference is "statistically significant" in the sense that it is very unlikely to have occurred by random chance alone. If explanation A is true, the population of all graduates of the preparation course is different from the entire population of LSAT writers. The sample did *not* come from a population with a mean LSAT score of 151.

The second explanation, or explanation B, is that the observed difference between sample and population means was caused by mere random chance. There is no important difference between graduates and the population of LSAT writers as a whole and the difference between the sample mean of 154 and the population mean of 151 is trivial and due to random chance. If explanation B is true, the population of LSAT preparation-course graduates is just like everyone else and has a mean LSAT score of 151.

Which explanation is correct? As long as we are working with a sample rather than the entire group, we cannot know the answer to this question for sure. However, we can set up a decision-making procedure so conservative that one of the two explanations can be chosen, with the knowledge that the probability of choosing the incorrect explanation is very low.

This decision-making process, in broad outline, begins with the assumption that explanation B is correct. Symbolically, the assumption that the mean LSAT score for all graduates of the preparation course is the same as the mean LSAT score for the population of LSAT writers as a whole can be stated as

$$\mu = 151$$

Remember that this μ refers to the mean for all LSAT preparation-course graduates, not just the 100 in the sample. This assumption, $\mu = 151$, can be tested statistically.

If explanation B (the population of graduates of the preparation course is not different from the population of LSAT writers as a whole and has a μ of 151) is true, then the probability of getting the observed sample outcome ($\overline{X} = 154$) can be found. Let us add an objective decision rule in advance. If the odds of getting the observed difference are less than 0.05 (5 out of 100, or 1 in 20), we will reject explanation B. If on the other hand, this explanation were true, a difference of this size (151 vs. 154) would be a very rare event, and in hypothesis testing, we always bet against rare events.

How can we estimate the probability of the observed sample outcome ($\overline{X} = 154$) if explanation B is correct? This value can be determined by using our knowledge of the sampling distribution of all possible sample outcomes. Looking back at the information we have and applying the Central Limit Theorem (see Chapter 5), we can assume that the sampling distribution is normal in shape, has a mean of 151 (because $\mu_{\overline{x}} = \mu$), and has a standard deviation of $9/\sqrt{100}$ because $\sigma_{\overline{x}} = \sigma/\sqrt{n}$. We also know that the standard normal distribution can be interpreted as a distribution of probabilities (see Chapter 4) and that the particular sample outcome noted above ($\overline{X} = 154$) is one of thousands of possible sample outcomes. The sampling distribution, with the sample outcome noted, is depicted in Figure 7.2.

Using our knowledge of the standardized normal distribution, we can add further useful information to this sampling distribution of sample

FIGURE 7.2 THE SAMPLING DISTRIBUTION OF ALL POSSIBLE SAMPLE MEANS

$\mu_{\overline{X}}$
(151)

154

FIGURE 7.3   THE SAMPLING DISTRIBUTION OF ALL POSSIBLE SAMPLE MEANS, WITH REJECTION AREAS IN SHADE

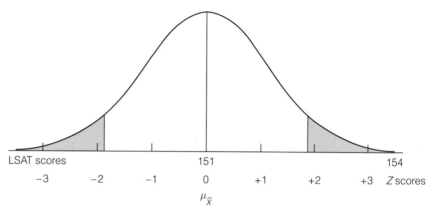

means. Specifically, with Z scores, we can depict the decision rule stated previously: any sample outcome with probability less than 0.05 (assuming that explanation B is true) will cause us to reject explanation B. The probability of 0.05 can be translated into an area and divided equally into the upper and lower tails of the sampling distribution. Using Appendix A, we find that the Z-score equivalent of this area is ± 1.96. The areas and Z scores are depicted in Figure 7.3.

The decision rule can now be rephrased. Any sample outcome falling in the shaded areas depicted in Figure 7.3 by definition has a probability of occurrence of less than 0.05. Such an outcome would be a rare event and would cause us to reject explanation B.

All that remains is to translate our sample outcome into a Z score so that we can see where it falls on the curve. To do this, we use the standard formula for locating any particular raw score under a normal distribution. When we use known or empirical distributions, this formula is expressed as

$$Z = \frac{X_i - \overline{X}}{s}$$

Or, to find the equivalent Z score for any raw score, subtract the mean of the distribution from the raw score and divide by the standard deviation of the distribution. Because we are now concerned with the sampling distribution of all sample means rather than an empirical distribution, the symbols in the formula will change, but the form remains exactly the same:

FORMULA 7.1
$$Z = \frac{\overline{X} - \mu}{\sigma/\sqrt{n}}$$

Or, to find the equivalent Z score for any sample mean, subtract the mean of the sampling distribution, which is equal to the population mean or μ, from the sample mean and divide by the standard deviation of the sampling distribution.

FIGURE 7.4   THE SAMPLING DISTRIBUTION OF SAMPLE MEANS WITH THE SAMPLE OUTCOME ($\overline{X}$ = 154)
NOTED IN Z SCORES, WITH REJECTION AREAS IN SHADE

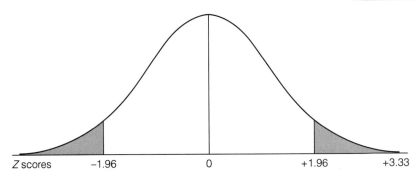

| Z scores | −1.96 | 0 | +1.96 | +3.33 |

Recalling the data given on this problem, we can now find the Z-score equivalent of the sample mean.

$$Z = \frac{154 - 151}{9/\sqrt{100}}$$

$$Z = \frac{3}{0.90}$$

$$Z = +3.33$$

In Figure 7.4, this Z score of +3.33 is noted on the distribution of all possible sample means and we see that the sample outcome does fall in the shaded area. If explanation B is true, this particular sample outcome has a probability of occurrence of less than 0.05. The sample outcome ($\overline{X}$ = 154 or Z = +3.33) would therefore be rare if explanation B was true, and the researcher may reject explanation B. If explanation B were true, this sample outcome would be extremely unlikely. The sample of 100 graduates of the LSAT preparation course comes from a population that is significantly different from the population of LSAT writers as a whole on LSAT scoring. Or, to put it another way, the sample does not come from a population that has a mean LSAT score of 151.

Keep in mind that our decisions in significance testing are based on information gathered from random samples. On rare occasions, a sample may not be representative of the population from which it was selected. The decision-making process outlined above has a very high probability of resulting in correct decisions, but, as long as we must work with samples rather than populations, we face an element of risk. That is, the decision to reject explanation B might be incorrect if this sample happens to be one of the few that is unrepresentative of the population of graduates of the LSAT training course. One important strength of hypothesis testing is that the probability of making an incorrect decision can be estimated. In the example at hand, explanation B was rejected and the probability of this decision being incorrect is 0.05—the decision rule established at the beginning of the process. To say that the probability of rejecting explanation B incorrectly is 0.05 means that, if we repeated this same test an infinite number of times, we would incorrectly reject explanation B only 5 times out of every 100.

7.3 THE FIVE-STEP MODEL FOR HYPOTHESIS TESTING

All the formal elements and concepts used in hypothesis testing were surreptitiously sneaked into the preceding discussion. This section presents their proper names and introduces a **five-step model** for organizing all hypothesis testing:

Step 1. Making assumptions and meeting test requirements

Step 2. Stating the null hypothesis

Step 3. Selecting the sampling distribution and establishing the critical region

Step 4. Computing the test statistic

Step 5. Making a decision and interpreting the results of the test

We will look at each step individually, using the LSAT problem from Section 7.2 as an example throughout.

Step 1. Making Assumptions and Meeting Test Requirements. Any application of statistics requires that certain assumptions be made, and all tests of hypotheses have certain requirements that must be met. Specifically, three criteria have to be satisfied when conducting a test of hypothesis with a single sample mean. First, all tests of hypothesis must be based on a random sample that has been selected according to the rules of EPSEM (see Chapter 5). Second, to justify computation of a mean, the variable being tested must be interval-ratio in level of measurement. Finally, we must assume that the sampling distribution of all possible sample means is normal in shape so that we may use the standardized normal distribution to find areas under the sampling distribution. We can be sure that this assumption is satisfied by using large samples (see the Central Limit Theorem in Chapter 5).

Usually, we will summarize these deliberations in abbreviated form as a mathematical model for the test. For example:

> Model: Random sampling
> Level of measurement is interval-ratio
> Sampling distribution is normal

Step 2. Stating the Null Hypothesis (H_0). The **null hypothesis** is the formal name for explanation B and is always a statement of "no difference." The exact form of the null hypothesis will vary depending on the test being conducted. In the single-sample case, the null hypothesis states that the sample comes from a population with a certain characteristic. In our example, the null hypothesis is that the population of LSAT preparation-course graduates is "no different" from the population of LSAT writers as a whole, that their average LSAT score is also 151, and that the difference between 151 and the sample mean of 154 is caused by random chance. Symbolically, the null hypothesis would be stated as

$$H_0: \mu = 151$$

where μ refers to the mean of the population of graduates of the LSAT preparation course. The null hypothesis is the central element in any test of hypothesis because the entire process is aimed at rejecting or failing to reject the H_0.

Usually, the researcher believes that the difference is significant and wants to reject the null hypothesis. At this point in the five-step model, the researcher's belief is stated in a **research hypothesis (H_1)**, a statement that directly contradicts the null hypothesis. Thus, the researcher's goal in hypothesis testing is often to gather evidence for the research hypothesis by rejecting the null hypothesis.

The research hypothesis can be stated in several ways. One form would simply assert that the population from which the sample was selected did not have a certain characteristic or, in terms of our example, had a mean that was not equal to a specific value

$$(H_1: \mu \neq 151)$$

where $\neq$ means "not equal to"

Symbolically, this statement asserts that the sample does not come from a population with a mean of 151, or that the population of graduates of the LSAT preparation course is different from the population of LSAT writers as a whole. The research hypothesis is enclosed in parentheses to emphasize that it has no formal standing or role in the hypothesis-testing process (except, as we shall see in the next section, in choosing between one-tailed and two-tailed tests). It serves as a reminder of what the researcher believes to be the truth.

Step 3. Selecting the Sampling Distribution and Establishing the Critical Region. The sampling distribution is the probabilistic yardstick against which a particular sample outcome is measured. By assuming that the null hypothesis is true (and *only* by this assumption), we can attach values to the mean and standard deviation of the sampling distribution and thus measure the probability of any specific sample outcome. There are several different sampling distributions, but for now we will confine our attention to the sampling distribution described by the standard normal curve as summarized in Appendix A.

The **critical region** consists of the areas under the sampling distribution that include unlikely sample outcomes. Prior to the test of hypothesis, we must define what we mean by *unlikely*. That is, we must specify in advance those sample outcomes so unlikely that they will lead us to reject the H_0. This decision rule will establish the critical region or **region of rejection**. The word *region* is used because, essentially, we are describing those areas under the sampling distribution that contain unlikely sample outcomes. In the example above, this area corresponded to a Z score of ± 1.96, called **Z (critical)**, which was graphically displayed in Figure 7.4. The shaded area is the critical region. Any sample outcome for which the Z-score equivalent fell in this area (i.e., below -1.96 or above $+1.96$) would have caused us to reject the null hypothesis.

By convention, the size of the critical region is reported as alpha (α), the proportion of all of the area included in the critical region. In the example above, our **alpha level** was 0.05. Other commonly used alphas are 0.10, 0.01, and 0.001.

In abbreviated form, all the decisions made in this step are noted below. The critical region is noted by the Z scores that mark its beginnings.

$$\text{Sampling distribution} = Z \text{ distribution}$$
$$\alpha = 0.05$$
$$Z(\text{critical}) = \pm 1.96$$

(For practice in finding Z (critical) scores, see problem 7.1a.)

Step 4. **Computing the Test Statistic.** To evaluate the probability of any given sample outcome, the sample value must be converted into a Z score. Solving the equation for Z-score equivalents is called computing the **test statistic**, and the resultant value will be referred to as **Z (obtained)** in order to differentiate the test statistic from the critical region. In our example above, we found a Z(obtained) of $+3.33$. *(For practice in computing obtained Z scores for means, see problems 7.1c, 7.2 to 7.7, and 7.15e and f.)*

Step 5. **Making a Decision and Interpreting the Results of the Test.** As the last step in the hypothesis-testing process, the test statistic is compared with the critical region. If the test statistic falls into the critical region, our decision will be to reject the null hypothesis. If the test statistic does not fall into the critical region, we fail to reject the null hypothesis. In our example, the two values were

$$Z(\text{critical}) = \pm 1.96$$
$$Z(\text{obtained}) = +3.33$$

and we saw that the Z(obtained) fell in the critical region (see Figure 7.4). Our decision was to reject the null hypothesis which stated that graduates of the LSAT preparation course have a mean LSAT score of 151 or that there is no difference between LSAT preparation-course graduates and LSAT writers as a whole. When we reject this null hypothesis, we are saying that graduates do *not* have a mean LSAT score of 151 and that there *is* a difference

Application 7.1

Despite many characteristics favourable to labour-market success, such as better than average education and health, studies show that recent immigrants to Canada (those who have been in Canada for less than 10 years) face many obstacles and challenges in the labour market. We know that, based on the 2001 Census, the mean income of the Canadian population of full-time workers (30 hours or more per week) was $38,728. A random sample of 336 recent immigrants employed full-time, from the Survey of Labour and Income Dynamics (a Statistics Canada–administered survey on labour-market activity and income), reveals an average income of $28,096 with a standard deviation of $18,410 in 2001. Are these earnings of recent immigrants significantly different from the population of full-time workers as a whole? We will use the five-step model to organize the decision-making process.

Step 1. Making Assumptions and Meeting Test Requirements.

Model: Random sampling
Level of measurement is interval-ratio
Sampling distribution is normal

From the information given (this is a large sample with $n > 100$ and income is an interval-ratio variable), we can conclude that the model assumptions and test requirements are satisfied.

Step 2. Stating the Null Hypothesis (H_0). The null hypothesis says that the average income of *all* recent immigrants to Canada is equal to the national average. In symbols:

$$H_0: \mu = 38{,}728$$

The question does not specify a direction: it only asks if the incomes of recent immigrants are "different from" (not higher or lower than) the national average. This suggests a two-tailed test:

$$(H_1: \mu \neq 38{,}728)$$

Step 3. Selecting the Sampling Distribution and Establishing the Critical Region.

$$\text{Sampling distribution} = Z \text{ distribution}$$
$$\alpha = 0.05$$
$$Z(\text{critical}) = \pm 1.96$$

Step 4. Computing the Test Statistic. The necessary information for conducting a test of the null hypothesis is

Recent Immigrants	Nation
$\overline{X} = 28{,}096$	$\mu = 38{,}728$
$s = 18{,}410$	
$n = 336$	

The test statistic, $Z(\text{obtained})$, would be

$$Z(\text{obtained}) = \frac{\overline{X} - \mu}{s/\sqrt{n - 1}}$$

$$Z(\text{obtained}) = \frac{28{,}096 - 38{,}728}{18{,}410/\sqrt{336 - 1}}$$

$$Z(\text{obtained}) = \frac{-10{,}632}{18{,}410/\sqrt{335}}$$

$$Z(\text{obtained}) = \frac{-10.632}{1{,}006}$$

$$Z(\text{obtained}) = -10.57$$

Step 5. Making a Decision and Interpreting the Results of the Test. With alpha set at 0.05, the critical region would begin at $Z(\text{critical}) = \pm 1.96$. With an obtained Z score of -10.57, the null would be rejected. This means that the difference between the incomes of recent immigrants to Canada and the incomes of Canadians as a whole is statistically significant. The difference is so large that we may conclude that it did not occur by random chance. The decision to reject the null hypothesis has a 0.05 probability of being wrong.

Source: Data from Statistics Canada, *2001 Canadian Census*, individual PUMF, and *2001 Survey of Labour and Income Dynamics*, individual PUMF.

between them and the population of LSAT writers as a whole. The difference between the sample mean of 154 and the mean of 151 for the entire population of LSAT writers is statistically significant or unlikely to be caused by random chance alone. In terms of LSAT score, graduates of the LSAT preparation course are different from the population of LSAT writers as a whole.

Note that there are two parts to step 5. First you make a decision about the null hypothesis: If the test statistic falls in the critical region, reject H_0. If the test statistic does not fall in the critical region, we fail to reject the H_0. Second, and just as importantly, you need to interpret the results of the test and say what your decision means. In this case, the null hypothesis was rejected: there is a significant difference between the sample mean and the mean for the entire population of LSAT writers and, therefore, graduates of the LSAT preparation course are different from the population of LSAT writers as a whole.

This five-step model will serve us as a framework for decision making throughout the hypothesis-testing chapters. The exact nature and method of expression for our decisions will be different for different situations. However, familiarity with the five-step model will assist you in mastering this material by providing a common frame of reference for all significance testing.

7.4 ONE-TAILED AND TWO-TAILED TESTS OF HYPOTHESIS

The five-step model for hypothesis testing is fairly rigid, and the researcher has little room for making choices. Nonetheless, the researcher must still make two crucial decisions. First, he or she must decide between a one-tailed and a two-tailed test. Second, an alpha level must be selected. In this section, we will discuss the former decision and, in Section 7.5, the latter.

The choice between a one- and two-tailed test is based on the researcher's expectations about the population from which the sample was selected. These expectations are reflected in the research hypothesis (H_1), which is contradictory to the null hypothesis and usually states what the researcher believes to be "the truth." In most situations, the researcher will wish to support the research hypothesis by rejecting the null hypothesis.

The format for the research hypothesis may take either of two forms, depending on the relationship between what the null hypothesis states and what the researcher believes to be the truth. The null hypothesis states that the population has a specific characteristic. In the example that has served us throughout this chapter, the null hypothesis stated that the "population of graduates of the LSAT preparation course have the *same* mean LSAT score (151) as the entire population of LSAT writers." The researcher might believe that the population of graduates actually scores *lower* on the LSAT (their population mean is *lower than* the value stated in the null hypothesis), *higher* on the LSAT (their population mean is *greater than* the value stated in the null hypothesis), or he or she might be unsure about the direction of the difference.

If the researcher is unsure about the direction, the research hypothesis states only that the population mean is "not equal" to the value stated in the null hypothesis. The research hypothesis stated in Section 7.3 ($\mu \neq 151$) was in this format. This is called a **two-tailed test** of significance because it means that the researcher will be equally concerned with the possibility that the true population value is greater than the value specified in the null hypothesis and the possibility that the true population value is less than the value specified in the null hypothesis.

In other situations, the researcher might be concerned only with differences in a specific direction. If the direction of the difference can be predicted, or if the researcher is concerned only with differences in one direction, a **one-tailed test** can be used. A one-tailed test may take one of two forms, depending on the researcher's expectations about the direction of the difference. If the researcher believes that the true population value is greater than the value specified in the null hypothesis, the research hypothesis would reflect that belief. In our example, if we had predicted that graduates of the LSAT preparation course had *higher* LSAT scores than the entire population of LSAT writers (or, an average LSAT score *greater than* 151) our research hypothesis would have been

$$(H_1: \mu > 151)$$

where $>$ signifies "greater than"

If we predicted that graduates had *lower* LSAT scores than the entire population of LSAT writers (or, an average LSAT score *less than* 151), our research hypothesis would have been

$$(H_1: \mu < 151)$$

where $<$ signifies "less than"

One-tailed tests are often appropriate when programs designed to solve a problem or improve a situation are being evaluated. If the LSAT training course resulted in lower LSAT scoring, for example, the course would be considered a failure. In a situation like this, the researcher may well focus only on outcomes that would indicate that the program is a success (i.e., when graduates of the LSAT preparation course have higher LSAT scores) and conduct a one-tailed test with a research hypothesis in the form: $H_1: \mu > 151$.

As another example, consider the evaluation of a program designed to increase youth employment. The evaluators would be concerned only with outcomes that show an increase in the youth employment rate. If the rate shows no change or if youth employment decreases, the program is a failure. Thus, the evaluators could legitimately use a one-tailed test that stated that youth employment rates for graduates of the program would be greater than ($>$) rates of employment among all youth.

In terms of the five-step model, the choice of a one-tailed or two-tailed test determines what we do with the critical region under the sampling distribution in step 3. In a two-tailed test, we split the critical region equally into the upper and lower tails of the sampling distribution. In a one-tailed test, we place the entire critical region in one tail of the sampling distribution. If we believe that the population characteristic is greater than the value stated in the null hypothesis (if the H_1 includes the > symbol), we place the entire critical region in the upper tail. If we believe that the characteristic is less than the value stated in the null hypothesis (if the H_1 includes the < symbol), the entire critical region goes in the lower tail.

For example, in a two-tailed test with alpha equal to 0.05, the critical region begins at Z(critical) = ±1.96. In a one-tailed test at the same alpha level, the Z(critical) is +1.65 if the upper tail is specified and −1.65 if the lower tail is specified. Table 7.1 summarizes the procedures to follow in terms of the nature of the research hypothesis. The difference in placing the critical region is graphically summarized in Figure 7.5, and the critical Z scores for the most common alpha levels are given in Table 7.2 for both one- and two-tailed tests.

Note that the critical Z values for one-tailed tests are always closer to the mean of the sampling distribution. Thus, a one-tailed test is more likely to reject the H_0 without changing the alpha level (assuming that we have specified the correct tail). One-tailed tests are a way of statistically both having and eating your cake and should be used whenever (1) the direction of the difference can be confidently predicted, or (2) the researcher is concerned only with differences in one tail of the sampling distribution.

An example will clarify how the one-tailed test is used. After many years of work, a sociologist has noted that sociology majors seem more sophisticated, charming, and cosmopolitan than the rest of the student body. A "Sophistication Scale" test has been administered to the entire student body and to a random sample of 100 sociology majors, and these results have been obtained

Student Body	Sociology Majors
$\mu = 17.3$	$\overline{X} = 19.2$
$\sigma = 7.4$	$n = 100$

We will use the five-step model to test the H_0 of no difference between sociology majors and the general student body.

TABLE 7.1   ONE- VS. TWO-TAILED TESTS, $\alpha = 0.05$

If the Research Hypothesis Uses	The Test Is	And Concern Is with	Z(critical) =
≠	Two-tailed	Both tails	±1.96
>	One-tailed	Upper tail	+1.65
<	One-tailed	Lower tail	−1.65

FIGURE 7.5 ESTABLISHING THE CRITICAL REGION, ONE-TAILED TESTS VERSUS TWO-TAILED TESTS, WITH REJECTION REGION FOR ALPHA = 0.05 IN SHADE

A. The two-tailed test, Z (critical) = ±1.96

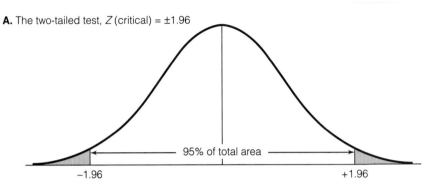

95% of total area

−1.96   +1.96

B. The one-tailed test for upper tail, Z (critical) = +1.65

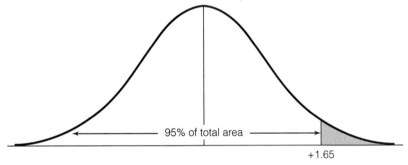

95% of total area

+1.65

C. The one-tailed test for lower tail, Z (critical) = −1.65

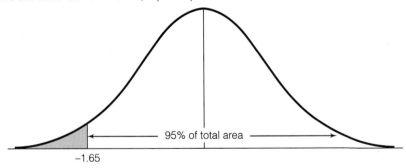

95% of total area

−1.65

TABLE 7.2 FINDING CRITICAL z SCORES FOR ONE-TAILED TESTS
(Single Sample Means)

		One-Tailed Value	
Alpha	Two-Tailed Value	Upper Tail	Lower Tail
0.10	±1.65	+1.29	−1.29
0.05	±1.96	+1.65	−1.65
0.01	±2.58	+2.33	−2.33
0.001	±3.29	+3.10	−3.10

Step 1. Making Assumptions and Meeting Test Requirements. Because we are using a mean to summarize the sample outcome, we must assume that the Sophistication Scale generates interval-ratio-level data. With a sample size of 100, the Central Limit Theorem applies, and we can assume that the sampling distribution is normal in shape.

Model: Random sampling
Level of measurement is interval-ratio
Sampling distribution is normal

Step 2. Stating the Null Hypothesis (H_0). The null hypothesis states that there is no difference between sociology majors and the general student body. The research hypothesis (H_1) will also be stated at this point. The researcher has predicted a direction for the difference ("Sociology majors are *more* sophisticated"), so a one-tailed test is justified. The two hypotheses may be stated as

$$H_0\text{: } \mu = 17.3$$
$$(H_1\text{: } \mu > 17.3)$$

Step 3. Selecting the Sampling Distribution and Establishing the Critical Region. We will use the standardized normal distribution (see Appendix A) to find areas under the sampling distribution. If alpha is set at 0.05, the critical region will begin at the Z score +1.65. That is, the researcher has predicted that sociology majors are *more* sophisticated and that this sample comes from a population that has a mean *greater than* 17.3, so he will be concerned only with sample outcomes in the upper tail of the sampling distribution. If sociology majors are *the same as* other students in terms of sophistication (if the H_0 is true), or if they are *less* sophisticated (and come from a population with a mean less than 17.3), the theory is disproved. These decisions may be summarized as

$$\text{Sampling distribution} = Z \text{ distribution}$$
$$\alpha = 0.05$$
$$Z(\text{critical}) = +1.65$$

FIGURE 7.6 Z(OBTAINED) VERSUS Z(CRITICAL) FOR THE ONE-TAILED TEST, WITH REJECTION REGION FOR ALPHA = 0.05 IN SHADE

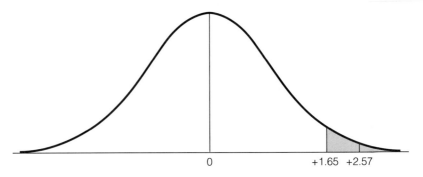

Step 4. Computing the Test Statistic.

$$Z(\text{obtained}) = \frac{\overline{X} - \mu}{\sigma/\sqrt{n}}$$

$$Z(\text{obtained}) = \frac{19.2 - 17.3}{7.4/\sqrt{100}}$$

$$Z(\text{obtained}) = +2.57$$

Step 5. Making a Decision and Interpreting the Results of the Test. Comparing the Z(obtained) with the Z(critical):

$$Z(\text{critical}) = +1.65$$
$$Z(\text{obtained}) = +2.57$$

We see that the test statistic falls into the critical region. This outcome is depicted graphically in Figure 7.6. We will reject the null hypothesis because, if the H_0 were true, a difference of this size would be very unlikely. There is a significant difference between sociology majors and the general student body in terms of sophistication. Because the null hypothesis has been rejected, the research hypothesis (sociology majors are more sophisticated) is supported. *(For practice in dealing with tests of significance for means that may call for one-tailed tests, see problems 7.2b, 7.3, 7.6, 7.8, and 7.17.)*

7.5 SELECTING AN ALPHA LEVEL

In addition to deciding between one-tailed and two-tailed tests, the researcher must also select an alpha level. We have seen that the alpha level plays a crucial role in hypothesis testing. When we assign a value to alpha, we define what we mean by an "unlikely" sample outcome. If the probability of the observed sample outcome is lower than the alpha level (if the test statistic falls into the critical region), we reject the null hypothesis as untrue. Thus, the alpha level will have important consequences for our decision in step 5.

How can reasonable decisions be made with respect to the value of alpha? Recall that, the alpha level defines what will be meant by *unlikely*. The alpha level also tells us the probability that the decision to reject the null hypothesis, if the test statistic falls into the critical region, will be incorrect. In hypothesis testing, the error of incorrectly rejecting the null hypothesis or rejecting a null hypothesis that is actually true is called **Type I error**, or **alpha error**. Type I error can be thought of as a "false positive" outcome of a criminal trial, such that a jury finds the accused *guilty* of the crime despite really being *not guilty*. The null hypothesis in this example is that the person is not guilty, and the research hypothesis is that the person is guilty. To minimize Type I error, use very small values for alpha.

To elaborate, when an alpha level is specified, the sampling distribution is divided into two sets of possible sample outcomes. The critical region includes all unlikely or rare sample outcomes. Outcomes in this region will cause us to reject the null hypothesis. The remainder of the area consists of all sample outcomes that are "nonrare." The lower the level of alpha, the smaller the critical region and the greater the distance between the mean of the sampling distribution and the beginnings of the critical region. Compare, for the sake of illustration, the following alpha levels and values for Z(critical) for two-tailed tests. As you may recall, this information was also presented in Table 6.1.

If Alpha Equals	The Two-Tailed Critical Region Will Begin at Z(critical) Equal to
0.10	±1.65
0.05	±1.96
0.01	±2.58
0.001	±3.29

As alpha goes down, the critical region becomes smaller and moves farther away from the mean of the sampling distribution. The lower the alpha level, the harder it will be to reject the null hypothesis and, because a Type I error can be made only if our decision in step 5 is to reject, the lower the probability of Type I error. To minimize the probability of rejecting a null hypothesis that is in fact true, use very low alpha levels. For instance, with an obtained Z score of +2.57 for the "sophistication" example in Section 7.4, we rejected the null hypothesis that there is no difference between sociology majors and the general student body in a one-tailed test at the 0.05 alpha level, where the critical region begins at +1.65. However, we would fail to reject the null hypothesis at the 0.001 level with a critical region of +3.10.

However, there is a complication. As the critical region decreases in size (as alpha levels decrease), the noncritical region—the area between the two Z(critical) scores in a two-tailed test—must become larger. All other things being equal, the lower the alpha level, the less likely that the sample outcome will fall into the critical region. This raises the possibility of a second type of incorrect decision, called **Type II error**, or **beta (β) error**: failing to reject a null hypothesis that is, in fact, false. Type II error is thus analogous to a "false negative" outcome of a criminal trial such that a jury finds a person *not guilty* of the crime despite actually being *guilty*.

In sum, the probability of Type I error decreases as the alpha level decreases, but the probability of Type II error increases. While the two types of error are inversely related, it is not possible to minimize both in the same test. That is, in conducting a hypothesis test we calculate the probability of committing Type I error, which we control by adjusting the alpha level, but not the probability of committing Type II error—Type II error remains unknown. Through additional computation, however, we can calculate the probability of not committing Type II error; in other words, the probability of correctly rejecting the null hypothesis, or making the right decision! This is referred to as the "power" of a hypothesis test. The routines for computing the power of a hypothesis test will not be considered in this textbook.

We must also be aware that there are different consequences associated with making each type of error. For example, in determining guilt during a criminal trial, sending an innocent person to jail (Type I error) has far different consequences than those that result from setting a guilty person free (Type II error). Which of these errors is more serious depends on the social costs related to them. Canadians tend to be distressed when Type II errors occur in the justice system, but outraged by Type I errors. The Canadian justice system, therefore, places great importance on decreasing Type I errors (sending innocent people to jail) at the expense of increasing Type II errors (letting guilty people go free).

It may be helpful to clarify the relationships between decision making and errors in table format. Table 7.3 lists the two decisions we can make in step 5 of the five-step model: we either reject or fail to reject the null hypothesis. The other dimension of Table 7.3 lists the two possible conditions of the null hypothesis: it is either actually true or actually false. The table combines these possibilities into a total of four possible combinations, two of which are desirable ("OK") and two of which are errors.

The two desirable outcomes are rejecting null hypotheses that are actually false and failing to reject null hypotheses that are actually true. The goal of any scientific investigation is to verify true statements and reject false statements.

TABLE 7.3   DECISION MAKING AND THE NULL HYPOTHESIS

The H_0 Is Actually:	Decision	
	Reject	Fail to Reject
True	Type I or α error	OK
False	OK	Type II or β error

The remaining two combinations are errors or situations that, naturally, we wish to avoid. If we reject a null hypothesis that is in fact true, we are saying that a true statement is false. Likewise, if we fail to reject a null hypothesis that is in fact false, we are saying that a false statement is true. We want to wind up in one of the boxes labelled "OK" in Table 7.3—to always reject false statements and accept the truth when we find it. Remember, however, that hypothesis testing always carries an element of risk and that it is not possible to minimize the chances of both Type I and Type II error simultaneously.

What all of this means, finally, is that you must think of selecting an alpha level as an attempt to balance the two types of error. Higher alpha levels will minimize the probability of Type II error (saying that false statements are true), and lower alpha levels will minimize the probability of Type I error (saying that true statements are false). Normally, in social science research, we will want to minimize Type I error, and lower alpha levels (0.05, 0.01, 0.001 or lower) will be used. The 0.05 level in particular has emerged as a generally recognized indicator of a significant result. However, the widespread use of the 0.05 level is simply a convention, and there is no reason that alpha cannot be set at virtually any sensible level (such as 0.04, 0.027, 0.083). The researcher has the responsibility of selecting the alpha level that seems most reasonable in terms of the goals of the research project.

7.6 THE STUDENT'S *t* DISTRIBUTION

To this point, we have considered only one type of hypothesis test. Specifically, we have focused on situations involving single sample means where the value of the population standard deviation (σ) was known. Needless to say, the value of σ will not be known in most research situations. However, a value for σ is required in order to compute the standard error of the mean ($\sigma/\sqrt{n}$), convert our sample outcome into a Z score, and place the Z(obtained) on the sampling distribution (step 4). How can a value for the population standard deviation reasonably be obtained?

It might seem sensible to estimate σ with s, the sample standard deviation. As we noted in Chapter 6, s is a biased estimator of σ, but the degree of bias decreases as sample size increases. For large samples (i.e., samples with 100 or more cases), the sample standard deviation yields an adequate estimate of σ. Thus, for large samples, we simply substitute s for σ in the formula for Z(obtained) in step 4, suitably corrected for bias using the the square root of $n - 1$ rather than the square root of n. We then continue on using the standard normal curve to find areas under the sampling distribution.

For smaller samples, however, when σ is unknown, an alternative distribution called the **Student's *t* distribution** must be used to find are⁄ under the sampling distribution and establish the critical region. The sh⁄ of the *t* distribution varies as a function of sample size, or more specif⁄

FIGURE 7.7 THE Z DISTRIBUTION AND THE t DISTRIBUTION FOR SELECTED DEGREES OF FREEDOM (df)

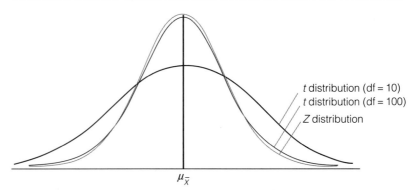

as a function of degrees of freedom (symbolized as df).* Degrees of freedom are equal to $n - 1$ in the case of a single-sample mean. Thus, there is a "family" of t sampling distributions, and the value of df defines a specific "member" of this family (i.e., it defines the shape of the t distribution).

The relative shapes of the Z distribution (in grey) and two specific t distributions (in black) are depicted in Figure 7.7. For the smaller sample (df = 10), the t distribution is flatter than the Z distribution, but, as sample size increases (df = 100), the t distribution comes to resemble the Z distribution more and more. The Z and t distributions are essentially identical when sample size is greater than 120. As n increases, the sample standard deviation (s) becomes a more and more adequate estimator of the population standard deviation (σ), and the t distribution becomes more and more like the Z distribution.

The t distribution is summarized in Appendix B. The t table differs from the Z table in several ways. First, there is a column on the left side of the table labelled Degrees of Freedom (df). As mentioned above, the exact shape of the t distribution—and thus the exact location of the critical region for any alpha level—varies as a function of sample size (degrees of freedom). Degrees of freedom must first be computed before the critical region for any alpha can be located. Second, alpha levels are arrayed across the top of Appendix B in two rows, one for one-tailed tests and one for two-tailed tests. To use the table, we should begin by locating the selected alpha level in the appropriate row.

The third difference is that the entries in the table are the actual scores, called t **(critical)**, that mark the beginnings of the critical regions and not

---

*Degrees of freedom are the number of values in a distribution that are free to vary. For a sample mean, a distribution has $n - 1$ degrees of freedom. This means that for a specific value of the mean, $n - 1$ scores are free to vary. For example, if the mean is 3 for a group of five scores, the distribution has $5 - 1$, or 4 degrees of freedom. When four of the scores are known, the fifth is fixed. If the four scores are 1, 2, 3, and 4, the fifth must be 5 and no other value.

areas under the sampling distribution. To illustrate the use of this table with single-sample means, find the critical region for alpha equal to 0.05, two-tailed test, for $n = 30$. The degrees of freedom will be $n - 1$, or 29; reading down the proper column, you should find a value of 2.045. Thus, the critical region for this test will begin at t(critical) $= \pm 2.045$.

Take a moment to notice some additional features of the t distribution. First, note that the t(critical) we found above is larger in value than the comparable Z(critical), which for a two-tailed test at an alpha of 0.05 would be ± 1.96. This relationship reflects the fact that the t distribution is flatter than the Z distribution (see Figure 7.7). When you use the t distribution, the critical regions will begin farther away from the mean of the sampling distribution and, therefore, the null hypothesis will be harder to reject. Furthermore, the smaller the sample size (the lower the degrees of freedom), the larger the value of t(obtained) necessary for a rejection of the H_0.

Second, scan the column for an alpha of 0.05, two-tailed test. Note that, for one degree of freedom, the t(critical) is ± 12.706 and that the value of t(critical) decreases as degrees of freedom increase. For degrees of freedom greater than 120, the value of t(critical) is the same as the comparable value of Z(critical), or ± 1.96. As sample size increases, the t distribution comes to resemble the Z distribution more and more until, with sample sizes greater than 120, the two distributions are essentially identical (again see Figure 7.7).*

To demonstrate the uses of the t distribution in more detail, we will work through an example problem. Note that, in terms of the five-step model, the changes required by using t scores occur mostly in steps 3 and 4. In step 3, the sampling distribution will be the t distribution, and degrees of freedom must be computed before locating the critical region as marked by t(critical). In step 4, a slightly different formula for computing the test statistic, **t(obtained)**, will be used. As compared with the formula for Z(obtained), s will replace σ and $n - 1$ will replace n.

Specifically,

FORMULA 7.2
$$t\text{(obtained)} = \frac{\overline{X} - \mu}{s/\sqrt{n-1}}$$

A researcher wonders if sociology students are different from the general student body in terms of academic achievement. She has gathered a random sample of 30 sociology students and has learned from the registrar that the mean grade-point average for all students is 2.50 ($\mu = 2.50$), but the standard

---

*Appendix B abbreviates the t distribution by presenting a limited number of critical t scores for degrees of freedom between 31 and 120. If the degrees of freedom for a specific problem equal 77 and alpha equals 0.05, two-tailed, we have a choice between a t(critical) of ± 2.000 (df $= 60$) and a t(critical) of ± 1.980 (df $= 120$). In situations such as these, take the larger table value as t(critical). This will make rejection of the H_0 less likely and is therefore the more conservative course of action.

deviation of the population (σ) has never been computed. Sample data are reported below. Is the sample from a population that has a mean of 2.50?

Student Body	Sociology Students
$\mu = 2.50 \; (= \mu_{\bar{X}})$	$\bar{X} = 2.78$
$\sigma = ?$	$s = 1.23$
	$n = 30$

Step 1. Making Assumptions and Meeting Test Requirements.

> Model: Random sampling
> Level of measurement is interval-ratio
> Sampling distribution is normal

Step 2. Stating the Null Hypothesis.

$$H_0: \mu = 2.50$$
$$(H_1: \mu \neq 2.50)$$

You can see from the research hypothesis that the researcher has not predicted a direction for the difference. This will be a two-tailed test.

Step 3. Selecting the Sampling Distribution and Establishing the Critical Region. Because σ is unknown and sample size is small, the t distribution will be used to find the critical region. Alpha will be set at 0.01.

> Sampling distribution = t distribution
> $\alpha = 0.01$, two-tailed test
> df $= (n - 1) = 29$
> t (critical) $= \pm 2.756$

Step 4. Computing the Test Statistic.

$$t(\text{obtained}) = \frac{\bar{X} - \mu}{s/\sqrt{n - 1}}$$

$$t(\text{obtained}) = \frac{2.78 - 2.50}{1.23/\sqrt{29}}$$

$$t(\text{obtained}) = \frac{0.28}{0.23}$$

$$t(\text{obtained}) = +1.22$$

Step 5. Making a Decision and Interpreting the Results of the Test. The test statistic does not fall into the critical region. Therefore, the researcher fails to reject the H_0. The difference between the sample mean (2.78) and the population mean (2.50) is no greater than what would be expected if only

FIGURE 7.8   SAMPLING DISTRIBUTION SHOWING t(OBTAINED) VERSUS t(CRITICAL) FOR THE TWO-TAILED TEST, WITH REJECTION REGION FOR ALPHA = 0.05 (df = 29) IN SHADE

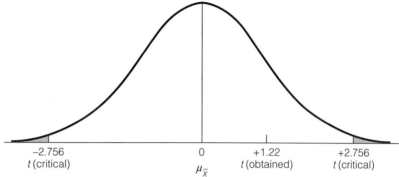

-2.756	0	$+1.22$	$+2.756$
t(critical)	$\mu_{\bar{X}}$	t(obtained)	t(critical)

random chance were operating. The test statistic and critical regions are displayed in Figure 7.8.

To summarize, when testing single-sample means we must make a choice regarding the theoretical distribution we will use to establish the critical region. The choice is straightforward. If the population standard deviation (σ) is known or sample size is large, the Z distribution (summarized in Appendix A) will be used. If σ is unknown and the sample is small, the t distribution (summarized in Appendix B) will be used. *(For practice in using the t distribution in a test of hypothesis, see problems 7.8 to 7.10 and 7.17.)*

7.7 TESTS OF HYPOTHESES FOR SINGLE-SAMPLE PROPORTIONS (LARGE SAMPLES)

In many cases, the sample variables we are interested in will not be measured in a way that justifies the assumption of interval-ratio level of measurement. One alternative in this situation would be to use a sample proportion (P_s) rather than a sample mean as the test statistic. As we shall see, the overall procedures for testing single-sample proportions are the same as those for testing means. The central question is still "Does the population from which the sample was drawn have a certain characteristic?" We still conduct the test based on the assumption that the null hypothesis is true, and we still evaluate the probability of the obtained sample outcome against a sampling distribution of all possible sample outcomes. Our decision at the end of the test is also the same. If the obtained test statistic falls into the critical region (is unlikely, given the assumption that the H_0 is true), we reject the H_0.

Having stressed the continuity in procedures and logic, we must hastily point out the important differences as well. These differences are best related in terms of the five-step model for hypothesis testing. In step 1, when working with sample proportions, we assume that the variable is measured at the nominal level of measurement. In step 2, the symbols used to state the null hypothesis are different even though the null is still a statement of "no difference."

In step 3, we will use only the standardized normal curve (the Z distribution) to find areas under the sampling distribution and locate the critical region. This will be appropriate as long as sample size is large. We will not consider small-sample tests of hypothesis for proportions in this textbook.

In step 4, computing the test statistic, the form of the formula remains the same. That is, the test statistic, Z(obtained), equals the sample statistic minus the mean of the sampling distribution, divided by the standard deviation of the sampling distribution. However, the symbols will change because we are basing the tests on sample proportions. The formula can be stated as

FORMULA 7.3

$$Z(\text{obtained}) = \frac{P_s - P_u}{\sqrt{P_u(1 - P_u)/n}}$$

Step 5 is exactly the same as before. If the test statistic, Z(obtained), falls into the critical region, as marked by Z(critical), reject the H_0.

An example should clarify these procedures. A random sample of 122 households in a low-income neighbourhood revealed that 53 (or a proportion of 0.43) of the households were headed by females. In the city as a whole, the proportion of female-headed households is 0.39. Are households in the low-income neighbourhood significantly different from the city as a whole in terms of this characteristic?

Step 1. **Making Assumptions and Meeting Test Requirements.**

Model: Random sampling
Level of measurement is nominal
Sampling distribution is normal in shape

Step 2. Stating the Null Hypothesis. The research question, as stated above, asks only if the sample proportion is different from the population proportion. Because no direction is predicted for the difference, a two-tailed test will be used.

$$H_0: P_u = 0.39$$
$$(H_1: P_u \neq 0.39)$$

Step 3. Selecting the Sampling Distribution and Establishing the Critical Region.

Sampling distribution $= Z$ distribution
$\alpha = 0.10$, two-tailed test
$Z(\text{critical}) = \pm 1.65$

Application 7.2

It was pointed out in Application 7.1 that immigrants arriving in Canada in recent years tend to be well educated. In a random sample from Statistics Canada's Survey of Labour and Income Dynamics, 22% of 645 recent immigrants (those who have been in Canada for less than 10 years) had a university degree in 2001. Census figures from that same year show that 18% of the Canadian population had a university degree. Are recent immigrants significantly more likely to have a university education than the population as a whole?

Step 1. Making Assumptions and Meeting Test Requirements.

> Model: Random sampling
> Level of measurement is nominal
> Sampling distribution is normal

This is a large sample, so we may assume a normal sampling distribution. The variable, percent with a university degree, is nominal in level of measurement.

Step 2. Stating the Null Hypothesis (H_0). The null hypothesis says that recent immigrants are not different from the nation as a whole.

$$H_0: P_u = 0.18$$

The original question ("are recent immigrants *more* likely to have a university education") suggests a one-tailed research hypothesis:

$$(H_1: P_u > 0.18)$$

The research hypothesis says that we will be concerned only with outcomes in which recent immigrants are more likely to hold a degree or with sample outcomes in the upper tail of the sampling distribution.

Step 3. Selecting the Sampling Distribution and Establishing the Critical Region.

$$\text{Sampling distribution} = Z \text{ distribution}$$
$$\alpha = 0.05$$
$$Z(\text{critical}) = +1.65$$

Step 4. Computing the Test Statistic. The information necessary for a test of the null hypothesis, expressed in the form of proportions, is

Recent Immigrants	Nation
$P_s = 0.22$	$P_u = 0.18$
$n = 645$	

The test statistic, $Z(\text{obtained})$, would be

$$Z(\text{obtained}) = \frac{P_s - P_u}{\sqrt{P_u(1 - P_u)/n}}$$

$$Z(\text{obtained}) = \frac{0.22 - 0.18}{\sqrt{(0.18)(1 - 0.18)/645}}$$

$$Z(\text{obtained}) = \frac{0.04}{\sqrt{(0.1476)/645}}$$

$$Z(\text{obtained}) = \frac{0.04}{0.015}$$

$$Z(\text{obtained}) = +2.67$$

Step 5. Making a Decision and Interpreting the Results of the Test. With alpha set at 0.05, one-tailed, the critical region would begin at $Z(\text{critical}) = +1.65$. With an obtained Z score of $+2.67$, the null hypothesis is rejected. The difference between recent immigrants and Canadians as a whole is statistically significant and in the predicted direction. Recent immigrants to Canada are significantly more likely to have a university degree.

Source: Data from Statistics Canada, *2001 Canadian Census*, individual PUMF, and *2001 Survey of Labour and Income Dynamics*, individual PUMF.

FIGURE 7.9   SAMPLING DISTRIBUTION SHOWING Z(OBTAINED) VERSUS Z(CRITICAL) FOR THE TWO-TAILED TEST, WITH REJECT REGION FOR ALPHA = 0.10 IN SHADE

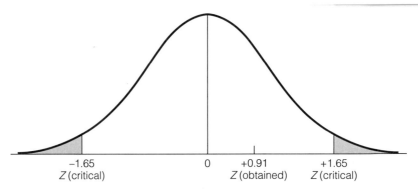

Step 4. Computing the Test Statistic.

$$Z(\text{obtained}) = \frac{P_s - P_u}{\sqrt{P_u(1 - P_u)/n}}$$

$$Z(\text{obtained}) = \frac{0.43 - 0.39}{\sqrt{0.39(0.61)/122}}$$

$$Z(\text{obtained}) = +0.91$$

Step 5. Making a Decision and Interpreting the Results of the Test. The test statistic, Z(obtained), does not fall into the critical region. Therefore, we fail to reject the H_0. There is no statistically significant difference between the low-income community and the city as a whole in terms of the proportion of households headed by females. Figure 7.9 displays the sampling distribution, the critical region, and the Z(obtained). *(For practice in tests of significance using sample proportions, see problems 7.1c, 7.11 to 7.14, 7.15 a to d, and 7.16.)*

7.8 HYPOTHESIS TESTING USING CONFIDENCE INTERVALS

Hypothesis testing and interval estimation (see Chapter 6) are the two main applications of inferential statistics. While the objective of each technique is different, *testing* a claim about a population parameter versus *estimating* a population parameter respectively, they are in reality just different ways of expressing the same information.

If an interval estimate (i.e., confidence interval) does not contain the value of the parameter specified by the null hypothesis, then a hypothesis test will reject the null hypothesis, and vice versa. That is, if the value of H_0 *is* contained within the confidence interval at a given alpha level, then H_0 *is not* rejected at that level. On the other hand, if the value of H_0 *is not* contained within the confidence interval at a given alpha level, then H_0 *is* rejected at that level. So, if a 99% confidence interval does not contain the value of the parameter given by the null hypothesis, then the null hypothesis is rejected at the 0.01 level; if a 95% confidence interval does not contain it, then the null hypothesis is rejected at the 0.05 level; and so on. The ability to use confidence intervals to test hypotheses applies to all situations, including means and proportions, and the one-sample case covered in this chapter and the two-sample case to be discussed in Chapter 8.

To see how the confidence interval for the sample mean corresponds to the hypothesis test for the sample mean, let us take another look at the LSAT example in Section 7.3. Recall that the null hypothesis stated that the population of graduates of the LSAT preparation course is just like everyone else and has a mean LSAT score of 151; that is, there is no difference in LSAT scoring between the graduates and LSAT writers as a whole, or

$$H_0: \mu = 151$$
$$(H_1: \mu \neq 151)$$

For a two-tailed test (the research hypothesis does not predict a direction for the difference) with alpha set at 0.05, the critical region begins at Z(critical) ± 1.96, or

$$\text{Sampling distribution} = Z \text{ distribution}$$
$$\alpha = 0.05, \text{ two-tailed test}$$
$$Z(\text{critical}) = \pm 1.96$$

We obtained a Z score of $+3.33$, or

$$Z = \frac{\overline{X} - \mu}{\sigma/\sqrt{n}}$$
$$Z = \frac{154 - 151}{9/\sqrt{100}}$$
$$Z = +3.33$$

Then, we reject the null hypothesis, H_0, because the test statistic, Z(obtained), falls into the critical region, as marked by Z(critical).

Next, let us construct a 95% confidence interval for the sample mean using Formula 6.1 (see Chapter 6):

$$\text{c.i.} = \overline{X} \pm Z\left(\frac{\sigma}{\sqrt{n}}\right)$$
$$\text{c.i.} = 154 \pm 1.96\left(\frac{9}{\sqrt{100}}\right)$$
$$\text{c.i.} = 154 \pm (1.96)(0.90)$$
$$\text{c.i.} = 154 \pm 1.76$$

Based on this result, we estimate that the population mean is greater than or equal to 152.24 and less than or equal to 155.76 at the 95% level of confidence.

The relationship between the confidence interval and hypothesis test can now be seen. Because this interval does not include the value of the parameter specified by the null hypothesis, 151, we would reject the null hypothesis. The difference between graduates of the LSAT training course and the entire population of LSAT writers is statistically significant at the 0.05 level. This is precisely the decision we made above using the formal hypothesis-testing approach. In sum, it will always be true that if the confidence interval contains the value of the parameter specified by the null hypothesis, then the null hypothesis cannot be rejected at the stated alpha level. If it does not, then the null hypothesis can be rejected.

SUMMARY

1. All the basic concepts and techniques for testing hypotheses were presented in this chapter. We saw how to test the null hypothesis of "no difference" for single sample means and proportions. In both cases, the central question is whether the population represented by the sample has a certain characteristic.

2. All tests of a hypothesis involve finding the probability of the observed sample outcome, given that the null hypothesis is true. If the outcome has a low probability, we reject the null hypothesis. In the usual research situation, we will wish to reject the null hypothesis and thereby support the research hypothesis.

3. The five-step model will be our framework for decision making throughout the hypothesis-testing chapters. What we do during each step, however, will vary, depending on the specific test being conducted.

4. If we can predict a direction for the difference in stating the research hypothesis, a one-tailed test is called for. If no direction can be predicted, a two-tailed test is appropriate. There are two kinds of errors in hypothesis testing. Type I, or alpha, error is rejecting a true null; Type II, or beta, error is failing to reject a false null. The probabilities of committing these two types of error are inversely related and cannot be simultaneously minimized in the same test. By selecting an alpha level, we try to balance the probability of these two kinds of error.

5. When testing sample means, the t distribution must be used to find the critical region when the population standard deviation is unknown and sample size is small.

6. Sample proportions can also be tested for significance. Tests are conducted using the five-step model. Compared to the test for the sample mean, the major differences lie in the level-of-measurement assumption (step 1), the statement of the null (step 2), and the computation of the test statistic (step 4).

7. Hypothesis testing and interval estimation (see Chapter 6) are just different ways of expressing the same information. If the confidence interval contains the value of the parameter specified by the null hypothesis in a one-sample test, then the null hypothesis is not rejected at the stated alpha level. Alternatively, the null hypothesis is rejected if the confidence interval does not contain the value.

8. If you are still confused about the uses of inferential statistics described in this chapter, don't be alarmed or discouraged. A sizable volume of rather complex material has been presented and only rarely will a beginning student fully comprehend the unique logic of hypothesis testing on the first exposure. After all, it is not every day that you learn how to test a statement you don't believe (the null hypothesis) against a distribution that doesn't exist (the sampling distribution)!

SUMMARY OF FORMULAS

Single-sample means, large samples:

7.1 $$Z(\text{obtained}) = \frac{\overline{X} - \mu}{\sigma/\sqrt{n}}$$

Single-sample means when samples are small and population standard deviation is unknown:

7.2 $$t(\text{obtained}) = \frac{\overline{X} - \mu}{s/\sqrt{n - 1}}$$

Single-sample proportions, large samples:

7.3 $$Z(\text{obtained}) = \frac{P_s - P_u}{\sqrt{P_u(1 - P_u)/n}}$$

GLOSSARY

Alpha level (α). The proportion of area under the sampling distribution that contains unlikely sample outcomes, given that the null hypothesis is true. Also, the probability of Type I error. (p. 191)

Critical region (region of rejection). The area under the sampling distribution that, in advance of the test itself, is defined as including unlikely sample outcomes, given that the null hypothesis is true. (p. 190)

Five-step model. A step-by-step guideline for conducting tests of hypotheses. A framework that organizes decisions and computations for all tests of significance. (p. 189)

Hypothesis testing. Statistical tests that estimate the probability of sample outcomes if assumptions about the population (the null hypothesis) are true. (p. 182)

Null hypothesis (H_0). A statement of "no difference." In the context of single-sample tests of significance, the population from which the sample was drawn is assumed to have a certain characteristic or value. (p. 189)

One-tailed test. A type of hypothesis test used when (1) the direction of the difference can be predicted or (2) concern focuses on outcomes in only one tail of the sampling distribution. (p. 194)

Research hypothesis (H_1). A statement that contradicts the null hypothesis. In the context of single-sample tests of significance, the research

hypothesis says that the population from which the sample was drawn does not have a certain characteristic or value. (p. 190)

Significance testing. See Hypothesis testing. (p. 182)

Student's t distribution. A distribution used to find the critical region for tests of sample means when σ is unknown and sample size is small. (p. 201)

t (critical). The t score that marks the beginning of the critical region of a t distribution. (p. 202)

t (obtained). The test statistic computed in step 4 of the five-step model. The sample outcome expressed as a t score. (p. 203)

Test statistic. The value computed in step 4 of the five-step model that converts the sample outcome into either a t score or a Z score. (p. 191)

Two-tailed test. A type of hypothesis test used when (1) the direction of the difference cannot be predicted or (2) concern focuses on outcomes in both tails of the sampling distribution. (p. 194)

Type I error (alpha error). The probability of rejecting a null hypothesis that is, in fact, true. (p. 199)

Type II error (beta error). The probability of failing to reject a null hypothesis that is, in fact, false. (p. 199)

Z (critical). The Z score that marks the beginnings of the critical region on a Z distribution. (p. 191)

Z (obtained). The test statistic computed in step 4 of the five-step model. The sample outcomes expressed as a Z score. (p. 191)

MULTIMEDIA RESOURCES

    http://www.healeystatistics.nelson.com

Visit the companion website for the second Canadian edition of *Statistics: A Tool for Social Research* to access a wide range of student resources. Begin by clicking on the Student Resources section of the textbook's website to access review quizzes, flashcards, and other study tools.

PROBLEMS

7.1 a. For each situation, find Z(critical).

Alpha	Form	Z(Critical)
0.05	One-tailed	
0.10	Two-tailed	
0.06	Two-tailed	
0.01	One-tailed	
0.02	Two-tailed	

b. For each situation, find the critical t score.

Alpha	Form	n	t(Critical)
0.10	Two-tailed	31	
0.02	Two-tailed	24	
0.01	Two-tailed	121	
0.01	One-tailed	31	
0.05	One-tailed	61	

c. Compute the appropriate test statistic (Z or t) for each situation:

1. $\mu = 2.40$ $\bar{X} = 2.20$
    $\sigma = 0.75$ $n = 200$

2. $\mu = 17.1$ $\bar{X} = 16.8$
              $s = 0.9$
              $n = 45$

3. $\mu = 10.2$ $\bar{X} = 9.4$
              $s = 1.7$
              $n = 150$

4. $P_u = 0.57$ $P_s = 0.60$
              $n = 117$

5. $P_u = 0.32$ $P_s = 0.30$
              $n = 322$

7.2 SOC **a.** The student body at Algebra University attends an average of 3.3 parties per month. A random sample of 117 sociology majors averages 3.8 parties per month with a standard deviation of 0.53. Are sociology majors significantly different from the student body as a whole? *(HINT: The wording of the research question suggests a two-tailed test. This means that the alternative or research hypothesis in step 2 will be stated as H_1: $\mu \neq 3.3$ and that the critical region will be split between the upper and lower tails of the sampling distribution. See Table 7.2 for values of Z (critical) for various alpha levels.)*

b. What if the research question were changed to "Do sociology majors attend a significantly *greater* number of parties"? How would the test conducted in 7.2a change? *(HINT: This wording implies a one-tailed test of significance. How would the research hypothesis change? For the alpha you used in problem 7.2a, what would the value of Z (critical) be?)*

7.3 SW **a.** Nationally, social workers average 10.2 years of experience. In a random sample, 203 social workers in the greater metropolitan area of Pearson, Ontario, average only 8.7 years with a standard deviation of 0.52. Are social workers in Pearson, Ontario, significantly less experienced? *(HINT: Note the wording of the research hypothesis. This situation may justify a one-tailed test of significance. If you chose a one-tailed test, what form would the research hypothesis take, and where would the critical region begin?)*

b. The same sample of social workers reports an average annual salary of $35,782 with a standard deviation of $622. Is this figure significantly higher than the national average of $34,509? (*HINT: The wording of the research hypothesis suggests a one-tailed test. What form would the research hypothesis take, and where would the critical region begin?*)

7.4 SOC Nationally, the average score on the GRE (Graduate Record Examinations) verbal test is 453 with a standard deviation of 95. A random sample of 152 first-year graduate students entering Algebra University shows a mean score of 502. Is there a significant difference?

7.5 SOC A random sample of 423 Albertans has finished an average of 12.7 years of formal education with a standard deviation of 1.7. Is this significantly different from the national average of 12.2 years?

7.6 SOC A sample of 105 workers in the Overkill Division of the Machismo Toy Factory earns an average of $24,375 per year. The average salary for all workers is $24,230 with a standard deviation of $523. Are workers in the Overkill Division overpaid? Conduct both one- and two-tailed tests.

7.7 GER **a.** Nationally, the population as a whole watches an average of 6.2 hours of TV per day. A random sample of 1,017 senior citizens reports watching an average of 5.9 hours per day with a standard deviation of 0.7. Is the difference significant?

b. The same sample of senior citizens reports that they belong to an average of 2.1 voluntary organizations and clubs with a standard deviation of 0.5. Nationally, the average is 1.7. Is the difference significant?

7.8 SOC A school system has assigned several hundred "chronic and severe underachievers" to an alternative educational experience. To assess the program, a random sample of 35 has been selected for comparison with all students in the system.

a. In terms of GPA, did the program work?

Systemwide GPA	Program GPA
$\mu = 2.47$	$\overline{X} = 2.55$
	$s = 0.70$
	$n = 35$

b. In terms of absenteeism (number of days missed per year), what can be said about the success of the program?

Systemwide	Program
$\mu = 6.13$	$\overline{X} = 4.78$
	$s = 1.11$
	$n = 35$

c. In terms of standardized test scores in math and reading, was the program a success?

Math Test Systemwide	Math Test Program
$\mu = 103$	$\overline{X} = 106$
	$s = 2.0$
	$n = 35$

Reading Test Systemwide	Reading Test Program
$\mu = 110$	$\overline{X} = 113$
	$s = 2.0$
	$n = 35$

(*HINT: Note the wording of the research questions. Is a one-tailed test justified? Is the program a success if the students in the program are no different from students systemwide? What if the program students were performing at lower levels? If a one-tailed test is used, what form should the research hypothesis take? Where will the critical region begin?*)

7.9 SOC A random sample of 26 sociology graduates in BC scored an average of 458 on the GRE advanced sociology test with a standard deviation of 20. Is this significantly different from the national average ($\mu = 440$)?

7.10 PA Nationally, the per capita property tax is $130 per month. A random sample of 36 western cities averages $98 per month with a standard deviation of $5. Is the difference significant? Summarize your conclusions in a sentence or two.

7.11 GER/CJ A survey shows that 10% of the population is victimized by property crime each year. A random sample of 527 older citizens (65 years or more of age) shows a victimization rate of 14%. Are older people more likely to be victimized? Conduct both one- and two-tailed tests of significance.

7.12 CJ A random sample of 113 convicted sex offenders in a provincial prison system completed a program designed to change their attitudes toward women, sex, and violence before being released on parole. Fifty-eight eventually became repeat sex offenders. Is this recidivism rate significantly different from the rate for all offenders (57%) in that province? Summarize your conclusions in a sentence or two. *(HINT: You must use the information given in the problem to compute a sample proportion. Remember to convert the population percentage to a proportion).*

7.13 PS In a recent provincial election, 55% of the voters rejected a proposal to institute a new provincial lottery. In a random sample of 150 voters from rural communities, 49% rejected the proposal. Is the difference significant? Summarize your conclusions in a sentence or two.

7.14 CJ Provincially, the police clear by arrest 35% of the robberies and 42% of the aggravated assaults reported to them. A researcher takes a random sample of all the robberies ($n = 207$) and aggravated assaults ($n = 178$) reported to a metropolitan police department in one year and finds that 83 of the robberies and 80 of the assaults were cleared by arrest. Are the local arrest rates significantly different from the provincial rate? Write a sentence or two interpreting your decision.

7.15 SOC/SW A researcher has compiled a file of information on a random sample of 317 families

in a city that has chronic, long-term patterns of child abuse. Below are reported some of the characteristics of the sample along with values for the city as a whole. For each trait, test the null hypothesis of "no difference" and summarize your findings.

a. Mothers' educational level (proportion completing high school):

City	Sample
$P_u = 0.63$	$P_s = 0.61$

b. Family size (proportion of families with four or more children):

City	Sample
$P_u = 0.21$	$P_s = 0.26$

c. Mothers' work status (proportion of mothers with jobs outside the home):

City	Sample
$P_u = 0.51$	$P_s = 0.27$

d. Relations with relatives (proportion of families that have contact with relatives at least once a week):

City	Sample
$P_u = 0.82$	$P_s = 0.43$

e. Fathers' educational achievement (average years of formal schooling):

City	Sample
$\mu = 12.3$	$\overline{X} = 12.5$
	$s = 1.7$

f. Fathers' occupational stability (average years in present job):

City	Sample
$\mu = 5.2$	$\overline{X} = 3.7$
	$s = 0.5$

7.16 SW You are the head of an agency seeking funding for a program to reduce unemployment among teenage males. Nationally, the unemployment rate for this group is 18%. A random sample of 323 teenage males in your area reveals an unemployment rate of 21.7%. Is the difference significant? Can you demonstrate a need for the program? Should you use a one-tailed test in this situation? Why? Explain the result of your test of significance as you would to a funding agency.

7.17 [PA] The city manager of Pearson, Ontario, has received a complaint from the local union of firefighters that they are underpaid. Not having much time, the city manager gathers the records of a random sample of 27 firefighters and finds that their average salary is $38,073 with a standard deviation of $575. If she knows that the average salary nationally is $38,202, how can she respond to the complaint? Should she use a one-tailed test in this situation? Why? What would she say in a memo to the union that would respond to the complaint?

7.18 The following essay questions review the basic principles and concepts of inferential statistics.

The order of the questions roughly follows the five-step model.

a. Hypothesis testing or significance testing can be conducted only with a random sample. Why?

b. Under what specific conditions can it be assumed that the sampling distribution is normal in shape?

c. Explain the role of the sampling distribution in a test of hypothesis.

d. The null hypothesis is an assumption about reality that makes it possible to test sample outcomes for their significance. Explain.

e. What is the critical region? How is the size of the critical region determined?

f. Describe a research situation in which a one-tailed test of hypothesis would be appropriate.

g. Thinking about the shape of the sampling distribution, why does use of the t distribution (as opposed to the Z distribution) make it more difficult to reject the null hypothesis?

h. What exactly can be concluded in the one-sample case when the test statistic falls into the critical region?

SPSS for Windows

Using SPSS for Windows to Conduct a One-Sample Test with the 2006 Census

The demonstration and exercise below use the shortened version of the 2006 Census data. Start SPSS for Windows and open the *Census.sav* file.

SPSS DEMONSTRATION 7.1 Using the Select Cases Command to Conduct a One-Sample Test

In this demonstration, we'll conduct a one-sample test to compare the income of a sample of persons with a Master's degree to the income of all Canadians, which according to Statistics Canada was $35,498 in 2006.* We predict that those with a Master's degree, with their advanced post-secondary education, skills, and training, will have a higher income than the general population. If we find that the average income for the sample of Master's degree graduates is significantly different than that of the general population, we can conclude that Master's degree graduates in Canada tend to have better incomes than the population as a whole.

*Source: Statistics Canada, 2007, Cat. No. 97-563-XCB2006005.

First, we need to use the **Select Cases** command to select Master's degree graduates for the analysis. Click **Data** from the menu bar of the **Data Editor** window and then click **Select Cases**. The **Select Cases** window appears and presents a number of different options. Click the button next to "If condition is satisfied" and then click on the **If** button. The **Select Cases: If** dialog box will open, where you specify the cases to be included in the analysis. Find and highlight *hdgree* (highest certificate, diploma, or degree) from the variable list on the left side of the dialog box, and then click the arrow to move *hdgree* into the text box. In this text box, type = **12** immediately to the right of the variable name *hdgree*. A value 12 on *hdgree* indicates a Master's degree graduate. The expression ***hdgree* = 12** should appear in the text box. Click **Continue**, and then **OK.**

The **Select Cases** command confines all subsequent analysis to this subset of cases, Master's degree graduates. This is easily verified, as the status bar at the bottom of the SPSS window displays the message "Filter On." It is important to note that the unselected cases in the data file, while not included in the analysis, do remain in the data set.

Because the sample of Master's degree graduates is small—with fewer than 100 cases—and the population standard deviation is unknown, we'll use the **One-Sample T Test** procedure, covered in Section 7.6, to test if the mean income of a Master's degree graduate differs from the mean income of all Canadians. From the main menu bar, click **Analyze, Compare Means**, and then **One-Sample T Test**. The **One-Sample T Test** dialog box will open with the usual list of variables on the left. Find and move the cursor over *totinc* (total income) and click the top arrow in the middle of the window to move *totinc* to the **Test Variable(s)** box. Next, click the **Test Value** box and type 35498. Click **OK** and the following output will be produced. Do not forget to turn filtering off after finishing the **One-Sample T Test** procedure. To do this, return to the **Select Cases** dialog box, select the "**All cases**" button, and then click **OK**.

One-Sample Statistics

	N	Mean	Std. Deviation	Std. Error Mean
Total income of individual	38	57105.26	60043.583	9740.355

One-Sample Test

					95% Confidence Interval of the Difference	
	t	df	Sig. (2-tailed)	Mean Difference	Lower	Upper
Total income of individual	2.218	37	.033	21607.263	1871.43	41343.10

In the first block of output ("One-Sample Statistics") are some descriptive statistics. There are 38 Master's degree graduates with a mean income of $57,105, which is different from the mean income of $35,498 for the general population.

Is the difference in means significant? The results of the test for significance are reported in the next block ("One-Sample Test") of output.

In the second output block, "One-Sample Test," we are given the values of t(obtained) (2.218) and degrees of freedom (37) needed to test if the difference between the sample mean of $57,105 and the population mean of $35,498 is statistically significant. To test for significance, we look up the t(critical) in the t table in Appendix B, and then compare the t(obtained) value to the t(critical) value as practised throughout this chapter.

Because we predicted a direction for this difference (Master's degree graduates have higher income than the general population), a one-tailed test in the upper tail of the sampling distribution is justified. With alpha equal to 0.05, our usual indicator of significance, and 37 degrees of freedom, we find the t(critical) is $+1.697$. (The t table does not include a value for 37 degrees of freedom, so we used the value for 30 degrees of freedom.)

The test statistic, t(obtained), of 2.218 falls into the critical region (i.e., 2.218 is greater than 1.697). We reject the null hypothesis. The difference is statistically significant, and the research hypothesis that Master's degree graduates have higher income than the general population is supported.

However, we could have more conveniently used the "Sig. (2-tailed)" value (.033) in the "One-Sample Test" output to test for significance. The value of .033 is an alpha level, except that it is the *exact* probability of getting the observed difference between the sample mean of $57,105 and the population mean of $35,498 if only chance is operating. This value is a two-tailed test of significance. Because we want the value for a one-tailed test, which SPSS does not provide, we simply divide the value by two, or $.033/2 = 0.0165$. This value, 0.0165, is the significance for a one-tailed test. With the exact probability of a one-tailed test now in hand, there is no need to look up the test statistic in the t table. This value, 0.0165, is less than .05 so we reject the null hypothesis.

Exercise (using *Census.sav*)

7.1 Statistics Canada reports that the average income of Canadians was $35,498 in 2006. Are Albertans different from Canadians in general in terms of this characteristic (i.e., do Albertans have lower or higher incomes than the national average)? Using Demonstration 7.1 as a guide, test for a significant difference between the mean income (*totinc*) of the sample of Albertans and the mean income of $35,498 for the Canadian population. Write a sentence or two summarizing the results of this test. (Make sure to use the **Select Cases** procedure to include only Albertans in the **One-Sample T Test** analysis, and use the two-tailed test.)

Hypothesis Testing II
The Two-Sample Case

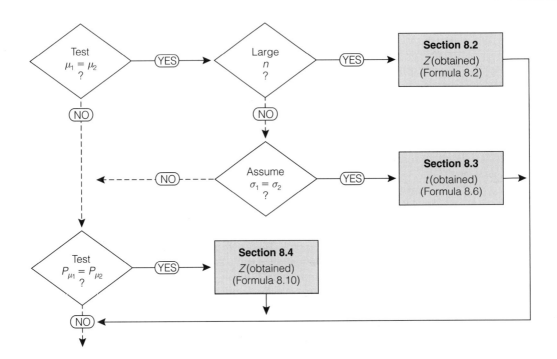

LEARNING OBJECTIVES

By the end of this chapter, you will be able to

1. Identify and cite examples of situations in which the two-sample test of hypothesis is appropriate.

2. Explain the logic of hypothesis testing as applied to the two-sample case.

3. Explain what an independent random sample is.

4. Perform a test of hypothesis for two-sample means or two-sample proportions following the five-step model and correctly interpret the results.

5. Conduct a two-sample hypothesis test using confidence intervals.

6. List and explain each of the factors (especially sample size) that affect the probability of rejecting the null hypothesis and explain the differences between statistical significance and importance.

8.1 INTRODUCTION

In Chapter 7, we dealt with hypothesis testing in the one-sample case. In that situation, our concern was with the significance of the difference between a sample value and a population value. In this chapter, we will consider research situations where we will be concerned with the significance of the difference between two separate populations. For example, in light of recent high-profile incidents of violence involving guns and controversies about the gun registry in Canada, we may ask, do men and women vary in their support for gun control? Obviously, we cannot ask every male and female for their opinions on gun control. Instead, we must draw random samples of both groups and use the information gathered from these samples to infer population patterns.

The central question asked in hypothesis testing in the two-sample case is "Is the difference between the samples large enough to allow us to conclude (with a known probability of error) that the populations represented by the samples are different?" Thus, if we find a large enough difference in support for gun control between random samples of men and women, we can argue that the difference between the samples did not occur by simple random chance but, rather, represents a real difference between men and women in the population.

In this chapter, we will consider tests for the significance of the difference between sample means and sample proportions. In both tests, the five-step model will serve as a framework for organizing our decision-making. The general flow of the hypothesis-testing process is very similar to the one followed in the one-sample case but we will also need to consider some important differences.

8.2 HYPOTHESIS TESTING WITH SAMPLE MEANS (LARGE SAMPLES)

One major difference between the one- and two-sample situations occurs in step 1 of the five-step model. The one-sample case (see Chapter 7) requires that the sample be selected following the principle of EPSEM (each case in the population must have an equal chance of being selected for the sample). The two-sample situation requires that the samples be selected independently as well as randomly. This requirement is met when the selection of a case for one sample has no effect on the probability that any particular case will be included in the other sample. In our example concerning gender differences in support of gun control, this would mean that the selection of a specific male for the sample would have no effect on the probability of selecting any particular female. This new requirement will be stated as **independent random sampling** in step 1.

The requirement of independent random sampling can be satisfied by drawing EPSEM samples from separate lists (e.g., one for females and one for males). It is usually more convenient, however, to draw a single EPSEM sample from a single list of the population and then subdivide the cases into separate groups (males and females, for example). As long as the original sample is selected randomly, any subsamples created by the researcher will meet the assumption of independent random samples.

The second important difference in the five-step model for the two-sample case is in the form of the null hypothesis. The null is still a statement of "no difference." Now, however, instead of saying that the population from which the sample is drawn has a certain characteristic, it will say that the two populations are no different. ("There is no significant difference between men and women in their support of gun control.") If the test statistic falls in the critical region, the null hypothesis of no difference between the populations can be rejected, and the argument that the populations are different based on the trait of interest will be supported.

A third important new element concerns the sampling distribution: the distribution of all possible sample outcomes. In Chapter 7, the sample outcome was either a mean or a proportion. Now, we are dealing with two samples (e.g., samples of men and women) and the sample outcome is the *difference between* the sample statistics. In terms of our example, the sampling distribution would include all possible differences in sample means for support of gun control between men and women. If the null hypothesis is true and men and women do *not* have different views about gun control, the difference between the population means would be zero, the mean of the sampling distribution will be zero, and the huge majority of differences between sample means would be zero (or, at any rate, very small in value). The greater the differences between the sample means, the further the sample outcome (the *difference* between the two sample means) will be from the mean of the sampling distribution (zero), and the more likely that the difference reflects a real difference between the two populations represented by the two samples.

To illustrate the procedure for testing sample means we will examine differences of opinion on gun control between men and women using actual data from the 2006 Canadian Election Study, an interuniversity project that regularly conducts a survey of a representative sample of Canadian voters on a variety of political issues. We divided the Canadian Election Study sample by sex, and then computed sample statistics for support of gun control for males and females. A scale was used to measure a person's overall attitude toward gun control, where higher scores indicated greater support of gun control in Canada. Assuming that the scale yields interval-ratio-level data, a test for the significance of the difference in sample means can be conducted.

As long as sample size is large (i.e., as long as the combined number of cases in the two samples is 100 or more), the sampling distribution of the differences in sample means will be normal, and the normal curve (see Appendix A) can be used to establish the critical regions. The test statistic, Z(obtained), will be computed by the usual formula: sample outcome (the difference between the sample means) minus the mean of the sampling distribution, divided by the standard deviation of the sampling distribution. The formula is presented as Formula 8.1. Note that numerical subscripts are used to identify the samples and the two populations they represent. The subscript attached to $\sigma\,(\sigma_{\bar{x}-\bar{x}})$ indicates that we are dealing with the sampling distribution of the *differences* in sample means.

FORMULA 8.1
$$Z(\text{obtained}) = \frac{(\overline{X}_1 - \overline{X}_2) - (\mu_1 - \mu_2)}{\sigma_{\bar{x}-\bar{x}}}$$

where $(\overline{X}_1 - \overline{X}_2)$ = the difference in the sample means
$(\mu_1 - \mu_2)$ = the difference in the population means
$\sigma_{\bar{x}-\bar{x}}$ = the standard deviation of the sampling distribution of the differences in sample means

The second term in the numerator $(\mu_1 - \mu_2)$, reduces to zero because we assume that the null hypothesis (which will be stated as H_0: $\mu_1 = \mu_2$) is true. Recall that tests of significance are always based on the assumption that the null hypothesis is true. If the means of the two populations are equal, then the term $(\mu_1 - \mu_2)$ will be zero and can be dropped from the equation. In effect, then, the formula we will actually use to compute the test statistic in step 4 will be

FORMULA 8.2
$$Z(\text{obtained}) = \frac{(\overline{X}_1 - \overline{X}_2)}{\sigma_{\bar{x}-\bar{x}}}$$

For large samples, the standard deviation of the sampling distribution of the difference in sample means is defined as

FORMULA 8.3
$$\sigma_{\bar{x}-\bar{x}} = \sqrt{\frac{\sigma_1^2}{n_1} + \frac{\sigma_2^2}{n_2}}$$

Because we will rarely, if ever, be in a position to know the values of the population standard deviations (σ_1 and σ_2), we must use the sample standard deviations, suitably corrected for bias, to estimate them. Formula 8.4 displays the equation used to estimate the standard deviation of the sampling distribution in this situation. This is called a **pooled estimate** because it combines information from both samples.

FORMULA 8.4
$$\sigma_{\bar{x}-\bar{x}} = \sqrt{\frac{s_1^2}{n_1 - 1} + \frac{s_2^2}{n_2 - 1}}$$

The sample outcomes for support of gun control are reported below, and a test for the significance of the difference can now be conducted.

Sample 1 (Men)	Sample 2 (Women)
$\overline{X}_1 = 6.9$	$\overline{X}_2 = 8.2$
$s_1 = 3.8$	$s_2 = 3.6$
$n_1 = 1,880$	$n_2 = 2,116$

Source: Data from 2006 Canadian Election Study.

We see from the sample statistics that men have a lower average score on the support for gun control scale and are thus less supportive of gun control. The test of hypothesis will tell us if this difference is large enough to justify the conclusion that it did not occur by random chance alone but rather reflects an actual difference between the populations of men and women on this issue.

Step 1. Making Assumptions and Meeting Test Requirements. Note that, although we now assume that the random samples are independent, the rest of the model is the same as in the one-sample case.

Model: Independent random samples
Level of measurement is interval-ratio
Sampling distribution is normal

Step 2. Stating the Null Hypothesis. The null hypothesis states that the *populations* represented by the samples are not different on this variable. No direction for the difference has been predicted, so a two-tailed test is called for, as reflected in the research hypothesis.

$$H_0: \mu_1 = \mu_2$$
$$(H_1: \mu_1 \neq \mu_2)$$

Step 3. Selecting the Sampling Distribution and Establishing the Critical Region. For large samples, the Z distribution can be used to find areas under the sampling distribution and establish the critical region. Alpha will be set at 0.05.

Sampling distribution = Z distribution
Alpha = 0.05
Z(critical) = ±1.96

Step 4. Computing the Test Statistic. Because the population standard deviations are unknown, Formula 8.4 will be used to estimate the standard deviation of the sampling distribution. This value will then be substituted into Formula 8.2 and Z(obtained) will be computed.

$$\sigma_{\bar{x}-\bar{x}} = \sqrt{\frac{s_1^2}{n_1 - 1} + \frac{s_2^2}{n_2 - 1}}$$

$$\sigma_{\bar{x}-\bar{x}} = \sqrt{\frac{(3.8)^2}{1,880 - 1} + \frac{(3.6)^2}{2,116 - 1}}$$

$$\sigma_{\bar{x}-\bar{x}} = \sqrt{(0.0077) + (0.0061)}$$

$$\sigma_{\bar{x}-\bar{x}} = \sqrt{0.0138}$$

$$\sigma_{\bar{x}-\bar{x}} = 0.117$$

$$Z(\text{obtained}) = \frac{(\bar{X}_1 - \bar{X}_2)}{\sigma_{\bar{x}-\bar{x}}}$$

$$Z(\text{obtained}) = \frac{6.9 - 8.2}{0.117}$$

$$Z(\text{obtained}) = \frac{-1.3}{0.117}$$

$$Z(\text{obtained}) = -11.11$$

Application 8.1

Most adult smokers started smoking in their teens. Here we will examine if there is a significant difference in the age that Canadians and Americans start smoking. We use real data from the 2002–2003 Joint Canada/United States Survey of Health, conducted by Statistics Canada and the U.S. Centers for Disease Control and Prevention, to compute the mean and standard deviation of age people start smoking ("How old were you when you first started to smoke every day?") for random samples of Canadian and American daily smokers. The sample information is:

Sample 1 (United States)	Sample 2 (Canada)
$\overline{X}_1 = 18.1$	$\overline{X}_2 = 17.4$
$s_1 = 5.0$	$s_2 = 4.7$
$n_1 = 812$	$n_2 = 682$

We can see from the sample results that the Americans initiated smoking at a later age. The significance of this difference will be tested following the five-step model.

Step 1. Making Assumptions and Meeting Test Requirements.

Model: Independent random samples
Level of measurement is interval-ratio
Sampling distribution is normal

Step 2. Stating the Null Hypothesis.

$$H_0: \mu_1 = \mu_2$$
$$(H_1: \mu_1 \neq \mu_2)$$

Step 3. Selecting the Sampling Distribution and Establishing the Critical Region.

Sampling distribution = Z distribution
Alpha = 0.05, two-tailed
Z(critical) = ±1.96

Step 4. Computing the Test Statistic.

$$\sigma_{\overline{x}-\overline{x}} = \sqrt{\frac{s_1^2}{n_1 - 1} + \frac{s_2^2}{n_2 - 1}}$$
$$\sigma_{\overline{x}-\overline{x}} = \sqrt{\frac{(5.0)^2}{812 - 1} + \frac{(4.7)^2}{682 - 1}}$$
$$\sigma_{\overline{x}-\overline{x}} = \sqrt{0.063}$$
$$\sigma_{\overline{x}-\overline{x}} = 0.25$$

$$Z(\text{obtained}) = \frac{(\overline{X}_1 - \overline{X}_2)}{\sigma_{\overline{x}-\overline{x}}}$$
$$Z(\text{obtained}) = \frac{18.1 - 17.4}{0.25}$$
$$Z(\text{obtained}) = \frac{0.70}{0.25}$$
$$Z(\text{obtained}) = 2.8$$

Step 5. Making a Decision and Interpreting the Results of the Test. Comparing the test statistic with the critical region,

$$Z(\text{obtained}) = 2.8$$
$$Z(\text{critical}) = ±1.96$$

we would reject the null hypothesis. This test supports the conclusion that Americans and Canadians are different with respect to age at which smoking is initiated. Given the direction of the difference, we also note that Americans are significantly older at smoking initiation.

Source: Data from Statistics Canada, 2002–2003 Joint Canada/United States Survey of Health.

Step 5. Making a Decision and Interpreting the Results of the Test. Comparing the test statistic with the critical region:

$$Z(\text{obtained}) = -11.11$$
$$Z(\text{critical}) = ±1.96$$

We see that the Z score clearly falls into the critical region. This outcome indicates that a difference as large as -1.3 ($6.9 - 8.2$) between the sample means is unlikely if the null hypothesis is true. The null hypothesis of no difference can be rejected, and the notion that Canadian men and women are different in terms of their support of gun control is supported. The decision to reject the null hypothesis has only a 0.05 probability (the alpha level) of being incorrect.

Note that the value for Z(obtained) is negative, indicating that men have significantly lower scores than women for support for gun control. The sign of the test statistics reflects our arbitrary decision to label men sample 1 and women sample 2. If we had reversed the labels and called women sample 1 and men sample 2, the sign of the Z(obtained) would have been positive, but its value (11.11) would have been exactly the same, as would our decision in step 5. *(For practice in testing the significance of the difference between sample means for large samples, see problems 8.1 to 8.6, 8.9, and 8.15d to f.)*

8.3 HYPOTHESIS TESTING WITH SAMPLE MEANS (SMALL SAMPLES)

As with single-sample means, when the population standard deviation is unknown and sample size is small (combined n's of less than 100), the Z distribution can no longer be used to find areas under the sampling distribution. Instead, we will use the t distribution to find the critical region and thus to identify unlikely sample outcomes. To utilize the t distribution for testing two sample means, we need to perform one additional calculation and make one additional assumption. The calculation is for degrees of freedom, a quantity required for proper use of the t table (see Appendix B). In the two-sample case, degrees of freedom are equal to $n_1 + n_2 - 2$.

The additional assumption is a more complex matter. When samples are small, we must assume that the variances of the populations of interest are equal in order to justify the assumption of a normal sampling distribution and to form a pooled estimate of the standard deviation of the sampling distribution. The assumption of equal variance in the population can be tested by an inferential statistical technique known as the analysis of variance or ANOVA (see Chapter 9). For our purposes here, however, we will simply assume equal population variances without formal testing. This assumption is safe as long as sample sizes are approximately equal.

To illustrate this procedure we will again use real data. Sponsored by the Canada Millennium Scholarship Foundation, the Student Financial Survey is one of the most comprehensive studies to date on the financial circumstances of Canadian post-secondary students. The survey collected information, via the Internet and telephone, from a random sample of 1,500 post-secondary students from across Canada during the 2001–2002 academic year. Here we will use these data to test for a significant difference in GPA (grade point average) between men and women enrolled in graduate programs at the master's level at Canadian universities. The sample statistics computed for random samples of male and female master's students are reported below.

Sample 1 (Men)	Sample 2 (Women)
$\overline{X}_1 = 83.74$	$\overline{X}_2 = 82.16$
$s_1 = 6.59$	$s_2 = 9.35$
$n_1 = 39$	$n_2 = 42$

Source: Data from *Making Ends Meet, 2001–2002 Student Financial Survey*, Canada Millennium Scholarship Foundation. March 2003.

With this information, and following the five-step model, a test for the significance of the difference in GPA can now be conducted.

Step 1. Making Assumptions and Meeting Test Requirements. Sample size is small, and the population standard deviation is unknown. Hence, we must assume equal population variances in the model.

Model: Independent random samples
Level of measurement is interval-ratio
Population variances are equal $(\sigma_1^2 = \sigma_2^2)$
Sampling distribution is normal

Step 2. Stating the Null Hypothesis. Because no direction for the difference has been predicted, a two-tailed test will be used as reflected in the research hypothesis.

$$H_0: \mu_1 = \mu_2$$
$$(H_1: \mu_1 \neq \mu_2)$$

Step 3. Selecting the Sampling Distribution and Establishing the Critical Region. With small samples, the t distribution is used to establish the critical region. Alpha will be set at 0.05, and a two-tailed test will be used.

Sampling distribution = t distribution
Alpha = 0.05, two-tailed
Degrees of freedom = $n_1 + n_2 - 2 = 39 + 42 - 2 = 79$
$t\,(\text{critical}) = \pm 2.000$

Step 4. Computing the Test Statistic. With small samples, a different formula (see Formula 8.5) is used for the pooled estimate of the standard deviation of the sampling distribution. This value is then substituted directly into the denominator of the formula for $t\,(\text{obtained})$ given in Formula 8.6.

FORMULA 8.5

$$\sigma_{\overline{x}-\overline{x}} = \sqrt{\frac{n_1 s_1^2 + n_2 s_2^2}{n_1 + n_2 - 2}} \sqrt{\frac{n_1 + n_2}{n_1 n_2}}$$

$$\sigma_{\overline{x}-\overline{x}} = \sqrt{\frac{(39)(6.59)^2 + (42)(9.35)^2}{39 + 42 - 2}} \sqrt{\frac{39 + 42}{(39)(42)}}$$

$$\sigma_{\overline{x}-\overline{x}} = \sqrt{\frac{5{,}365}{79}} \sqrt{\frac{81}{1{,}638}}$$

$$\sigma_{\overline{x}-\overline{x}} = (8.24)(.22)$$

$$\sigma_{\overline{x}-\overline{x}} = 1.81$$

FORMULA 8.6

$$t(\text{obtained}) = \frac{(\overline{X}_1 - \overline{X}_2)}{\sigma_{\overline{x}-\overline{x}}}$$

$$t(\text{obtained}) = \frac{83.74 - 82.16}{1.81}$$

$$t(\text{obtained}) = \frac{1.58}{1.81}$$

$$t(\text{obtained}) = 0.87$$

Step 5. Making a Decision and Interpreting the Results of the Test. Comparing the test statistic with the critical region,

$$t(\text{obtained}) = 0.87$$
$$t(\text{critical}) = \pm 2.00$$

we can see that the test statistic $t(\text{obtained}) = 0.87$ does not fall into the critical region as marked by the $t(\text{critical})$ of ± 2.00. Thus, we fail to reject the null hypothesis. The difference between the sample means is trivial and no greater than what would be expected if the null hypothesis were true and only random chance were operating. Male and female master's students are not significantly different in GPA. The test statistic and sampling distribution are depicted in Figure 8.1. *(For practice in testing the significance of the difference between sample means for small samples, see problems 8.7 and 8.8.)*

FIGURE 8.1   THE SAMPLING DISTRIBUTION WITH CRITICAL REGION AND TEST STATISTIC DISPLAYED

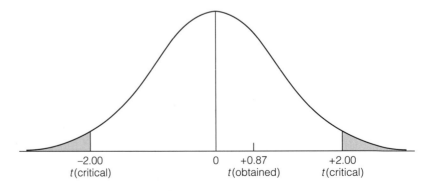

−2.00		0	+0.87	+2.00
t(critical)			*t*(obtained)	*t*(critical)

8.4 HYPOTHESIS TESTING WITH SAMPLE PROPORTIONS (LARGE SAMPLES)

Testing for the significance of the difference between two sample proportions is analogous to testing for two sample means. The null hypothesis states that no difference exists between the populations from which the samples are drawn on the trait being tested. The sample proportions form the basis of the test statistic computed in step 4, which is then compared with the critical region. When sample sizes are large (combined n's of 100 or more), the Z distribution may be used to find the critical region. We will not consider tests of significance for proportions based on small samples in this textbook.

In order to find the value of the test statistics, several preliminary equations must be solved. Formula 8.7 uses the values of the two sample proportions (P_s) to give us an estimate of the population proportion (P_u), the proportion of cases in the population that have the trait under consideration assuming the null hypothesis is true.

FORMULA 8.7

$$P_u = \frac{n_1 P_{s1} + n_2 P_{s2}}{n_1 + n_2}$$

The estimated value of P_u is then used to determine a value for the standard deviation of the sampling distribution of the difference in sample proportions in Formula 8.8:

FORMULA 8.8

$$\sigma_{p-p} = \sqrt{P_u(1 - P_u)} \sqrt{\frac{(n_1 + n_2)}{n_1 n_2}}$$

This value is then substituted into the formula for computing the test statistic, presented as Formula 8.9:

FORMULA 8.9

$$Z(\text{obtained}) = \frac{(P_{s1} - P_{s2}) - (P_{u1} - P_{u2})}{\sigma_{p-p}}$$

where $(P_{s1} - P_{s2})$ = the difference between the sample proportions
$(P_{u1} - P_{u2})$ = the difference between the population proportions
σ_{p-p} = the standard deviation of the sampling distribution of the difference between sample proportions

As was the case with sample means, the second term in the numerator is assumed to be zero by the null hypothesis. Therefore, the formula reduces to

FORMULA 8.10

$$Z(\text{obtained}) = \frac{(P_{s1} - P_{s2})}{\sigma_{p-p}}$$

Remember to solve these equations in order, starting with Formula 8.7 (and skipping Formula 8.9).

An example, with actual data, will make these procedures clearer. The prevalence of unmet health care needs is about the same in Canada and the United States: About one in ten adults in each country reports having a recent health care need that went unmet. We speculate, however, that the *reasons* for unmet health care needs are different in each country, and predict that Canadians are significantly more likely than Americans to have an unmet need due to long waiting times for care (waiting times to see a medical specialist or to have a diagnostic test, elective surgery, etc.). Using random samples from the 2002–2003 Joint Canada/United States Survey of Health (a Statistics Canada health survey conducted in partnership with the U.S. Centers for Disease Control and Prevention), the proportion of persons with an unmet health care need due to a waiting time problem in each country is reported below.

Sample 1 (United States)	Sample 2 (Canada)
$P_{s1} = 0.06$	$P_{s2} = 0.31$
$n_1 = 643$	$n_2 = 390$

The sample data reveal a difference in the predicted direction. Of the 643 Americans with unmet health care needs, just 40 (or a proportion of 0.06) reported long waiting times as the reason for their unmet needs. For the 390 Canadians with unmet health care needs, the proportion is 0.31. The significance of this observed difference can be tested with the five-step model.

Step 1. Making Assumptions and Meeting Test Requirements.

Model: Independent random samples
Level of measurement is nominal
Sampling distribution is normal

Step 2. Stating the Null Hypothesis. Because a direction has been predicted (Canadians are more likely to have their needs unmet because of waiting times), a one-tailed test will be used, and the research hypothesis is stated in accordance with this decision.

$$H_0: P_{u1} = P_{u2}$$

$$(H_1: P_{u1} < P_{u2})$$

Step 3. Selecting the Sampling Distribution and Establishing the Critical Region. Because the sample size is large, the Z distribution will be used to establish the critical region. Alpha will be set at 0.05 for a one-tailed test.

Sampling distribution = Z distribution
Alpha = 0.05, one-tailed
Z (critical) = -1.65

Step 4. Computing the Test Statistic. Begin with the formula for estimating P_u (see Formula 8.7), substitute the resultant value into Formula 8.8, and then solve for Z(obtained) with Formula 8.10.

$$P_u = \frac{n_1 P_{s1} + n_2 P_{s2}}{n_1 + n_2}$$

$$P_u = \frac{(643)(0.06) + (390)(0.31)}{643 + 390}$$

$$P_u = 0.15$$

$$\sigma_{p-p} = \sqrt{P_u(1 - P_u)} \sqrt{\frac{n_1 + n_2}{n_1 n_2}}$$

$$\sigma_{p-p} = \sqrt{(0.15)(0.85)} \sqrt{\frac{643 + 390}{(643)(390)}}$$

$$\sigma_{p-p} = (0.36)(0.06)$$

$$\sigma_{p-p} = 0.02$$

$$Z(\text{obtained}) = \frac{(P_{s1} - P_{s2})}{\sigma_{p-p}}$$

$$Z(\text{obtained}) = \frac{0.06 - 0.31}{0.02}$$

$$Z(\text{obtained}) = -12.5$$

Step 5. **Making a Decision and Interpreting the Results of the Test.** Comparing the test statistic with the critical region,

$$Z(\text{obtained}) = -12.5$$
$$Z(\text{critical}) = -1.65$$

we clearly see that the test statistic falls into the critical region. If the null ($P_{u1} = P_{u2}$) were true, this would be a very unlikely outcome, so the null can be rejected. There is a statistically significant difference between Americans and Canadians (a difference so large that it is unlikely to be due to random chance) in the proportion of those with an unmet health care need due to long waiting times. Specifically, in 2002–2003, Canadians were significantly more likely than Americans to report this problem. *(For practice in testing the significance of the difference between sample proportions, see problems 8.10 to 8.14 and 8.15a to c.)*

8.5 HYPOTHESIS TESTING USING INDIVIDUAL CONFIDENCE INTERVALS

In Chapter 7 we discussed the direct relationship between the confidence interval and hypothesis testing in the one-sample case. While the objective of each technique is different, they are indeed just different ways of expressing the same information about a single sample. For this reason, a confidence interval can be used as a convenient substitute for hypothesis testing.

In the two-sample case, there is a close, but not direct, relationship between the techniques. We can assess if the difference between two means (or proportions) is statistically significant by examining the overlap of the confidence interval for each mean (or proportion). However, confidence interval overlap is only an approximation of the formal hypothesis testing method discussed in Sections 8.2 through 8.4, and it is not equal to a formal hypothesis test.

For example, when the 95% confidence intervals for two means *do not overlap*, then the two means *will be* significantly different from one another at the 0.05 level. If the 95% confidence intervals *overlap*, then the difference between the means *will not be* statistically significant at the 0.05 level, most of the time! In other words, the confidence intervals for two means can overlap and yet the two means can be significantly different. The reason you can have an overlap in the individual confidence intervals, yet still find a statistically significant difference, is because each confidence interval takes into account just one sample size and one measure of variability, the single standard deviation, while the formal hypothesis test for the difference between two samples takes into consideration the larger (pooled) variance and sample size of the two samples together. Thus, in the case of an overlap we cannot rely on this method, and instead we must conduct a formal hypothesis test.

As an example of how to assess quickly the significance of the difference between sample means using the overlap of confidence intervals, let us take another look at the gun control example of Section 8.2. Recall that actual data from the Canadian Election Study was used to compute sample statistics for attitudes toward gun control for males and females, where higher scores indicate greater support of gun control, as follows:

Males	Females
$\overline{X}_1 = 6.9$	$\overline{X}_2 = 8.2$
$s_1 = 3.8$	$s_2 = 3.6$
$n_1 = 1,880$	$n_2 = 2,116$

Source: Data from 2006 Canadian Election Study.

Also recall that the decision was to reject the null hypothesis of no difference: Men and women are different in terms of their support of gun control.

Now, let us construct a 95% confidence interval for each sample mean using Formula 6.2 (see Chapter 6) as follows.

For males:

$$\text{c.i.} = \overline{X} \pm Z\left(\frac{s}{\sqrt{n-1}}\right)$$

$$\text{c.i.} = 6.9 \pm 1.96\left(\frac{3.8}{\sqrt{1,879}}\right)$$

$$\text{c.i.} = 6.9 \pm (1.96)(0.088)$$

$$\text{c.i.} = 6.9 \pm 0.17$$

For females:

$$c.i. = \bar{X} \pm z\left(\frac{s}{\sqrt{n-1}}\right)$$

$$c.i. = 8.2 \pm 1.96\left(\frac{3.6}{\sqrt{2,115}}\right)$$

$$c.i. = 8.2 \pm (1.96)(0.078)$$

$$c.i. = 8.2 \pm 0.15$$

Based on these results, we estimate, at the 95% level of confidence, that the population mean for males is greater than or equal to 6.73 and less than or equal to 7.07, and for females is greater than or equal to 8.05 and less than or equal to 8.35. Because the 95% confidence intervals for the two means do not overlap, we can reject the null hypothesis of no difference at the 0.05 level. The two means are significantly different from one another—precisely the decision we made above using formal hypothesis testing.

In summary, when confidence intervals do not overlap, the "confidence interval" and the formal hypothesis testing method always lead to the same decision, so either approach can be used as a test for the significance of the difference between sample means or sample proportions. By contrast, when confidence intervals overlap, then the difference between the sample means or sample proportions is most likely (most of the time) not statistically significant. In the case of an overlap we cannot rely on confidence interval overlap to determine statistical significance, and instead must use formal hypothesis testing. To put it briefly, the overlap of confidence intervals should be used only to "eyeball," or roughly estimate, the significance of the difference between sample means or proportions.

8.6 THE LIMITATIONS OF HYPOTHESIS TESTING: SIGNIFICANCE VS. IMPORTANCE

Given that we are usually interested in rejecting the null hypothesis, we should take a moment to consider systematically the factors that affect our decision in step 5. Generally speaking, the probability of rejecting the null hypothesis is a function of four independent factors:

1. The size of the observed difference(s)
2. The alpha level
3. The use of one- or two-tailed tests
4. The size of the sample

Only the first of these four is not under the direct control of the researcher. The size of the difference (either between the sample outcome and the population value or between two sample outcomes) is partly a function of the testing procedures (i.e., how variables are measured) but should generally reflect the underlying realities we are trying to probe.

The relationship between alpha level and the probability of rejection is straightforward. The higher the alpha level, the larger the critical region, the

---

Application 8.2

Over the past two decades, there has been a dramatic increase in obesity throughout the world. In this application we ask whether obesity rates differ between Canada and the United States? Once again, we will use data from the 2002–2003 Joint Canada/United States Survey of Health to compute the proportion of obese persons for each country.

United States	Canada
$P_{s1} = 0.21$	$P_{s2} = 0.15$
$n_1 = 4,971$	$n_2 = 3,369$

This is all the information we will need to conduct a test of the null hypothesis following the familiar five-step model with alpha set at 0.05, two-tailed test.

Step 1. Making Assumptions and Meeting Test Requirements.

Model: Independent random samples
Level of measurement is nominal
Sampling distribution is normal

Step 2. Stating the Null Hypothesis.

$$H_0: P_{u1} = P_{u2}$$
$$(H_1: P_{u1} \neq P_{u2})$$

Step 3. Selecting the Sampling Distribution and Establishing the Critical Region.

Sampling distribution = Z distribution
Alpha = 0.05, two-tailed
Z(critical) = ±1.96

Step 4. Computing the Test Statistic. Remember to start with Formula 8.7, substitute the value for P_u into Formula 8.8, and then substitute that value into Formula 8.10 to solve for Z(obtained).

$$P_u = \frac{n_1 P_{s1} + n_2 P_{s2}}{n_1 + n_2}$$

$$P_u = \frac{(4,971)(0.21) + (3,369)(0.15)}{4,971 + 3,369}$$

$$P_u = \frac{1,549.26}{8,340}$$

$$P_u = 0.19$$

$$\sigma_{p-p} = \sqrt{P_u(1 - P_u)} \sqrt{\frac{n_1 + n_2}{n_1 n_2}}$$

$$\sigma_{p-p} = \sqrt{(0.19)(0.81)} \sqrt{\frac{4,971 + 3,369}{(4,971)(3,369)}}$$

$$\sigma_{p-p} = \sqrt{0.1539} \sqrt{\frac{8,340}{16,747,299}}$$

$$\sigma_{p-p} = \sqrt{0.1539} \sqrt{0.0005}$$

$$\sigma_{p-p} = (0.39)(0.022)$$

$$\sigma_{p-p} = 0.009$$

$$Z(\text{obtained}) = \frac{(P_{s1} - P_{s2})}{\sigma_{p-p}}$$

$$Z(\text{obtained}) = \frac{0.21 - 0.15}{0.009}$$

$$Z(\text{obtained}) = \frac{0.06}{0.009}$$

$$Z(\text{obtained}) = 6.67$$

Step 5. Making a Decision and Interpreting the Results of the Test. With an obtained Z score of 6.67, we would reject the null hypothesis. There is a statistically significant difference between the United States and Canada in their obesity rates.

Source: Data from Statistics Canada, 2002–2003 Joint Canada/United States Survey of Health.

higher the percentage of all possible sample outcomes that fall in the critical region, and the greater the probability of rejection. Thus, it is easier to reject the H_0 at the 0.05 level than at the 0.01 level, and easier still at the 0.10 level. The danger here, of course, is that higher alpha levels will lead to more frequent Type I errors, and we might find ourselves declaring small differences to be statistically significant. In similar fashion, using a one-tailed test will increase the probability of rejection (assuming that the proper direction has been predicted).

The final factor is sample size: With all other factors constant, the probability of rejecting H_0 increases with sample size. In other words, the larger the sample, the more likely we are to reject the null hypothesis and, with very large samples (say samples with thousands of cases), we may declare small, unimportant differences to be statistically significant.

This relationship may appear to be surprising but the reasons for it can be appreciated with a brief consideration of the formulas used to compute test statistics in step 4. In all these formulas, for all tests of significance, sample size (n) is in the "denominator of the denominator." Algebraically, this is equivalent to being in the numerator of the formula and means that the value of the test statistic is directly proportional to n and that the two will increase together. To illustrate, consider Table 8.1, which shows the value of the test statistic for single sample means from samples of various sizes. The value of the test statistic, Z(obtained), increases as n increases even though none of the other terms in the formula changes. This pattern of higher probabilities for rejecting H_0 with larger samples holds for all tests of significance.

On one hand, the relationship between sample size and the probability of rejecting the null should not alarm us unduly. Larger samples are, after all, better approximations of the populations they represent. Thus, decisions based on larger samples can be trusted more than decisions based on small samples.

On the other hand, this relationship clearly underlines what is perhaps the most significant limitation of hypothesis testing. Simply because a difference is statistically significant does not guarantee that it is important in any other sense. Particularly with very large samples, relatively small differences may be statistically significant. Even with small samples, of course, differences that are otherwise trivial or uninteresting may be statistically significant. The crucial point is that statistical significance and theoretical or practical importance can be two very different things. Statistical significance is a necessary but not sufficient condition for theoretical or practical importance. A difference that is not statistically significant is almost certainly unimportant. However, significance by itself does not guarantee importance. Even when it is clear that the research results were not produced by random chance, the researcher must still assess their importance. Do they firmly support a theory or hypothesis? Are they clearly consistent with a prediction or analysis? Do they strongly indicate a line of action in solving some problem? These are the kinds of questions a researcher must ask when assessing the importance of the results of a statistical test.

Also, we should note that researchers have access to some very powerful ways of analyzing the importance (vs. the statistical significance) of research results. These statistics, including bivariate measures of association and multivariate statistical techniques, will be introduced in Parts III and IV of this textbook.

TABLE 8.1 TEST STATISTICS FOR SINGLE-SAMPLE MEANS COMPUTED FROM SAMPLES OF VARIOUS SIZES ($\overline{X} = 80$, $\mu = 79$, $s = 5$ throughout)

Sample Size	Test Statistic, Z(Obtained)
100	1.99
200	2.82
500	4.47

8.7 INTERPRETING STATISTICS: ARE THERE SIGNIFICANT DIFFERENCES IN INCOME BETWEEN MEN AND WOMEN?

In Canada, as in many other nations around the globe, concerted efforts have been made to equalize working conditions for men and women. How successful have these efforts been? Do significant differences in the income of men and women persist? Is there a "gender gap" in income?

We will investigate the relationship between gender and personal income using randomly selected samples of men and women from the full 2001 Census of Canada database. If the difference between the samples of men and women is large enough, we can infer that there is a difference in average income between men and women in the population.

Before conducting the test, we need to deal with an important issue. We should not compare the personal incomes of all men and all women because some difference could be caused by the fact that women are less likely to be in the paid labour market (i.e., they may be occupied as wives and mothers) and, thus, less likely to have an income. We will deal with this by restricting the comparison to respondents who work full-time.

To test for the significance of the difference in personal income, the following sample information was calculated:

Males	Females
$\overline{X}_1 = 43{,}681$	$\overline{X}_2 = 31{,}875$
$s_1 = 33{,}038$	$s_2 = 20{,}952$
$n_1 = 200{,}706$	$n_2 = 145{,}108$

Source: Data from Statistics Canada, *2001 Census of Canada*, individual PUMF.

It appears that there is a gender gap and that, on the average, males earn more than females. Is this difference in sample means between males and females significant? Could it have occurred by random chance?

Because we are dealing with large samples, we use the test of significance described in Section 8.2. The null hypothesis is that males and females have the same average income in the population ($\mu_1 = \mu_2$). We will skip the customary trip through the five-step model and simply report that the Z(obtained) calculated with Formula 8.2 (step 4) is 119.81, much greater than the customary Z(critical) score of ± 1.96 associated with an alpha level of 0.05. The difference in sample means is so large that we must reject the null hypothesis and conclude (with a probability of error of 0.05) that the population means are different: Males earn significantly more than females.

The large obtained Z score reflects in part the large sample size of the 2001 Census. We explained in the previous section that the probability of rejecting the null hypothesis increases with sample size. The obtained Z score and probability of rejecting the null hypothesis are further influenced by the size of the observed difference in means, and the census data show that men earn much more on average than women. We can conclude, then, the results are significant, and that they are likely to be important given that males earn on the average almost $12,000 a year more than females.

Why does a significant gender gap in income exist? Is it the result of differences in levels of education? If females were significantly less educated than males, this would account for at least some of the difference in income. We will again use the 2001 Census of Canada to get information on years of education for random samples of males and females.

The census measures education with a series of categories rather than in actual years. Respondents were asked to choose from a list of education ranges, for example, less than grade 5, 5 to 8 years, and so forth. Education is measured at the ordinal level, and we need an interval-ratio dependent variable to test for the significance of the difference between sample means.

One way to deal with this problem is simply to treat the ordinal variable as an interval-ratio variable. Another approach, the one used here, is to convert the variable to a form that more closely approximates interval-ratio data by substituting the midpoints for each interval of the variable. Instead of working with the interval "less than grade 5," we let the midpoint (i.e., 2 years) stand for the interval. The midpoint 6.5 is used for the "5 to 8 years" interval, and so on.

While this technique makes education a more numerical variable, it creates possible inaccuracies. Estimates of the population parameters from this modified variable should be treated only as gross approximations. Because we are concerned with difference in education rather than actual education itself, we should nonetheless be able to develop some conclusions:

Males	Females
$\overline{X}_1 = 13.67$	$\overline{X}_2 = 14.05$
$s_1 = 3.54$	$s_2 = 3.28$
$n_1 = 200{,}706$	$n_2 = 145{,}108$

Source: Data from Statistics Canada, *2001 Census of Canada*, individual PUMF.

We can see that both males and females average more than 13 years of schooling (one-and-a-half to two years more than a high school education) and that the average for females is actually higher than the average for males. The test statistic computed in step 4 is a Z(obtained) of -59.9. The test statistic is in the critical region, as marked by a Z(critical) score of ± 1.96 at the 0.05 level, so we reject the null hypothesis of no difference. Males and females differ in levels of schooling in the population: Females are significantly better educated than males. These results suggest that females are getting a lower return in income for their education, and that education is unlikely to account for the difference in income.

If not education, what else might explain the significant income gap between males and females? To answer this question entirely is far beyond the bounds of this statistics textbook. We can suggest that one important part of the answer lies in the fact that men and women pursue different kinds of careers and jobs. Men tend to dominate the more lucrative, higher-prestige occupations while women are concentrated in jobs that have lower levels of remuneration. According to the 2001 Census of Canada, over half of all women in the paid labour force work in either clerical or unskilled sales and service jobs, which tend to provide low wages. Just over 20% of all men work in these occupations.

READING STATISTICS 5: Hypothesis Testing

Professional researchers use a vocabulary that is much terser than ours when presenting the results of tests of significance. This is partly because of space limitations in scientific journals and partly because professional researchers can assume a certain level of statistical literacy in their audiences. Thus, they omit many of the elements—such as the null hypothesis or the critical region—that we have been so careful to state.

Instead, researchers report only the sample values (e.g., means or proportion), the value of the test statistic (e.g., a Z or t score), the alpha level, the degrees of freedom (if applicable), and sample size. The results of a study on number of children in suburban vs. centre-city families might be reported as "the difference between the sample means of 2.37 (suburban families) and 2.78 (centre-city families) was tested and found to be significant ($t = -2.16$, df $= 77$, $p < 0.05$)." Note that the alpha level is reported as "$p < 0.05$." This is shorthand for "the probability of a difference of this magnitude occurring by chance alone, if the null hypothesis of no difference is true, is less than 0.05" and is a good illustration of how researchers can convey a great deal of information in just a few symbols. In a similar fashion, our somewhat long-winded phrase "the test statistic falls in the critical region and, therefore, the null hypothesis is rejected" is rendered tersely and simply: "the difference ... was ... found to be significant."

When researchers need to report the results of many tests of significance, they will often use a summary table to report the sample information and whether the difference is significant at a certain alpha level. If you read the researcher's description and analysis of such tables, you should have little difficulty interpreting and understanding them. As a final note, these comments about how significance tests are reported in the literature apply to all of the tests of hypotheses covered in Part II of this textbook.

Statistics in the Professional Literature

Canadian education researcher J. Douglas Willms examined reading performances of youth in Canada and the United States using data from PISA (Programme for International Student Assessment). PISA is an international study of literacy skills of 15-year-old students. Students are selected following the principles of EPSEM. For more information on PISA, see Chapter 3.

Table 1 shows that Canadian youth outperform their American counterparts. The average PISA test score in overall reading literacy is 534 for Canadian students compared to 504 for U.S. students. Willms reports that the difference is statistically significant at $p < 0.05$.

Willms points out that the difference is also meaningful and important. A mean difference in reading scores of 30 points between Canadian and U.S. youth (534 vs. 504) is equivalent to almost one full year of schooling. Canadian 15-year-olds are a full year ahead of American 15-year-olds in reading literacy skills.

TABLE 1 TEST SCORES FOR READING LITERACY, BY COUNTRY

Canada	United States
$\overline{X}_1 = 534^*$	$\overline{X}_2 = 504^*$
$s_1 = 95$	$s_2 = 105$
$n_1 = 29{,}461$	$n_2 = 3{,}700$

$^*p < 0.05$

Source: Data from Willms, J. D. 2004. *Reading Achievement in Canada and the United States: Findings from the OECD Programme for International Student Assessment.* Human Resources Skills and Development Canada. Catalogue Number: HS28-3/2004E. http://www.hrsdc.gc.ca/en/cs/sp/lp/publications/2004-002611/page00.shtml.

SUMMARY

1. A common research situation is to test for the significance of the difference between two populations. Sample statistics are calculated for random samples of each population, and then we test for the significance of the difference between the samples as a way of inferring differences between the specified populations.

2. When sample information is summarized in the form of sample means, and n is large, the Z distribution is used to find the critical region. When n is small, the t distribution is used to establish the critical region. In the latter circumstance, we must also assume equal population variances before forming a pooled estimate of the standard deviation of the sampling distribution.

3. Differences in sample proportions may also be tested for significance. For large samples, the Z distribution is used to find the critical region.

4. A two-sample hypothesis test can be approximated using confidence intervals. When the confidence intervals for two samples do not overlap, then the null hypothesis of no difference between the populations will be rejected at the stated alpha level. If the confidence intervals overlap, then the difference will not be statistically significant most of the time. Hence, in the case of an overlap, we must further conduct the two-sample hypothesis test described in this chapter.

5. In all tests of hypothesis, a number of factors affect the probability of rejecting the null: the size of the difference, the alpha level, the use of one- vs. two-tailed tests, and sample size. Statistical significance is not the same thing as theoretical or practical importance. Even after a difference is found to be statistically significant, the researcher must still demonstrate the relevance or importance of his or her findings. The statistics presented in Parts III and IV of this textbook will give us the tools we need to deal directly with issues beyond statistical significance.

SUMMARY OF FORMULAS

Test statistic for two sample means, large samples:

8.1 $\qquad Z(\text{obtained}) = \dfrac{(\overline{X}_1 - \overline{X}_2) - (\mu_1 - \mu_2)}{\sigma_{\overline{x}-\overline{x}}}$

Test statistic for two sample means, large samples (simplified formula):

8.2 $\qquad Z(\text{obtained}) = \dfrac{(\overline{X}_1 - \overline{X}_2)}{\sigma_{\overline{x}-\overline{x}}}$

Standard deviation of the sampling distribution of the difference in sample means, large samples:

8.3 $\qquad \sigma_{\overline{x}-\overline{x}} = \sqrt{\dfrac{\sigma_1^2}{n_1} + \dfrac{\sigma_2^2}{n_2}}$

Pooled estimate of the standard deviation of the sampling distribution of the difference in sample means, large samples:

8.4 $\qquad \sigma_{\overline{x}-\overline{x}} = \sqrt{\dfrac{s_1^2}{n_1 - 1} + \dfrac{s_2^2}{n_2 - 1}}$

Pooled estimate of the standard deviation of the sampling distribution of the difference in sample means, small samples:

8.5 $\qquad \sigma_{\overline{x}-\overline{x}} = \sqrt{\dfrac{n_1 s_1^2 + n_2 s_2^2}{n_1 + n_2 - 2}} \sqrt{\dfrac{n_1 + n_2}{n_1 n_2}}$

Test statistic for two sample means, small samples:

8.6 $\qquad t(\text{obtained}) = \dfrac{(\overline{X}_1 - \overline{X}_2)}{\sigma_{\overline{x}-\overline{x}}}$

Pooled estimate of population proportion, large samples:

8.7 $\qquad P_u = \dfrac{n_1 P_{s1} + n_2 P_{s2}}{n_1 + n_2}$

Standard deviation of the sampling distribution of the difference in sample proportions, large samples:

8.8 $\qquad \sigma_{p-p} = \sqrt{P_u(1 - P_u)} \sqrt{\dfrac{n_1 + n_2}{n_1 n_2}}$

Test statistic for two sample proportions, large samples:

8.9 $\quad Z(\text{obtained}) = \dfrac{(P_{s1} - P_{s2}) - (P_{u1} - P_{u2})}{\sigma_{p-p}}$

Test statistic for two sample proportions, large samples (simplified formula):

8.10 $\quad Z(\text{obtained}) = \dfrac{(P_{s1} - P_{s2})}{\sigma_{p-p}}$

GLOSSARY

Independent random samples. Random samples gathered in such a way that the selection of a particular case for one sample has no effect on the probability that any particular case will be selected for the other samples. (p. 219)

Pooled estimate. An estimate of the standard deviation of the sampling distribution of the difference in sample means based on the standard deviations of both samples. (p. 221)

MULTIMEDIA RESOURCES

 http://www.healeystatistics.nelson.com

Visit the companion website for the second Canadian edition of *Statistics: A Tool for Social Research* to access a wide range of student resources. Begin by clicking on the Student Resources section of the textbook's website to access review quizzes, flashcards, and other study tools.

PROBLEMS

8.1 For each problem below, test for the significance of the difference in sample statistics using the five-step model. *(HINT: Remember to solve Formula 8.4 before attempting to solve Formula 8.2. Also, in Formula 8.4, perform the mathematical operations in the proper sequence. First square each sample standard deviation, then divide by $n - 1$, add the resultant values, and then find the square root of the sum.)*

a. Sample 1	Sample 2
$\bar{X}_1 = 72.5$	$\bar{X}_2 = 76.0$
$s_1 = 14.3$	$s_2 = 10.2$
$n_1 = 136$	$n_2 = 257$

b. Sample 1	Sample 2
$\bar{X}_1 = 107$	$\bar{X}_2 = 103$
$s_1 = 14$	$s_2 = 17$
$n_1 = 175$	$n_2 = 200$

8.2 SOC Questionnaires were administered to samples of undergraduate students. Among other things, the questionnaires contained a scale that measured attitudes toward interpersonal violence (higher scores indicate greater approval of interpersonal violence). Test the results as reported below for differences in sex and social-class background.

a. Sample 1 (Males)	Sample 2 (Females)
$\bar{X}_1 = 2.99$	$\bar{X}_2 = 2.99$
$s_1 = 0.88$	$s_2 = 0.91$
$n_1 = 122$	$n_2 = 251$

b. Sample 1 (White Collar)	Sample 2 (Blue Collar)
$\bar{X}_1 = 2.46$	$\bar{X}_2 = 2.67$
$s_1 = 0.91$	$s_2 = 0.87$
$n_1 = 249$	$n_2 = 97$

c. Summarize your results in terms of the significance and the direction of the differences. Which of these two factors seems to make the biggest difference in attitudes toward interpersonal violence?

8.3 SOC Do athletes in different sports vary in terms of intelligence? Below are aptitude test scores of random samples of university varsity hockey and soccer players. Is there a significant difference? Write a sentence or two explaining the difference.

a.

Sample 1 (Hockey Players)	Sample 2 (Soccer Players)
$\bar{X}_1 = 460$	$\bar{X}_2 = 442$
$s_1 = 92$	$s_2 = 57$
$n_1 = 102$	$n_2 = 117$

What about male and female university athletes?

b.

Sample 1 (Males)	Sample 2 (Females)
$\bar{X}_1 = 452$	$\bar{X}_2 = 480$
$s_1 = 88$	$s_2 = 75$
$n_1 = 107$	$n_2 = 105$

8.4 PA A number of years ago, the fire department in Pearson, Ontario began recruiting females through an employment equity program. In terms of efficiency ratings as compiled by their superiors, how do the employment equity employees rate? The ratings of random samples of both groups were collected, and the results are reported below (higher ratings indicate greater efficiency).

Sample 1 (Employment Equity)	Sample 2 (Regular)
$\bar{X}_1 = 15.2$	$\bar{X}_2 = 15.5$
$s_1 = 3.9$	$s_2 = 2.0$
$n_1 = 97$	$n_2 = 100$

Write a sentence or two of interpretation.

8.5 SOC Are middle-class families more likely than working-class families to maintain contact with relatives? Write a paragraph summarizing the results of these tests.

a. A sample of middle-class families reported an average of 7.3 visits per year with close relatives while a sample of working-class families averaged 8.2 visits. Is the difference significant?

Visits

Sample 1 (Middle Class)	Sample 2 (Working Class)
$\bar{X}_1 = 7.3$	$\bar{X}_2 = 8.2$
$s_1 = 0.3$	$s_2 = 0.5$
$n_1 = 89$	$n_2 = 55$

b. The middle-class families averaged 2.3 phone calls and 8.7 e-mail messages per month with close relatives. The working-class families averaged 2.7 calls and 5.7 e-mail messages per month. Are these differences significant?

Phone Calls

Sample 1 (Middle Class)	Sample 2 (Working Class)
$\bar{X}_1 = 3$	$\bar{X}_2 = 2.7$
$s_1 = 0.5$	$s_2 = 0.8$
$n_1 = 89$	$n_2 = 55$

E-mail Messages

Sample 1 (Middle Class)	Sample 2 (Working Class)
$\bar{X}_1 = 8.7$	$\bar{X}_2 = 5.7$
$s_1 = 0.3$	$s_2 = 1.1$
$n_1 = 89$	$n_2 = 55$

8.6 SOC Are university students who live in residence significantly more involved in campus life than students who commute to campus? The data below report the average number of hours per week students devote to extracurricular activities. Is the difference between these randomly selected samples of commuter and residential students significant?

Sample 1 (Residential)	Sample 2 (Commuter)
$\bar{X}_1 = 12.4$	$\bar{X}_2 = 10.2$
$s_1 = 2.0$	$s_2 = 1.9$
$n_1 = 158$	$n_2 = 173$

8.7 SOC Are senior citizens who live in retirement communities more socially active than those who live in age-integrated communities? Write a sentence or two explaining the results of these tests. (*HINT: Remember to use the proper formulas for small sample sizes.*)

a. A random sample of senior citizens living in a retirement village reported that they had an average of 1.42 face-to-face interactions per day with their neighbours. A random sample of those living in age-Integrated communities reported 1.58 interactions. Is the difference significant?

Sample 1 (Retirement Community)	Sample 2 (Age-Integrated Neighbourhood)
$\bar{X}_1 = 1.42$	$\bar{X}_2 = 1.58$
$s_1 = 0.10$	$s_2 = 0.78$
$n_1 = 43$	$n_2 = 37$

b. Senior citizens living in the retirement village reported that they had 7.43 telephone calls with friends and relatives each week while those in the age-integrated communities reported 5.50 calls. Is the difference significant?

Sample 1 (Retirement Community)	Sample 2 (Age-Integrated Neighbourhood)
$\bar{X}_1 = 7.43$	$\bar{X}_2 = 5.50$
$s_1 = 0.75$	$s_2 = 0.25$
$n_1 = 43$	$n_2 = 37$

8.8 SW As the director of the local Youth Club, you have claimed for years that membership in your club reduces juvenile delinquency. Now, a cynical member of your funding agency has demanded proof of your claim. Fortunately, your local sociology department is on your side and springs to your aid with student assistants, computers, and hand calculators at the ready. Random samples of members and non-members are gathered and interviewed with respect to their involvement in delinquent activities. Each respondent is asked to enumerate the number of delinquent acts he or she has engaged in over the past year. The results are in and reported below (the average number of admitted acts of delinquency). What can you tell the funding agency?

Sample 1 (Members)	Sample 2 (Non-Members)
$\bar{X}_1 = 10.3$	$\bar{X}_2 = 12.3$
$s_1 = 2.7$	$s_2 = 4.2$
$n_1 = 40$	$n_2 = 55$

8.9 SOC A survey has been administered to random samples of respondents in each of five nations. For each nation, are men and women significantly different in terms of their reported levels of satisfaction? Respondents were asked: "How satisfied are you with your life as a whole?" Responses varied from 1 (very dissatisfied) to 10 (very satisfied). Conduct a test for the significance of the difference in mean scores for each nation.

Canada

Males	Females
$\bar{X}_1 = 7.4$	$\bar{X}_2 = 7.7$
$s_1 = 0.20$	$s_2 = 0.25$
$n_1 = 1,005$	$n_2 = 1,234$

Nigeria

Males	Females
$\bar{X}_1 = 6.7$	$\bar{X}_2 = 7.8$
$s_1 = 0.16$	$s_2 = 0.23$
$n_1 = 1,825$	$n_2 = 1,256$

China

Males	Females
$\bar{X}_1 = 7.6$	$\bar{X}_2 = 7.1$
$s_1 = 0.21$	$s_2 = 0.11$
$n_1 = 1,400$	$n_2 = 1,200$

Mexico

Males	Females
$\bar{X}_1 = 8.3$	$\bar{X}_2 = 9.1$
$s_1 = 0.29$	$s_2 = 0.30$
$n_1 = 1,645$	$n_2 = 1,432$

Japan

Males	Females
$\bar{X}_1 = 8.8$	$\bar{X}_2 = 9.3$
$s_1 = 0.34$	$s_2 = 0.32$
$n_1 = 1,621$	$n_2 = 1,683$

8.10 For each problem, test the sample statistics for the significance of the difference. (*HINT: In testing proportions, remember to begin with Formula 8.7, then solve Formulas 8.8 and 8.10.*)

a.

Sample 1	Sample 2
$P_{s1} = 0.17$	$P_{s2} = 0.20$
$n_1 = 101$	$n_2 = 114$

b.

Sample 1	Sample 2
$P_{s1} = 0.62$	$P_{s2} = 0.60$
$n_1 = 532$	$n_2 = 478$

8.11 | CJ | About half of the police officers in Pearson, Ontario have completed a special course in investigative procedures. Has the course increased their efficiency in clearing crimes by arrest? The proportions of cases cleared by arrest for samples of trained and untrained officers are reported below.

Trained	Untrained
$P_{s1} = 0.47$	$P_{s2} = 0.43$
$n_1 = 157$	$n_2 = 113$

8.12 | SW | A large counselling centre needs to evaluate several experimental programs. Write a paragraph summarizing the results of these tests. Did the new programs work?

a. One program is designed for divorce counselling; the key feature of the program is its counsellors, who are married couples working in teams. About half of all clients have been randomly assigned to this special program and half to the regular program, and the proportion of cases that eventually ended in divorce was recorded for both. The results for random samples of couples from both programs are reported below. In terms of preventing divorce, did the new program work?

Special Program	Regular Program
$P_{s1} = 0.53$	$P_{s2} = 0.59$
$n_1 = 78$	$n_2 = 82$

b. The agency is also experimenting with peer counselling for depressed children. About half of all clients were randomly assigned to peer counselling. After the program had run for a year, a random sample of children from the new program was compared with a random sample of children who did not receive peer counselling. In terms of the percentage who were judged to be "much improved," did the new program work?

Peer Counselling	No Peer Counselling
$P_{s1} = 0.10$	$P_{s2} = 0.15$
$n_1 = 52$	$n_2 = 56$

8.13 | SOC | At Algebra University, the sociology and psychology departments have been feuding for years about the respective quality of their programs. In an attempt to resolve the dispute, you have gathered data about the graduate school experience of random samples of both groups of majors. The results are presented below: the proportion of majors who applied to graduate schools, the proportion of majors accepted into their preferred programs, and the proportion of these groups who completed their programs. As measured by these data, is there a significant difference in program quality?

a. Proportion of majors who applied to graduate school:

Sociology	Psychology
$P_{s1} = 0.53$	$P_{s2} = 0.40$
$n_1 = 150$	$n_2 = 175$

b. Proportion accepted by program of first choice:

Sociology	Psychology
$P_{s1} = 0.75$	$P_{s2} = 0.85$
$n_1 = 80$	$n_2 = 70$

c. Proportion completing the programs:

Sociology	Psychology
$P_{s1} = 0.75$	$P_{s2} = 0.69$
$n_1 = 60$	$n_2 = 60$

8.14 | CJ | The local police chief started a "crimeline" program some years ago and wonders if it's really working. The program publicizes unsolved violent crimes in the local media and offers cash rewards for information leading to arrests. Are "featured" crimes more likely to be cleared by arrest than other violent crimes? Results from random samples of both types of crimes are reported as follows:

Crimeline Crimes Cleared by Arrest	Non-Crimeline Crimes Cleared by Arrest
$P_{s1} = 0.35$	$P_{s2} = 0.25$
$n_1 = 178$	$n_2 = 212$

8.15 | SOC | Some results from a recent social survey administered to a random sample of adults are reported below in terms of differences by sex. Which of these differences, if any, are significant? Write a sentence or two of interpretation for each test.

a. Proportion favouring the legalization of marijuana:

Sample 1 (Males)	Sample 2 (Females)
$P_{s1} = 0.37$	$P_{s2} = 0.31$
$n_1 = 202$	$n_2 = 246$

b. Proportion strongly agreeing that "kids are life's greatest joy":

Sample 1 (Males)	Sample 2 (Females)
$P_{s1} = 0.47$	$P_{s2} = 0.58$
$n_1 = 251$	$n_2 = 351$

c. Proportion voting in the last federal election:

Sample 1 (Males)	Sample 2 (Females)
$P_{s1} = 0.59$	$P_{s2} = 0.47$
$n_1 = 399$	$n_2 = 509$

d. Average hours spent on e-mail each week:

Sample 1 (Males)	Sample 2 (Females)
$\bar{X}_1 = 4.18$	$\bar{X}_2 = 3.38$
$s_1 = 7.21$	$s_2 = 5.92$
$n_1 = 431$	$n_2 = 535$

e. Average number of times religious service attended each month:

Sample 1 (Males)	Sample 2 (Females)
$\bar{X}_1 = 3.19$	$\bar{X}_2 = 3.99$
$s_1 = 2.60$	$s_2 = 2.72$
$n_1 = 641$	$n_2 = 808$

f. Average number of children:

Sample 1 (Males)	Sample 2 (Females)
$\bar{X}_1 = 1.49$	$\bar{X}_2 = 1.93$
$s_1 = 1.50$	$s_2 = 1.50$
$n_1 = 635$	$n_2 = 803$

SPSS for Windows

Using SPSS for Windows to Test the Significance of the Difference between Two Means with the 2009 GSS

The demonstrations and exercises below use the shortened version of the 2009 GSS data set supplied with this textbook.

SPSS DEMONSTRATION 8.1 Do Men and Women Differ in Social Activity?

SPSS for Windows includes several tests for the significance of the difference between means. In this demonstration, we'll use the **Independent-Samples T Test**, to test for the significance of the difference between men and women in how often they go out in the evening to engage in leisure activities such as visiting friends or going to a bar, restaurant, movie, casino, shopping mall, or gym? If there is a statistically significant difference between the sample means for men and women, we can conclude that the populations (all Canadian adult men and women) are different on this variable.

Start SPSS for Windows and load the 2009 GSS database (*GSS.sav*). From the main menu bar, click **Analyze**, then **Compare Means**, and then **Independent-Samples T Test**. The Independent-Samples T Test dialog box will open with the usual list of variables on the left. Find and move the cursor over *numevact_c* (average number of evening activities respondent goes out for in a month) and click the top arrow in the middle of the window to move *numevact_c* to the **Test Variable(s)** box. Next, find and highlight *sex* and click the button arrow in the middle of the window to move *sex* to the **Grouping Variable** box. Two question marks will appear in the **Grouping Variable** box, and the **Define Groups** button will become active. SPSS needs to know which cases go in which groups, and in the case at hand, the instructions we need to supply are straightforward. Males (indicated by a score of 1 on *sex*) go into group 1 and females (a score of 2) will go into group 2.

Click the **Define Groups** button, and the **Define Groups** window will appear. The cursor will be blinking in the box beside Group 1—SPSS is asking for the score that will determine which cases go into this group. Type a 1 in this box (for males) and then click the box next to Group 2 and type a 2 (for females). Click **Continue** to return to the **Independent-Samples T Test** window and click **OK** and the output below will be produced.

Group Statistics

	Sex of respondent	*N*	Mean	Std. Deviation	Std. Error Mean
Average number of evening activities respondent goes out for	Male	747	28.64	17.233	.631
	Female	765	23.68	16.938	.613

Independent Samples Test

		Levene's Test for Equality of Variances		*t*-test for Equality of Means						95% Confidence Interval of the Difference	
		F	Sig.	*t*	df	Sig. (2-tailed)	Mean Difference	Std. Error Difference	Lower	Upper
Average number of evening activities respondent goes out for	Equal variances assumed	2.251	.134	5.647	1510	.000	4.963	.879	3.239	6.687
	Equal variances not assumed			5.646	1507.260	.000	4.963	.879	3.238	6.687

In the first block of output ("Group Statistics") there are some descriptive statistics. There were 747 males in the sample, and they participated in 28.64 activities during the evening in an average month, with a standard deviation of 17.233. The 765 females went out an average of 23.68 times per month with a standard deviation of 16.938.

We can see from this output that the sample means are different and that, on the average, males go out in the evening more often. Is the difference in sample means significant? The results of the test for significance are reported in the next block ("Independent Samples Test") of output.

For now, we will skip over the first two columns which report the results of a test for equality of the population variances. Results in the remaining columns in the row labelled "Equal variances assumed" are based on the same model used in this chapter. To test the significance of the difference between two means we can either manually look up the t value (5.647) in the t table (see Appendix B), as practised throughout this chapter, or more conveniently use the "Sig. (2-tailed)" value (.000), where "Sig." means significance. The value of .000 is the alpha level, except it is the *exact probability* of getting the observed difference in sample means if only chance is operating. Thus it is often called the "p" level (see the Reading Statistics 5 box). However, do not interpret .000 as a zero probability. It simply means that the exact probability value is less than .0005. The exact value is revealed by double-clicking on the "Sig. (2-tailed)" value in the output, but to save space, SPSS cuts it off at three decimal places, or .000.

Because SPSS provides the exact probability (cut off at three decimal places), there is no need to look up the test statistic in a t table. This value (.000) is less than .05, our usual indicator of significance, so we reject the null hypothesis and conclude that the difference in means is statistically significant. On the average, men and women do differ significantly in how often they go out in the evening.

These results are based on the assumption that the population variances are equal. In Section 8.3 we noted that this assumption is safe as long as sample sizes are approximately equal, as they are in this case. However, SPSS for Windows provides a *formal* test for equal variances in the population: Levene's Test for Equality of Variances. If the Levene's Test for Equality of Variances is significant (i.e., if the value under the "Sig." column is less than .05, as per our usual indicator of significance), the variances are significantly different. If this is the case, a modified t test should be used, which appears in the row labelled "Equal variances not assumed." A value *greater* than .05 indicates that the assumption of equal variances has been met and that the t test in that row can be used.

The last two columns report the 95% confidence interval for the difference in means. Recall from our discussion in Section 7.8 that a hypothesis test will reject a null hypothesis if a confidence interval does not contain the value of the parameter specified by the null hypothesis, and vice versa. Using the conventional hypothesis test approach, we rejected the null hypothesis that males and females on average go out the same number of times in the population ($\mu_1 - \mu_2 = 0$) because the significance value of .000 was less than .05. We would make exactly the same decision using the 95% confidence interval for the difference in means. Because the interval, with a range of 3.239 to 6.687, does not contain the hypothesized null value, 0, the hypothesis is rejected at the 0.05 level.

SPSS DEMONSTRATION 8.2 The Error Bar Graph

In Demonstration 6.2, we produced an error bar graph for the confidence interval for the mean. As we will demonstrate here, the error bar graph is especially useful when two (or more) groups are being compared because we can quickly assess if there is a statistically significant difference between two means by examining if the two confidence intervals overlap.

It is very important to note, as discussed in Section 8.5, that using the overlap of confidence intervals for *each mean* provides only an approximation of the statistical significance of the difference between sample means. The confidence interval for the *difference in means* illustrated in Demonstration 8.1, on the other hand, provides a precise test for the significance of the difference. The latter is equal to formal hypothesis testing, the former is not.

To produce an error bar graph of the 95% confidence interval of each mean, click **Graphs, Legacy Dialogs,** and then **Error Bar**. The **Error Bars** dialog box appears, with the **Simple** and **Summaries for Groups of Cases** buttons already highlighted. These are the ones we want, so just click **Define**. The **Define Simple Error Bar** dialog box appears. Transfer the dependent variable, *numevact_c*, to the **Variable** box and the independent variable, *sex*, to the **Category Axis** box, and then click **OK**, and the following error bars will be produced:

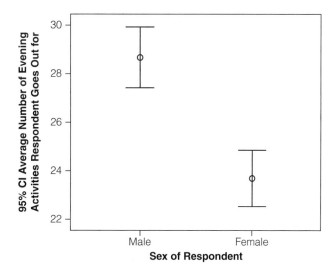

The error bars show that the sample means (marked by the small circles on each bar), are different and that, on the average, males go out in the evening more often than females. Further, the confidence intervals (indicated by the length of each bar) do not overlap, so the two means are significantly different from one another. This approximates the decision we made in Demonstration 8.1.

SPSS DEMONSTRATION 8.3 Using the COMPUTE Command to Test for Gender Differences in Perception of Criminal Courts

SPSS provides a variety of tools to transform and manipulate variables. One of these tools is the SPSS **Compute** command. Appendix F.5 provides a step-by-step demonstration of the **Compute** command to create a summary scale of perception of criminal courts (*crtscale*) by adding the scores on the three constituent items (*pcc_q120, pcc_q130,* and *pcc_q140*). You can quickly create the *crtscale* variable by following that demonstration.

Here we will test *crtscale* for the significance of the difference by gender. Our question is: "Do men and women have different perceptions of the job done by criminal courts?" If the difference in the sample means is large enough, we can reject the null hypothesis and conclude that the populations are different.

To answer the question follow the instructions in Demonstration 8.1 for using the **Independent-Samples T Test** command, and move *crtscale* rather than *numevact_c* to the **Test Variable(s)** box. If necessary, repeat the procedure for making *sex* the grouping variable. Your output will be as shown:

Group Statistics

	Sex of respondent	N	Mean	Std. Deviation	Std. Error Mean
crtscale	Male	747	5.3189	1.60994	.05890
	Female	765	5.4024	1.61268	.05832

Independent Samples Test

		Levene's Test for Equality of Variances		t-test for Equality of Means							
								Std. Error Difference	95% Confidence Interval of the Difference	
		F	Sig.	t	df	Sig. (2-tailed)	Mean Difference		Lower	Upper
crtscale	Equal variances assumed	.015	.902	-1.007	1510	.314	-.08350	.08289	-.24609	.07910
	Equal variances not assumed			-1.007	1509.045	.314	-.08350	.08289	-.24608	.07909

We can assume equal variances because the Levene's Test for Equality of Variances is not significant—the value under the "Sig." column is *greater* than .05. Next, the results show that the sample means are very close in value (5.3189 vs. 5.4024) and the test statistic ($t = -1.007$) is not significant, as indicated by the "Sig. (2-tailed)" value of .314. There is no significant gender difference in attitude toward criminal courts. We should point out that *crtscale* is only ordinal in level of measurement. Scales like this are often treated as interval-ratio variables, but we should still be cautious in interpreting the results.

Exercises (using *GSS.sav*)

8.1 Does the level of alcohol consumption significantly differ between males and females? Using Demonstration 8.1 as a guide, test for a significant difference in alcohol consumption levels (variable name *drr_q120*) between males and females. Write a sentence or two summarizing the results of this test.

8.2 Using Demonstration 8.3 as a guide, construct a summary scale for "perception of police" using *plp_q130, plp_q150,* and *plp_q160* in place of *pcc_q120, pcc_q130,* and *pcc_q140.* Test for the significance of the difference using *sex* as the independent variable. Write a sentence or two summarizing the results of this test.

8.3 What other independent variables might explain differences in the "perception of police scale" constructed in Exercise 8.2? Select three more independent variables besides *sex* and conduct additional *t* tests with this scale as the dependent variable. Write a sentence or two summarizing the results of these tests.*

---

*The *t* test requires the independent variable to have only two categories, but you can use a variable with more than two categories (e.g., marital status) and just restrict the *t* test to any two groups (e.g., married vs. single, married vs. divorced, widowed versus separated). To do this, open the **Independent-Samples T Test** dialog box, put *marstat* (marital status) in the **Grouping Variable** box, and then click the **Define Groups** button to indicate the two groups you wish to compare (e.g., to compare married and single persons, type the value 1 [married] in the **Group 1** textbox and value 6 [single] in the **Group 2** textbox, or vice-versa because the *t* test results will be exactly the same if you define single as group 1 and married as group 2).

9

Hypothesis Testing III
The Analysis of Variance

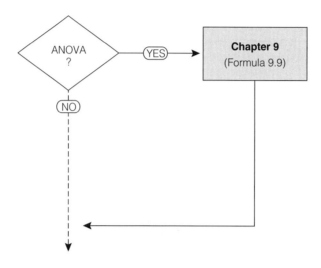

9.1 INTRODUCTION

In this chapter, we will examine a very flexible and widely used test of significance called the **analysis of variance** (often abbreviated as **ANOVA**). This test can be used in a number of situations where previously discussed tests are less than optimum or entirely inappropriate. ANOVA is designed to be used with interval-ratio-level dependent variables and is a powerful tool for analyzing the most sophisticated and precise measurements you are likely to encounter.

It is perhaps easiest to think of ANOVA as an extension of the *t* test for the significance of the difference between two sample means, which was presented in Chapter 8. The *t* test can be used only in situations in which our independent variable has exactly two categories (e.g., immigrants and non-immigrants). The analysis of variance, on the other hand, is appropriate for independent variables with more than two categories (e.g., married/common-law, single, widowed, separated, and divorced).

To illustrate, suppose we conducted an experiment in teaching introductory biology at a large university. One section was taught by the traditional "lecture-lab" method, a second was taught by an "all-lab" approach with no lectures, and a third was taught entirely by a series of "videotaped" lectures and demonstrations that the students were free to view at any time and as often as they wanted. Students were randomly assigned to one of three sections, and at the end of the semester, random samples of final exam scores were collected from each section. Is there a significant difference in student performance on the final exam by teaching method? Because the independent variable (teaching method) has three categories and the dependent variable (final exam score) is measured at the interval-ratio level, analysis of variance provides a very useful statistical context in which this question can be addressed.

9.2 THE LOGIC OF THE ANALYSIS OF VARIANCE

For ANOVA, the null hypothesis is that the populations from which the samples are drawn are equal on the characteristic of interest. As applied to our problem, the null hypothesis could be phrased as "Students in the three different sections of introductory biology at the university do not vary in their final exam scores," or symbolically as $\mu_1 = \mu_2 = \mu_3$. (Note that this is an extended version of the null hypothesis for the two-sample *t* test.) As usual, the researcher will normally be interested in rejecting the null and, in this case, showing that final exam grades are related to teaching method.

If the null hypothesis of "no difference" in the populations is true, then any means calculated from randomly selected samples should be roughly equal in value. The average final exam score for the "lecture-lab" sample should be about the same as the average score for the "all-lab" sample and the "videotaped" sample. Note that the averages are unlikely to be exactly the same value even if the null hypothesis really is true, as we will always encounter some error or chance fluctuations in the measurement process. We are *not* asking: "Are there differences between the samples or categories of the independent variable (or, in our example, the sections of the introductory biology course)?" Rather, we are asking: "Are the differences between the samples large enough to reject the null hypothesis and justify the conclusion that the populations are different?"

Now, consider what kinds of outcomes we might encounter when conducting the teaching method experiment. Of the infinite variety of

TABLE 9.1   FINAL EXAM SCORES BY TEACHING METHOD

	Lecture-Lab	All-Lab	Videotaped
Mean =	70.3	71.0	70.1
Standard Deviation =	12.4	11.9	12.2

TABLE 9.2   FINAL EXAM SCORES BY TEACHING METHOD

	Lecture-Lab	All-Lab	Videotaped
Mean =	84.7	71.3	65.7
Standard Deviation =	12.4	11.9	12.2

possibilities, let's focus on two extreme outcomes as exemplified by Tables 9.1 and 9.2. In the first set of hypothetical results (Table 9.1), we see that the means and standard deviations of the groups are quite similar. The average scores are about the same for every group of students and all three groups exhibit about the same dispersion. These results would be quite consistent with the null hypothesis of no difference. Neither the average score nor the dispersion of the scores changes in any important way by section.

Now consider another set of fictitious results as displayed in Table 9.2. Here we see substantial differences in average score from category to category, with the "Videotaped" group having the lowest average score and the "Lecture-Lab" group having the highest. Also, the standard deviations are low and similar from group to group, indicating that there is not much variation within the groups of students. Table 9.2 shows marked differences *between* groups of students combined with homogeneity *within* groups of students, as indicated by the low values of the standard deviations. In other words, there are marked differences from group to group but little difference within each group. These results would contradict the null hypothesis and support the notion that final exam scores do vary by teaching method.

In principle, ANOVA makes the kinds of comparisons outlined above. The test compares the amount of variation between categories (e.g., from the "Lecture-Lab" group to the "All-Lab" group to the "Videotaped" group) with the amount of variation within categories (among the "Lecture-Lab" group, among the "All-Lab" group, and among the "Videotaped" group). The greater the differences between categories, relative to the differences within categories, the more likely that the null hypothesis of "no difference" is false and can be rejected. If exam scores truly vary by teaching method, then the sample mean for each group of students should be quite different from the others and dispersion within the groups should be relatively low and similar.

9.3 THE COMPUTATION OF ANOVA

Even though we have been thinking of ANOVA as a test for the significance of the difference between sample means, the computational routine actually involves developing two separate estimates of the population variance, σ^2 (hence the name "analysis of variance"). Recall from Chapter 3 that the variance and standard deviation both measure dispersion and that the variance is simply the standard deviation squared. One estimate of the population variance is based on the amount of variation within each of the categories of the independent variable and the other is based on the amount of variation between categories.

Before constructing these estimates, we need to introduce some new concepts and statistics. The first new concept is the total variation of the scores, which is measured by a quantity called the **total sum of squares** or **SST**.

FORMULA 9.1
$$\text{SST} = \sum (X_i - \overline{X})^2$$

To find this quantity, we would take each score, subtract the mean, square the difference, and then add to get the total of the squared differences. If this formula seems vaguely familiar, it's because the same expression appears in the numerator of the formula for the sample variance and the standard deviation (see Chapter 3). This redundancy is not surprising, considering that the SST is also a way of measuring dispersion.

To construct the two separate estimates of the population variance, the total variation (SST) is divided into two components. One of these reflects the pattern of variation within the categories and is called the **sum of squares within (SSW)**. The other component is based on the variation between categories and is called the **sum of squares between (SSB)**. SSW and SSB are components of SST, as reflected in Formula 9.2:

FORMULA 9.2
$$\text{SST} = \text{SSB} + \text{SSW}$$

The sum of squares within is defined as

FORMULA 9.3
$$\text{SSW} = \sum (X_i - \overline{X}_k)^2$$

where SSW = the sum of the squares within the categories
$\overline{X}_k$ = the mean of a category

This formula directs us to take each score, subtract the mean of the category from the score, square the result, and then sum the squared differences. We will do this for each category separately and then sum the squared differences for all categories to find SSW.

The sum of squares between reflects the variation between the samples, with the category means serving as summary statistics for each category. Each category mean will be treated as a "case" for purposes of this estimate, and the formula for the sum of squares between is

FORMULA 9.4
$$\text{SSB} = \sum n_k (\overline{X}_k - \overline{X})^2$$

where SSB = the sum of squares between the categories
n_k = the number of cases in a category
$\overline{X}_k$ = the mean of a category

To find SSB, subtract the overall mean of all scores from each category mean, square the difference, multiply by the number of cases in the category, and add the results across all the categories.

Let's pause for a second to remember what we are after here. If the null hypothesis is true, then there should not be much variation from category to category, relative to the variation within categories, and the two estimates to the population variance based on SSW and SSB should be roughly equal. The larger the difference between the two estimates, the more likely we will be to reject the null hypothesis. If the category means are about the same value, the differences will not be significant. The larger the differences between category means and the more homogeneous the categories, the more likely that the differences are statistically significant.

The next step in the computational routine is to construct the estimates of the population variance. To do this, we will divide each sum of squares by its respective degrees of freedom. To find the degrees of freedom associated with SSW, subtract the number of categories (k) from the number of cases (n). The degrees of freedom associated with SSB are the number of categories minus one. In summary,

FORMULA 9.5
$$\text{dfw} = n - k$$

where dfw = degrees of freedom associated with SSW
n = total number of cases
k = number of categories

FORMULA 9.6
$$\text{dfb} = k - 1$$

where dfb = degrees of freedom associated with SSB
k = number of categories

The actual estimates of the population variance, called the **mean square estimates**, are calculated by dividing each sum of squares by its respective degrees of freedom:

FORMULA 9.7
$$\text{Mean square within} = \frac{\text{SSW}}{\text{dfw}}$$

FORMULA 9.8
$$\text{Mean square between} = \frac{\text{SSB}}{\text{dfb}}$$

The test statistic calculated in step 4 of the five-step model is called the ***F* ratio**, and its value is determined by the following formula:

FORMULA 9.9
$$F = \frac{\text{Mean square between}}{\text{Mean square within}}$$

As you can see, the value of the F ratio will be a function of the amount of variation between categories to the amount of variation within the categories. The greater the variation between the categories relative to the variation within, the higher the value of the F ratio and the more likely we will reject the null hypothesis.

9.4 A COMPUTA-
TIONAL SHORTCUT

The computational routine for ANOVA, as summarized in the previous section, requires a number of separate steps and different formulas and will surely seem complicated the first time you see it. As is almost always the case, if you proceed systematically from formula to formula (in the correct order, of course), you will see that the computations aren't nearly as formidable as they appear at first glance. Unfortunately, they will still be lengthy and time-consuming. So, at the risk of stretching your patience, let us introduce a way to save some time and computational effort. This will require the introduction of even more formulas, but the eventual savings in time will be worth the effort. Formula 9.10 shows a quicker, more convenient way to calculate SST:

FORMULA 9.10

$$SST = \sum X^2 - n\bar{X}^2$$

To solve this formula, first find the sum of the squared scores (in other words, square each score and then add up the squared scores). Next, square the overall mean, multiply that value by the total number of cases in the sample (n), and subtract that quantity from the sum of the squared scores.

Once we have the values of SST and SSB, we can find SSW by manipulating Formula 9.2 and doing some simple subtraction:

FORMULA 9.11

$$SSW = SST - SSB$$

The computational routine for ANOVA can be summarized as follows:

1. Find SST by Formula 9.10.
2. Find SSB by Formula 9.4.
3. Find SSW by subtraction (see Formula 9.11).
4. Calculate the degrees of freedom (see Formulas 9.5 and 9.6).
5. Construct the two mean square estimates to the population variance by dividing SSB and SSW by their respective degrees of freedom (see Formulas 9.7 and 9.8).
6. Find the obtained F ratio by dividing the between estimate by the within estimate (see Formula 9.9).

These computations and the actual test of significance will be illustrated in the next sections.

9.5 A COMPUTA-
TIONAL EXAMPLE

Continuing with our teaching method problem, let us assume that we have final exam scores (where a score is the percent of correct answers on the final exam) from a random sample of 27 students, equally divided into the three sections. All scores are reported in Table 9.3 along with the squared scores, the category means, and the overall mean.

TABLE 9.3 FINAL EXAM SCORES BY TEACHING METHOD FOR 27 STUDENTS

	Lecture-Lab		All-Lab		Videotaped	
	X	X^2	X	X^2	X	X^2
	55	3,025	56	3,136	50	2,500
	57	3,249	60	3,600	52	2,704
	60	3,600	62	3,844	60	3,600
	63	3,969	67	4,489	61	3,721
	72	5,184	70	4,900	63	3,969
	73	5,329	71	5,041	69	4,761
	79	6,241	82	6,724	71	5,041
	85	7,225	88	7,744	80	6,400
	92	8,464	95	9,025	82	6,724
$\sum X =$	636		651		588	
$\sum X^2 =$		46,286		48,503		39,420
$\overline{X}_k =$	70.67		72.33		65.33	
			$\overline{X} = 1{,}875/27 = 69.44$			

To organize our computations, we will follow the routine summarized at the end of Section 9.4. We begin by finding SST with Formula 9.10:

$$\text{SST} = \sum X^2 - n\overline{X}^2$$
$$= 134{,}209 - (27)(69.44)^2$$
$$= 4{,}017.33$$

The sum of squares between is found by Formula 9.4:

$$\text{SSB} = \sum n_k(\overline{X}_k - \overline{X})^2$$
$$= (9)(70.67 - 69.44)^2 + (9)(72.33 - 69.44)^2$$
$$+ (9)(65.33 - 69.44)^2$$
$$= 13.62 + 75.17 + 152.03$$
$$= 240.82$$

Now SSW can be found by subtraction (see Formula 9.11):

$$\text{SSW} = \text{SST} - \text{SSB}$$
$$= 4{,}017.33 - 240.82$$
$$= 3{,}776.51$$

To find the degrees of freedom for the two sums of squares, we use Formulas 9.5 and 9.6:

$$\text{dfw} = n - k = 27 - 3 = 24$$
$$\text{dfb} = k - 1 = 3 - 1 = 2$$

Finally, we are ready to construct the mean square estimates to the population variance. For the estimate based on SSW, we use Formula 9.7:

$$\text{Mean square within} = \frac{\text{SSW}}{\text{dfw}} = \frac{3{,}776.51}{24} = 157.36$$

For the between estimate, we use Formula 9.8:

$$\text{Mean square between} = \frac{\text{SSB}}{\text{dfb}} = \frac{240.82}{2} = 120.41$$

The test statistic, or obtained F ratio, is found by Formula 9.9:

$$F = \frac{\text{Mean square between}}{\text{Mean square within}}$$

$$F = \frac{120.41}{157.36}$$

$$F = 0.77$$

This statistic must still be evaluated for its significance. *(For practice in computing these quantities and solving these formulas, solve any of the end-of-chapter problems.)*

9.6 A TEST OF SIGNIFICANCE FOR ANOVA

In this section, we will see how to test an F ratio for significance and also take a look at some of the assumptions underlying the ANOVA test. As usual, we will follow the five-step model as a convenient way of organizing the decision-making process.

Step 1. Making Assumptions and Meeting Test Requirements.

> Model: Independent random samples
> Level of measurement is interval-ratio
> Populations are normally distributed
> Population variances are equal

The model assumptions are quite stringent and underscore the fact that ANOVA should be used only with dependent variables that have been carefully and precisely measured. However, as long as sample sizes are equal (or nearly so), ANOVA can tolerate some violation of the model assumptions. In situations where you are uncertain or have samples of very different size, it is probably advisable to use an alternative test. (We will not consider any such alternative test in this textbook.)

Step 2. Stating the Null Hypothesis. For ANOVA, the null hypothesis always states that the means of the populations from which the samples were drawn are equal. For our example problem, we are concerned with three different populations or categories, so our null hypothesis would be

$$H_0: \mu_1 = \mu_2 = \mu_3$$

where μ_1 represents the mean for students in the "Lecture-Lab" section, μ_2, the mean for students in the "All-Lab" section, and, μ_3, the mean for students in the "Videotaped" section.

The research hypothesis states simply that at least one of the population means is different. The wording here is important. If we reject the null,

ANOVA does not identify which mean or means are significantly different. In the final section of the chapter, we will briefly discuss some advanced tests that can help us identify which pairs of means are significantly different.

(H_1: At least one of the population means is different.)

Step 3. Selecting the Sampling Distribution and Establishing the Critical Region. The sampling distribution for ANOVA is the F distribution, which is summarized in Appendix D. Note that there are separate tables for alphas of 0.05 and 0.01, respectively. As with the t table, the value of the critical F score will vary by degrees of freedom. For ANOVA, there are two separate degrees of freedom, one for each estimate of the population variance. The numbers across the top of the table are the degrees of freedom associated with the between estimate (dfb), and the numbers down the side of the table are those associated with the within estimate (dfw). In our example, dfb is ($k - 1$), or 2, and dfw is ($n - k$), or 24 (see Formulas 9.5 and 9.6). So, if we set alpha at 0.05, our critical F score will be 3.40.

Summarizing these considerations:

$$\text{Sampling distribution} = F \text{ distribution}$$
$$\text{Alpha} = 0.05$$
$$\text{Degrees of freedom (within)} = (n - k) = 24$$
$$\text{Degrees of freedom (between)} = (k - 1) = 2$$
$$F(\text{critical}) = 3.40$$

Taking a moment to inspect the two F tables, you will notice that all the values are greater than 1.00. This is because ANOVA is a one-tailed test, and we are concerned only with outcomes in which there is more variance between categories than within categories. F values of less than 1.00 would indicate that the between estimate was lower in value than the within estimate and, because we would always fail to reject the null in such cases, we simply ignore this class of outcomes.

Step 4. Computing the Test Statistic. This was done in the previous section, where we found an obtained F ratio of 0.77.

Step 5. Making a Decision and Interpreting the Results of the Test. Compare the test statistic with the critical value:

$$F(\text{critical}) = 3.40$$
$$F(\text{obtained}) = 0.77$$

Because the test statistic does not fall into the critical region, our decision would be to fail to reject the null. Student performance does not differ significantly by teaching method, and the variation we observed in the sample means is unimportant. *(For practice in conducting the ANOVA test, see problems 9.2 to 9.9. Begin with the lower-numbered problems as they have smaller data sets and fewer categories, and, therefore, the simplest calculations.)*

9.7 AN ADDITIONAL EXAMPLE FOR COMPUTING AND TESTING THE ANALYSIS OF VARIANCE

In this section, we will work through an additional example of the computation and interpretation of the ANOVA test. We will first review matters of computation, then find the obtained F ratio, and then test the statistic for its significance. In the computational section, we will follow the step-by-step guidelines presented at the end of Section 9.4.

We have gathered real data on the life expectancy (the number of years the average citizen can expect to live at birth) for a random sample of 15 nations at three levels of economic development. "Least developed" nations are largely agricultural and have the lowest quality of life, "developed" nations are industrial and the most affluent and modern, and "developing" nations are between these extremes. Is there a significant difference in life expectancy between countries at different levels of development? The data are reported in Table 9.4, which also includes some additional information we will need to complete our calculations.

To find SST by the computational Formula 9.10:

$$SST = \sum X^2 - n\overline{X}^2$$
$$= (113{,}790.65 + 24{,}223.23 + 29{,}578.78) - 15(66.11)^2$$
$$= 67{,}592.66 - 65{,}557.98$$
$$= 2{,}034.68$$

To find SSB by Formula 9.4:

$$SSB = \sum n_k(\overline{X}_k - \overline{X})^2$$
$$= (5)(52.10 - 66.11)^2 + (5)(69.46 - 66.11)^2 + (5)(76.76 - 66.11)^2$$
$$= 981.40 + 56.11 + 567.11$$
$$= 1{,}604.62$$

TABLE 9.4 LIFE EXPECTANCY BY LEVEL OF DEVELOPMENT

Least Developed			Developing			Developed		
Nation	X	X^2	Nation	X	X^2	Nation	X	X^2
Cambodia	56.8	3,226.24	China	71.6	5,126.56	Belgium	78.0	6,084.00
Mali	47.0	2,209.00	Indonesia	68.3	4,664.89	Canada	79.9	6,384.01
Nepal	58.2	3,387.24	Pakistan	61.5	3,782.25	Japan	80.8	6,528.64
Niger	41.6	1,730.56	Chile	74.7	5,580.09	Russia	67.3	4,529.29
Sudan	56.9	3,237.61	Turkey	71.2	5,069.44	U.K.	77.8	6,052.84
$\sum X =$	260.5			347.3			383.8	
$\sum X^2 =$		13,790.65			24,223.23			29,578.78
$\overline{X}_k =$		52.10			69.46			76.76

$$\overline{X} = 991.6/15 = 66.11$$

Source: U.S Bureau of the Census. 2003. *Statistical Abstract of the United States*, 2002. p 829. Washington, DC: U.S. Government Printing Office.

Now we can find SSW by Formula 9.11:

$$SSW = SST - SSB$$
$$= 2{,}034.68 - 1{,}604.62$$
$$= 430.06$$

The degrees of freedom are found by Formulas 9.5 and 9.6:

$$dfw = n - k = 15 - 3 = 12$$
$$dfb = k - 1 = 3 - 1 = 2$$

The estimates to the population variances are found by Formulas 9.7 and 9.8:

$$\text{Mean square within} = \frac{SSW}{dfw} = \frac{430.06}{12} = 35.84$$

$$\text{Mean square between} = \frac{SSB}{dfb} = \frac{1{,}604.62}{2} = 802.31$$

The F ratio (see Formula 9.9) is

$$F(\text{obtained}) = \frac{\text{Mean square between}}{\text{Mean square within}}$$

$$F(\text{obtained}) = \frac{802.31}{35.84}$$

$$F(\text{obtained}) = 22.39$$

And we can now test this value for its significance.

Step 1. **Making Assumptions and Meeting Test Requirements.**

> Model: Independent random samples
> Level of measurement is interval-ratio
> Populations are normally distributed
> Population variances are equal

The researcher will always be in a position to judge the adequacy of the first two assumptions in the model. The second two assumptions are more problematical, but remember that ANOVA will tolerate some deviation from its assumptions as long as sample sizes are roughly equal.

Step 2. **Stating the Null Hypothesis.**

> $H_0: \mu_1 = \mu_2 = \mu_3$
> (H_1: At least one of the population means is different.)

Step 3. **Selecting the Sampling Distribution and Establishing the Critical Region.**

> Sampling distribution = F distribution
> Alpha = 0.05
> Degrees of freedom (within) = $(n - k) = (15 - 3) = 12$
> Degrees of freedom (between) = $(k - 1) = (3 - 1) = 2$
> $F(\text{critical}) = 3.88$

Step 4. **Computing the Test Statistic.** We found an obtained F ratio of 22.39.

Step 5. **Making a Decision and Interpreting the Results of the Test.** Compare the test statistic with the critical value:

$$F(\text{critical}) = 3.88$$
$$F(\text{obtained}) = 22.39$$

The test statistic is in the critical region, and we would reject the null of no difference. The differences between the three groupings are very unlikely to have occurred by chance alone. There is a significant difference in life expectancy between nations at the three levels of economic development.

9.8 THE LIMITATIONS OF THE TEST

ANOVA is appropriate whenever you want to test differences between the means of an interval-ratio-level variable across three or more categories of an independent variable. This application is called **one-way analysis of variance**, as it involves the effect of a single variable (e.g., teaching method) on another (e.g., final exam grade). This is the simplest application of ANOVA, and you should be aware that the technique has numerous more advanced and complex forms. For example, you may encounter research projects in which the effects of two separate variables on some third variable were observed. This application is called *two-way analysis of variance.*

One important limitation of ANOVA is that it requires interval-ratio measurement of the dependent variable and roughly equal numbers of cases in each of the categories of the independent variable. The former condition may be difficult to meet with complete confidence for many variables of interest to the social sciences. The latter condition may create problems when the research hypothesis calls for comparisons between groups that are, by their nature, unequal in numbers (e.g., number of people in each province) and may call for some unusual sampling schemes in the data-gathering phase of a research project. Neither of these limitations should be particularly crippling, because ANOVA can tolerate some deviation from its model assumptions, but you should be aware of these limitations in planning your own research as well as in judging the adequacy of research conducted by others.

A second limitation of ANOVA actually applies to all forms of significance testing and was introduced in Section 8.6. These tests are designed to detect non-random differences—differences so large that they are very unlikely to be produced by random chance alone. The problem is that differences that are statistically significant are not necessarily important in any other sense. The last two parts of this textbook will provide statistical techniques that can assess the importance of results directly.

A final limitation of ANOVA relates to the research hypothesis. As you recall, when the null hypothesis is rejected, the research hypothesis is supported. The limitation is that the research hypothesis is not specific; it simply asserts that at least one of the population means is different from the others. Obviously, we would like to know which differences are significant. We can sometimes make this determination by simple inspection. In our problem involving the economic development of nations, for example, it is pretty clear from Table 9.4 that the "least developed" group is the source of most of the differences. This informal, "eyeball" method can be misleading, however, and you should exercise caution in making conclusions about which means are significantly different. There is a statistical technique called post hoc, or "after the fact" analysis, that can be used to reliably identify which pairs of means are significantly different. The computational routines for post hoc analysis are beyond the scope of this textbook, but the tests are commonly available in computerized statistical packages such as SPSS.

SUMMARY

1. One-way analysis of variance is a powerful test of significance that is commonly used when comparisons across more than two categories or samples are of interest. It is perhaps easiest to conceptualize ANOVA as an extension of the test for the difference in sample means.

2. ANOVA compares the amount of variation within categories to the amount of variation between categories. If the null of no difference is false, there should be relatively great variation between categories and relatively little variation within categories. The greater the differences from category to category relative to the differences within the categories, the more likely we will be able to reject the null.

3. The computational routine for even simple applications of ANOVA can quickly become quite complex. The basic process is to construct separate estimates to the population variance based on the variation within the

categories and the variation between the categories. The test statistic is the F ratio, which is based on a comparison of these two estimates. The basic computational routine is summarized at the end of Section 9.4, and this is probably an appropriate time to mention the widespread availability of statistical packages such as SPSS, the purpose of which is to perform complex calculations such as these accurately and quickly. If you haven't yet learned how to use such programs, ANOVA may provide you with the necessary incentive.

4. The ANOVA test can be organized into the familiar five-step model for testing the significance of sample outcomes. Although the model assumptions (step 1) require high-quality data, the test can tolerate some deviation as long as sample sizes are roughly equal. The null takes the familiar form of stating that there is no difference of any importance among the population values, while the

research hypothesis asserts that at least one population mean is different. The sampling distribution is the F distribution, and the test is always one-tailed. The decision to reject or to fail to reject the null is based on a comparison of the obtained F ratio with the critical F ratio as determined for a given alpha level and degrees of freedom. The decision to reject the null indicates only that one or more of the population means is different from the others. We can often determine which sample mean(s) account for the difference by inspecting the sample data, but this informal method should be used with caution, and post hoc tests are more reliable indicators of significant differences.

SUMMARY OF FORMULAS

Total sum of squares:

9.1 $\text{SST} = \sum (X_i - \overline{X})^2$

The two components of the total sum of squares:

9.2 $\text{SST} = \text{SSB} + \text{SSW}$

Sum of squares within:

9.3 $\text{SSW} = \sum (X_i - \overline{X}_k)^2$

Sum of squares between:

9.4 $\text{SSB} = \sum n_k (\overline{X}_k - \overline{X})^2$

Degrees of freedom for SSW:

9.5 $\text{dfw} = n - k$

Degrees of freedom for SSB:

9.6 $\text{dfb} = k - 1$

Mean square within:

9.7 $\text{Mean square within} = \dfrac{\text{SSW}}{\text{dfw}}$

Mean square between:

9.8 $\text{Mean square between} = \dfrac{\text{SSB}}{\text{dfb}}$

F ratio:

9.9 $F = \dfrac{\text{Mean square between}}{\text{Mean square within}}$

Computational formula for SST:

9.10 $\text{SST} = \sum X^2 - n\overline{X}^2$

Finding SSW by subtraction:

9.11 $\text{SSW} = \text{SST} - \text{SSB}$

GLOSSARY

Analysis of variance. A test of significance appropriate for situations in which we are concerned with the differences among more than two sample means. (p. 248)

ANOVA. See Analysis of variance. (p. 248)

F ratio. The test statistic computed in step 4 of the ANOVA test. (p. 252)

Mean square estimate. An estimate of the variance calculated by dividing the sum of squares within (SSW) or the sum of squares between (SSB) by the proper degrees of freedom. (p. 252)

One-way analysis of variance. Application of ANOVA in which the effect of a single independent variable on a dependent variable is observed. (p. 259)

Sum of squares between (SSB). The sum of the squared deviations of the sample means from the overall mean, weighted by sample size. (p. 251)

Sum of squares within (SSW). The sum of the squared deviations of scores from the category means. (p. 251)

Total sum of squares (SST). The sum of the squared deviations of the scores from the overall mean. (p. 251)

MULTIMEDIA RESOURCES

http://www.healeystatistics.nelson.com

Visit the companion website for the second Canadian edition of *Statistics: A Tool for Social Research* to access a wide range of student resources. Begin by clicking on the Student Resources section of the textbook's website to access review quizzes, flashcards, and other study tools.

PROBLEMS

(NOTE: The number of cases in these problems is very low—a fraction of the sample size necessary for any serious research—in order to simplify computations.)

9.1 Calculate the obtained *F* ratio for each set of scores below. *(HINT: Follow the computational short-cut outlined in Section 9.4 and keep track of all sums and means by constructing computational tables like Table 9.3 or 9.4.)*

a. Category

A	B	C
5	10	12
7	12	16
8	14	18
9	15	20

b. Category

A	B	C
1	2	3
10	12	10
9	2	7
20	3	14
8	1	1

c. Category

A	B	C	D
13	45	23	10
15	40	78	20
10	47	80	25
11	50	34	27
10	45	30	20

9.2 SOC What type of person is most involved in the neighbourhood and community? Who is more likely to volunteer for organizations such as Scouts, Big Sisters, or the United Way? A random sample of 15 people has been asked for their number of memberships in community voluntary organizations and some other information. Which differences are significant?

a. Membership by education:

Less Than High School	High School	College/ University
0	1	0
1	3	3
2	3	4
3	4	4
4	5	4

b. Membership by length of residence in present community:

Less Than 2 Years	2–5 Years	More Than 5 Years
0	0	1
1	2	3
3	3	3
4	4	4
4	5	4

c. Membership by extent of television watching:

Little or None	Moderate	High
0	3	4
0	3	4
1	3	4
1	3	4
2	4	5

d. Membership by number of children:

None	One Child	More Than One Child
0	2	0
1	3	3
1	4	4
3	4	4
3	4	5

9.3 SOC In a local community, a random sample of 18 couples has been assessed on a scale that measures the extent to which power and decision making are shared (lower scores) or monopolized by one party (higher scores) and on marital happiness (lower scores indicate lower levels of unhappiness). The couples were also classified by type of relationship: traditional (only the husband works outside the home), dual-career (both parties work), and cohabitational (parties living together but not legally married, regardless of work patterns). Does decision making or happiness vary significantly by type of relationship?

a.

	Decision Making	
Traditional	Dual-Career	Cohabitational
7	8	2
8	5	1
2	4	3
5	4	4
7	5	1
6	5	2

b.

	Happiness	
Traditional	Dual-Career	Cohabitational
10	12	12
14	12	14
20	12	15
22	14	17
23	15	18
24	20	22

9.4 CJ Two separate crime-reduction programs have been implemented in the city of Pearson, Ontario. One involves a neighbourhood watch program with citizens actively involved in crime prevention. The second involves officers patrolling the neighbourhoods on foot rather than in patrol cars. In terms of the percentage reduction in crimes reported to the police over a one-year period, were the programs successful? The results are for random samples of 18 neighbourhoods drawn from the entire city.

Neighbourhood Watch	Foot Patrol	No Program
−10	−21	+30
−20	−15	−10
+10	−80	+14
+20	−10	+80
+70	−50	+50
+10	−10	−20

9.5 SOC Are sexually active teenagers any better informed about AIDS and other potential health problems related to sex than teenagers who are sexually inactive? A 15-item test of general knowledge about sex and health was administered to random samples of teens who are sexually inactive, teens who are sexually active but with only a single partner ("going steady"), and teens who are sexually active with more than one partner. Is there any significant difference in the test scores?

Inactive	Active— One Partner	Active— More Than One Partner
10	11	12
12	11	12
8	6	10
10	5	4
8	15	3
5	10	15

9.6 PS Does the rate of voter turnout vary significantly by the type of election? A random sample of electoral districts displays the following pattern of voter turnout by election type. Assess the results for significance.

Municipal	Provincial	Federal
33	35	42
78	56	40
32	35	52
28	40	66
10	45	78
12	42	62
61	65	57
28	62	75
29	25	72
45	47	51
44	52	69
41	55	59

9.7 GER Do older citizens lose interest in politics and current affairs? A brief quiz on recent headline stories was administered to random samples of respondents from each of four different age groups.

Is there a significant difference? The data below represent numbers of correct responses.

High School (15–18)	Young Adult (21–30)	Middle-Aged (40–55)	Retired (65+)
0	0	2	5
1	0	3	6
1	2	3	6
2	2	4	6
2	4	4	7
2	4	5	7
3	4	6	8
5	6	7	10
5	7	7	10
7	7	8	10
7	7	8	10
9	10	10	10

9.8 SOC A social survey was administered to a random sample of adults. A subsample of these adults, selected randomly, is shown below. Each respondent has been classified as either a city dweller, a suburbanite, or a rural dweller. Are there statistically significant differences by place of residence for any of the variables listed below?

a. Occupational Prestige (higher scores indicate greater prestige)

Urban	Suburban	Rural
32	40	30
45	48	40
42	50	40
47	55	45
48	55	45
50	60	50
51	65	52
55	70	55
60	75	55
65	75	60

b. Number of Children

Urban	Suburban	Rural
1	0	1
1	1	4
0	0	2
2	0	3
1	2	3
0	2	2
2	3	5
2	2	0
1	2	4
0	1	6

c. Monthly Family Income (in thousands of dollars)

Urban	Suburban	Rural
5	6	5
7	8	5
8	11	11
11	12	10
8	12	9
9	11	6
8	11	10
3	9	7
9	10	9
10	12	8

d. Number of Times Religious Service Attended per Month

Urban	Suburban	Rural
0	0	1
7	0	5
0	2	4
4	5	4
5	8	0
8	5	4
7	8	8
5	7	8
7	2	8
4	6	5

e. Hours of TV Watching per Day

Urban	Suburban	Rural
5	5	3
3	7	7
12	10	5
2	2	0
0	3	1
2	0	8
3	1	5
4	3	10
5	4	3
9	1	1

9.9 SOC Does support for suicide ("death with dignity") vary by social class? Is this relationship different in different nations? Small samples in three nations were asked if it is ever justified for a person with an incurable disease to take their own lives. Respondents answered in terms of a 10-point scale on which 10 was "always justified" (the strongest support for "death with dignity") and 1 was "never justified" (the lowest level of support). Results are reported on the next page.

Mexico					United States			
Lower Class	Working Class	Middle Class	Upper Class		Lower Class	Working Class	Middle Class	Upper Class
5	2	1	2		4	4	4	1
2	2	1	4		5	5	6	5
4	1	3	5		6	1	7	8
5	1	4	7		1	4	5	9
4	6	1	8		3	3	8	9
2	5	2	10		3	3	9	9
3	7	1	10		3	4	9	8
1	2	5	9		5	2	8	6
1	3	1	8		3	1	7	9
3	1	1	8		6	1	2	9

Canada			
Lower Class	Working Class	Middle Class	Upper Class
7	5	1	5
7	6	3	7
6	7	4	8
4	8	5	9
7	8	7	10
8	9	8	10
9	5	8	8
9	6	9	5
6	7	9	8
5	8	5	9

SPSS for Windows

Using SPSS for Windows to Conduct Analysis of Variance with the 2006 Census

The demonstrations and exercises below use the shortened version of the 2006 Census data. Start SPSS for Windows and open the *Census.sav* file.

SPSS DEMONSTRATION 9.1 Using the RECODE Command to Test for Regional Differences in Monthly Rent Payments

SPSS provides several different ways of conducting the analysis of variance test. We'll use the **One-Way ANOVA** procedure, which is the most accessible way to conduct the analysis of variance test, to answer the question "Is there a significant difference in average monthly rent payments by province?"

Before we do the analysis of variance, smaller provinces should be collapsed into groups or regions to create more equal sample sizes. We'll use the SPSS **Recode** command, a commonly used tool to transform and manipulate variables, to collapse *pr* (province) into six regions. (The original scores for *pr* are given in Appendix G, or they can be viewed by clicking **Utilities** and then **Variables** from the SPSS main menu bar.)

First, click **Transform** from the main menu and choose **Recode into Different Variables**. The **Recode into Different Variables** dialog box will open. Highlight *pr* and click on the arrow button to move the variable to the **Input Variable** → **Output**

Variable box. In the **Output Variable** box on the right, click in the **Name** text box and type a name for the new (output) variable: We suggest *region*. Click the **Change** button.

Second, click on the **Old and New Values** button in the middle of the screen to open the **Recode into Different: Old and New Values** dialog box. Read down the left-hand column until you find the **Range** button. Click on the button, and the cursor will move to the small box immediately below. Type 10 into the first **Range** text box and then click on the second text box and type 13. Then, in the **New Value** box in the upper-right-hand corner of the screen, click the **Value** button and then type 1 in the adjacent text box. Finally, click the **Add** button. The expression "10 thru 13 → 1" will appear in the **Old → New** text box. This completes the first recode instruction to SPSS.

For the second recode instruction, click the **Value** button in the **Old Value** box. Move the cursor to the small text box immediately under the **Value** button. Type 24 in the text box. Next, in the **New Value** box, click the **Value** button and type 2 in the adjacent text box. Click the **Add** button. The expression "24 → 2" appears in the **Old → New** box. Continue this sequence of operations until all old values of *pr* have been recoded into new values. The recoding instructions that need to be added in the **Old → New** box should contain all of the following expressions (the order is not important):

$$
\begin{array}{ll}
10 \text{ thru } 13 & \rightarrow \ 1 \\
24 & \rightarrow \ 2 \\
35 & \rightarrow \ 3 \\
46 \text{ thru } 47 & \rightarrow \ 4 \\
48 & \rightarrow \ 5 \\
59 & \rightarrow \ 6 \\
\end{array}
$$

This scheme groups all respondents with: scores 10 (Nfld/Labrador), 11 (PEI), 12 (Nova Scotia), or 13 (New Brunswick) on *pr* together into a score of 1 on *region*; score 24 (Quebec) on *pr* into a score of 2 on *region*; score 35 (Ontario) on *pr* into a score of 3 on *region*; scores 46 (Manitoba) or 47 (Saskatchewan) on *pr* together into a score of 4 on *region*; score 48 (Alberta) on *pr* into a score of 5 on *region*; and score 59 (BC) on *pr* into a score of 6 on *region*.

Third, click the **Continue** button at the bottom of the screen, and you will return to the **Recode into Different Variables** dialog box. Click **OK**, and SPSS will execute the transformation. It is always a good idea to check the frequency distribution of the recoded variable to make sure that the computations were carried out correctly.

We have attached value labels to each score of *region* (1 = Atlantic Canada, 2 = Quebec, etc.) to make the SPSS output easier to read. For more practice using the recode command, including how to add value labels, see Appendix F.5.

To use the **One-Way ANOVA** procedure, click **Analyze**, **Compare Means**, and then **One-Way ANOVA**. The **One-Way ANOVA** window appears. Find *grosrt* (gross rent) in the variable list on the left and click the arrow to move the variable name into the **Dependent List** box. Next, find *region* (it may appear at the end of the variable list) and click the arrow to move the variable name into the **Factor** box. To request means and standard deviations along with the analysis of variance, click **Options** and then click the checkbox next to **Descriptive** in the **Statistics** section. Click **Continue** and then **OK**, and the output below, slightly edited for clarity, will be produced.

Descriptives

Gross rent

	N	Mean	Std. Deviation	Std. Error	Lower Bound	Upper Bound	95% Confidence Interval for Mean	
							Minimum	Maximum
Atlantic Canada	19	686.11	304.877	69.944	539.16	833.05	300	1488
Quebec	138	645.55	297.120	25.293	595.54	695.57	0	1319
Ontario	131	870.56	394.191	34.441	802.43	938.70	0	1880
Manitoba/ Saskatchewan	25	600.24	210.993	42.199	513.15	687.33	200	1306
Alberta	36	909.94	412.151	68.692	770.49	1049.40	0	1751
British Columbia	52	861.87	375.258	52.039	757.39	966.34	0	2052
Total	401	769.94	366.141	18.284	734.00	805.89	0	2052

ANOVA

Gross rent

	Sum of Squares	df	Mean Square	F	Sig.
Between Groups	5460203.041	5	1092040.608	8.956	.000
Within Groups	48163356.64	395	121932.548		
Total	53623559.68	400			

The "Descriptives" report displays various summary statistics. The results indicate that rent is distributed differently across the regions. The mean rent for the sample as a whole (all provinces) is 769.94. Manitobans/Saskatchewanians tend to pay the lowest amount for rent and Albertans the highest in Canada.

The output box labelled "ANOVA" includes sums of squares, degrees of freedom (*df*), mean square estimates, *F* ratio (8.956), and, at the far right "Sig." value (.000), the exact probability of getting these results if the null hypothesis is true. (As discussed in Demonstration 8.1, when the exact probability value is less than .0005, SPSS cuts it off at three decimal places, or .000, to save space.) There is no need to look up the *F* ratio in the *F* table, Appendix D, when the exact probability is provided. Because the value .000 is less than .05, our usual indicator of significance, we reject the null hypothesis. The difference in mean rent between the regions is statistically significant.

SPSS DEMONSTRATION 9.2 The Error Bar Graph

ANOVA results, as shown in Demonstration 9.1, tell us if *any* of the group means differ significantly from each other. It does not tell us, however, *which* groups differ significantly from each other. In Demonstration 8.2, the overlap of error bars for individual confidence intervals was used to judge the significance of the difference between two samples. We can use the error bar graph in a similar manner to get an indication of which pairs of means are significantly different.

To produce error bar graphs of the 95% confidence interval of each mean, click **Graphs**, **Legacy Dialogs**, and then **Error Bar**. The **Error Bar** dialog box appears,

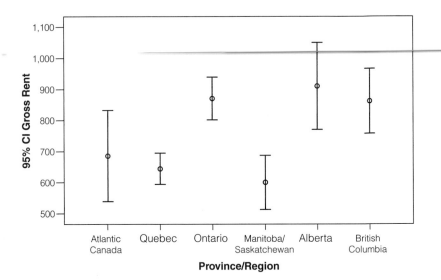

with the **Simple** and **Summaries for Groups of Cases** buttons already highlighted. These are the ones we want, so just click **Define**. The **Define Simple Error Bar** dialog box appears. Transfer the dependent variable, *grosrt*, to the **Variable** box and the independent variable, *region*, to the **Category Axis** box, and click **OK**.

The error bar graph shows the mean rent for each region. The 95% confidence interval for each mean is also presented. By "eyeballing" the overlap of confidence intervals for each mean, we can get a sense of which means are significantly different. For example, there appears to be a significant difference in average rent between Ontario and Manitoba/Saskatchewan populations, but not between Ontario and Alberta populations. An exact method to determine which pairs of means are significantly different is the post hoc test discussed in Section 9.8. The post hoc test is a multiple comparison test for the significance of the difference between two sample means. It is equivalent to the *t* test covered in Chapter 8, except all possible pairs of sample means are tested. The post hoc test is like performing a series of *t* tests.

Exercises (using *Census.sav*)

9.1 Use the **Recode** command illustrated in Demonstration 9.1 to collapse *pr* into the following three regions: 1) Atlantic Canada and Quebec, 2) Ontario, and 3) Manitoba, Saskatchewan, Alberta, and BC. The recoding instructions that should appear in the **Old** → **New** box are as follows:

$$10 \text{ thru } 24 \rightarrow 1$$
$$35 \qquad\quad \rightarrow 2$$
$$46 \text{ thru } 59 \rightarrow 3$$

Next, use the **One-Way ANOVA** procedure to test for a significant difference between recoded *pr* as the independent variable (factor) and *grosrt* as the dependent variable. Write a sentence or two summarizing the results of this test.

9.2 Using Demonstration 9.2 as a guide, get an error bar graph for the variables in Exercise 9.1. Write a sentence or two of interpretation for the graph. Which regions appear to differ significantly from each other?

Hypothesis Testing IV
Chi Square

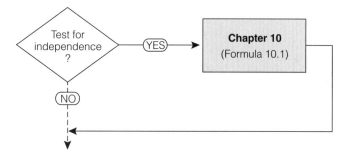

10.1 INTRODUCTION

The **chi square (χ^2) test** has probably been the most frequently used test of hypothesis in the social sciences, a popularity that is due largely to the fact that the assumptions and requirements in step 1 of the five-step model are easy to satisfy. Specifically, the test can be conducted with variables measured at any level of measurement and, because it is a **non-parametric** or "distribution-free" test, it requires no assumption at all about the shape of the population or sampling distribution. While the website for this textbook provides discussion of other non-parametric tests of significance such as the Mann–Whitney U test, the chi square test is the focus of this chapter.

Why is it an advantage to have assumptions and requirements that are easy to satisfy? The decision to reject the null hypothesis (step 5) is not specific: It means only that one statement in the model (step 1) or the null hypothesis (step 2) is wrong. Usually, of course, we single out the null hypothesis for rejection. The more certain we are of the model, the greater our confidence that the null hypothesis is the faulty assumption. A "weak" or easily satisfied model means that our decision to reject the null hypothesis can be made with even greater certainty.

Chi square has also been popular for its flexibility. Not only can it be used with variables at any level of measurement, it can be used with variables that have many categories or scores. For example, in Chapter 8, we tested the significance of the difference in the proportions of Americans and Canadians with an unmet health care need due to long waiting times. What if the researcher wished to expand the test to include British persons? The two-sample test would no longer be applicable, but chi square handles the more complex variable easily. However, while chi square can be used at any level of measurement, it is most appropriate for nominal level variables. As we will see in Chapters 12 and 13 respectively, it is more appropriate to use a different kind of significance test for ordinal and interval-ratio level variables.

10.2 BIVARIATE TABLES

Chi square is computed from **bivariate tables**, so called because they display the scores of cases on two different variables at the same time. Bivariate tables are used to ascertain if there is a significant relationship between the variables and for other purposes that we will investigate in later chapters. In fact, these tables are very commonly used in research, and a detailed examination of them is in order.

First of all, bivariate tables have (of course) two dimensions. The horizontal (across) dimension is referred to in terms as **rows**, and the vertical dimension (up and down) is referred to in terms of **columns**. Each column or row represents a score on a variable, and the intersections of the row and columns **(cells)** represent the various combined scores on both variables.

Let's use an example to clarify. Suppose a researcher is interested in the relationship between sex and participation in voluntary groups, community-service organizations, and so forth. Is there a difference in the level of involvement in volunteer groups between the sexes? We have two variables (sex and number of memberships) and, for the sake of simplicity, assume that number of memberships is a simple dichotomy. That is, people have been classified as either male or female and as either high or low in their level of involvement in voluntary associations.

By convention, the independent variable (the variable that is taken to be the cause) is placed in the columns and the dependent variable in the rows. In the example at hand, sex is the causal variable (the question was "is membership *affected by* sex?"), and each column will represent a score on this variable. Each row, on the other hand, will represent a score on level

TABLE 10.1   RATES OF PARTICIPATION IN VOLUNTARY ASSOCIATIONS
BY SEX FOR 100 CITIZENS

Participation Rates	Sex		
	Male	Female	
High			50
Low			50
	50	50	100

of membership (high or low). Table 10.1 displays the outline of the bivariate table for a sample of 100 people.

Note some further details of the table. First, subtotals have been added to each column and row. These are called the row or column **marginals**, and, in this case, they tell us that 50 members of the sample were male and 50 were female (the column marginals) and 50 were rated as high in participation and 50 were rated low (the row marginals). Second, the total number of cases in the sample ($n = 100$) is reported at the intersection of the row and column marginals. Finally, take careful note of the labelling of the table. Each row and column is identified and the table has a descriptive title that includes the names of the variables with the dependent variable listed first. Clear, complete labels and concise titles should be included in *all* tables, graphs, and charts.

As you probably noticed, Table 10.1 lacks one piece of crucial information: the numbers of each sex that rated high or low on the dependent variable. To finish the table, we need to classify each member of the sample in terms of both their sex and their level of participation, keep count of how often each combination of scores occurs, and record these numbers in the appropriate cell of the table. Because each of our variables (sex and participation rates) has two scores, there are four possible combinations of scores, each corresponding to a cell in the table. For example, males with high levels of participation would be counted in the upper-left-hand cell, females with low levels of participation would be counted in the lower-right-hand cell, and so forth. When we are finished counting, each cell will display the number of times each combination of scores occurred.

Finally, note how the bivariate table could be expanded to accommodate variables with more scores. For instance, if we had measured participation rates with three categories (e.g., high, moderate, and low) rather than two, we would simply add an additional row to the table.

10.3 THE LOGIC OF CHI SQUARE

The chi square test has several different uses. This chapter will deal with an application called the chi square test for **independence**. We have encountered the term *independence* in connection with the requirements for the two-sample case (see Chapter 8) and for the ANOVA test (see Chapter 9). In those situations, we noted that independent random samples are gathered such that the selection of a particular case for one sample has no effect on the probability that any particular case will be selected for the other sample (see Section 8.2).

In the context of chi square, the concept of independence takes on a slightly different meaning because it refers to the relationship between the variables, not the samples. Two variables are independent if the classification of a case into a particular category of one variable has no effect on the probability that the case will fall into any particular category of the second variable. For example, sex and participation in voluntary associations would be independent of each other if the classification of a case as male or female has no effect on the classification of the case as high or low on participation. In other words, the variables would be independent if level of participation and sex were completely unrelated to each other.

Consider Table 10.1 again. If these two variables are truly independent, the cell frequencies will be determined solely by random chance and we would find that, just as an honest coin will show heads about 50% of the time when flipped, about half of the male respondents will rank high on participation and half will rank low. The same pattern would hold for the 50 female respondents and, therefore, each of the four cells would have about 25 cases in it, as illustrated in Table 10.2. This pattern of cell frequencies indicates that the sex of the subjects has no effect on the probability that they would be either high or low in participation. The probability of being classified as high or low would be 0.5 for both males and females, and the variables would therefore be independent.

The null hypothesis for chi square is that the variables are independent. Under the assumption that the null hypothesis is true, the cell frequencies we would expect to find if only random chance were operating are computed. These frequencies, called **expected frequencies** (symbolized f_e), are then compared, cell-by-cell, with the frequencies actually observed (**observed frequencies,** symbolized f_o) and recorded in a table. If the null hypothesis is true and the variables are independent, then there should be little difference between the expected and observed frequencies. If the null is false, however, there should be large differences between the two. The greater the differences between expected (f_e) and observed (f_o) frequencies, the less likely that the variables are independent and the more likely that we will be able to reject the null hypothesis.

TABLE 10.2 THE CELL FREQUENCIES THAT WOULD BE EXPECTED IF RATES OF PARTICIPATION AND SEX WERE INDEPENDENT

	Sex		
Participation Rates	Male	Female	
High	25	25	50
Low	25	25	50
	50	50	100

10.4 THE COMPUTA-TION OF CHI SQUARE

As with all tests of hypothesis, with chi square we compute a test statistic, χ^2**(obtained)** from the sample data and then place that value on the sampling distribution of all possible sample outcomes. Specifically, the χ^2(obtained) will be compared with the value of χ^2**(critical)** that will be determined by consulting a chi square table (Appendix C) for a particular alpha level and degrees of freedom. Prior to conducting the formal test of hypothesis, let us take a moment to consider the calculation of chi square, as defined by Formula 10.1.

FORMULA 10.1

$$\chi^2(\text{obtained}) = \sum \frac{(f_o - f_e)^2}{f_e}$$

where f_o = the cell frequencies observed in the bivariate table
f_e = the cell frequencies that would be expected if the variables were independent

We must work on a cell-by-cell basis to solve this formula. To compute chi square, subtract the expected frequency from the observed frequency for each cell, square the result, divide by the expected frequency for that cell, and then sum the resultant values for all cells.

This formula requires an expected frequency for each cell in the table. In Table 10.2, the marginals are the same value for all rows and columns, and the expected frequencies are obvious by intuition: f_e = 25 for all four cells. In the more usual case, the expected frequencies will not be obvious, marginals will be unequal, and we must use Formula 10.2 to find the expected frequency for each cell:

FORMULA 10.2

$$f_e = \frac{\text{Row marginal} \times \text{Column marginal}}{n}$$

That is, the expected frequency for any cell is equal to the total number of cases in the row (the row marginal) times the total number of cases in the column (the column marginal) divided by the total number of cases in the table (n).

An example using Table 10.3 should clarify these procedures. A random sample of 100 social work graduates has been classified in terms of whether the Canadian Association of Schools of Social Work (CASSW) has accredited their undergraduate programs (the column or independent variable) and whether they were hired in social work positions within three months of graduation (the row or dependent variable).

Beginning with the upper-left-hand cell (graduates of CASSW-accredited programs who are working as social workers), the expected frequency for this cell, using Formula 10.2, is (40)(55)/100, or 22. For the other cell in this row (graduates of non-accredited programs who are working as social workers), the expected frequency is (40)(45)/100, or 18. For the two cells in the bottom row, the expected frequencies are (60)(55)/100, or 33, and (60)(45)/100, or 27, respectively. The expected frequencies for all four cells are displayed in Table 10.4.

TABLE 10.3   EMPLOYMENT OF 100 SOCIAL WORK GRADUATES BY CASSW-ACCREDITATION STATUS OF UNDERGRADUATE PROGRAM (fictitious data)

	Accreditation Status		
Employment Status	Accredited	Not Accredited	Totals
Working as a social worker	30	10	40
Not working as a social worker	25	35	60
Totals	55	45	100

TABLE 10.4   EXPECTED FREQUENCIES FOR TABLE 10.3

	Accreditation Status		
Employment Status	Accredited	Not Accredited	Totals
Working as a social worker	22	18	40
Not working as a social worker	33	27	60
Totals	55	45	100

TABLE 10.5   COMPUTATIONAL TABLE FOR TABLE 10.3

(1)	(2)	(3)	(4)	(5)
f_o	f_e	$f_o - f_e$	$(f_o - f_e)^2$	$(f_o - f_e)^2 / f_e$
30	22	8	64	2.91
10	18	−8	64	3.56
25	33	−8	64	1.94
35	27	8	64	2.37
$n = 100$	$n = 100$	0		χ^2(obtained) = 10.78

Note that the row and column marginals as well as the total number of cases in Table 10.4 are exactly the same as those in Table 10.3. The row and column marginals for the expected frequencies must *always* equal those of the observed frequencies, a relationship that provides a convenient way of checking your arithmetic to this point.

The value for chi square for these data can now be found by solving Formula 10.1. It will be helpful to use a computing table, such as Table 10.5, to organize the several steps required to compute chi square. The table lists the observed frequencies (f_o) in column 1 in order from the upper-left-hand cell to the lower-right-hand cell, moving left to right across the table and top to bottom. Column 2 lists the expected frequencies (f_e) in exactly the same order. Double-check to make sure that you have listed the cell frequencies in the same order for both of these columns.

The next step is to subtract the expected frequency from the observed frequency for each cell and list these values in column 3. To complete column 4, square the value in column 3 and then, in column 5, divide the column 4 value by the expected frequency for that cell. Finally, add up column 5. The sum of this column is χ^2(obtained).

$$\chi^2(\text{obtained}) = 10.78$$

Note that the totals for columns 1 and 2 (f_o and f_e) are exactly the same. This will always be the case, and, if the totals do not match, you have probably made a mistake in the calculation of the expected frequencies. Also note that the sum of column 3 will always be zero, another convenient way to check your math to this point.

This sample value for chi square must still be tested for its significance. *(For practice in computing chi square, see any of the end-of-chapter problems.)*

10.5 THE CHI SQUARE TEST FOR INDEPENDENCE

As always, the five-step model for significance testing will provide the framework for organizing our decision making. The data presented in Table 10.3 will serve as our example.

Step 1. **Making Assumptions and Meeting Test Requirements.** Note that we make no assumptions at all about the shape of the sampling distribution.

Model: Independent random samples
Level of measurement is nominal

Step 2. **Stating the Null Hypothesis.** As stated previously, the null hypothesis in the case of chi square states that the two variables are independent. If the null is true, the differences between the observed and expected frequencies will be small. As usual, the research hypothesis directly contradicts the null. Thus, if we reject H_0, the research hypothesis will be supported.

H_0: The two variables are independent
(H_1: The two variables are dependent)

Step 3. **Selecting the Sampling Distribution and Establishing the Critical Region.** The sampling distribution of sample chi squares, unlike the Z and t distributions, is positively skewed, with higher values of sample chi squares in the upper tail of the distribution (to the right). Thus, with the chi square test, the critical region is established in the upper tail of the sampling distribution.

Values for χ^2(critical) are given in Appendix C. This table is similar to the t table, with alpha levels arrayed across the top and degrees of freedom down the side. A major difference, however, is that degrees of freedom (df) for chi square are found by the following formula:

FIGURE 10.1 THE CHI SQUARE DISTRIBUTION, WITH REJECTION REGION FOR ALPHA 0.05, (df = 1) IN SHADE

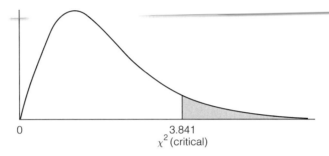

$$0 \qquad\qquad\qquad \begin{array}{c} 3.841 \\ \chi^2 \text{(critical)} \end{array}$$

FORMULA 10.3 $$df = (r - 1)(c - 1)$$

A table with two rows and two columns (a 2 × 2 table) has one degree of freedom regardless of the number of cases in the sample.* A table with two rows and three columns would have $(2 - 1)(3 - 1)$, or two degrees of freedom. Our sample problem involves a 2 × 2 table with df = 1, so if we set alpha at 0.05, the critical chi square score would be 3.841. Summarizing these decisions, we have

$$\text{Sampling distribution} = \chi^2 \text{ distribution}$$
$$\text{Alpha} = 0.05$$
$$\text{Degrees of freedom} = 1$$
$$\chi^2\text{(critical)} = 3.841$$

The sampling distribution of χ^2 is depicted in Figure 10.1.

Step 4. Computing the Test Statistic. The mechanics of these computations were introduced in Section 10.4. As you recall, we had

$$\chi^2\text{(obtained)} = \sum \frac{(f_o - f_e)^2}{f_e}$$

$$\chi^2\text{(obtained)} = 10.78$$

Step 5. Making a Decision and Interpreting the Results of the Test. Comparing the test statistic with the critical region,

$$\chi^2\text{(obtained)} = 10.78$$
$$\chi^2\text{(critical)} = 3.841$$

---

*Degrees of freedom are the number of values in a distribution that are free to vary for any particular statistic. A 2 × 2 table has one degree of freedom because, for a given set of marginals, once one cell frequency is determined, all other cell frequencies are fixed (i.e., they are no longer free to vary). In Table 10.3, for example, if any cell frequency is known, all others are determined. If the upper-left-hand cell is known to be 30, the remaining cell in that row must be 10, because there are 40 cases total in the row and $40 - 30 = 10$. Once the frequencies of the cells in the top row are established, cell frequencies for the bottom row are determined by subtraction from the column marginals. Incidentally, this relationship can be used to good advantage when computing expected frequencies. For example, in a 2 × 2 table, only one expected frequency needs to be computed. The f_e's for all other cells can then be found by subtraction.

we see that the test statistic falls into the critical region and, therefore, we reject the null hypothesis of independence. The pattern of cell frequencies observed in Table 10.3 is unlikely to have occurred by chance alone. The variables are dependent. Specifically, based on these sample data, the probability of securing employment in the field of social work is dependent on the CASSW-accreditation status of the program. *(For practice in conducting and interpreting the chi square test for independence, see problems 10.3 to 10.15.)*

Let's take a moment to stress exactly what the chi square test does and does not tell us. A significant chi square means that the variables are (probably) dependent on each other in the population: CASSW-accreditation status makes a difference in whether or not a person is working as a social worker. Chi square does not give us any detail about the relationship, however. In our example, it does not tell us if it's the graduates of the accredited programs or the non-accredited programs that are more likely to be working as social workers. To compare these two groups, we must perform some additional calculations. We can figure out how the independent variable (CASSW-accreditation status) is affecting the dependent variable (employment as a social worker) by computing **column percentages** which is done by calculating percentages within each column of the bivariate table. This procedure is analogous to calculating percentages for frequency distributions (see Chapter 2).

To calculate column percentages, divide each cell frequency by the total number of cases in the column (the column marginal). For Table 10.3, starting in the upper-left-hand cell, we see that there are 30 cases in this cell and 55 cases in the column. In other words, 30 of the 55 graduates of CASSW-accredited programs are working as social workers. The column percentage for this cell is therefore: $(30/55) \times 100 = 54.55\%$. For the lower-left-hand cell, the column percentage is $(25/55) \times 100 = 45.45\%$. For the two cells in the right-hand column (graduates of non-accredited programs), the column percentages are $(10/45) \times 100 = 22.22$ and $(35/45) \times 100 = 77.78$. All column percentages are displayed in Table 10.6.

Column percentages help to make the relationship between the two variables more obvious and we can see easily from Table 10.6 that students from CASSW-accredited programs are more likely to be working as social

TABLE 10.6   COLUMN PERCENTAGES FOR TABLE 10.3

Employment Status	Accreditation Status		Totals
	Accredited	Not Accredited	
Working as a social worker	54.55%	22.22%	40.00%
Not working as a social worker	45.45%	77.78%	60.00%
Totals	100.00% (55)	100.00% (45)	100.00%

workers. Nearly 55% of these students are working as social workers versus less than 25% of the students from non-accredited programs. We already knew that this relationship is significant (unlikely to be caused by random chance) and now, with the aid of column percentages, we know how the two variables are related. According to these results, graduating from a CASSW-accredited program would be a decided advantage for people seeking to enter the social work profession.

Let's highlight two points in summary:

1. Chi square is a test of statistical significance. It tests the null hypothesis that the variables are independent in the population. If we reject the null hypothesis, we are concluding, with a known probability of error (determined by the alpha level), that the variables are dependent on each other in the population. In the terms of our example, this means that CASSW-accreditation status makes a difference in the likelihood of finding work as a social worker. By itself, however, chi square does not tell us the exact nature of the relationship.

2. Computing column percentages allows us to examine the bivariate relationship in more detail. By comparing the column percentages for the various scores of the independent variable, we can see exactly how the independent variable affects the dependent variable. In this case, the column percentages reveal that graduates of CASSW-accredited programs are more likely to find work as social workers. We will explore column percentages more extensively when we discuss bivariate association in Chapters 11 and 12.

10.6 THE CHI SQUARE TEST: AN EXAMPLE

To this point, we have confined our attention to 2 × 2 tables. For purposes of illustration, we will work through the computational routines and decision-making process for larger (4 × 2) tables using data from the World Values Survey. As you will see, larger tables require more computations (because they have more cells); in all other essentials, they are dealt with in the same way as 2 × 2 tables.

The World Values Survey is administered by a network of social scientists about every five years to randomly selected samples of citizens from around the globe. It is designed to allow cross-national comparisons of values and norms on a wide variety of topics including opinions on life, family, work, traditional values, morality, religion, politics, the environment, and other contemporary social issues. World Values Survey data can be downloaded for free on the Internet at http://www.worldvaluessurvey.org.

We will use the World Values Survey to examine the relationship between the respondent's country of residence—the independent variable—and the importance of politics in the life of the respondent—the dependent variable. The analysis is limited to residents of Canada and the United States. Table 10.7 displays the bivariate table for this relationship.

TABLE 10.7   IMPORTANCE OF POLITICS BY COUNTRY

	Country		
Importance of Politics	Canada	U.S.	Totals
Very important	174	188	362
Rather important	609	492	1,101
Not very important	807	421	1,228
Not at all important	333	93	426
Totals	1,923	1,194	3,117

Source: Data from EUROPEAN AND WORLD VALUES SURVEYS FOUR-WAVE INTEGRATED DATA FILE, 1981–2004, v.20060423, 2006. The European Values Study Foundation and World Values Survey Association. Aggregate File Producers: ASEP/JDS, Madrid, Spain/Tilburg University, Tilburg, the Netherlands. Aggregate File Distributors: ASEP/JDS and ZA, Cologne, Germany.

The World Values Survey is administered to random samples of individuals selected in accordance with the rules of EPSEM (see Chapter 5), so we can assume that the results apply to the general populations of Canada and the United States.

Our first step in conducting a chi square test is to compute the expected frequency for each cell in the bivariate table. To do so we use Formula 10.2. In the first row, the expected frequency for the left-hand cell is (362)(1,923)/3,117, or 223.3; the expected frequency for the middle cell is (362)(1,194)/3,117, or 138.7. In the second row, the expected frequencies for the left-hand cell is (1,101)(1,923)/3,117, or 679.3; the expected frequency for the middle cell is (1,101)(1,194)/3,117, or 421.7. In the third row, the expected frequency for the left-hand cell is (1,228)(1,923)/3,117, or 757.6; the expected frequency for the middle cell is (1,228)(1,194)/3,117, or 470.4. Finally, for the fourth row, the expected frequency for the left-hand cell is (426)(1,923)/3,117, or 262.8; the expected frequency for the middle cell is (426)(1,194)/3,117, or 163.2. These results are displayed in Table 10.8.

The next step involves solving the formula for χ^2 (obtained) for the bivariate table, being very careful to be certain that we are using the proper f_o's and f_e's for each cell. We use a computational table, Table 10.9, to organize

TABLE 10.8   EXPECTED FREQUENCIES FOR TABLE 10.7

	Country		
Importance of Politics	Canada	U.S.	Totals
Very important	223.33	138.67	362
Rather important	679.25	421.75	1,101
Not very important	757.60	470.40	1,228
Not at all important	262.82	163.18	426
Totals	1,923.00	1,194.00	3,117

TABLE 10.9   COMPUTATIONAL TABLE FOR TABLE 10.7

		Importance of Politics by Country		
(1)	(2)	(3)	(4)	(5)
f_o	f_e	$f_o - f_e$	$(f_o - f_e)^2$	$(f_o - f_e)^2/f_e$
174	223.33	−49.33	2,433.45	10.90
188	138.67	49.33	2,433.45	17.55
609	679.25	−70.25	4,935.06	7.27
492	421.75	70.25	4,935.06	11.70
807	757.60	49.40	2,440.36	3.22
421	470.40	−49.40	2,440.36	5.19
333	262.82	70.18	4,925.23	18.74
931	163.18	−70.18	4,925.23	30.18
$n = 3,117$	$n = 3,117.00$		χ^2 (obtained) $= 104.75$	

the calculations. We see here, in the total of column 5, that the value of the obtained chi square is 104.75.

In our next step we test the obtained chi square for its statistical significance. The five-step model for significance testing will provide the framework for organizing our decision making.

Step 1. **Making Assumptions and Meeting Test Requirements.**

Model: Independent random samples
Level of measurement is nominal

Step 2. **Stating the Null Hypothesis.**

H_0: The two variables are independent
(H_1: The two variables are dependent)

Step 3. **Selecting the Sampling Distribution and Establishing the Critical Region.**

Sampling distribution $= \chi^2$ distribution
Alpha $= 0.05$
Degrees of freedom $= (r - 1)(c - 1) = (4 - 1)(2 - 1) = 3$
χ^2(critical) $= 7.815$

Step 4. **Computing the Test Statistic.**

$$\chi^2(\text{obtained}) = \sum \frac{(f_o - f_e)^2}{f_e}$$

$\chi^2(\text{obtained}) = 104.75$

TABLE 10.10   COLUMN PERCENTAGES FOR TABLE 10.7

Importance of Politics	Country		Totals
	Canada	U.S.	
Very important	9.05	15.75	11.61
Rather important	31.67	41.21	35.32
Not very important	41.97	35.26	39.40
Not at all important	17.31	7.78	13.67
Totals	100.00%	100.00%	100.00%

Step 5. **Making a Decision and Interpreting the Results of the Test.** The test statistic, χ^2(obtained) = 104.75, falls into the critical region, which, for alpha = 0.05, df = 3, begins at χ^2(critical) = 7.815. We therefore reject the null hypothesis. The observed frequencies are significantly different from the frequencies we would expect to find if the variables were independent. We can conclude that the importance of politics in peoples' lives is dependent on country or residence.

To complete the analysis, it would be useful to know exactly how the two variables are related. We can determine this by computing and analyzing column percentages. The column percentages in Table 10.10 show that almost 60% of Americans said that politics are either very or rather important in their lives. Just over 40% of Canadians said the same. We have already concluded that the relationship is significant and now we know the pattern of the relationship: Politics tend to be more important in the lives of Americans than Canadians.

10.7 THE LIMITATIONS OF THE CHI SQUARE TEST

Like any other test, chi square has limits, and you should be aware of several potential difficulties. First, even though chi square is very flexible and handles many different types of variables, it becomes difficult to interpret when the variables have many categories. For example, two variables with five categories each would generate a 5 × 5 table with 25 cells—far too many combinations of scores to be easily absorbed or understood. As a very rough rule of thumb, the chi square test is easiest to interpret and understand when both variables have four or fewer scores.

Two further limitations of the test are related to sample size. When sample size is small, it can no longer be assumed that the sampling distribution of all possible sample outcomes is accurately described by the chi square distribution. For chi square, a small sample is defined as one where a high percentage of the cells have expected frequencies (f_e) of 5 or less. Various rules of thumb have been developed to help the researcher decide what constitutes a "high percentage of cells." Probably the safest course is to take corrective action whenever *any* of the cells have expected frequencies of 5 or less.

There has been a good deal of public debate, particularly in the last decade, over privatization of the Canadian health care system. Do attitudes toward privatization of health care vary by region of residence? Is attitude on privatization dependent on region? We will examine this issue with an actual random sample of 369 Canadians from the 2006 Canadian Election Study, and classify respondents by their region of residence—Atlantic Canada, Quebec, Ontario, and Western Canada—and, as a measure of privatization, by whether they favour or oppose having some private hospitals in Canada. (The Canadian Election Study surveyed adults in the 10 provinces only, thus excluding the territories.) The 2 × 4 table below shows these results:

Attitude	Region Atlantic	Quebec	Ontario	Western	Totals
Favour	15	58	46	69	188
Oppose	21	38	65	57	181
Totals	36	96	111	126	369

The frequencies we would expect to find if the null hypothesis (H_0: the variables are independent) were true are

Attitude	Region Atlantic	Quebec	Ontario	Western	Totals
Favour	18.34	48.91	56.55	64.19	188.00
Oppose	17.66	47.09	54.45	61.81	181.00
Totals	36.00	96.00	111.00	126.00	369.00

Expected frequencies are found on a cell-by-cell basis by the formula

$$\frac{\text{Row marginal} \times \text{Column marginal}}{n}$$

And, the calculation of chi square will be organized into a computational table.

(1) f_o	(2) f_e	(3) $f_o - f_e$	(4) $(f_o - f_e)^2$	(5) $(f_o - f_e)^2/f_e$
15	18.34	−3.34	11.15	0.61
58	48.91	9.09	82.63	1.69
46	56.55	−10.55	111.30	1.97
69	64.19	4.81	23.14	0.36
21	17.66	3.34	11.15	0.63
38	47.09	−9.09	82.63	1.75
65	54.45	10.55	111.30	2.04
57	61.81	−4.81	23.14	0.37
$n = 369$	$n = 369.00$			χ^2 (obtained) = 9.42

Step 1. Making Assumptions and Meeting Test Requirements.
   Model: Independent random samples
   Level of measurement is nominal

Step 2. Stating the Null Hypothesis.
   H_0: The two variables are independent
   (H_1: The two variables are dependent)

Step 3. Selecting the Sampling Distribution and Establishing the Critical Region.

Sampling distribution = χ^2 distribution
Alpha = 0.05
Degrees of freedom = $(r - 1)(c - 1)$
   $= (2 - 1)(4 - 1) = 3$
χ^2(critical) = 7.815

Step 4. Computing the Test Statistic.

$$\chi^2(\text{obtained}) = \sum \frac{(f_o - f_e)^2}{f_e}$$

$\chi^2(\text{obtained}) = 9.42$

Step 5. Making a Decision and Interpreting the Results of the Test. With an obtained χ^2 of 9.42, we would reject the null hypothesis of independence. For this sample, there is a statistically significant relationship between region of residence and attitude toward health care privatization.

   To complete the analysis, it would be useful to know exactly how the two variables are related. We can determine this by computing and analyzing column percentages:

Attitude	Region Atlantic	Quebec	Ontario	Western	Totals
Favour	41.67	60.42	41.44	54.76	50.95
Oppose	58.33	39.58	58.56	45.24	49.05
Totals	100.00%	100.00%	100.00%	100.00%	100.00%

The column percentages show that just 41% of persons from the Atlantic provinces and Ontario favour having some private hospitals in Canada. By comparison, about 55% and 60% of persons from Western Canada and Quebec, respectively, favour the privatization of some hospitals. We have already concluded that the relationship is significant and now we know the pattern of the relationship.

Source: All data from 2006 Canadian Election Study.

READING STATISTICS 6: Gender Differences in Health

In this section, we will examine a study on gender and health among Canadian university students. The research was conducted by a group of scholars in the Department of Kinesiology and Physical Education at Wilfrid Laurier University.

The research team selected a sample of 166 male and 472 female undergraduate students. Each student answered questions about their overall health and health-related behaviours during the current school year. The bivariate tables below show relationship between gender and participation in physical activity, hours per day engaged in social activities, and general state of health. Chi square was used to assess each relationship for statistical significance at the 0.05 alpha level. Significant relationships are symbolized as $p < 0.05$ in the tables. This tells us that the relationship would occur by chance alone less than 1 in 20 times, or 5% of the time (see the discussion of the "p" format in Reading Statistics 5).

The first and second bivariate tables reveal that gender is significantly related to both physical and social activity at the 0.05 level. Looking at the column percentages, we see how these variables are related. Almost three out of ten (27%) male respondents participated five or more times per week in physical activity. The comparable figure for females is about two out of ten (19%). Males are also more socially active: about 21% spent five to six hours per day in social activity compared to less than 15% of female respondents.

HEALTH BEHAVIOURS AND HEALTH STATUS BY GENDER: Frequencies and Percentages*

1. Participation in physical activity

1. Participation in physical activity	Gender	
	Male	Female
Never	6 (3.6%)	28 (5.9%)
1–2 times/week	48 (29.1%)	198 (41.9%)
3–4 times/week	66 (40.0%)	155 (32.8%)
5+ times/week	45 (27.3%)	91 (19.3%)
Totals	165 (100.0%)	472 (99.9%)

$$\chi^2 = 11.9, \, p < 0.05$$

2. Hours/day engaged in social activities

2. Hours/day engaged in social activities	Gender	
	Male	Female
0–2	25 (15.2%)	108 (23.0%)
3–4	92 (55.8%)	273 (58.2%)
5–6	35 (21.2%)	67 (14.3%)
6+	13 (7.9%)	21 (4.5%)
Totals	165 (100.1%)	469 (100.0%)

$$\chi^2 = 10.0, \, p < 0.05$$

3. General state of health

3. General state of health	Gender	
	Male	Female
Excellent	53 (32.5%)	104 (22.2%)
Good	96 (58.9%)	320 (68.2%)
Poor/Fair	14 (8.6%)	45 (9.5%)
Totals	163 (100.0%)	469 (99.9%)

$$\chi^2 = 6.9, \, p < 0.05$$

* Percentages may not total to 100% because of rounding error.

Turning to the third bivariate table, we see that the relationship between gender and general health state is statistically significant at the 0.05 level. Further, almost 33% of males in the sample have excellent health compared to 22% of females. According to the authors, the relationship between gender and general health state among Canadian university students reflects differences in disease prevention and health promotion between males and females:

Although Canadian male university students engaged in negative health-related behaviors more frequently than females, this study also revealed that male students were engaging in two key positive and preventive health measures more than their female counterparts. First, male students were engaging more frequently than female students in physical activity. . . . This is important as regular exercise has been identified by numerous health

(continued next page)

READING STATISTICS 6: *(continued)*

organizations as reducing the risk of cardiovascular illnesses and various cancers, as well as increasing quality of life. . . . [Second], male students also engaged in significantly greater amounts of social activity per day than females. . . . Social activity may serve as a buffer for college life stress for Canadian male

students and therefore act as a health promoting behavior." (pp. 40–41)

Source: Dawson, K., Schneider, M., Fletcher, P., & Bryden, "Examining Gender Differences in the Health Behaviors of Canadian University Students." *Journal of the Royal Society for the Promotion of Health* (127: 38–44, Jan 2007). Reprinted by permission of SAGE.

In the case of 2 × 2 tables, the value of χ^2(obtained) can be adjusted by applying Yates' correction for continuity, the formula for which is

FORMULA 10.4

$$\chi_c^2 = \sum \frac{(|f_o - f_e| - 0.5)^2}{f_e}$$

where χ_c^2 = corrected chi square
$|f_o - f_e|$ = the absolute values of the difference between the observed and expected frequency for each cell

The correction factor is applied by reducing the absolute value* of the term $(f_o - f_e)$ by 0.5 before squaring the difference and dividing by the expected frequency for the cell.

For tables larger than 2 × 2, there is no correction formula for computing χ^2(obtained) for small samples. It may be possible to combine some of the categories of the variables and thereby increase cell sizes. Obviously, however, this course of action should be taken only when it is sensible to do so. In other words, distinctions that have clear theoretical justifications should not be erased merely to conform to the requirements of a statistical test. When you feel that categories cannot be combined to build up cell frequencies, and the percentage of cells with expected frequencies of 5 or less is small, it is probably justifiable to continue with the uncorrected chi square test as long as the results are regarded with a suitable amount of caution.

A second potential problem related to sample size occurs with large samples. We pointed out in Chapter 8 that all tests of hypothesis are sensitive to sample size. That is, the probability of rejecting the null hypothesis increases as the number of cases increases, regardless of any other factor. It turns out that chi square is especially sensitive to sample size and that larger samples may lead to the decision to reject the null when the actual relationship is trivial. In fact, chi square is more responsive to changes in sample size than other test statistics, because the value of χ^2(obtained) will increase

---

*Absolute values ignore plus and minus signs.

at the same rate as sample size. That is, if sample size is doubled, the value of χ^2(obtained) will be doubled. *(For an illustration of this principle,' see problem 10.14.)*

Our major purpose in stressing the relationship between sample size and the value of chi square is really to point out, once again, the distinction between statistical significance and theoretical importance. On one hand, tests of significance play a crucial role in research. As long as we are working with random samples, we must know if our research results could have been produced by mere random chance.

On the other hand, like any other statistical technique, tests of hypothesis are limited in the range of questions they can answer. Specifically, these tests will tell us whether our results are statistically significant or not. They will not necessarily tell us if the results are important in any other sense. To deal more directly with questions of importance, we must use an additional set of statistical techniques called measures of association. We previewed these techniques in this chapter when we used column percentages, and measures of association will be the subject of Part III of this textbook.

SUMMARY

1. The chi square test for independence is appropriate for situations in which the variables of interest have been organized into table format. The null hypothesis is that the variables are independent or that the classification of a case into a particular category on one variable has no effect on the probability that the case will be classified into any particular category of the second variable.

2. Because chi square is non-parametric and requires only nominally measured variables, its model assumptions are easily satisfied. Furthermore, because it is computed from bivariate tables, in which the number of rows and columns can be easily expanded, the chi square test can be used in many situations in which other tests are inapplicable.

3. In the chi square test, we first find the frequencies that would appear in the cells if the variables were independent (f_e) and then compare those frequencies, cell by cell,

with the frequencies actually observed in the cells (f_o). If the null is true, expected and observed frequencies should be quite close in value. The greater the difference between the observed and expected frequencies, the greater the possibility of rejecting the null.

4. The chi square test has several important limitations. It is often difficult to interpret when tables have many (more than four or five) dimensions. Also, as sample size (n) decreases, the chi square test becomes less trustworthy, and corrective action may be required. Finally, with very large samples, we might declare relatively trivial relationships to be statistically significant. As is the case with all tests of hypothesis, statistical significance is not the same thing as "importance" in any other sense. As a general rule, statistical significance is a necessary but not sufficient condition for theoretical or practical importance.

SUMMARY OF FORMULAS

Chi square (obtained):

10.1 $\chi^2(\text{obtained}) = \sum \dfrac{(f_o - f_e)^2}{f_e}$

Expected frequencies:

10.2 $f_e = \dfrac{(\text{Row marginal} \times \text{Column marginal})}{n}$

Degrees of freedom, bivariate tables:

10.3 $df = (r - 1)(c - 1)$

Yates' correction for continuity:

10.4 $\chi_c^2 = \sum \dfrac{(|f_o - f_e| - 0.5)^2}{f_e}$

GLOSSARY

Bivariate table. A table that displays the joint frequency distributions of two variables. (p. 270)

Cells. The cross-classification categories of the variables in a bivariate table. (p. 270)

χ^2 (critical). The score on the sampling distribution of all possible sample chi squares that marks the beginning of the critical region. (p. 273)

χ^2 (obtained). The test statistic as computed from sample results. (p. 273)

Chi square test. A non-parametric test of hypothesis for variables that have been organized into a bivariate table. (p. 269)

Column. The vertical dimension of a bivariate table. By convention, each column represents a score on the independent variable. (p. 270)

Column percentages. Percentages computed within each column of a bivariate table. (p. 277)

Expected frequency (f_e). The cell frequencies that would be expected in a bivariate table if the variables were independent. (p. 272)

Independence. The null hypothesis in the chi square test. Two variables are independent if, for all cases, the classification of a case on one variable has no effect on the probability that the case will be classified in any particular category of the second variable. (p. 271)

Marginals. The row and column subtotals in a bivariate table. (p. 271)

Non-parametric. A "distribution-free" test. These tests do not assume a normal sampling distribution. (p. 269)

Observed frequency (f_o). The cell frequencies actually observed and recorded in a bivariate table. (p. 272)

Row. The horizontal dimension of a bivariate table, conventionally representing a score on the dependent variable. (p. 270)

MULTIMEDIA RESOURCES

   http://www.healeystatistics.nelson.com

Visit the companion website for the second Canadian edition of *Statistics: A Tool for Social Research* to access a wide range of student resources. Begin by clicking on the Student Resources section of the textbook's website to access review quizzes, flashcards, and other study tools.

PROBLEMS

10.1 For each table below, calculate the obtained chi square. (*HINT: Calculate the expected frequencies for each cell with Formula 10.2. Double-check to make sure you are using the correct row and column marginals for each cell. It may be helpful to record the expected frequencies in table format as well—see Tables 10.2, 10.4, and 10.8. Next, use a computational table to organize the calculation for Formula 10.1—see Tables 10.5 and 10.9. For* *each cell, subtract expected frequency from observed frequency and record the result in column 3. Square the value in column 3 and record the result in column 4, and then divide the value in column 4 by the expected frequency for that cell and record the result in column 5. Remember that the sum of column 5 in the computational table is obtained chi square. As you proceed, check to make sure that you are using the correct values for each cell.)*

a.

20	25	45
20	25	45
45	45	90

b.

10	15	25
20	30	50
30	45	75

c.

20	25	45
30	30	60
55	45	100

d.

10	15	25
20	30	50
35	65	25

10.2 SOC A sample of 25 cities have been classified as high or low on their homicide rates and on the number of guns sold within the city limits. Calculate the obtained chi square for these data.

Volume of Gun Sales	Homicide Rate		
	Low	High	Totals
High	8	5	13
Low	4	8	12
Totals	12	13	25

10.3 SW A local politician is concerned that a program for the homeless in her city is discriminating against females. The data below were taken from random samples of female and male homeless people.

Received Services?	Sex		
	Female	Male	Totals
Yes	6	7	13
No	4	9	13
Totals	10	16	26

a. Is there a statistically significant relationship between sex and whether the person has received services from the program?

b. Compute column percentages for the table to determine the pattern of the relationship. Which group is more likely to get services?

10.4 Is there a "gender gap" in support of the Liberal Party of Canada among university faculty? To answer this question, a sample of university faculty has been asked about their political party preference.

Party Preference	Sex		
	Male	Female	Totals
Liberal	10	15	25
Other	15	10	25
Totals	25	25	50

a. Is there a statistically significant relationship between sex and party preference?

b. Compute column percentages for the table to determine the pattern of the relationship. Which sex is more likely to prefer the Liberals?

10.5 PA Is there a relationship between salary levels and unionization for public employees? The data below represent this relationship for fire departments in a random sample of 100 cities of roughly the same size. Salary data have been dichotomized at the median. Summarize your findings.

Salary	Status		
	Union	Non-union	Totals
High	21	29	50
Low	14	36	50
Totals	35	65	100

a. Is there a statistically significant relationship between these variables?

b. Compute column percentages for the table to determine the pattern of the relationship. Which group is more likely to get high salaries?

10.6 SOC A program of pet therapy has been running at a local nursing home. Are the participants in the program more alert and responsive than non-participants? The results, drawn from a random sample of residents, are reported below.

Alertness	Status		Totals
	Participants	Non-participants	
High	23	15	38
Low	11	18	29
Totals	34	33	67

a. Is there a statistically significant relationship between participation and alertness?
b. Compute column percentages for the table to determine the pattern of the relationship. Which group is more likely to be alert?

10.7 SOC The provincial Ministry of Education has rated a sample of local school boards for compliance with province-mandated guidelines for quality. Is the quality of a school board significantly related to the affluence of the community as measured by per capita income?

Quality	Per Capita Income		Totals
	Low	High	
Low	16	8	24
High	9	17	26
Totals	25	25	50

a. Is there a statistically significant relationship between these variables?
b. Compute column percentages for the table to determine the pattern of the relationship. Are high- or low-income communities more likely to have high-quality schools?

10.8 CJ A local judge has been allowing some individuals convicted of "driving under the influence" to work in a hospital emergency room as an alternative to fines, suspensions, and other penalties. A random sample of offenders has been drawn. Do participants in this program have lower rates of recidivism for this offence?

Recidivist?	Status		Totals
	Participants	Non-participants	
Yes	60	123	183
No	55	108	163
Totals	115	231	346

a. Is there a statistically significant relationship between these variables?
b. Compute column percentages for the table to determine the pattern of the relationship. Which group is more likely to be arrested again for driving under the influence?

10.9 SOC Is there a relationship between length of marriage and satisfaction with marriage? The necessary information has been collected from a random sample of 100 respondents drawn from a local community.

Satisfaction	Length of Marriage (in years)			Totals
	Less than 5	5–10	More than 10	
Low	10	20	20	50
High	20	20	10	50
Totals	30	40	30	100

a. Is there a statistically significant relationship between these variables? Write a sentence or two explaining your decision.
b. Compute column percentages for the table to determine the pattern of the relationship. Which group is more likely to be highly satisfied?

10.10 PS Is there a relationship between political ideology and class standing? Are upperclass persons significantly different from lowerclass individuals on this variable? The table below reports the relationship between these two variables for a random sample of 267 adult Canadians.

Political Ideology	Class Standing		Totals
	Lowerclass	Upperclass	
Liberal	43	40	83
Moderate	50	50	100
Conservative	40	44	84
Totals	133	134	267

a. Is there a statistically significant relationship between these variables?
b. Compute column percentages for the table to determine the pattern of the relationship. Which group is more likely to be conservative?

10.11 SOC At a large urban university, about half of the students live off campus in various arrangements, and the other half live in residence on campus. Is academic performance dependent on living arrangements? The results based on a random sample of 300 students are presented below.

	Residential Status			
GPA	Off Campus with Roommates	Off Campus with Parent	On Campus	Totals
Low	22	20	48	90
Moderate	36	40	54	130
High	32	10	38	80
Totals	90	70	140	300

a. Is there a statistically significant relationship between these variables?

b. Compute column percentages for the table to determine the pattern of the relationship. Which group is more likely to have a high GPA?

10.12 SOC An urban sociologist has built up a database describing a sample of the neighbourhoods in her city and has developed a scale by which each area can be rated for the "quality of life" (this includes measures of pollution, noise, open space, services available, and so on). She has also asked samples of residents of these areas about their level of satisfaction with their neighbourhoods.

	Quality of Life			
Satisfaction	Low	Moderate	High	Totals
Low	21	15	6	42
Moderate	12	25	21	58
High	8	17	32	57
Totals	41	57	59	157

a. Is there significant agreement between the sociologist's objective ratings of quality of life and the respondents' self-reports of satisfaction?

b. Compute column percentages for the table to determine the pattern of the relationship. Which group is most likely to say that their satisfaction is high?

10.13 SOC Does support for the legalization of marijuana vary by region of Canada? The table displays the relationship between the two variables for a random sample of 1,020 adult Canadians.

	Region				
Legalize?	Atlantic	Central	Western	Northern	Totals
Yes	60	65	42	78	245
No	245	200	180	150	775
Totals	305	265	222	228	1,020

a. Is there a statistically significant relationship between these variables?

b. Compute column percentages for the table to determine the pattern of the relationship. Which region is most likely to favour the legalization of marijuana?

10.14 SOC A researcher is concerned with the relationship between attitudes toward violence and violent behaviour. If attitudes "cause" behaviour (a very debatable proposition), then people who have positive attitudes toward violence should have high rates of violent behaviour. A pretest was conducted on 70 respondents and, among other things, the respondents were asked, "Have you been involved in a violent incident of any kind over the past six months?" The researcher established the following relationship:

	Attitude toward Violence		
Involvement	Favourable	Unfavourable	Totals
Yes	16	19	35
No	14	21	35
Totals	30	40	70

The chi square calculated on these data is 0.23, which is not significant at the 0.05 level (confirm this conclusion with your own calculations). Undeterred by this result, the researcher proceeded with the project and gathered a random sample of 7,000. In terms of percentage distributions, the results for the full sample were exactly the same as for the pretest:

	Attitude toward Violence		
Involvement	Favourable	Unfavourable	Totals
Yes	1,600	1,900	3,500
No	1,400	2,100	3,500
Totals	3,000	4,000	7,000

However, the chi square obtained is a very healthy 23.4 (confirm with your own calculations). Why is the full-sample chi square significant when the pretest was not? What happened? Do you think that the second result is important?

10.15 SOC Some results from a survey given to a random sample of Canadians are presented below. For each table, conduct the chi square test of significance and compute column percentages. Write a sentence or two of interpretation for each test.

a. Support for the same-sex marriage by age:

| Support? | Age | | | |
	Younger than 30	30–49	50 and Older	Totals
Yes	154	360	213	727
No	179	441	429	1,049
Totals	333	801	642	1,776

b. Support for gun control by age:

| Support? | Age | | | |
	Younger than 30	30–49	50 and Older	Totals
Favour	361	867	675	1,903
Oppose	144	297	252	693
Totals	505	1,164	927	2,596

c. Fear of walking alone at night by age:

| Fear? | Age | | | |
	Younger than 30	30–49	50 and Older	Totals
Yes	147	325	300	772
No	202	507	368	1,077
Totals	349	832	668	1,849

d. Support for legalizing marijuana by age:

| Legalize? | Age | | | |
	Younger than 30	30–49	50 and Older	Totals
Should	128	254	142	524
Should not	224	534	504	1,262
Totals	352	788	646	1,786

e. Support for suicide when a person has an incurable disease by age:

| Support? | Age | | | |
	Younger than 30	30–49	50 and Older	Totals
Yes	225	537	367	1,129
No	107	270	266	643
Totals	332	807	633	1,772

SPSS for Windows

Using SPSS for Windows to Conduct the Chi Square Test with the 2009 GSS

The demonstrations and exercises below use the shortened version of the 2009 GSS data set supplied with this textbook.

SPSS DEMONSTRATION 10.1 Does Criminal Victimization Vary by Area of Residence?

The **Crosstabs** procedure in SPSS produces bivariate tables and a wide variety of statistics. This procedure is commonly used in social science research at all levels, and you will see many references to **Crosstabs** in chapters to come. We will introduce the command here, and we will return to it often in later sessions.

In this demonstration we ask two questions: "Is area of residence significantly related to criminal victimization?" and, if so, "Are persons residing in urban areas or in rural areas most likely to be a victim of crime?" We can answer these questions, at least for the 2009 GSS sample, by constructing a bivariate table to display the relationship between *luc_rst* (urban/rural indicator) and *lifevict* (ever been a victim of crime). We will also request a chi square test for the table.

Start SPSS for Windows and load the 2009 GSS database (GSS.sav). From the main menu bar, click **Analyze**, **Descriptive Statistics**, and then **Crosstabs**. The **Crosstabs** dialog box will appear with the variables listed in a box on the left. Highlight *lifevict* and click the arrow to move the variable name into the **Row(s)** box, and then highlight *luc_rst* and move it into the **Column(s)** box. Click the **Statistics** button at the top of the window and click the box next to **Chi-square**. Click **Continue**. Then, click the **Cells** button and check the boxes next to "**Expected**" in the **Counts** box and "**Column**" in the **Percentages** box. This will generate the expected frequencies and column percentages, respectively, for the table. Click **Continue** and **OK**, and the output below will be produced. (Note, the output has been slightly edited for clarity, and will not exactly match the output on your screen.)

Victim of crime – lifetime * Urban/Rural indicator. Crosstabulation

			Urban/Rural indicator.		
			Urban	Rural	Total
Victim of crime-lifetime	Yes	Count	787	157	944
		Expected Count	756.1	187.9	944.0
		% within Urban/Rural	65.0%	52.2%	62.4%
	No	Count	424	144	568
		Expected Count	454.9	113.1	568.0
		% within Urban/Rural	35.0%	47.8%	37.6%
Total		Count	1211	301	1512
		Expected Count	1211.0	301.0	1512.0
		% within Urban/Rural	100.0%	100.0%	100.0%

Chi-Square Tests

	Value	df	Asymp. Sig. (2-sided)	Exact Sig. (2-sided)	Exact Sig. (1-sided)
Pearson Chi-Square	16.915[a]	1	.000		
Continuity Correction[b]	16.372	1	.000		
Likelihood Ratio	16.572	1	.000		
Fisher's Exact Test				.000	.000
Linear-by-Linear Association	16.904	1	.000		
N of Valid Cases	1512				

a. 0 cells (0.0%) have expected count less than 5. The minimum expected count is 113.07.
b. Computed only for a 2 × 2 table.

The crosstabulation table is small (2 × 2), and the information is straightforward. Let's begin with the cells. Each cell displays the observed frequency, or the number of cases, in the cell ("Count") and the column percentage for that cell ("% within Urban/Rural"). For example, there were 787 respondents who lived in an urban area and who had answered "yes" to being a victim of crime, and these were 65.0% of all respondents residing in an urban area. By contrast, there were 157 respondents residing in a rural area, or 52.2%, who reported being a victim. Persons living in an urban area are generally more likely than those living in a rural area to have been a victim of crime at some point in the past.

The table also displays the expected frequency for each cell. The greater the differences between expected frequencies ("Expected Count") and observed frequencies ("Count"), the less likely that the variables are independent and the more likely that we will be able to reject the null hypothesis. The results of the chi square test are formally reported in the output block that follows the crosstabulation table.

The value of chi square (obtained) is found in the row "Pearson Chi-Square." The value of the obtained chi square is 16.915, the degree of freedom is 1, and the exact significance of the chi square is .000 (i.e., the exact probability of getting these results if only random chance is operating). Recall that when the exact probability value is less than .0005, SPSS cuts it off at three decimal places, or .000, to save space.

To test if there is a significant relationship between the variables we can manually compare the value of chi square (obtained) to the value of chi square (critical), determined by consulting the chi square table in Appendix C for a particular alpha level and degrees of freedom as we have practised throughout this chapter. Because SPSS provides the exact probability, there is no need to look up the test statistic in the chi-square table. The exact probability value, .000, is well below the standard indicator of a significant result (alpha = .05), so we reject the null hypothesis that the variables are independent and conclude that there is a statistically significant relationship between area of residence and victimization. Being a victim of crime is dependent on area of residence, and those residing in an urban area are more likely to be a victim. In Exercise 10.1, you will have the opportunity to investigate other variables that might be significantly related to victimization.

As a final note, the number of the cells with expected frequencies less than five is provided at the bottom of the "Chi-Square Tests" output box. Yates' correction for continuity, labelled "Continuity Correction," should be used in any 2 × 2 table where one or more cells have expected counts less than five. When this is the case for tables larger than 2 × 2, consider collapsing categories of the variables to increase cell sizes.

SPSS DEMONSTRATION 10.2 Does Spirituality Vary by Sex?

In this demonstration we will examine the relationship between sex and importance of religious or spiritual beliefs. Specifically, "Is spirituality higher for males or females?" Run the **Crosstabs** procedure again with *rlr_q110* (how important are your religious or spiritual beliefs) as the row variable and *sex* as the column variable. Don't forget to request chi square, expected frequencies, and column percentages. The output, slightly edited for clarity, is shown below.

How important are your religious or spiritual beliefs to the * Sex of respondent. Crosstabulation

			Sex of respondent.		
			Male	Female	Total
How important are your religious or spiritual beliefs	. . . very important?	Count	218	268	486
		Expected Count	240.1	245.9	486.0
		% within Sex	29.2%	35.0%	32.1%
	. . . some what important?	Count	227	251	478
		Expected Count	236.2	241.8	478.0
		% within Sex	30.4%	32.8%	31.6%
	. . . not very important?	Count	152	128	280
		Expected Count	138.3	141.7	280.0
		% within Sex	20.3%	16.7%	18.5%
	. . . not at all important?	Count	150	118	268
		Expected Count	132.4	135.6	268.0
		% within Sex	20.1%	15.4%	17.7%
Total		Count	747	765	1512
		Expected Count	747.0	765.0	1512.0
		% within Sex	100.0%	100.0%	100.0%

Chi-Square Tests

	Value	df	Asymp. Sig. (2-sided)
Pearson Chi-Square	12.015[a]	3	.007
Likelihood Ratio	12.034	3	.007
Linear-by-Linear Association	11.401	1	.001
N of Valid Cases	1512		

a. 0 cells (0.0%) have expected count less than 5. The minimum expected count is 132.40.

Chi square is 12.015, degrees of freedom are 3, and the exact probability of getting this pattern of cell frequencies by random chance alone is .007. There is a significant relationship between the variables. The column percentages show that spirituality increases from males to females. Focusing on the bottom row, we see that 20.1% of males thought that religious or spiritual beliefs are not at all important. Just 15.4% of females said the same. Exercise 10.2 provides an opportunity to look at other variables that might be significantly related to *rlr_q110*.

Exercises (using *GSS.sav*)

10.1 For a follow-up to Demonstration 10.1, find two more variables that might be related to *lifevict*. Run the **Crosstabs** procedure with *lifevict* as the row variable and your other variables as the column variables.* Write a paragraph summarizing the results of these two tests. Which relationships are significant at the .05 alpha level?

10.2 As a follow-up to Demonstration 10.2, find two more variables that might be related to *rlr_q110*. Use the **Crosstabs** procedure to see if any of your variables have a significant relationship with *rlr_q110*.* Which of the variables had the most significant relationship?

---

*If necessary, use the recode procedure shown in Appendix F.5 to reduce the number of categories in the independent (column) variables.

PART II CUMULATIVE EXERCISES

1. Conduct the appropriate test of significance for each research situation. Problems are stated in no particular order and include research situations from each chapter in Part II. (Use alpha = 0.05 throughout.)

   a. Is there a gender gap in use of the Internet? Random samples of men and women have been questioned about the average number of minutes they spend each week on the Internet for any purpose. Is the difference significant?

Women	Men
$\overline{X}_1 = 55$	$\overline{X}_2 = 60$
$s_1 = 2.5$	$s_2 = 2.0$
$n_1 = 520$	$n_2 = 515$

   b. For high school students, is there a relationship between social class and involvement in activities such as clubs and sports? Data have been gathered for a random sample of students. Is the relationship significant?

	Class		
Involvement	Higher	Lower	Totals
High	11	19	30
Moderate	19	21	40
Low	8	12	20
Totals	38	52	90

   c. A social survey was administered to a random sample of adults. One question asked respondents how many total sex partners they have had over their lifetimes. The data for a subsample of 23 of these respondents are shown below. Does the number vary significantly by educational level?

Less than High School	High School	At Least Some College/University
1	1	2
1	2	1
2	3	5
1	8	9
9	10	11
2	5	2
9	4	1
	3	1

d. A sample of Canadians selected at random was asked how many times they had moved since they were 18 years of age. The results are presented below. On the average, how many times do Canadians move?

$$\overline{X} = 3.5$$
$$s = 0.4$$
$$n = 1,450$$

e. On the average, school boards in a province receive budget support from the provincial government of $623 per student. A random sample of 107 rural schools reports that they received an average of $605 per pupil. Is the difference significant?

$$\mu = 623 \quad \overline{X} = 605$$
$$s = 74$$
$$n = 107$$

2. Below are a number of research questions that can be answered by the techniques presented in Chapters 6 through 10. For each question, select the most appropriate test, compute the necessary statistics, and state your conclusions.

In order to complete some problems, you must first calculate the sample statistics (for example, means or proportions) that are used in the test of hypothesis. Use alpha = 0.05 throughout. The questions are presented in random order. There is at least one problem for each chapter, but we have not included a research situation for every statistical procedure covered in the chapters.

In selecting tests and procedures, you need to consider the question, the number of samples or categories being compared, and the level of measurement of the variables. These problems are based on social survey data, shown below, collected from a random sample of 25 Canadian adults, and you may have to violate some assumptions about sample size in order to complete this exercise. Abbreviated versions of the survey questions along with the meanings of the codes are also presented.

a. Is there a statistically significant difference in average hours of TV watching by income level? By sex?

b. Is there a statistically significant relationship between age and happiness?

c. Estimate the average number of hours spent watching TV for the entire population.

d. If Canadians currently average 2.3 children, is this sample representative of the population?

e. Are the educational levels of political conservatives and political liberals significantly different?

f. Does average hours of TV watching vary by level of happiness?

g. Based on the sample data, estimate the proportion of female Canadians in the population.

SURVEY ITEMS

1. How many children have you ever had? Scores are actual numbers.
2. Respondent's educational level
   0. Less than high school
   1. High school
   2. At least some college or university

3. Sex
   1. Male
   2. Female
4. Age
   1. Younger than 35
   2. 35 and older
5. Number of hours of TV watched per day. Values are actual number of hours.
6. What is your political ideology?
   1. Liberal
   2. Conservative
7. Respondent's income
   1. $24,999 or less
   2. $25,000 or more
8. Respondent's overall level of happiness
   1. Very happy
   2. Pretty happy
   3. Not too happy

Case	No. of Children	Educational Level	Sex	Age	TV Hours	Political Ideology	Income	Happiness
1	3	1	1	1	3	1	1	2
2	2	0	1	1	1	1	2	3
3	4	2	1	2	3	1	1	1
4	0	2	1	1	2	1	1	1
5	5	1	1	1	2	1	2	2
6	1	1	1	2	3	1	2	1
7	9	0	1	1	6	1	1	1
8	6	1	1	2	4	1	1	2
9	4	2	1	1	2	2	2	2
10	2	1	1	1	1	1	2	3
11	2	0	1	2	4	1	1	3
12	4	1	2	1	5	2	1	2
13	0	1	1	2	2	2	1	2
14	2	1	1	2	2	1	1	2
15	3	1	2	2	4	1	1	1
16	2	0	1	2	2	1	2	1
17	2	1	1	2	2	1	2	3
18	0	2	1	2	2	1	2	1
19	3	0	1	2	5	2	1	1
20	2	1	2	1	10	1	1	3
21	2	1	1	2	4	1	2	1
22	1	0	1	2	5	1	2	1
23	0	2	1	1	2	2	1	1
24	0	1	1	2	0	2	2	1
25	2	2	1	1	1	2	2	1

Bivariate Measures of Association

The chapters in this part cover the computation and analysis of a class of statistics known as measures of association. These statistics are extremely useful in scientific research and commonly reported in the professional literature. They provide, in a single number, an indication of the strength and—if applicable—direction of a bivariate relationship.

It is important to remember the difference between statistical significance, covered in Part II, and association, the topic of this section. Tests for statistical significance provide answers to certain questions: Were the differences or relationships observed in the sample caused by mere random chance? What is the probability that the sample results reflect patterns in the population(s) from which the sample(s) was selected? Measures of association address a different set of questions: How strong is the relationship between the variables? What is the direction or pattern of the relationship? Thus, measures of association provide information complementary to tests of significance. Association and significance are two different things and, while the most satisfying results are those that are *both* statistically significant and strong, it is common to find mixed results: relationships that are statistically significant but weak, not statistically significant but strong, and so forth.

Chapter 11 introduces the basic ideas behind the analysis of association in terms of bivariate tables and column percentages then presents measures of association appropriate for nominal-level variables. Chapter 12 presents measures of association for variables measured at the ordinal level, and Chapter 13 presents Pearson's *r*, the most important measure of association and the only one designed for interval-ratio-level variables.

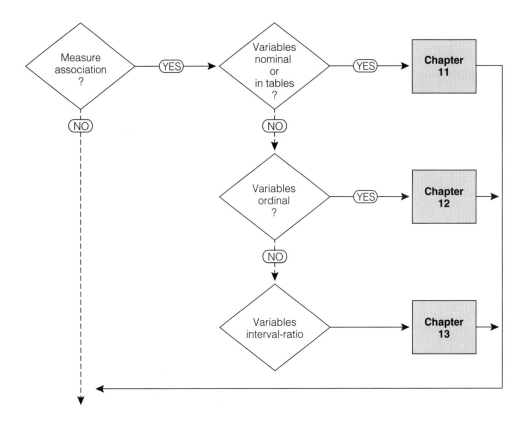

Introduction to Bivariate Association and Measures of Association for Variables Measured at the Nominal Level

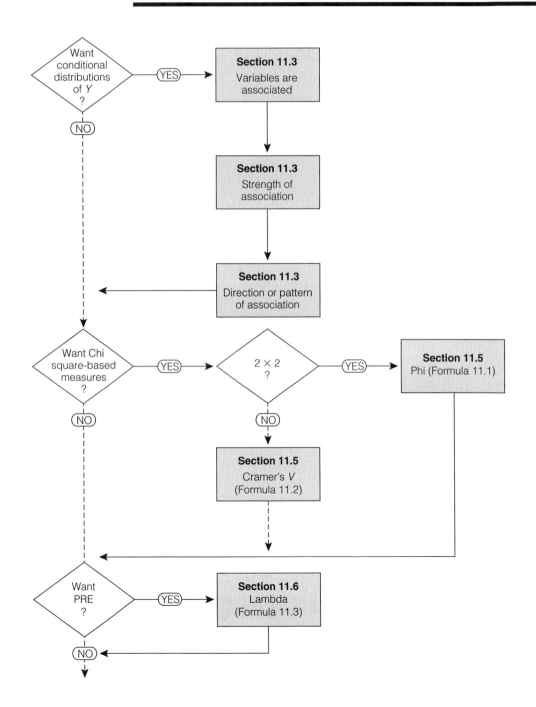

LEARNING OBJECTIVES

By the end of this chapter, you will be able to

1. Explain how we can use measures of association to describe and analyze the importance of relationships (versus their statistical significance).

2. Define "association" in the context of bivariate tables and in terms of changing conditional distributions.

3. List and explain the three characteristics of a bivariate relationship: existence, strength, and pattern or direction.

4. Investigate a bivariate association by properly calculating percentages for a bivariate table and interpreting the results.

5. Compute and interpret three measures of association for variables measured at the nominal level: phi, Cramer's V, and lambda.

11.1 STATISTICAL SIGNIFICANCE AND THEORETICAL IMPORTANCE

As we have seen over the past several chapters, tests of statistical significance are extremely important in social science research. As long as social scientists must work with random samples rather than populations, these tests are indispensable for dealing with the possibility that our research results are the products of mere random chance. However, tests of significance are often merely the first step in the analysis of research results. These tests do have limitations, and statistical significance is not necessarily the same thing as relevance or importance. Furthermore, all tests of significance are affected by sample size; tests performed on large samples may result in decisions to reject the null hypothesis when, in fact, the observed differences are quite minor.

Beginning with this chapter, we will be working with **measures of association**. Whereas tests of significance detect non-random relationships, measures of association provide information about the strength and direction of relationships, information that is more directly relevant for assessing the importance of relationships and testing the power and validity of our theories. The theories that guide scientific research are almost always stated in cause-and-effect terms (e.g., "variable X causes variable Y"). As an example, recall our discussion of the materialistic hypothesis in Chapter 1. In that theory, the causal (or independent) variable was social class and the effect (or dependent) variable was health status. The theory asserts that social class *causes* health. Measures of association help us trace causal relationships among variables, and they are our most important and powerful statistical tools for documenting, measuring, and analyzing cause-and-effect relationships.

As useful as they are, measures of association, like any class of statistics, do have their limitations. Most importantly, these statistics cannot *prove* that two variables are causally related. Even if there is a strong (and significant) statistical association between two variables, we cannot necessarily conclude that one variable is a cause of the other. We will explore causation in more detail in Part IV, but for now you should keep in mind that causation and association are two different things. We can use a statistical association between variables as evidence for a causal relationship, but association by itself is not proof that a causal relationship exists.

Another important use for measures of association is prediction. If two variables are associated, we can predict the score of a case on one variable from the score of that case on the other variable. For example, if social class and health are associated, we can predict that people who have high social class will be healthier than those with low social class. Note that prediction and causation can be two separate matters. If variables are associated, we can predict from one to the other even if the variables are not causally related.

This chapter will introduce the concept of **association** between variables in the context of bivariate tables and will stress the use of percentages to analyze associations between variables. We will then proceed to the logic, calculation, and interpretation of some widely used measures of association. By the end of the chapter, you will have an array of statistical tools you can use to analyze the strength and direction of associations between variables.

11.2 ASSOCIATION BETWEEN VARIABLES AND THE BIVARIATE TABLE

Most generally, two variables are said to be associated if the distribution of one of them changes under the various categories or scores of the other. For example, suppose that an industrial sociologist was concerned with the relationship between job satisfaction and productivity for assembly-line workers. If these two variables are associated, then scores on productivity will change under the different conditions of satisfaction. Highly satisfied workers will have different scores on productivity than workers who are low on satisfaction, and levels of productivity will vary by levels of satisfaction.

This relationship will become clearer with the use of bivariate tables. As you recall (see Chapter 10), bivariate tables display the scores of cases on two different variables. By convention, the **independent** or **X variable** (i.e., the variable taken as causal) is arrayed in the columns, and the **dependent** or **Y variable** in the rows (for the sake of brevity, we will often refer to the independent variable as X and the dependent variable as Y in the material that follows). Each column of the table (the vertical dimension) represents a score or category of the independent variable (X), and each row (the horizontal dimension) represents a score or category of the dependent variable (Y).*

---

*While it is conventional to construct a bivariate table in this format, the opposite is equally acceptable where the columns are scores of the dependent variable and rows are scores of the independent variable.

Table 11.1 displays a relationship between productivity and job satisfaction for a fictitious sample of 173 factory workers. We focus on the columns to detect the presence of an association between variables displayed in table format. Each column shows the pattern of scores on the dependent variable for each score on the independent variable. For example, the left-hand column indicates that 30 of the 60 workers who were low on job satisfaction were low on productivity, 20 were moderately productive, and 10 were high on productivity. The middle column shows that 21 of the 61 moderately satisfied workers were low on productivity, 25 were moderately productive, and 15 were high on productivity. Of the 52 workers who are highly satisfied (the right-hand column), 7 were low on productivity, 18 were moderate, and 27 were high.

By inspecting the table from column to column we can observe the effects of the independent variable on the dependent variable (provided, of course, that the table is constructed with the independent variable in the columns). These "within-column" frequency distributions are called the **conditional distributions of Y**; they display the distribution of scores on the dependent variable for each condition (or score) of the independent variable.

Table 11.1 indicates that productivity and satisfaction are associated: The distribution of scores on Y (productivity) changes across the various conditions of X (satisfaction). For example, half of the workers who were low on satisfaction were also low on productivity (30 out of 60), and over half of the workers who were high on satisfaction were high on productivity (27 out of 52).

Although it is intended to be a test of significance, the chi square statistic provides another way to detect the existence of an association between two variables that have been organized into table format. Any non-zero value for obtained chi square indicates that the variables are associated. For example, the obtained chi square for Table 11.1 is 24.2, a value that affirms our previous conclusion, based on the conditional distributions of Y, that an association of some sort exists between job satisfaction and productivity.

Often, the researcher will have already conducted a chi square test before considering matters of association. In such cases, it will not be necessary to inspect the conditional distributions of Y to ascertain whether or not the two variables are associated. If the obtained chi square is zero, the two variables are independent and not associated. Any value other than zero indicates some association between the variables. Remember, however, that

TABLE 11.1   PRODUCTIVITY BY JOB SATISFACTION (frequencies)

Productivity (Y)	Job Satisfaction (X)			Totals
	Low	Moderate	High	
Low	30	21	7	58
Moderate	20	25	18	63
High	10	15	27	52
Totals	60	61	52	173

statistical significance and association are two different things. It is perfectly possible for two variables to be associated (as indicated by a non-zero chi square) but still independent (if we fail to reject the null hypothesis).

In this section, we have defined, in a general way, the concept of association between two variables. We have also shown two different ways to detect the presence of an association. In the next section, we will extend the analysis beyond questions of the mere presence or absence of an association and, in a systematic way, see how we can develop additional, very useful information about the relationship between two variables.

11.3 THREE CHARACTERISTICS OF BIVARIATE ASSOCIATIONS

Bivariate associations possess three different characteristics, each of which must be analyzed for a full investigation of the relationship. Investigating these characteristics may be thought of as a process of finding answers to three questions:

1. Does an association exist?
2. If an association does exist, how strong is it?
3. What is the pattern and/or the direction of the association?

We will consider each of these questions separately.

Does an Association Exist?   We have already discussed the general definition of association, and we have seen that we can detect an association by observing the conditional distributions of Y in a table or by using chi square. In Table 11.1, we know that the two variables are associated to some extent because the conditional distributions of productivity (Y) are different across the various categories of satisfaction (X) and because the chi square statistic is a non-zero value.

Comparisons from column to column in Table 11.1 are relatively easy to make because the column totals are roughly equal. This will not usually be the case and it is helpful to compute percentages to control for varying column totals. These column percentages, introduced in Chapter 10, are computed within each column separately and make the pattern of association more visible.

The general procedure for detecting association with bivariate tables is to compute percentages within the columns (vertically or down each column) and then compare column to column across the table (horizontally or across the rows). We can conveniently remember this procedure with the following statement: "Percentage Down, Compare Across." Table 11.2 presents column percentages calculated from the data in Table 11.1. Note that this table reports the row and column marginals in parentheses. Besides controlling for any differences in column totals, tables in percentage form are usually easier to read because changes in the conditional distributions of Y are easier to detect.

In Table 11.2, we can see that the largest cell changes position from column to column. For workers who are low on satisfaction, the single

TABLE 11.2   PRODUCTIVITY BY JOB SATISFACTION (percentages)

| | Job Satisfaction (X) | | | |
Productivity (Y)	Low	Moderate	High	Totals
Low	50.00%	34.43%	13.46%	33.53%
Moderate	33.33%	40.98%	34.62%	36.42%
High	16.67%	24.59%	51.92%	30.05%
Totals	100.00%	100.00%	100.00%	100.00%
	(60)	(61)	(52)	(173)

TABLE 11.3   PRODUCTIVITY BY HEIGHT (an illustration of no association)

| | Height (X) | | |
Productivity (Y)	Short	Medium	Tall
Low	33.33%	33.33%	33.33%
Moderate	33.33%	33.33%	33.33%
High	33.33%	33.33%	33.33%
	100.00%	100.00%	100.00%

largest cell is in the top row (low on productivity). For the middle column (moderate on satisfaction), the largest cell is in the middle row (moderate on productivity), and, for the right-hand column (high on satisfaction), it is in the bottom row (high on productivity). Even a cursory glance at the conditional distributions of Y in Table 11.2 reinforces our conclusion that an association does exist between these two variables.

If two variables are not associated, then the conditional distributions of Y will not change across the columns. The distribution of Y would be the same for each condition of X. Table 11.3 illustrates a "perfect nonassociation" between height and productivity. Table 11.3 is only one of many patterns that indicate "no association." The important point is that the conditional distributions of Y are the same. Levels of productivity do not change at all for the various heights and, therefore, no association exists between these variables. Also, the obtained chi square computed from this table would have a value of zero, again indicating no association.

How Strong Is the Association?   Once we establish the existence of the association, we need to develop some idea of how strong the association is. This is essentially a matter of determining the amount of change in the conditional distributions of Y. At one extreme, of course, there is the case of "no association" where the conditional distributions of Y do not change at all (see Table 11.3). At the other extreme is a perfect association, the strongest

Application 11.1

Early retirement from the workforce is more common today than it was a few decades ago, with the average Canadian retiring at about age 62. Many Canadians, however, feel that they will not be able to afford to retire early. We would expect that persons with lower levels of education, who tend to have lower earnings and are less likely to have a private pension plan, are more likely to believe that early retirement will not happen for them, compared to those with higher education.

This section will examine the association between highest level of education completed and age at which one plans to retire. The following table reports the joint frequency distributions of education and planned retirement age in percentages for a sample of 1,426 Canadians from the Survey of Financial Security, a survey administered by Statistics Canada to collect information on the economic well-being of Canadians.

PLANNED RETIREMENT AGE BY LEVEL OF EDUCATION (percentages)

Age	Education		
	< High School	High School	College/University
65+	69	52	46
60–64	19	27	30
<60	12	21	24
	100%	100%	100%
	(215)	(325)	(886)

Source: Statistics Canada, 2005 Survey of Financial Security, PUMF.

Conditional distributions of planned retirement age (Y) change across the values of education (X), so these variables are associated. The clustering of cases in the diagonal from upper left to lower right suggests a substantial relationship in the predicted direction. People who are low on education are more likely to plan for retirement at age 65 or later, and people who are high on education are more likely to plan for early retirement (i.e., plan to retire before the age of 65). Because the maximum difference in column percentages in the table is 23% (69% − 46% = 23%), the relationship can be characterized as moderate. The results support our causal argument that better-educated people feel that they will have the financial security necessary to facilitate an early retirement from the workforce (X causes Y).

possible relationship. In general, a perfect association exists between two variables if each value of the dependent variable is associated with one and only one value of the independent variable. In a bivariate table, all cases in each column would be located in a single cell and there would be no variation in Y for a given value of X (see Table 11.4).

A perfect relationship would be taken as very strong evidence of a causal relationship between the variables, at least for the sample at hand. In

TABLE 11.4   PRODUCTIVITY BY HEIGHT (an illustration of perfect association)

Productivity (Y)	Height (X)		
	Short	Medium	Tall
Low	0%	0%	100%
Moderate	0%	100%	0%
High	100%	0%	0%
	100%	100%	100%

fact, the results presented in Table 11.4 would indicate that, for this sample, height is the sole cause of productivity. Also, in the case of a perfect relationship, predictions from one variable to the other could be made without error. If we knew that a particular worker was short, for example, we could be sure that he or she is highly productive.

Of course, the huge majority of relationships will fall somewhere between the two extremes of no association and perfect association. We need to develop some way of describing these intermediate relationships consistently and meaningfully. For example, Tables 11.1 and 11.2 show that there is an association between productivity and job satisfaction. How could this relationship be described in terms of strength? How close is the relationship to perfect? How far away from no association?

To answer these questions, researchers rely on statistics called measures of association, a variety of which are presented later in this chapter and in the chapters to follow. Measures of association provide precise, objective indicators of the strength of a relationship. Virtually all of these statistics are designed so that they have a lower limit of 0.00 and an upper limit of 1.00 (± 1.00 for ordinal and interval-ratio measures of association). A measure that equals 0.00 indicates no association between the variables (the conditional distributions of Y do not vary), and a measure of 1.00 (± 1.00 in the case of ordinal and interval-ratio measures) indicates a perfect relationship. The exact meaning of values between 0.00 and 1.00 varies from measure to measure, but for all measures, the closer the value is to 1.00, the stronger the relationship (the greater the change in the conditional distributions of Y).

We will begin to consider measures of association used in social research later in this chapter. At this point, let's consider the **maximum difference**, a less formal way of assessing the strength of a relationship based on comparing column percentages across the rows. This technique is "quick and easy": easy to apply (at least for small tables) but limited in its usefulness. To calculate the maximum difference, compute the column percentages as usual and then skim the table across *each* of the rows to find the largest difference in *any* row between column percentages. For example, the largest difference in column percentages in Table 11.2 is in the top row between the "Low" column and the "High" column: 50.00% − 13.46% = 36.54%. The maximum difference in the middle row is between "moderates" and "lows" (40.98% − 33.33% = 7.65%), and in the bottom row, it is between "highs" and "lows" (51.92% − 16.67% = 35.25%). Both of the latter values are less than the maximum difference in the top row.

Once you have found the maximum difference in the table, the scale presented in Table 11.5 can be used to describe the strength of the relationship. Using this scale, we can describe the relationship between productivity and job satisfaction in Table 11.2 as strong.

You should be aware that the relationships between the size of the maximum difference and the descriptive terms (weak, moderate, and strong) in Table 11.5 are arbitrary and approximate. We will get more precise and useful information when we compute and analyze measures of association, beginning later in this chapter. Also, maximum differences are easiest to find and most useful for smaller tables. In large tables, with many (say, more than three) columns and rows, it can be cumbersome to find the high and low percentages and it is advisable to consider only measures of association as indicators of the strength of relationships for these tables. Finally, note that the maximum difference is based on only two values (the high and low column percentages within any row). Like the range (see Chapter 3), this statistic can give a misleading impression of the overall strength of the relationship. Within these limits, however, the maximum difference can provide a useful, quick, and easy way of characterizing the strength of relationships (at least for smaller tables).

As a final caution, do not mistake chi square as an indicator of the strength of a relationship. Even very large values for chi square do not necessarily mean that the relationship is strong. Remember that significance and association are two separate matters, and chi square, by itself, is not a measure of association. While a non-zero value indicates that there is some association between the variables, the magnitude of chi square bears no particular relationship to the strength of the association. However, as we will see later in this chapter, there are ways to transform chi square into other statistics that do measure the strength of the association between two variables. *(For practice in computing percentages and judging the existence and strength of an association, see any of the problems at the end of this chapter.)*

What Is the Pattern and/or the Direction of the Association? Investigating the pattern of the association requires that we ascertain which values

TABLE 11.5 THE RELATIONSHIP BETWEEN THE MAXIMUM DIFFERENCE
AND THE STRENGTH OF THE RELATIONSHIP

Maximum Difference	Strength
If the maximum difference is:	*The strength of the relationship is:*
between 0 and 10 percentage points	weak
between 11 and 30 percentage points	moderate
more than 30 percentage points	strong

or categories of one variable are associated with which values or categories of the other. We have already remarked on the pattern of the relationship between productivity and satisfaction. Table 11.2 indicates that low scores on satisfaction are associated with low scores on productivity, moderate satisfaction with moderate productivity, and high satisfaction with high productivity.

When both variables are at least ordinal in level of measurement, the association between the variables may also be described in terms of direction.* The direction of the association can be either positive or negative. An association is positive if the variables vary in the same direction. That is, in a **positive association**, high scores on one variable are associated with high scores on the other variable, and low scores on one variable are associated with low scores on the other. In a positive association, as one variable increases in value, the other also increases; and as one variable decreases, the other also decreases. Table 11.6 displays, with fictitious data, a positive relationship between education and use of public libraries. As education increases (as you move from left to right across the table), library use also increases (the percentage of "high" users increases). The association between job satisfaction and productivity, as displayed in Tables 11.1 and 11.2, is also a positive association.

In a **negative association**, the variables vary in opposite directions. High scores on one variable are associated with low scores on the other, and increases in one variable are accompanied by decreases in the other. Table 11.7 displays a negative relationship, again with fictitious data, between education and television viewing. The amount of television viewing decreases as education increases. In other words, as you move from left to right across the top of the table (as education increases), the percentage of heavy viewers decreases.

Measures of association for ordinal and interval-ratio variables are designed so that they will take on positive values for positive associations and negative values for negative associations. Thus, a measure of association preceded by a plus sign indicates a positive relationship between the two

TABLE 11.6 LIBRARY USE BY EDUCATION
(an illustration of a positive relationship)

Library Use	Education		
	Low	Moderate	High
Low	60%	20%	10%
Moderate	30	60	30
High	10	20	60
Totals	100%	100%	100%

TABLE 11.7 AMOUNT OF TELEVISION VIEWING BY EDUCATION (an illustration of a negative relationship)

Television Viewing	Education		
	Low	Moderate	High
Low	10%	20%	60%
Moderate	30	60	30
High	60	20	10
Totals	100%	100%	100%

*Variables measured at the nominal level have no numerical order to them (by definition). Therefore, associations including nominal-level variables, while they may have a pattern, cannot be said to have a direction.

variables, with the value +1.00 indicating a perfect positive relationship. A negative sign indicates a negative relationship, with −1.00 indicating a perfect negative relationship. We will consider the direction of relationships in more detail in Chapters 12 and 13. *(For practice in determining the pattern of an association, see any of the end-of-chapter problems. For practice in determining the direction of a relationship, see problems 11.1 and 11.7.)*

11.4 INTRODUCTION TO MEASURES OF ASSOCIATION

Conditional distributions, column percentages, and the maximum difference provide very useful information about the bivariate association, and should always be computed and analyzed. However, they can be awkward and cumbersome to use, especially for larger tables. Measures of association, on the other hand, characterize the strength (and for ordinal- and interval-ratio-level variables, the direction) of bivariate relationships in a single number, a more compact and convenient format for interpretation and discussion.

There are many measures of association but we will confine our attention to a few of those most widely used. We will cover these statistics by the level of measurement for which they are most appropriate. In this chapter, we will consider measures appropriate for nominally measured variables. In the next chapter, we will cover measures of association for ordinal-level variables, and finally, in Chapter 13, we will consider Pearson's r, a measure of association or correlation for interval-ratio-level variables. You will note that several of the research situations used as examples involve variables measured at different levels (e.g., one nominal-level variable and one ordinal-level variable). The general procedure in the situation of "mixed levels" is to be conservative and select measures of association appropriate for the lower of the two levels of measurement.

11.5 CHI SQUARE–BASED MEASURES OF ASSOCIATION

When working with nominal-level variables, social science researchers rely heavily on measures of association based on the value of chi square. While chi square per se is a test of statistical significance, it can be transformed into other statistics that measure the strength of the association between two variables. When the value of chi square is already known, these measures are easy to calculate. To illustrate, let us reconsider Table 10.3, which displayed, with fictitious data, a relationship between CASSW (Canadian Association of Schools of Social Work) accreditation and employment for social work graduates. For the sake of convenience, this table is reproduced here as Table 11.8.

We saw in Chapter 10 that this relationship is statistically significant ($\chi^2 = 10.78$, which is significant at $\alpha = 0.05$), but the question now concerns the *strength* of the association. A brief glance at Table 11.8 shows that the conditional distributions of employment status do change, so the variables are associated. To emphasize this point, it is always helpful to calculate column percentages, as in Table 11.9.

TABLE 11.8   EMPLOYMENT STATUS OF 100 SOCIAL WORK GRADUATES BY CASSW-ACCREDITATION STATUS OF UNDERGRADUATE PROGRAM

| | Accreditation Status | | |
Employment Status	Accredited	Not Accredited	Totals
Working as a social worker	30	10	40
Not working as a social worker	25	35	60
Totals	55	45	100

TABLE 11.9   EMPLOYMENT STATUS BY CASSW-ACCREDITATION STATUS (percentages)

| | Accreditation Status | | |
Employment Status	Accredited	Not Accredited	Totals
Working as a social worker	54.55%	22.22%	40.00%
Not working as a social worker	45.45%	77.78%	60.00%
	100.00%	100.00%	100.00%

So far, we know that the relationship between these two variables is statistically significant and that there is an association of some kind between CASSW accreditation and employment. To assess the strength of the association, we will compute a **phi (ϕ)**. This statistic is a frequently used chi square–based measure of association appropriate for 2 × 2 tables (i.e., tables with two rows and two columns).

Calculating Phi.   One of the attractions of phi is that it is easy to calculate. Simply divide the value of the obtained chi square by the total number of cases in the sample (n) and take the square root of the result. Expressed in symbols, the formula for phi is

FORMULA 11.1

$$\phi = \sqrt{\frac{\chi^2}{n}}$$

For the data displayed in Table 11.8, the chi square is 10.78. Therefore, phi is

$$\phi = \sqrt{\frac{\chi^2}{n}}$$

$$\phi = \sqrt{\frac{10.78}{100}}$$

$$\phi = 0.33$$

For a 2 × 2 table, phi ranges in value from 0 (no association) to 1.00 (perfect association). The closer to 1.00, the stronger the relationship; the closer to 0.00, the weaker the relationship. For Table 11.8, we already knew that the relationship was statistically significant at the 0.05 level. Phi, as a measure of association, adds information about the strength of the relationship. As for the pattern of the association, the column percentages in Table 11.9 show that graduates of CASSW-accredited programs were more often employed as social workers.

Calculating Cramer's V. For tables larger than 2 × 2 (specifically, for tables with more than two columns and more than two rows), the upper limit of phi can exceed 1.00. This makes phi difficult to interpret, and a more general form of the statistic called **Cramer's V** must be used for larger tables. The formula for Cramer's V is

FORMULA 11.2

$$V = \sqrt{\frac{x^2}{(n)(\min r - 1, c - 1)}}$$

where $(\min r - 1, c - 1)$ = the minimum value of $r - 1$ (number of rows minus 1) or $c - 1$ (number of columns minus 1)

In words: To calculate V, find the lesser of the number of rows minus 1 $(r - 1)$ or the number of columns minus 1 $(c - 1)$, multiply this value by n, divide the result into the value of chi square, and then find the square root. Cramer's V has an upper limit of 1.00 for any size table and will be the same value as phi if the table has either two rows or two columns. Like phi, Cramer's V can be interpreted as an index that measures the strength of the association between two variables.

To illustrate the computation of V, suppose you had gathered the data displayed in Table 11.10, which shows the relationship between membership in student clubs or organizations and academic achievement for a sample of university students. The obtained chi square for this table is 31.5, a value that is significant at the 0.05 level. Cramer's V is

$$V = \sqrt{\frac{x^2}{(n)(\min r - 1, c - 1)}}$$

$$V = \sqrt{\frac{31.50}{(75)(2)}}$$

$$V = \sqrt{\frac{31.50}{150}}$$

$$V = \sqrt{0.21}$$

$$V = 0.46$$

Because Table 11.10 has the same number of rows and columns, we may use either $(r - 1)$ or $(c - 1)$ in the denominator. In either case, the value of the

TABLE 11.10   ACADEMIC ACHIEVEMENT BY STUDENT-CLUB MEMBERSHIP (fictitious data)

| Academic Achievement | Club Membership | | | Totals |
	Varsity or Intramural Sports Club	Non-Sports Club	No Membership	
Low	4	4	17	25
Moderate	15	6	4	25
High	4	16	5	25
Totals	23	26	26	75

TABLE 11.11   ACADEMIC ACHIEVEMENT BY STUDENT-CLUB MEMBERSHIP (percentages)

| Academic Achievement | Club Membership | | | Totals |
	Varsity or Intramural Sports Club	Non-Sports Club	No Membership	
Low	17.39	15.38	65.38	33.33
Moderate	65.22	23.08	15.39	33.33
High	17.39	61.54	19.23	33.33
Totals	100.00	100.00	100.00	100.00

denominator is n multiplied by $(3 - 1)$, or 2. Column percentages are presented in Table 11.11 to help identify the pattern of this relationship. Members of sports clubs tend to be moderate, members of non-sports clubs tend to be high, and non-members tend to be low in academic achievement.

Interpreting Phi and Cramer's V.   It will be helpful to have some general guidelines for interpreting the value of measures of association for nominal variables, similar to the guidelines we used for interpreting the maximum difference in column percentages. Table 11.12 presents the general relationship between the value of the statistic and the strength of the relationship for phi and Cramer's V. As was the case with Table 11.5, the relationships in Table 11.12 are arbitrary and meant as general guidelines only. Using these guidelines, we can characterize the relationship in Table 11.8 (phi = 0.33) and Table 11.10 (Cramer's $V = 0.46$) as strong.

Limitations Phi and Cramer's V.   One limitation of phi and Cramer's V is that they are only general indicators of the strength of the relationship. Of course, the closer these measures are to 0.00, the weaker the relationship, and the closer to 1.00, the stronger the relationship. Values between 0.00 and 1.00 can be described as weak, moderate, or strong according to the general guidelines presented in Table 11.12 but have no direct or meaningful interpretation. On the other hand, phi and V are easy to calculate (once the value of chi square has been obtained) and are commonly used indicators of the

TABLE 11.12 THE RELATIONSHIP BETWEEN THE VALUE OF NOMINAL-LEVEL MEASURES OF ASSOCIATION AND THE STRENGTH OF THE RELATIONSHIP

Value	Strength
If the value is	*The strength of the relationship is*
between 0.00 and 0.10	weak
between 0.11 and 0.30	moderate
greater than 0.30	strong

importance of an association. *(For practice in computing phi and Cramer's V, see any of the problems at the end of this chapter. Problems with 2 × 2 tables will minimize computations. Remember that for tables with either two rows or two columns, phi and Cramer's V will have the same value.)*

11.6 LAMBDA: A PROPORTIONAL REDUCTION IN ERROR MEASURE OF ASSOCIATION

The Logic of Proportional Reduction in Error. In recent years, measures based on a logic known as **proportional reduction in error (PRE)** have been developed to complement the older chi square–based measures of association. Specifically, unlike their chi square–based counterparts, PRE-based measures of association provide a direct, meaningful interpretation.

Most generally stated, the logic of PRE measures requires us to make two different predictions about the scores of cases. In the first prediction, we ignore information about the independent variable and, therefore, make many errors in predicting the score on the dependent variable. In the second prediction, we take account of the score of the case on the independent variable to help predict the score on the dependent variable. If there is an association between the variables, we will make fewer errors when taking the independent variable into account. Hence, the value of a PRE-based measure of association has a precise, meaningful interpretation in the sense that it quantitatively measures the proportional reduction in errors between the two predictions. Applying these general thoughts to the case of nominal-level variables will make the logic clearer.

For nominal-level variables, we first predict the category into which each case will fall on the dependent variable (Y) while ignoring the independent variable (X). Because we would, in effect, be predicting blindly in this case, we would make many errors (i.e., we would often incorrectly predict the category of a case on the dependent variable).

The second prediction allows us to take the independent variable into account. If the two variables are associated, the additional information supplied by the independent variable will reduce our errors of prediction (i.e., we should misclassify fewer cases). The stronger the association between the variables, the greater the reduction in errors. In the case of a perfect association, we would make no errors at all when predicting the score on Y from the score on X. But when there is no association between the variables, knowledge of the independent variable will not improve the accuracy of our predictions. We would make just as many errors of prediction with knowledge of the independent variable as we would without knowledge of it.

An illustration should make these principles clearer. Suppose you were placed in the rather unusual position of having to predict whether each of the next 100 people you meet will be shorter or taller than 5 feet 9 inches under the condition that you would have no knowledge of these people at all. With absolutely no information about these people, your predictions will be wrong quite often (you will frequently misclassify a tall person as short and vice versa).

Now assume that you must go through this ordeal twice, but on the second round, you know the sex of the person whose height you must predict. Because height is associated with sex and females are, on the average, shorter than males, the optimal strategy would be to predict that all females are short and all males are tall. Of course, you will still make errors on this second round, but if the variables are associated, the number of errors on the second round will be less than the number of errors on the first. That is, using information about the independent variable will reduce the number of errors (if, of course, the two variables are related). How can these unusual thoughts be translated into a useful statistic?

Lambda.   One hundred individuals have been categorized by gender and height, and the data are displayed in Table 11.13. It is clear, even without percentages, that the two variables are associated. To measure the strength of this association, a PRE measure called **lambda** (symbolized by the Greek letter λ) will be calculated. Following the logic introduced in the previous section, we must find two quantities. First, the number of prediction errors made while ignoring the independent variable (gender) must be found. Then, we will find the number of prediction errors made while taking gender into account. These two sums will then be compared to derive the statistic.

First, the information given by the independent variable (gender) can be ignored, in effect, by working only with the row marginals. Two different predictions can be made about height (the dependent variable) by using these marginals. We can predict either that all subjects are tall or that all subjects are short.* For the first prediction (all subjects are tall), 48 errors will be made. That is, for this prediction, all 100 cases would be placed in the first row. Because only 52 of the cases actually belong in this row, this prediction would result in (100 − 52), or 48, errors. If we had predicted that all subjects were short, on the

TABLE 11.13   HEIGHT BY GENDER

Height	Gender		Totals
	Male	Female	
Tall	44	8	52
Short	6	42	48
Totals	50	50	100

*Other predictions are, of course, possible, but these are the only two permitted by lambda.

other hand, we would have made 52 errors (100 − 48 = 52). We will take the *lesser* of these two numbers and refer to this quantity as "E_1" for the number of errors made while ignoring the independent variable. So, $E_1 = 48$.

In the second step in the computation of lambda, we predict the score on Y (height) again but this time we take X (gender) into account. To do this, follow the same procedure as in the first step but this time move from column to column. Because each column is a category of X, we thus take X into account in making our predictions. For the left-hand column (males), we predict that all 50 cases will be tall and make six errors (50 − 44 = 6). For the second column (females), our prediction is that all females are short, and eight errors will be made. By moving from column to column, we have taken X into account and have made a total of 14 errors of prediction, a quantity we will label "E_2" ($E_2 = 6 + 8 = 14$).

If the variables are associated, we will make fewer errors under the second procedure than under the first. In other words, E_2 will be smaller than E_1. In this case, we made fewer errors of prediction while taking gender into account ($E_2 = 14$) than while ignoring gender ($E_1 = 48$), so gender and height are clearly associated. Our errors were reduced from 48 to only 14. To find the *proportional* reduction in error, use Formula 11.3:

FORMULA 11.3

$$\lambda = \frac{E_1 - E_2}{E_1}$$

where E_1 = the total number of cases minus the largest row total

E_2 = the sum of the following: for each column, the column total minus the largest cell frequency

For the sample problem, the value of lambda would be

$$\lambda = \frac{E_1 - E_2}{E_1}$$

$$\lambda = \frac{48 - 14}{48}$$

$$\lambda = \frac{34}{48}$$

$$\lambda = 0.71$$

The value of lambda ranges from 0.00 to 1.00. Of course, a value of 0.00 means that the variables are not associated at all (E_1 is the same as E_2) and a value of 1.00 means that the association is perfect (E_2 is zero and scores on the dependent variable can be predicted without error from the independent variable). Unlike phi or V, however, the numerical value of lambda between the extremes of 0.00 and 1.00 has a precise meaning: It is an index of the extent to which the independent variable (X) helps us to predict (or, more loosely, understand) the dependent variable (Y). When multiplied by

---

Application 11.2

A random sample of students from the Canadian Internet Use Survey, conducted by Statistics Canada to measure the extent and scope to which Canadians use the Internet, was asked about using the Internet to play games in the last year. The table below displays the actual data for this variable by sex of respondent. Is online gaming related to sex?

	Sex		
Online Gaming	Male	Female	Totals
Yes	407	438	845
No	253	590	843
Totals	660	1,028	1,688

Because this is a 2 × 2 table, we can compute phi as a measure of association. The chi square for the table is 58.41, so phi is

$$\phi = \sqrt{\frac{\chi^2}{n}}$$

$$\phi = \sqrt{\frac{58.41}{1,688}}$$

$$\phi = \sqrt{0.035}$$

$$\phi = 0.19$$

which indicates a moderate relationship between the two variables.

A lambda can also be computed as an additional measure of association:

$$E_1 = 1,688 - 845 = 843$$

$$E_2 = (660 - 407) + (1,028 - 590)$$

$$= 253 + 438 = 691$$

$$\lambda = \frac{E_1 - E_2}{E_1}$$

$$\lambda = \frac{843 - 691}{843}$$

$$\lambda = \frac{152}{843}$$

$$\lambda = 0.18$$

A lambda of 0.18 indicates that we would make 18% fewer errors in predicting use of the Internet to play games (Y) from sex (X), as opposed to predicting use of the Internet to play games while ignoring sex. The association is moderate and, by inspection of the table, we can see that male students are more likely to play games online (62%), and female students are more likely not to use the Internet to play games (57%).

Source: Data from Statistics Canada, 2005 Canadian Internet Use Survey, PUMF.

100, the value of lambda indicates the strength of the association in terms of the percentage reduction in error. Thus, the lambda above would be interpreted by concluding that knowledge of gender improves our ability to predict height by 71%. Or, we are 71% better off knowing gender when attempting to predict height.

Calculating Lambda: Another Example.   In this section, we will work through another example, based on actual data, to state the computational routine for lambda in more general terms. Implemented in 1994, the North American Free Trade Agreement (NAFTA) removed most barriers to trade, and increased cross-border trade among the United States, Canada, and Mexico. Since that time, public opinion on NAFTA in Canada has been mixed.

We will use data from the 2006 Canadian Election Study, shown in Table 11.14, to examine whether public opinion toward free trade varies by region. (The Canadian Election Study surveyed adults in the 10 provinces only, thus excluding the territories). To make the number of cases in this example more manageable, yet still representative, we randomly selected about 10% of cases (or 379 respondents) from the full sample of about 4,000 respondents.

Step 1. To find E_1, the number of errors made while ignoring X (region, in this case), subtract the largest row total from n. For Table 11.14, E_1 will be

$$E_1 = n - \text{(Largest row total)}$$
$$E_1 = 379 - 145$$
$$E_1 = 234$$

Thus, we will misclassify 234 cases on opinion toward free trade while ignoring region.

Step 2. Next, E_2—the number of errors made when taking the independent variable into account—must be found. For each column, subtract the largest cell frequency from the column total and then add the subtotals together. For the data presented in Table 11.14:

$$\text{For Atlantic Canada: } 41 - 21 = 20$$
$$\text{For Quebec: } 92 - 40 = 52$$
$$\text{For Ontario: } 117 - 48 = 69$$
$$\text{For Western Canada: } 129 - 60 = 69$$
$$E_2 = 210$$

A total of 210 errors are made when predicting opinion toward free trade while taking region into account.

TABLE 11.14 OPINION TOWARD FREE TRADE* BY REGION

| | Region | | | | |
Opinion on Free Trade	Atlantic	Quebec	Ontario	Western	Totals
Somewhat/Strongly Disagree	10	40	29	60	139
Somewhat Agree	21	33	48	43	145
Strongly Agree	10	19	40	26	95
Totals	41	92	117	129	379

*Based on the question, "Do you strongly agree, somewhat agree, somewhat disagree, or strongly disagree that, overall, free trade with the U.S. has been good for the Canadian economy?"

Source: Data from 2006 Canadian Election Study.

Step 3. In step 1, 234 errors of prediction were made as compared to 210 errors in step 2. Because the number of errors has been reduced, the variables are associated. To find the proportional reduction in error, the values for E_1 and E_2 can be directly substituted into Formula 11.3:

$$\lambda = \frac{234 - 210}{234}$$

$$\lambda = \frac{24}{234}$$

$$\lambda = 0.10$$

Using our conventional labels (see Table 11.12), we would call this a weak relationship. Using PRE logic, we can add more detail to the characterization: When attempting to predict opinion toward free trade, we would make 10% fewer errors by taking region into account. Knowledge of a respondent's region of residence improves the accuracy of our predictions by a factor of 10%. The weak strength of lambda indicates that factors other than region are associated with the dependent variable.

Limitations of Lambda.   As a measure of association, lambda has two characteristics that should be stressed. First, lambda is asymmetric. This means that the value of the statistic will vary, depending on which variable is taken as dependent. For example, in Table 11.14, the value of lambda would be about 0.07 if region had been taken as the dependent variable (verify this with your own computation). Thus, you should exercise some caution in the designation of a dependent variable. If you consistently follow the convention of arraying the independent variable in the columns and the dependent variable in the rows and compute lambda as outlined above, the asymmetry of the statistic should not be confusing.

Second, when one of the row totals is much larger than the others, lambda can be misleading. It can be 0.00 even when other measures of association are greater than 0.00 and the conditional distributions for the table indicate that there is an association between the variables. This anomaly is a function of the way lambda is calculated and suggests that great caution should be exercised in the interpretation of lambda when the row marginals are very unequal. In fact, in the case of very unequal row marginals, a chi square–based measure of association would be the preferred measure of association. *(For practice in computing lambda, see any of the problems at the end of this chapter. As with phi and Cramer's V, it's probably a good idea to start with small samples and 2 × 2 tables.)*

READING STATISTICS 7: Bivariate Tables and Associated Statistics

In this chapter and the next one, our primary concern is with measures of association for bivariate tables. These statistics are very useful for summarizing the strength and—as we will see in the next chapter—the direction of relationships. The statistics associated with any bivariate table will usually be reported directly below the table itself. This information would include the name of the measure of association and its value. Also, if the research involves a random sample, the results of the chi square test or a test for the significance of the measure itself (as we will see in Section 12.7) will be reported. Thus, the information would look something like this:

$$\lambda = 0.47$$
$$\chi^2 = 13.23 \ (2\text{df}, \ p < 0.05)$$

Note that the alpha level is reported in the "$p <$" format.

Besides reporting the value of these statistics, researchers also interpret them in the text of their studies. The preceding statistics might be characterized by the following statement: "The association between the variables is statistically significant and strong." Again, we see that researchers will avoid our rather wordy (but more careful) style of presenting results. Where we might say "a lambda of 0.47 indicates that we will reduce our errors of prediction by 47% when predicting the dependent variable from the independent variable, as opposed to predicting the dependent while ignoring the independent," the researcher will simply report the value of lambda and characterize that value in a word or two (e.g., "The association is strong"). The researcher assumes that his or her audience is statistically literate and can make the more detailed interpretations themselves.

However, the first step in examining a bivariate table for a relationship is to apply the techniques introduced earlier in this chapter. Column percentages and conditional distributions will give you more detail about the relationship than measures of association. As useful as they are, the latter should be regarded as summary statements rather than analysis in depth. In this installment of Reading Statistics we will review a study that looks at the relationship between ethnicity and politics using both sets of techniques.

Statistics in the Professional Literature

Heterogeneity in ethnicity and culture is a growing characteristic of Canadian society. Many aspects of Canadian society reflect this ethnocultural diversity. Yet as Tossutti and Najem (2002) highlight, there is a considerable gap between ethnocultural minorities in the general population and their representation in federal politics.

Tossutti and Najem look specifically at the association between federal political party affiliation and ethnocultural origin of political candidates. Party affiliation is categorized as follows: Liberal Party, Canadian Alliance, Progressive Conservative Party (PC), New Democratic Party (NDP), and Bloc Québécois (BQ). Ethnocultural origin is divided into two categories: those who trace their origins to the Aboriginal, French, and British founding groups ("non-minority") and those who do not ("minority"). Tossutti and Najem examine a number of relationships between politics and ethnocultural origin.

We focus here on two of these relationships, based on data from the 2000 federal election. Both bivariate tables are constructed in conventional format, with the independent variable in the columns, the dependent variable in the rows, and percentages calculated in the columns. The Cramer's V associated with each table is reported directly below it.

Table 1 shows the relationship between federal election candidates' party affiliation (independent variable) and ethnocultural origin (dependent variable). A Cramer's V of 0.11 indicates a weak

(continued next page)

READING STATISTICS 7:   *(continued)*

moderate association. The column percentages show that political parties differed in minority candidate recruitment in the 2000 federal election, with the Liberals fielding the most and the BQ the least minority candidates in the election, yet the Alliance was not far behind the Liberals. This was an unexpected finding, the authors note, given the Alliance's perceived "anti-immigrant" image versus the Liberal's image of openness to minorities.

TABLE 1   PARTY AFFILIATION AND ETHNOCULTURAL ORIGIN OF CANDIDATES
IN THE 2000 FEDERAL ELECTION, PERCENTAGES (*N*'S IN PARENTHESES)

Ethnocultural Origin	Party Affiliation				
	Liberal	Alliance	PC	NDP	BQ
Minority	26.6	23.5	19.2	24.7	6.7
Non-minority	73.4	76.5	80.8	75.3	93.3
Totals	100.0	100.0	100.0	100.0	100.0
	(301)	(298)	(292)	(300)	(75)

Cramer's $V = 0.11$

Looking at minority candidates only, Table 2 examines the relationship between party affiliation (independent variable) and election success of candidates (dependent variable) in the 2000 federal election. Cramer's V (0.52) indicates a strong association. Conditional distributions show that minority candidates representing the Liberals, followed by the Alliance, had the highest success rates at the ballot box. PC, NDP, and BQ minority candidates had the lowest election victory rates. If you want to learn more about this study, the reference is provided at the end of this box.

TABLE 2   PARTY AFFILIATION AND VICTORY RATES OF ETHNIC MINORITY CANDIDATES
IN THE 2000 FEDERAL ELECTION, PERCENTAGES (*N*'S IN PARENTHESES)

Election Success	Party Affiliation				
	Liberal	Alliance	PC	NDP	BQ
Elected	57.0	28.6	1.8	5.5	0.0
Not elected	43.0	71.4	98.2	94.5	100.0
Totals	100.0	100.0	100.0	100.0	100.0
	(80)	(70)	(56)	(74)	(5)

Cramer's $V = 0.52$

Source: Tossutti, L. and Najem, T. "Minorities and Elections in Canada's Four Party System: Macro and Micro Constraints and Opportunities." *Canadian Ethnic Studies* (34: 84–111, 2002).

SUMMARY

1. Analyzing the association between variables provides information that is complementary to tests of significance. The latter are designed to detect non-random relationships, whereas measures of association are designed to quantify the importance or strength of a relationship.

2. Relationships between variables have three characteristics: the existence of an association, the strength of the association, and the direction or pattern of the association. These three characteristics can be investigated by calculating percentages for a bivariate table in the direction of the independent variable (vertically) and then comparing in the other direction (horizontally). This procedure can be summarized in the following statement: "Percentage Down, Compare Across." It is often useful (as well as quick and easy) to assess the strength of a relationship by finding the maximum difference in column percentages in any row of the table.

3. Tables 11.1 and 11.2 can be analyzed in terms of these three characteristics. Clearly, a relationship does exist between job satisfaction and productivity, because the conditional distributions of the dependent variable (productivity) are different for the three different conditions of the independent variable (job satisfaction). Even without a measure of association, we can see that the association is substantial in that the change in Y (productivity) across the three categories of X (satisfaction) is marked. The maximum difference of 36.54% confirms that the relationship is

substantial (strong). Furthermore, the relationship is positive in direction. Productivity increases as job satisfaction rises, and workers who report high job satisfaction tend also to be high on productivity. Workers with little job satisfaction tend to be low on productivity.

4. Given the nature and strength of the relationship, it could be predicted with fair accuracy that highly satisfied workers tend to be highly productive ("happy workers are busy workers"). These results might be taken as evidence of a causal relationship between these two variables, but they cannot, by themselves, prove that a causal relationship exists: Association is not the same thing as causation. In fact, although we have presumed that job satisfaction is the independent variable, we could have argued the reverse causal sequence ("busy workers are happy workers"). The results presented in Tables 11.1 and 11.2 are consistent with both causal arguments.

5. Phi, Cramer's V, and lambda are measures of association and each is appropriate for a specific situation. We use phi for 2 × 2 tables and Cramer's V for tables larger than 2 × 2. While phi and Cramer's V are chi square–based measures, lambda is a PRE-based measure and provides a more direct interpretation for values between the extremes of 0.00 and 1.00. These statistics express information about the strength of relationship *only*. In all cases, be sure to analyze the column percentages as well as the measures of association to maximize the information you have about the relationship.

SUMMARY OF FORMULAS

Phi	11.1	$\phi = \sqrt{\dfrac{\chi^2}{n}}$
Cramer's V	11.2	$V = \sqrt{\dfrac{\chi^2}{(n)(\min r - 1,\, c - 1)}}$
Lambda	11.3	$\lambda = \dfrac{E_1 - E_2}{E_1}$

GLOSSARY

Association. The relationship between two (or more) variables. Two variables are said to be associated if the distribution of one variable changes for the various categories or scores of the other variable. (p. 302)

Conditional distribution of Y. The distribution of scores on the dependent variable for a specific score or category of the independent variable when the variables have been organized into table format. (p. 303)

Cramer's V. A chi square–based measure of association. Appropriate for nominally measured variables that have been organized into a bivariate table of any number of rows and columns. (p. 312)

Dependent variable. In a bivariate relationship, the variable that is taken as the effect. (p. 302)

Independent variable. In a bivariate relationship, the variable that is taken as the cause. (p. 302)

Lambda (λ). A measure of association appropriate for nominally measured variables that have been organized into a bivariate table. Lambda is based on the logic of proportional reduction in error (PRE). (p. 315)

Maximum difference. A way to assess the strength of an association between variables that have been organized into a bivariate table. The maximum difference is the largest difference between column percentages for any row of the table. (p. 307)

Measures of association. Statistic that quantifies the strength of the association between variables. (p. 301)

Negative association. A bivariate relationship where the variables vary in opposite directions. As one variable increases, the other decreases, and high scores on one variable are associated with low scores on the other. (p. 309)

Phi (ϕ). A chi square–based measure of association. Appropriate for nominally measured variables that have been organized into a 2 × 2 bivariate table. (p. 311)

Positive association. A bivariate relationship where the variables vary in the same direction. As one variable increases, the other also increases, and high scores on one variable are associated with high scores on the other. (p. 309)

Proportional reduction in error (PRE). The logic that underlies the definition and computation of lambda. The statistic compares the number of errors made when predicting the dependent variable while ignoring the independent variable (E_1) with the number of errors made while taking the independent variable into account (E_2). (p. 314)

X. Symbol used for any independent variable. (p. 302)

Y. Symbol used for any dependent variable. (p. 302)

MULTIMEDIA RESOURCES

http://www.healeystatistics.nelson.com

Visit the companion website for the second Canadian edition of *Statistics: A Tool for Social Research* to access a wide range of student resources. Begin by clicking on the Student Resources section of the textbook's website to access review quizzes, flashcards, and other study tools.

PROBLEMS

11.1 | PA | Various supervisors in the municipal government of Pearson, Ontario, have been rated on the extent to which they practise authoritarian styles of leadership and decision making. The efficiency of each department has also been rated, and the results are summarized below. Calculate percentages for the table so that it shows the effect of leadership style on efficiency. Is there an association between these two variables? Describe the strength and direction of the relationship.

	Authoritarianism		
Efficiency	Low	High	Totals
Low	10	12	22
High	17	5	22
Totals	27	17	44

	2004 Election		
2006 Election	Voted	Didn't Vote	Totals
Voted	117	23	140
Didn't Vote	17	178	195
Totals	134	201	335

11.2 SOC The administration of a university has proposed an increase in the mandatory student fee in order to finance an upgrading of the varsity football program. A sample of the faculty has completed a survey on the issue. Is there any association between support for raising fees and the sex, discipline, or tenured status of the faculty? Calculate percentages for each table, then describe the strength and pattern of the association.

a. Support for raising fees by sex:

	Sex		
Support	Males	Females	Totals
For	12	8	20
Against	15	12	27
Totals	27	20	47

b. Support for raising fees by discipline:

	Discipline		
Support	Social Sciences & Arts	Science & Business	Totals
For	6	13	19
Against	14	14	28
Totals	20	27	47

c. Support for raising fees by tenured status:

	Status		
Support	Tenured	Non-tenured	Total
For	15	4	19
Against	18	10	28
Total	33	14	47

11.3 PS How consistent are people in their voting habits? Do the same people vote from election to election? Below are the results of a poll in which people were asked if they had voted in each of the last two federal elections. Calculate percentages for the table, and assess the strength and pattern of this relationship.

11.4 SOC A needs assessment survey has been distributed in a large retirement community. Residents were asked to check off the services or programs they thought should be added. Is there any association between sex and the perception of a need for more social occasions? Calculate percentages for the table, and assess the strength and pattern of this relationship.

	Sex		
More Parties?	Male	Female	Totals
Yes	321	426	747
No	175	251	426
Totals	496	677	1,173

11.5 Compute a phi and a lambda for problems 11.1–11.4. Compare the value of the measure of association with your impressions of the strength of the relationships based solely on the percentages you calculated for those problems.

11.6 In any social science journal, find an article that includes a bivariate table. Inspect the table and the related text carefully and answer the following questions:

a. Identify the variables in the table. What values (categories) does each possess? What is the level of measurement for each variable?

b. Is the table in percentage form? In what direction are the percentages calculated? Are comparisons made between columns or rows?

c. Is one of the variables identified by the author as independent?

d. How is the relationship characterized by the author in terms of the strength of the association? In terms of the direction (if any) of the association?

e. Find the measure of association (if any) calculated for the table. What is the numerical value of the measure? What is the sign (if any) of the measure?

11.7 SOC If a person's political ideology (liberal, moderate, or conservative) is known, can we predict their position on issues? If liberals are generally progressive and conservatives are generally traditional (with moderates in between), what relationships would you expect to find between political ideology and these issues?

  a. Support for same-sex marriage
  b. The death penalty
  c. The legal right to commit suicide for people with incurable diseases
  d. Support for traditional gender roles
  e. Support for the legalization of marijuana

The tables below show the results of a recent public opinion survey. For each table, compute column percentages and the maximum difference. Summarize the strength and direction of each relationship in a brief paragraph. Were your expectations confirmed?

  a. Support for same-sex marriage by political ideology:

Supports Same-sex Marriage?	Political Ideology			Totals
	Liberal	Moderate	Conservative	
Favour	309	234	154	697
Oppose	211	360	419	990
Totals	520	594	573	1,687

  b. Support for capital punishment by political ideology:

Supports Capital Punishment?	Political Ideology			Totals
	Liberal	Moderate	Conservative	
Favour	440	693	693	1,826
Oppose	265	214	186	665
Totals	705	907	879	2,491

  c. Support for the right of people with an incurable disease to commit suicide by political ideology:

Supports the Right to Suicide?	Political Ideology			Totals
	Liberal	Moderate	Conservative	
Favour	381	394	319	1,094
Oppose	120	229	261	610
Totals	501	623	580	1,704

  d. Support for traditional gender roles by political ideology:

Supports Traditional Gender Roles?	Political Ideology			Totals
	Liberal	Moderate	Conservative	
Favour	59	90	108	257
Oppose	454	548	484	1,486
Totals	513	8	592	1,743

  e. Support for legalizing marijuana by political ideology.

Should Marijuana Be Legalized?	Political Ideology			Totals
	Liberals	Moderates	Conservatives	
Favour	132	78	52	262
Oppose	101	87	109	297
Totals	233	165	161	559

11.8 Problem 11.7 analyzed the bivariate relationships between political ideology, the independent variable, and five different dependent variables using only percentages. Now, with the aid of measures of association, these characterizations should be easier to develop. Compute a phi and a lambda for each table in problem 11.7. Compare the measures of association with your characterizations based on the percentages.

Using SPSS for Windows to Analyze Bivariate Association with the 2009 GSS

The demonstrations and exercises below use the shortened version of the 2009 GSS data set supplied with this textbook. Start SPSS for Windows and open the *GSS.sav* file.

SPSS DEMONSTRATION 11.1 Does Health Vary by Income?

What's the relationship between income and health? To answer this question we'll run a **Crosstabs** on *incmhsd* (total household income) and *srh_q110* (state of health). We must first recode *incmhsd* because it has too many (13) categories (see Appendix G) to be used in a bivariate table. We will provide only a brief review here; a detailed guide on recoding *incmhsd,* including adding labels to the values of the recoded variable, is given in Appendix F.5.

Click **Transform** from the main menu and choose **Recode into Different Variables**. Next, move the variable *incmhsd* to the **Input Variable → Output Variable** box, then type a name—we suggest *income4*—in the **Output Variable** box. Click the **Change** button. Next, click on the **Old and New Values** button. We have decided to collapse the values of *incmhsd* into four categories. The recoding instructions that should appear in the **Old → New** dialog box are:

$$1 \text{ thru } 6 \rightarrow 1$$
$$7 \text{ thru } 9 \rightarrow 2$$
$$10 \text{ thru } 11 \rightarrow 3$$
$$12 \text{ thru } 13 \rightarrow 4$$

Click **Continue,** and then **OK** after inputting these recode instructions.

We will also recode state of health, *srh_q110.* As a rule of thumb, it is best to collapse a variable into logical groups. We decided to collapse *srh_q110* into a dichotomized variable: good health versus poor health. Click **Transform** and then **Recode into Different Variables**. Next, click the **Reset** button to reset all specifications in the dialog and sub-dialog boxes to their default state. Move the variable *srh_q110* to the **Input Variable → Output Variable** box. Give the recoded variable a new name in the **Output Variable** box (we used *health*), then click the **Change** button. Click the **Old and New Values** button, and follow these recoding instructions:

$$1 \text{ thru } 3 \rightarrow 1$$
$$4 \text{ thru } 5 \rightarrow 2$$

Click **Continue,** and then **OK**. Scores 1 (excellent), 2 (very good), or 3 (good) on *srh_q110* are grouped together into a score of 1 on *health,* and scores 4 (fair) or 5 (poor) on *srh_q110* into a score of 2 on *health.*

We highly recommend that both new variables be added to the permanent data file because they will be used in future SPSS demonstrations and exercises. To do so, click **Save** from the **File** menu, and the updated data set with *income4* and *health* added will be saved to disk. If you are using the student version of SPSS, remember that your data set is limited to 50 variables.

To examine the effect of *income4* on *health,* click **Analyze, Descriptive Statistics**, and **Crosstabs**, and then input *health* as the row variable and *income4* as the column variable. Click the **Cells** button and request column percentages by clicking the box next to **Column** in the **Percentages** box. With the dependent variable in the rows and the independent variable in the columns and with percentages calculated within columns, we will be able to read the table by following the rules developed in this chapter. Click the **Continue** button to return to the **Crosstabs** dialog box. Also, request chi square by clicking the **Statistics** button. Click **Continue**, and then **OK**, and the following output will be produced. (The output has been modified slightly, including adding labels to the values of *income4* and *health* as illustrated in Appendix F.5, to improve readability.)

Health * Income4 Crosstabulation

			Income4				
			<$30,000	$30,000–$59,999	$60,000–99,999	$100,000+	Total
Health	Good	Count	92	264	337	446	1139
		% within income4	74.8%	89.5%	91.1%	95.1%	90.6%
	Poor	Count	31	31	33	23	118
		% within income4	25.2%	10.5%	8.9%	4.9%	9.4%
Total		Count	123	295	370	469	1257
		% within income4	100.0%	100.0%	100.0%	100.0%	100.0%

Chi-Square Tests

	Value	df	Asymp. Sig. (2-sided)
Pearson Chi-Square	47.785[a]	3	.000
Likelihood Ratio	39.664	3	.000
Linear-by-Linear Association	37.528	1	.000
N of Valid Cases	1257		

a. 0 cells (0.0%) have expected count less than 5. The minimum expected count is 11.55.

Inspecting the table column by column, you will see that there is a relationship, and that it is moderate in strength. The maximum difference in the bottom row, poor health, is between the lowest and highest income groups: 25.2% − 4.9% = 20.3%.

Both variables are measured at the ordinal level, so we can also describe the direction. Is this relationship positive or negative? Remember that in a positive association, high scores on one variable will be associated with high scores on the other and low scores will be associated with low. In a negative relationship, high scores on one variable are associated with low scores on the other. Looking at the table again, we see that the relationship is negative: As income increases, poor health decreases.

The exact probability value of chi square, .000, is well below the standard indicator of a significant result, .05, so we reject the null hypothesis that the variables are independent and conclude that there is a statistically significant relationship between income and health.

As a final point, let us direct your attention to the "Total" (or total number of cases) column in the "Crosstabulation" output. There are a total of 1,257 people in the analysis. The original sample included over 1,500 people. What happened to all those "missing cases"? These missing cases are respondents who did not provide information on income. All statistics produced by the crosstabs command apply to only those that provide information on both variables; all other cases are deleted from the analysis. This is called *pairwise* deletion of missing data as only those cases that have non-missing values for *both* variables are included in the crosstab. The phenomenon of diminishing sample size is a common problem in survey research that, at some point, may jeopardize the integrity of the inquiry.

SPSS DEMONSTRATION 11.2   Does Criminal Victimization Vary by Area of Residence? Another Look

In Demonstration 10.1, we used the **Crosstabs** procedure to examine the relationship between *lifevict* (ever been a victim of crime) and *luc_rst* (urban/rural indicator). We saw that the relationship was statistically significant, and that persons living in an urban area were more likely than those living in a rural area to have been a victim of crime. In this demonstration, we will re-examine the relationship and have SPSS compute some measures of association.

Click **Analyze**, then **Descriptive Statistics**, and then **Crosstabs**. Move *lifevict* into the **Row(s)** box and *luc_rst* into the **Column(s)** box. Click the **Cells** button and request column percentages. Click the **Statistics** button and request chi square, phi, Cramer's *V*, and lambda. Click **Continue**, and then **OK**, and the following output, slightly edited to improve readability, will be produced.

The measures of association are reported below the output for the chi square tests. Three values for lambda are reported in the "Directional Measures" output block. Remember that lambda is asymmetric and will change value depending on which variable is taken as dependent. (Symmetric lambda is more or less an average of the two asymmetric lambda values.) In this case, *lifevict* (ever been a victim of crime) is the dependent variable, so lambda is .000, a value that indicates no relationship between the variables. Looking at the first block in the output "Crosstabulation," we see, however, that the conditional distributions do change, indicating that there actually is a relationship. The problem here is that the row totals are very unequal, and lambda is misleading and should be disregarded (see Section 11.6). (Goodman and Kruskal tau is similar to lambda, and is based on the logic of proportional reduction in error. It is also an asymmetric measure of association.)

Phi and Cramer's *V* are reported in the "Symmetric Measures" output block. The statistics are identical in value, .106, as they will be whenever the table has either two rows or two columns. The measures reveal an association between the variables, albeit a weak one.

Victim of crime – lifetime * Urban/Rural indicator. Crosstabulation

| | | | Urban/Rural indicator. | | Total |
			Urban	Rural	
Victim of crime – lifetime	Yes	Count % within Urban/Rural indicator.	787 65.0%	157 52.2%	944 62.4%
	No	Count % within Urban/Rural indicator.	424 35.0%	144 47.8%	568 37.6%
Total		Count % within Urban/Rural indicator.	1211 100.0%	301 100.0%	1512 100.0%

Chi-Square Tests

	Value	df	Asymp. Sig. (2-sided)	Exact Sig. (2-sided)	Exact Sig. (1-sided)
Pearson Chi-Square	16.915[a]	1	.000		
Continuity Correction[b]	16.372	1	.000		
Likelihood Ratio	16.572	1	.000		
Fisher's Exact Test				.000	.000
Linear-by-Linear Association	16.904	1	.000		
N of Valid Cases	1512				

a. 0 cells (0.0%) have expected count less than 5. The minimum expected count is 113.07.
b. Computed only for a 2 × 2 table.

Directional Measures

			Value	Asymp. Std. Error[a]	Approx. T	Approx. Sig.
Nominal by Nominal	Lambda	Symmetric	.000	.000	.[b]	.[b]
		Victim of crime – lifetime Dependent	.000	.000	.[b]	.[b]
		Urban/Rural indicator. Dependent	.000	.000	.[b]	.[b]
	Goodman and Kruskal tau	Victim of crime – lifetime Dependent	.011	.006		.000[c]
		Urban/Rural indicator. Dependent	.011	.006		.000[c]

a. Not assuming the null hypothesis.
b. Cannot be computed because the asymptotic standard error equals zero.
c. Based on chi-square approximation.

Symmetric Measures

		Value	Approx. Sig.
Nominal by Nominal	Phi	.106	.000
	Cramer's V	.106	.000
N of Valid Cases		1512	

a. Not assuming the null hypothesis.
b. Using the asymptotic standard error assuming the null hypothesis.

The significance value of chi square, .000, reported in the "Chi-Square Tests" output block, is lower than .05, so we reject the null hypothesis and conclude that the relationship between area of residence and victimization is statistically significant. Even though Phi and Cramer's *V* tell us that the relationship between area of residence and victimization is rather weak, chi square indicates that it is statistically significant. This reminds us once again that association and statistical significance are two different things.

Exercises (using *GSS.sav*)

11.1 As long as *srh_q110* has already been recoded, examine the relationship between recoded *srh_q110* as dependent or row variable and *luc_rst* (urban/rural indicator) as the independent or column variable using the **Crosstabs** procedure. Be sure to request column percentage in the cells and the chi square test. Write a paragraph summarizing the results. Describe the relationships in terms of strength and pattern.

11.2 Following up on Demonstration 11.2, select two more variables that you think might be related to *lifevict*. Run the **Crosstabs** procedure with *lifevict* as dependent or row variable and your other variables as the independent or column variables. Be sure to request column percentage in the cells, as well as phi and lambda. Write a few sentences describing each relationship.

Association Between Variables Measured at the Ordinal Level

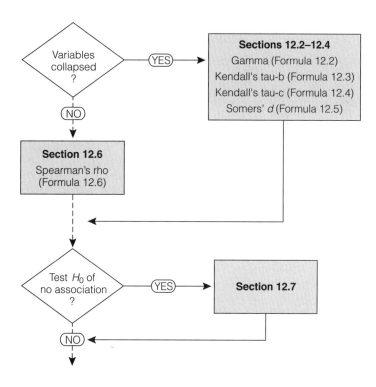

By the end of this chapter, you will be able to

1. Calculate and interpret gamma, Kendall's tau-b and tau-c, Somers' d, and Spearman's rho.

2. Explain the logic of pairs as it relates to measuring association.

3. Use gamma, Kendall's tau-b and tau-c, Somers' d, and Spearman's rho to analyze and describe a bivariate relationship in terms of the three questions introduced in Chapter 11.

4. Test gamma and Spearman's rho for significance.

12.1 INTRODUCTION

There are two common types of ordinal-level variables. Some have many possible scores and look, at least at first glance, like interval-ratio-level variables. We will call these "continuous ordinal variables." An attitude scale that incorporated many different items and, therefore, had many possible values would produce this type of variable.

The second type, which we will call a "collapsed ordinal variable," has only a few (no more than five or six) values or scores and can be created either by collecting data in collapsed form or by collapsing a continuous ordinal scale. For example, we would produce collapsed ordinal variables by measuring social class as upper, middle, or lower or by reducing the scores on an attitude scale into just a few categories (such as high, moderate, and low).

A number of measures of association have been developed for use with collapsed ordinal-level variables. The most commonly used statistics in this group include **gamma (G)**, **Somers' d (d_{yx})**, **Kendall's tau-b (τ_b)**, and a variant of Kendall's tau-b called **Kendall's tau-c (τ_c)**. These statistics are covered in the first part of this chapter. For continuous ordinal variables, a statistic called **Spearman's rho (r_s)** is typically used. We will cover this measure of association toward the end of the chapter.

This chapter will expand your understanding of how bivariate associations can be described and analyzed, but it is important to remember that we are still trying to answer the three questions raised in Chapter 11: Are the variables associated? How strong is the association? What is the direction of the association?

12.2 THE LOGIC OF PAIRS

Gamma, Kendall's tau-b and tau-c, and Somers' d are conceptually similar to each other. They each measure strength and direction of association by comparing each respondent to every other respondent, called a "pair of respondents" or more simply a "pair," in terms of their rankings on the independent and dependent variable. The total number of unique pairs of respondents in a data set can be found by the following formula:

FORMULA 12.1

$$\frac{n(n-1)}{2}$$

where n = the total number of respondents

Pairs can be further divided into five sub-groups. A pair of respondents is "similar" if the respondent with the larger value on the independent variable also has the larger value on the dependent variable. A pair is "dissimilar" if the respondent with the larger value on the independent variable has the smaller value on the dependent variable. A pair is "tied" if respondents have the same value on either the independent or dependent variable, or on both. Specifically, a pair is "tied on the independent variable" if both respondents have the same score on the independent but not dependent variable; a pair is "tied on the dependent variable" if both respondents have the same score on the dependent but not independent variable; and a pair is "tied on both variables" if both respondents have the same independent and dependent variable scores.

TABLE 12.1   DATA ON LENGTH OF SERVICE AND BURNOUT FOR FIVE TEACHERS

Teacher	Length (X)	Burnout (Y)
Omar	1	1
Camil	2	2
Joseph	2	3
Karina	3	3
Steven	3	3

For Length of Service: 1 = low, 2 = moderate, 3 = high.
For Burnout: 1 = low, 2 = moderate, 3 = high.

As an example, let's assume that a researcher is concerned about the causes of "burnout" (i.e., demoralization and loss of commitment) among elementary school teachers and wonders about the relationship between years of service (independent or X variable) and level of burnout (dependent or Y variable). To examine this relationship, five elementary school teachers were sampled and asked about number of years employed as a teacher (1 = low, 2 = moderate, or 3 = high) and level of teacher-burnout (1 = low, 2 = moderate, or 3 = high). Their scores are reported in Table 12.1.

Using Formula 12.1 we find that there are 10 unique pairs among the five teachers:

$$\frac{5(5-1)}{2} = \frac{20}{2} = 10$$

Table 12.2 lists each of the 10 pairs by type of pair. So, for example, looking at Camil and Steven in Table 12.1, we see that Steven is ranked above Camil on length of service. Steven is also ranked above Camil on burnout. Camil-Steven is therefore a similar pair. On the other hand, Joseph-Steven is a tied pair on the dependent variable, since they each have the same score on burnout but not length of service. We also see that Karina-Steven is a

TABLE 12.2   PAIRS OF TEACHERS BY TYPE OF PAIR

Pair	Type of Pair
Omar-Camil	Similar
Omar-Joseph	Similar
Omar-Karina	Similar
Omar-Steven	Similar
Camil-Joseph	Tied on the independent variable
Camil-Karina	Similar
Camil-Steven	Similar
Joseph-Karina	Tied on the dependent variable
Joseph-Steven	Tied on the dependent variable
Karina-Steven	Tied on both variables

tied pair on both variables as both respondents have the same independent and dependent variable scores.

12.3 ANALYZING RELATIONSHIPS WITH GAMMA, KENDALL'S TAU-B AND TAU-C, AND SOMERS' *D*

Determining Strength of Relationships. Gamma, Kendall's tau-b and tau-c, and Somers' *d* measure the strength of association between variables by considering the number of similar versus dissimilar pairs. When there are an equal number of similar and dissimilar pairs, the value of these statistics will be equal to 0.00 indicating no association between the independent and dependent variables. As the number of similar relative to dissimilar *or* dissimilar relative to similar pairs increases, the value moves closer to 1.00. Thus, the larger the difference between the number of similar and dissimilar pairs, the stronger the association. When all pairs are either similar *or* dissimilar, the value of these statistics will be equal to 1.00, indicating a perfect relationship.

Table 12.3 provides some additional assistance with interpreting the values of gamma, Kendall's tau-b and tau-c, and Somers' *d* in a format similar to Tables 11.5 and 11.12. As with the latter tables, the relationship between the values and the descriptive terms is arbitrary, so the outline presented in Table 12.3 is intended as a general guideline only.

Determining Direction of Relationships. Nominal measures of association, like phi and lambda, measure only the strength of a bivariate association. Ordinal measures of association are more sophisticated and add information about the overall direction of the relationship (positive or negative). It is also relatively easy to determine direction: If the sign of the statistic is a plus, the direction is positive; a minus sign indicates a negative relationship. So, for example, a value of +1.00 indicates a perfect *positive* relationship between the variables, while a value of −1.00 indicates a perfect *negative* relationship. (Note that the strength of a relationship is independent of its direction. That is, a value of −1.00 would be exactly as strong as a value of +1.00 but opposite in direction.)

A positive relationship means that the scores of respondents tend to be ranked in the same order on both variables. In more general terms, a positive relationship means that the variables change in the same direction. That

TABLE 12.3 THE RELATIONSHIP BETWEEN THE VALUE OF ORDINAL-LEVEL MEASURES OF ASSOCIATION AND THE STRENGTH OF THE RELATIONSHIP

Value	Strength
If the value is	The strength of the relationship is
between 0.00 and 0.10	weak
between 0.11 and 0.30	moderate
greater than 0.30	strong

is, as scores on one variable increase (or decrease), scores on the other variable also increase (or decrease). Table 12.4 illustrates the general shape of a positive relationship. In a positive relationship, the scores of respondents tend to fall along a diagonal from upper left to lower right (assuming, of course, that the tables have been constructed with the column variable increasing from left to right and the row variable increasing from top to bottom).

Negative relationships are the opposite of positive relationships. Low scores on one variable are associated with high scores on the other and high scores with low scores. This pattern means that the cases will tend to fall along a diagonal from lower left to upper right (at least for all tables in this textbook). Table 12.5 illustrates a generalized negative relationship.

You should be aware of an additional complication. The coding for ordinal-level variables is arbitrary, and a higher score may mean *more* or *less* of the variable being measured. For example, if we measured social class as upper, middle, and lower, we could assign scores to the categories in either of two ways:

A	B
(1) Upper	(3) Upper
(2) Middle	(2) Middle
(3) Lower	(1) Lower

While coding according to scheme "B" might seem preferable (because higher scores go with higher class position), both schemes are perfectly legitimate and the direction of a relationship will change, depending on which scheme is selected. Using scheme "B," we would find positive relationships between social class and education: As education increased, so would class.

Using scheme "A," however, the same relationship would appear to be negative because the numerical scores (1, 2, 3) are coded in reverse order: The highest social class is assigned the lowest score, and so forth. If you didn't check the coding scheme, you might conclude that a negative gamma, Kendall's tau-b or tau-c, or Somers' *d* means that class decreases as education increases when, actually, the opposite is true.

TABLE 12.4 A GENERALIZED POSITIVE RELATIONSHIP

Variable Y	Variable X		
	Low	Moderate	High
Low	X		
Moderate		X	
High			X

TABLE 12.5 A GENERALIZED NEGATIVE RELATIONSHIP

Variable Y	Variable X		
	Low	Moderate	High
Low			X
Moderate		X	
High	X		

Unfortunately, this source of confusion cannot be avoided when working with ordinal-level variables. Coding schemes will always be arbitrary for these variables and you need to exercise additional caution when interpreting the direction of ordinal-level variables.

Gamma. Gamma, Kendall's tau-b, and Somers' d are computed by subtracting the number of similar pairs from dissimilar pairs, then dividing this result by the total number of pairs. Where these statistics differ is in how they treat tied pairs—each deals with tied pairs in a different way. (Note that the value of these statistics will be identical when there are no tied pairs.)

Gamma is the number of similar over dissimilar pairs as a proportion of all pairs excluding ties. The formula for gamma is:

FORMULA 12.2

$$G = \frac{n_s - n_d}{n_s + n_d}$$

where n_s = number of pairs of respondents ranked the same on both variables (i.e., similar pairs).

n_d = number of pairs of respondents ranked differently on the two variables (i.e., dissimilar pairs).

Gamma ranges from -1.00 for a negative relationship to $+1.00$ for a positive relationship. A value of zero indicates no relationship. Gamma is a symmetrical measure of association, so its value will be the same regardless of which variable is taken as the dependent.

To illustrate the computation of G, let's consider the relationship between levels of burnout and years of service for the five elementary school teachers in Table 12.1. To compute gamma, we must find the number of similar pairs, n_s, and dissimilar pairs, n_d. Turning to Table 12.2, we see that there are a total of six (6) similar pairs and zero (0) dissimilar pairs. Next, we substitute these numbers into the numerator and denominator of the formula:

$$G = \frac{n_s - n_d}{n_s + n_d}$$

$$G = \frac{6 - 0}{6 + 0}$$

$$G = \frac{6}{6}$$

$$G = +1.00$$

Thus, ignoring ties, there is perfect agreement between the teachers: a teacher with a *higher* length of service also has a *higher* level of burnout. That is, there is a perfect positive association between the variables.

Gamma as a PRE Measure.   In addition to interpretation of strength and direction of association, gamma has a PRE (proportional reduction in error) interpretation. In Chapter 11, we saw that for nominal-level variables the logic of PRE was based on two different "predictions" of the scores of cases on the dependent variable (Y): one that ignored the independent variable (X) and a second that took the independent variable into account. We also saw that the value of lambda showed the extent to which taking the independent variable into account improved accuracy when predicting the score of the dependent variable.

The PRE logic for variables measured at the ordinal level is similar, and gamma, like lambda, measures the proportional reduction in error gained by predicting one variable while taking the other into account. The major difference lies in the way predictions are made. In the case of gamma, we predict the *order* of pairs of respondents rather than a score on the dependent variable. That is, we predict whether one respondent will have a higher or lower score than the other. First, we predict the order of a pair of respondents on one variable while ignoring their order on the other. Second, we predict the order on one variable while taking order on the other variable into account.

As an illustration, let's look at the question of burnout and years of service among elementary school teachers. One way to state this question is to ask if teachers with more years of service have higher levels of burnout. Another way to ask the same question is: Do teachers who rank higher on years of service also rank higher on burnout? If we knew that teacher A had more years of service than teacher B, would we be able to predict that teacher A is also more burned-out than teacher B? That is, would knowledge of the order of this pair of teachers on one variable help us predict their order on the other?

If the two variables are associated, we will reduce our errors when our predictions about one of the variables are based on knowledge of the other variable. Furthermore, the stronger the association, the fewer the errors we will make. When there is no association between the variables, gamma will be 0.00, and knowledge of the order of a pair of respondents on one variable will not improve our ability to predict their order on the other. A gamma of ±1.00 denotes a perfect relationship: the order of all pairs of respondents on one variable would be predictable without error from their order on the other variable, as is the case for the length of service and level of burnout example.

Limitation of Gamma.   Gamma ignores tied pairs of cases, and is based only on pairs (similar and dissimilar) that inherently reflect a relationship between the variables. (As an example, just six of the 10 unique pairs shown in Table 12.2 are used in calculating gamma.) Thus, it can *exaggerate* the strength of association between two ordinal variables. Kendall's tau-b and tau-c (named after British statistician, Maurice Kendall) and Somers' d (developed by the sociologist Robert H. Somers) were designed to correct this problem.

Kendall's tau-b and tau-c and Somers' d are extensions or modifications of gamma. Like gamma, they contain the same quantity in the numerator, $n_s - n_d$. However, their denominator is more complex.

Kendall's tau-b includes both pairs tied on the independent variable and pairs tied on the dependent variable. Kendall's tau-c is used as an alternative to Kendall's tau-b in certain circumstances. Somers' d includes only pairs tied on the dependent variable. Kendall's tau-b and tau-c are symmetrical measures of association (the same value is produced regardless of which variable is considered the dependent), while Somers' d is designed specifically as an asymmetric measure, and assumes that you can identify one of the variables as the dependent variable. Thus, Somers' d corrects only for pairs tied on the dependent variable. These statistics will always be lower than gamma, except when there are no ties, because their denominators will be larger than the denominator of gamma.

Kendall's tau-b.   The formula for computing Kendall's tau-b is

FORMULA 12.3
$$\tau_b = \frac{n_s - n_d}{\sqrt{(n_s + n_d + t_x)(n_s + n_d + t_y)}}$$

where n_s = number of similar pairs
n_d = number of dissimilar pairs
t_x = number of pairs tied on the independent variable, X
t_y = number of pairs tied on the dependent variable, Y

Kendall's tau-b ranges from -1.00 to $+1.00$. Kendall's tau-b does *not* have a PRE interpretation.

Let's again consider the relationship between burnout and years of service. In addition to the number of similar and dissimilar pairs, to compute tau-b we must find the number of pairs tied on the independent variable and the number of pairs tied on the dependent variable. Looking at Table 12.2, we see that there are a total of six (6) similar pairs, one (1) pair tied on the independent, and two (2) pairs tied on the dependent. Substituting these numbers into the numerator and denominator of Formula 12.3, the value of Kendall's tau-b is

$$\tau_b = \frac{n_s - n_d}{\sqrt{(n_s + n_d + t_x)(n_s + n_d + t_y)}}$$

$$\tau_b = \frac{6 - 0}{\sqrt{(6 + 0 + 1)(6 + 0 + 2)}}$$

$$\tau_b = \frac{6}{\sqrt{(7)(8)}}$$

$$\tau_b = \frac{6}{\sqrt{56}}$$

$$\tau_b = \frac{6}{7.48}$$

$$\tau_b = +0.80$$

The computed value of tau-b of $+0.80$ means that there is a strong, positive relationship between the variables.

Kendall's tau-c.   Kendall's tau-b is limited in that it can reach a maximum of 1.00 only when the independent and dependent variables have the same number of categories. In the example above, tau-b is an appropriate measure of association since each variable (teacher-burnout and years of service) contains three categories (i.e., low, moderate, and high). When the independent and dependent variables do not have the same number of categories, Kendall's tau-c a variant of Kendall's tau-b, should be used instead. Kendall's tau-c adjusts for number of categories. It is designed to reach a maximum of 1.00 for variables with different numbers of categories. Therefore, tau-b is used when there are an equal number of categories in the independent and dependent variables and tau-c when the numbers of categories are not the same.

The formula for Kendall's tau-c is

FORMULA 12.4
$$\tau_c = \frac{2m(n_s - n_d)}{n^2(m - 1)}$$

where n_s = number of similar pairs
n_d = number of dissimilar pairs
n = number of respondents
m = minimum value, whichever is less of the number of categories on the independent variable or the number of categories on the dependent variable.

Like tau-b, tau-c ranges from -1.00 to $+1.00$, is a symmetrical measure, and does *not* have a PRE interpretation.

While tau-b is the appropriate measure for the burnout and years of service data in Table 12.1, we will compute tau-c for purposes of illustration. There is a total of six (6) similar pairs, five (5) cases, and a minimum value of three (3) (because the variables have the same number of categories, we may use the number of categories on either the independent or dependent variable as the minimum value). Therefore,

$$\tau_c = \frac{2m(n_s - n_d)}{n^2(m - 1)}$$

$$\tau_c = \frac{(2 \times 3)(6 - 0)}{5^2(3 - 1)}$$

$$\tau_c = \frac{(6)(6)}{25(2)}$$

$$\tau_c = \frac{36}{50}$$

$$\tau_c = +0.72$$

The computed value of tau-c of $+0.72$ means that there is a strong, positive relationship between the variables.

Somers' d. The formula for computing Somers' d is

FORMULA 12.5

$$d_{yx} = \frac{n_s - n_d}{n_s + n_d + t_y}$$

where n_s = number of similar pairs
n_d = number of dissimilar pairs
t_y = number of pairs tied on the dependent variable, Y

Somers' d ranges from -1.00 (for negative relationships) to $+1.00$ (for positive relationships). It is an asymmetric measure. Thus, two values of Somers' d can be computed: d_{yx} where Y is treated as the dependent variable and d_{xy} where X is treated as the dependent. In the example to follow, we assume Y is the dependent. Somers' d does *not* have a PRE interpretation.

For the data displayed in Table 12.1, there are a total of six (6) similar pairs and two (2) pairs tied on the dependent. Therefore, Somers' d is

$$d_{yx} = \frac{n_s - n_d}{n_s + n_d + t_y}$$

$$d_{yx} = \frac{6 - 0}{6 + 0 + 2}$$

$$d_{yx} = \frac{6}{8}$$

$$d_{yx} = +0.75$$

Somers' d equals $+0.75$, and, like Kendall's tau-b ($+0.80$), is lower than gamma ($+1.00$). As previously mentioned, this will always be the case because the denominators of these statistics will be larger than the denominator of gamma, except when there are no ties. Nonetheless, each measure indicates a very strong and positive association between length of service and burnout.

Which Measure to Use? There is no hard and fast rule on which ordinal measure of association to use. When there are relatively few ties, gamma should be used because it has a PRE interpretation and the others do not. When there are many ties (which becomes more likely as table size decreases), gamma tends to exaggerate the strength of relationship, so an adjusted measure (one that takes ties into account) should be used. Use Kendall's tau-b when the independent and dependent variables have the same number of categories; use Kendall's tau-c when the variables have an unequal number of categories; or alternatively, use Somers' d when one of the variables is specifically identified as the dependent.

12.4 GAMMA, KENDALL'S TAU-B AND TAU-C, SOMERS' *D* FOR BIVARIATE TABLES

In the previous section, just a handful of cases were used to compute gamma, Kendall's tau-b and tau-c, and Somers' *d*. Keeping the number of respondents to a minimum helped to simplify the logic of pairs underlying these statistics and their calculations. In most situations, however, we have a relatively large number of cases, which have been grouped into a bivariate table. While it is still possible to list all pairs of respondents, as we did in Table 12.2, in such situations, it becomes cumbersome to do so and, in fact, unnecessary. This is because there is an easy and direct method for finding the number of similar, dissimilar, and tied pairs in a bivariate table.

Gamma.   Let's suppose that 100 elementary school teachers were sampled and asked about their number of years employed as a teacher and level of teacher-burnout, and then their scores were organized into a bivariate table as shown in Table 12.6. Recall that to compute gamma, we must find the number of pairs of respondents that are ranked the same, n_s, and ranked differently, n_d, on the variables. We find these numbers by working with the cell frequencies in the bivariate table.

To find the number of pairs of respondents ranked the same (n_s), begin with the cell containing the respondents that were ranked the lowest on both variables. In Table 12.6, this would be the upper-left-hand cell. (Note that not all tables are constructed with values increasing from left to right across the columns and from top to bottom down the rows. When using other tables, always check that you have located the proper cell.) The 20 respondents in the upper-left-hand cell all rank low on both burnout and length of service. Now, form a pair of respondents by selecting one respondent from this cell and one from any other cell—for example, the middle cell in the table. All 15 respondents in this cell are moderate on both variables. Any pair of respondents formed between these two cells will be ranked the same on both variables. The total number of pairs of respondents is given by multiplying the cell frequencies. So, the contribution of these two cells to the total n_s is (20)(15), or 300.

Following this logic, to find the total number of pairs of cases ranked the same on both variables, multiply the number of cases in each cell by the total of all frequencies below and to the right of that cell. Repeat this procedure for each cell and add the resultant products. The total of these

TABLE 12.6   BURNOUT BY LENGTH OF SERVICE FOR 100 TEACHERS

	Length of Service			
Burnout	Low	Moderate	High	Totals
Low	20	6	4	30
Moderate	10	15	5	30
High	8	11	21	40
Totals	38	32	30	100

products is n_s. Remember that gamma ignores all pairs of respondents that are tied on one or both variables, that is, pairs formed within the same row, column, or cell. This means that, in computing n_s, we will work with only the pairs of respondents that can be formed between each cell and the cells below and to the right of it.

Figure 12.1, which reproduces the data from Table 12.6, shows the direction of multiplication for each of the four cells that, in a 3 × 3 table, can contribute to n_s. (Note that none of the cells in the bottom row or the right-hand column can contribute to n_s because they have no cells below and to the right of them.) The frequency in the darker-shaded cell is multiplied by the product of the frequencies in the lighter-shaded cells. In this example, we find that a total of 1,831 (1,040 + 156 + 320 + 315) pairs of cases are ranked the same on both variables; that is, $n_s = 1,831$.

Our next step is to find the number of pairs of cases ranked differently (n_d) on both variables. To do so, we begin with the upper-right-hand cell and multiply the number of cases in the cell by the total frequency of cases below and to the left; that is, the four respondents in the upper-right-hand cell are low on Y and high on X; if a pair is formed with any respondent from this cell and any cell below and to the left, the respondents will be ranked differently on the two variables. Repeat this procedure for each cell and add the resultant products. The total of these products is n_d. Note that the pattern for computing n_d is the reverse of the pattern for n_s.

The computation of n_d for a 3 × 3 table is shown in Figure 12.2. Again, the frequency in the darker-shaded cell is multiplied by the product of the frequencies in the lighter-shaded cells. We find that the total number of pairs of cases ranked in different order on the variables is 499 (176 + 108 + 95 + 120).

FIGURE 12.1 COMPUTING n_s IN A 3 × 3 TABLE

	LOW	MODERATE	HIGH
LOW	20	6	4
MODERATE	10	15	5
HIGH	8	11	21

20(15 + 5 + 11 + 21) = 1,040

	LOW	MODERATE	HIGH
LOW	20	6	4
MODERATE	10	15	5
HIGH	8	11	21

6(5 + 21) = 156

	LOW	MODERATE	HIGH
LOW	20	6	4
MODERATE	10	15	5
HIGH	8	11	21

10(11 + 21) = 320

	LOW	MODERATE	HIGH
LOW	20	6	4
MODERATE	10	15	5
HIGH	8	11	21

15(21) = 315

FIGURE 12.2   COMPUTING n_d IN A 3 × 3 TABLE

	LOW	MODERATE	HIGH
LOW	20	6	4
MODERATE	10	15	5
HIGH	8	11	21

4(10 + 15 + 8 + 11) = 176

	LOW	MODERATE	HIGH
LOW	20	6	4
MODERATE	10	15	5
HIGH	8	11	21

6(10 + 8) = 108

	LOW	MODERATE	HIGH
LOW	20	6	4
MODERATE	10	15	5
HIGH	8	11	21

5(8 + 11) = 95

	LOW	MODERATE	HIGH
LOW	20	6	4
MODERATE	10	15	5
HIGH	8	11	21

15(8) = 120

Since there are many more cases of similar relative to dissimilar pairs (1,831 versus 499) for Table 12.6, we know the value of gamma will be positive. Using Formula 12.2 the value of gamma is

$$G = \frac{n_s - n_d}{n_s + n_d}$$

$$G = \frac{1,831 - 499}{1,831 + 499}$$

$$G = \frac{1,332}{2,330}$$

$$G = +0.57$$

A gamma of +0.57 indicates that length of service has a strong and positive association with degree of burnout. Since gamma also has a PRE interpretation, a value of 0.57 indicates that we would make 57% fewer errors if we predicted the order of pairs of cases on one variable from the order of pairs of cases on the other (as opposed to predicting order while ignoring the other variable). Knowing the respective ordering of two teachers on length of service will help us predict their ordering on burnout.

Kendall's tau-b and tau-c.   In computing gamma for the data in Table 12.6, only 2,330 ($n_s + n_d$) of the 4,950 possible pairs were used. (Formula 12.1 shows there are ($n(n - 1))/2$ or 4,950 unique pairs to work with when n equals 100.) The rest (tied pairs) were ignored.

Kendall's tau-b, on the other hand, includes pairs tied on the dependent, t_y, and independent, t_x, variables. To find t_y, begin with the cell containing the cases ranked the lowest on both variables (the upper-left-hand cell in Table 12.6). Next, multiply the frequency in that cell by the total of all frequencies immediately to the right of that cell. Repeat this procedure for each cell and add the products together.

Figure 12.3, again produced from the data in Table 12.6, shows the direction of multiplication for each of the six cells in a 3 × 3 table that can contribute to t_y. The frequency in the darker-shaded cell is multiplied by the product of the frequencies in the lighter-shaded cells. Hence, $t_y = 200 + 200 + 256 + 24 + 75 + 231 = 986$. There are 986 pairs tied on the dependent variable "burnout."

To find t_x, we follow the same logic, but in the opposite direction. As, shown in Figure 12.4, $t_x = 360 + 156 + 104 + 80 + 165 + 105 = 970$. There are 970 pairs tied on the independent variable "length of service."

FIGURE 12.3 COMPUTING t_y IN A 3 × 3 TABLE

	LOW	MODERATE	HIGH
LOW	20	6	4
MODERATE	10	15	5
HIGH	8	11	21

20(6 + 4) = 200

	LOW	MODERATE	HIGH
LOW	20	6	4
MODERATE	10	15	5
HIGH	8	11	21

6(4) = 24

	LOW	MODERATE	HIGH
LOW	20	6	4
MODERATE	10	15	5
HIGH	8	11	21

10(15 + 5) = 200

	LOW	MODERATE	HIGH
LOW	20	6	4
MODERATE	10	15	5
HIGH	8	11	21

15(5) = 75

	LOW	MODERATE	HIGH
LOW	20	6	4
MODERATE	10	15	5
HIGH	8	11	21

8(11 + 21) = 256

	LOW	MODERATE	HIGH
LOW	20	6	4
MODERATE	10	15	5
HIGH	8	11	21

11(21) = 231

FIGURE 12.4   COMPUTING t_x IN A 3 × 3 TABLE

	LOW	MODERATE	HIGH
LOW	20	6	4
MODERATE	10	15	5
HIGH	8	11	21

20(10 + 8) = 360

	LOW	MODERATE	HIGH
LOW	20	6	4
MODERATE	10	15	5
HIGH	8	11	21

10(8) = 80

	LOW	MODERATE	HIGH
LOW	20	6	4
MODERATE	10	15	5
HIGH	8	11	21

6(15 + 11) = 156

	LOW	MODERATE	HIGH
LOW	20	6	4
MODERATE	10	15	5
HIGH	8	11	21

15(11) = 165

	LOW	MODERATE	HIGH
LOW	20	6	4
MODERATE	10	15	5
HIGH	8	11	21

4(5 + 21) = 104

	LOW	MODERATE	HIGH
LOW	20	6	4
MODERATE	10	15	5
HIGH	8	11	21

5(21) = 105

So, for the burnout and years of service problem, the value of Kendall's tau-b (using Formula 12.3) is

$$\tau_b = \frac{n_s - n_d}{\sqrt{(n_s + n_d + t_x)(n_s + n_d + t_y)}}$$

$$\tau_b = \frac{1{,}831 - 499}{\sqrt{(1{,}831 + 499 + 970)(1{,}831 + 499 + 986)}}$$

$$\tau_b = \frac{1{,}332}{3{,}308}$$

$$\tau_b = +0.40$$

Since there are an equal number of categories on independent and dependent variables, tau-b is more appropriate than tau-c for this problem. (Remember, tau-b is used when there are an equal number of categories on the variables and tau-c when the variables have an unequal number of categories.) However, we will compute tau-c for purposes of demonstration. Substituting the appropriate numbers into the numerator and denominator of Formula 12.4, the value of Kendall's tau-c is

$$\tau_c = \frac{2m(n_s - n_d)}{n^2(m - 1)}$$

$$\tau_c = \frac{(2 \times 3)(1,831 - 499)}{100^2(3 - 1)}$$

$$\tau_c = \frac{(6)(1,332)}{(10,000)(2)}$$

$$\tau_c = \frac{7,992}{20,000}$$

$$\tau_c = +0.40$$

The computed values for Kendall's tau-b and tau-c are virtually identical, and both indicate a strong and positive association between the variables.

Somers' d. While Kendall's tau-b includes pairs tied on both variables, Somers' d uses ties only on the dependent, t_y. Using Formula 12.5 the value of Somers' d is

$$d_{yx} = \frac{n_s - n_d}{n_s + n_d + t_y}$$

$$d_{yx} = \frac{1,831 - 499}{1,831 + 499 + 986}$$

$$d_{yx} = \frac{1,332}{3,316}$$

$$d_{yx} = 0.40$$

Somers' d, like gamma and Kendall's tau-b and tau-c, indicates a strong and positive association between length of service and burnout.

Summary. Gamma, Kendall's tau-b and tau-c, and Somers' d measure association by comparing respondents to each other, called pairs of respondents, in terms of their rankings on the independent and dependent variable. As such, these statistics can be calculated for variables measured at the ordinal level or higher. Gamma ignores tied pairs of cases, and tends to exaggerate the strength of association, especially for small tables where there are many ties. Alternatively, Kendall's tau-b (when bivariate tables have an equal number of rows and columns), Kendall's tau-c (when tables have an unequal number of rows and columns), or Somers' d (when one of the variables can be identified as the dependent variable) should be used instead of gamma in such situations.

As a final note, it is important to stress that to use the computational routines for these statistics presented in Figures 12.1 to 12.4, you must arrange the table in the manner of Table 12.6, with the column variable increasing in value as you move from left to right and the row variable increasing in value from top to bottom. Be careful to construct your tables according to this format. If you are working with data already in table format, you may have to rearrange the table or rethink the direction of patterns. *(To practise computing and interpreting gamma, Kendall's tau-b or tau-c, and Somers' d see problems 12.1 to 12.10 and 12.15. Begin with some of the smaller, 2 × 2 tables until you are comfortable with these procedures.)*

Application 12.1

A group of 40 nations have been rated as high or low on religiosity (based on the percentage of a random sample of citizens who described themselves as "a religious person") and as high or low in their support for single mothers (based on the percentage of a random sample of citizens who said they would approve of a woman choosing to be a single parent). Are more religious nations less approving of single mothers?

	Religiosity		
Approval	Low	High	Totals
Low	4	9	13
High	11	16	27
Totals	15	25	40

We will compute a gamma, Kendall's tau-b (since there is an equal number of categories on independent and dependent variables), and Somers' *d* to summarize the strength and direction of the association. First, we must find the number of similar, n_s, and dissimilar pairs, n_d, and the number of pairs tied on the dependent (approval), t_y, and independent (religiosity), t_x, variables.

The number of pairs of cases ranked in the same order on both variables (n_s) is

$$n_s = 4(16) = 64$$

The number of pairs of cases ranked in a different order on both variables (n_d) is

$$n_d = 9(11) = 99$$

The number of pairs tied on the dependent variable (t_y) is

$$t_y = 4(9) + 11(16) = 36 + 176 = 212$$

The number of pairs tied on the independent variable (t_x) is $t_x = 4(11) + 9(16) = 44 + 144 = 188$

Gamma is

$$G = \frac{n_s - n_d}{n_s + n_d} = \frac{64 - 99}{64 + 99} = \frac{-35}{163} = -0.21$$

Kendall's tau-b is

$$\tau_b = \frac{n_s - n_d}{\sqrt{(n_s + n_d + t_x)(n_s + n_d + t_y)}}$$

$$= \frac{64 - 99}{\sqrt{(64 + 99 + 188)(64 + 99 + 212)}}$$

$$= \frac{-35}{363} = -0.10$$

Somers' *d* is

$$d_{yx} = \frac{n_s - n_d}{n_s + n_d + t_y}$$

$$= \frac{64 - 99}{64 + 99 + 212} = \frac{-35}{375} = -0.09$$

A gamma of −0.21 means that, when predicting the order of pairs of cases on the dependent variable (approval of single mothers), we would make 21% fewer errors by taking the independent variable (religiosity) into account. The values for gamma, Kendall's tau-b, and Somers' *d* show that there is a moderate to weak, negative association between these two variables. As religiosity increases, approval decreases (or, more religious nations are less approving of single mothers).

Application 12.2

There is no age at which individuals are immune to stress. However, do levels of stress vary by age? Are younger Canadians more stressed out than older Canadians? We will examine the relationship between age and stress using an actual random sample of 1,000 respondents from the Canadian Mental Health and Well-being Survey. Age has been grouped as 15 to 44 years of age, 45 to 64 years of age, and 65 years of age and older. Stress was measured in the survey with the following question, "Thinking about the amount of stress in your life, would you say that most days are: not stressful ('low' stress) or stressful ('high' stress)?"

	Age			
Stress	15–44	45–64	65+	Totals
Low	154	121	125	400
High	346	179	75	600
Totals	500	300	200	1,000

We will compute a gamma, Kendall's tau-c (since there is an unequal number of categories on the independent and dependent variables), and Somers' *d* to summarize the strength and direction of the association. To calculate the statistics, we must find the number of similar and dissimilar pairs, and the number of pairs tied on the dependent (stress) variable.

The number of pairs of cases ranked in the same order on both variables (n_s) is

$$n_s = 154(179 + 75) + 121(75)$$
$$= 39,116 + 9,075 = 48,191$$

The number of pairs of cases ranked in different order on both variables (n_d) is

$$n_d = 125(179 + 346) + 121(346)$$
$$= 65,625 + 41,866 = 107,491$$

The number of pairs tied on the dependent variable (t_y) is

$$t_y = 154(121 + 125) + 121(125)$$
$$+ 346(179 + 75) + 179(75)$$
$$= 37,884 + 15,125 + 87,884 + 13,425$$
$$= 154,318$$

Gamma is

$$G = \frac{n_s - n_d}{n_s + n_d} = \frac{48,191 - 107,491}{48,191 + 107,491} = \frac{-59,300}{155,682}$$
$$= -0.38$$

Kendall's tau-c is

$$\tau_c = \frac{2m(n_s - n_d)}{n^2(m - 1)} = \frac{(2 \times 2)(48,191 - 107,491)}{1,000^2(2 - 1)}$$
$$= \frac{-237,200}{1,000,000} = -0.24$$

Somers' *d* is

$$d_{yx} = \frac{n_s - n_d}{n_s + n_d + t_y}$$
$$= \frac{48,191, - 107,491}{48,191 + 107,491 + 154,318}$$
$$= \frac{-59,300}{310,000} = -0.19$$

A gamma of −0.38 means that, when predicting the order of pairs of cases on stress level, we would make 38% fewer errors by taking age into account, as opposed to ignoring it. The values for gamma, tau-c, and Somers' *d* indicate a strong to moderate, negative association between these two variables. As age increases, stress level decreases: Older Canadians are less likely to report high levels of stress.

Source: Data from Statistics Canada, 2002 *Mental Health and Well-being* - Canadian Community Health Survey, PUMF.

12.5 INTERPRETING STATISTICS: WHAT ARE THE SOURCES OF VOLUNTEERISM IN CANADA?

In this section, we will examine an important feature of Canadian life: community participation and civic engagement. We will look specifically at what kind of person is most engaged in volunteerism. Put differently, what factors are related to volunteerism?

We will use data from the 2004 Canada Survey of Giving, Volunteering and Participating (CSGVP) to answer this question. The CSGVP, which began in 1997, is conducted every few years by Statistics Canada to collect information on how and why Canadians donate their money, time, and other resources to charitable and non-profit organizations. The 2004 CSGVP was administered to a randomly selected sample of approximately 21,000 adult Canadians.

To measure volunteerism (the dependent variable), we used a series of variables that asked people whether they had engaged, without pay on behalf of a group(s) or an organization(s), over the past 12 months in the following activities: canvassing, fundraising, committee membership, mentoring, event organization, administrative duties, coaching, counselling, health care support, food collection, facilities/grounds maintenance, volunteer driving, first aid, conservation, or other unpaid activities. We created a composite variable that counted the number of activities undertaken by each respondent. Their level of volunteerism was then rated as high, moderate, or low. People rated as low had been engaged in no activities in the previous year, and those rated as moderate had volunteered for one or two activities. Individuals volunteering for three or more activities in the past year were coded as high.

This simple variable will not be a perfectly accurate measurement of volunteerism. For example, people might help others directly on their own (e.g., visiting the elderly or unpaid babysitting) or be involved in the daily life of their community but not actually belong to any formal groups or organizations. This kind of "informal" volunteering will not be captured by the variable we created. Or, some people might be involved in many volunteer activities but actually spend very little time (e.g., just a few hours once or twice a year) on each activity. These people will be classified as highly involved on the variable we created, even though their involvement is actually minimal. Like almost all variables of interest to the social sciences, volunteerism is complex and subtle and cannot be adequately captured with a single measurement. Nonetheless, we should be able to develop some insight into the issue, even if the variable is not perfect. Researchers typically have to settle for partial or incomplete measurement of their concepts.

What should we use as independent variables? In other words, what factors might have causal relationships with volunteerism? In this section, we investigate three possibilities. First, we predict that health has a positive impact on volunteerism as good health facilitates one's ability to do volunteer work. Second, because studies show that education is positively related to job performance, we predict that it has a similar relationship with volunteer work. Finally, we argue that religiosity, measured by frequency of religious service attendance, is an important predictor of charitable activity because most religious faiths and organizations encourage—and provide the mechanisms for—volunteering, altruistic giving, and civic participation.

The level of measurement of each of these independent variables, as well as the dependent variable, is ordinal; the categories can be distinguished in terms of "more or less." We will use tables, column percentages, and gamma (although we could have just as easily used Kendall's tau-b, Kendall's tau-c, or Somers' d) to examine which of these arguments has support and to compare the strength and direction of each relationship.

Table 12.7 shows that the relationship between health status and volunteering is strong and positive in direction (gamma = 0.38), and is statistically significant ($p < 0.05$). The column percentages in the table show that volunteerism increases as health status increases: Only 22.2% of people with poor health are highly involved in volunteer activities compared to 39.3% of people with good health.

The relationship between volunteering and education in Table 12.8 is significant at the 0.05 level, moderate in strength, and in the predicted direction. Looking at the bottom row of the table, we see that the percentage of each education group that is highly involved in volunteer activities increases as education increases. The column percentages show

TABLE 12.7   VOLUNTEERISM BY HEALTH STATUS*

	Health Status		
Volunteerism	Poor	Good	Totals
Low	1,685 (55.4%)	5,640 (32.8%)	7,325 (36.2%)
Moderate	679 (22.3%)	4,802 (27.9%)	5,481 (27.1%)
High	675 (22.2%)	6,770 (39.3%)	7,445 (36.8%)
Totals	3,039 (99.9%)	17,212 (100.0%)	20,251 (100.1%)

Gamma = 0.38, $p < 0.05$
*Percentages may not total to 100% because of rounding error.

Source: Data from Statistics Canada, *2004 Canada Survey of Giving, Volunteering and Participating*, PUMF.

TABLE 12.8   VOLUNTEERISM BY EDUCATION*

	Education				
Volunteerism	Less Than High School	High School	Other Post-Secondary	University	Totals
Low	1,719 (51.0%)	1,330 (40.2%)	2,833 (34.2%)	1,010 (22.3%)	6,892 (35.4%)
Moderate	852 (25.3%)	958 (28.9%)	1,416 (27.8%)	1,212 (26.7%)	5,319 (27.3%)
High	799 (23.7%)	1,022 (30.9%)	3,144 (38.0%)	2,310 (51.0%)	7,275 (37.3%)
Totals	3,370 (100.0%)	3,310 (100.0%)	8,274 (100.0%)	4,532 (100.0%)	19,486 (100.0%)

Gamma = 0.27, $p < 0.05$
*Percentages may not total to 100% because of rounding error.

Source: Data from Statistics Canada, *2004 Canada Survey of Giving, Volunteering and Participating*, PUMF.

TABLE 12.9   VOLUNTEERISM BY RELIGIOUS SERVICE ATTENDANCE*

| | Religious Service Attendance | | | |
Volunteerism	Never	Yearly or Monthly	Daily or Weekly	Totals
Low	2,097 (47.1%)	1,539 (38.0%)	1,822 (25.5%)	5,458 (34.9%)
Moderate	1,198 (26.9%)	1,117 (27.6%)	1,951 (27.3%)	4,266 (27.2%)
High	1,159 (26.0%)	1,396 (34.5%)	3,380 (47.3%)	5,935 (37.9%)
Totals	4,454 (100.0%)	4,052 (100.1%)	7,153 (100.1%)	15,659 (100.0%)

Gamma = 0.29, $p < 0.05$
*Percentages may not total to 100% because of rounding error.
Source: Data from Statistics Canada, *2004 Canada Survey of Giving, Volunteering and Participating*, PUMF.

that just 23.7% of respondents with less than a high school education are high on volunteerism versus 51.0% of those with a university education.

Table 12.9 shows the relationship between volunteering and religiosity. The relationship is significant, and changes in the column percentages are rather large. Persons that attend religious service daily or weekly are more likely to be highly involved in volunteer activities (47.3%) than those that never attend (26.0%). As indicated by gamma, this is a positive relationship (as frequency of religious service attendance increases, volunteering increases) that is more or less strong.

In summary, we can see that people in good health, those with higher education, and frequent attendees of religious services are more actively involved in volunteer activities. Health, education, and religiosity seem to be relatively important causes of volunteerism. While these bivariate results cannot show which variable is cause and which is effect (remember that association is not the same thing as causation), they are worthy of additional investigation. Multivariate techniques designed to be used with nominal- and ordinal-level variables, covered on the website for this textbook, might be a logical next step in the process of analyzing each of the relationships.

12.6 SPEARMAN'S RHO (r_s)

To this point, we have considered ordinal variables that have a limited number of categories (possible values) and are presented in tables. However, many ordinal-level variables have a broad range of scores and many distinct values. Such data may be collapsed into a few broad categories (such as high, moderate, and low), organized into a bivariate table, and analyzed with gamma or any of the other measures of association discussed above. Collapsing scores in this manner may be beneficial and desirable in many instances, but some important distinctions between cases may be obscured or lost as a consequence.

For example, suppose a researcher wished to test the claim that jogging is beneficial not only physically but also psychologically. Do joggers have an enhanced sense of self-esteem? To deal with this issue, 10 female joggers are measured on two scales, the first measuring involvement in jogging and the other measuring self-esteem. Scores are reported in Table 12.10.

TABLE 12.10   THE SCORES OF 10 SUBJECTS ON INVOLVEMENT IN JOGGING AND A MEASURE OF SELF-ESTEEM

Joggers	Involvement in Jogging (X)	Self-esteem (Y)
Wendy	18	15
Debbie	17	18
Alicia	15	12
Ava	12	16
Evelyn	10	6
Camille	9	10
Tori	8	8
Isabel	8	7
Maxine	5	5
Lynn	1	2

These data could be collapsed and a bivariate table produced. We could, for example, dichotomize both variables to create only two values (high and low) for both variables. Although collapsing scores in this way is certainly legitimate and often necessary,* two difficulties with this practice must be noted. First, the scores seem continuous, and there are no obvious or natural division points in the distribution that would allow us to distinguish, in a non-arbitrary fashion, between high scores and low ones. Second, and more important, grouping these cases into broader categories will cause us to lose information. That is, if both Wendy and Debbie are placed in the category "high" on involvement, the fact that they had different scores on the variable would be obscured. If differences like this are important and meaningful, then we should opt for a measure of association that permits the retention of as much detail and precision in the scores as possible.

Spearman's rho (r_s) is a measure of association for ordinal-level variables that have a broad range of many different scores and few ties between cases on either variable. Scores on ordinal-level variables cannot, of course, be manipulated mathematically except for judgments of "greater than" or "less than." To compute Spearman's rho, cases are first ranked from high to low on each variable and then the ranks (not the scores) are manipulated to produce the final measure. Table 12.11 displays the original scores and the rankings of the cases on both variables.

To rank the cases, first find the highest score on each variable and assign it rank 1. Wendy has the high score on X (18) and is thus ranked number 1. Debbie, on the other hand, is highest on Y and is ranked first on that variable. All other cases are then ranked in descending order of scores. If any cases have the same score on a variable, assign them the average of the ranks they would have used up had they not been tied. Tori and Isabel have identical scores of 8 on involvement. Had they not been tied, they

---

*For example, collapsing scores may be advisable when the researcher is not sure that fine distinctions between scores are meaningful.

TABLE 12.11   COMPUTING SPEARMAN'S RHO

	Involvement (X)	Rank	Self-Image (Y)	Rank	D	D^2
Wendy	18	1	15	3	−2	4
Debbie	17	2	18	1	1	1
Alicia	15	3	12	4	−1	1
Ava	12	4	16	2	2	4
Evelyn	10	5	6	8	−3	9
Camille	9	6	10	5	1	1
Tori	8	7.5	8	6	1.5	2.25
Isabel	8	7.5	7	7	0.5	0.25
Maxine	5	9	5	9	0	0
Lynn	1	10	2	10	0	0
					$\sum D = 0$	$\sum D^2 = 22.50$

would have used up ranks 7 and 8. The average of these two ranks is 7.5, and this average of used ranks is assigned to all tied cases. (For example, if Maxine had also had a score of 8, three ranks—7, 8, and 9—would have been used, and all three tied cases would have been ranked eighth.)

The formula for Spearman's rho is

FORMULA 12.6

$$r_s = 1 - \frac{6 \sum D^2}{n(n^2 - 1)}$$

where $\sum D^2$ = the sum of the differences in ranks, the quantity squared

To compute $\sum D^2$, the rank of each case on Y is subtracted from its rank on X (D is the difference between rank on Y and rank on X). A column has been provided in Table 12.11 so that these differences may be recorded on a case-by-case basis. Note that the sum of this column ($\sum D$) is 0. That is, the negative differences in rank are equal to the positive differences, as will always be the case, and you should use the total of this column as a check on your computations to this point. If the $\sum D$ is not equal to 0, you have made a mistake either in ranking the cases or in subtracting the differences.

In the column headed D^2, each difference is squared to eliminate negative signs. The sum of this column is $\sum D^2$ and this quantity is entered directly into the formula. For our sample problem:

$$r_s = 1 - \frac{6 \sum D^2}{n(n^2 - 1)}$$

$$r_s = 1 - \frac{6(22.5)}{10(100 - 1)}$$

$$r_s = 1 - \frac{135}{990}$$

$$r_s = 1 - 0.14$$

$$r_s = +0.86$$

Spearman's rho is an index of the strength of association between the variables; it ranges from 0.00 (no association) to ± 1.00 (perfect association). A perfect positive association ($r_s = +1.00$) would exist if there were no disagreements in ranks between the two variables (if cases were ranked in exactly the same order on both variables). A perfect negative relationship ($r_s = -1.00$) would exist if the ranks were in perfect disagreement (if the case ranked highest on one variable were lowest on the other, and so forth). A Spearman's rho of 0.86 indicates a strong, positive relationship between these two variables. The respondents who were highly involved in jogging also ranked high on self-image. These results are supportive of claims regarding the psychological benefits of jogging.

Spearman's rho is an index of the relative strength of a relationship, and values between 0.00 and ± 1.00 have no direct interpretation. However, if the value of rho is squared, a PRE interpretation is possible. Rho squared (r_s^2) represents the proportional reduction in errors of prediction when predicting rank on one variable from rank on the other variable, as compared to predicting rank while ignoring the other variable. In the example above, r_s was 0.86 and r_s^2 would be 0.74. Thus, our errors of prediction would be reduced by 74% if, when predicting the rank of a subject on self-image, the rank of the subject on involvement in jogging were taken into account. *(For practice in computing and interpreting Spearman's rho, see problems 12.11 to 12.14. Problem 12.11 has the fewest number of cases and is probably a good choice for a first attempt at these procedures.)*

12.7 TESTING THE NULL HYPOTHESIS OF "NO ASSOCIATION" WITH GAMMA AND SPEARMAN'S RHO

Whenever a researcher is working with EPSEM, or random samples, he or she will need to ascertain if the sample findings can be generalized to the population. In Part II of this textbook, we considered various ways that information taken from samples—for example, the difference between two sample means—could be generalized to the populations from which the samples were drawn. A test of the null hypothesis, regardless of the form or specific test used, asks essentially if the patterns (or differences, or relationships) that have been observed in the samples can be assumed to exist in the population. Measures of association can also be tested for significance. When data have been collected from a random sample, we will not only need to measure the existence, strength, and direction of the association, but we will also want to know if we can assume that the variables are related in the population.

For nominal-level variables, the statistical significance of a relationship is usually judged by the chi square test. Chi square tests could also be conducted on tables displaying the relationship between ordinal-level variables. However, chi square tests deal with the probability that the observed cell frequencies occurred by chance alone and are therefore not a direct test of the significance of the measure of association itself. In this section we will look at tests of significance for two measures: gamma and Spearman's rho. The computational routines for testing Kendall's tau-b and tau-c and Somers' *d* for significance are beyond the scope of this textbook, but are available in most computerized statistical packages such as SPSS.

Application 12.3

The Human Development Index (HDI) is a measure of a country's "human development" achievements in health (life expectancy), literacy (educational attainment), and standard of living (income). United Nations member states are ranked annually according to their computed HDI score. The higher the HDI score, the higher the level of "human development" in a country. The table below lists the top five ranked (i.e., most developed) countries in 2008 according to the HDI (note that only ranks, not actual HDI scores, are provided in the table). Canada, for example, ranked fourth out of the 177 countries in 2008.

The table also shows how these five countries rank *among themselves* according to the United Nations' Gender Empowerment Measure (GEM) index, which measures the level of gender equality in countries (i.e., percentage of seats in a country's national legislative body held by females, percentage of female legislators and senior officials, percentage of females in professional jobs, and ratio of female to male earnings). The higher the GEM score, the higher the level of gender equality in the country. Again, we only show how these five nations ranked among themselves, not their actual GEM scores or ranking among all nations.

Overall, the HDI and GEM provide powerful measures of human well-being. However, are they related? Do countries with higher human development have more gender equality? We have the ranks of the HDI and GEM scores for each country, so we will compute Spearman's rho to summarize the strength and direction of the association.

Country	HDI Rank	GEM Rank	D	D^2
Iceland	1	2	-1	1
Norway	2	1	1	1
Australia	3	3	0	0
Canada	4	4	0	0
Ireland	5	5	0	0
			$\sum D = 0$	$\sum D^2 = 2$

Spearman's rho for these variables is

$$r_s = 1 - \frac{6 \sum D^2}{n(n^2 - 1)}$$

$$r_s = 1 - \frac{(6)(2)}{5(25 - 1)}$$

$$r_s = 1 - \left(\frac{12}{120}\right)$$

$$r_s = 1 - 0.1$$

$$r_s = +0.90$$

For these five countries, the variables have a strong, positive association. The higher the human development, the greater the gender equality within a country. The value of r_s^2 is 0.81 ($0.90^2 = 0.81$), which indicates that we will make 81% fewer errors when predicting rank on one variable from rank on the other, as opposed to ignoring rank on the other variable, for these five nations.

Source: Data from United Nations (2008). http://hdr.undp.org/en/statistics/.

When testing gamma and Spearman's rho for statistical significance, the null hypothesis will state that there is no association between the variables in the population and that, therefore, the population value for the measure is 0.00. Population values will be denoted by the Greek letters gamma (γ) and rho (ρ_s). For both measures, the test procedures will be organized around the familiar five-step model (see Chapter 7).

Testing Gamma for Significance   To illustrate the test of significance for gamma, we will use Table 12.6, where gamma was 0.57.

Step 1. Making Assumptions and Meeting Test Requirements. When sample size is greater than 10, the sampling distribution of all possible sample gammas can be assumed to be normal in shape.

> Model: Random sampling
>> Level of measurement is ordinal
>> Sampling distribution is normal

Step 2. Stating the Null Hypothesis.

$$H_0: \gamma = 0.0$$
$$(H_1: \gamma \neq 0.0)$$

Step 3. Selecting the Sampling Distribution and Establishing the Critical Region. For samples of 10 or more, the Z distribution (Appendix A) can be used to find areas under the sampling distribution:

> Sampling distribution $= Z$ distribution
> Alpha $= 0.05$
> Z(critical) $= \pm 1.96$

Step 4. Computing the Test Statistic.

FORMULA 12.7
$$Z(\text{obtained}) = G\sqrt{\frac{n_s + n_d}{n(1 - G^2)}}$$

$$Z(\text{obtained}) = G\sqrt{\frac{n_s + n_d}{n(1 - G^2)}} = 0.57\sqrt{\frac{1{,}831 + 499}{100(1 - 0.33)}} = 0.57\sqrt{\frac{2{,}330}{100(0.67)}}$$

$$Z(\text{obtained}) = 0.57\sqrt{34.78} = 3.36$$

Step 5. Making a Decision and Interpreting the Results of the Test. Comparing the Z (obtained) with the Z (critical):

$$Z(\text{obtained}) = 3.36$$
$$Z(\text{critical}) = \pm 1.96$$

We see that the null hypothesis can be rejected. The sample gamma is unlikely to have occurred by chance alone, and we may conclude that these variables are related in the population from which the sample was drawn.

(For practice in conducting and interpreting the test of significance for gamma, see problems 12.2, 12.7, and 12.10.)

Testing Spearman's Rho for Significance   When testing Spearman's rho, the null hypothesis states that the population value (ρ_s) is actually 0 and, therefore, that the value of the sample Spearman's rho (r_s) is the result of mere random chance. When the number of cases in the sample is 10 or more, the sampling distribution of Spearman's rho approximates the t distribution, and we will use this distribution to conduct the test. To illustrate, the Spearman's rho computed in Section 12.6 will be used.

Step 1. **Making Assumptions and Meeting Test Requirements.**

> Model: Random sampling
> Level of measurement is ordinal
> Sampling distribution is normal

Step 2. **Stating the Null Hypothesis.**

$$H_0: \rho_s = 0.0$$
$$(H_1: \rho_s \neq 0.0)$$

Step 3. **Selecting the Sampling Distribution and Establishing the Critical Region.**

> Sampling distribution $= t$ distribution
> Alpha $= 0.05$
> Degrees of freedom $= n - 2 = 8$
> t (critical) $= \pm 2.306$

Step 4. **Computing the Test Statistic.**

FORMULA 12.8
$$t \, (\text{obtained}) = r_s\sqrt{\frac{n - 2}{1 - r_s^2}}$$

$$t \, (\text{obtained}) = r_s\sqrt{\frac{n - 2}{1 - r_s^2}} = 0.86\sqrt{\frac{8}{1 - 0.74}} = 0.86\sqrt{\frac{8}{0.26}}$$

$$t(\text{obtained}) = 0.86\sqrt{30.77} = (0.86)(5.55) = 4.77$$

Step 5. **Making a Decision and Interpreting the Results of the Test.** Comparing the test statistic with the critical region:

$$t \, (\text{obtained}) = 4.77$$
$$t \, (\text{critical}) = \pm 2.306$$

We see that the null hypothesis can be rejected. We may conclude, with a 0.05 chance of making an error, that the variables are related in the population from which the samples were drawn. *(For practice in conducting and interpreting the test of significance for Spearman's rho, see problems 12.11 and 12.14.)*

SUMMARY

1. Measures of association for variables with collapsed ordinal scales (gamma, Kendall's tau-b and tau-c, and Somers' d) were covered along with a measure (Spearman's rho) appropriate for "continuous" ordinal variables. These measures summarize the overall strength and direction of the association between the variables. Gamma and Spearman's rho-squared also have PRE interpretations.

2. Gamma, Kendall's tau-b and tau-c, and Somers' d are based on the concept of pairs. They measure association by comparing each respondent to every other respondent (i.e., a pair) on their rankings on the independent and dependent variable, then counting the number of various types of pairs (similar, dissimilar, or tied).

3. Spearman's rho is computed from the ranks of the scores of the cases on two "continuous" ordinal variables.

4. Both gamma and Spearman's rho can be directly tested for their statistical significance when computed for a random sample drawn from a defined population. The null hypothesis is that the variables are not related in the population, and the test can be organized by using the familiar five-step model.

SUMMARY OF FORMULAS

Gamma	12.2	$G = \dfrac{n_s - n_d}{n_s + n_d}$
Kendall's tau-b	12.3	$\tau_b = \dfrac{n_s - n_d}{\sqrt{(n_s + n_d + t_x)(n_s + n_d + t_y)}}$
Kendall's tau-c	12.4	$\tau_c = \dfrac{2m(n_s - n_d)}{n^2(m - 1)}$
Somers' d	12.5	$d_{yx} = \dfrac{n_s - n_d}{n_s + n_d + t_y}$
Spearman's rho	12.6	$r_s = 1 - \dfrac{6 \sum D^2}{n(n^2 - 1)}$
Z (obtained) for gamma	12.7	$Z(\text{obtained}) = G\sqrt{\dfrac{n_s + n_d}{n(1 - G^2)}}$
t (obtained) for Spearman's rho	12.8	$t(\text{obtained}) = r_s\sqrt{\dfrac{n - 2}{1 - r_s^2}}$

GLOSSARY

Gamma (G). A measure of association appropriate for any two variables measured with "collapsed" ordinal scales. (p. 334)

Kendall's tau-b (τ_b). A measure of association appropriate for two variables measured with "collapsed" ordinal scales with an equal number of categories. (p. 334)

Kendall's tau-c (τ_c). A measure of association appropriate for two variables measured with "collapsed" ordinal scales with an unequal number of categories. (p. 334)

Somers' *d* (*d*$_{yx}$). A measure of association appropriate for two variables measured with "collapsed" ordinal scales where one variable is identified as the dependent. (p. 334)

Spearman's rho (*r*$_s$). A measure of association appropriate for two ordinally-measured variables that are "continuous" in form. (p. 334)

MULTIMEDIA RESOURCES

http://www.healeystatistics.nelson.com

Visit the companion website for the second Canadian edition of *Statistics: A Tool for Social Research* to access a wide range of student resources. Begin by clicking on the Student Resources section of the textbook's website to access review quizzes, flashcards, and other study tools.

PROBLEMS

For problems 12.1 to 12.10 and 12.15 calculate percentages for the bivariate tables as described in Chapter 11. Use the percentages to help analyze the strength and direction of the association.

12.1 SOC A small sample of immigrants to Canada, none of whom speak either of the nation's two official languages, has been interviewed about their level of adjustment. Is the pattern of adjustment affected by length of residence in Canada? For each table compute gamma and summarize the relationship in terms of strength and direction. *(HINT: In 2 × 2 tables, only two cells can contribute to n_s or n_d. To compute n_s, multiply the number of cases in the upper-left-hand cell by the number of cases in the lower-right-hand cell. For n_d, multiply the number of cases in the upper-right-hand cell by the number of cases in the lower-left-hand cell.)*

a. Facility in English or French:

| English/ French Facility | Length of Residence | | |
	Less than Five Years (Low)	More than Five Years (High)	Totals
Low	20	10	30
High	5	15	20
Totals	25	25	50

b. Total family income:

| Income | Length of Residence | | |
	Less than Five Years (Low)	More than Five Years (High)	Totals
Below national average	18	8	26
Above national average	7	17	24
Totals	25	25	50

c. Extent of contact with country of origin:

| Contact | Length of Residence | | |
	Less than Five Years (Low)	More than Five Years (High)	Totals
Rare	5	20	25
Frequent	20	5	25
Totals	25	25	50

12.2 Compute gamma for the tables presented in problems 10.2, 10.6, 10.7, 10.9, 10.10, and 10.12. Because these tables are based on random samples, test the gammas you computed for significance.

12.3 Compute gamma for the table presented in problem 11.1. Summarize the relationship in terms of strength and direction.

12.4 CJ A random sample of 150 cities has been classified as small, medium, or large by population and as high or low on crime rate. Compute gamma, Kendall's tau-c, and Somers' *d*. Compare the measures of association. Are they similar in value? Do they characterize the strength of the association in the same way? *(NOTE: Make sure to compute Kendall's tau-c, and not tau-b, since the table has an unequal number of rows and columns.)*

Crime Rate	City Size			
	Small	Medium	Large	Totals
Low	21	17	8	46
High	29	33	42	104
Totals	50	50	50	150

12.5 SOC Some research has shown that families vary by how they socialize their children to sports, games, and other leisure-time activities. In middle-class families, such activities are carefully monitored by parents and are, in general, dominated by adults (e.g., minor league hockey). In working-class families, children more often organize and initiate such activities themselves, and parents are much less involved (e.g., sandlot or playground baseball games). Are the data below consistent with these findings? Compute gamma and summarize the relationship in a few sentences.

As a Child, Did You Play Mostly Organized or Sandlot Sports?	Social Class Background		
	White-collar	Blue-collar	Totals
Organized	155	123	278
Sandlot	101	138	239
Totals	256	261	517

12.6 Is support for sexual freedom related to age? Is the relationship between the variables different for different nations? The World Values Survey has been administered to random samples drawn from Canada, the United States, and Mexico. Respondents were asked if they agree or disagree that "individuals should have the chance to enjoy complete sexual freedom without being restricted." Compute gamma for each table. Is there a relationship? Describe the strength and direction of the relationship. Which age group is most supportive of sexual freedom? How does the relationship change from nation to nation?

a. Canada

People Should Enjoy Sexual Freedom	Age			
	18–34	35–54	55+	Totals
Agree	378	174	66	618
Neither agree nor disagree	626	710	586	1,922
Disagree	163	101	74	338
Totals	1,167	985	726	2,878

b. United States

People Should Enjoy Sexual Freedom	Age			
	18–34	35–54	55+	Totals
Agree	583	288	147	1,018
Neither agree nor disagree	877	982	1,061	2,920
Disagree	113	72	53	238
Totals	1,573	1,342	1,261	4,176

c. Mexico

People Should Enjoy Sexual Freedom	Age			
	18–34	35–54	55+	Totals
Agree	780	284	61	1,125
Neither agree nor disagree	1,300	847	275	2,422
Disagree	317	148	43	508
Totals	2,397	1,279	379	4,055

Source: Data from EUROPEAN AND WORLD VALUES SURVEYS FOUR-WAVE INTEGRATED DATA FILE, 1981-2004, v.20060423, 2006. The European Values Study Foundation and World Values Survey Association. Aggregate File Producers: ASEP/JDS, Madrid, Spain/Tilburg University, Tilburg, the Netherlands. Aggregate File Distributors: ASEP/JDS and ZA, Cologne, Germany.

12.7 PA All applicants for municipal jobs in Pearson, Ontario, are given an aptitude test, but the test has never been evaluated to see if test scores are in any way related to job performance. The following table reports aptitude test scores and job performance ratings for a random sample of 75 city employees.

Efficiency Ratings	Test Scores			Totals
	Low	Moderate	High	
Low	11	6	7	24
Moderate	9	10	9	28
High	5	9	9	23
Totals	25	25	25	75

a. Are these two variables associated? Compute gamma, then describe the strength and direction of the relationship in a sentence or two.
b. Is gamma statistically significant?
c. Should the aptitude test continue to be administered? Why or why not?

12.8 SW A sample of children has been observed and rated for symptoms of depression. Their parents have been rated for authoritarianism. Compute gamma, Kendall's tau-b, and Somers' *d*. Compare the measures of association. Do they characterize the strength of the association in the same way? *(NOTE: Make sure to compute Kendall's tau-b, and not tau-c, since the table has an equal number of rows and columns.)*

Symptoms of Depression	Authoritarianism			Totals
	Low	Moderate	High	
Few	7	8	9	24
Some	15	10	18	43
Many	8	12	3	23
Totals	30	30	30	90

12.9 SOC Are levels of stress and education related? Compute gamma, and describe the strength and direction of the relationship.

Stress Level	Level of Education				Totals
	Less than High School	High School	Some College/ University	College/ University Graduate	
Low	48	50	61	42	201
High	45	43	33	27	148
Totals	93	93	94	69	349

12.10 SOC In a recent survey, a random sample of respondents was asked to indicate how happy they were with their situations in life. Are their responses related to income level?

Happiness	Income			Totals
	Low	Moderate	High	
Not happy	101	82	36	219
Pretty happy	40	227	100	367
Very happy	216	198	203	617
Totals	357	507	339	1,203

a. Compute gamma to describe the strength and direction of the relationship.
b. Is the relationship statistically significant?

12.11 SOC A random sample of 11 neighbourhoods in Pearson, Ontario, has been rated by an urban sociologist on a "quality-of-life" scale (which includes measures of affluence, availability of medical care, and recreational facilities) and a social cohesion scale. The results are presented below in scores. Higher scores indicate higher "quality of life" and greater social cohesion.

Neighbourhood	Quality of Life	Social Cohesion
Queens Lake	17	8.8
North End	40	3.9
Mountaintop	47	4.0
Lakeside	90	3.1
Blossom Park	35	7.5
Kingswood	52	3.5
Cambridge Shores	23	6.3
Windsor Forest	67	1.7
College Park	65	9.2
Uplands	63	3.0
Riverview	100	5.3

a. Are the two variables associated? What is the strength and direction of the association? Summarize the relationship in a sentence or two. *(HINT: Don't forget to square the value of Spearman's rho for a PRE interpretation.)*
b. Conduct a test of significance for this relationship. Summarize your findings.

12.12 SW Several years ago, a job-training program began, and a team of social workers screened the candidates for suitability for employment. Now the screening process is being evaluated, and the actual work performance of a sample of hired candidates has been rated. Did the screening process work? Is there a relationship between the original scores and performance evaluation on the job?

Case	Original Score	Performance Evaluation
A	17	78
B	17	85
C	15	82
D	13	92
E	13	75
F	13	72
G	11	70
H	10	75
I	10	92
J	10	70
K	9	32
L	8	55
M	7	21
N	5	45
O	2	25

12.13 SOC Below are the scores of a sample of 15 countries on a measure of ethnic diversity (the higher the number, the greater the diversity) and a measure of economic inequality (the higher the score, the greater the inequality). Are these variables related? Are ethnically diverse countries more economically unequal?

Country	Diversity	Inequality
A	91	29.7
B	87	58.4
C	83	57.5
D	75	31.5
E	72	48.4
F	69	32.7
G	65	32.0
H	63	41.0
I	57	30.1
J	50	50.3
K	44	32.5
L	31	33.7
M	16	25.6
N	4	35.9
O	3	27.2

12.14 Random samples of foreign-born and non-foreign-born citizens from 20 countries were rated on a Social Distance Scale. Lower scores represent less social distance and less prejudice. How similar are these rankings? Is the relationship statistically significant?

	Average Social Distance Scale Score	
Country	Non-foreign Born	Foreign Born
A	1.2	2.6
B	1.4	2.9
C	1.5	3.6
D	1.6	3.6
E	1.8	3.9
F	1.9	3.3
G	2.0	3.8
H	2.1	2.7
I	2.2	3.0
J	2.3	3.3
K	2.4	4.2
L	2.4	1.3
M	2.8	3.5
N	2.9	3.4
O	3.4	3.7
P	3.7	5.1
Q	3.9	3.9
R	3.9	4.1
S	4.2	4.4
T	5.3	5.4

12.15 In problem 11.7, we looked at the relationships between five dependent variables and the independent variable political ideology. In this problem, we'll use income as an independent variable and assess its relationship with the same set of variables. For each table, calculate gamma. Describe the strength and direction of each relationship in a few sentences. *Be careful in interpreting direction.*

a. Support for same-sex marriage by income:

	Income			
Same-sex Marriage?	Less than $24,900	$24,900 to $50,000	More than $50,000	Totals
Favour	220	218	226	664
Oppose	366	299	250	915
Totals	586	517	476	1,579

b. Support for capital punishment by income:

	Income			
Capital Punishment?	Less than $24,900	$24,900 to $50,000	More than $50,000	Totals
Favour	567	574	552	1,693
Oppose	270	183	160	613
Totals	837	757	712	2,306

c. Approval of suicide for people with an incurable disease by income:

Right to Suicide?	Income			
	Less than $24,900	$24,900 to $50,000	More than $50,000	Totals
Favour	343	341	338	1,022
Oppose	227	194	147	568
Totals	570	535	485	1,590

d. Support for traditional gender roles by income:

Traditional Gender Roles?	Income			
	Less than $24,900	$24,900 to $50,000	More than $50,000	Totals
Favour	130	71	39	240
Oppose	448	479	461	1,388
Totals	578	550	500	1,628

e. Support for legalizing marijuana by income:

Legalize Marijuana?	Income			
	Less than $24,900	$24,900 to $50,000	More than $50,000	Totals
Favour	492	478	451	1,421
Oppose	85	68	53	206
Totals	577	546	504	1,627

SPSS for Windows

Using SPSS for Windows to Produce Ordinal-Level Measures of Association with the 2009 GSS

The demonstrations and exercises below use the shortened version of the 2009 GSS data set supplied with this textbook. Start SPSS for Windows and open the *GSS.sav* file.

SPSS DEMONSTRATION 12.1 Interpreting the Direction of Relationships— Another Look at Income and Health

In Demonstration 11.1, we used percentages to look at the relationship between recoded *srh_q110* (state of health) and recoded *incmhsd* (total household income). Let's re-examine this relationship and find out whether gamma, Kendall's tau-c, and Somers' *d* can add any new information. We will use the **Crosstabs** program with *income4* (recoded *incmhsd*) as the independent (column) variable and *health* (recoded *srh_q110*) as the dependent (row) variable. If you no longer have access to the recoded version of these variables, follow the directions in Demonstration 11.1.

In the **Crosstabs** dialog box, click the **Statistics** button and request gamma, Somers' *d*, and Kendall's tau-c (we have selected Kendall's tau-c given the unequal number of categories on the independent and dependent variables). Don't forget to click the **Cells** button and request column percentages. Click **OK**, and the output (slightly edited for readability) should look like this:

Health * Income4 Crosstabulation

			Income				
			<$30,000	$30,000-$59,999	$60,000-$99,999	$100,000+	Total
Health	Good	Count	92	264	337	446	1139
		% within income4	74.8%	89.5%	91.1%	95.1%	90.6%
	Poor	Count	31	31	33	23	118
		% within income4	25.2%	10.5%	8.9%	4.9%	9.4%
Total		Count	123	295	370	469	1257
		% within income4	100.0%	100.0%	100.0%	100.0%	100.0%

Directional Measures

			Value	Asymp. Std. Error[a]	Approx. T^b	Approx. Sig.
Ordinal by Ordinal	Somers'd	Symmetric	−.118	.021	−5.274	.000
		Health Dependent	−.073	.014	−5.274	.000
		Income4 Dependent	−.304	.053	−5.274	.000

a. Not assuming the null hypothesis.
b. Using the asymptotic standard error assuming the null hypothesis.

Symmetric Measures

		Value	Asymp. Std. Error[a]	Approx. T^b	Approx. Sig.
Ordinal by Ordinal	Kendall's tau-c	−.104	.020	−5.274	.000
	Gamma	−.401	.064	−5.274	.000
N of Valid Cases		1257			

a. Not assuming the null hypothesis.
b. Using the asymptotic standard error assuming the null hypothesis.

Let's look first at gamma in the "Symmetric Measures" output box, a value of −.401 indicates a strong and negative relationship. So, the higher the income, the lower the health, right? Wrong. Look at the codes for health. A low score indicates a high level of health. The negative sign for gamma is telling us that higher scores on *income4* are associated with a low score (a score of 1 or good) on health. Despite the negative sign, this is really a "positive" relationship in the sense that health improves with income. Always inspect tables carefully to make sure that you are interpreting the direction of the relationship properly.

Looking next at Kendall's tau-c, a value of −.104 indicates a weak to moderate relationship. This value is much lower than gamma, as is Somers' *d* reported in the "Directional Measures" output box. Also, notice that there are three values of Somers' *d*. The "Symmetric" version of Somers' *d* (−.118) is a type of average of the two asymmetrical (i.e., directional) versions of Somers' *d*: d_{yx} (−.073) ("HEALTH Dependent") and d_{xy} (−.304) ("INCOME4 Dependent").

So, which of these statistics should we use? Gamma tends to exaggerate the strength of relationship, so either Kendall's tau-c or Somers' *d* will likely offer a more realistic picture of the strength of association between income and health. Further, if one of the variables is specifically identified as the dependent variable (e.g., health), then asymmetrical Somers' *d* (−.073) is likely the most appropriate measure of association.

SPSS DEMONSTRATION 12.2 Does Disability Vary by Age?

Let's take another look at a relationship between two ordinal-level variables: *hal_q410* (are your daily activities at home, work, school limited by a physical condition?) as the dependent variable and *agegr5* (age) as the independent variable. The latter has too many categories (15) to be used in a bivariate table (see Appendix G), so we must first recode the variable. We have decided to collapse the values of *agegr5* into three categories.

Click **Transform** and **Recode into Different Variables**. Next, move the variable *agegr5* to the **Input Variable → Output Variable** box, then type a name— we suggest *age3*—in the **Output Variable** box. Click the **Change** button. Next, click on the **Old and New Values** button. The recoding instructions that should appear in the **Old → New** box of the **Recode into Different Variables: Old and New Values** window should be:

$$1 \text{ thru } 6 \rightarrow 1$$
$$7 \text{ thru } 10 \rightarrow 2$$
$$11 \text{ thru } 15 \rightarrow 3$$

Click **Continue**, and then **OK** after inputting these recode instructions. This scheme groups all respondents with scores 1 thru 6 on *agegr5* (15–39) together into a score of 1 on *age3*, scores 7 thru 10 on *agegr5* (40–59) together into a score of 2 on *age3*, and scores 11 thru 15 on *agegr5* (60+) together into a score of 3 on *age3*.

Again, we highly recommend that this variable be added to the permanent data file as it will be used in subsequent demonstrations and exercises. Click **Save** from the **File** menu, and the updated data set with *age3* added will be saved to disk. Remember that your data set is limited to 50 variables in the SPSS student version.

Let's now examine the relationship between *hal_q410* and *age3* with gamma, Kendall's tau-b, and Somers' *d*. Use **Crosstabs** once again with *age3* as the independent (column) variable. The dependent variable *hal_q410* will go in the rows. Request gamma, Kendall's tau-b (since the independent and dependent variables have an equal number of categories), Somers' *d*, and column percentages. The output, slightly edited for readability, should look like this:

Are your daily activities at home, work, school or any other * age3 Crosstabulation

			age3			
			15–39	40–59	60+	Total
Are your daily activities at home, work, school or any other	No	Count	712	444	204	1360
		% within age3	95.8%	87.2%	78.5%	89.9%
	Sometimes	Count	21	28	26	75
		% within age3	2.8%	5.5%	10.0%	5.0%
	Often or always	Count	10	37	30	77
		% within age3	1.3%	7.3%	11.5%	5.1%
Total		Count	743	509	260	1512
		% within age3	100.0%	100.0%	100.0%	100.0%

Directional Measures

			Value	Asymp. Std. Error[a]	Approx. T^b	Approx. Sig.
Ordinal by Ordinal	Somers'd	Symmetric	.171	.019	7.801	.000
		Are your daily activities at home, work, school or any other Dependent	.111	.014	7.801	.000
		age3 Dependent	.369	.040	7.801	.000

a. Not assuming the null hypothesis.
b. Using the asymptotic standard error assuming the null hypothesis.

Symmetric Measures

		Value	Asymp. Std. Error[a]	Approx. T^b	Approx. Sig.
Ordinal by Ordinal	Kendall's tau-b	.203	.023	7.801	.000
	Gamma	.529	.049	7.801	.000
N of Valid Cases		1512			

a. Not assuming the null hypothesis.
b. Using the asymptotic standard error assuming the null hypothesis.

A gamma of .529 indicates a strong, positive relationship. Older respondents (a score of 3 on *age3*) had the highest percentage who reported "Often or always" (has daily activities limited by a physical condition), and younger respondents had the highest percentage who reported "No" (daily activities limited by a physical condition). As age increases, having a disability (the percentage who say "Often or always") increases.

Not surprisingly, Kendall's tau-b, with a value of .203, is much lower than gamma, and indicates a moderate relationship. Similarly, if we take *hal_q410* as the dependent variable, then Somers' *d* (.111) also offers a more modest picture of the strength of relationship between age and disability.

Exercise (using *GSS.sav*)

12.1 Use gamma, Kendall's tau (tau-b when a bivariate table has an equal number of rows and columns, otherwise tau-c), and Somers' *d* to analyze and describe the relationship between any two ordinal-level variables.* Summarize the strength and direction of the relationship in a few sentences.

12.2 Follow up on Demonstration 12.2 with two new ordinal-level independent variables. What other factors might affect *hal_q410*? As a suggestion, try *drr_q110* and *drr_q120* as independent variables.* Summarize the strength and direction of the relationships in a few sentences. Are these relationships stronger or weaker than those with recoded *agegr5*? Be careful in interpreting the direction of the relationships.

*If necessary, use the **Recode** command illustrated in Appendix F.5 to reduce the number of categories in your variables.

Association Between Variables Measured at the Interval-Ratio Level

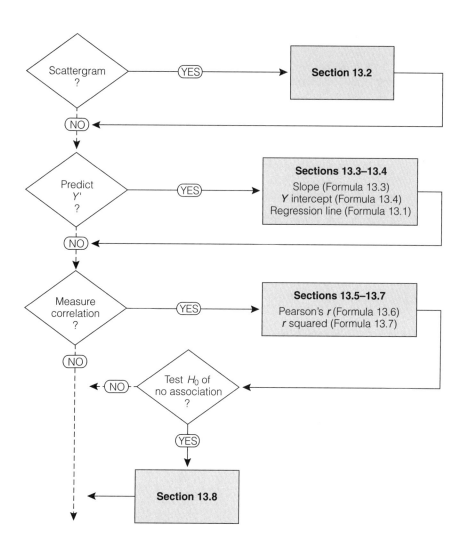

LEARNING OBJECTIVES

By the end of this chapter, you will be able to

1. Interpret a scattergram.
2. Calculate and interpret slope (b), Y intercept (a), and Pearson's r and r^2.

3. Find and explain the least-squares regression line and use it to predict values of Y.

4. Explain the concepts of total, explained, and unexplained variance.

5. Use regression and correlation techniques to analyze and describe a bivariate relationship in terms of the three questions introduced in Chapter 11.

6. Test Pearson's r for significance.

13.1 INTRODUCTION

This chapter presents a set of statistical techniques for analyzing the association or correlation between variables measured at the interval-ratio level.* As we shall see, these techniques are rather different in their logic and computation from those covered in Chapters 11 and 12. Let us stress at the outset, therefore, that we are still asking the same three questions: Is there a relationship between the variables? How strong is the relationship? What is the direction of the relationship? You might become preoccupied with some of the technical details and computational routines in this chapter, so remind yourself occasionally that our ultimate goals are unchanged: We are trying to understand bivariate relationships, explore possible causal ties between variables, and improve our ability to predict scores.

13.2 SCATTERGRAMS

As we have seen over the past several chapters, properly percentaged tables provide important information about bivariate associations between nominal- and ordinal-level variables. In addition to measures of association like phi or gamma, the conditional distributions and patterns of cell frequency almost always provide useful information and a better understanding of the relationship between variables.

By the same token, the usual first step in analyzing a relationship between interval-ratio variables is to construct and examine a **scattergram**. Like bivariate tables, these graphs allow us to quickly identify several important features of the relationship. An example will illustrate the construction and use of scattergrams. Suppose a researcher is interested in analyzing how dual-wage-earner families (i.e., families where both husband and wife have jobs outside the home) cope with housework. Specifically, the researcher wonders if the number of children in the family is related to the amount of time the husband contributes to housekeeping chores. The relevant data for a sample of 12 dual-wage-earner families are displayed in Table 13.1.

A scattergram, like a bivariate table, has two dimensions. The scores of the independent (X) variable are arrayed along the horizontal axis, and the

---

*The term *correlation* is commonly used instead of *association* when discussing the relationship between interval-ratio variables. We will use the two terms interchangeably.

TABLE 13.1 NUMBER OF CHILDREN AND HUSBAND'S CONTRIBUTION TO HOUSEWORK (fictitious data)

Family	Number of Children	Hours per Week Husband Spends on Housework
A	1	1
B	1	2
C	1	3
D	1	5
E	2	3
F	2	1
G	3	5
H	3	0
I	4	6
J	4	3
K	5	7
L	5	4

FIGURE 13.1 HUSBAND'S HOUSEWORK BY NUMBER OF CHILDREN

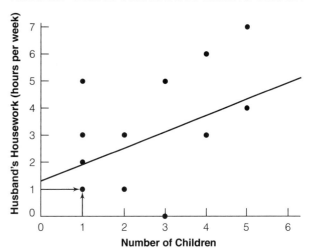

scores of the dependent (Y) variable along the vertical axis. Each dot on the scattergram represents a case in the sample and is located at a point determined by the scores of the case. Figure 13.1 shows a scattergram displaying the relationship between "number of children" and "husband's housework" for the sample of 12 families presented in Table 13.1. Family A has a score of 1 on the X variable (number of children) and 1 on the Y variable (husband's housework) and is represented by the dot above the score of 1 on the X axis and directly to the right of the score of 1 on the Y axis. All 12 cases are similarly represented by dots on Figure 13.1. Also note that, as always, the scattergram is clearly titled and both axes are labelled.

The overall pattern of the dots or cases summarizes the nature of the relationship between the two variables. The clarity of the pattern can be enhanced by drawing a straight line through the cluster of dots such that the line touches every dot or comes as close to doing so as possible. In Section 13.3, a precise technique for fitting this line to the pattern of the dots will be explained. For now, an "eyeball" approximation will suffice. This summarizing line is called the **regression line** and has already been added to the scattergram.

Scattergrams, even when they are crudely drawn, can be used for a variety of purposes. They provide at least impressionistic information about the existence, strength, and direction of the relationship and can also be used to check the relationship for linearity (i.e., how well the pattern of dots can be approximated with a straight line). Finally, the scattergram can be used to predict the score of a case on one variable from the score of that case on the other variable. We will briefly examine each of these uses.

To determine the existence of a relationship, we can return to the basic definition of an association stated in Chapter 11. Two variables are associated if the distributions of Y (the dependent variable) change for the various conditions of X (the independent variable). In Figure 13.1, scores on X (number of children) are arrayed along the horizontal axis. The dots above each score on X are the scores (or conditional distributions) of Y. That is, the dots represent scores on Y for each value of X. Figure 13.1 shows that there is a relationship between these variables because these conditional distributions of Y (the dots above each score on X) change as X changes. The existence of an association is further reinforced by the fact that the regression line lies at an angle to the X axis. If these two variables had not been associated, the conditional distributions of Y would not have changed, and the regression line would have been parallel to the horizontal axis.

The strength of the bivariate association can be judged by observing the spread of the dots around the regression line. In a perfect association, all dots would lie on the regression line. The more the dots are clustered around the regression line, the stronger the association.

The direction of the relationship can be detected by observing the angle of the regression line. Figure 13.1 shows a positive relationship: As X (number of children) increases, husband's housework (Y) also increases. Husbands in families with more children tend to do more housework. If the relationship had been negative, the regression line would have sloped in the opposite direction to indicate that high scores on one variable were associated with low scores on the other.

To summarize these points about the existence, strength, and direction of the relationship, Figure 13.2 shows a perfect positive and a perfect negative relationship and a "zero relationship," or "non-relationship," between two variables.

One key assumption underlying the statistical techniques to be introduced later in this chapter is that the two variables have an essentially **linear**

FIGURE 13.2   POSITIVE, NEGATIVE, AND ZERO RELATIONSHIPS

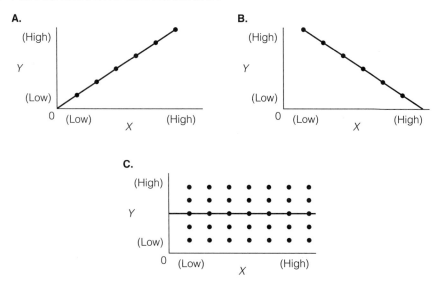

FIGURE 13.3   SOME NON-LINEAR RELATIONSHIPS

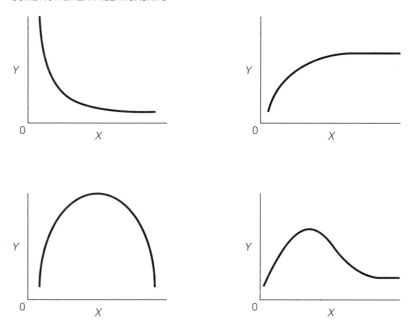

relationship. In other words, the observation points or dots in the scattergram must form a pattern that can be approximated with a straight line. Significant departures from linearity would require the use of statistical techniques beyond the scope of this textbook. Examples of some common curvilinear relationships are presented in Figure 13.3. If the scattergram shows that the variables have a non-linear relationship, the techniques described in this chapter should be used with great caution or not at all. Checking for the linearity of the relationship is perhaps the most important reason for constructing at least a crude, hand-drawn scattergram before proceeding with the statistical analysis. If the relationship is non-linear, you might need to treat the variables as if they were ordinal rather than interval-ratio in level of measurement. *(For practice in constructing and interpreting scattergrams, see problems 13.1 to 13.5.)*

13.3 REGRESSION AND PREDICTION

A final use of the scattergram is to predict scores of cases on one variable from their score on the other. To illustrate, suppose that, based on the relationship between number of children and husband's housework displayed in Figure 13.1, we wish to predict the number of hours of housework a husband with a family of six children would do each week. The sample has no families with six children, but if we extend the axes and regression line in Figure 13.1 to incorporate this score, a prediction is possible. Figure 13.4 reproduces the scattergram and illustrates how the prediction would be made.

The predicted score on Y—which is symbolized as Y' to distinguish predictions of Y from actual Y scores—is found by first locating the relevant

FIGURE 13.4 PREDICTING HUSBAND'S HOUSEWORK

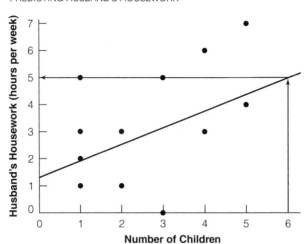

score on X ($X = 6$ in this case) and then drawing a straight line from that point to the regression line. From the regression line, another straight line parallel to the X axis is drawn across to the Y axis. The predicted Y score (Y') is found at the point where the line crosses the Y axis. In our example, we would predict that, in a dual-wage-earner family with six children, the husband would devote about five hours per week to housework.

Of course, this prediction technique is crude, and the value of Y' can change depending on how accurately the freehand regression line is drawn. One way to eliminate this source of error would be to find the straight line that most accurately summarizes the pattern of the observation points and therefore best describes the relationship between the two variables. Is there such a "best-fitting" straight line? If there is, how is it defined?

Recall that our criterion for the freehand regression line was that it touch all the dots or come as close to doing so as possible. Also, recall that the dots above each value of X can be thought of as conditional distributions of Y, the dependent variable. Within each conditional distribution of Y, the mean is the point around which the variation of the scores is at a minimum. In Chapter 3, we noted that the mean of any distribution of scores is the point around which the variation of the scores, as measured by squared deviations, is minimized:

$$\sum(X_i - \overline{X})^2 = \text{minimum}$$

Thus, if the regression line is drawn so that it touches each **conditional mean of Y**, it would be the straight line that comes as close as possible to all the scores.

Conditional means are found by summing all Y values for each value of X and then dividing by the number of cases. For example, four families had one child ($X = 1$), and the husbands of these four families devoted 1, 2, 3, and 5 hours per week to housework. Thus, for $X = 1$, $Y = 1, 2, 3$, and 5, and the conditional mean of Y for $X = 1$ is 2.75 ($11/4 = 2.75$). Husbands in

FIGURE 13.5 CONDITIONAL MEANS OF Y

TABLE 13.2 CONDITIONAL MEANS OF Y
(husband's housework) FOR VARIOUS VALUES OF X
(number of children)

Number of Children (X)	Husband's Housework (Y)	Conditional Means of Y
1	1,2,3,5	2.75
2	3,1	2.00
3	5,0	2.50
4	6,3	4.50
5	7,4	5.50

families with one child worked an average of 2.75 hours per week doing housekeeping chores. Conditional means of Y are computed in the same way for each value of X displayed in Table 13.2 and plotted in Figure 13.5.

Let us quickly remind ourselves of the reason for these calculations. We are seeking the single best-fitting regression line for summarizing the relationship between X and Y, and we have seen that a line drawn through the conditional means of Y will minimize the spread of the observation points. It will come as close to all the scores as possible and will therefore be the single best-fitting regression line.

Now, a line drawn through the points on Figure 13.5 (the conditional means of Y) will be the best-fitting line we are seeking, but you can see from the scattergram that the line will not be straight. In fact, only rarely (when there is a perfect relationship between X and Y) will conditional means fall in a perfectly straight line. Because we still must meet the condition of linearity, let us revise our criterion and define the regression line as the unique straight line that touches all conditional means of Y or comes as close to doing so as possible. Formula 13.1 defines the "least-squares" regression line, or the single straight regression line that best fits the pattern of the data points.

FORMULA 13.1
$$Y = a + bX$$

where Y = score on the dependent variable
a = the Y intercept or the point where the regression line crosses the Y axis
b = the slope of the regression line or the amount of change produced in Y by a unit change in X
X = score on the independent variable

The formula introduces two new concepts. First, the **Y intercept (a)** is the point at which the regression line crosses the vertical, or Y, axis. This means that the intercept is equal to the value of Y when X is zero. Second, the

slope (*b*) of the least-squares regression line is the amount of change produced in the dependent variable (*Y*) by a unit change in the independent variable (*X*). Think of the slope of the regression line as a measure of the effect of the *X* variable on the *Y* variable. If the variables have a strong association, then changes in the value of *X* will be accompanied by substantial changes in the value of *Y*, and the slope (*b*) will have a high value. The weaker the effect of *X* on *Y* (the weaker the association between the variables), the lower the value of the slope (*b*). If the two variables are unrelated, the least-squares regression line would be parallel to the *X* axis, and *b* would be 0.00 (the line would have no slope). As a final point, the intercept and the slope are both expressed in the *units* of the dependent variable (e.g., number of *hours* per week the husband spends on housework), and thus provide a direct and intuitive interpretation.

With the least-squares formula (Formula 13.1), we can predict values of *Y* in a much less arbitrary and impressionistic way than through mere eyeballing. This will be so, remember, because the least-squares regression line as defined by Formula 13.1 is the single straight line that best fits the data because it comes as close as possible to all of the conditional means of *Y*. To see how predictions of *Y* can be made, however, we must first calculate *a* and *b*. (*For practice in using the regression line to predict scores on Y from scores on X, see problems 13.1 to 13.3 and 13.5.)*

13.4 THE COMPUTATION OF *a* AND *b*

Because the value of *b* is needed to solve for *a*, we will begin with the computation of the slope of the least-squares regression line. The definitional formula for the slope is

FORMULA 13.2

$$b = \frac{\Sigma(X - \overline{X})(Y - \overline{Y})}{\Sigma(X - \overline{X})^2}$$

The numerator of this formula is called the *covariation* of *X* and *Y*. It is a measure of how *X* and *Y* vary together, and its value will reflect both the direction and strength of the relationship. These days, of course, computers and statistical packages like SPSS are used to compute complex statistics like *b*. However, for smaller samples (and for the end-of-chapter problems in this textbook), *b* is sometimes still calculated using handheld calculators. In these situations, Formula 13.2 is awkward to use and the following computational formula, which can be derived from Formula 13.2, can be used instead:

FORMULA 13.3

$$b = \frac{n \Sigma XY - (\Sigma X)(\Sigma Y)}{n \Sigma X^2 - (\Sigma X)^2}$$

where b = the slope
n = the number of cases
ΣXY = the summation of the crossproducts of the scores
ΣX = the summation of the *X* scores
ΣY = the summation of the *Y* scores
ΣX^2 = the summation of the squared scores on *X*

Admittedly, this formula appears formidable at first glance, but it can be solved without too much difficulty if computations are organized into table format. The computing table displayed in Table 13.3 has a column for each of the four quantities needed to solve the formula. The data are from the dual-wage-earner family sample (see Table 13.1).

In Table 13.3, the first two columns list the original X and Y scores for each case. The third column contains the squared scores on X, and the fourth lists the squared scores on Y. The fifth column lists the crossproducts of the scores for each case. In other words, the entries in the last column are determined by multiplying both scores for each case. We can now replace the symbols in Formula 13.3 with the proper sums:

$$b = \frac{n\,\Sigma XY - (\Sigma X)(\Sigma Y)}{n\,\Sigma X^2 - (\Sigma X)^2}$$

$$b = \frac{(12)(125) - (32)(40)}{(12)(112) - (32)^2}$$

$$b = \frac{(1,500 - 1,280)}{(1,344 - 1,024)}$$

$$b = \frac{220}{320}$$

$$b = 0.69$$

A slope of 0.69 indicates that, for each unit change in X, there is an increase of 0.69 units in Y. For our example, the addition of each child (an increase

TABLE 13.3   COMPUTATION OF THE SLOPE (b)

X	Y	X^2	Y^{2}*	XY
1	1	1	1	1
1	2	1	4	2
1	3	1	9	3
1	5	1	25	5
2	3	4	9	6
2	1	4	1	2
3	5	9	25	15
3	0	9	0	0
4	6	16	36	24
4	3	16	9	12
5	7	25	49	35
5	4	25	16	20
$\Sigma X = 32$	$\Sigma Y = 40$	$\Sigma X^2 = 112$	$\Sigma Y^2 = 184$	$\Sigma XY = 125$

$$\bar{X} = \frac{32}{12} = 2.67$$

$$\bar{Y} = \frac{40}{12} = 3.33$$

*The quantity ΣY^2 is not used in the computation of b. We will need it later, however, when we compute Pearson's r (see Section 13.5).

of one unit in X) results in an increase of 0.69 hour of housework being done by the husband (an increase of 0.69 units—or hours—in Y).

Once the slope has been calculated, finding the intercept (a) is relatively easy. To compute the mean of X and the mean of Y, divide the sums of columns 1 and 2 of Table 13.3 by n and enter these figures into Formula 13.4:

FORMULA 13.4

$$a = \overline{Y} - b\overline{X}$$

For our sample problem, the value of a would be

$$a = \overline{Y} - b\overline{X}$$
$$a = 3.33 - (0.69)(2.67)$$
$$a = 3.33 - 1.84$$
$$a = 1.49$$

Thus, the least-squares regression line will cross the Y axis at the point where Y equals 1.49.

The full least-squares regression line for our sample data can now be specified:

$$Y = a + bX$$
$$Y = (1.49) + (0.69)X$$

This formula can be used to estimate or predict scores on Y for any value of X. In Section 13.3, we used the freehand regression line to predict a score on Y (husband's housework) for a family with six children ($X = 6$). Our prediction was that, in families of six children, husbands would contribute about five hours per week to housekeeping chores. By using the least-squares regression line, we can see how close our impressionistic, eyeball prediction was.

$$Y' = a + bX$$
$$Y' = (1.49) + (0.69)(6)$$
$$Y' = (1.49) + (4.14)$$
$$Y' = 5.63$$

Based on the least-squares regression line, we would predict that in a dual-wage-earner family with six children, husbands would devote 5.63 hours a week to housework. What would our prediction of husband's housework be for a family of seven children ($X = 7$)?

Note that our predictions of Y scores are basically "educated guesses." We will be unlikely to predict values of Y exactly except in the (relatively rare) case where the bivariate relationship is perfect and perfectly linear. Note also, however, that the accuracy of our predictions will increase as relationships become stronger. This is because the dots are more clustered around the least-squares regression line in stronger relationships. (*The slope and Y intercept may be computed for any problem at the end of this chapter, but see problems 13.1 to 13.5 in particular. These problems have smaller data sets and will provide good practice until you are comfortable with these calculations.*)

13.5 THE CORRELA-
TION COEFFICIENT
(PEARSON'S r)

We pointed out in Section 13.4 that the slope (*b*) of the least-squares regression line is a measure of the effect of *X* on *Y*. Because the slope is the amount of change produced in *Y* by a unit change in *X*, *b* will increase in value as the relationship increases in strength. However, *b* does not vary between zero and one and is therefore awkward to use as a measure of association. Instead, researchers rely heavily (almost exclusively) on a statistic called **Pearson's r**, or the correlation coefficient, to measure association between interval-ratio variables. Like the ordinal measures of association discussed in Chapter 12, Pearson's *r* varies from 0.00 to ±1.00, with 0.00 indicating no association and +1.00 and −1.00 indicating perfect positive and perfect negative relationships, respectively. The definitional formula for Pearson's *r* is

FORMULA 13.5

$$r = \frac{\Sigma(X - \overline{X})(Y - \overline{Y})}{\sqrt{[\Sigma(X - \overline{X})^2][\Sigma(Y - \overline{Y})^2]}}$$

Note that the numerator of this formula is the covariation of *X* and *Y*, as was the case with Formula 13.2. When computing with a handheld calculator, computational Formula 13.6 is preferred over the definitional formula.

FORMULA 13.6

$$r = \frac{n\,\Sigma XY - (\Sigma X)(\Sigma Y)}{\sqrt{[n\,\Sigma X^2 - (\Sigma X)^2][n\,\Sigma Y^2 - (\Sigma Y)^2]}}$$

A computing table such as Table 13.3 is strongly recommended as a way of organizing the quantities needed to solve this equation. For our sample problem involving dual-wage-earner families, the quantities displayed in Table 13.3 can be substituted directly into Formula 13.6:

$$r = \frac{(12)(125) - (32)(40)}{\sqrt{[(12)(112) - (32)^2][(12)(184) - (40)^2]}}$$

$$r = \frac{1{,}500 - 1{,}280}{\sqrt{(1{,}344 - 1{,}024)(2{,}208 - 1{,}600)}}$$

$$r = \frac{220}{\sqrt{194{,}560}}$$

$$r = +0.50$$

An *r* value of +0.50 indicates a strong, positive linear relationship between the variables. As the number of children in the family increases, the hourly contribution of husbands to housekeeping duties also increases. *(Every problem at the end of this chapter requires the computation of Pearson's r. It is probably a good idea to practise with smaller data sets and easier computations first—see problem 13.1 in particular.)*

Application 13.1

Five students were randomly selected from a larger sample of 1,500 students in the Student Financial Survey, a comprehensive study on the financial circumstances of Canadian post-secondary students sponsored by the Canada Millennium Scholarship Foundation. The table below shows data for these five students on their GPA (grade point average) and the average number of hours worked per week in the last semester. (While the data in this application are real, the number of cases is far too small to draw any serious conclusions, and thus, this is intended only for purposes of illustration and to simplify computations.) Are these variables associated? Columns have been added for all necessary sums.

Student	Hours Worked (per week) (X)	GPA (Y)	X^2	Y^2	XY
1	25	61	625	3,721	1,525
2	20	72	400	5,184	1,440
3	15	82	225	6,724	1,230
4	8	87	64	7,569	696
5	0	67	0	4,489	0
	68	369	1,314	27,687	4,891

The slope (b) is

$$b = \frac{n \sum XY - (\sum X)(\sum Y)}{n \sum X^2 - (\sum X)^2}$$

$$b = \frac{(5)(4,891) - (68)(369)}{(5)(1,314) - (68)^2}$$

$$b = \frac{-637}{1,946}$$

$$b = -0.33$$

A slope of −0.33 means that for every unit change in X (for every 1 hour increase in work per week), there was a change of −0.33 units in Y (grade point average decreased by 0.33, or by one-third of a point). The Y intercept (a) is

$$a = \overline{Y} - b\overline{X}$$

$$a = \frac{369}{5} - (-0.33)\left(\frac{68}{5}\right)$$

$$a = 73.8 - (-0.33)(13.6)$$

$$a = 73.8 + 4.5$$

$$a = 78.3$$

The least-squares regression equation is

$$Y = a + bX = 78.3 + (-0.33)X$$

The correlation coefficient is

$$r = \frac{n \sum XY - (\sum X)(\sum Y)}{\sqrt{[n \sum X^2 - (\sum X)^2][n \sum Y^2 - (\sum Y)^2]}}$$

$$r = \frac{(5)(4,891) - (68)(369)}{\sqrt{[(5)(1,314) - (68)^2][(5)(27,687) - (369)^2]}}$$

$$r = \frac{-637}{\sqrt{(1,946)(2,274)}}$$

$$r = \frac{-637}{\sqrt{442,5204}}$$

$$r = \frac{-637}{2,103.62}$$

$$r = -0.30$$

For these five students, GPA and hours worked have a moderate to strong, negative relationship. Grade point average decreases as the number of hours worked per week increases. The coefficient of determination, r^2, is $(-0.30)^2$, or 0.09. This indicates that 9% of the variance in GPA is explained by hours worked for this sample of five students.

Source: Data from *Making Ends Meet, 2001–2002 Student Financial Survey*, Canada Millennium Scholarship Foundation. March 2003.

13.6 INTERPRETING THE CORRELATION COEFFICIENT: r^2

Pearson's r is an index of the strength of the linear relationship between two variables. While a value of 0.00 indicates no linear relationship and a value of ± 1.00 indicates a perfect linear relationship, values between these extremes have no direct interpretation. We can, of course, describe relationships in terms of how closely they approach the extremes (e.g., coefficients approaching 0.00 can be described as "weak" and those approaching ± 1.00 as "strong"), but this description is somewhat subjective. Also, we can use the guidelines stated in Table 12.3 for ordinal-level measures of association to attach descriptive words to the specific values of Pearson's r. In other words, values between 0.00 and 0.10 would be described as weak, values between 0.11 and 0.30 would be moderate, and values greater than 0.30 would be strong. Remember, of course, that these labels are arbitrary guidelines and will not be appropriate or useful in all possible research situations.

Fortunately, we can develop a less arbitrary, more direct interpretation of r by calculating an additional statistic called the **coefficient of determination**. This statistic, which is simply the square of Pearson's $r(r^2)$, can be interpreted with a logic akin to proportional reduction in error (PRE). As you recall, the logic of PRE measures of association is to predict the value of the dependent variable under two different conditions. First, Y is predicted while ignoring the information supplied by X and, second, the independent variable X is taken into account. With r^2, both the method of prediction and the construction of the final statistic are somewhat different and require the introduction of some new concepts.

When working with variables measured at the interval-ratio level, the predictions of the Y scores under the first condition (while ignoring X) will be the mean of Y. Given no information on X, this prediction strategy will be optimal because we know that the mean of any distribution is closer to all the scores than any other point in the distribution. We remind you of the principle of minimized variation introduced in Chapter 3 and expressed as

$$\sum (Y - \overline{Y})^2 = minimum$$

The scores of any variable vary less around the mean than around any other point. If we predict the mean of Y for every case, we will make fewer errors of prediction than if we predict any other value for Y.

Of course, we will still make many errors in predicting Y even if we faithfully follow this strategy. The amount of error is represented in Figure 13.6, which displays the relationship between number of children and husband's housework with the mean of Y noted. The vertical lines from the actual scores to the predicted score represent the amount of error we would make when predicting Y while ignoring X.

We can define the extent of our prediction error under the first condition (while ignoring X) by subtracting the mean of Y from each actual Y score and squaring and summing these deviations. The resulting figure, which can be denoted as $\sum (Y - \overline{Y})^2$, is called the **total variation** in Y. We

FIGURE 13.6   PREDICTING *Y* WITHOUT *X* (dual-career families)

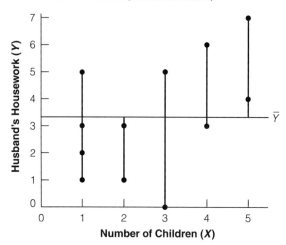

now have a visual representation (Figure 13.6) and a method for calculating the error we incur by predicting *Y* without knowledge of *X*. As we shall see below, we do not need to actually calculate the total variation to find the value of the coefficient of determination, r^2.

Our next step will be to determine the extent to which knowledge of *X* improves our ability to predict *Y*. If the two variables have a linear relationship, then predicting scores on *Y* from the least-squares regression equation will incorporate knowledge of *X* and reduce our errors of prediction. So, under the second condition, our predicted *Y* score for each value of *X* will be

$$Y' = a + bX$$

Figure 13.7 displays the data from the dual-career families with the regression line, as determined by the above formula, drawn in. The vertical lines from each data point to the regression line represent the amount of error in predicting *Y* that remains even after *X* has been taken into account.

As was the case under the first condition, we can precisely define the reduction in error that results from taking *X* into account. Specifically, two different sums can be found and then compared with the total variation of *Y* to construct a statistic that will indicate the improvement in prediction.

The first sum, called the **explained variation**, represents the improvement in our ability to predict *Y* when taking *X* into account. This sum is found by subtracting $\overline{Y}$ (our predicted *Y* score without *X*) from the score predicted by the regression equation (*Y'*, or the *Y* score predicted with knowledge of *X*) for each case and then squaring and summing these differences. These operations can be summarized as $\Sigma(Y' - \overline{Y})^2$ and the resulting figure could then be compared with the total variation in *Y* to determine the extent to which our knowledge of *X* improves our ability to predict *Y*. Specifically, it can be shown mathematically that

FIGURE 13.7   PREDICTING Y WITH X (dual-career families)

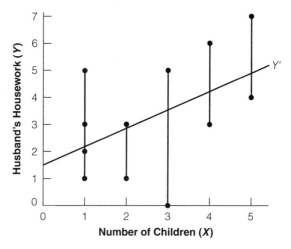

FORMULA 13.7

$$r^2 = \frac{\Sigma(Y' - \overline{Y})^2}{\Sigma(Y - \overline{Y})^2} = \frac{\text{Explained variation}}{\text{Total variation}}$$

Thus, the coefficient of determination, or r^2, is the proportion of the total variation in Y attributable to or explained by X. Like other PRE measures, r^2 indicates precisely the extent to which X helps us predict, understand, or explain Y.

Above, we refer to the improvement in predicting Y with X as the explained variation. The use of this term suggests that some of the variation in Y will be "unexplained" or not attributable to the influence of X. In fact, the vertical lines in Figure 13.7 represent the **unexplained variation**, or the difference between our best prediction of Y with X and the actual scores. The unexplained variation is thus the scattering of the actual scores around the regression line and can be found by subtracting the predicted Y scores from the actual Y scores for each case and then squaring and summing the differences. These operations can be summarized as $\Sigma(Y - Y')^2$ and the resulting sum would measure the amount of error in predicting Y that remains even after X has been taken into account. The proportion of the total variation in Y unexplained by X can be found by subtracting the value of r^2 from 1.00. Unexplained variation is usually attributed to the influence of some combination of other variables, measurement error, and random chance.

As you may have recognized by this time, the explained and unexplained variations bear a reciprocal relationship with each other. As one of these sums increases in value, the other decreases. Furthermore, the stronger the linear relationship between X and Y, the greater the value of the explained variation and the lower the unexplained variation. In the case of a perfect relationship ($r = \pm 1.00$), the unexplained variation would be 0 and r^2 would be 1.00. This would indicate that X explains or accounts for all the variation in Y and that we could predict Y from X without error. On the other hand, when X and Y

are not linearly related ($r = 0.00$), the explained variation would be 0 and r^2 would be 0.00. In such a case, we would conclude that X explains none of the variation in Y and does not improve our ability to predict Y.

Relationships intermediate between these two extremes can be interpreted in terms of how much X increases our ability to predict or explain Y. For the dual-career families, we calculated an r of 0.50. Squaring this value yields a coefficient of determination of 0.25 ($r^2 = 0.25$), which indicates that number of children (X) explains 25% of the total variation in husband's housework (Y). When predicting the number of hours per week that husbands in such families would devote to housework, we will make 25% fewer errors by basing the predictions on number of children and predicting from the regression line, as opposed to ignoring this variable and predicting the mean of Y for every case. Also, 75% of the variation in Y is unexplained by X and presumably due to some combination of the influence of other variables, measurement error, and random chance. (*For practice in the interpretation of r^2, see any of the problems at the end of this chapter.*)

13.7 THE CORRELATION MATRIX

Social science research projects usually include many variables and the data analysis phase of a project often begins with the examination of a correlation matrix, a table that shows the relationships between all possible pairs of variables. The correlation matrix gives a quick, easy-to-read overview of the interrelationships in the data set and may suggest strategies or "leads" for further analysis. These tables are commonly included in the professional research literature and it will be useful to have some experience reading them.

An example of a correlation matrix, using cross-national data, is presented in Table 13.4. The matrix uses variable names as rows and columns and the cells in the table show the bivariate correlation (usually a Pearson's r) for each combination of variables. Note that the row headings duplicate the column headings. To read the table, begin with GDP per capita, the variable in the far left-hand column (column 1) and top row (row 1). Read down column 1 or across row 1 to see the correlations of this variable with all other variables, including the correlation of GDP per capita with itself (1.00) in the top cell. To see the relationships between other variables, move from column to column or row to row.

Note that the diagonal from upper left to lower right of the matrix presents the correlation of each variable with itself. Values along this diagonal will always be exactly 1.00 and, because this information is not useful, it could easily be deleted from the table.

Also note that the cells below and to the left of the diagonal are redundant with the cells above and to the right of the diagonal. For example, look at the second cell down (row 2) in column 1. This cell displays the correlation between GDP per capita and inequality, as does the cell in the top row (row 1) of column 2. In other words, the lower-left-hand part of the table is

TABLE 13.4   A CORRELATION MATRIX SHOWING INTERRELATIONSHIPS
FOR FIVE VARIABLES ACROSS 161 NATIONS

	(1)	(2)	(3)	(4)	(5)
	GDP per Capita	Inequality	Unemployment Rate	Literacy	Voter Turnout
(1) GDP per Capita	1.00	−0.43	−0.34	0.46	0.28
(2) Inequality	−0.43	1.00	0.33	−0.15	−0.36
(3) Unemployment Rate	−0.34	0.33	1.00	−0.48	−0.28
(4) Literacy	0.46	−0.15	−0.48	1.00	0.40
(5) Voter Turnout	0.28	−0.36	−0.28	0.40	1.00

VARIABLES:

(1) *GDP per Capita:* Gross Domestic Product (the total value of all goods and services) divided by population size. This variable is an indicator of the level of affluence and prosperity in the society. Higher scores mean greater prosperity.
(2) *Inequality:* An index of income inequality. Higher scores mean greater inequality.
(3) *Unemployment Rate:* The annual rate of joblessness.
(4) *Literacy:* Number of people over age 15 able to read and write per 1,000 population.
(5) *Voter Turnout:* Percentage of eligible voters who participated in the most recent election.

a mirror image of the upper-right-hand part. Commonly, research articles in the professional literature will delete the redundant cells in order to make the table more readable.

What does this matrix tell us? Starting at the upper left of the table (column 1), we can see that GDP per capita has a strong negative relationship with inequality and unemployment rate, which means that more affluent nations tend to have less inequality and lower rates of joblessness. GDP per capita also has a strong positive relationship with literacy (more affluent nations have higher levels of literacy) and a moderate positive relationship with voter turnout (more affluent nations tend to have higher levels of participation in the electoral process).

To assess the other relationships in the data set, move from column to column and row to row, one variable at a time. For each subsequent variable, there will be one less cell of new information. For example, consider inequality, the variable in column 2 and row 2. We have already noted its strong negative relationship with GDP per capita and, of course, we can ignore the correlation of the variable with itself. This leaves only three new relationships, which can be read by moving down column 2 or across row 2. Inequality has a strong positive relationship with unemployment (the greater the inequality, the greater the unemployment), a moderate negative relationship with literacy (nations with more inequality tend to have lower literacy rates), and a strong negative relationship with voter turnout (the greater the inequality, the lower the turnout).

For unemployment, the variable in column 3, there are only two new relationships: a strong negative correlation with literacy (the higher the

Application 13.2

Are nations that have more educated populations more tolerant? Are more educated nations therefore less likely to see homosexuality as wrong? Random samples from 10 nations have been asked if they agree that homosexuality is "never acceptable."

Information has also been gathered on the average years of school completed for people over 25 in each nation. How are these variables related? The data are presented in the table below. Columns have been added for all necessary sums.

Nation	Average Years of Schooling (X)	Percentage Agreeing that Homosexuality Is "Always Wrong" (Y)	X^2	Y^2	XY
China	6	88	36	7,744	528
Brazil	5	56	25	3,136	280
United States	12	45	144	2,025	540
Japan	10	42	100	1,764	420
Mexico	7	55	49	3,025	385
India	5	77	25	5,929	385
South Africa	6	61	36	3,721	366
Finland	10	37	100	1,369	370
Canada	11	26	121	676	286
Germany	10	15	100	225	150
Totals	82	502	736	29,614	3,710

Source: Data from *World Values Survey and United Nations Human Development Report.*

(continued next page)

unemployment, the lower the literacy) and a moderate negative relationship with voter turnout (the higher the unemployment rate, the lower the turnout). For literacy, the variable in column 4, there is only one new relationship. Literacy has a strong positive relationship with voter turnout (turnout increases as literacy goes up).

In closing, we should note that the cells in a correlation matrix will often include other information in addition to the bivariate correlations. It is common, for example, to include the number of cases on which the correlation is based and, if relevant, an indication of the statistical significance of the relationship.

Application 13.2: *(continued)*

The slope (*b*) is

$$b = \frac{n \sum XY - (\sum X)(\sum Y)}{n \sum X^2 - (\sum X)^2}$$

$$b = \frac{(10)(3,710) - (82)(502)}{(10)(736) - (82)^2}$$

$$b = \frac{37,100 - 41,164}{7,360 - 6,724}$$

$$b = \frac{-4,064}{636}$$

$$b = -6.39$$

A slope of −6.39 means that for every increase in years of education (a unit change in *X*), there is a decrease of 6.39 points in the percentage of people who feel that homosexuality is never justified.

The *Y* intercept (*a*) is

$$a = \overline{Y} - b\overline{X}$$

$$a = \frac{502}{10} - (-6.39)\left(\frac{82}{10}\right)$$

$$a = 50.2 - (-6.39)(8.2)$$

$$a = 50.2 + 52.4$$

$$a = 102.6$$

The least-squares regression equation is

$$Y = a + bX = 102.6 + (-6.39)X$$

The correlation coefficient is

$$r = \frac{n \sum XY - (\sum X)(\sum Y)}{\sqrt{[n \sum X^2 - (\sum X)^2][n \sum Y^2 - (\sum Y)^2]}}$$

$$r = \frac{(10)(3,710) - (82)(502)}{\sqrt{[(10)(736) - (82)^2][(10)(29,614) - (502)^2]}}$$

$$r = \frac{37,100 - 41,164}{\sqrt{(7,360 - 6,724)(296,140 - 252,004)}}$$

$$r = \frac{-4,064}{\sqrt{(636)(44,136)}}$$

$$r = \frac{-4,064}{\sqrt{28,070,7496}}$$

$$r = \frac{-4,064}{5,298.16}$$

$$r = -0.77$$

For these 10 nations, education and disapproval of homosexuality have a strong, negative relationship. Disapproval of homosexuality decreases as education increases. The coefficient of determination, r^2, is $(0.77)^2$, or 0.59. This indicates that 59% of the variance in attitude toward homosexuality is explained by education for this sample of 10 nations.

13.8 TESTING PEARSON'S *r* FOR SIGNIFICANCE

When the relationship measured by Pearson's *r* is based on data from a random sample, it will usually be necessary to test *r* for its statistical significance. That is, we will need to know if a relationship between the variables can be assumed to exist in the population from which the sample was drawn. To illustrate this test, the *r* of 0.50 from the dual-wage-earner family sample will be used. As was the case when testing gamma and Spearman's rho, the null hypothesis states that there is no linear association between the two variables in the population from which the sample was drawn. The population parameter is symbolized as ρ (rho), and the appropriate sampling distribution is the *t* distribution.

To conduct this test, we need to make a number of assumptions in step 1. Most should be quite familiar, but several are new. First, we must assume that both variables are normal in distribution **(bivariate normal distributions)**. Second, we must assume that the relationship between the two variables is roughly linear in form.

The third assumption involves a new concept: **homoscedasticity**. Basically, a homoscedastic relationship is one where the variance of the Y scores is uniform for all values of X. That is, if the Y scores are evenly spread above and below the regression line for the entire length of the line, the relationship is homoscedastic.

A visual inspection of the scattergram will usually be sufficient to appraise the extent to which the relationship conforms to the assumptions of linearity and homoscedasticity. As a rule of thumb, if the data points fall in a roughly symmetrical, cigar-shaped pattern, whose shape can be approximated with a straight line, then it is appropriate to proceed with this test of significance. Any significant evidence of non-linearity or marked departures from homoscedasticity may indicate the need for an alternative measure of association and thus a different test of significance.

Step 1. Making Assumptions and Meeting Test Requirements.

> Model: Random sampling
> Level of measurement is interval-ratio
> Bivariate normal distributions
> Linear relationship
> Homoscedasticity
> Sampling distribution is normal

Step 2. Stating the Null Hypothesis.

$$H_0: \rho = 0.0$$
$$(H_1: \rho \neq 0.0)$$

Step 3. Selecting the Sampling Distribution and Establishing the Critical Region. With the null of "no relationship" in the population, the sampling distribution of all possible sample r's is approximated by the t distribution. Degrees of freedom are equal to $(n - 2)$.

> Sampling distribution = t distribution
> Alpha = 0.05
> Degrees of freedom = $n - 2 = 10$
> t(critical) = ± 2.28

Step 4. Computing the Test Statistic. The formula for computing the test statistic is given in Formula 13.8.

FORMULA 13.8

$$t(\text{obtained}) = r\sqrt{\frac{n - 2}{1 - r^2}}$$

Substituting the values into the formula, we would have:

$$t(\text{obtained}) = (0.50)\sqrt{\frac{12 - 2}{1 - (0.50)^2}}$$

$$t(\text{obtained}) = (0.50)\sqrt{\frac{10}{0.75}}$$

$$t(\text{obtained}) = (0.50)(3.65)$$

$$t(\text{obtained}) = 1.83$$

Step 5. **Making a Decision and Interpreting the Results of the Test.** Because the test statistic does not fall into the critical region as marked by t(critical), we fail to reject the null hypothesis. We do not have sufficient evidence to conclude that the variables are related in the population. The test indicates that the sample value of $r = 0.50$ could have occurred by chance alone if the null hypothesis is true and the variables are unrelated in the population. *(For practice in conducting and interpreting tests of significance with Pearson's r, see problems 13.1, 13.2, 13.4, 13.5, 13.8, and 13.9.)*

13.9 REGRESSION WITH NOMINAL- AND ORDINAL-LEVEL VARIABLES

A key assumption underlying the regression techniques discussed in this chapter is that both the independent and dependent variables are measured at the interval-ratio level. Still, there is a way to include nominal- or ordinal-level independent variables in the regression analysis. The solution is to treat these variables as dummy variables—variables with only two values (0 and 1). We do not use this approach, however, when the dependent variable is nominal or ordinal. Instead, we can use a technique related to least-squares regression called logistic regression. The logic and computational routines for the dummy variable solution and logistic regression are covered in detail on the website for this textbook.

13.10 INTERPRETING STATISTICS: THE CORRELATES OF CRIME

What causes crime? Sociologists have been researching this question since the discipline was founded. While we cannot contribute to this voluminous body of work in a textbook devoted to statistical analysis, we can investigate some of the relationships and correlations that are of continuing interest to criminologists.

One school of criminological thought argues that crime is related to poverty. A central proposition of this approach might be phrased as: "Crime rates will be highest among the most disadvantaged and impoverished groups, those with the highest rates of unemployment and the lowest levels of 'economic viability' (job skills, levels of education) in the legitimate economy." In this installment of Interpreting Statistics, we will take a look at the empirical relationship between a measure of criminality and a measure of poverty in Canada.

The units of analysis will be Canada's largest cities, called CMAs or Census Metropolitan Areas. A CMA is defined as an area consisting of one or more adjacent municipalities surrounding a major urban core with a population of at least 100,000. To make the data comparable, only those CMAs with populations of 500,000 and over are examined.

We will use the police-reported crime rate (i.e., criminal offences reported to police per 100,000 population) in the year 2000 as an indicator of criminal activity as the dependent variable. Police-reported crime data are gathered by the Uniform Crime Reporting survey of the Canadian Centre for Justice Statistics at Statistics Canada. The reader should note that police-reported crime is not a perfect measure of crime. Victimization surveys usually produce higher rates of criminal activity than police-reported statistics. This is because victimization surveys collect crime information directly from the population, whether or not it has been reported to police. (There are various reasons why victims of criminal incidents do not report incidents to the police, including the seriousness of the incident, the victim's reluctance to get police involved, the belief that police cannot or will not do much, and fear of reprisals.) As the independent variable of our exercise, we will use the percentage of the population living below the poverty line in the year 2000.

The scores and basic descriptive statistics for the variables are reported in Table 13.5. On crime, cities range from a high of 11,210 offences per 100,000 population in Vancouver to a low of 5,108 per 100,000 population in Quebec City. Poverty rates range from a high of 22.3% in Montreal to a low of 14.3% in Calgary.

The first step in assessing an association between interval-ratio-level variables is to produce a scattergram. Figure 13.8 plots the crime rate on the vertical or Y axis and the poverty rate along the horizontal or X axis. What can we say

TABLE 13.5 SCORES ON POVERTY AND CRIME FOR NINE CANADIAN CITIES, WITH DESCRIPTIVE STATISTICS

City	Crime Rate[1] (Y)	Poverty Rate[2] (X)
Calgary	7,115	14.3
Edmonton	8,377	16.5
Hamilton	6,565	17.0
Montreal	7,234	22.3
Ottawa	5,680	15.0
Quebec	5,108	18.9
Toronto	5,290	16.7
Vancouver	11,210	20.8
Winnipeg	10,377	19.8
Mean	7,449	17.9
Standard Deviation	2,173	2.7
Range	6,102	8.0

[1]Number of criminal offences per 100,000 population, 2000.
[2]Percentage of population living below the poverty line, 2000.

Source: Data from Statistics Canada, *Crime Statistics in Canada*, 2000 (2001). Catalogue no. 85-002-XIE (Crime rate); and Statistics Canada, *2001 Canadian Census*, individual PUMF (Poverty rate).

FIGURE 13.8   CRIME RATE BY POVERTY RATE FOR NINE CANADIAN CITIES

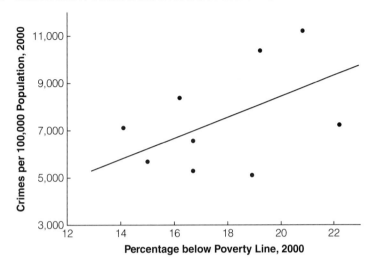

about this relationship? The regression line is not horizontal, so there is a relationship between these variables. The dots (cities) are fairly well scattered around the regression line, and we can see immediately that this will be, at best, a moderately strong relationship. The regression line slopes up from left to right, so this is a positive relationship: Cities that have higher poverty rates tend to have higher crime rates (or, crime rates tend to increase as poverty rates increase).

The second step in assessing this relationship is to specify the regression line. We will skip the mechanics of computation here and simply report the values for the regression coefficients (a and b).

$$Y = a + bX$$
$$Y = 744 + (374)X$$

The regression line will cross the Y axis at the point where $Y = 744$. In other words, when the poverty rate is 0%, the number of criminal offences per 100,000 population is 744. The slope of the regression, b, is 374. That is, every unit (i.e., percentage) increase in X (poverty rate) increases the number of criminal offences by 374 per 100,000 population.

Next, we will calculate and interpret Pearson's r. Again, we will skip the details of the computation and report that $r = 0.47$, which reinforces the impression that there is a moderately strong relationship between crime and poverty rates. The coefficient of determination (r^2) is about 0.22, which means that poverty rate, by itself, explains about 22% of the variation in the crime rate.

In sum, the linear regression equation, the correlation coefficient, and the coefficient of determination suggest that there is a moderately strong relationship between poverty and crime. The amount of unexplained variation (78%) suggests that many other variables besides poverty have an influence on the crime rate.

We should also note two other limitations of this simple test. First, correlation is not the same thing as causation. Just because two variables are correlated does not mean that they have a causal relationship. Second, a related point, a criminal offence is by definition an individual act of behaviour, but the data we used in this test was collected from cities. Just because there is an association between the variables at the macro (city) level does not necessarily mean that the variables are related in the same way at the micro (individual) level. (This problem is called the *ecological fallacy*.) All we know from our analysis is that cities with higher rates of poverty tend to have higher rates of crime. Our theory would lead us to assume that it is the victims of poverty (poor people) who are the offenders, but this conclusion is not proven by this analysis. It may also be the wealthier residents of the poorer cities who are committing the crimes. We would need much more information—on both the micro and macro levels—before we develop final conclusions on the relation between poverty and crime.

SUMMARY

This summary is based on the example used throughout the chapter.

1. We began with a question: Is the number of children in dual-wage-earner families related to the number of hours per week husbands devote to housework? We presented the observations in a scattergram (see Figure 13.1), and our visual impression was that the variables were associated in a positive direction. The pattern formed by the observation points in the scattergram could be approximated with a straight line, thus, the relationship was roughly linear.

2. Values of Y can be predicted with the free-hand regression line, but predictions are more accurate if the least-squares regression line is used. The least-squares regression line is the line that best fits the data by minimizing the variation in Y. Using the formula that defines the least-squares regression line ($Y = a + bX$), we found a slope (b) of 0.69, which indicates that each additional child (a unit change in X) is accompanied by an increase of 0.69 hour of housework per week for the husbands. We also predicted, based on this formula, that in a dual-wage-earner family with six children ($X = 6$), husbands would contribute 5.63 hours of housework a week ($Y' = 5.63$ for $X = 6$).

3. Pearson's r is a statistic that measures the overall linear association between X and Y. Our impression from the scattergram of a substantial positive relationship was confirmed by the computed r of 0.50. We also saw that this relationship yields an r^2 of 0.25, which indicates that 25% of the total variation in Y (husband's housework) is accounted for or explained by X (number of children).

4. Assuming that the 12 families represented a random sample, we tested the Pearson's r for its statistical significance and found that, at the 0.05 level, we could not assume that these two variables were also related in the population.

5. We acquired a great deal of information about this bivariate relationship. We know the strength and direction of the relationship and have also identified the regression line that best summarizes the effect of X on Y. We know the amount of change we can expect in Y for a unit change in X. In short, we have a greater volume of more precise information

about this association between interval-ratio variables than we ever did about associations between ordinal or nominal variables. This is possible, of course, because the data generated by interval-ratio measurement are more precise and flexible than those produced by ordinal or nominal measurement techniques.

SUMMARY OF FORMULAS

Least-squares regression line:

13.1 $Y = a + bX$

Definitional formula for the slope:

13.2 $b = \dfrac{\Sigma(X - \overline{X})(Y - \overline{Y})}{\Sigma(X - \overline{X})^2}$

Computational formula for the slope:

13.3 $b = \dfrac{n\,\Sigma XY - (\Sigma X)(\Sigma Y)}{n\,\Sigma X^2 - (\Sigma X)^2}$

Y intercept:

13.4 $a = \overline{Y} - b\overline{X}$

Definitional formula for Pearson's r:

13.5 $r = \dfrac{\Sigma(X - \overline{X})(Y - \overline{Y})}{\sqrt{[\Sigma(X - \overline{X})^2][\Sigma(Y - \overline{Y})^2]}}$

Computational formula for Pearson's r:

13.6 $r = \dfrac{n\,\Sigma XY - (\Sigma X)(\Sigma Y)}{\sqrt{[n\,\Sigma X^2 - (\Sigma X)^2][n\,\Sigma Y^2 - (\Sigma Y)^2]}}$

Coefficient of determination:

13.7 $r^2 = \dfrac{\Sigma(Y' - \overline{Y})^2}{\Sigma(Y - \overline{Y})^2}$

13.8 $t(\text{obtained}) = r\sqrt{\dfrac{n - 2}{1 - r^2}}$

GLOSSARY

Bivariate normal distributions. The model assumption in the test of significance for Pearson's r that both variables are normally distributed. (p. 388)

Coefficient of determination (r^2). The proportion of all variation in Y that is explained by X. Found by squaring the value of Pearson's r. (p. 381)

Conditional means of Y. The mean of all scores on Y for each value of X. (p. 374)

Explained variation. The proportion of all variation in Y that is attributed to the effect of X. Equal to $\Sigma(Y' - \overline{Y})^2$. (p. 382)

Homoscedasticity. The model assumption in the test of significance for Pearson's r that the variance of the Y scores is uniform across all values of X. (p. 388)

Linear relationship. A relationship between two variables in which the observation points (dots) in the scattergram can be approximated with a straight line. (p. 372)

Pearson's r (r). A measure of association for variables that have been measured at the interval-ratio level; ρ (Greek letter rho) is the symbol for the population value of Pearson's r. (p. 379)

Regression line. The single best-fitting straight line that summarizes the relationship between two variables. Regression lines are fitted to the data points by the least-squares criterion, whereby the line touches all conditional means of Y or comes as close to doing so as possible. (p. 371)

Scattergram. Graphic display device that depicts the relationship between two variables. (p. 370)

Slope (b). The amount of change in one variable per unit change in the other; b is the symbol for the slope of a regression line. (p. 376)

Total variation. The spread of the Y scores around the mean of Y. Equal to $\Sigma(Y - \overline{Y})^2$. (p. 381)

Unexplained variation. The proportion of the total variation in Y that is not accounted for by X. Equal to $\Sigma(Y - Y')^2$. (p. 383)

Y intercept (a). The point where the regression line crosses the Y axis. (p. 375)

Y'. Symbol for predicted score on Y. (p. 373)

MULTIMEDIA RESOURCES

http://www.healeystatistics.nelson.com

Visit the companion website for the second Canadian edition of *Statistics: A Tool for Social Research* to access a wide range of student resources. Begin by clicking on the Student Resources section of the textbook's website to access review quizzes, flashcards, and other study tools.

PROBLEMS

13.1 PS Why does voter turnout vary from election to election? For municipal elections in five different cities, information has been gathered on the percentage of eligible voters who actually voted, unemployment rate, average years of education for the city, and the percentage of all political ads that used "negative campaigning" (personal attacks, negative portrayals of the opponent's record, etc.). For each relationship:

a. Draw a scattergram and a freehand regression line.

b. Compute the slope (b) and find the Y intercept (a). (*HINT: Remember to compute b before computing a. A computing table such as Table 13.3 is highly recommended.*)

c. State the least-squares regression line and predict the voter turnout for a city in which the unemployment rate was 12, a city in which the average years of schooling was 11, and an election in which 90% of the ads were negative.

d. Compute r and r^2. (*HINT: A computing table such as Table 13.3 is highly recommended. If you constructed one for computing b, you already have most of the quantities you will need to solve for r.*)

e. Assume these cities are a random sample and conduct a test of significance for each relationship.

f. Describe the strength and direction of the relationships in a sentence or two. Which

(if any) relationships were significant? Which factor had the strongest effect on turnout?

TURNOUT AND UNEMPLOYMENT

City	Turnout	Unemployment Rate
A	55	5
B	60	8
C	65	9
D	68	9
E	70	10

TURNOUT AND LEVEL OF EDUCATION

City	Turnout	Average Years of School
A	55	11.9
B	60	12.1
C	65	12.7
D	68	12.8
E	70	13.0

TURNOUT AND NEGATIVE CAMPAIGNING

City	Turnout	Percentage of Negative Advertisements
A	55	60
B	60	63
C	65	55
D	68	53
E	70	48

13.2 SOC Occupational prestige scores (higher scores indicate greater prestige) for a sample of fathers and their oldest son and oldest daughter are shown in the table.

Family	Father's Prestige	Son's Prestige	Daughter's Prestige
A	80	85	82
B	78	80	77
C	75	70	68
D	70	75	77
E	69	72	60
F	66	60	52
G	64	48	48
H	52	55	57

Analyze the relationship between father's and son's prestige and the relationship between father's and daughter's prestige. For each relationship:

a. Draw a scattergram and a freehand regression line.

b. Compute the slope (b) and find the Y intercept (a).

c. State the least-squares regression line. What prestige score would you predict for a son whose father had a prestige score of 72? What prestige score would you predict for a daughter whose father had a prestige score of 72?

d. Compute r and r^2.

e. Assume these families are a random sample and conduct a test of significance for both relationships.

f. Describe the strength and direction of the relationships in a sentence or two. Does the occupational prestige of the father have an impact on his children? Does it have the same impact for daughters as it does for sons?

13.3 GER The residents of a housing development for senior citizens have completed a survey on which they indicated how physically active they are and how many visitors they receive each week. Are these two variables related for the 10 cases reported on the following table? Draw a scattergram and compute r and r^2. Find the least-squares regression line. What would be the predicted number of visitors for a person whose level of activity was a 5? How about a person who scored 18 on level of activity?

Case	Level of Activity	Number of Visitors
A	10	14
B	11	12
C	12	10
D	10	9
E	15	8
F	9	7
G	7	10
H	3	15
I	10	12
J	9	2

13.4 PS The variables below were collected for a random sample of 10 electoral districts during the last federal election. Draw scattergrams and compute r and r^2 for each combination of variables and test the correlations for their significance. Write a paragraph interpreting the relationship between these variables.

District	Percentage Working-class	Unemployment Rate	Voter Turnout
A	50	10	56
B	45	12	55
C	56	8	52
D	78	15	60
E	13	5	89
F	85	20	25
G	62	18	64
H	33	9	88
I	25	0	42
J	49	9	36

13.5 SOC/CJ The table below presents the scores of 10 randomly selected Canadian cities on each of six variables: three measures of criminal activity and three measures of population structure. Crime rates are the number of incidents per 100,000 population. For each combination of crime rate and population characteristic:

a. Draw a scattergram and a freehand regression line.

b. Compute the slope (b) and find the Y intercept (a).

c. State the least-squares regression line. What homicide rate would you predict for a city with a growth rate of -1? What robbery rate would you predict for a city with a population density of 250? What auto theft rate would you predict for a city in which 50% of the population lived in the urban core?

City	Crime Rates			Population		
	Homicide	Robbery	Auto Theft	Growth[1]	Density[2]	Urbanization[3]
A	1	19	104	3.8	41.7	52.6
B	5	214	286	5.5	402.7	92.1
C	4	138	344	4.7	277.8	81.2
D	2	37	184	5.4	52.3	45.3
E	6	89	252	14.4	181.5	78.1
F	5	81	230	9.6	102.3	48.8
G	6	145	447	22.8	81.5	84.8
H	7	146	842	40.0	46.7	88.2
I	3	99	594	21.1	90.0	83.1
J	6	178	537	13.6	221.2	96.7

[1]Percentage change in population over the last 10 years.
[2]Population per square kilometre of land area.
[3]Percentage of population living in urban core.

Source: Data from U.S. Bureau of the Census, *Statistical Abstracts of the United States: 2001*, (Washington, DC, 2002).

d. Compute r and r^2.

e. Since these cities come from a random sample, conduct a test of significance for both relationships.

f. Describe the strength and direction of each of these relationships in a sentence or two.

13.6 SOC Data on three variables have been collected for 15 nations. The variables are fertility rate (average number of children born to each woman), average education for females (expressed as a percentage of average education for men), and maternal mortality (death rate for mothers per 100,000 live births). On female education, a value of 100 means that men and women have equal levels of education, values over 100 mean that women have more education and values less than 100 mean that women have less education than men.

Nation	Fertility	Education of Females	Maternal Mortality
Niger	7.2	50	590
Cambodia	4.8	74	470
Guatemala	4.7	86	190
Ghana	4.0	46	210
Bolivia	3.7	60	390
Egypt	3.2	41	170
Dominican Republic	3.0	87	230
Mexico	2.7	96	55
Vietnam	2.5	59	130
Turkey	2.2	49	130
United States	2.1	102	8

(continued in next column)

(continued)

Nation	Fertility	Education of Females	Maternal Mortality
China	1.8	60	55
Canada	1.7	102	7
Japan	1.4	98	8
Italy	1.2	99	7

a. Compute r and r^2 for each combination of variables.

b. Summarize these relationships in terms of strength and direction.

13.7 SOC The basketball coach at a university believes that his team plays better and scores more points in front of larger crowds. The number of points scored and attendance for all home games last season are reported below. Do these data support the coach's argument?

Game	Points Scored	Attendance
1	54	378
2	57	350
3	59	320
4	80	478
5	82	451
6	75	250
7	73	489
8	53	451
9	67	410
10	78	215
11	67	113
12	56	250
13	85	450
14	101	489
15	99	472

13.8 SOC The table below presents the scores of 15 large Canadian cities on three variables. Compute r and r^2 for each combination of variables. Assume that these 15 cities are a random sample of Canada's 50 largest cities and test the correlations for their significance. Write a paragraph interpreting the relationship among these three variables.

City	Per Capita Expenditures on Education	Percentage High School Graduates[1]	Rank in Per Capita Income
A	1,102	82	48
B	1,339	90	7
C	1,907	88	1
D	1,171	84	25
E	1,621	86	9
F	1,276	88	24
G	1,159	81	45
H	1,412	86	5
I	1,487	86	18
J	1,041	80	50
K	1,194	90	22
L	1,262	88	6
M	1,163	79	32
N	1,223	86	15
O	1,549	90	20

[1]Based on percentage of population age 25 and older.

13.9 SOC A social survey was administered to a random sample of adults. Fifteen individuals were then randomly selected from the sample. Their scores on five of the variables in the survey are reproduced below. Is there a relationship between occupational prestige (higher scores indicate greater prestige) and age? Between number of times religious service attended (per month) and number of children? Between number of children and hours of TV watching (per day)? Between age and hours of TV watching? Between age and number of children? Between hours of TV watching and occupational prestige? Which of these relationships are significant?

Occupational Prestige	Number of Children	Age	Religious Service Attendance per Month	Hours of TV per Day
32	3	34	3	1
50	0	41	0	3
17	0	52	7	2
69	3	67	0	5
17	0	40	0	5
52	0	22	2	3
32	3	31	0	4
50	0	23	8	4
19	9	64	1	6
37	4	55	0	2
14	3	66	5	5
51	0	22	6	0
45	0	19	3	7
44	0	21	4	1
46	4	58	2	0

SPSS for Windows

Using SPSS for Windows to Produce Pearson's *r* and the Regression Line with the 2006 Census

The demonstrations and exercises below use the shortened version of the 2006 Census data. Start SPSS for Windows and open the *Census.sav* file.

SPSS DEMONSTRATION 13.1 The Scattergram

The scattergram provides a convenient look at the relationship between two variables. Here we will examine the effect of *hhsize* (number of persons in household) on *value* (value of dwelling) with the scattergram. Click **Graphs**, **Legacy Dialogs**, and then **Scatter/Dot**. The **Scatter/Dot** dialog box appears with five choices. We want the **Simple Scatter**, so highlight this option and click **Define**. The **Simple Scatterplot** dialog box appears. Transfer the dependent variable, *value*, to the **Y Axis** box, and the independent variable, *hhsize,* to the **X Axis** box. Click **OK**, and the following scattergram will be produced.

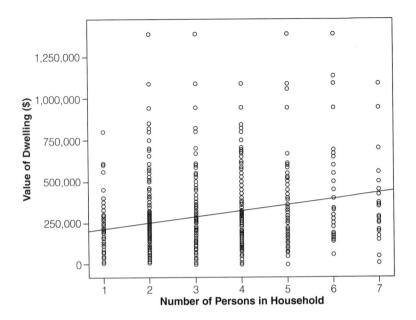

We added the least-squares regression line to the scattergram to provide a better sense of the relationship between the variables. To do this, double-click on any part of the scattergram to open the **Chart Editor** window. Then, click the **Elements** menu and choose **Fit Line at Total**. Close the **Chart Editor** window to return to the **Output** window.

The regression line tells us that a relationship exists, and that it is positive in direction. As household size increases, house value increases. However, the strength and linearity (whether the data points approximate a straight line) of this relationship are more difficult to detect because the overall pattern of the dots around the regression line is obscured by overlapping data points (respondents with identical values on both the independent and dependent variable).

It is difficult to eliminate completely the problem of overplotting. One way to reduce the problem is to "jitter" the data, that is, to subtract or add a small random quantity to each value of the independent and dependent variable. Data points will be separated by this quantity, reducing the overlap and making it easier to assess the strength and linearity of the relationship in the scattergram. Jittering disentangles overlapping data points and, in many cases, makes it possible to assess the nature of a relationship.

A second and more practical way to reduce overlap and assess the strength and linearity of a relationship is to take a random sample from the larger sample, and then get a scattergram from that sample. This will greatly reduce the number of cases and make the scattergram easier to read. To do this, click **Data** from the menu bar of the **Data Editor** window and click **Select Cases**. Next, click the **Random sample of cases** button and then the **Sample** button. Request a 2% random sample by typing 2 into the box on the first line. (You can request a smaller or larger sample, but 2% should work well in most cases.) Click **Continue**, and then

OK to draw the random sample. Then, use the **Simple Scatter** procedure once again, and the output will look similar to this:

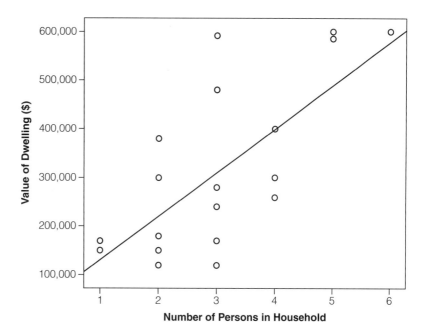

The nature of the relationship between the two variables is now exposed. The pattern of dots on the scattergram indicates a moderate, positive linear relationship between the value of the house and the number of people residing in a house. The scores of Y are also evenly spread at each value of X, indicating the relationship is homoscedastic.

If you carry out this demonstration, your output will be based on a different set of randomly selected cases, so your scattergram will look slightly different. You may wish to repeat the steps above several times to get a better sense of the nature of the relationship; each time you want to produce a new random sample and scatterplot, go back to the **Select Cases** dialog box and click the **OK** button.

SPSS DEMONSTRATION 13.2 Assessing the Effect of Household Size on the Value of a House with Linear Regression

After assessing the nature and verifying the linearity of the relationship with the scattergram, we can proceed to find the slope (b) and the Y intercept (a) of the least-squares regression line. In this demonstration, we will continue to examine the relationship between household size and house price. (Make sure that the random sample filter is turned off by clicking the **Reset** button and then **OK** in the **Select Cases** dialog box.) Click **Analyze**, **Regression**, and **Linear**. In the **Linear Regression** window, move *value* into the **Dependent** box and *hhsize* into the **Independent(s)** box. Click **OK**, and the following output will appear.

Model Summary

Model	R	R Square	Adjusted R Square	Std. Error of the Estimate
1	.210[a]	.044	.043	236154.516

a. Predictors: (Constant), Number of persons in household

ANOVA[a]

Model		Sum of Squares	df	Mean Square	F	Sig.
1	Regression	2.796E + 12	1	2.796E + 12	50.144	.000[b]
	Residual	6.068E + 13	1088	55768955275		
	Total	6.347E + 13	1089			

a. Dependent Variable: Value of dwelling
b. Predictors: (Constant), Number of persons in household

Coefficients[a]

Model		Unstandardized Coefficients		Standardized Coefficients	t	Sig.
		B	Std. Error	Beta		
1	(Constant)	179039.520	17579.807		10.184	.000
	Number of persons in household	36359.876	5134.674	.210	7.081	.000

a. Dependent Variable: Value of dwelling

The "Model Summary" block reports Pearson's r (.210) and r square (.044). The "ANOVA" output block shows the significance of the relationship (Sig. = .000). Recall that when the exact probability value is less than .0005, SPSS cuts it off at three decimal places, or .000, to save space. Because we have the exact probability, there is no need to look up the test statistic in a table. The exact probability value, .000, is well below the standard indicator of a significant result (alpha = .05), so we reject the null hypothesis and conclude that there is a statistically significant relationship between household size and house value. (See Demonstration 6.1 for an explanation about why some values in the output contain numbers with the letter "E".)

So far, we know that the independent variable explains 4.4% of the variance in *value* and that this result is statistically significant. In the last output block, we see the slope (B) is 36359.876 and the Y intercept (labelled as Constant) is 179039.520. A slope of 36359.876 means that for every increase of one person in household size, the average price of a house increases by $36,360. Accordingly, the value of a two-person house is worth on average $36,360 more than a one-person house, the value of a three-person house is worth on average $36,360 more than a two-person house, and so on. The Y intercept tells us that the average value of a house is $179,040 when household size is zero. Y intercept has no meaningful interpretation because household size cannot be zero. Finally, we can use the least-squares regression line $Y = a + bX$, or $Y = (179{,}040) + (36{,}360)X$, to predict scores on *value* for any value of *hhsize*.

Exercises (using *Census.sav*)

13.1 Use the **Select Cases** command illustrated in Demonstration 13.1 to take a 2% random sample from the larger sample.

Next, use the **Scatter/Dot** procedure to examine the relationship between *hhsize*, the independent variable or "X Axis," and *grosrt*, the dependent variable or "Y Axis." What does the scattergram reveal about the nature (linearity, strength, and direction) of the relationship between the number of persons in the household and what tenants pay in monthly rent? Write up your results.

13.2 Conduct the analysis in Demonstration 13.2 again, but with *grosrt* (rent) as the dependent variable. Does *hhsize* (household size) have an effect on *grosrt* as it did with *value*?

1. For each situation, compute and interpret the appropriate measure of association. Also, compute and interpret percentages for bivariate tables. Describe relationships in terms of the strength and pattern or direction.

   a. For 10 Canadian cities data has been gathered on rates of property crime (theft, breaking and entering, fraud) per 100,000 population and the percentage of people who are new immigrants (arrived in Canada within the past five years). Are the variables related?

City	Property Crime Rate	Percentage Immigrants
A	1,500	10
B	1,200	18
C	2,000	9
D	1,700	11
E	1,600	15
F	1,000	20
G	1,700	9
H	1,300	22
I	900	10
J	700	15

   b. There is some evidence that people's involvement in their communities (membership in voluntary organizations, participation in local politics, and so forth) has been declining, and television has been cited as the cause. Do the data below support the idea that TV is responsible for the decline?

Hours of Community Service	Television Viewing			Totals
	Low	Moderate	High	
Low	5	10	18	33
Moderate	10	12	10	32
High	15	8	7	30
Totals	30	30	35	95

   c. An international magazine has rated countries in terms of "quality of life" (a scale that includes health care, availability of leisure facilities, unemployment rate, and a number of other variables) and quality of the system of higher education. Both scales range from 1 (low) to 20 (high). Is there a correlation between these two variables for the 10 countries listed below?

Country	Quality of Life	Quality of Higher Education
A	10	10
B	12	13
C	15	18

(*continued*)

Country	Quality of Life	Quality of Higher Education
D	18	20
E	10	15
F	9	11
G	11	12
H	8	6
I	13	9
J	6	8

d. The number of Canadian employees doing telework—scheduled work from home—has grown sharply over the last decade, with advancements in information technology and telecommunications. The table below shows the relationship between marital status and telework arrangement, if any, for a random sample of Canadian employees. Is there a relationship between these variables?

Do You Work from Home?	Marital Status			
	Married/ Common-law	Separated/ Divorced/ Widowed	Single	Totals
Yes, but not regularly	2	0	3	5
Yes, 1–2 days each week	8	4	0	12
Yes, 3 or more days each week	0	3	3	6
No	10	8	4	22
Totals	20	15	10	45

2. A number of research questions are stated below. Each can be answered by at least one of the techniques presented in Chapters 11 through 13. For each research situation, use the social survey data collected from 25 respondents shown below to compute the most appropriate measure of association and write a sentence or two of response to the question. The questions are presented in random order. In selecting a measure of association, you need to consider the number of possible values and the level of measurement of the variables.

a. Are scores on "number of sex partners over the past year" associated with education or age? Compute a measure of association, assuming that the variables are interval-ratio in level of measurement.

b. Is fear of walking alone at night associated with sex? Is it associated with marital status?

c. Is support for spanking associated with religious service attendance? Is it associated with marital status?

Survey Items:

1. Marital status of respondent:
   1. Married
   2. Not married (includes widowed, divorced, etc.)
2. How often do you attend religious service?
   0. Never
   1. Rarely
   2. Often
3. Age.
4. Respondent's years of education.
5. Sex:
   1. Male
   2. Female
6. It is sometimes necessary to discipline a child with a spanking:
   1. Support
   2. Oppose
7. Fear of walking alone at night:
   1. Yes
   2. No
8. Number of sex partners over the past year.

Case	Marital Status	Religious Service Attendance	Age	Education	Sex	Spanking	Fear	Number of Sex Partners
1	2	0	22	12	2	1	2	5
2	1	0	52	13	1	1	2	2
3	1	2	44	16	1	2	1	3
4	1	0	56	10	1	1	2	1
5	1	2	61	8	2	2	2	0
6	1	0	28	19	2	1	2	5
7	2	1	59	9	1	2	1	0
8	1	1	69	11	1	2	2	5
9	2	0	23	4	1	1	2	6
10	2	2	31	20	2	1	1	6
11	1	2	67	21	2	2	1	1
12	1	1	46	9	1	1	1	2
13	2	0	19	10	2	1	1	5
14	1	2	34	11	1	2	2	2
15	2	0	29	18	2	1	1	4
16	1	1	31	16	1	1	1	5
17	2	1	88	6	2	2	2	1
18	1	0	24	15	2	1	1	4
19	2	2	69	11	1	1	1	2
20	1	2	60	14	1	2	2	3
21	1	1	29	12	2	1	2	4
22	1	2	43	13	2	2	1	2
23	1	0	35	20	1	1	1	4
24	2	2	38	9	2	2	2	4
25	2	0	83	19	1	2	1	0

Multivariate Techniques

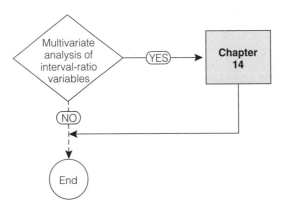

Few research questions can be answered by a statistical analysis of only two variables, and therefore, the typical research project will include many variables. In Chapters 11 through 13, we saw how various statistical techniques can be applied to bivariate relationships. In Chapter 14, we will see how the regression techniques presented in Chapter 13 can be extended to probe the relationships among three or more variables measured at the interval-ratio level of measurement. (Techniques presented in Chapters 11 and 12 can also be extended to probe the relationships among three or more nominal- or ordinal-level variables. These multivariate techniques are covered on the website for this textbook.)

The multivariate techniques presented in Chapter 14 produce some of the most powerful and useful statistics available to social science researchers. The mathematics underlying these statistics can become very complicated, and the chapter focuses on the simplest possible applications. Furthermore, clearly labelled subsections divide the presentation of basic concepts and interpretation from the computations.

Before considering the techniques themselves, we should consider why they are important and what they might be able to tell us. There are two general reasons for utilizing multivariate techniques. First, and most fundamental, is the goal of simply gathering additional information about a specific bivariate relationship by observing how that relationship is affected (if at all) by the presence of a third variable (or a fourth or a fifth variable). Multivariate techniques will increase the amount of information we have on the basic bivariate relationship and (we hope) enhance our understanding of that relationship. A second and strongly related rationale for multivariate statistics involves the issue of causation. While multivariate statistical techniques cannot prove the existence of causal connections between variables, they can provide valuable evidence in support of causal arguments and are very important tools for testing and revising theory.

14

Partial Correlation and Multiple Regression and Correlation

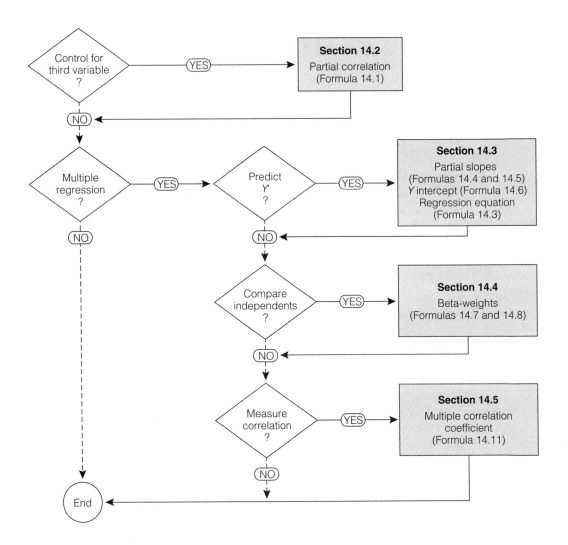

LEARNING OBJECTIVES

By the end of this chapter, you will be able to

1. Compute and interpret partial correlation coefficients.
2. Recognize and interpret direct or spurious and intervening relationships.

3. Find and interpret the least-squares multiple regression equation with partial slopes.
4. Calculate and interpret the multiple correlation coefficient (R^2).
5. Explain the limitations of partial and multiple regression analysis.

14.1 INTRODUCTION

Very few (if any) worthwhile research questions can be answered through a statistical analysis of only two variables. Social science research is, by nature, multivariate and often involves the simultaneous analysis of scores of variables. Some of the most powerful and widely used statistical tools for multivariate analysis of interval-ratio variables are introduced in this chapter. (Other techniques, namely those designed to be used with nominal- and ordinal-level variables, are covered on the website for this textbook.) We will cover techniques that are used to analyze causal relationships and to make predictions, both crucial endeavours in any science.

These techniques are based on the regression and correlation techniques presented in Chapter 13. We will first consider partial correlation analysis, a technique that allows us to examine a bivariate relationship while controlling for a third variable. The second technique involves multiple regression and correlation and allows the researcher to assess the effects, separately and in combination, of more than one independent variable on the dependent variable.

Throughout this chapter, we will focus on research situations involving three variables. This is the least complex application of these techniques but extensions to situations involving four or more variables are relatively straightforward. To deal efficiently with the computations required by the more complex applications, we refer you to any of the computerized statistical packages (such as SPSS) probably available on your campus.

14.2 PARTIAL CORRELATION

In Chapter 13, we used Pearson's r to measure the strength and direction of bivariate relationships. To provide an example, we looked at the relationship between number of children (X) and husband's contribution to housework (Y) for a sample of 12 families. We found a positive relationship of moderate strength ($r = +0.50$), and concluded that husbands tend to make a larger contribution to housework as the number of children increases.

You might wonder, as researchers commonly do, if this relationship always holds true for *all* types of families? For example, might husbands in strongly religious families respond differently from those in less religious families? Would husbands from families that were politically conservative behave differently from husbands in more liberal families? How about educated husbands? Would they respond differently from less educated husbands? We can address these kinds of issues by a technique called **partial correlation** in which we observe how the bivariate relationship changes when a third variable like religion, political ideology, or education is introduced. Third variables are often referred to as Z variables or **control variables**.

Partial correlation is done by first computing Pearson's r for the bivariate (or zero-order) relationship and then computing the partial (or first-order) correlation coefficient. If the partial correlation coefficient differs from the zero-order correlation coefficient, we can conclude that the third variable does affect the bivariate relationship. If, for example, well-educated husbands respond differently to an additional child compared to less well-educated husbands, the partial correlation coefficient will differ in strength (and, perhaps, in direction) from the bivariate correlation coefficient.

Before considering matters of computation, we'll consider the relationships between the partial and bivariate correlation coefficients and what they might mean. We will examine each of three possible patterns in turn.

Types of Relationships. One possible outcome is that the partial correlation coefficient is essentially the same as the bivariate correlation coefficient. Imagine, for example, that after we controlled for husband's education, we found a partial correlation coefficient of $+0.49$ compared to the zero-order Pearson's r of $+0.50$. This would mean that the third variable (husband's education) has no effect on the relationship between number of children and husband's hours of housework. In other words, regardless of their education, husbands respond in a similar way to additional children. This outcome is consistent with the

FIGURE 14.1 A DIRECT RELATIONSHIP BETWEEN TWO VARIABLES

conclusion that there is a causal, or **direct relationship**, between X and Y and that the third variable (Z) is irrelevant to the investigation as illustrated in Figure 14.1. In this case, the researcher would discard that particular Z variable from further consideration but might run additional tests with the other likely control variables (e.g., the religion of the family).

A second possible outcome occurs when the partial correlation coefficient is much weaker than the bivariate coefficient, perhaps dropping to zero. This outcome is consistent with two different relationships between the variables. The first is called a **spurious relationship**: The control variable (Z) is a cause of both the independent (X) and the dependent (Y) variable as illustrated in Figure 14.2. This outcome would mean that there is no actual relationship between X and Y and that they appear to be related only because both depend on a common cause (Z). Once Z is taken into account, the apparent relationship between X and Y disappears.

FIGURE 14.2 A SPURIOUS RELATIONSHIP BETWEEN X AND Y

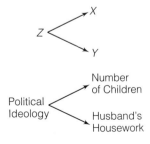

What would a spurious relationship look like? Imagine that we controlled for the political ideology of the parents in our 12-family sample and found that the partial correlation coefficient was much weaker than bivariate Pearson's r. This would indicate that the number of children does not actually change the husband's contribution to housework (i.e., the relationship between X and Y is not direct). Rather, political ideology is the mutual cause of both of the other variables: More conservative families would be more likely to follow traditional gender role patterns (in which husbands contribute less to housework) *and* have more children.

This pattern, in which the partial correlation is much weaker than the bivariate correlation, is also consistent with an **intervening relationship** between the variables as illustrated in Figure 14.3. In this situation, X and Y are not linked directly but are causally connected through the Z variable. Again, once Z is controlled, the apparent relationship between X and Y disappears.

How can we tell the difference between spurious and intervening relationships? This distinction cannot be made on statistical grounds: Spurious and intervening relationships look exactly the same in terms of statistics. The researcher may be able to distinguish between these two relationships in terms of the order of the variables (i.e., which came first) or on theoretical grounds, but not on statistical grounds.

FIGURE 14.3 AN INTERVENING RELATIONSHIP BETWEEN X AND Y

Terminology and Formula. The formula for partial correlation requires some new terminology. We will be dealing with more than one bivariate relationship and need to differentiate them with subscripts. Thus, the symbol r_{yx} will refer to the correlation coefficient between variable Y and variable X, r_{yz} will refer to the correlation coefficient between Y and Z, and r_{xz} will refer to the correlation coefficient between X and Z. As previously mentioned, correlation coefficients calculated for bivariate relationships are referred to as **zero-order correlations.**

Partial correlation coefficients, when controlling for a single variable, are called first-order partials and are symbolized as $r_{yx.z}$. The variable to the right of the dot is the control variable. Thus, $r_{yx.z}$ refers to the partial correlation coefficient that measures the relationship between variables X and Y while controlling for variable Z. The formula for the first-order partial is

FORMULA 14.1
$$r_{yx.z} = \frac{r_{yx} - (r_{yz})(r_{xz})}{\sqrt{1 - r_{yz}^2}\,\sqrt{1 - r_{xz}^2}}$$

Note that you must first calculate the zero-order coefficients between all possible pairs of variables (variables X and Y, X and Z, and Y and Z) before solving this formula.

Computation. To illustrate the computation of a first-order partial, we will return to the relationship between number of children (X) and husband's contribution to housework (Y) for 12 dual-career families. The zero-order r between these two variables ($r_{yx} = 0.50$) indicated a strong, positive relationship. Suppose the researcher wished to investigate the possible effects of husband's education on the bivariate relationship. The original data (from Table 13.1) and the scores of the 12 families on the new variable (years of education completed by the husband) are presented in Table 14.1.

TABLE 14.1 SCORES ON THREE VARIABLES FOR 12 DUAL-WAGE-EARNER FAMILIES

Family	Husband's Housework (Y)	Number of Children (X)	Husband's Years of Education (Z)
A	1	1	12
B	2	1	14
C	3	1	16
D	5	1	16
E	3	2	18
F	1	2	16
G	5	3	12
H	0	3	12
I	6	4	10
J	3	4	12
K	7	5	10
L	4	5	16

The zero-order correlations, as presented in Table 14.2, indicate that the husband's contribution to housework is positively related to number of children ($r_{yx} = 0.50$), that better-educated husbands tend to do less housework ($r_{yz} = -0.30$), and that families with better-educated husbands have fewer children ($r_{xz} = -0.47$). *(NOTE: zero-order correlations are calculated using Formula 13.6 for Pearson's r.)*

Is the relationship between husband's housework and number of children affected by husband's education? Substituting the zero-order correlations into Formula 14.1, we would have

$$r_{yx.z} = \frac{r_{yx} - (r_{yz})(r_{xz})}{\sqrt{1 - r_{yz}^2}\ \sqrt{1 - r_{xz}^2}}$$

$$r_{yx.z} = \frac{(0.50) - (-0.30)(-0.47)}{\sqrt{1 - (-0.30)^2}\ \sqrt{1 - (0.47)^2}}$$

$$r_{yx.z} = \frac{(0.50) - (0.14)}{\sqrt{1 - 0.09}\ \sqrt{1 - 0.22}}$$

$$r_{yx.z} = \frac{0.36}{\sqrt{0.91}\ \sqrt{0.78}}$$

$$r_{yx.z} = \frac{0.36}{(0.95)(0.88)}$$

$$r_{yx.z} = \frac{0.36}{0.84}$$

$$r_{yx.z} = 0.43$$

Interpretation. The first-order partial ($r_{yx.z} = 0.43$) measures the strength of relationship between husband's housework (Y) and number of children (X)

TABLE 14.2   ZERO-ORDER CORRELATIONS

	Husband's Housework (Y)	Number of Children (X)	Husband's Years of Education (Z)
Husband's Housework (Y)	1.00	0.50	−0.30
Number of Children (X)		1.00	−0.47
Husband's Years of Education (Z)			1.00

while controlling for husband's education (Z). It is lower in value than the zero-order coefficient ($r_{yx} = 0.50$), but the difference in the two values is not great. This result suggests a direct relationship between variables X and Y (see Figure 14.1). That is, when controlling for husband's education, the statistical relationship between husband's housework and number of children is essentially unchanged. Regardless of education, husband's hours of housework increases with the number of children.

Our next step in statistical analysis would probably be to discard this control variable (husband's education) and select another. The more the bivariate relationship retains its strength across a series of controls for third variables (Zs), the stronger the evidence for a direct relationship between X and Y.

Summary. The possible outcomes of controlling for a third variable were introduced in this section. By observing the partial correlation coefficients, we can identify direct or spurious and intervening relationships. In a direct relationship, the partial correlation coefficient is more or less equal to the zero-order correlation coefficient (as demonstrated above with the problem involving number of children, husband's contribution to housework, and husband's education). If, however, the partial correlation coefficient is much lower in value than the zero-order coefficient, the bivariate relationship between X and Y is either spurious or intervening.* That is, there is no direct association between X and Y, and the zero-order relationship is due mainly to the effects of Z. In a spurious relationship, X and Y are both caused by Z, whereas an intervening relationship means that X and Y are linked by Z (see Figures 14.2 and 14.3, respectively). In either case, the relationship between X and Y disappears once the effect of Z is controlled, and the next step in the statistical analysis would be to incorporate the control variable

---

*Since this outcome, where the partial correlation coefficient is much weaker than the zero-order coefficient, is consistent with *both* a spurious relationship *and* an intervening relationship, partial correlation techniques do not allow a researcher to distinguish between the relationships. Instead of statistical grounds, the differentiation between these two types of causal patterns must be made on the grounds of temporal ordering among the variables and/or theory.

TABLE 14.3 A SUMMARY OF THE POSSIBLE RESULTS OF CONTROLLING FOR THIRD VARIABLES

Partial Coefficient (compared with bivariate coefficient) Shows	Pattern	Implications for Further Analysis	Likely Next Step in Statistical Analysis	Theoretical Implications
Same relationship between X and Y	Direct relationship	Disregard Z	Analyze another control variable	Theory that X causes Y is supported
Weaker relationship between X and Y	Spurious relationship	Incorporate Z	Focus on relationship between Z and Y	Theory that X causes Y is not supported
	Intervening relationship	Incorporate Z	Focus on relationships between X, Y, and Z	Theory that X causes Y is partially supported but must be revised to take Z into account

into the analysis as an independent variable. A guideline for decision making for each of the outcomes is provided in Table 14.3. *(For practice in computing and interpreting partial correlation coefficients, see problems 14.1 to 14.3.)*

14.3 MULTIPLE REGRESSION: PREDICTING THE DEPENDENT VARIABLE

Partial correlation techniques are used when a researcher wants to observe how a specific relationship between an independent variable, X, and a dependent variable, Y, behaves in the presence of a control variable, Z. By observing the partial correlation coefficients, we can identify direct, spurious, or intervening relationships. However, it is often the case that a researcher wants to assess a causal model in which the variable taken as the independent variable (X) and the control variable (Z) each has a separate effect on the dependent variable (Y) and are uncorrelated with each other. This relationship is depicted in Figure 14.4. The absence of an arrow between X and Z indicates that they have no mutual relationship. This pattern means that both X and Z should be treated as independent variables, and the statistical analysis would probably involve multiple regression and correlation. As we shall see in this section and in the next one, these techniques enable the researcher to isolate the separate effects of several independent variables on the dependent variable, and thus to make judgments about which independent has the stronger effect on the dependent.

FIGURE 14.4 A CASUAL RELATIONSHIP AMONG THREE VARIABLES X, Z, AND Y

In Chapter 13, the least-squares regression line was introduced as a way of describing the overall linear relationship between two interval-ratio variables and of predicting scores on Y from scores on X. This line was the best-fitting line to summarize the bivariate relationship and was defined by the formula:

FORMULA 14.2

$$Y = a + bX$$

where $a =$ the Y intercept
$b =$ the slope

The least-squares regression line can be modified to include (theoretically) any number of independent variables. This technique is called **multiple regression**. For ease of explication, we will confine our attention to the case involving two independent variables. The least-squares multiple regression equation is

FORMULA 14.3

$$Y = a + b_1X_1 + b_2X_2$$

where $b_1 =$ the partial slope of the linear relationship between the first independent variable and Y
$b_2 =$ the partial slope of the linear relationship between the second independent variable and Y

Some new notation and some new concepts are introduced in this formula. First, while the dependent variable is still symbolized as Y, the independent variables are differentiated by subscripts. Thus, X_1 identifies the first independent variable and X_2 the second. The symbol for the slope (b) is also subscripted to identify the independent variable with which it is associated.

Partial Slopes. A major difference between the multiple and bivariate regression equations concerns the slopes (b's). In the case of multiple regression, the b's are called **partial slopes**, and they show the amount of change in Y for a unit change in the independent while controlling for the effects of the other independent(s) in the equation. The partial slopes are thus analogous to partial correlation coefficients (see Section 14.2) and represent the direct effect of the associated independent variable on Y.

Computing and Interpreting Partial Slopes. We use Formulas 14.4 and 14.5 to determine the partial slopes for the independent variables. The subscripts attached to the symbols (b, s, r) in the formulas identify the variables: "Y" is the dependent variable, "1" refers to the first independent variable, and "2" refers to the second independent variable.*

---

*Partial slopes can be computed from zero-order slopes but Formulas 14.4 and 14.5 are somewhat easier to use.

FORMULA 14.4
$$b_1 = \left(\frac{s_y}{s_1}\right)\left(\frac{r_{y1} - r_{y2}r_{12}}{1 - r_{12}^2}\right)$$

FORMULA 14.5
$$b_2 = \left(\frac{s_y}{s_2}\right)\left(\frac{r_{y2} - r_{y1}r_{12}}{1 - r_{12}^2}\right)$$

where b_1 = the partial slope of X_1 on Y
b_2 = the partial slope of X_2 on Y
s_y = the standard deviation of Y
s_1 = the standard deviation of the first independent variable (X_1)
s_2 = the standard deviation of the second independent variable (X_2)
r_{y1} = the bivariate correlation between Y and X_1
r_{y2} = the bivariate correlation between Y and X_2
r_{12} = the bivariate correlation between X_1 and X_2

To illustrate the computation of the partial slopes, we will assess the combined effects of number of children (X_1) and husband's education (X_2) on husband's contribution to housework. All the relevant information can be calculated from Table 14.1 and is reproduced below:

Husband's Housework	Number of Children	Husband's Education
$\overline{Y} = 3.3$	$\overline{X_1} = 2.7$	$\overline{X_2} = 13.7$
$s_y = 2.1$	$s_1 = 1.5$	$s_2 = 2.6$

Zero-order correlations
$r_{y1} = 0.50$
$r_{y2} = -0.30$
$r_{12} = -0.47$

The partial slope for the first independent variable, number of children or X_1, is

$$b_1 = \left(\frac{s_y}{s_1}\right)\left(\frac{r_{y1} - r_{y2}r_{12}}{1 - r_{12}^2}\right)$$

$$b_1 = \left(\frac{2.1}{1.5}\right)\left(\frac{0.50 - (-0.30)(-0.47)}{1 - (-0.47)^2}\right)$$

$$b_1 = (1.4)\left(\frac{0.50 - 0.14}{1 - 0.22}\right)$$

$$b_1 = (1.4)\left(\frac{0.36}{0.78}\right)$$

$$b_1 = (1.4)(0.46)$$

$$b_1 = 0.65$$

A slope of 0.65 indicates that there is an increase of .65 units in Y for each unit change in X_1, while controlling for the effects of X_2. That is, there is an increase of .65 hour of housework per week being done by husbands with each additional child, regardless of their years of education.

For the second independent variable, husband's education or X_2, the partial slope is

$$b_2 = \left(\frac{s_y}{s_2}\right)\left(\frac{r_{y2} - r_{y1}r_{12}}{1 - r_{12}^2}\right)$$

$$b_2 = \left(\frac{2.1}{2.6}\right)\left(\frac{-0.30 - (-0.24)}{1 - 0.22}\right)$$

$$b_2 = (0.81)\left(\frac{-0.30 + 0.24}{0.78}\right)$$

$$b_2 = (0.81)\left(\frac{-0.06}{0.78}\right)$$

$$b_2 = (0.81)(-0.08)$$

$$b_2 = -0.07$$

This value of -0.07 means that contribution to housekeeping duties by husbands decreases by .07 hour per week with each additional year of education, regardless of number of children in the family.

Finding and Interpreting the Y Intercept.   Now that partial slopes have been determined for both independent variables, the Y intercept (a) can be found. Note that a is calculated from the mean of the dependent variable (symbolized as $\overline{Y}$) and the means of the two independent variables ($\overline{X}_1$ and $\overline{X}_2$).

FORMULA 14.6
$$a = \overline{Y} - b_1\overline{X}_1 - b_2\overline{X}_2$$

Substituting the proper values for the example problem at hand, we would have

$$a = \overline{Y} - b_1\overline{X}_1 - b_2\overline{X}_2$$

$$a = 3.3 - (0.65)(2.7) - (-0.07)(13.7)$$

$$a = 3.3 - (1.8) - (-1.0)$$

$$a = 3.3 - 1.8 + 1.0$$

$$a = 2.5$$

The Y intercept is the point where the regression line crosses the Y axis and is equal to the mean of Y when all independents equal 0. Thus, husbands with no children and no years of eduction contribute an average of 2.5 hours per week to housekeeping chores.

The Least Squares Multiple Regression Line and Predicting Y′.   For our example problem, the full least-squares multiple regression equation is

$$Y = a + b_1X_1 + b_2X_2$$

$$Y = 2.5 + (0.65)X_1 + (-0.07)X_2$$

As was the case with the bivariate regression line, this formula can be used to predict scores on the dependent variable from scores on the independent variables. For example, what would be our best prediction of husband's housework (Y') for a family of four children ($X_1 = 4$) where the husband had completed 11 years of schooling ($X_2 = 11$)? Substituting these values into the least-squares formula, we would have

$$Y' = 2.5 + (0.65)(4) + (-0.07)(11)$$
$$Y' = 2.5 + 2.6 - 0.8$$
$$Y' = 4.3$$

Our prediction would be that this husband would contribute 4.3 hours per week to housework. This prediction is, of course, a kind of "educated guess," which is unlikely to be perfectly accurate. However, we will make fewer errors of prediction using the least-squares line (and, thus, incorporating information from the independent variables) than we would using any other method of prediction (assuming, of course, that there is a linear association between the independent and the dependent variables). *(For practice in predicting Y scores and in computing slopes and the Y intercept, see problems 14.1 to 14.6.)*

14.4 MULTIPLE REGRESSION: ASSESSING THE EFFECTS OF THE INDEPENDENT VARIABLES

The least-squares multiple regression equation (see Formula 14.3) is used to isolate the separate effects of the independents and to predict scores on the dependent variable. However, in many situations, using this formula to determine the relative importance of the various independent variables will be awkward—especially when the independent variables differ in terms of units of measurement (e.g., number of children vs. years of education). When the units of measurement differ, a comparison of the partial slopes will not necessarily tell us which independent variable has the strongest effect and is thus the most important variable. Comparing the partial slopes of variables that differ in units of measurement is a little like comparing apples and oranges.

The comparability of the independent variables can be increased converting all variables in the equation to a common scale, and thereby eliminating variations in the values of the partial slopes that are solely a function of differences in units of measurement. We can, for example, standardize all distributions by changing the scores of all variables to Z scores. Each distribution of scores would then have a mean of 0 and a standard deviation of 1 (see Chapter 4), and comparisons between the independent variables would be much more meaningful.

Beta-weights. To standardize the variables to the normal curve, we could actually convert all scores into the equivalent Z scores and then recompute the slopes and the Y intercept. This would require a good deal of work, and, fortunately, a shortcut is available for directly computing the slopes of the standardized scores. These **standardized partial slopes** are called **beta-weights** and are symbolized b^*. The beta-weights show the amount of change in the standardized scores of Y for a one-unit change in the standardized scores of each independent variable while controlling for the effects of all other independent variables.

Formulas and Computation for Beta-weights.   When we have two independent variables, the beta-weight for each is found by using Formula 14.7 and Formula 14.8:

FORMULA 14.7
$$b_1^* = b_1\left(\frac{s_1}{s_y}\right)$$

FORMULA 14.8
$$b_2^* = b_2\left(\frac{s_2}{s_y}\right)$$

We can now compute the beta-weights for our sample problem to see which of the two independents has the stronger effect on the dependent. For the first independent variable, number of children (X_1):

$$b_1^* = b_1\left(\frac{s_1}{s_y}\right)$$

$$b_1^* = (0.65)\left(\frac{1.5}{2.1}\right)$$

$$b_1^* = (0.65)(0.71)$$

$$b_1^* = 0.46$$

For the second independent variable, husband's years of education (X_2):

$$b_2^* = b_2\left(\frac{s_2}{s_y}\right)$$

$$b_2^* = (-0.07)\left(\frac{2.6}{2.1}\right)$$

$$b_2^* = (-0.07)(1.24)$$

$$b_2^* = -0.09$$

Interpreting Beta-Weights.   Comparing the value of the beta-weights for our example problem, we see that number of children ($b_1^* = 0.46$) has a stronger effect than husband's education ($b_2^* = -0.09$) on husband's housework. Furthermore, the net effect (after controlling for the effect of education) of the first independent variable is positive while the net effect of the second independent variable (after controlling for the effect of number of children) is negative. We can conclude that number of children is the more important of the two variables and that husband's contribution to housework increases as the number of children increases regardless of husband's years of education.

The Standardized Least-Squares Regression Line.   Using standardized scores, the least-squares regression equation can be written as

FORMULA 14.9
$$Z_y = a_z + b_1^* Z_1 + b_2^* Z_2$$

where Z indicates that all scores have been standardized to the normal curve.

The standardized regression equation can be further simplified by dropping the term for the Y intercept; this term will always be zero when scores have been standardized.

Because the mean of any standardized distribution of scores is zero, the mean of the standardized Y scores will be zero and the Y intercept will also be zero ($a = \bar{Y} = 0$). Thus, Formula 14.9 simplifies to

FORMULA 14.10
$$Z_y = b_1^* Z_1 + b_2^* Z_2$$

The standardized regression equation, with beta-weights noted, would be

$$Z_y = (0.46)Z_1 + (-0.09)Z_2$$

and it is immediately obvious that the first independent variable has a much stronger direct effect on Y than the second independent variable.

Summary. Multiple regression analysis permits the researcher to summarize the linear relationship among two or more independents and a dependent variable. The unstandardized regression equation (see Formula 14.3) permits values of Y to be predicted from the independent variables in the original units of the variables. The standardized regression equation (see Formula 14.10) allows the researcher to easily assess the relative importance of the various independent variables by comparing the beta-weights. (see For practice in computing and interpreting beta-weights, see any of the problems at the end of this chapter. It is probably a good idea to start with problem 14.1 as it has the smallest data set and the least complex computations.)

14.5 MULTIPLE CORRELATION

We use the multiple regression equations to disentangle the *separate* direct effects of each independent variable on the dependent. Using **multiple correlation** techniques, we can also determine the *combined* effects of all independents on the dependent variable. We do so by computing the **multiple correlation coefficient (R)** and the **coefficient of multiple determination (R^2)**. The value of the latter statistic represents the proportion of the variance in Y that is explained by all the independent variables combined.

In terms of zero-order correlation, we have seen that "number of children" (X_1) explains a proportion of 0.25 of the variance in Y ($r_{y1}^2 = (0.50)^2 = 0.25$) by itself and that husband's education explains a proportion of 0.09 of the variance in Y ($r_{y2}^2 = (-0.30)^2 = 0.09$). The two zero-order correlations cannot be simply added together to determine their combined effect on Y, because the two independents are also correlated with each other and, therefore, they will "overlap" in their effects on Y and explain some of the same variance. This overlap is eliminated in Formula 14.11:

FORMULA 14.11
$$R^2 = r_{y1}^2 + r_{y2.1}^2(1 - r_{y1}^2)$$

where R^2 = the multiple correlation coefficient

$\quad r_{y1}^2$ = the zero-order correlation between Y and X_1, the quantity squared

$\quad r_{y2.1}^2$ = the partial correlation of Y and X_2, while controlling for X_1, the quantity squared

Application 14.1

Five recently divorced men were asked about their dating behaviour (i.e., the number of dates they went on) in the last month. Is number of dates related to the length of time married? Is number of dates related to socio-economic status as measured by yearly income?

Case	Number of Dates (Y)	Years Married (X_1)	Income (dollars) (X_2)
A	5	5	30,000
B	4	7	45,000
C	4	10	25,000
D	3	2	27,000
E	1	15	17,000

$$\overline{Y} = 3.4 \quad \overline{X}_1 = 7.8 \quad \overline{X}_2 = 28,800.00$$
$$s = 1.4 \quad s = 4.5 \quad s = 9,173.88$$

The zero-order correlations among these three variables are

	Years Married (X_1)	Income (X_2)
Number of Dates (Y)	−0.62	0.62
Years married (X_1)		−0.49

These results suggest strong but opposite relationships between each independent and number of dates. Number of dates decreases as years married increases, and increases as income increases.

To find the multiple regression equation, we must find the partial slopes.

For years married (X_1):

$$b_1 = \left(\frac{s_y}{s_1}\right)\left(\frac{r_{y1} - r_{y2}r_{12}}{1 - r_{12}^2}\right)$$

$$b_1 = \frac{1.4}{4.5}\left(\frac{(-0.62) - (0.62)(-0.49)}{1 - (-0.49)^2}\right)$$

$$b_1 = (0.31)\left(\frac{(-0.62) - (-0.30)}{1 - 0.24}\right)$$

$$b_1 = (0.31)\left(\frac{-0.32}{0.76}\right)$$

$$b_1 = (0.31)(-0.42)$$

$$b_1 = -0.13$$

For income (X_2):

$$b_2 = \left(\frac{s_y}{s_2}\right)\left(\frac{r_{y2} - r_{y1}r_{12}}{1 - r_{12}^2}\right)$$

$$b_2 = \left(\frac{1.4}{9173.88}\right)\left(\frac{(0.62) - (-0.62)(-0.49)}{1 - (-0.49)^2}\right)$$

$$b_2 = (0.00015)\left(\frac{(0.62) - (0.30)}{1 - 0.24}\right)$$

$$b_2 = (0.00015)\left(\frac{0.32}{0.76}\right)$$

$$b_2 = (0.00015)(0.42)$$
$$b_2 = 0.000063$$

(continued next page)

The first term in this formula (r_{y1}^2) is the coefficient of determination for the relationship between Y and X_1. It represents the amount of variation in Y explained by X_1 by itself. To this quantity we add the amount of the variation remaining in Y (given by $1 - r_{y1}^2$) that can be explained by X_2 after the effect of X_1 is controlled ($r_{y2.1}^2$). Basically, Formula 14.11 allows X_1 to explain as much of Y as it can and then adds in the effect of X_2 after X_1 is controlled (thus eliminating the "overlap" in the variance of Y that X_1 and X_2 have in common).

Application 14.1: (*continued*)

The Y intercept would be

$a = \overline{Y} - b_1\overline{X_1} - b_2\overline{X_2}$
$a = 3.4 - (-0.13)(7.8) - (0.000063)(28,800)$
$a = 3.4 - (-1.01) - (1.81)$
$a = 3.4 + 1.01 - 1.81$
$a = 2.60$

The multiple regression equation is

$Y = a + b_1X_1 + b_2X_2$
$Y = 2.60 + (-0.13)X_1 + (0.000063)X_2$

What is the number of dates we could predict for a male who had been married 30 years ($X_1 = 30$) and had an income of \$50,000 ($X_2 = 50,000$)?

$Y' = 2.60 + (-0.13)(30) + (0.000063)(50,000)$
$Y' = 2.60 + (-3.9) + (3.15)$
$Y' = 1.85$

To assess which of the two independents has the stronger effect on number of dates, the standardized partial slopes must be computed.
For years married (X_1):

$$b_1^* = b_1\left(\frac{s_1}{s_y}\right)$$

$$b_1^* = (-0.13)\left(\frac{4.5}{1.4}\right)$$

$$b_1^* = -0.42$$

For income (X_2):

$$b_2^* = b_2\left(\frac{s_2}{s_y}\right)$$

$$b_2^* = (0.000063)\left(\frac{9173.88}{1.4}\right)$$

$$b_2^* = 0.41$$

The standardized regression equation is

$$Z_y = b_1^*Z_1 + b_2^*Z_2$$
$$Z_y = (-0.42)Z_1 + (0.41)Z_2$$

and the independents have nearly equal but opposite effects on number of dates. To assess the combined effects of the two independents on number of dates, the coefficient of multiple determination must be computed.

$$R^2 = r_{y1}^2 + r_{y2.1}^2(1 - r_{y1}^2)$$
$$R^2 = (-0.62)^2 + (0.46)^2(1 - (-0.62)^2)$$
$$R^2 = 0.38 + (0.21)(1 - 0.38)$$
$$R^2 = 0.38 + (0.21)(0.62)$$
$$R^2 = 0.38 + 0.13$$
$$R^2 = 0.51$$

The first independent, years married, explains 38% of the variation in number of dates by itself. To this quantity, income explains an additional 13% of the variation in number of dates. Taken together, the two independents explain a total of 51% of the variation in number of dates.

Computing and Interpreting R and R^2. To observe the combined effects of number of children (X_1) and husband's years of education (X_2) on husband's housework (Y), we need two quantities. The correlation between X_1 and Y ($r_{y1} = 0.50$) has already been found. Before we can solve Formula 14.11, we must first calculate the partial correlation of Y and X_2 while controlling for X_1 ($r_{y2.1}$):

$$r_{y2.1} = \frac{r_{y2} - (r_{y1})(r_{12})}{\sqrt{1 - r_{y1}^2}\,\sqrt{1 - r_{12}^2}}$$

$$r_{y2.1} = \frac{(-0.30) - (0.50)(-0.47)}{\sqrt{1 - (0.50)^2}\ \sqrt{1 - (-0.47)^2}}$$

$$r_{y2.1} = \frac{(-0.30) - (-0.24)}{\sqrt{0.75}\ \sqrt{0.78}}$$

$$r_{y2.1} = \frac{-0.06}{0.77}$$

$$r_{y2.1} = -0.08$$

Formula 14.11 can now be solved for our sample problem:

$$R^2 = r_{y1}^2 + r_{y2.1}^2(1 - r_{y1}^2)$$
$$R^2 = (0.50)^2 + (-0.08)^2(1 - 0.50^2)$$
$$R^2 = 0.25 + (0.006)(1 - 0.25)$$
$$R^2 = 0.25 + 0.005$$
$$R^2 = 0.255$$

The first independent variable (X_1), number of children, explains 25% of the variance in Y by itself. To this total, the second independent (X_2), husband's education, adds only half a percent, for a total explained variance of 25.5%. In combination, the two independents explain a total of 25.5% of the variation in the dependent variable. *(For practice in computing and interpreting R and R^2, see any of the problems at the end of this chapter. It is probably a good idea to start with problem 14.1 as it has the smallest data set and the least complex computations.)*

14.6 INTERPRETING STATISTICS: ANOTHER LOOK AT THE CORRELATES OF CRIME

In Chapter 13, we assessed the association between poverty and crime. We found a strong and positive relationship ($r = 0.47$) between a measure of poverty and the crime rate for Canada's largest cities, an indication that there is an important relationship between these two variables. In this installment of Interpreting Statistics, we will return to this relationship and add several independent variables to the analysis.*

Our first new independent variable is a measure of age: the percentage of the population less than 25. The rates for some crimes are strongly related to age: They are highest for people in their teens and twenties but decline dramatically as age rises. Thus, we can expect that there will be a substantial positive relationship between this measure of age and the crime rate (the higher the proportion of younger people in a population, the higher the crime rate).

---

*This analysis considers the effects of three independent variables, one more than was included in previous examples in this chapter. As you will see, the addition of an independent variable will not complicate interpretation and analysis unduly. However, the mathematics underlying multiple regression with three independent variables is complex and should be performed with the aid of a computerized statistics packages such as SPSS. We will not show the underlying computations in this analysis.

Our second new independent variable comes from research showing that crime rates follow a regional pattern in Canada, rising from east to west.*

Thus, we should expect to find higher rates of crime in western cities (Calgary, Edmonton, Winnipeg, and Vancouver) compared to eastern cities (Hamilton, Montreal, Ottawa, Quebec, and Toronto).

Although it is reasonable to include region in this analysis, we must first confront an important problem. Region is a nominal-level variable but regression analysis requires that all variables be interval-ratio in level of measurement. We can resolve this problem by treating region as a "dummy variable," a variable that can be treated as interval-ratio regardless of its actual level of measurement.

Dummy variables have exactly two categories, one coded as a score of zero and the other as a score of one. Treated this way, nominal-level variables such as gender (e.g., with males coded as 0 and females coded as 1) or immigration status (e.g., Canadian-born coded as 0 and foreign-born coded as 1) are commonly included as independent variables in regression equations. In this case, we will create a variable that is coded so that western cities are scored as "1" and non-western cities as "0." Coded this way, region should have a positive relationship with crime—as region "increases" (as we increase from a score of 0, non-western cities, to a score of 1, western cities), the crime rate also increases.

It is important to note that we could have as easily coded eastern cities as "1" and non-eastern cities as "0," with identical results. Correlation coefficients, slopes, and R^2 values would be the same regardless of which region we coded as 1 and 0. The only difference would be the direction of the relationship. If we instead decided to score eastern cities as "1" and non-eastern cities as "0," we would expect region to have a negative relationship (i.e., correlation coefficients and slopes would be negative) with crime. Coding of dummy variables is therefore a subjective decision made by the researcher. (Dummy variables are covered in more detail on the website for this textbook.)

Before beginning the multivariate analysis, we should examine the correlation coefficients between all possible pairs of variables. Zero-order correlations, and the scores used in computing them, for the variables are reported in Table 14.4. As we saw in Chapter 13, there is a strong, positive relationship between poverty and crime: Cities with higher rates of poverty have higher rates of crime. Crime rate has a weak to moderate, positive relationship with age: Cities with younger populations tend to have slightly higher crime rates. Finally, crime rate has a very strong, positive relationship with region: Western Canadian cities have higher rates of crime than non-western cities.

The results of the multivariate analysis are provided in Table 14.5. Looking at the unstandardized partial slopes (b), we see that the number

---

*Source: Statistics Canada. 2001. *Crime comparisons between Canada and the United States.* Catalogue no. 85-002-XPE.

TABLE 14.4   SCORES ON POVERTY, AGE, REGION, AND CRIME FOR NINE CANADIAN CITIES AND ZERO-ORDER CORRELATIONS

Scores

City	Crime[1]	Poverty[2]	Age[3]	Region[4]
Calgary	7,115	14.3	34.1	1
Edmonton	8,377	16.5	35.5	1
Hamilton	6,565	17.0	32.4	0
Montreal	7,234	22.3	31.4	0
Ottawa	5,680	15.0	32.9	0
Quebec	5,108	18.9	30.0	0
Toronto	5,290	16.7	32.8	0
Vancouver	11,210	20.8	30.9	1
Winnipeg	10,377	19.8	33.4	1

Zero-Order Correlations

	Crime	Poverty	Age	Region
Crime	1.00	0.47	0.12	0.80
Poverty		1.00	−0.60	−0.03
Age			1.00	0.49
Region				1.00

[1]Number of criminal offences per 100,000 population, 2000.
[2]Percentage of population living below the poverty line, 2000.
[3]Percentage of population under age 25, 2000.
[4]Western cities coded as 1; non-western cities coded as 0.

Source: Data from Statistics Canada, *Crime Statistics in Canada, 2000* (2001), Catalogue no. 85-002-XIE (Crime rate) and Statistics Canada, *2001 Canadian Census*, individual PUMF (Age and Poverty rate).

TABLE 14.5   MULTIPLE REGRESSION ANALYSIS OF THE CRIME RATE

Variable	b	b^*
Poverty	403	0.50
Age	35	0.03
Region	3,278	0.80
Intercept (a)	−2,367	
	$R^2 = 0.87$	

b = partial slope
b^* = standardized partial slopes

of criminal offences per 100,000 people increases on average by 403 for each percentage increase in the poverty rate, while controlling for the effects of age and region. The slope for age is also positive—cities with younger populations tend to have higher crime rates. Crime also increases with region. On average, western Canadian cities experience 3,278 more criminal offences per 100,000 people compared to eastern Canadian cities, controlling for poverty and age. The standardized partial slopes (b^*) in Table 14.5 tell us that crime is more affected by region than poverty or

READING STATISTICS 8: Multiple Regression and Partial Correlation

Research projects that analyze the interrelationships among many variables are particularly likely to employ multiple regression and correlation as central statistical techniques. The results of these projects will typically be presented in summary tables that report the multiple correlations, slopes, and, if applicable, the significance of the results. The zero-order correlations are often presented in the form of a matrix that displays the value of Pearson's r for every possible bivariate relationship in the data set. An example of such a matrix can be found in Section 14.6.

Usually, tables that summarize the multivariate analysis will report R^2 and the slope for each independent variable in the regression equation. An example of this kind of summary table would look like this:

Independent Variables	Multiple R^2	Beta-weights
X_1	0.17	0.47
X_2	0.23	0.32
X_3	0.27	0.16
⋮	⋮	⋮

This table reports that the first independent variable, X_1, has the strongest direct relationship with the dependent variable and explains 17% of the variance in the dependent by itself ($R^2 = 0.17$). The second independent, X_2, adds 6% to the explained variance ($R^2 = 0.23$ after X_2 is entered into the equation). The third independent, X_3, adds 4% to the explained variance of the dependent ($R^2 = 0.27$ after X_3 is entered into the

equation). Table 14.5 provides an alternative example of how the results of a multiple regression analysis may be reported.

In addition to multiple regression, partial correlation is also frequently used in research. As we will now see, partial correlation allows researchers to observe how a bivariate relationship behaves in the presence of a third variable.

Statistics in the Professional Literature

There are a great number of cross-national comparative studies on the topic of income inequality and population health. Reviews of the literature reveal that the majority of international studies support the hypothesis that income inequality has a negative effect on population health. In other words, the greater the dispersion of income in a country, the lower its life expectancy. According to this hypothesis, the United States would have a lower life expectancy than Canada, for example, because the former has more income inequality than the latter.

Income inequality as a determinant of population health, however, has become an increasingly contentious issue. It is argued that evidence of a population-level association between income inequality and health is slowly dissipating. To shed light on this issue, Canadian social scientists Rob Brown and Steven Prus tested the income inequality–population health hypothesis with the most currently available data at the time of their publication—data from the year 2000.

(*continued next page*)

age. In fact, the effect of region on crime is 1.6 times that of poverty ($0.80/0.50 = 1.6$).

By itself, poverty explains 22% ($r = 0.47$, so $(0.47)^2 = 0.22$) of the variance in crime rates among the cities (see Table 14.4). To this, age and region add another 65% for a total of 87% ($R^2 = 0.87$). These three variables, together, account for over 80% of the variation in crime rates from city to city. This is a very substantial percentage, with only 13% of the variation

READING STATISTICS 8: (*continued*)

TABLE 1 CORRELATION COEFFICIENT FOR INCOME INEQUALITY (GINI) AND LIFE EXPECTANCY FOR 18 COUNTRIES, BY SEX, BEFORE AND AFTER CONTROLLING FOR AVERAGE POPULATION INCOME.*

	Zero-order Correlation	Partial Correlation
	r	r
Male	$-.603$[†]	$-.207$
Female	$-.605$[†]	$.024$

*These countries are Australia, Austria, Belgium, Canada, Denmark, Finland, France, Germany, Greece, Ireland, Israel, Netherlands, Norway, Spain, Sweden, Switzerland, the United Kingdom, and the United States.

[†] $p < .01$

Source: From Prus, S. and R. Brown, "Age-specific Income Inequality and Life Expectancy: New Evidence," *2008 Living to 100 Symposium Monograph, The Society of Actuaries*. Copyright © 2008 by The Society of Actuaries, Schaumburg Illinois. Reprinted with permission.

The correlation coefficient was used to examine the relationship between income inequality (Gini coefficient) and life expectancy, separately for males and females. The Gini coefficient, introduced in Chapter 3, is a measure of inequality that ranges from 0 to 1. If everyone in a given country had the same income, there would be no income inequality, and the Gini coefficient would be 0. If one individual held all income in a given country, the Gini coefficient would be equal to 1. So, the Gini coefficient increases as inequality increases. Life expectancy is the expected number of years to be lived at birth in a given country.

The correlation coefficient was calculated before (zero-order) and after (partial) controlling for average income of the entire population to gauge the extent to which average population income changes the original relationship between income inequality and life expectancy. The results of their multivariate analysis are reported in Table 1.

Brown and Prus found that life expectancy is negatively and significantly related to income inequality regardless of sex. The zero-order correlation coefficients for males and females are approximately -0.60. That is, as income inequality increases, life expectancy decreases.

After controlling for average population income, the partial correlations are noticeably weaker and statistically insignificant compared to the zero-order correlations. The coefficients are reduced to -0.207 for males and 0.024 for females after removing the effect of average population income. This outcome weakens the hypothesis that there is a direct causal relationship between income inequality and life expectancy. Brown and Prus conclude that the zero-order relationship is spurious and due to the effects of average population income rather than income inequality itself.

remaining unaccounted for or unexplained. We might be able to raise the value of R^2 by adding more independent variables to the equation. However, it is common to find that additional independent variables will explain smaller and smaller proportions of the variance and have a diminishing effect on R^2. This phenomenon can be caused by many factors including the fact that the independent variables will usually be correlated with each other (e.g., see the relationship between region and age in Table 14.4) and will overlap in their effect on the dependent variable.

In summary, the multivariate analysis indicates that poverty and region have important, positive effects on crime rate. The effect of age is positive, but of little importance. The standardized partial slopes show that region is clearly the most important of the three independent variables in understanding crime rates. Taken together, the three variables account for 87% of the variance in crime rate from city to city. However, with only nine cases (cities) in this analysis, we must be particularly cautious in interpreting and drawing conclusions from these findings.

14.7 THE LIMITATIONS OF PARTIAL CORRELATION AND MULTIPLE REGRESSION AND CORRELATION

Partial correlation and multiple regression and correlation are very powerful tools for analyzing the interrelationships among three or more variables. The techniques presented in this chapter permit the researcher to observe how a bivariate relationship behaves in the presence of a control variable(s), to predict scores on one variable from two or more other variables, to distinguish between independent variables in terms of the importance of their direct effects on a dependent variable, and to determine the total effect of a set of independent variables on a dependent variable. In terms of the flexibility of these techniques and the volume of information they can supply, partial correlation and multiple regression and correlation represent some of the most powerful statistical techniques available to social science researchers.

Powerful tools are not cheap. They demand high-quality data, and measurement at the interval-ratio level is difficult to accomplish at this stage in the development of the social sciences (though as illustrated in Section 14.6, we can resolve this problem for a nominal- or ordinal-level independent variable by treating it as a dummy variable). Furthermore, these techniques assume that the interrelationships among the variables follow a particular form. First, they assume that each independent variable has a linear relationship with the dependent variable.

Second, the techniques of multiple regression and correlation further assume that the effects of the independent variables are "additive." This means that we must assume that the best prediction of the dependent variable (Y) can be obtained by simply adding up the scores of the independent variables, as reflected by the plus signs in Formula 14.3. Not all combinations of variables will conform to this assumption. For example, some variables have "interactive" relationships with each other. These are relationships in which some of the scores of the variables combine in unusual, nonadditive ways. For example, consider a health survey that found positive and linear bivariate relationships between years of age (X_1), body weight (X_2), and number of health problems (Y). When combined in a regression analysis, however, certain combinations of scores on the independent variables (for example, old age combined with high body weight) produced an especially high number of health problems. In other words, age and weight interact with each other, and persons who were old *and* high in body weight had more health problems than those persons who were old but did not have high body weight or those persons who had high body weight but were not old.

If there is interaction among the variables, we cannot accurately estimate or predict the dependent variable by simply adding the effects of the independent variables. There are techniques for handling interaction among the variables in the set, but these techniques are beyond the scope of this textbook.

Third, multiple regression and correlation techniques also assume that the independent variables are uncorrelated with each other. Strictly speaking, this condition means that the zero-order correlation among all pairs of independents should be zero, but practically, we act as if this assumption has been met if the intercorrelations among the independents are low.

To the extent that these assumptions are violated, the statistics introduced in this chapter become less and less trustworthy and the techniques less and less useful. A careful inspection of the bivariate scattergrams will help to assess the reasonableness of the assumptions of partial and multiple correlation and regression.

Finally, we should note that we have covered only the simplest applications of partial correlation and multiple regression and correlation. In terms of logic and interpretation, the extensions to situations involving more variables are relatively straightforward. However, the computations for these situations are extremely complex. If you are faced with a situation involving more than three variables, turn to one of the computerized statistical packages that are commonly available on university campuses (e.g., SPSS). These programs require minimal computer literacy and can handle complex calculations in, literally, the blink of an eye. Efficient use of these packages will enable you to avoid drudgery and will free you to do what social scientists everywhere enjoy doing most: pondering the meaning of your results and, by extension, the nature of social life.

SUMMARY

1. Partial correlation involves controlling for the effect of a third variable (Z) on a bivariate relationship. Partial correlations permit the detection of direct and spurious or intervening relationships among X, Y, and Z.

2. Multiple regression includes statistical techniques by which predictions of the dependent variable from more than one independent variable can be made (by using partial slopes and the multiple regression equation) and by which we can disentangle the relative importance of the independent variables (by using standardized partial slopes).

3. The multiple correlation coefficient (R^2) summarizes the combined effects of all independent variables on the dependent variable in terms of the proportion of the total variation in Y that is explained by all of the independent variables.

4. Partial correlation and multiple regression and correlation are some of the most powerful tools available to the researcher and demand high-quality measurement and relationships among the variables that are linear and noninteractive. Further, correlations among the independents must be low (preferably zero). Although the price is high, these techniques pay considerable dividends in the volume of precise and detailed information they generate about the interrelationships among the variables.

SUMMARY OF FORMULAS

Partial correlation coefficient:

14.1 $$r_{yx.z} = \frac{r_{yx} - (r_{yz})(r_{xz})}{\sqrt{1 - r_{yz}^2}\ \sqrt{1 - r_{xz}^2}}$$

Least-squares regression line (bivariate):

14.2 $$Y = a + bX$$

Least-squares multiple regression line:

14.3 $$Y = a + b_1X_1 + b_2X_2$$

Partial slope for X_1:

14.4 $$b_1 = \left(\frac{s_y}{s_1}\right)\left(\frac{r_{y1} - r_{y2}r_{12}}{1 - r_{12}^2}\right)$$

Partial slope for X_2:

14.5 $$b_2 = \left(\frac{s_y}{s_2}\right)\left(\frac{r_{y2} - r_{y1}r_{12}}{1 - r_{12}^2}\right)$$

Y intercept:

14.6 $$a = \overline{Y} - b_1\overline{X}_1 - b_2\overline{X}_2$$

Standardized partial slope (beta-weight) for X_1:

14.7 $$b_1^* = b_1\left(\frac{s_1}{s_y}\right)$$

Standardized partial slope (beta-weight) for X_2:

14.8 $$b_2^* = b_2\left(\frac{s_2}{s_y}\right)$$

Standardized least-squares regression line:

14.9 $$Z_y = a_z + b_1^*Z_1 + b_2^*Z_2$$

Standardized least-squares regression line (simplified):

14.10 $$Z_y = b_1^*Z_1 + b_2^*Z_2$$

Coefficient of multiple determination:

14.11 $$R^2 = r_{y1}^2 + r_{y2.1}^2(1 - r_{y1}^2)$$

GLOSSARY

Beta-weights (b^*). Standardized partial slopes. (p. 418)

Coefficient of multiple determination (R^2). A statistic that equals the total variation explained in the dependent variable by all independent variables combined. (p. 420)

Control variable. A "third variable" (Z) that might affect a bivariate relationship. (p. 410)

Direct relationship. A multivariate relationship in which the control variable has no effect on the bivariate relationship. (p. 410)

Intervening relationship. A multivariate relationship in which the bivariate relationship becomes substantially weaker after controlling for a third variable. The independent (X) and the dependent (Y) variables are linked primarily through the control variable (Z). (p. 411)

Multiple correlation. A multivariate technique for examining the combined effects of more than one independent variable on a dependent variable. (p. 420)

Multiple correlation coefficient (R). A statistic that indicates the strength of the correlation between a dependent variable and two or more independent variables. (p. 420)

Multiple regression. A multivariate technique that breaks down the separate effects of the independent variables on the dependent variable; used to make predictions of the dependent variable. (p. 415)

Partial correlation. A multivariate technique for examining a bivariate relationship while controlling for other variables. (p. 410)

Partial correlation coefficient. A statistic that shows the relationship between two variables while controlling for other variables; $r_{yx.z}$ is the symbol for the partial correlation coefficient when controlling for one variable. (p. 411)

Partial slopes. In a multiple regression equation, the slope of the relationship between a particular independent variable and the dependent variable while controlling for all other independents in the equation. (p. 415)

Spurious relationship. A multivariate relationship in which the bivariate relationship becomes substantially weaker after controlling for a third variable.

The independent (X) and dependent (Y) variables are not causally linked. Rather, both are caused by the control variable (Z). (p. 410)

Standardized partial slopes (beta-weights). The slope of the relationship between a particular

independent variable and the dependent when all scores have been normalized. (p. 418)

Zero-order correlations. Correlation coefficients for bivariate relationships. (p. 411)

MULTIMEDIA RESOURCES

http://www.healeystatistics.nelson.com

Visit the companion website for the second Canadian edition of *Statistics: A Tool for Social Research* to access a wide range of student resources. Begin by clicking on the Student Resources section of the textbook's website to access review quizzes, flashcards, and other study tools.

PROBLEMS

14.1 PS In problem 13.1 data regarding voter turnout in five cities were presented. For the sake of convenience, the data for three of the variables are presented again here along with descriptive statistics and zero-order correlations.

City	Turnout	Unemployment Rate	% Negative Ads
A	55	5	60
B	60	8	63
C	65	9	55
D	68	9	53
E	70	10	48
Mean =	63.6	8.2	55.8
s =	5.5	1.7	5.3

	Unemployment	Negative Ads
Turnout	0.95	−0.87
Unemployment		−0.70

a. Compute the partial correlation coefficient for the relationship between turnout (Y) and unemployment (X) while controlling for the effect of negative advertising (Z). What effect does this control variable have on the bivariate relationship? Is the relationship between turnout and unemployment direct? *(HINT: Use Formula 14.1 and see Section 14.2.)*

b. Compute the partial correlation coefficient for the relationship between turnout (Y) and negative advertising (X) while controlling for the effect of unemployment (Z). What effect does this have on the bivariate relationship? Is the relationship between turnout and negative advertising direct? *(HINT: Use Formula 14.1 and see Section 14.2. You will need this partial correlation to compute the multiple correlation coefficient.)*

c. Find the unstandardized multiple regression equation with unemployment (X_1) and negative ads (X_2) as the independent variables. What turnout would be expected in a city in which the unemployment rate was 10% and 75% of the campaign ads were negative? *(HINT: Use Formulas 14.4 and 14.5 to compute the partial slopes and then use Formula 14.6 to find a, the Y intercept. The regression line is stated in Formula 14.3. Substitute 10 for X_1 and 75 for X_2 to compute predicted Y.)*

d. Compute beta-weights for each independent variable. Which has the stronger impact on turnout? *(HINT: Use Formulas 14.7 and 14.8 to calculate the beta-weights.)*

e. Compute the multiple correlation coefficient (R) and the coefficient of multiple determination (R^2). How much of the variance in voter turnout is explained by the two independent variables? *(HINT: Use Formula 14.11. You calculated the partial correlation coefficient in part b of this problem.)*

f. Write a paragraph summarizing your conclusions about the relationships among these three variables.

14.2 SOC A scale measuring support for increases in the national defence budget has been administered to a sample. The respondents have also been asked to indicate how many years of school they have completed and how many years, if any, they served in the Canadian military. Take "support" as the dependent variable.

Case	Support	Years of School	Years of Service
A	20	12	2
B	15	12	4
C	20	16	20
D	10	10	10
E	10	16	20
F	5	8	0
G	8	14	2
H	20	12	20
I	10	10	4
J	20	16	0

a. Compute r for all three relationships (Support and Years of School, Support and Years of Service, and Years of School and Years of Service). Compute the partial correlation coefficient for the relationship between support (Y) and years of school (X) while controlling for the effect of years of service (Z). What effect does the third variable (years of service or Z) have on the bivariate relationship? Is the relationship between support and years of school direct?

b. Compute the partial correlation coefficient for the relationship between support (Y) and years of service (X) while controlling for the effect of years of school (Z). What effect does Z have on the bivariate relationship? Is the relationship between support and years of service direct? *(HINT: You will need this partial correlation to compute the multiple correlation coefficient.)*

c. Find the unstandardized multiple regression equation with school (X_1) and service (X_2) as the independent variables. What level of

support would be expected in a person with 13 years of school and 15 years of service?

d. Compute beta-weights for each independent variable. Which has the stronger impact on support?

e. Compute the multiple correlation coefficient (R) and the coefficient of multiple determination (R^2). How much of the variance in support is explained by the two independent variables? *(HINT: You calculated the partial correlation coefficient in part b of this problem.)*

f. Write a paragraph summarizing your conclusions about the relationships among these three variables.

14.3 SOC Data on civil strife (number of incidents), unemployment, and urbanization have been gathered for 10 nations. Take civil strife as the dependent variable. Compute the zero-order correlations among all three variables.

Number of Incidents of Civil Strife	Unemployment Rate	Percentage of Population Living in Urban Areas
0	5.3	60
1	1.0	65
5	2.7	55
7	2.8	68
10	3.0	69
23	2.5	70
25	6.0	45
26	5.2	40
30	7.8	75
53	9.2	80

a. Compute the partial correlation coefficient for the relationship between strife (Y) and unemployment (X) while controlling for the effect of urbanization (Z). What effect does this have on the bivariate relationship? Is the relationship between strife and unemployment direct?

b. Compute the partial correlation coefficient for the relationship between strife (Y) and urbanization (X) while controlling for the effect of unemployment (Z). What effect does this have on the bivariate relationship? Is the relationship between strife and urbanization direct? *(HINT: You will need this partial correlation to compute the multiple correlation coefficient.)*

CHAPTER 14   PARTIAL CORRELATION AND MULTIPLE REGRESSION AND CORRELATION   **433**

c. Find the unstandardized multiple regression equation with unemployment (X_1) and urbanization (X_2) as the independent variables. What level of strife would be expected in a nation in which the unemployment rate was 10% and 90% of the population lived in urban areas?

d. Compute beta-weights for each independent variable. Which has the stronger impact on strife?

e. Compute the multiple correlation coefficient (R) and the coefficient of multiple determination (R^2). How much of the variance in strife is explained by the two independent variables?

f. Write a paragraph summarizing your conclusions about the relationships among these three variables.

14.4 SOC/CJ In problem 13.5, crime and population data were presented for each of 10 Canadian cities. The data are reproduced here.

14.5 PS Problem 13.4 presented data on 10 electoral districts. The information is reproduced here.

District	Percentage Working-Class	Unemployment Rate	Voter Turnout
A	50	10	56
B	45	12	55
C	56	8	52
D	78	15	60
E	13	5	89
F	85	20	25
G	62	18	64
H	33	9	88
I	25	0	42
J	49	9	36

	Crime Rate			Population		
City	Homicide	Robbery	Auto Theft	Growth	Density	Urbanization
A	1	19	104	3.8	41.7	52.6
B	5	214	286	5.5	402.7	92.1
C	4	138	344	4.7	277.8	81.2
D	2	37	184	5.4	52.3	45.3
E	6	89	252	14.4	181.5	78.1
F	5	81	230	9.6	102.3	48.8
G	6	145	447	22.8	81.5	84.8
H	7	146	842	40.0	46.7	88.2
I	3	99	594	21.1	90.0	83.1
J	6	178	537	13.6	221.2	96.7

Take the three crime variables as the dependent variables (one at a time) and

a. Find the multiple regression equations (unstandardized) with growth and urbanization as independent variables.

b. Make a prediction for each crime variable for a city with a 5% growth rate and a population that is 90% urbanized.

c. Compute beta-weights for each independent variable in each equation and compare their relative effect on each dependent.

d. Compute R and R^2 for each crime variable, using the population variables as independent variables.

e. Write a paragraph summarizing your findings.

Take voter turnout as the dependent variable and

a. Find the multiple regression equations (unstandardized).

b. What turnout would you expect for a district in which 0% of the voters were working-class and 5% were unemployed?

c. Compute beta-weights for each independent variable and compare their relative effect on turnout. Which is the more important factor?

d. Compute R and R^2.

e. Write a paragraph summarizing your findings.

14.6 SW Twelve families have been referred to a counsellor, and she has rated each of them on a cohesiveness scale. Also, she has information on family income and number of children currently

NEL

living at home. Take family cohesion as the dependent variable.

Family	Cohesion Score	Family Income	Number of Children
A	10	30,000	5
B	10	70,000	4
C	9	35,000	4
D	5	25,000	0
E	1	55,000	3
F	7	40,000	0
G	2	60,000	2
H	5	30,000	3
I	8	50,000	5
J	3	25,000	4
K	2	45,000	3
L	4	50,000	0

a. Find the multiple regression equations (unstandardized).

b. What level of cohesion would be expected in a family with an income of $20,000 and 6 children?

c. Compute beta-weights for each independent variable and compare their relative effect on cohesion. Which is the more important factor?

d. Compute R and R^2.

e. Write a paragraph summarizing your findings.

14.7 Problem 13.8 presented per capita expenditures on education for 15 large Canadian cities, along with rank on income per capita and the percentage of the population that has graduated from high school. The data are reproduced below. Take educational expenditures as the dependent variable.

City	Per Capita Expenditures on Education	Percentage High School Graduates	Rank in per Capita Income
A	1,102	82	48
B	1,339	90	7
C	1,907	88	1
D	1,171	84	25
E	1,621	86	9
F	1,276	88	24
G	1,159	81	45
H	1,412	86	5
I	1,487	86	18
J	1,041	80	50
K	1,194	90	22
L	1,262	88	6
M	1,163	79	32
N	1,223	86	15
O	1,549	90	20

a. Compute beta-weights for each independent variable and compare their relative effect on expenditures. Which is the more important factor?

b. Compute R and R^2.

c. Write a paragraph summarizing your findings.

14.8 SOC The scores on four variables for 20 individuals are reported below: hours of TV (number of hours of TV viewing each day), occupational prestige (higher scores indicate greater prestige), number of children, and age. Take TV viewing as the dependent variable and select two of the remaining variables as independents.

Hours of TV	Occupational Prestige	Number of Children	Age
4	50	2	43
3	36	3	58
3	36	1	34
4	50	2	42
2	45	2	27
3	50	5	60
4	50	0	28
7	40	3	55
1	57	2	46
3	33	2	65
1	46	3	56
3	31	1	29
1	19	2	41
0	52	0	50
2	48	1	62
4	36	1	24
3	48	0	25
1	62	1	87
5	50	0	45
1	27	3	62

a. Compute beta-weights for each of the independent variables you selected and compare their relative effect on the hours of television watching. Which is the more important factor?

b. Compute R and R^2.

c. Write a paragraph summarizing your findings.

Using SPSS for Windows for Regression Analysis with the 2006 Census

The demonstration and exercise below use the shortened version of the 2006 Census data. Start SPSS for Windows and open the *Census.sav* file.

SPSS DEMONSTRATION 14.1 What Are the Effects of Hours Worked and Sex on Income?

We will use the **Linear Regression** procedure to examine the effects of number of hours worked per week (*hrswrk*) and sex (*sex*) on total annual income (*totinc*). This demonstration represents a very sparing use of the power of the regression command and an extremely economical use of all the options available. We urge you to explore some of the variations and capabilities of this powerful data-analysis procedure.

Ideally, the independent variables in a linear regression analysis should be interval-ratio in level of measurement, but sex is a nominal-level variable, and its inclusion in a regression procedure may be surprising. However, nominal variables with only two categories—sometimes called "dummy variables"—are commonly used in regression (see Section 14.6).

With the 2006 Census loaded, click **Analyze**, **Regression**, and **Linear**, and the **Linear Regression** window will appear. Move *totinc* into the **Dependent** box and *hrswrk* and *sex* into the **Independent(s)** box. If you wish, you can click the **Statistics** button and then click **Descriptives** to get zero-order correlations, means, and standard deviations for the variables. Click **Continue**, and then **OK**, and the following output will appear (descriptive information about the variables and the zero-order correlations are omitted here to conserve space).

Model Summary

Model	R	R Square	Adjusted R Square	Std. Error of the Estimate
1	.289[a]	.084	.083	46921.397

a. Predictors: (Constant), Sex, Hours worked for pay or in self-employment

ANOVA[a]

Model		Sum of Squares	df	Mean Square	F	Sig.
1	Regression	3.015E + 11	2	1.507E + 11	68.462	.000[b]
	Residual	3.296E + 12	1497	2201617479		
	Total	3.597E + 12	1499			

a. Dependent Variable: Total income of individual
b. Predictors: (Constant), Sex, Hours worked for pay or in self-employment

Coefficients[a]

Model		Unstandardized Coefficients		Standardized Coefficients		
		B	Std. Error	Beta	t	Sig.
1	(Constant)	5179.789	3864.528		1.340	.180
	Hours worked for pay or in self-employment	562.345	55.830	.253	10.072	.000
	Sex	10431.339	2456.455	.106	4.247	.000

a. Dependent Variable: Total income of individual

The "Model Summary" output block reports the multiple R (.289) and R square (.084), which indicates that the independent variables combined account for 8.4% of the variation in total annual income. The "ANOVA" block shows the relationship between the variables is statistically significance (Sig. = .000). (See Demonstration 6.1 for an explanation about why some values in the output contain numbers with the letter "E.")

In the last output block, we see the slopes (B) of the independent variables on *totinc*, the standardized partial slopes (Beta), and the Y intercept (reported as a constant of 5179.789). The slope for hours worked indicates that annual income increases by $562 on average with each one hour increase in work per week while controlling for the effects of sex. The slope for sex is also positive (10431.339). In other words, income increases as sex *increases*, that is, income is higher for people with the *higher* score on sex. Because a female is coded as 1 and a male as 2, the average income for males is $10,431 higher than the average income for females, even after controlling for hours worked. From this information, we can build a regression equation to predict scores on *totinc*.

The beta for *hrswrk* (.253) is much larger than the beta for *sex* (.106). What does this mean? At least for this sample, a person's income is more affected by how many hours worked per week than by sex.

Exercise (using *Census.sav*)

14.1 Conduct the analysis in Demonstration 14.1 again with *sempi* (self-employment income) as the dependent variable. Compare and contrast with the analysis of *totinc*.

PART IV CUMULATIVE EXERCISES

1. For a sample of 20 recently graduated students planning to go into a master's degree program, data have been gathered on overall undergraduate GPA, average number of hours worked each week during the school year, and Graduate Record Examinations (GRE) score (a measure of preparedness for graduate-level work). Using the techniques presented in Chapter 14, test the hypothesis that GPA will decrease with hours worked and increase with GRE score, but hours worked will have the strongest effect.

GPA	Hours Worked per Week	GRE
3.14	13	550
2.00	20	375
2.11	22	450
3.00	10	575
3.75	0	600
3.11	21	650
3.22	7	605
2.75	25	630
2.50	30	680
2.10	32	610
2.45	20	580
2.01	40	590
3.90	0	675
3.45	0	650
2.30	25	550
2.20	18	470
2.60	25	600
3.10	15	525
2.60	27	480
2.20	20	500

2. A brief survey has been conducted to test the hypothesis that the amount of time devoted to watching television will increase with age and decrease with education, but age will have the strongest effect. Use the techniques presented in Chapter 14 to test the hypothesis on the following data:

Hours Watching TV per Week	Age in Years	Years of Education
14	52	10
10	45	12
8	18	12
5	45	12
10	57	10
14	65	8
3	23	12
12	47	11
2	30	14
1	20	16
21	60	16
15	55	12
12	47	9
8	32	14
15	50	12
10	45	10
20	72	16
12	40	16
14	42	14
10	38	12

Appendix A   Area Under the Normal Curve

Column (a) lists Z scores from 0.00 to 4.00. Only positive scores are displayed, but because the normal curve is symmetrical, the areas for negative scores will be exactly the same as areas for positive scores. Column (b) lists the proportion of the total area between the Z score and the mean. Figure A.1 displays areas of this type. Column (c) lists the proportion of the area beyond the Z score, and Figure A.2 displays this type of area.

FIGURE A.1   AREA BETWEEN MEAN AND Z

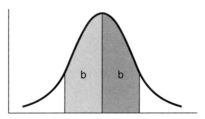

FIGURE A.2   AREA BEYOND Z

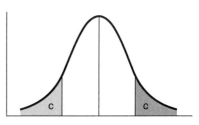

(a) Z	(b) Area between Mean and Z	(c) Area beyond Z	(a) Z	(b) Area between Mean and Z	(c) Area beyond Z
0.00	0.0000	0.5000	0.27	0.1064	0.3936
0.01	0.0040	0.4960	0.28	0.1103	0.3897
0.02	0.0080	0.4920	0.29	0.1141	0.3859
0.03	0.0120	0.4880	0.30	0.1179	0.3821
0.04	0.0160	0.4840			
0.05	0.0199	0.4801	0.31	0.1217	0.3783
0.06	0.0239	0.4761	0.32	0.1255	0.3745
0.07	0.0279	0.4721	0.33	0.1293	0.3707
0.08	0.0319	0.4681	0.34	0.1331	0.3669
0.09	0.0359	0.4641	0.35	0.1368	0.3632
0.10	0.0398	0.4602	0.36	0.1406	0.3594
			0.37	0.1443	0.3557
0.11	0.0438	0.4562	0.38	0.1480	0.3520
0.12	0.0478	0.4522	0.39	0.1517	0.3483
0.13	0.0517	0.4483	0.40	0.1554	0.3446
0.14	0.0557	0.4443			
0.15	0.0596	0.4404	0.41	0.1591	0.3409
0.16	0.0636	0.4364	0.42	0.1628	0.3372
0.17	0.0675	0.4325	0.43	0.1664	0.3336
0.18	0.0714	0.4286	0.44	0.1700	0.3300
0.19	0.0753	0.4247	0.45	0.1736	0.3264
0.20	0.0793	0.4207	0.46	0.1772	0.3228
			0.47	0.1808	0.3192
0.21	0.0832	0.4168	0.48	0.1844	0.3156
0.22	0.0871	0.4129	0.49	0.1879	0.3121
0.23	0.0910	0.4090	0.50	0.1915	0.3085
0.24	0.0948	0.4052			
0.25	0.0987	0.4013	0.51	0.1950	0.3050
0.26	0.1026	0.3974	0.52	0.1985	0.3015

(a) Z	(b) Area between Mean and Z	(c) Area beyond Z	(a) Z	(b) Area between Mean and Z	(c) Area beyond Z
0.53	0.2019	0.2981	1.05	0.3531	0.1469
0.54	0.2054	0.2946	1.06	0.3554	0.1446
0.55	0.2088	0.2912	1.07	0.3577	0.1423
0.56	0.2123	0.2877	1.08	0.3599	0.1401
0.57	0.2157	0.2843	1.09	0.3621	0.1379
0.58	0.2190	0.2810	1.10	0.3643	0.1357
0.59	0.2224	0.2776	1.11	0.3665	0.1335
0.60	0.2257	0.2743	1.12	0.3686	0.1314
0.61	0.2291	0.2709	1.13	0.3708	0.1292
0.62	0.2324	0.2676	1.14	0.3729	0.1271
0.63	0.2357	0.2643	1.15	0.3749	0.1251
0.64	0.2389	0.2611	1.16	0.3770	0.1230
0.65	0.2422	0.2578	1.17	0.3790	0.1210
0.66	0.2454	0.2546	1.18	0.3810	0.1190
0.67	0.2486	0.2514	1.19	0.3830	0.1170
0.68	0.2517	0.2483	1.20	0.3849	0.1151
0.69	0.2549	0.2451	1.21	0.3869	0.1131
0.70	0.2580	0.2420	1.22	0.3888	0.1112
0.71	0.2611	0.2389	1.23	0.3907	0.1093
0.72	0.2642	0.2358	1.24	0.3925	0.1075
0.73	0.2673	0.2327	1.25	0.3944	0.1056
0.74	0.2703	0.2297	1.26	0.3962	0.1038
0.75	0.2734	0.2266	1.27	0.3980	0.1020
0.76	0.2764	0.2236	1.28	0.3997	0.1003
0.77	0.2794	0.2206	1.29	0.4015	0.0985
0.78	0.2823	0.2177	1.30	0.4032	0.0968
0.79	0.2852	0.2148	1.31	0.4049	0.0951
0.80	0.2881	0.2119	1.32	0.4066	0.0934
0.81	0.2910	0.2090	1.33	0.4082	0.0918
0.82	0.2939	0.2061	1.34	0.4099	0.0901
0.83	0.2967	0.2033	1.35	0.4115	0.0885
0.84	0.2995	0.2005	1.36	0.4131	0.0869
0.85	0.3023	0.1977	1.37	0.4147	0.0853
0.86	0.3051	0.1949	1.38	0.4162	0.0838
0.87	0.3078	0.1922	1.39	0.4177	0.0823
0.88	0.3106	0.1894	1.40	0.4192	0.0808
0.89	0.3133	0.1867	1.41	0.4207	0.0793
0.90	0.3159	0.1841	1.42	0.4222	0.0778
0.91	0.3186	0.1814	1.43	0.4236	0.0764
0.92	0.3212	0.1788	1.44	0.4251	0.0749
0.93	0.3238	0.1762	1.45	0.4265	0.0735
0.94	0.3264	0.1736	1.46	0.4279	0.0721
0.95	0.3289	0.1711	1.47	0.4292	0.0708
0.96	0.3315	0.1685	1.48	0.4306	0.0694
0.97	0.3340	0.1660	1.49	0.4319	0.0681
0.98	0.3365	0.1635	1.50	0.4332	0.0668
0.99	0.3389	0.1611	1.51	0.4345	0.0655
1.00	0.3413	0.1587	1.52	0.4357	0.0643
1.01	0.3438	0.1562	1.53	0.4370	0.0630
1.02	0.3461	0.1539	1.54	0.4382	0.0618
1.03	0.3485	0.1515	1.55	0.4394	0.0606
1.04	0.3508	0.1492	1.56	0.4406	0.0594

(a)	(b) Area between	(c) Area beyond	(a)	(b) Area between	(c) Area beyond
Z	Mean and Z	Z	Z	Mean and Z	Z
1.57	0.4418	0.0582	2.09	0.4817	0.0183
1.58	0.4429	0.0571	2.10	0.4821	0.0179
1.59	0.4441	0.0559	2.11	0.4826	0.0174
1.60	0.4452	0.0548	2.12	0.4830	0.0170
1.61	0.4463	0.0537	2.13	0.4834	0.0166
1.62	0.4474	0.0526	2.14	0.4838	0.0162
1.63	0.4484	0.0516	2.15	0.4842	0.0158
1.64	0.4495	0.0505	2.16	0.4846	0.0154
1.65	0.4505	0.0495	2.17	0.4850	0.0150
1.66	0.4515	0.0485	2.18	0.4854	0.0146
1.67	0.4525	0.0475	2.19	0.4857	0.0143
1.68	0.4535	0.0465	2.20	0.4861	0.0139
1.69	0.4545	0.0455	2.21	0.4864	0.0136
1.70	0.4554	0.0446	2.22	0.4868	0.0132
1.71	0.4564	0.0436	2.23	0.4871	0.0129
1.72	0.4573	0.0427	2.24	0.4875	0.0125
1.73	0.4582	0.0418	2.25	0.4878	0.0122
1.74	0.4591	0.0409	2.26	0.4881	0.0119
1.75	0.4599	0.0401	2.27	0.4884	0.0116
1.76	0.4608	0.0392	2.28	0.4887	0.0113
1.77	0.4616	0.0384	2.29	0.4890	0.0110
1.78	0.4625	0.0375	2.30	0.4893	0.0107
1.79	0.4633	0.0367	2.31	0.4896	0.0104
1.80	0.4641	0.0359	2.32	0.4898	0.0102
1.81	0.4649	0.0351	2.33	0.4901	0.0099
1.82	0.4656	0.0344	2.34	0.4904	0.0096
1.83	0.4664	0.0336	2.35	0.4906	0.0094
1.84	0.4671	0.0329	2.36	0.4909	0.0091
1.85	0.4678	0.0322	2.37	0.4911	0.0089
1.86	0.4686	0.0314	2.38	0.4913	0.0087
1.87	0.4693	0.0307	2.39	0.4916	0.0084
1.88	0.4699	0.0301	2.40	0.4918	0.0082
1.89	0.4706	0.0294	2.41	0.4920	0.0080
1.90	0.4713	0.0287	2.42	0.4922	0.0078
1.91	0.4719	0.0281	2.43	0.4925	0.0075
1.92	0.4726	0.0274	2.44	0.4927	0.0073
1.93	0.4732	0.0268	2.45	0.4929	0.0071
1.94	0.4738	0.0262	2.46	0.4931	0.0069
1.95	0.4744	0.0256	2.47	0.4932	0.0068
1.96	0.4750	0.0250	2.48	0.4934	0.0066
1.97	0.4756	0.0244	2.49	0.4936	0.0064
1.98	0.4761	0.0239	2.50	0.4938	0.0062
1.99	0.4767	0.0233	2.51	0.4940	0.0060
2.00	0.4772	0.0228	2.52	0.4941	0.0059
2.01	0.4778	0.0222	2.53	0.4943	0.0057
2.02	0.4783	0.0217	2.54	0.4945	0.0055
2.03	0.4788	0.0212	2.55	0.4946	0.0054
2.04	0.4793	0.0207	2.56	0.4948	0.0052
2.05	0.4798	0.0202	2.57	0.4949	0.0051
2.06	0.4803	0.0197	2.58	0.4951	0.0049
2.07	0.4808	0.0192	2.59	0.4952	0.0048
2.08	0.4812	0.0188	2.60	0.4953	0.0047

(a) Z	(b) Area between Mean and Z	(c) Area beyond Z	(a) Z	(b) Area between Mean and Z	(c) Area beyond Z
2.61	0.4955	0.0045	3.11	0.4991	0.0009
2.62	0.4956	0.0044	3.12	0.4991	0.0009
2.63	0.4957	0.0043	3.13	0.4991	0.0009
2.64	0.4959	0.0041	3.14	0.4992	0.0008
2.65	0.4960	0.0040	3.15	0.4992	0.0008
2.66	0.4961	0.0039	3.16	0.4992	0.0008
2.67	0.4962	0.0038	3.17	0.4992	0.0008
2.68	0.4963	0.0037	3.18	0.4993	0.0007
2.69	0.4964	0.0036	3.19	0.4993	0.0007
2.70	0.4965	0.0035	3.20	0.4993	0.0007
2.71	0.4966	0.0034	3.21	0.4993	0.0007
2.72	0.4967	0.0033	3.22	0.4994	0.0006
2.73	0.4968	0.0032	3.23	0.4994	0.0006
2.74	0.4969	0.0031	3.24	0.4994	0.0006
2.75	0.4970	0.0030	3.25	0.4994	0.0006
2.76	0.4971	0.0029	3.26	0.4994	0.0006
2.77	0.4972	0.0028	3.27	0.4995	0.0005
2.78	0.4973	0.0027	3.28	0.4995	0.0005
2.79	0.4974	0.0026	3.29	0.4995	0.0005
2.80	0.4974	0.0026	3.30	0.4995	0.0005
2.81	0.4975	0.0025	3.31	0.4995	0.0005
2.82	0.4976	0.0024	3.32	0.4995	0.0005
2.83	0.4977	0.0023	3.33	0.4996	0.0004
2.84	0.4977	0.0023	3.34	0.4996	0.0004
2.85	0.4978	0.0022	3.35	0.4996	0.0004
2.86	0.4979	0.0021	3.36	0.4996	0.0004
2.87	0.4979	0.0021	3.37	0.4996	0.0004
2.88	0.4980	0.0020	3.38	0.4996	0.0004
2.89	0.4981	0.0019	3.39	0.4997	0.0003
2.90	0.4981	0.0019	3.40	0.4997	0.0003
2.91	0.4982	0.0018	3.41	0.4997	0.0003
2.92	0.4982	0.0018	3.42	0.4997	0.0003
2.93	0.4983	0.0017	3.43	0.4997	0.0003
2.94	0.4984	0.0016	3.44	0.4997	0.0003
2.95	0.4984	0.0016	3.45	0.4997	0.0003
2.96	0.4985	0.0015	3.46	0.4997	0.0003
2.97	0.4985	0.0015	3.47	0.4997	0.0003
2.98	0.4986	0.0014	3.48	0.4997	0.0003
2.99	0.4986	0.0014	3.49	0.4998	0.0002
3.00	0.4986	0.0014	3.50	0.4998	0.0002
3.01	0.4987	0.0013	3.60	0.4998	0.0002
3.02	0.4987	0.0013	3.70	0.4999	0.0001
3.03	0.4988	0.0012			
3.04	0.4988	0.0012	3.80	0.4999	0.0001
3.05	0.4989	0.0011			
3.06	0.4989	0.0011	3.90	0.4999	<0.0001
3.07	0.4989	0.0011	4.00	0.4999	<0.0001
3.08	0.4990	0.0010			
3.09	0.4990	0.0010			
3.10	0.4990	0.0010			

Appendix B   Distribution of *t*

Degrees of Freedom (df)	Level of Significance for One-tailed Test					
	.10	.05	.025	.01	.005	.0005
	Level of Significance for Two-tailed Test					
	.20	.10	.05	.02	.01	.001
1	3.078	6.314	12.706	31.821	63.657	636.619
2	1.886	2.920	4.303	6.965	9.925	31.598
3	1.638	2.353	3.182	4.541	5.841	12.941
4	1.533	2.132	2.776	3.747	4.604	8.610
5	1.476	2.015	2.571	3.365	4.032	6.859
6	1.440	1.943	2.447	3.143	3.707	5.959
7	1.415	1.895	2.365	2.998	3.499	5.405
8	1.397	1.860	2.306	2.896	3.355	5.041
9	1.383	1.833	2.262	2.821	3.250	4.781
10	1.372	1.812	2.228	2.764	3.169	4.587
11	1.363	1.796	2.201	2.718	3.106	4.437
12	1.356	1.782	2.179	2.681	3.055	4.318
13	1.350	1.771	2.160	2.650	3.012	4.221
14	1.345	1.761	2.145	2.624	2.977	4.140
15	1.341	1.753	2.131	2.602	2.947	4.073
16	1.337	1.746	2.120	2.583	2.921	4.015
17	1.333	1.740	2.110	2.567	2.898	3.965
18	1.330	1.734	2.101	2.552	2.878	3.922
19	1.328	1.729	2.093	2.539	2.861	3.883
20	1.325	1.725	2.086	2.528	2.845	3.850
21	1.323	1.721	2.080	2.518	2.831	3.819
22	1.321	1.717	2.074	2.508	2.819	3.792
23	1.319	1.714	2.069	2.500	2.807	3.767
24	1.318	1.711	2.064	2.492	2.797	3.745
25	1.316	1.708	2.060	2.485	2.787	3.725
26	1.315	1.706	2.056	2.479	2.779	3.707
27	1.314	1.703	2.052	2.473	2.771	3.690
28	1.313	1.701	2.048	2.467	2.763	3.674
29	1.311	1.699	2.045	2.462	2.756	3.659
30	1.310	1.697	2.042	2.457	2.750	3.646
40	1.303	1.684	2.021	2.423	2.704	3.551
60	1.296	1.671	2.000	2.390	2.660	3.460
120	1.289	1.658	1.980	2.358	2.617	3.373
∞	1.282	1.645	1.960	2.326	2.576	3.291

Source: Table III of Fisher & Yates: *Statistical Tables for Biological, Agricultural and Medical Research*, published by Longman Group Ltd., London (1974), 6th edition (previously published by Oliver & Boyd Ltd., Edinburgh). Reprinted by permission of Pearson Education Limited.

Appendix C   Distribution of Chi Square

df	.99	.98	.95	.90	.80	.70	.50	.30	.20	.10	.05	.02	.01	.001
1	.000	.001	.004	.016	.064	.148	.455	1.074	1.642	2.706	3.841	5.412	6.635	10.827
2	.0201	.0404	.103	.211	.446	.713	1.386	2.408	3.219	4.605	5.991	7.824	9.210	13.815
3	.115	.185	.352	.584	1.005	1.424	2.366	3.665	4.642	6.251	7.815	9.837	11.341	16.268
4	.297	.429	.711	1.064	1.649	2.195	3.357	4.878	5.989	7.779	9.488	11.668	13.277	18.465
5	.554	.752	1.145	1.610	2.343	3.000	4.351	6.064	7.289	9.236	11.070	13.388	15.086	20.517
6	.872	1.134	1.635	2.204	3.070	3.828	5.348	7.231	8.558	10.645	12.592	15.033	16.812	22.457
7	1.239	1.564	2.167	2.833	3.822	4.671	6.346	8.383	9.803	12.017	14.067	16.622	18.475	24.322
8	1.646	2.032	2.733	3.490	4.594	5.527	7.344	9.524	11.030	13.362	15.507	18.168	20.090	26.125
9	2.088	2.532	3.325	4.168	5.380	6.393	8.343	10.656	12.242	14.684	16.919	19.679	21.666	27.877
10	2.558	3.059	3.940	4.865	6.179	7.267	9.342	11.781	13.442	15.987	18.307	21.161	23.209	29.588
11	3.053	3.609	4.575	5.578	6.989	8.148	10.341	12.899	14.631	17.275	19.675	22.618	24.725	31.264
12	3.571	4.178	5.226	6.304	7.807	9.034	11.340	14.011	15.812	18.549	21.026	24.054	26.217	32.909
13	4.107	4.765	5.892	7.042	8.634	9.926	12.340	15.119	16.985	19.812	22.362	25.472	27.688	34.528
14	4.660	5.368	6.571	7.790	9.467	10.821	13.339	16.222	18.151	21.064	23.685	26.873	29.141	36.123
15	5.229	5.985	7.261	8.547	10.307	11.721	14.339	17.322	19.311	22.307	24.996	28.259	30.578	37.697
16	5.812	6.614	7.962	9.312	11.152	12.624	15.338	18.418	20.465	23.542	26.296	29.633	32.000	39.252
17	6.408	7.255	8.672	10.085	12.002	13.531	16.338	19.511	21.615	24.769	27.587	30.995	33.409	40.790
18	7.015	7.906	9.390	10.865	12.857	14.440	17.338	20.601	22.760	25.989	28.869	32.346	34.805	42.312
19	7.633	8.567	10.117	11.651	13.716	15.352	18.338	21.689	23.900	27.204	30.144	33.687	36.191	43.820
20	8.260	9.237	10.851	12.443	14.578	16.266	19.337	22.775	25.038	28.412	31.410	35.020	37.566	45.315
21	8.897	9.915	11.591	13.240	15.445	17.182	20.337	23.858	26.171	29.615	32.671	36.343	38.932	46.797
22	9.542	10.600	12.338	14.041	16.314	18.101	21.337	24.939	27.301	30.813	33.924	37.659	40.289	48.268
23	10.196	11.293	13.091	14.848	17.187	19.021	22.337	26.018	28.429	32.007	35.172	38.968	41.638	49.728
24	10.856	11.992	13.848	15.659	18.062	19.943	23.337	27.096	29.553	33.196	36.415	40.270	42.980	51.179
25	11.524	12.697	14.611	16.473	18.940	20.867	24.337	28.172	30.675	34.382	37.652	41.566	44.314	52.620
26	12.198	13.409	15.379	17.292	19.820	21.792	25.336	29.246	31.795	35.563	38.885	42.856	45.642	54.052
27	12.879	14.125	16.151	18.114	20.703	22.719	26.336	30.319	32.912	36.741	40.113	44.140	46.963	55.476
28	13.565	14.847	16.928	18.939	21.588	23.647	27.336	31.391	34.027	37.916	41.337	45.419	48.278	56.893
29	14.256	15.574	17.708	19.768	22.475	24.577	28.336	32.461	35.139	39.087	42.557	46.693	49.588	58.302
30	14.953	16.306	18.493	20.599	23.364	25.508	29.336	33.530	36.250	40.256	43.773	47.962	50.892	59.703

Source: Table IV of Fisher & Yates: *Statistical Tables for Biological, Agricultural and Medical Research*, published by Longman Group Ltd., London (1974), 6th edition (previously published by Oliver & Boyd Ltd., Edinburgh). Reprinted by permission of Pearson Education Limited.

Appendix D   Distribution of F

$$p = .05$$

n_1 \ n_2	1	2	3	4	5	6	8	12	24	∞
1	161.4	199.5	215.7	224.6	230.2	234.0	238.9	243.9	249.0	254.3
2	18.51	19.00	19.16	19.25	19.30	19.33	19.37	19.41	19.45	19.50
3	10.13	9.55	9.28	9.12	9.01	8.94	8.84	8.74	8.64	8.53
4	7.71	6.94	6.59	6.39	6.26	6.16	6.04	5.91	5.77	5.63
5	6.61	5.79	5.41	5.19	5.05	4.95	4.82	4.68	4.53	4.36
6	5.99	5.14	4.76	4.53	4.39	4.28	4.15	4.00	3.84	3.67
7	5.59	4.74	4.35	4.12	3.97	3.87	3.73	3.57	3.41	3.23
8	5.32	4.46	4.07	3.84	3.69	3.58	3.44	3.28	3.12	2.93
9	5.12	4.26	3.86	3.63	3.48	3.37	3.23	3.07	2.90	2.71
10	4.96	4.10	3.71	3.48	3.33	3.22	3.07	2.91	2.74	2.54
11	4.84	3.98	3.59	3.36	3.20	3.09	2.95	2.79	2.61	2.40
12	4.75	3.88	3.49	3.26	3.11	3.00	2.85	2.69	2.50	2.30
13	4.67	3.80	3.41	3.18	3.02	2.92	2.77	2.60	2.42	2.21
14	4.60	3.74	3.34	3.11	2.96	2.85	2.70	2.53	2.35	2.13
15	4.54	3.68	3.29	3.06	2.90	2.79	2.64	2.48	2.29	2.07
16	4.49	3.63	3.24	3.01	2.85	2.74	2.59	2.42	2.24	2.01
17	4.45	3.59	3.20	2.96	2.81	2.70	2.55	2.38	2.19	1.96
18	4.41	3.55	3.16	2.93	2.77	2.66	2.51	2.34	2.15	1.92
19	4.38	3.52	3.13	2.90	2.74	2.63	2.48	2.31	2.11	1.88
20	4.35	3.49	3.10	2.87	2.71	2.60	2.45	2.28	2.08	1.84
21	4.32	3.47	3.07	2.84	2.68	2.57	2.42	2.25	2.05	1.81
22	4.30	3.44	3.05	2.82	2.66	2.55	2.40	2.23	2.03	1.78
23	4.28	3.42	3.03	2.80	2.64	2.53	2.38	2.20	2.00	1.76
24	4.26	3.40	3.01	2.78	2.62	2.51	2.36	2.18	1.98	1.73
25	4.24	3.38	2.99	2.76	2.60	2.49	2.34	2.16	1.96	1.71
26	4.22	3.37	2.98	2.74	2.59	2.47	2.32	2.15	1.95	1.69
27	4.21	3.35	2.96	2.73	2.57	2.46	2.30	2.13	1.93	1.67
28	4.20	3.34	2.95	2.71	2.56	2.44	2.29	2.12	1.91	1.65
29	4.18	3.33	2.93	2.70	2.54	2.43	2.28	2.10	1.90	1.64
30	4.17	3.32	2.92	2.69	2.53	2.42	2.27	2.09	1.89	1.62
40	4.08	3.23	2.84	2.61	2.45	2.34	2.18	2.00	1.79	1.51
60	4.00	3.15	2.76	2.52	2.37	2.25	2.10	1.92	1.70	1.39
120	3.92	3.07	2.68	2.45	2.29	2.17	2.02	1.83	1.61	1.25
∞	3.84	2.99	2.60	2.37	2.21	2.09	1.94	1.75	1.52	1.00

Values of n_1 and n_2 represent the degrees of freedom associated with the between and within estimates of variance, respectively.

Source: Table V of Fisher & Yates: *Statistical Tables for Biological, Agricultural and Medical Research*, published by Longman Group Ltd., London (1974), 6th edition (previously published by Oliver & Boyd Ltd., Edinburgh). Reprinted by permission of Pearson Education Limited.

$p = .01$

n_1 n_2	1	2	3	4	5	6	8	12	24	∞
1	4052	4999	5403	5625	5764	5859	5981	6106	6234	6366
2	98.49	99.01	99.17	99.25	99.30	99.33	99.36	99.42	99.46	99.50
3	34.12	30.81	29.46	28.71	28.24	27.91	27.49	27.05	26.60	26.12
4	21.20	18.00	16.69	15.98	15.52	15.21	14.80	14.37	13.93	13.46
5	16.26	13.27	12.06	11.39	10.97	10.67	10.27	9.89	9.47	9.02
6	13.74	10.92	9.78	9.15	8.75	8.47	8.10	7.72	7.31	6.88
7	12.25	9.55	8.45	7.85	7.46	7.19	6.84	6.47	6.07	5.65
8	11.26	8.65	7.59	7.01	6.63	6.37	6.03	5.67	5.28	4.86
9	10.56	8.02	6.99	6.42	6.06	5.80	5.47	5.11	4.73	4.31
10	10.04	7.56	6.55	5.99	5.64	5.39	5.06	4.71	4.33	3.91
11	9.65	7.20	6.22	5.67	5.32	5.07	4.74	4.40	4.02	3.60
12	9.33	6.93	5.95	5.41	5.06	4.82	4.50	4.16	3.78	3.36
13	9.07	6.70	5.74	5.20	4.86	4.62	4.30	3.96	3.59	3.16
14	8.86	6.51	5.56	5.03	4.69	4.46	4.14	3.80	3.43	3.00
15	8.68	6.36	5.42	4.89	4.56	4.32	4.00	3.67	3.29	2.87
16	8.53	6.23	5.29	4.77	4.44	4.20	3.89	3.55	3.18	2.75
17	8.40	6.11	5.18	4.67	4.34	4.10	3.79	3.45	3.08	2.65
18	8.28	6.01	5.09	4.58	4.25	4.01	3.71	3.37	3.00	2.57
19	8.18	5.93	5.01	4.50	4.17	3.94	3.63	3.30	2.92	2.49
20	8.10	5.85	4.94	4.43	4.10	3.87	3.56	3.23	2.86	2.42
21	8.02	5.78	4.87	4.37	4.04	3.81	3.51	3.17	2.80	2.36
22	7.94	5.72	4.82	4.31	3.99	3.76	3.45	3.12	2.75	2.31
23	7.88	5.66	4.76	4.26	3.94	3.71	3.41	3.07	2.70	2.26
24	7.82	5.61	4.72	4.22	3.90	3.67	3.36	3.03	2.66	2.21
25	7.77	5.57	4.68	4.18	3.86	3.63	3.32	2.99	2.62	2.17
26	7.72	5.53	4.64	4.14	3.82	3.59	3.29	2.96	2.58	2.13
27	7.68	5.49	4.60	4.11	3.78	3.56	3.26	2.93	2.55	2.10
28	7.64	5.45	4.57	4.07	3.75	3.53	3.23	2.90	2.52	2.06
29	7.60	5.42	4.54	4.04	3.73	3.50	3.20	2.87	2.49	2.03
30	7.56	5.39	4.51	4.02	3.70	3.47	3.17	2.84	2.47	2.01
40	7.31	5.18	4.31	3.83	3.51	3.29	2.99	2.66	2.29	1.80
60	7.08	4.98	4.13	3.65	3.34	3.12	2.82	2.50	2.12	1.60
120	6.85	4.79	3.95	3.48	3.17	2.96	2.66	2.34	1.95	1.38
∞	6.64	4.60	3.78	3.32	3.02	2.80	2.51	2.18	1.79	1.00

Values of n_1 and n_2 represent the degrees of freedom associated with the between and within estimates of variance, respectively.

Appendix E   Using Statistics: Ideas for Research Projects

This appendix presents outlines for four research projects, each of which requires the use of SPSS to analyze the 2006 Census or the 2009 GSS data used throughout this textbook, though most of the projects can be done with other data sets that may be available to your instructor. The research projects should be completed at various intervals during the course, and each project permits a great deal of choice on the part of the student. The first project stresses description and should be done after completing Chapters 2 and 3. The second involves estimation and should be completed in conjunction with Chapter 6. The third project uses hypothesis testing and should be done after completing Part II, and the fourth combines inferential statistics with measures of association (with an option for multivariate analysis) and should be done after Part III (or IV).

**PROJECT 1—
DESCRIPTIVE
STATISTICS**

1. From either the 2006 Census (short version, *Census.sav*, or full version, *CensusFull.sav*) or the 2009 GSS (short version, *GSS.sav*, or full version, *GSSFull.sav*) data set, select five variables and use the **Frequencies** command to get frequency distributions and summary statistics. *(NOTE: Select at least one variable from each level of measurement.)* Click the **Statistics** button and request the mean, median, mode, standard deviation, and range. See Demonstration 3.1 for guidelines and examples. Make a note of all relevant information when it appears on screen or make a hard copy. See Appendix G for a list of variables available in the Census and GSS.

2. For each variable, get a bar chart or histogram to summarize the overall shape of the distribution of the variable. See Demonstrations 2.2 and 4.1 for guidelines and examples.

3. Inspect the frequency distributions and graphs and choose appropriate measures of central tendency and, for ordinal- and interval-ratio-level variables, dispersion. Also, for interval-ratio variables check for skew both by using the histogram and by comparing the mean and median (see Section 3.4). Write a sentence or two of description for each variable, being careful to include a description of the overall shape of the distribution (see Chapter 2) and central tendency and dispersion (see Chapter 3).

4. Below are examples of *minimal* summary sentences, using fictitious data:

   For a nominal-level variable (e.g., marital status), report the mode and some detail about the overall distribution. For example:

"Most respondents were married (57.5%), but divorced (17.4%) and single (21.3%) individuals were also common."

For an ordinal-level variable (e.g., occupational prestige), use the median (and, perhaps, the mode) and the range.

"The median prestige score was 44.3, and the range extended from 34 to 87. The most common score was 42."

For an interval-ratio level variable (e.g., population density for 124 nations), use the mean (and, perhaps, the median or mode) and the standard deviation (and, perhaps, the range).

"For these nations, population density (population per square kilometre) ranged from a low of 4.00 to a high of 12,000. The standard deviation was 1,000. The nations averaged 351 people per square kilometre, and the median density was 193. The distribution is positively skewed, and some nations have very high population density."

PROJECT 2— ESTIMATION

In this exercise, you will use the 2006 Census (short version: *Census.sav*) sample to estimate the characteristics of the Canadian population. You will use SPSS to generate the sample statistics to find the confidence interval and state each interval in words.

A. Estimating Means

1. There are relatively few interval-ratio variables in the 2006 Census, and for this part of the project, you may use ordinal variables that have *at least* three categories or scores. Choose a total of three variables that fit this description *other than* the variables you used in Exercise 6.1. *(NOTE: Your instructor may specify a different number of variables.)*

2. Use the **Explore** command to get the 95% confidence interval for the first of your variables. Repeat this procedure for the remaining variables.

3. For each variable, write a summary sentence reporting the variable, the interval itself, the confidence level, and sample size. Write in plain English, as if you were reporting results in a newspaper. Most importantly, you should make it clear that you are estimating characteristics of the entire Canadian population. For example, a summary sentence might look like this:

"Based on a random sample of 1,500, I estimate at the 95% level that Canadian drivers average between 98.46 and 102.22 kilometres per hour when driving on highways."

B. Estimating Proportions

1. Choose three variables that are nominal or ordinal with *two or three* categories *other than* the variables you used in Exercise 6.3. *(NOTE: Your instructor may specify a different number of variables.)*

2. Use the **Frequencies** command to get the percentage of the sample in the various categories of each variable. Change the percentages (remember to use the "valid percents" column) to find proportions and construct confidence intervals for one category of each variable (e.g., the % female for *sex*) using Formula 6.3.

3. For each variable, write a summary sentence reporting the variable, the interval, the confidence level, and sample size. Write in plain English, as if you were reporting results in a newspaper. Remember to make it clear that you are estimating a characteristic of the Canadian population.

4. For any one of the intervals you constructed, identify each of the following concepts and terms and briefly explain their role in estimation: sample, population, statistic, parameter, EPSEM, representative, confidence level.

**PROJECT 3 —
SIGNIFICANCE
TESTING**

Use the 2006 Census (short version: *Census.sav*) data set for this project.

A. Two-Sample *t* Test (Chapter 8)

1. Choose two different dependent variables that are measured at the interval-ratio level (since there are relatively few interval-ratio variables in the 2006 Census, you may instead use ordinal variables that have *at least* three scores). Choose independent variables that might logically be a cause of your dependent variables. Remember that, for a *t* test, independent variables can have *only* two categories. Independent variables can be any level of measurement, and you may use the same independent variable for both tests.

2. Click **Analyze, Compare Means,** and then **Independent Samples T Test**. Put your dependent variable(s) in the **Test Variable(s)** box and your independent variable in the **Grouping Variable** box. You will also need to specify the scores used to define the groups on the independent variable. See SPSS Demonstration 8.1 for an example. Make a note of the test results (group means, obtained *t* score, significance, sample size) or keep a hard copy. Repeat the procedure for the second dependent variable.

3. Write up the results of the test. At a minimum, your report should clearly identify the independent and dependent variables, the sample statistics, the value of the test statistic (step 4), the results of the test (step 5), and the alpha level you used.

B. Analysis of Variance (Chapter 9)

1. Choose two different interval-ratio dependent variables (again, given the small number of interval-ratio variables in the 2006 Census, you may instead use ordinal variables that have three or more scores). Choose independent variables that might logically be a cause of your dependent variables and that have between three and five categories. You may use the same independent variables for both tests.

2. Click **Analyze, Compare Means**, and then **One-way Anova**. The **One-way Anova** window will appear. Find your dependent variable in the variable list on the left and click the arrow to move the variable name into the **Dependent List** box. Note that you can request more than one dependent variable at a time. Next, find the name of your independent variable and move it to the **Factor** box. Click **Options** and then click the box next to **Descriptive** in the **Statistics** box to request means and standard deviations. Click **Continue** and **OK**. Make a note of the test results or keep a hard copy. Repeat, if necessary, for your second dependent variable.

3. Write up the results of the test. At a minimum, your report should clearly identify the independent and dependent variables, the sample statistics (category means), the value of the test statistic (step 4), the results of the test (step 5), the degrees of freedom, and the alpha level you used.

C. Chi Square (Chapter 10)

1. Choose two different dependent variables of any level of measurement that have five or fewer (preferably 2–3) scores. For each dependent variable, choose an independent variable that might logically be a cause. Independent variables can be any level of measurement as long as they have five or fewer (preferably 2–3) categories. Output will be easier to analyze if you use variables with few categories. You may use the same independent variable for both tests.

2. Click **Analyze, Descriptive Statistics**, and then **Crosstabs**. The **Crosstabs** dialog box will appear. Highlight your first dependent variable and move it into the **Rows** box. Next, highlight your independent variable and move it into the **Columns** box. Click the **Statistics** button at the bottom of the window and click the box next to **Chi square**. Click **Continue** and **OK**. Make a note of the results or keep a hard copy. Repeat for your second dependent variable.

3. Write up the results of the test. At a minimum, your report should clearly identify the independent and dependent variables, the value of the test statistic (step 4), the results of the test (step 5), the degrees of freedom, and the alpha level you used. It is almost always desirable to also report the column percentages (see Section 10.5).

**PROJECT 4—
ANALYZING THE
STRENGTH AND
SIGNIFICANCE OF
RELATIONSHIPS**

A. Using Bivariate Tables

1. From the 2009 GSS data set (short version, *GSS.sav*, or full version, *GSSFull.sav*), select either

   a. One dependent variable and three independent variables (possible causes) or

   b. One independent variable and three possible dependent variables (possible effects).

   Variables can be from any level of measurement but must have only a few (2–5) categories or "scores." Develop research questions or hypotheses about the relationships between variables. Make sure that the causal links you suggest are sensible and logical.

2. Use the **Crosstabs** procedure to generate bivariate tables. See any of the Demonstrations at the end of Chapters 11 or 12 for examples. Click **Analyze**, **Descriptive Statistics**, and **Crosstabs** and place your dependent variable(s) in the rows and independent variable(s) in the columns. On the **Crosstabs** dialog box, click the **Statistics** button and choose chi square, phi or V, and gamma for every table you request. On the **Crosstabs** dialog box, click the **Cells** button and get column percentages for every table you request. Make a note of results as they appear on the screen or get hard copies.

3. Write a report that presents and analyzes these relationships. Be clear about which variables are dependent and which are independent. For each combination of variables, report the test of significance and measure of association. In addition, for each relationship, report and discuss column percentages, pattern or direction of the relationship, and strength of the relationship.

4. *OPTIONAL MULTIVARIATE ANALYSIS* (*NOTE: Multivariate analysis for variables organized in table format is covered on the website for this textbook*). Pick one of the bivariate relationships you produced in step 2 and find a logical control variable for this relationship. Run **Crosstabs** for the bivariate relationship again while controlling for the third variable. Compare the partial tables with each other and with the bivariate table. Is the original bivariate relationship direct? Is there evidence of a spurious or intervening relationship? Do the variables have an interactive relationship? Write up the results of this analysis and include them in your summary paper for this project.

B. Using Interval-Ratio Variables

1. From the 2006 Census (short version: *Census.sav*; or full version: *CensusFull.sav*), select either

   a. One dependent variable and three independent variables (possible causes) or

b. One independent variable and three possible dependent variables (possible effects).

Variables should be interval-ratio in level of measurement, but you may use ordinal-level variables as long as they have more than (preferably many more than) two scores. Develop research questions or hypotheses about the relationships between variables. Make sure that the causal links you suggest are sensible and logical.

2. Use the **Regression** and **Scatterplot** (click **Graphs**, **Legacy Dialogs**, then **Scatter/Dot**) procedures to analyze the bivariate relationships. Make a note of results (including r, r^2, slope, beta-weights, and a) as they appear on the screen or print hard copies.

3. Write a report that presents and analyzes these relationships. Be clear about which variables are dependent and which are independent. For each combination of variables, report the significance of the relationship (if relevant) and the strength and direction of the relationship. Include r, r^2, and the beta-weights in your report.

4. *OPTIONAL MULTIVARIATE ANALYSIS.* Pick one of the bivariate relationships you produced in step 2 and find another logical independent variable. Run **Regression** again with both independent variables and analyze the results. How much improvement is there in the explained variance after the second independent variable is included? Write up the results of this analysis and include them in your summary paper for this project.

Appendix F   An Introduction to SPSS for Windows

Computers have affected virtually every aspect of human society, and, as you would expect, their impact on the conduct of social research has been profound. Researchers routinely use computers to organize data and compute statistics—activities that humans often find dull, tedious, and difficult but which computers accomplish with accuracy and ease. This division of labour allows social scientists to spend more time on analysis and interpretation—activities that humans typically enjoy but which are beyond the power of computers (so far, at least).

These days, the skills needed to use computers successfully are quite accessible, even for people with little or no experience. This appendix will prepare you to use a statistics program called SPSS for Windows (SPSS stands for "Statistical Package for the Social Sciences"). We use Version 20, though Versions 10 to 19 of SPSS are completely compatible with the information and instructions presented here and throughout the textbook. If you have used a mouse to "point and click" and run a computer program, you are ready to learn how to use this program. Even if you are completely unfamiliar with computers, you will find this program accessible. After you finish this appendix, you will be ready to do the exercises found at the end of most chapters of this textbook.

A word of caution before we begin: This appendix is intended only as an *introduction* to SPSS. It will give you an overview of the program and enough information so that you can complete the assignments in the textbook. It is unlikely, however, that this appendix will answer all your questions or provide solutions to all the problems you might encounter. So, this is a good place to tell you that SPSS has an extensive and easy-to-use "help" facility that will provide assistance as you request it. You should familiarize yourself with this feature and use it as needed. To get help, simply click on the **Help** command on the toolbar across the top of the screen.

SPSS is a **statistical package** (or **statpak**), a set of computer programs that work with data and compute statistics as requested by the user (you). Once you have entered the data for a particular group of observations, you can easily and quickly produce an abundance of statistical information without doing any computations yourself. Also, you can access the power of the computer without having to write computer programs yourself.

Why bother to learn this technology? The truth is that the labour-saving capacity of computers is sometimes exaggerated, and there are research situations in which they are unnecessary. If you are working with a small number of observations or need only a few, uncomplicated statistics, then statistical packages are probably not going to be helpful. However, as the number of cases increases and as your requirements for statistics become more sophisticated, computers and statpaks will become more and more useful.

An example should make this point clearer. Suppose you have gathered a sample of 150 respondents and the *only* thing you want to know about these people is their average age. To compute an average, as you know, you add the scores and divide by the total number of cases. How long do you think it would take you to add 150 two-digit numbers (ages) with a hand calculator? (Don't even think about doing it by hand.) If you entered the scores at the (pretty fast) rate of one per second, or sixty scores a minute, it would take about three or four minutes to enter the ages and get the average. Even if you worked slowly and carefully and did the addition a second and third time to check your math, you could probably complete all calculations in less than 20 minutes. If this were all the information you needed, computers and statpaks would not save you any time.

Such a simple research project is not very realistic, however. Typically, researchers deal with not one but scores or even hundreds of variables, and samples have hundreds or thousands of cases. While you could add 150 numbers in perhaps three or four minutes, how long would it take to add the scores for 1,500 cases? What are the chances of processing 1,500 numbers without making significant errors of arithmetic? The more complex the research situation, the more valuable and useful statpaks become. SPSS can produce statistical information in a few keystrokes or clicks of the mouse that might take you minutes, hours, or even days to produce with a hand calculator.

Clearly, this is technology worth mastering by any social researcher. With SPSS, you can avoid the drudgery of mere computation, spend more time on analysis and interpretation, and conduct research projects with very large data sets. Mastery of this technology might be very handy indeed in your upper-level courses, in a wide variety of jobs, or in graduate school.

F.1 GETTING STARTED—DATABASES AND COMPUTER FILES

Before statistics can be calculated, SPSS must first have some data to process. A **database** is an organized collection of related information such as the responses to a survey. For purposes of computer analysis, a database is organized into a **file**, a collection of information that is stored under the same name in the memory of the computer; on a diskette, CD-ROM, or DVD-ROM; or in some other medium. Words as well as numbers can be saved in files. If you've ever used a word processing program to type a letter or term paper, you probably saved your work in a file so that you could update or make corrections at a later time. Data can be stored in files indefinitely. Because it can take months to conduct a thorough data analysis, the ability to save a database is another advantage of using computers.

For the SPSS exercises in this textbook, we will use data from two well-established Canadian social surveys, the Census of Canada and the Canadian General Social Survey (GSS). Both surveys contain questions on a large variety of issues from a sample of Canadians. The Census and GSS are conducted regularly and have been the basis for hundreds of research projects by professional social researchers. The GSS is a rich source of information about public opinion in Canada and includes data on everything from attitudes about crime to self-evaluation of one's health. The Census provides information on the demographic, social, and economic characteristics of Canadians.

The Census and GSS are especially valuable because the respondents are chosen so that the samples as a whole are representative of the entire Canadian population. A representative sample reproduces, in miniature form, the characteristics of the population from which it was taken (see Chapter 5). So, when you analyze either the Census or GSS database, you are in effect analyzing Canadian society. The data are real, and the relationships you will analyze reflect some of the most important and sensitive issues in Canadian life.

The 2006 and 2009 versions of the Census and General Social Survey, respectively, are provided with this textbook. The complete 2006 Census and 2009 GSS databases each contain hundreds of items of information for thousands of respondents. Some of you will be using a student version of SPSS for Windows, which is limited in the number of cases and variables it can process. To accommodate these limits, we have reduced the databases to about 50 items of information and 1,500 respondents.

The 2006 Census and 2009 GSS data files are summarized in Appendix G. Please turn to this appendix and familiarize yourself with it. Note that the variables are listed alphabetically by their variable names. In many cases, the variable names (e.g., *sex*) are easy to figure out. In other cases, variable names (like *msvic*) are not so obvious. Appendix G also shows the wording of the item that generated the variable. For example, the *msvic* variable consists of responses to a question about victimization: What is the most serious *victimization* (reported by respondent) in the past 12 months? Note that the variable name is formed from the question: *most* serious *victimization* reported by the respondent? Appendix G is a code book; it lists all the codes (or scores) for each survey item along with their meanings.

It's important that you understand the difference between a statpak (SPSS) and a database (like the Census or GSS) and what we are ultimately after here. A database consists of information. A statpak organizes the information in the database and produces statistics. Our goal is to apply the statpak to the database to produce output (e.g., statistics and graphs) that we can analyze and use to answer questions. The process might be diagrammed as in Figure F.1.

FIGURE F.1   THE DATA ANALYSIS PROCESS

Database	$\rightarrow$	**Statpak**	$\rightarrow$	**Output**	$\rightarrow$	**Analysis**
(raw information)		(computer programs)		(statistics and graphs)		(interpretation)

Statpaks like SPSS are general research tools that can be used to analyze databases of all sorts; they are not limited to the 2006 Census or 2009 GSS. In the same way, the 2006 Census or 2009 GSS could be analyzed with statpaks other than those used in this textbook. Other widely used statpaks include SAS and Stata—each of which may be available on your campus.

F.2 STARTING SPSS FOR WINDOWS AND LOADING THE 2009 GSS

If you are using the complete, professional version of SPSS for Windows, you will probably be working in a computer lab, and you can begin running the program immediately. If you are using the student version of the program on your personal computer, the first thing you need to do is install the software. Follow the instructions that came with the program and return to this appendix when installation is complete.

To start SPSS for Windows, find the icon (or picture) on the screen of your monitor that has an "SPSS" label attached to it. Use the computer mouse to move the arrow on the monitor screen over this icon and then double-click the left button on the mouse. This will start up the SPSS program.

After a few seconds the SPSS for Windows screen will appear and ask, in the middle of the screen, "What would you like to do?" Of the choices listed, the button next to "Open an existing data source" will be checked (or pre-selected), and there will probably be a number of data sets listed in the window at the bottom of the screen. Find the 2009 General Social Survey data set, labelled *GSS.sav*, which we will work with in the remainder of this appendix. If you have the data set on a diskette or other medium, you will need to specify the correct drive. Check with your instructor to make sure that you know where to find the 2009 GSS.

Once you've located the data set, click on the name of the file with the left-hand button on the mouse, and SPSS will load the data. The next screen you will see is the SPSS Data Editor screen.

Note that there is a list of commands across the very top of the screen. These commands begin with **File** at the far left and end with **Help** at the far right. This is the main menu bar for SPSS. When you click any of these words, a **menu** of commands and choices will drop down. Basically, you tell SPSS what to do by clicking on your desired choices from these menus. Sometimes, submenus will appear, and you will need to specify your choices further.

SPSS provides the user with a variety of options for displaying information about the data file and output on the screen. We highly recommend that you tell the program to display lists of variables by name (e.g., *actlimit*) rather than labels (e.g., Are you limited in the amount or kind of activity you can do). Lists displayed this way will be easier to read and compare to Appendix G. To do this, click **Edit** on the main menu bar and then click **Options** from the drop-down submenu. A dialog box labelled "Options" will appear with a series of "tabs" along the top. The "General" options should be displayed but,

TABLE F.1 SUMMARY OF COMMANDS

To start SPSS for Windows	Click the SPSS icon on the screen of the computer monitor
To open a data file	Double-click on the data file name
To set display options for lists of variables	Click **Edit** from the main menu bar, then click **Options**. On the "General" tab make sure that "Display names" and "Alphabetical" are selected and then click **OK**.

if not, click on this tab. On the "General" screen, find the box labelled "Variable Lists" and, if they are not already selected, click "Display names" and "Alphabetical" and then click **OK**. If you make changes, a message may appear on the screen that tells you that changes will take effect the next time a data file is opened.

In this section, you learned how to start up SPSS for Windows, load a data file, and set some of the display options for this program. These procedures are summarized in Table F.1.

F.3 WORKING WITH THE 2009 GSS DATABASE

Note that in the SPSS Data Editor window the data are organized into a two-dimensional grid with columns running up and down (vertically) and rows running across (horizontally). Each column is a variable or item of information from the survey. The names of the variables are listed at the tops of the columns. Remember that you can find the meaning of these variable names in the GSS 2009 code book in Appendix G.

Another way to decipher the meaning of variable names is to click **Utilities** on the menu bar and then click **Variables**. The Variables window opens. This window has two parts. On the left is a list of all variables in the database arranged in alphabetical order with the first variable highlighted. On the right is the Variable Information window with information about the highlighted variable. The second variable listed, for example, is *actlimit*. The Variable Information window displays a fragment of the question that was actually asked during the survey ("Are you limited in the amount or kind of activity you can do") and shows the possible scores on this variable (a score of 1 = yes and a score of 2 = no) along with some other information.

The same information can be displayed for any variable in the data set. For example, find the variable *sex* in the list. You can do this by using the arrow keys on your keyboard or the slider bar on the right of the variable list window. You can also move through the list by typing the first letter of the variable name you are interested in. For example, type "s" and you will be moved to the first variable name in the list that begins with that letter. Now you can see that the variable measures sex and that a score of "1" indicates that the respondent is male and "2" is female. What do *relig6* and *marstat* measure? Close this window by clicking the **Close** button at the bottom of the window.

TABLE F.2   SUMMARY OF COMMANDS

To move around in the Data window	1. Click the cell you want to highlight or 2. Use the arrow keys on your keyboard or 3. Move the slider buttons or 4. Click the arrows on the right-hand and bottom margins
To get information about a variable	1. From the menu bar, click **Utilities** and then click **Variables**. Scroll through the list of variable names until you highlight the name of the variable in which you are interested. Variable information will appear in the window on the right 2. See Appendix G

Examine the window displaying the 2009 GSS a little more. Each row of the window (reading across or from left to right) contains the scores of a particular respondent on all the variables in the database. Note that the upper-left-hand cell is highlighted (shaded a darker colour than the other cells). This cell contains the score of respondent #1 on the first variable. The second row contains the scores of respondent #2, and so forth. You can move around in this window with the arrow keys on your keyboard. The highlight moves in the direction of the arrow, one cell at a time.

In this section, you learned to read information in the Data Editor window and to decipher the meaning of variable names and scores. These commands are summarized in Table F.2, and we are now prepared to actually perform some statistical operations with the 2009 GSS database.

F.4 PUTTING SPSS TO WORK ON THE 2009 GSS DATABASE: PRODUCING STATISTICS

At this point, the database on the screen is just a mass of numbers with little meaning for you. That's okay because you will not have to actually read any information from this screen. Virtually all of the statistical operations you will conduct will begin by clicking the **Analyze** command from the menu bar, selecting a procedure and statistics, and then naming the variable or variables you would like to process.

To illustrate, let's have SPSS for Windows produce a frequency distribution for the variable *sex*. Frequency distributions are tables that display the number of times each score of a variable occurred in the sample (see Chapter 2). So, when we complete this procedure, we will know the number of males and females in the 2009 GSS sample.

With the 2009 GSS loaded, begin by clicking the **Analyze** command on the menu bar. From the menu that drops down, click **Descriptive Statistics** and then **Frequencies**. The Frequencies window appears with the variables listed in alphabetical order in the box on the left. The first variable (*acmyr*) will be highlighted. Use the slider button or the arrow keys on the right-hand margin of this box to scroll through the variable list until you highlight the variable *sex*, or type "s" to move to the approximate location.

Once the variable you want to process has been highlighted, click the arrow button in the middle of the screen to move the variable name to the

TABLE F.3 AN EXAMPLE OF SPSS OUTPUT (RESPONDENTS' SEX)

		Frequency	Percent	Valid Percent	Cumulative Percent
Valid	Male	747	49.4	49.4	49.4
	Female	765	50.6	50.6	100.0
	Total	1,512	100.0	100.0	

box on the right-hand side of the screen. SPSS will produce frequency distributions for all variables listed in this box, but, for now, we will confine our attention to *sex*. Click the **OK** button in the upper-right-hand corner of the Frequencies window and, in seconds, a frequency distribution will be produced.

SPSS sends all tables and statistics to the Output window or SPSS viewer. This window is now "closest" to you, and the Data Editor window is "behind" the Output window. If you wanted to return to the Data Editor, click on any part of it if it is visible, and it will move to the "front" and the Output window will be "behind" it. To display the Data Editor window if it is not visible, minimize the Output window by clicking the "-" box in the upper-right-hand corner.

Frequencies The output from SPSS, slightly modified, is reproduced as Table F.3. What can we tell from this table? The score labels (male and female) are printed at the left with the number of cases (frequency) in each category of the variable one column to the right. As you can see, there are 747 males and 765 females in the sample. The next two columns give information about percentages and the last column to the right displays cumulative percentages. We will defer a discussion of this last column until a later exercise.

One of the percentage columns is labelled Percent and the other is labelled Valid Percent. The difference between these two columns lies in the handling of missing values. The Percent column is based on all cases, including people who did not respond to the item and people who said they did not have the requested information. The Valid Percent column excludes all missing scores. Because we will almost always want to ignore missing scores, we will pay attention only to the Valid Percent column. Note that for sex, there are no missing scores (gender was determined by the interviewer), and the two columns are identical.

F.5 COMPUTING, RECODING, AND LABELLING VARIABLES

SPSS provides a variety of ways to transform and manipulate variables. This section demonstrates how to use SPSS to create and recode variables. We will use the SPSS compute command to create a *new* variable and the SPSS recode command to transform the values of an *existing* variable.

We will also demonstrate how to add labels to make variables more meaningful.

Creating a New Variable with the Compute Command   In this demonstration, we will use the SPSS **Compute** command to create new variables and summary scales. Let's begin by considering three of the questions from the 2009 GSS that measure perception of criminal courts in Canada: *pcc_q120*, *pcc_q130*, and *pcc_q140*. Each item examines a unique aspect of attitude toward criminal courts. Specifically, the questions ask about the type of job that courts are doing in helping victims (*pcc_q120*), determining guilt (*pcc_q130*), and ensuring a fair trial (*pcc_q140*). Because these three situations are distinct, each item should be analyzed in its own right. Suppose, however, that you wanted to create a summary scale that indicated a person's *overall* feelings about Canadian criminal courts.

One way to do this would be to add the scores on the three variables together. This would create a new variable, which we will call *crtscale*, with nine possible scores since each of the three variables contain three scores (1, 2, and 3).

A respondent that consistently answered "good job" (coded as "1") to all three items would receive a score of 3 on the new summary variable. We might label this as a "highly positive" view of the overall job done by criminal courts. A score of 4 would occur when a respondent answered "good job" to any two items and "average job" (coded as "2") to the remaining item, and would indicate an overall "positive" perception. The other scores on this scale would be 5, 6, 7, 8, and 9, the highest possible score which is given to a respondent that answered "poor job" (coded as "3") to all items. This would be consistent with a "highly negative" perception of the overall work done by criminal courts. Once created, *crtscale* could be analyzed, transformed, and manipulated exactly like a variable actually recorded in the data file.

To create this scale, use the **Compute** command. Click **Transform** and then **Compute Variable** from the main menu. The **Compute Variable** window will appear. Find the **Target Variable** box in the upper-left-hand corner of this window. The first thing we need to do is assign a name to the new variable we are about to compute (*crtscale*) and type that name in this box.

Next, we need to tell SPSS how to compute the new variable. In this case, *crtscale* will be computed by adding the scores of *pcc_q120*, *pcc_q130*, and *pcc_q140*. Find *pcc_q120* in the variable list on the left and click the arrow button in the middle of the screen to transfer the variable name to the **Numeric Expression** box. Next, click the plus sign (+) on the calculator pad under the **Numeric Expression** box, and the sign will appear next to *pcc_q120*. Then, highlight *pcc_q130* in the variable list and click the arrow button to transfer the variable name to the **Numeric Expression** box. Again click the plus sign (+). Finally highlight and transfer the last variable, *pcc_q140*, into the **Numeric Expression** box.

The expression in the **Numeric Expression** box should now read *pcc_q120 + pcc_q130 + pcc_q140*. Click **OK**, and *crtscale* will be created and added to the data set. If you want to keep this new variable permanently, click **Save** from the **File** menu, and the updated data set with *crtscale* added will be saved to disk. If you are using the student version of SPSS, remember that your data set is limited to 50 variables.

We now have a new variable that measures perception of criminal courts—a more general summary item that was created from three existing items related to specific aspects of the work done by criminal courts. It is always a good idea to check the frequency distribution for computed and recoded variables to make sure that the computations were carried out correctly. Use the **Frequencies** procedure (click **Analyze**, **Descriptive Statistics**, and **Frequencies**) to get tables for *pcc_q120*, *pcc_q130*, *pcc_q140*, and *crtscale*. Your output will look like this:

Criminal courts help victims

		Frequency	Percent	Valid Percent	Cumulative Percent
Valid	Good job	373	24.7	24.7	24.7
	Average job	743	49.2	49.2	73.8
	Poor job	395	26.2	26.2	100.0
	Total	1512	100.0	100.0	

Criminal courts good at sentencing

		Frequency	Percent	Valid Percent	Cumulative Percent
Valid	Good job	525	34.7	34.7	34.7
	Average job	775	51.3	51.3	86.0
	Poor job	212	14.0	14.0	100.0
	Total	1512	100.0	100.0	

Criminal courts ensure a fair trial

		Frequency	Percent	Valid Percent	Cumulative Percent
Valid	Good job	783	51.8	51.8	51.8
	Average job	620	41.0	41.0	92.8
	Poor job	108	7.2	7.2	100.0
	Total	1512	100.0	100.0	

crtscale

		Frequency	Percent	Valid Percent	Cumulative Percent
Valid	3.00 (highly positive)	261	17.3	17.3	17.3
	4.00	229	15.2	15.2	32.4
	5.00	248	16.4	16.4	48.8
	6.00	435	28.8	28.8	77.6
	7.00	217	14.4	14.4	92.0
	8.00	57	3.8	3.8	95.7
	9.00 (highly negative)	64	4.3	4.3	100.0
	Total	1512	100.0	100.0	

Looking at the first three tables we see that the level of approval varies by item. Only about 25% of respondents feel that criminal courts do a good job at helping victims, while more than half (52%) feel that criminal courts do a good job at ensuring a fair trial.

The new variable, *crtscale* shown in the final table above, summarizes each respondent's overall position on the issue. (Note, as a convenience we added labels to the first and last values to improve the readability of this table. We will demonstrate how to add labels at the end of this section.)

We see that about 17% of the sample believe that the courts do a good job in all three areas (scored 3), while less than 5% believe the courts do a poor job (scored 9). Thus, there are many more Canadians who have a "highly positive" view of the overall job done by criminal courts than there those that have a "highly negative" perception. Most Canadians, however, fall somewhere in between these two extremes. In fact, about 29% of the sample scored a 6, meaning that they approved of the work done in some situations but not in all cases.

Notice that the total number of respondents (1,512) is equal for all three questions, and therefore, this number is equal to the number of cases included in the combined scale *crtscale*. This means there are no missing values in the variables measured. In most practical settings, however, researchers encounter missing values in some or all of their questions. Let's assume such a situation. If, for example, only 1,000 respondents answered the question about "criminal courts ensuring a fair trial" but all 1,512 respondents answered the other two questions, the number of cases included in the computed scale, *crtscale*, would be 1,000. That is, when SPSS executes a **Compute** statement, it automatically eliminates any cases that are missing scores on any of the constituent items. If these cases were not eliminated, a variety of errors and misclassifications could result.

Collapsing Categories with the Recode Command   We often need to make a variable more compact by collapsing its scores into fewer categories. SPSS provides a number of ways to change the scores of a variable, and one of the most useful of these is the **Recode** command.

As an example of using this command, we will create a new version of the variable *incmhsd* (total household income) that has fewer categories and is more suitable for display in a frequency distribution. When we are finished, we will have two different versions of the same variable in the data set: the original version and a new version with collapsed categories. We recommend that the new version be added to the permanent data file because it will be used in future demonstrations.

We have decided to collapse the values of *incmhsd* into four categories. We begin by collapsing all respondents with values 1 (no income) through 6 ($20,000–$29,999) on *incmhsd* into a value of 1. Hence, this collapsed category includes all respondents with total household incomes of $29,999 or less. The next recodes involve collapsing values 7 ($30,000–$39,999) through 9 ($50,000–$59,999) on *incmhsd* into a value of 2, values 10 ($60,000–$79,999) through 11 ($80,000–$99,999) on *incmhsd* into a value of 3, and finally values 12 ($100,000 –$149,999) through 13 ($150,000 or more) on *incmhsd* into a value of 4. As you will see, recoding requires many small steps, so please be patient and execute the commands as they are discussed.

1. In the **SPSS Data Editor** window, click **Transform** from the menu bar where you can find two types of recode commands: **Recode into Same Variables** and **Recode into Different Variables**. If we choose the former (**Recode into Same Variables**), the new version of the variable will replace the old version—the original version of *incmhsd* (total household income) would disappear. We definitely do not want this to happen, so we will choose (click on) **Recode into Different Variables**. This option will allow us to keep both the old and new versions of the variable.

2. The **Recode into Different Variables** dialog box will open. A list box containing an alphabetical list of variables is on the left. Use your mouse to highlight *incmhsd* and then click on the arrow button to move the variable to the **Input Variable → Output Variable** box. The input variable is the old version of *incmhsd,* and the output variable is the new, recoded version we will soon create.

3. In the **Output Variable** box on the right, click in the **Name** text box and type a name for the new (output) variable. We suggest *income4* (total household income grouped into four categories) for the new variable, but you can assign any name as long as it does not duplicate the name of some other variable in the data set. Click the **Change** button and the expression *incmhsd → income4* will appear in the **Input Variable → Output Variable** box.

4. Click on the **Old and New Values** button in the middle of the screen, and a new dialog box will open.

5. Read down the left-hand column in the **Old Value** box until you find the **Range** button. Click on the button, and the cursor will move to the small text box immediately below. Type 1 into the first **Range** text box and then click on the second text box and type 6. In the **New Value** box in the upper-right-hand corner of the screen, click the **Value** button. Type 1 in the **Value** text box and then click the **Add** button directly below. The expression "1 thru 6 → 1" will appear in the **Old → New** dialog box. This completes the first recode instruction to SPSS.

   Note, alternatively, for the first category, you can choose the **Range, LOWEST through value** button. The cursor will move to the small box immediately below. Then type 6 in the text box. Do not forget to type 1 in the **New Value** box and click the **Add** button. The expression "Lowest thru 6 → 1" appears in the **Old → New** box.

6. Continue recoding by returning to the **Range** text boxes on the left. Type 7 in the first box under the **Range** option and 9 in the second box, and then click the **Value** button in the **New Values** box. Type 2 in the **Value** text box and then click the **Add** button. The expression "7 thru 9 → 2" appears in the **Old → New** box.

7. Return again to the **Range** text boxes, and specify the low and high points of next interval. Type 10 in the first box under the **Range** option and 11 in the second box and then click the **Value** button in the **New Values** box. Type 3 in the **Value** text box and then click the **Add** button. The expression "10 thru 11 → 3" appears in the **Old → New** box.

8. For the last recode, return to the **Range** text boxes. Type 12 in the first box under the **Range** option and 13 in the second box and then click the **Value** button in the **New Values** box. Type 4 in the **Value** text box and then click the **Add** button. The expression "12 thru 13 → 4" appears in the **Old → New** box.

   Note, the values 98 and 99 are defined as missing in the original variable *incmhsd*, and are automatically redefined during the recode procedure as missing and re-labeled as "." [period] in the new variable *income4*. Because this is done automatically by SPSS, these cases are referred to as "system" missing values.

9. Now click the **Continue** button at the bottom of the screen, and you will return to the **Recode into Different Variable** dialog box. Click **OK**, and SPSS will execute the transformation.

You now have a data set with one more variable named *income4* (or whatever name you gave the recoded variable). SPSS adds the new variable to the data set, and you can find it in the last column to the right in the data window. You can make the new variable a permanent part of the data set by saving the data file at the end of the session. If you do not wish to save the new, expanded data file, click **No** when you are asked if you want to save the data file. Remember that if you are using the student version of SPSS for Windows you are limited to a maximum of 50 variables, and you will not be able to save more than two new variables (unless you delete other variables to make space) because there are already 48 variables in the 2009 GSS data set.

Finally, to make sure that no mistakes were made in the recoding process, produce a frequency distribution for *income4* using the **Frequencies** command. The table should look like this:

Income4

		Frequency	Percent	Valid Percent	Cumulative Percent
Valid	1	122	8.1	9.8	9.8
	2	295	19.5	23.5	33.2
	3	370	24.5	29.5	62.7
	4	469	31.0	37.3	100.0
	Total	1256	83.1	100.0	
Missing	System	256	16.9		
Total		1512	100.0		

The sample is particularly clustered around categories 3 and 4, or between $60,000 to $99,999 and $100,000 or more—over 65% of the sample is in these category. There are relatively fewer respondents in the lowest income group, category 1, or <$30,000.

Adding Labels   This table can be made easier to read and more meaningful by attaching labels. There are two types of labels that can be attached to a variable.

First, a "variable label" provides a description of the variable. For example we may decide to label our new variable *income4* "recode version of total household income." To do this, click the **Variable View** tab located at the bottom of the SPSS Data Editor screen. The first column, **Name**, in the variable view window contains the names of the variables in the data file. Scroll up or down this window until you locate the variable name *income4*, which will be in the last row. Next, click on the cell in the **Label** column and type: recode version of total household income (or any other label that you want to use for the variable). SPSS output for this variable will now display both the name and label.

Second, labels can be applied to the values of a variable. Thus, whereas a "variable label" provides a description of the entire variable, a "value label" describes the meaning of each value of a variable. To add value labels to *income4*, click the **Variable View** tab located at the bottom of the SPSS Data

Editor screen, and scroll to the row containing the variable name (*income4*). Next, click on the cell in the **Values** column, which initially indicates "**None**" of the values has been labelled, then click on the button with the three dots in it. The **Value Labels** dialog box will open. Type the first value (1) into the **Value** text box and its label into the **Value Label** text box (<$30,000, or any other label that you want to use for the value). Then click **Add**. Next, enter the second value (2) into the **Value** text box and its label into the **Value Label** text box ($30,000–$59,999). Repeat this exercise for each value, making sure to click **Add** after each entry. (You can fix or delete any entry by highlighting it in the large display box and clicking **Change** or **Remove**.) Click **OK** after all values labels have been added.

SPSS output will now display all labels. For example, the **Frequencies** command will produce a frequency distribution for *income4* as follows:

Income4

recode version of total household income

		Frequency	Percent	Valid Percent	Cumulative Percent
Valid	<$30,000	122	8.1	9.8	9.8
	$30,000–$59,999	295	19.5	23.5	33.2
	$60,000–$99,999	370	24.5	29.5	62.7
	$100,000+	469	31.0	37.3	100.0
	Total	1256	83.1	100.0	
Missing	System	256	16.9		
Total		1512	100.0		

F.6 EDITING OUTPUT

SPSS output can be edited directly in the **Output** window. To edit a table, double-click on any part of the table. Next, double-click the exact area of the table to be edited, and make the appropriate revision. To edit a graph, double-click on any part of the graph in the **Output** window and the SPSS **Chart Editor** window will appear. This window gives you a wide array of options for the final appearance of the chart.

For example, if you want to change the colour of some elements (e.g., bars or background) in the chart, first you need to click on the elements to be highlighted, then click on the **Edit** menu and choose **Properties**. (Alternatively, you can directly open the **Properties** dialog box by right clicking anywhere on the highlighted elements then choosing **Properties Window**.) The **Properties** dialog box will appear where you can find different options under each tab. For example, the options for changing the colour of the elements is the **Fill & Border** tab. Explore these options at your leisure using the **Help** button at the bottom of the window as necessary. You need to close the **SPSS Chart Editor** window and return to the **Output** window to see the changes you have made.

F.7 PRINTING, SAVING, PASTING, AND EXPORTING OUTPUT

Once you've gone to the trouble of producing statistics, a table, or a graph, you will probably want to keep a permanent record. There are three ways to do this. First, you can print a copy of the contents of the SPSS Viewer to take with you. To do this, click on **File** and then click **Print** from the **File** menu. Alternatively, find the icon of a printer (third from the left) in the row of icons just below the menu bar and click on it.

The second way to create a permanent record of SPSS output is to save the window to the computer's memory or to a diskette or other medium. To do this, click **Save** from the **File** menu. The Save dialog box opens. Give the output a name (some abbreviation such as "freqsex" might do) and, if necessary, specify the name of the drive in which your diskette is located. Click **OK**, and the table will be permanently saved.

Third, tables and charts in the Output window can be used in many applications, including word processors. Specifically, SPSS output tables and charts can be pasted into a word processing document. Formats are retained and can be edited in the word processor. (Note that charts are pasted in graph format and tables in table format.)

To paste, click on any part of the table or chart in the SPSS Output window, then click **Copy** from the **Edit** menu. Next, open your word processor, and click **Paste** from the **Edit** menu. Repeat this process separately for each table or chart that you want to paste into the word processor document.

Alternatively, SPSS output tables and charts can be exported to a document. From the SPSS Output window, click **Export** from the **File** menu. Next, select **Word/RTF file (*.doc)** from the **File Type** drop-down list, and click **OK**. Then, open your word processor, click **Open** from the **Edit** menu, and double-click the file name to open it. You may have to change the folder specification to locate the file. By default, SPSS names the file OUTPUT and saves it in the SPSS program folder.

F.8 ENDING YOUR SPSS FOR WINDOWS SESSION

Once you have saved or printed your work, you may end your SPSS session. Click on **File** from the menu bar and then click **Exit**. If you haven't already done so, you will be asked if you want to save the contents of the Output window. You may save the frequency distribution at this point if you wish. Otherwise, click **NO**. The program will close, and you will be returned to the screen from which you began.

Appendix G   Information and Code Books for the 2006 Census and 2009 General Social Survey

G.1 INTRODUCTION TO CENSUS AND GSS

Four data sets from two social surveys, the 2006 Census of Canada and the 2009 Canadian General Social Survey (GSS), are provided on the website for the textbook. The data sets are named *CensusFull.sav*, *Census.sav*, *GSSFull.sav*, and *GSS.sav*. SPSS uses the file extension ".sav" as a saved data format. These files will load easily into most versions of SPSS.

The Census and GSS are conducted by Statistics Canada. The GSS is a public-opinion poll that has been conducted annually since 1985 on representative samples of Canadians aged 15 years and older living in private households in the 10 provinces. The content and focus of the survey change each year. The 2009 GSS contained items on the nature and extent of criminal victimization in Canada, as well as demographic and background characteristics of the respondents.

The Census, on the other hand, is an enumeration of the entire Canadian population, and is conducted every five years. It collects information on the demographic, social, and economic characteristics of Canadians.

The Census data set that is supplied with this textbook is based on a random sample, called the Public Use Microdata File for individuals, or PUMF, of all persons in the population enumerated in the 2006 Census. The 2006 Census PUMF for individuals contains 140 variables, including family composition, labour-force activity, and income. Because many of these variables are not applicable to younger Canadians, we restricted the sample to adults (i.e., persons 15 and over).

G.2 CENSUS AND GSS DATA SETS

The original Census and GSS data sets each contain dozens of variables on a sample of thousands of cases. We have shortened the Census (*Census.sav*) and GSS (*GSS.sav*) data sets to about 50 variables and 1,500 randomly selected cases to be compatible with the student version of SPSS. (SPSS Student Version, created for classroom instruction, is in essence the full version of the SPSS base software but limited to a maximum of 50 variables and 1,500 cases.) These shortened data sets are used for all of the end-of-chapter exercises.

For those using the full, professional version of SPSS for Windows, we additionally provide the complete Census and GSS data sets (*CensusFull.sav* and *GSSFull.sav*). They include the original random samples for the variables in the shortened Census and GSS data sets.

Variables in the Census and GSS data sets were selected to best meet the objectives of this textbook, and to provide students with the ability to examine issues of current and emerging interest. The code book for the Census and GSS data sets are provided below. The variable names, shown in the left margin, are those used in the data file to identify the variables. A description or the exact question as it was asked on the Census and GSS questionnaires for each variable is provided. The numbers beside each response are the scores recorded in each data set.

The website for the textbook provides further information on the Census and GSS. Detailed descriptions and frequency distributions for all variables in the full sample, as well as information on other issues such as sampling design and data collection, are contained in the files named *Census_guide.pdf* and *GSS_guide.pdf* on the website.

In sum, the four data sets provided with, and used throughout, this textbook are:

1. *CensusFull.sav*. The full (complete sample) version of the 2006 Census of Canada.
2. *Census.sav*. The short (1,500 randomly selected cases) version of the 2006 Census of Canada.
3. *GSSFull.sav*. The full (complete sample) version of the 2009 General Social Survey (GSS).
4. *GSS.sav*. The short (1,500 randomly selected cases) version of the 2009 General Social Survey (GSS).

G.3 SPSS STUDENT VERSION

The SPSS Student Version is available at many campus bookstores.

G.4 MISSING DATA AND SAMPLE DESIGN IN THE CENSUS AND GSS

It is important to comment on two features of the data sets. First, social survey data like the Census and GSS typically contain "missing data." Missing data occur when a respondent did not (e.g., refused to) or could not (e.g., lacked the information to) answer a specific question. Most variables in the original Census and GSS data sets had relatively few missing cases. The missing cases for these variables were simply excluded from the data files supplied with this textbook.

On the other hand, a few other variables (e.g., income) contained significantly more missing cases. Deleting these cases may produce biased data and results, so for these variables, missing data were retained but defined as missing in data sets. For example, missing cases for the variable *incm* (annual personal income) in the GSS data set were assigned the numeric values of 98 and 99, and then defined as missing. These missing data will be automatically eliminated from all statistical analysis, unless SPSS is commanded to do otherwise. Missing data are a common problem in survey research that, if significant in number, may jeopardize the integrity of the inquiry.

Second, the sample data in the Census file were selected according to the principles of EPSEM as discussed in Chapter 5. The GSS, like the vast majority of Statistics Canada surveys, uses a "complex" sampling design that is ultimately based on the principle of EPSEM. It is said to be "complex" as opposed to "simple" (as in "simple" random sampling) because of the types and combinations of sampling methods used—the GSS uses a stratified, multi-stage cluster design with probability sampling at all stages to select a representative sample of persons 15 years of age and older in Canada (excluding residents of the Yukon, Northwest Territories, Nunavut, and full-time residents of institutions).

However, the GSS uses an *unequal* probability of selection method. That is, it under- and over-samples various groups of individuals to ensure that subpopulations of interest to the survey, such as persons 65 and older, are represented in the sample. Because individuals do not have an equal probability of selection, it is necessary to "weight" (correct) the sample to approximate an EPSEM sample. A weight variable, called *wght_per*, was calculated by Statistics Canada. It is included in the GSS data file, and once you open the GSS file in SPSS, the weight variable is automatically "turned on" to correct for this bias. In the *GSS.sav* data file, for example, with the weight turned on, the sample of 1,500 cases actually converts to a sample size of 1,512.

G.5 GSS CODE BOOK

acmyr

Main activity of the respondent in the last 12 months.
1. Working at a paid job or business
2. Looking for paid work
3. Going to school
4. Caring for children
5. Household work
6. Retired
7. Maternity/paternity leave
8. Long term illness
9. Volunteering or care-giving other than for children
10. Other

actlimit

Are you limited in the amount or kind of activity you can do at home, at work, or at school or in other activities because of a long-term physical or mental condition or health problem?
1. Yes
2. No

agegr5	Age group of the respondent.

1. 15 to 17	2. 18 to 19
3. 20 to 24	4. 25 to 29
5. 30 to 34	6. 35 to 39
7. 40 to 44	8. 45 to 49
9. 50 to 54	10. 55 to 59
11. 60 to 64	12. 65 to 69
13. 70 to 74	14. 75 to 79
15. 80 years and over	

discrim — Respondent has been a victim of discrimination (because of his/her sex, ethnicity, race, religion, sexual orientation, age, disability, or language) in the past five years.
1. Yes
2. No

drr_q110 — In the past month, how often did you drink alcoholic beverages? Was it:
1. ...every day
2. ...4 to 6 times a week
3. ...2 to 3 times a week
4. ...once a week
5. ...once or twice in the past month
6. ...never in the past month
7. ...never drinks

drr_q120 — How many times in the past month have you had 5 or more drinks on the same occasion?

   97 Not asked: never drinks or did not drink (***defined as missing in the data set***)

dwelc — Dwelling type of the respondent.
1. Single detached house
2. Low-rise apartment ($<$5 stories)
3. High-rise apartment (5+ stories)
4. Other

dwellown — Dwelling owned by a member of the household?
1. Yes
2. No

edu10 — Highest level of education obtained by the respondent—10 groups.
1. Doctorate/masters/some graduate
2. Bachelor's degree
3. Diploma/certificate from community college
4. Diploma/certificate from trade/technical
5. Some university
6. Some community college/CEGEP/nursing
7. Some trade/technical

8. High school diploma
9. Some secondary/high school
10. Elementary school/no schooling

famtype Respondent's type of family structure.
1. Couple only
2. Intact family
3. Stepfamily with common child
4. Stepfamily without a common child
5. Lone-parent family
7. Not asked; no spouse/partner or children in household

hal_q410 Are your daily activities at home, work, school or any other area limited by a physical condition?
1. No
2. Sometimes
3. Often or always

hsdsizec Household size of respondent.
1. One household member
2. Two household members
3. Three household members
4. Four household members
5. Five household members
6. Six household members or more

incm Annual personal income of the respondent
1. No income
2. Less than $5,000
3. $5,000 to $9,999
4. $10,000 to $14,999
5. $15,000 to $19,999
6. $20,000 to $29,999
7. $30,000 to $39,999
8. $40,000 to $49,999
9. $50,000 to $59,999
10. $60,000 to $79,999
11. $80,000 to $99,999
12. $100,000 or more
98. Not stated (*defined as missing in the data set*)
99. Don't know (*defined as missing in the data set*)

incmhsd Total household income.
1. No income or loss
2. Less than $5,000
3. $5,000 to $9,999

4. $10,000 to $14,999
5. $15,000 to $19,999
6. $20,000 to $29,999
7. $30,000 to $39,999
8. $40,000 to $49,999
9. $50,000 to $59,999
10. $60,000 to $79,999
11. $80,000 to $99,999
12. $100,000 to $149,999
13. $150,000 or more
98. Not stated (*defined as missing in the data set*)
99. Don't know (*defined as missing in the data set*)

lanhsdc   Respondent's household language.
1. English only
2. French only
3. Other language

lifevict   Victim of crime—lifetime.
1. Yes
2. No

live_neigh   Length of time respondent has lived in current neighbourhood.
1. Less than 6 months
2. 6 months to less than 1 year
3. 1 year to less than 3 years
4. 3 years to less than 5 years
5. 5 years to less than 10 years
6. 10 years and over

luc_rst   Urban/rural indicator.
1. Urban
2. Rural

marstat   Marital status of the respondent.
1. Married
2. Living common-law
3. Widowed
4. Separated
5. Divorced
6. Single (Never married)

med_depress   Medication of respondent—to help you get out of depression.
1. Yes
2. No

msvic	Most serious victimization reported by respondent in the past 12 months— excludes spousal and ex-spousal abuse.

       101. Sexual assault
       202. Robbery
       203. Attempted robbery
       304. Assault
       405. Break and enter
       406. Attempted break and enter
       507. Motor vehicle theft
       508. Part of a motor vehicle theft
       509. Attempted motor vehicle (parts) theft
       610. Theft of personal property
       611. Attempted theft of personal property
       712. Theft of household property
       713. Attempted theft of household property
       814. Vandalism
       997. Not applicable (No crime reported)
       999. Unclassifiable

numevact_c   Average number of evening activities respondent goes out for in a month.
       62. 62 and more

oce_q180   Respondent has reported stalking incident(s).
       1. Yes
       2. No

pcc_q120   Are the Canadian criminal courts doing a good job, an average job, or a poor job: ... of helping the victim?
       1. Good job
       2. Average job
       3. Poor job

pcc_q130   Are the Canadian criminal courts doing a good job, an average job, or a poor job: ... of determining whether the accused or the person charged is guilty or not?
       1. Good job
       2. Average job
       3. Poor job

pcc_q140   Are the Canadian criminal courts doing a good job, an average job, or a poor job: ... of ensuring a fair trial for the accused?
       1. Good job
       2. Average job
       3. Poor job

pcc_q150   In general, would you say that sentences handed down by the courts are too severe, about right, or not severe enough?
       1. Too severe
       2. About right
       3. Not severe enough

phr_q110   Compared to other areas in Canada, do you think your neighbourhood has a higher amount of crime, about the same, or a lower amount of crime?
1. Higher
2. About the same
3. Lower

phr_q120   During the last 5 years, do you think that crime in your neighbourhood has increased, decreased, or remained about the same?
1. Increased
2. Decreased
3. About the same

phr_q135   How safe do you feel from crime walking ALONE in your area after dark? Do you feel:
1. very safe?   2. reasonably safe?
3. somewhat unsafe?   4. very unsafe?
5. does not walk alone

phr_q190   When alone in your home in the evening or at night, do you feel:
1. ... very worried?
2. ... somewhat worried?
3. ... not at all worried about your safety from crime?
4. ... never alone

phr_q200   In general, how satisfied are you with your personal safety from crime? Are you:
1. ... very satisfied?
2. ... somewhat satisfied?
3. ... somewhat dissatisfied?
4. ... very dissatisfied?
5. ... No opinion

plp_q130   Do you think your local police force does a good job, an average job, or a poor job: ... of being approachable and easy to talk to?
1. Good job
2. Average job
3. Poor job

plp_q150   Do you think your local police force does a good job, an average job, or a poor job: ... of ensuring the safety of the citizens in your area?
1. Good job
2. Average job
3. Poor job

plp_q160   Do you think your local police force does a good job, an average job, or a poor job: ... of treating people fairly?
1. Good job
2. Average job
3. Poor job

ppp_q110 | Do you think that the prison system does a good job, an average job, or a poor job: ... of supervising and controlling prisoners while in prison?
1. Good job
2. Average job
3. Poor job

ppp_q120 | Do you think that the prison system does a good job, an average job, or a poor job: ... of helping prisoners become law-abiding citizens?
1. Good job
2. Average job
3. Poor job

ppp_q160 | Do you think that the parole system does a good job, an average job, or a poor job: ... of releasing offenders who are not likely to commit another crime?
1. Good job
2. Average job
3. Poor job

ppp_q170 | Do you think that the parole system does a good job, an average job, or a poor job: ... of supervising offenders on parole?
1. Good job
2. Average job
3. Poor job

prv | Province of residence of the respondent.
10. Newfoundland and Labrador
11. Prince Edward Island
12. Nova Scotia
13. New Brunswick
24. Quebec
35. Ontario
46. Manitoba
47. Saskatchewan
48. Alberta
59. British Columbia

relig6 | Religion of respondent. In six categories.
1. No religion
2. Roman Catholic
3. United Church
4. Protestant
5. Other
6. Para-religious groups or unknown

rlr_q110 | How important are your religious or spiritual beliefs to the way that you live your life? Would you say it is:
1. ... very important?
2. ... somewhat important?
3. ... not very important?
4. ... not at all important?

sex Sex of the respondent.
1. Male
2. Female

srh_q110 In general, would you say your health is:
1. Excellent? 2. Very good?
3. Good? 4. Fair?
5. Poor?

vismin Visible minority status.
1. Visible minority
2. Non-visible minority

wght_per Person Weight

wkwehr_c Number of hours usually worked at all jobs in a week.
0. Not asked (Not working at a paid job or business)
75. 75 and more hours

yrarri Range of years when the respondent came to live permanently in Canada.
1. Before 1946
2. 1946 to 1959
3. 1960 to 1964
4. 1965 to 1969
5. 1970 to 1974
6. 1975 to 1979
7. 1980 to 1984
8. 1985 to 1989
9. 1990 to 1994
10. 1995 to 1999
11. 2000 to 2004
12. 2005 to 2009
97. Not asked; Born in Canada/Canadian citizen by birth

G.6 CENSUS CODE BOOK

agegrp Age group of the respondent.
6. 15 to 17 7. 18 to 19
8. 20 to 24 9. 25 to 29
10. 30 to 34 11. 35 to 39
12. 40 to 44 13. 45 to 49
14. 50 to 54 15. 55 to 59
16. 60 to 64 17. 65 to 69
18. 70 to 74 19. 75 to 79
20. 80 to 84 21. 85 years and over

attsch	Refers to either full-time or part-time (day or evening) attendance at school, college or university during the nine-month period between September 2005 and May 16, 2006.

    1. Did not attend school
    2. Attended school

citizen	Legal citizenship status of the respondent.

    1. Canadian, by birth
    2. Canadian naturalization
    3. Not Canadian citizen

cma	Area (census metropolitan area or CMA) of residence of the respondent.

    205. Halifax
    399. Moncton - Saint John
    421. Québec
    462. Montréal
    499. Sherbrooke - Trois-Rivières
    505. Ottawa - Gatineau
    532. Oshawa
    535. Toronto
    537. Hamilton
    539. St. Catharines - Niagara
    541. Kitchener
    555. London
    559. Windsor
    577. Brantford - Guelph - Barrie
    588. Kingston - Peterborough
    599. Greater Sudbury/Grand Sudbury - Thunder Bay
    602. Winnipeg
    799. Regina - Saskatoon
    825. Calgary
    835. Edmonton
    933. Vancouver
    935. Victoria
    988. Kelowna - Abbotsford
    999. Other census metropolitan areas, Census Agglomerations and other geographies

dist	Refers to the distance, in kilometres, between the respondent's residence and his or her usual workplace location

    1. Less than 5 km
    2. 5 to 9.9 km
    3. 10 to 14.9 km
    4. 15 to 19.9 km
    5. 20 to 24.9 km

6. 25 to 29.9 km
7. 30 km or more
9. Not in the Labour Force or Work at Home

ethder   Refers to the ethnic or cultural group(s) to which the respondent's ancestors belong.

1. Canadian
2. Provincial or regional origins
3. Aboriginal origins
4. French origins
5. English
6. Irish
7. Scottish
8. Welsh
9. Other British origins
10. Jamaican
11. Other Caribbean origins
12. Latin, Central and South American origins
13. Dutch (Netherlands)
14. German
15. Other Western European origins
16. Swedish
17. Norwegian
18. Danish
19. Finnish
20. Other Northern European origins
21. Hungarian (Magyar)
22. Polish
23. Russian
24. Ukrainian
25. Romanian
26. Other Eastern European origins
27. Greek
28. Italian
29. Portuguese
30. Spanish
31. Other Southern European origins
32. Jewish
33. African origins
34. Lebanese
35. Other Arab origins
36. West Asian origins
37. East Indian
38. Other South Asian origins
39. Chinese

40. Filipino
41. Korean
42. Vietnamese
43. Other East and Southeast Asian origins
44. All other single response origins
45. Canadian, British, French and provincial origins only
46. Canadian, British, French and provincial and other origins only
47. Aboriginal origins only
48. Aboriginal and Canadian, British, French and provincial origins only
49. Aboriginal and Canadian, British, French and provincial and other origins
50. Aboriginal and other origins only

fol   First official language spoken
1. English
2. French
3. Both English and French
4. Neither English nor French

fptwk   Refers to persons who worked for pay or in self-employment in 2005.
1. Worked mainly full-time weeks in 2005
2. Worked mainly part-time weeks in 2005
9. Not in the Labour Force

genstat   Generation status of the respondent.
1. 1st generation
2. 2nd: Parents not born in Canada
3. 2nd: One parent born in Canada
4. 3rd and over

grosrt   Refers to the total average monthly payments paid by tenant households to secure shelter.
9999. Persons in owner occupied dwellings (*defined as missing in the data set*)

gtrfs   Refers to total income from all transfer payments received by respondent from federal, provincial, territorial or municipal governments during calendar year 2005.

hdgree   Highest certificate, diploma or degree
1. None
2. High school graduation certificate or equivalency certificate
3. Other trades certificate or diploma
4. Registered apprenticeship certificate

5. College, CEGEP or other non-university certificate or diploma from a program of 3 months to less than 1 year
6. College, CEGEP or other non-university certificate or diploma from a program of 1 year to 2 years
7. College, CEGEP or other non-university certificate or diploma from a program of more than 2 years
8. University certificate or diploma below bachelor level
9. Bachelor's degree
10. University certificate or diploma above bachelor level
11. Degree in medicine, dentistry, veterinary medicine or optometry
12. Master's degree
13. Earned doctorate degree

hhinc　　Refers to the total income of a household (i.e., sum of the total incomes of all members of that household).

1. Under $2,000	2. $2,000 to $4,999
3. $5,000 to $6,999	4. $7,000 to $9,999
5. $10,000 to $11,999	6. $12,000 to $14,999
7. $15,000 to $16,999	8. $17,000 to $19,999
9. $20,000 to $24,999	10. $25,000 to $29,999
11. $30,000 to $34,999	12. $35,000 to $39,999
13. $40,000 to $44,999	14. $45,000 to $49,999
15. $50,000 to $54,999	16. $55,000 to $59,999
17. $60,000 to $64,999	18. $65,000 to $69,999
19. $70,000 to $74,999	20. $75,000 to $79,999
21. $80,000 to $89,999	22. $90,000 to $99,999
23. $100,000 to $124,999	24. $125,000 to $149,999
25. $150,000 to $174,999	26. $175,000 to $199,999
27. $200,000 to $249,999	28. $250,000 and over

hhsize　　Number of persons in a household.
7. 7+ persons

hhtype　　Type of household
1. One family, married couple
2. One family, common-law couple
3. One family, lone parent family
4. More than one family
5. Person living alone
6. Two or more persons not in census families

hrswrk　　Refers to the actual number of hours that persons worked for pay or in self-employment at all jobs held in the week (Sunday to Saturday) prior to Census Day (May 16, 2006).
0. Not in the Labour Force
84. 84 hrs+

invst   Refers to interest or other investment income received during calendar year 2005 by the respondent.

lfact   Refers to the labour market activity of the respondent in the week (Sunday to Saturday) prior to Census Day (May 16, 2006).
1. Employed - Worked in reference week
2. Employed - Absent in reference week
3. Unemployed - Temporary layoff - Did not look for work
4. Unemployed - Temporary layoff - Looked for full-time work
5. Unemployed - Temporary layoff - Looked for part-time work
6. Unemployed - New job - Did not look for work
7. Unemployed - New job - Looked for full-time work
8. Unemployed - New job - Looked for part-time work
9. Unemployed - Looked for full-time work
10. Unemployed - Looked for part-time work
11. Not in the labour force - Last worked in 2006
12. Not in the labour force - Last worked in 2005
13. Not in the labour force - Last worked before 2005
14. Not in the labour force - Never worked

lico   The income status of the respondent in relation to Statistics Canada's low income cut-offs (LICOs) (i.e., poverty line).
1. Above LICO
2. Below LICO

marst   Legal marital status
1. Divorced
2. Legally married (and not separated)
3. Separated, but still legally married
4. Never legally married (single)
5. Widowed

mfs   Refers to the predominant discipline or area of learning or training of a person's highest postsecondary degree, certificate or diploma.
1. Educational, recreational and counselling services
2. Fine and applied arts
3. Humanities and related fields
4. Social sciences and related fields
5. Commerce, management and business administration
6. Agricultural, biological, nutritional, and food sciences
7. Engineering and applied sciences
8. Applied science technologies and trades
9. Health professions and related technologies
10. Mathematics, computer and physical sciences
11. No postsecondary qualifications

mode   Refers to the mode of transportation to work by the respondent.
1. Bicycle
2. Car, truck, van as driver
3. Motorcycle
4. Other mode
5. Car, truck, van as passenger
6. Taxicab
7. Public transit
8. Walked
9. Not in the Labour Force or Work at Home

mrkinc   Refers to the sum of employment income, investment income, retirement pensions, superannuation and annuities, and other money income received by the respondent during calendar year 2005.

nochrd   Occupation of the respondent.
1. Managers
2. Professionals
3. Semi-professionals and technicians
4. Supervisors
5. Administrative and senior clerical personnel
6. Skilled sales and service personnel
7. Skilled crafts and trades workers
8. Clerical personnel
9. Intermediate sales and service personnel
10. Semi-skilled manual workers
11. Other sales and service personnel
12. Other manual workers
99. Not in the Labour Force

omp   Refers to the total average monthly payments made by owner of households to secure shelter.
9999. Persons in tenant occupied dwellings (***defined as missing in the data set***)

otinc   Refers to all regular cash income received by the respondent during calendar year 2005 and not reported in any of the other sources listed in the data set.

pr   Province or territory of residence of the respondent.
10. Newfoundland and Labrador
11. Prince Edward Island
12. Nova Scotia
13. New Brunswick

24. Quebec
35. Ontario
46. Manitoba
47. Saskatchewan
48. Alberta
59. British Columbia

retir   Refers to all regular income received by the respondent during calendar year 2005 as the result of having been a member of a pension plan of one or more employers.

sempi   Refers to the total income received by respondent during calendar year 2005 as net income from self-employment.

sex   Gender of the respondent.
1. Female
2. Male

tenur   Refers to whether some member of the household owns or rents the dwelling.
1. Owned
2. Rented

totinc   Refers to the total money income received from all sources during calendar year 2005 by the respondent.

uphwrk   Refers to the number of hours persons spent doing unpaid housework, yard work or home maintenance in the week (Sunday to Saturday) prior to Census Day (May 16, 2006).

1. None	2. Less than 5 hours
3. 5 to 14 hours	4. 15 to 29 hours
5. 30 to 59 hours	6. 60 hours or more

upkid   Refers to the number of hours persons spent looking after children without pay in the week (Sunday to Saturday) prior to Census Day (May 16, 2006).

1. None	2. Less than 5 hours
3. 5 to 14 hours	4. 15 to 29 hours
5. 30 to 59 hours	6. 60 hours or more

upsr   Refers to the number of hours persons spent providing unpaid care or assistance to seniors in the week (Sunday to Saturday) prior to Census Day (May 16, 2006).

1. None	2. Less than 5 hours
3. 5 to 9 hours	4. 10 to 19 hours
5. 20 hours or more	

value   The dollar amount expected by the owner if the dwelling were to be sold. 9999999. Persons in tenant occupied dwellings (***defined as missing in the data set***)

vismin   Refers to whether the person is a member of a visible minority in Canada.

1. Chinese
2. South Asian
3. Black
4. Filipino
5. Latin American
6. Southeast Asian
7. Arab
8. West Asian
9. Korean
10. Japanese
11. Visible minority, n.i.e.
12. Multiple visible minority
13. Not a visible minority

wages   Refers to gross wages and salaries before deductions received by the respondent during calendar year 2005.

wkswrk   Refers to the number of weeks in 2005 during which persons worked for pay or in self-employment at all jobs held.

0. Not in the Labour Force

yrimm   The year in which landed immigrant status was first obtained.

1. before 1950
2. 1950 to 1954
3. 1955 to 1959
4. 1960 to 1964
5. 1965 to 1969
6. 1970 to 1974
7. 1975 to 1979
1980 1980
1981 1981
1982 1982
1983 1983
1984 1984
1985 1985
1986 1986
1987 1987
1988 1988
1989 1989
1990 1990
1991 1991
1992 1992
1993 1993
1994 1994
1995 1995

1996 1996
1997 1997
1998 1998
1999 1999
2000 2000
2001 2001
2002 2002
2003 2003
2004 2004
2005 2005
2006 2006
9999 Canadian-born

Answers to Odd-Numbered Computational Problems

In addition to answers, this section suggests some problem-solving strategies and provides examples of how to interpret the numerical answers. You should try to solve and interpret the problems on your own before consulting this section.

In solving these problems, we let our calculators or computers do most of the work. We worked with whatever level of precision these devices permitted and, generally, didn't round off until the end or until we had to record an intermediate sum. We always rounded off to two places of accuracy (or, two places beyond the decimal point, or to 100ths). If you follow these same conventions, your answers will almost always match our answers. However, there is no guarantee that our answers will always be exact matches, and you should be aware that small discrepancies might occur and that they are almost always trivial. If the difference between your answer and our answer doesn't seem trivial, you should double-check to make sure you haven't made an error or solve the problem again using a greater degree of precision.

Finally, please allow us a brief disclaimer about mathematical errors in this section. Let us assure you, first of all, that we know how important this section is for most students and that we worked hard to be certain that these answers are correct. Human fallibility being what it is, however, we know that we cannot make absolute guarantees. Should you find any errors, please let us know so that we can make corrections in the future.

Chapter 2

2.1 **a.** Complex A: $(5/20) \times 100 = 25.00\%$
Complex B: $(10/20) \times 100 = 50.00\%$
b. Complex A: $4:5 = 0.80$
Complex B: $6:10 = 0.60$
c. Complex A: $(0/20) = 0.00$
Complex B: $(1/20) = 0.05$
d. $(6/(4 + 6)) = (6/10) = 60.00\%$
e. Complex A: $8:5 = 1.60$
Complex B: $2:10 = 0.20$

2.3 Bank robbery rate =
$(47/211,732) \times 100,000 = 22.20$
Homicide rate = $(13/211,732) \times 100,000 = 6.14$
Auto theft rate = $(23/211,732) \times 100,000 = 10.86$

Chapter 3

3.1 "Region of birth" is a nominal-level variable, "support for legalization" and "opinion of food" are ordinal, and "expenses" and "number of movies" are interval-ratio. The mode, the most common score, is the only measure of central tendency available for nominal-level variables. For the ordinal-level variables, *don't forget to array the scores from high to low* before locating the median. There are ten lower-year students (n is even), so the median will be the score halfway between the scores of the two middle cases. There are 11 upper-year students (n is odd), so the median will be the score of the middle case. To find the mean for the interval-ratio variables, add the scores and divide by the number of cases.

Variable	Lower Year	Upper Year
Region of birth:	Mode = Atlantic	Mode = Atlantic
Legalization:	Median = 3	Median = 5
Expenses:	Mean = 48.50	Mean = 63.00
Movies:	Mean = 5.8	Mean = 5.18
Food:	Median = 6	Median = 4

3.3

Variable	Level of Measurement	Measure of Central Tendency
Sex	Nominal	Mode = male
Social class	Ordinal	Median = "medium" (the middle case is in this category)
Number of years in the party	I-R	Mean = 26.15
Education	Ordinal	Median = high school
Marital status	Nominal	Mode = married
Number of children	I-R	Mean = 2.39

3.5

Variable	Level of Measurement	Measure of Central Tendency
Marital status	Nominal	Mode = married
Sex	Nominal	Mode = female
Age	I-R	Mean = 27.53
Attitude on legalization of marijuana	Ordinal	Median = 7

3.7 The median is 27.5 and the mean 26.9. Since, Q_1 is 15 (the median of the lower half of the data) and Q_3 is 35 (the median of the upper half of the data), the interquartile range is $35 - 15$, or 20. The standard deviation is 12.28.

3.9

Statistic	2000	2005
Standard deviation	40.86	29.46

The standard deviation becomes smaller over the time period. This indicates that the dispersion in the group (the differences in income from province to province) decreased.

3.11 Mean = 40.25, Median = 44.5. The lower value for the mean indicates a negative skew or a few very *low* scores. For this small group of nations, the skew is caused by the score of Mexico (10), which is much lower than the scores of the other seven nations (which are grouped between 37 and 51).

3.13 To find the median, the scores for both groups first must be ranked from high to low. Both groups have 25 cases ($n = $ odd), so the median is the score of the 13th case. For first-year students, the median is 35 and, for final-year students, the median is 30. The mean score for first-year students is 31.72. For final-year students, the mean is 28.60.

Chapter 4

4.1

X_i	Z score	% Area Above	% Area Below
5	−1.67	95.25	4.75
6	−1.33	90.82	9.18
7	−1.00	84.13	15.87
8	−0.67	74.86	25.14
9	−0.33	62.93	37.07
11	0.33	37.07	62.93
12	0.67	25.14	74.86
14	1.33	9.18	90.82
15	1.67	4.75	95.25
16	2.00	2.28	97.72
18	2.67	0.38	99.62

4.3

	Z scores	Area
a.	0.10 & 1.10	32.45%
b.	0.60 & 1.10	13.86%
c.	0.60	27.43%
d.	0.90	18.41%
e.	0.60 & −0.40	38.11%
f.	0.10 & −0.40	19.52%
g.	0.10	53.98%
h.	0.30	61.79%
i.	0.60	72.57%
j.	1.10	86.43%

4.5

X_i	Z Score	Number of Students Above	Number of Students Below
60	−2.00	195	5
57	−2.50	199	1
55	−2.83	199	1
67	−0.83	159	41
70	−0.33	126	74
72	0.00	100	100
78	1.00	32	168
82	1.67	10	190
90	3.00	1	199
95	3.83	1	199

Note: Number of students (a discrete variable) has been rounded off to the nearest whole number.

4.7

	Z score	Area
a.	−2.20	1.39%
b.	1.80	96.41%
c.	−0.20 & 1.80	54.34%
d.	0.80 & 2.80	20.93%
e.	−1.20	88.49%
f.	0.80	21.19%

4.9

	Z score	Area
a.	−1.00 & 1.50	0.7745
b.	0.25 & 1.50	0.3345
c.	1.50	0.0668
d.	0.25 & −2.25	0.5865
e.	−1.00 & −2.25	0.1465
f.	−1.00	0.1587

4.11 Yes. The raw score of 110 translates into a Z score of +2.88. 99.80% of the area lies below this score, so this individual was in the top 1% on this test.

4.13 For the first event, the probability is 0.0919 and, for the second, the probability is 0.0655. The first event is more likely.

Part I Cumulative Exercises

1. The level of measurement is the most important criteria for selecting descriptive statistics. The table below presents all relevant statistics for each variable. Statistics which are not appropriate for a variable are noted with an "X."

Religion is nominal so the only statistics available are the mode and the variation ratio (v). For the two ordinal-level variables ("strength" and "comfort"), the median and the range are the appropriate choices. For interval-ratio variables like "pray" and "age," the mean and standard deviation are the preferred summary statistics.

Level of measurement	Religion Nominal	Strength Ordinal	Pray I-R	Comfort Ordinal	Age I-R
Mode	Protestant				
Median	X	7		1	
Mean	X	X	1.40	X	41.53
v	0.67				
Range	X	9		4	
Stnd. dev.	X	X	1.62	X	12.54

3. As always, the level of measurement is the primary guideline for choosing descriptive statistics and the most appropriate statistics are noted in the table below. Statistics which are not appropriate for a variable are noted with an "X."

Level of measurement	Children I-R	School Ordinal	Sex Nominal	Spanking Ordinal	TV I-R	Age Ordinal
Mode			Male			
Median		1.00	X	2		1
Mean	2.44	X	X	X	3.08	X
v			0.20			
Range		4	X	3		2
Stnd. dev.	2.06	X	X	X	2.04	X

Chapter 6

6.1 **a.** 5.2 ± 0.11   **b.** 100 ± 0.71
c. 20 ± 0.40   **d.** 1,020 ± 5.41
e. 7.3 ± 0.23   **f.** 33 ± 0.80

6.5 **a.** 2.30 ± 0.04   **b.** 2.10 ± 0.01, 0.78 ± 0.07
c. 6.00 ± 0.37

6.7 **a.** 178.23 ± 1.97. The estimate is that students spent between $176.26 and $180.20 on books.

b. 1.5 ± 0.04 The estimate is that students visited the clinic between 1.46 and 1.54 times on the average.

c. 2.8 ± 0.13 **d.** 3.5 ± 0.19

6.9. 14 ± 0.07 The estimate is that between 7% and 21% of the population consists of unmarried couples living together.

6.11 a. $P_s = (823/1,496) = 0.55$
Confidence interval: 0.55 ± 0.02
Between 53% and 57% of the population agrees with the statement.
b. $P_s = (650/1,496) = 0.44$
Confidence interval: 0.44 ± 0.02
c. $P_s = (375/1,496) = 0.25$
Confidence interval: 0.25 ± 0.02
d. $P_s = (1,023/1,496) = 0.68$
Confidence interval: 0.68 ± 0.02
e. $P_s = (800/1,496) = 0.54$
Confidence interval: 0.54 ± 0.02

6.13

Alpha (α)	Confidence Level	Confidence Interval
0.10	90%	100 ± 0.74
0.05	95%	100 ± 0.88
0.01	99%	100 ± 1.16
0.001	99.9%	100 ± 1.47

6.15 The confidence interval is 0.51 ± 0.05. The estimate would be that between 46% and 56% of the population prefer candidate A. The population parameter (P_u) is equally likely to be anywhere in the interval (i.e., it's just as likely to be 46% as it is to be 56%), so a winner cannot be predicted.

6.17 The confidence interval is 0.23 ± 0.08. At the 95% confidence level, the estimate would be that between 240 (15%) and 496 (31%) of the 1,600 incoming students would be extremely interested. The estimated numbers are found by multiplying n (1,600) by the upper (0.31) and lower (0.15) limits of the interval.

6.19 a. 43.87 ± 0.49
b. 2.86 ± 0.08
c. 1.81 ± 0.06
d. 0.29 ± 0.02
e. 0.18 ± 0.02
f. 0.36 ± 0.02
g. 0.81 ± 0.02

Chapter 7

7.3 **a.** Z (obtained) $= -41.00$
b. Z (obtained) $= 29.09$

7.5 Z (obtained) $= 6.04$

7.7 **a.** Z (obtained) $= -13.66$
b. Z (obtained) $= 25.50$

7.9 t (obtained) $= 4.50$

7.11 Z (obtained) $= 3.06$

7.13 Z (obtained) $= -1.48$

7.15 **a.** Z (obtained) $= -0.74$
b. Z (obtained) $= 2.19$
c. Z (obtained) $= -8.55$
d. Z (obtained) $= -18.07$
e. Z (obtained) $= 2.09$
f. Z (obtained) $= -53.33$

7.17 t (obtained) $= -1.14$

Chapter 8

8.1 **a.** $\sigma = 1.39$, Z (obtained) $= -2.52$
b. $\sigma = 1.61$, Z (obtained) $= 2.49$

8.3 **a.** Z (obtained) $= 1.70$
b. Z (obtained) $= -2.48$

8.5 **a.** $\sigma = 0.08$ Z (obtained) $= 11.25$
b. Phone calls: $\sigma = 0.12$ Z(obtained) $= -3.33$
E-mail messages: $\sigma = 0.15$ Z(obtained) $= 20.00$

8.7 These are small samples (combined n's of less than 100), so be sure to use Formulas 8.5 and 8.6 in step 4.
a. $\sigma = 0.12$, t (obtained) $= -1.33$
b. $\sigma = 0.13$, t (obtained) $= 14.85$

8.9 (Canada) $\sigma = 0.0095$, Z (obtained) $= -31.58$
(Nigeria) $\sigma = 0.0075$, Z (obtained) $= -146.67$
(China) $\sigma = 0.0065$, Z (obtained) $= 76.92$

(Mexico) $\sigma = 0.0107$, Z (obtained) $= -74.77$
(Japan) $\sigma = 0.012$, Z (obtained) $= -41.67$

The large values for the Z scores indicate that the differences are significant at very low alpha levels (i.e., they are extremely unlikely to have been caused by random chance alone). Note that women are significantly happier than men in every nation except China where men are significantly happier.

8.11 $P_u = 0.45$, $\sigma_p = 0.06$, Z (obtained) $= 0.67$

8.13 a. $P_u = 0.46$, $\sigma_p = 0.06$, Z (obtained) $= 2.17$
 b. $P_u = 0.80$, $\sigma_p = 0.07$, Z (obtained) $= -1.43$
 c. $P_u = 0.72$, $\sigma_p = 0.08$, Z (obtained) $= 0.75$

8.15 a. Z (obtained) $= 1.50$
 b. Z (obtained) $= -2.75$
 c. Z (obtained) $= 4.00$
 d. Z (obtained) $= 1.86$
 e. Z (obtained) $= -5.71$
 f. Z (obtained) $= -5.50$

Chapter 9

9.1

Problem	Grand Mean	SST	SSB	SSW	F ratio
a.	12.17	231.67	173.17	58.5	13.32
b.	6.87	455.73	78.53	377.20	1.25
c.	31.65	8,362.55	5,053.35	3,309.2	8.14

9.3

Problem	Grand Mean	SST	SSB	SSW	F ratio
a.	4.39	86.28	45.78	40.50	8.48
b.	16.44	332.44	65.44	267.00	1.84

For problem 9.3a, with alpha $= 0.05$ and df $= 2$, 15, the critical F ratio would be 3.68. We would reject the null hypothesis and conclude that decision making *does* vary significantly by type of relationship. By inspection of the group means, it seems that the "cohabitational" category accounts for most of the differences.

9.5 SST $= 213.61$, SSB $= 2.11$, SSW $= 211.50$
 F (obtained) $= 0.08$

9.7 SST $= 429.48$, SSB $= 124.06$, SSW $= 305.42$
 F (obtained) $= 5.96$

9.9

Nation	Grand Mean	SST	SSB	SSW	F ratio
Mexico	3.78	300.98	154.08	146.90	12.59
Canada	6.88	156.38	20.08	136.30	1.78
United States	5.13	286.38	135.28	151.10	10.74

At alpha $= 0.05$ and df $= 3$, 36, the critical F ratio is 2.92. There is a significant difference in support for suicide by class in Mexico and the United States but not in Canada. The category means for Mexico suggest that the upper class accounts for most of the differences. For the United States, there is more variation across the category means and the working class seems to account for most of the differences. Going beyond the ANOVA test and comparing the grand means, support is highest in Canada and lowest in Mexico.

Chapter 10

10.1 a. 1.11   **b.** 0.00   **c.** 1.52   **d.** 1.46

10.3 A computing table is highly recommended as a way of organizing the computations for chi square:

Computational Table for Problem 10.3

(1)	(2)	(3)	(4)	(5)
f_o	f_e	$f_o - f_e$	$(f_o - f_e)^2$	$(f_o - f_e)^2/f_e$
6	5	1	1	0.20
7	8	−1	1	0.13
4	5	−1	1	0.20
9	8	1	1	0.13
$n = 26$	$n = 26$	0	χ^2 (obtained) $= 0.65$	

There is 1 degree of freedom in a 2×2 table. With alpha set at 0.05, the critical value for the chi square would be 3.841. The obtained chi square is 0.65, so we fail to reject the null hypothesis of independence between the variables. There is no statistically significant relationship between sex and services received.

10.5

Computational Table for Problem 10.5

(1)	(2)	(3)	(4)	(5)
f_o	f_e	$f_o - f_e$	$(f_o - f_e)^2$	$(f_o - f_e)^2 / f_e$
21	17.5	3.5	12.25	0.70
29	32.5	−3.5	12.25	0.38
14	17.5	−3.5	12.25	0.70
36	32.5	3.5	12.25	0.38
$n = 100$	$n = 100.0$	0		χ^2 (obtained) = 2.15

With 1 degree of freedom and alpha set at 0.05, the critical region will begin at 3.841. The obtained chi square of 2.15 does not fall within this area, so the null hypothesis cannot be rejected. There is no statistically significant relationship between unionization and salary.

10.7 The obtained chi square is 5.12, which is significant (df = 1, alpha = 0.05).

10.9 The obtained chi square is 6.67.

10.11 The obtained chi square is 12.59.

10.13 The obtained chi square is 19.33.

10.15

Problem	Chi Square	Significant at α = 0.05?
a.	25.19	Yes
b.	1.80	No
c.	5.23	No
d.	28.43	Yes
e.	14.17	Yes

Part II Cumulative Exercises

1. One of the challenges of empirical research is to make reasonable decisions about which estimation procedure or statistical test to use in which situation. You can minimize the confusion and ambiguity by approaching the decision systematically. We'll use the first problem of this exercise to consider some ways in which reasonable decisions can be made. The situation call for a test of hypothesis ("Is the difference significant?"), so our choice of procedures will be limited to Chapters 7–10. Next, determine the types of variables you are working with. Number of minutes is an interval-ratio-level variable, and gender is nominal and has only two categories. Which test should we use? The techniques in Chapter 7 (one-sample tests) and Chapter 9 (tests involving more than two samples or categories) are not relevant. Chi square (see Chapter 10) won't work unless we collapse the scores on Internet use into a few categories. This leaves Chapter 8. A test of sample means fits the situation, and we have a large sample (combined n's greater than 100), so it looks like we're going to wind up in Section 8.2.

Another way to approach test selection would be to use the flowcharts presented at the beginning of each part and chapter. The flowcharts would quickly lead to Chapter 8, where we would answer: YES, we want to test for the significance of the difference between means, and YES, sample size is large. These answers will also lead to Section 8.2.

a. $\sigma = 0.14$, Z (obtained) = −35.71

The difference in Internet minutes is significant. Men, on the average, use this technology more frequently.

b. The table format is a sure tip-off that the chi square test is appropriate. The obtained chi square is 0.87, which is not significant at the 0.05 level. There is no statistically significant relationship between involvement and social class.

c. "Number of partners" sounds like an interval-ratio-level variable, and education has three categories. Analysis of variance is an appropriate test for this situation. The F ratio is 0.13—not at all significant—so we must conclude that this dimension of sexuality does not vary by level of education.

d. The problem asks for a characteristic of a population ("How many times do adult Canadians move?") but gives information only for a "random sample." The estimation procedures presented in Chapter 6 fit the situation and, because the information is presented in the form of a mean, you should use Formula 6.2 to form the estimate. At an alpha level of 0.05, the confidence interval would be 3.5 ± 0.02.

e. The research question focuses on the difference between a single sample and a population, so Chapter 7 is relevant. Because the population standard deviation is unknown, and we have a large sample, Sections 7.1–7.5 and Formula 7.1 will be relevant. Z (obtained) is −2.50, which would be significant at alpha = 0.05. The sample is significantly different from the population—rural school districts are different from the universe of school districts in this province.

Chapter 11

Tables display conditional distributions (or column percentages).

11.1

Efficiency	Authoritarianism	
	Low	High
Low	37.04	70.59
High	62.96	29.41
Totals	100.00	100.00

The conditional distributions change, so there is a relationship between the variables. The change from column to column is quite large and the maximum difference is (70.59 − 37.04) = 33.55. Using Table 11.5 as a guideline, we can say that this relationship is strong. From inspection of the percentages, we can see that efficiency decreases as authoritarianism increases—workers with dictatorial bosses are less productive (or, maybe, bosses become more dictatorial when workers are inefficient), so this relationship is negative in direction.

11.3

2006 Election	2004 Election	
	Voted	Didn't Vote
Voted	87.31	11.44
Didn't Vote	12.69	88.56
Totals	100.00	100.00

The maximum difference for this table is (87.31 − 11.44) or 75.87. This is a very strong relationship. People are very consistent in their voting habits.

11.5

Problem	ϕ	λ
11.1	0.33	0.32
11.2 a.	0.04	0.00
b.	0.18	0.00
c.	0.16	0.00
11.3	0.75	0.71
11.4	0.02	0.00

11.7 a.

Supports Same-sex Marriage?	Political Ideology		
	Liberal	Moderate	Conservative
Favour	59.42	39.39	26.88
Oppose	40.58	60.31	73.12
Totals	100.00	100.00	100.00

The maximum difference of 32.54 indicates a strong relationship. Liberals support same-sex marriage, conservatives are opposed, and moderates are intermediate.

Chapter 12

12.1 **a.** $G = 0.71$ **b.** $G = 0.69$ **c.** $G = -0.88$
These relationships are strong. Facility in English/French and income increase with length of residence. Use the percentages to help interpret the direction of a relationship. In the first table, 80% of recent immigrants were "Low" in English/French facility while 60% of long-term immigrants were "High." In this relationship, low scores on one variable are associated with low scores on the other, and scores increase together (as one increases, the other increases), so this is a positive relationship. In contrast, contact with country of origin decreases with length of residence (−0.88). Most recent immigrants have higher levels of contact, and most long-term immigrants have lower levels.

12.3 $G = -0.61$ This is a strong negative relationship. As authoritarianism increases, efficiency decreases.

12.5 $G = 0.27$ Be careful interpreting the direction of this relationship. The positive sign of gamma means that cases tend to fall along the diagonal from upper left to lower right. In this case, white-collar families are more associated with organized sports and blue-collar families with sandlot sports. Computing percentages will help you identify the direction of the relationship.

12.7 $G = 0.22$, Z (obtained) = 0.92

12.9 $G = -0.14$

12.11 $r_s = -0.46$, t (obtained) = −1.55

12.13 $r_s = 0.33$

For these nations, there is a moderate positive relationship between diversity and inequality. The greater the diversity, the greater the inequality.

12.15 a. $G = -0.14$ **b.** $G = -0.17$
c. $G = -0.14$ **d.** $G = 0.39$
e. $G = -0.13$

Income has moderate negative relationships with the first three and the last dependent variables. Be careful in interpreting direction for these tables and remember that a negative gamma means that cases tend to be clustered along the diagonal from lower left to upper right. Computing percentages will clarify direction. For example, for the first table, low income is associated with opposition to same-sex marriage (62% of the people in this column said "Oppose") and high income is associated with support (47% of the people in this column said "Favour" and this is the highest percentage of support across the three income groups).

Income has a strong positive relationship with support for traditional gender roles. Note the way in which the dependent variable is coded: "Favour" means support for traditional gender roles. A positive relationship means that cases tend to fall along the diagonal from upper left to lower right. In this case, favouring is greater for low income and declines as income increases. Is this truly a "positive" relationship? As always, percentages will help clarify the direction of the relationship.

Chapter 13

13.1 *(HINT: When finding the slope, remember that "Turnout" is the dependent or Y variable.)*

13.3 *(HINT: When finding the slope, remember that "Number of visitors" is the dependent or Y variable.)*

Slope (b)	-0.37
Y intercept (a)	13.42
r	-0.31
r^2	0.09

13.5

Dependent Variables		Independent Variables		
		Density	Growth	Urbanization
Auto theft	a	417.08	135.47	-215.46
	b	-0.23	17.50	7.96
	r	-0.13	0.89	0.67
	r^2	0.02	0.79	0.45
Robbery	a	59.97	94.38	-96.71
	b	0.37	1.44	2.81
	r	0.72	0.27	0.87
	r^2	0.52	0.07	0.76
Homicide	a	3.87	3.01	-0.58
	b	0.00	0.11	0.07
	r	0.26	0.62	0.65
	r^2	0.07	0.38	0.42

c. For a growth rate of -1, the predicted homicide rate would be 2.90. For a population density of 250, the predicted robbery rate would be 152.47. For a city with 50% urbanization, the predicted rate of auto theft would be 182.54.

13.7 $b = 0.05$, $a = 53.18$, $r = 0.40$, $r^2 = 0.16$

13.9

Relationship	r	r^2	t (obtained)
Prestige and age	-0.30	0.09	-1.13
Attendance and number of children	-0.39	0.15	-1.53
Number of children and hours of TV	0.18	0.03	0.66
Age and hours of TV	0.16	0.03	0.58
Age and number of children	0.67	0.45	3.25
Hours of TV and prestige	-0.19	0.04	0.70

	For Turnout (Y) and		
	Unemployment	Education	Neg. Campaigning
Slope (b)	3.00	12.67	-0.90
Y intercept (a)	39.00	-94.73	114.01
Reg. Eq.	$Y = (39) + (3)X$	$Y = (-94.73) + (12.67)X$	$Y = (114.01) + (-0.90)X$
r	0.95	0.98	-0.87
r^2	0.90	0.96	0.76
t (obtained)	5.00	9.05	-3.08

Part III Cumulative Exercises

1. a. Assuming that crime rates and "percentage immigrant" are both measured at the interval-ratio level, Pearson's r would be the appropriate measure of association. This is a moderate negative relationship ($r = -0.47$) and percentage of immigrants explains 22% of the variation in crime rate for these 10 cities. As the percentage of immigrants increases, the crime rate decreases.

b. These variables are ordinal in level of measurement, so gamma would be the appropriate measure of association. Gamma is -0.43, indicating a moderate negative relationship. As TV viewing increases, involvement decreases.

c. The appropriate measure for these variables is Spearman's rho, which is 0.74. This is a strong positive relationship and countries with higher quality of life have superior systems of higher education.

d. Marital status is a nominal-level variable, and the table is larger than 2 × 2. Cramer's V is 0.40, indicating a strong relationship between the variables. Because of the uneven row totals, lambda is zero even though there is an association between these variables.

Chapter 14

14.1 a. For turnout (Y) and unemployment (X) while controlling for negative advertising (Z), $r_{yx.z} = 0.95$. The relationship between X and Y is not affected by the control variable Z.

b. For turnout (Y) and negative advertising (X) while controlling for unemployment (Z), $r_{yx.z} = -0.89$. The bivariate relationship is not affected by the control variable.

c. Turnout (Y) = 70.25 + (2.09) unemployment (X_1) + (-0.43) negative advertising (X_2). For unemployment (X_1) = 10 and negative advertising (X_2) = 75, turnout (Y) = 58.90.

d. For unemployment (X_1): $b_1^* = 0.66$. For negative advertising (X_2): $b_2^* = -0.41$. Unemployment has a stronger effect on turnout than negative advertising. Note that the independent variables' effect on turnout is in opposite directions.

e. $R^2 = 0.98$

14.3 a. For strife (Y) and unemployment (X), controlling for urbanization (Z), $r_{yx.z} = 0.79$.

b. For strife (Y) and urbanization (X), controlling for unemployment (Z), $r_{yx.z} = 0.20$.

c. Strife (Y) = (-14.60) + (4.94) unemployment (X_1) + (0.16) urbanization (X_2). With unemployment = 10 and urbanization = 90, strife (Y') would be 49.19.

d. For unemployment (X_1): $b_1^* = 0.78$. For urbanization (X_2): $b_2^* = 0.13$.

e. $R^2 = 0.65$

14.5 a. Turnout (Y) = 83.80 + (-1.16) working-class (X_1) + (2.89) unemployment (X_2).

b. For $X_1 = 0$ and $X_2 = 5$, $Y' = 98.25$

c. $Z_y = (-1.27)Z_1 + (0.84)Z_2$

d. $R^2 = 0.51$

14.7 a. $Z_y = (-0.001)$ HS grads (Z_1) + (-0.71) Rank (Z_2)

b. $R^2 = 0.51$

Part IV Cumulative Exercises

1. In this situation, we have three variables: GPA, hours of work, and GRE score. GPA is the dependent variable, and the zero-order correlation with "hours worked" is -0.83, a strong and negative relationship, which indicates that having a job did interfere with academic success for this sample. The zero-order correlation between GPA and GRE score is 0.55, a relationship that is consistent with the idea that GRE scores predict success in university.

The results of the regression analysis with "hours worked" (X_1) and GRE score (X_2) as independents:

$$Y = 1.71 + (-0.04)X_1 + (0.003)X_2$$
$$Z_y = (-0.75)Z_1 + (0.43)Z_2$$
$$R^2 = 0.86$$

The beta-weights indicate that "hours worked" has a stronger direct effect on GPA than GRE score. Even for students who were well prepared for graduate school and had high GRE scores, having a job had a negative impact on GPA. The high value for R^2 means that only a small percentage of the variance in GPA (14%) is left unexplained by these two independent variables.

Glossary

Each entry includes a brief definition and refers to the page number where the term was introduced.

Alpha. The probability that a confidence interval does not contain the population value. (p. 152)

Alpha error. See *Type I error.* (p. 199)

Alpha level. The proportion of the area under the sampling distribution that contains unlikely sample outcomes if the null is true. Also, the probability of Type I error. (p. 191)

Analysis of variance. A test of significance appropriate when testing for the differences among more than two sample means. (p. 248)

ANOVA. See *Analysis of variance.* (p. 248)

Association. The relationship between two (or more) variables. Two variables are said to be associated if the distribution of one variable changes for the various categories or scores of the other variable. (p. 302)

Average deviation. The average of the absolute deviations of the scores around the mean. (p. 80)

Bar chart. A graphic display device for nominal- and ordinal-level variables. (p. 51)

Beta error. See *Type II error.* (p. 199)

Beta-weights (b^*). Standardized partial slopes. (p. 418)

Bias. A criterion used to select sample statistics for estimation procedures. A statistic is unbiased if the mean of its sampling distribution is equal to the population value of interest. (p. 149)

Bivariate normal distributions. The model assumption in the test of significance for Pearson's r that both variables are normally distributed. (p. 388)

Bivariate table. A table that displays the joint frequency distribution of two variables. (p. 286)

Cells. The cross-classification categories of the variables in a bivariate table. (p. 270)

Central Limit Theorem. A theorem that specifies the mean, standard deviation, and shape of the sampling distribution, given that the sample is large. (p. 136)

χ^2(critical). The chi square score that marks the beginnings of the critical region of the chi square sampling distribution. (p. 273)

χ^2(obtained). The test statistic computed in step 4 of the five-step model. (p. 273)

Chi square test. A non-parametric test of hypothesis for variables organized in a bivariate table. (p. 269)

Coefficient of determination (r^2). The proportion of all variation in Y that is explained by X. (p. 381)

Coefficient of multiple determination (R^2). A statistic that equals the total variation explained in the dependent variable by all independent variables combined. (p. 420)

Column. The vertical dimension of a bivariate table. (p. 270)

Column percentages. Percentages computed within each column of a bivariate table. (p. 277)

Conditional distribution of Y. The distribution of scores on the dependent variable for a specific score or category of the independent variable. (p. 303)

Conditional means of Y. The mean of all scores on Y for each value of X. (p. 374)

Confidence interval. An estimate of a population value in which a range of values is specified. (p. 149)

Confidence level. An alternative way to express alpha, the probability that a confidence interval will not contain the population value. (p. 152)

Continuous variable. A variable with a unit of measurement that can be subdivided infinitely. (p. 18)

Control variable. A "third variable" (Z) that might affect a bivariate relationship. (p. 410)

Cramer's V. (V) A chi square–based measure of association. (p. 312)

Critical region (region of rejection). The area under the sampling distribution that includes all unlikely sample outcomes. (p. 190)

Cumulative frequency. A column in a frequency distribution that displays the number of cases in an interval and all preceding intervals. (p. 46)

Cumulative percentage. A column in a frequency distribution that displays the percentage of cases in an interval and all preceding intervals. (p. 46)

Data. In social science research, information that is represented by numbers. (p. 9)

Database. An organized collection of related information. (p. 454)

Data reduction. Summarizing many scores with a few statistics. (p. 16)

Dependent variable. A variable that is identified as an effect, result, or outcome variable. The dependent variable is thought to be caused by the independent variable. (pp. 11, 302)

Descriptive statistics. The branch of statistics concerned with (1) summarizing the distribution of a single variable or (2) measuring the relationship between two or more variables. (p. 15)

Deviations. The distances between the scores and the mean. (p. 80)

Direct relationship. A multivariate relationship in which a control variable has no effect on the bivariate relationship. (p. 410)

Discrete variable. A variable with a basic unit of measurement that cannot be subdivided. (p. 18)

Dispersion. The amount of variety or heterogeneity in a distribution of scores. (p. 66)

Efficiency. The extent to which sample outcomes are clustered around the mean of the sampling distribution. (p. 149)

EPSEM. Equal probability of selection method. A technique for selecting samples in which every element or case in the population has an equal probability of being selected for the sample. (p. 131)

Error bar. A graphic display device used to illustrate the confidence interval of a sample mean. (p. 157)

Expected frequency (f_e). The cell frequencies that would be expected in a bivariate table if the variables were independent. (p. 286)

Explained variation. The proportion of all variation in Y that is attributed to the effect of X. (p. 382)

F ratio. For the analysis of variance, the test statistic computed in step 4 of the five-step model. (p. 252)

File. A database (or any other information) that is stored under the same name in the memory of the computer or other storage media. (p. 434)

Five-step model. A step-by-step guideline for conducting tests of hypotheses. (p. 189)

Frequency distribution. A table that displays the number of cases in each category of a variable. (p. 55)

Frequency polygon. A graphic display device for interval-ratio variables. (p. 53)

Gamma (G). A measure of association for ordinal variables organized in table format. (p. 334)

Histogram. A graphic display device for interval-ratio variables. (p. 51)

Homoscedasticity. The model assumption in the test of significance for Pearson's r that the variance of the Y scores is uniform across all values of X. (p. 388)

Hypothesis. A statement about the relationship between variables that is derived from a theory. Hypotheses are more specific than theories, and all terms and concepts are fully defined. (p. 12)

Hypothesis testing. Statistical tests that estimate the probability of sample outcomes if assumptions about the population (the null hypothesis) are true. (p. 182)

Independence. The null hypothesis in the chi square test. Two variables are independent if the classification of a case on one variable has no effect on the probability that the case will be classified in any particular category of the second variable. (p. 286)

Independent random samples. Random samples gathered so that the selection of a case for one sample has no effect on the probability that any particular case will be selected for the other samples. (p. 219)

Independent variable. A variable that is identified as a causal variable. The independent variable is thought to cause the dependent variable. (pp. 11, 302)

Inferential statistics. The branch of statistics concerned with making generalizations from samples to populations. (p. 17)

Interquartile range (Q). The distance from the third quartile to the first. (p. 73)

Intervals. The categories used in frequency distributions for interval-ratio-level variables. (p. 43)

Intervening relationship. A multivariate relationship in which the independent and dependent variables are linked primarily through the control variable. (p. 411)

Kendall's tau-b (τ_b). A measure of association appropriate for two variables measured with "collapsed" ordinal scales with an equal number of categories. (p. 334)

Kendall's tau-c (τ_c). A measure of association appropriate for two variables measured with "collapsed" ordinal scales with an unequal number of categories. (p. 334)

Lambda (λ). A measure of association for nominal-level variables that have been organized into a bivariate table. Lambda is based on the logic of PRE. (p. 315)

Level of measurement. The mathematical characteristics of a variable as determined by the measurement process. A major criterion for selecting statistical techniques. (p. 18)

Linear relationship. A relationship between two variables in which the observation points (dots) in the scattergram can be approximated with a straight line. (p. 372)

Marginals. The row and column subtotals of a bivariate table. (p. 271)

Margin of error. The size of a confidence interval for a sample mean or sample proportion. It is also called the margin of sampling error, or just sampling error. (p. 149)

Maximum difference. The largest difference between column percentages for any row of a bivariate table. A way to assess the strength of the association, most useful for smaller tables. (p. 307)

Mean ($\overline{X}$ or μ). The arithmetic average of the scores; $\overline{X}$ represents the mean of a sample, and μ represents the mean of a population. (p. 75).

Mean square estimate. In the analysis of variance, an estimate of the variance calculated by dividing the sum of squares within (SSW) or the sum of squares between (SSB) by the appropriate degrees of freedom. (p. 252)

Measures of association. Statistics that summarize the strength and direction of the relationship between variables. (pp. 16, 301)

Measures of central tendency. Statistics that summarize a distribution of scores by reporting the most typical, average, or central value of the distribution. (p. 66)

Measures of dispersion. Statistics that indicate the amount of variety or heterogeneity in a distribution of scores. (p. 66)

Median (Md). The point in a distribution of scores above and below which half of the cases fall. (p. 71)

Menu. A list of options in a statistical package. (p. 456)

Midpoint. The point halfway between the upper and lower limits of a class interval. (p. 44)

Mode. The most common value in a distribution or the largest category of a variable. (p. 68)

Multiple correlation. A multivariate technique for examining the combined effects of more than one independent variable on a dependent variable. (p. 420)

Multiple correlation coefficient (R). A statistic that indicates the strength of the correlation between a dependent variable and two or more independent variables. (p. 420)

Multiple regression. A multivariate technique that breaks down the separate effects of the independent variables on the dependent variable. (p. 415)

Negative association. A bivariate relationship in which the variables vary in opposite directions. As one variable increases, the other decreases, and high scores on one variable are associated with low scores on the other. (p. 309)

Nonparametric test. A type of significance test in which no assumptions about the shape of the sampling distribution are made. (p. 269)

Normal curve. A theoretical distribution of scores that is symmetrical, unimodal, and bell shaped. The standard normal curve always has a mean of 0 and a standard deviation of 1. (p. 102)

Normal curve table. Appendix A; a detailed description of the area between a Z score and the mean of a standardized normal distribution. (p. 106)

Null hypothesis (H_0). A statement of "no difference." The specific form varies from test to test. (p. 189)

Observed frequency (f_o). The cell frequencies actually observed and recorded in a bivariate table. (p. 272)

One-tailed test. A type of hypothesis test that can be used when (1) the direction of the difference can be predicted or (2) concern is focused on only one tail of the sampling distribution. (p. 194)

One-way analysis of variance. An application of ANOVA in which the effect of a single variable on another is observed. (p. 259)

Outliers. Extreme high or low scores in a distribution. (p. 73)

Parameter. A characteristic of a population. (p. 130)

Partial correlation. A multivariate technique for examining a bivariate relationship while controlling for other variables. (p. 410)

Partial correlation coefficient. A statistic that shows the relationship between two variables while controlling for other variables; $r_{yx.z}$ is the symbol for the partial correlation coefficient when controlling for one variable. (p. 411)

Partial slopes. In a multiple regression equation, the slope of the relationship between a particular independent variable and the dependent variable while controlling for all other independents in the equation. (p. 415)

Pearson's r (r). A measure of association for variables that have been measured at the interval-ratio level. (p. 379)

Percentage (%). The number of cases in a category divided by the number of cases in all categories, the entire quantity multiplied by 100. (p. 33)

Phi (ϕ). A chi square–based measure of association. (p. 311)

Pie chart. A graphic display device for nominal- and ordinal-level variables. (p. 55)

Point estimate. An estimate of a population value in which a single value is specified. (p. 148)

Pooled estimate. An estimate of the standard deviation of the sampling distribution of the difference in sample means based on the standard deviations of both samples. (p. 221)

Population. The total collection of all cases in which the researcher is interested. (p. 17)

Positive association. A bivariate relationship in which the variables vary in the same direction. As one variable increases, the other also increases, and high scores on one variable are associated with high scores on the other. (p. 309)

Proportion (p). The number of cases in a category divided by the number of cases in all categories. (p. 33)

Proportional reduction in error (PRE). The logic that underlies the definition and computation of several different measures of association. Statistics are derived by comparing the number of errors made in predicting the dependent variable while ignoring the independent variable with the number of errors made while taking the independent variable into account. (p. 314)

Range (R). A measure of variation in a set of scores. The range is equal to the highest score minus the lowest score. (p. 72)

Rate. The number of actual occurrences divided by the number of possible occurrences per some unit of time. (p. 38)

Ratio. The number of cases in one category divided by the number of cases in another category. (p. 37)

Real limits. The upper and lower limits of an interval in a frequency distribution when the variable is treated as continuous. (p. 45)

Region of rejection. See *Critical region.* (p. 190)

Regression line. The best-fitting straight line that summarizes the relationship between two variables. The regression line is fitted to the data points by the least-squares criterion whereby the line touches all conditional means of Y or comes as close to doing so as possible. (p. 371)

Representative. A characteristic of a random sample or a sample drawn according to the rule of EPSEM. A sample that accurately reproduces the major characteristics of the population from which it was drawn is said to be representative of the population. (p. 131)

Research. Any process of gathering information systematically and carefully to answer questions or test theories. Statistics are useful for research projects in which the information is represented in numerical form or as data. (p. 9)

Research hypothesis (H_1). A statement that contradicts the null hypothesis. The specific form varies from test to test. (p. 190)

Row. The horizontal dimension of a table. (p. 270)

Sample. A subset of a population. In inferential statistics, information is gathered from random or EPSEM samples and then generalized to populations. (p. 17)

Sampling distribution. The distribution of all possible sample outcomes of a given statistic. (p. 133)

Scattergram. A graphic display device that depicts the relationship between two variables. (p. 370)

Significance testing. See *Hypothesis testing.* (p. 182)

Simple random sample. A sample drawn from a population so that every case has an equal chance of being included. (p. 132)

Skew. The extent to which a distribution of scores has a few cases that are extremely high (positive skew) or extremely low (negative skew). (p. 92)

Slope (b). The amount of change in a variable per unit change in the other variable. (p. 376)

Somers' d (d_{yx}). A measure of association appropriate for two variables measured with "collapsed" ordinal scales where one variable is identified as the dependent. (p. 334)

Spearman's rho (r_s). A measure of association for ordinal variables that are in "continuous" format. (p. 334)

Spurious relationship. A multivariate relationship in which both the independent and dependent variables are actually caused by the control variable. The independent and dependent are not causally related. (p. 410)

Standard deviation (*s* or *σ*). The square root of the squared deviations of the scores around the mean, divided by the number of cases. The most commonly used measure of dispersion; *s* represents the standard deviation of a sample, and *σ* represents the standard deviation of a population. (p. 92)

Standard error of the mean. The standard deviation of a sampling distribution of sample means. (p. 136)

Standardized partial slopes (beta-weights). The slope of the relationship between a particular independent variable and the dependent when all scores are expressed as *Z* scores. (p. 418)

Stated limits. The intervals of a frequency distribution when stated as discrete categories. (p. 45)

Statistical package (statpak). A set of computer programs designed to manipulate and statistically analyze data. (p. 453)

Statistics. A set of mathematical techniques for organizing and analyzing data. (p. 9)

Student's *t* distribution. A distribution used to find the critical region for tests of sample means when *σ* is unknown and sample size is small. (p. 201)

Sum of squares between (SSB). The sum of the squared deviations of the sample means from the overall mean, weighted by sample size. (p. 251)

Sum of squares within (SSW). The sum of the squared deviations from the category means. (p. 251)

_t_ (critical). The *t* score that marks the beginnings of the critical region of a *t* distribution. (p. 211)

_t_ (obtained). The test statistic computed in step 4 of the five-step model for tests of sample means when *n* is small and population standard deviation is unknown. (p. 203)

Test statistic. The value computed in step 4 of the five-step model that places the sample outcome on the sampling distribution. (p. 191)

Theory. A generalized explanation of the relationship between two or more variables. (p. 10)

Total sum of squares (SST). The sum of the squared deviations of the scores from the overall mean. (p. 251)

Total variation. The spread of the *Y* scores around the mean of *Y*. (p. 381)

Two-tailed test. A type of hypothesis test that can be used when (1) the direction of the difference cannot be predicted or (2) concern is focused on both tails of the sampling distribution. (p. 194)

Type I error (alpha error). The probability of rejecting a null hypothesis that is true. (p. 199)

Type II error (beta error). The probability of failing to reject a null hypothesis that is false. (p. 199)

Unexplained variation. The proportion of the total variation in *Y* that is not accounted for by *X*. (p. 383)

Variable. Any trait that can change values from case to case. (p. 11)

Variance (*s²* or *σ²*). The squared deviations of the scores around the mean, divided by the number of cases. A measure of dispersion used in inferential statistics and in regression techniques; s^2 represents the variance of a sample, and σ^2 represents the variance of a population. (p. 92)

Variation ratio (*v*). The proportion of cases that are not in the modal category (mode) of a variable. (p. 92)

_X_. Symbol used for any independent variable. (p. 302)

_Y_. Symbol used for any dependent variable. (p. 302)

_Y′_. Symbol for predicted score on *Y*. (p. 373)

_Y_ intercept (*a*). The point where the regression line crosses the *Y* axis. (p. 375)

_Z_ (critical). The *Z* score that marks the beginnings of the critical region of a *Z* distribution. (p. 191)

_Z_ (obtained). The test statistic computed in step 4 of the five-step model. (p. 191)

_Z_ scores. Standard scores; the way scores are expressed after they have been standardized to the theoretical normal curve. (p. 105)

Zero-order correlations. Correlation coefficients for bivariate relationships. (p. 411)

Index

GLOSSARY OF SYMBOLS

The number in parentheses indicates the chapter in which the symbol is introduced.

a — Point at which the regression line crosses the Y axis (13)

ANOVA — The analysis of variance (9)

b — Slope of the regression line (13)

b_i — Partial slope of the linear relationship between the ith independent variable and the dependent variable (14)

b_i^* — Standardized partial slope of the linear relationship between the ith independent variable and the dependent variable (14)

df — Degrees of freedom (7)

d_{yx} — Somers' d (12)

f — Frequency (2)

F — The F ratio (9)

f_e — Expected frequency (10)

f_o — Observed frequency (10)

G — Gamma for a sample (12)

H_0 — Null hypothesis (7)

H_1 — Research or alternate hypothesis (7)

Md — Median (3)

Mo — Mode (3)

N — Number of cases in the population (2)

n — Number of cases in the sample (2)

n_d — Number of pairs of cases ranked in different order on two variables (12)

n_s — Number of pairs of cases ranked in the same order on two variables (12)

% — Percentage (2)

p — Proportion (2)

P_s — A sample proportion (6)

P_u — A population proportion (6)

PRE — Proportional reduction in error (11)

Q — Interquartile range (3)

r — Pearson's correlation coefficient for a sample (13)

r^2 — Coefficient of determination (13)

R — Range (3)

r_s — Spearman's rho for a sample (12)

$r_{xy.z}$ — Partial correlation coefficient (14)

R^2 — Multiple correlation coefficient (14)

s — Sample standard deviation (3)

SSB — The sum of squares between (9)

SST — The total sum of squares (9)

SSW — The sum of squares within (9)

s^2 — Sample variance (3)

t — Student's t score (7)

V — Cramer's V (11)

v — Variation Ratio (3)

X — Any independent variable (11)

$\overline{X}$ — Mean of a sample (3)

X_i — Any score in a distribution (3)

Y — Any dependent variable (11)

Y' — A predicted score on Y (13)

Z scores — Standard scores (4)